Remembering the Year of the French

Irish Folk History and Social Memory

GUY BEINER

THE UNIVERSITY OF WISCONSIN PRESS

This book was originally published with the support of the Anonymous Fund for the Humanities of the University of Wisconsin–Madison.

The University of Wisconsin Press
1930 Monroe Street, 3rd Floor
Madison, Wisconsin 53711-2059

www.wisc.edu/wisconsinpress/

3 Henrietta Street
London WC2E 8LU, England

5   4   3   2

Printed in the United States of America

Library of Congress Cataloging-in-Publication Data

Beiner, Guy, 1968–
Remembering the year of the French: Irish folk history and social memory / Guy Beiner.
p.   cm.
Includes bibliographical references and index.
ISBN 0-299-21820-1 (cloth: alk. paper)
1. Ireland—History—Rebellion of 1798. 2. Ireland—History—Rebellion of 1798—Historiography. 3. Ireland—History—Rebellion of 1798—Public opinion. 4. French Expedition to Ireland, 1796–1797. 5. Folklore and history—Ireland. 6. Popular culture—Ireland—History. I. Title.
DA949.B45   2006
941.507—dc22   2006008619

ISBN 978-0-299-21824-9 (pbk.: alk. paper)

Cover illustration: Unpublished illustration by Jack B. Yeats of the 1798 Centennial celebration at the battlefield of Carricknagat outside Collooney, in County Sligo, in 1898, during which the foundation stone was laid for a monument to the United Irishman Bartholomew Teeling. Courtesy of Martin Naughton.

Cover design: Judy Gilats

The treasured finds have crumbled away, the traces have been obliterated. The past has received back what was its own to keep and what it has lent us for a while. But already memory has gone to work, searching, gathering evidence in the uncertain stillness of the no-man's land.

Siegfried Lenz
The Heritage (1981)

Table of Contents

Illustrations

(ix)

Preface

ONE DREARY DAY, in the autumn of 1997, I stepped out of the Modern Irish History Department at University College Dublin, to which I had recently arrived, walked down the corridors of the Arts Faculty and opened a door into Aladdin's cave. Inside I found not only a thousand and one tales, but also many more—each waiting to take me on a magic carpet ride and show me wonders beyond belief. I had discovered the archive of the Department of Irish Folklore. Once the door closed behind me, nothing would ever be the same.

Unwittingly, I had embarked on a quest, and many obstacles lay ahead. My instincts told me that Irish folklore was laden with riches for those interested in history of popular culture, but the treasures proved to be inaccessible. They were mostly expressed in a tongue not known to me, and so I first had to familiarize myself with the Irish language. Even then, once I delved into the labyrinths of folklore, my training in history was undermined. I was soon haunted by heretical thoughts, which challenged deep-rooted orthodoxies that had been instilled in me.

I was bewildered in a strange land, in need of tools to map the way. Perhaps what is most amazing about the long hours I spent over the years meandering in the folklore archive is this: apart from a couple of stray passersby, I cannot recall meeting other historians. They were all too busy studying *History*. To find my bearings, I grappled and eventually came to terms with oral history and oral tradition. It was then that I fathomed the importance of memory and had to apply myself to the study of psychology, sociology, anthropology, . . . the list grew longer and longer. The more I read, the more I realized how much more I needed to learn. The demands were excessive and yet there was no turning back.

I must confess that, before commencing my studies, I knew little about Ireland's history, culture, politics, and society. Fortunately, within reach, there were magnificent libraries and archives waiting to be mined. Enlightenment, however, is not to be found in the written word alone. The true pleasure of research in Ireland is that there are many wise people who are generously willing to share their knowledge. Conversations often took place over tall glasses of stout in the congenial environment of smoke-filled lounges and pub booths. Then there were the back roads. Whenever I could spare the time, I traveled through the west of Ireland taking any available mode of transportation—car, bus, train, bicycle, boat, or simply on foot. Only in the great outdoors did history become real.

This book—the outcome of these explorations and adventures—was never intended to be a standard historical monograph. It audaciously proposes to turn modern Irish history (and, by extension, history at large) on its head. Its gestation was arduous and frustrating. I could not have completed it without the support of my partner Anikó Takács, who tolerated incessant mumblings of obscure terms such as "folk historiography" and "vernacular landscape," alongside incoherent recitations of fragments of Irish folk poetry. The original manuscript was finished in 2002, following the birth of our daughter, Daniella, at a time when my homeland was despairingly troubled with violent conflict. This combination of circumstances poignantly brought home the significance of subjective perceptions of historical events, as pithily expressed in the traditional Irish saying "cogadh beag i bhfad ó bhaile agus páiste a bheith ag Bríd" (a small war is far from home and Bríd will have a child). By coincidence, the text was revised in the most peaceful of Dublin neighborhoods, Sandymount, sixty-six years after Richard Hayes completed there *The Last Invasion of Ireland,* a historiographical landmark from which this study has benefited immensely. Final touches were made during the bicentennial of the Rising of 1803 when, once again, historians commemorated a national hero and completely ignored the memory of the "common people" who flocked to the standard and paid the price. Prolonged delays were incurred, the manuscript languished unpublished for several years, and in the interim our sons Adam and David were born. Having left Ireland, I observed from afar with some satisfaction the emergence of remembrance as a key topic in Irish Studies. I have since redirected my attention from memory to the study of forgetting. "The road goes ever on and on."

Acknowledgments

THIS BOOK WAS written with the help of numerous people. It originated in an interdisciplinary program directed by Angela Bourke at the Faculty of Arts in UCD. The research was thoughtfully supervised by Thomas Bartlett at the Department of Modern Irish History in UCD, whose guidance was invaluable. Throughout my studies, Séamas Ó Catháin and Dáithí Ó hÓgáin of the Department of Irish Folklore at UCD offered continuous instruction. Specialization in Irish Studies also benefited from an invitation to attend the Inaugural Summer Session of the Notre Dame Keough Center's Irish Seminar on "Memory, History and Fiction: The Creation of Ireland 1500–2000," which was extended by the institution's director Kevin Whelan, who offered insightful commentary on many aspects of this study. The incisive critique of David Fitzpatrick of the Department of Modern History in TCD proved to be most helpful. If truth be told, the book would not have seen the light of day had it not received a vote of confidence from James Donnelly, Jr. of the University of Wisconsin, who gave me a shot in the arm just when I was about to throw the manuscript into the dustbin.

In addition to those named above, various aspects of work in progress were critiqued by academic experts, who generously offered advice and suggested useful references. These include Richard Aylmer (British Columbia), Avner Ben-Amos (Tel Aviv University), Dan Ben-Amos (University of Pennsylvania), Mícheál Briody (University of Helsinki), Michael Brown (TCD), Peter Burke (Emmanuel College Cambridge), Marc Caball (formerly Irish Research Council for the Humanities and Social Sciences), Peter Collins (St. Mary's University College, Belfast), Sean J. Connolly (QUB), Maura Cronin (Mary Immaculate College, Limerick), Michael Cronin (Dublin City University), Seamus Deane (University of Notre Dame), David Dickson (TCD), Tom Dunne (UCC), Anne Fogarty (UCD), Roy Foster (Hertford College, Oxford), Tom Garvin (UCD), Luke Gibbons (University of Notre Dame), John Horgan (Dublin City University), John Horne (TCD), Margaret Kelleher (NUI

Maynooth), James Kelly (St. Patrick's College, Drumcondra), Dáire Keogh (St. Patrick's College, Drumcondra), Declan Kiberd (UCD), Michael Laffan (UCD), Joep Leerssen (University of Amsterdam), Ronit Lentin (TCD), James Livesey (formerly TCD), David Lowenthal (University College, London), Ian McBride (King's College, London), Vincent Morely (UCD), William Nolan (UCD), Breandán Mac Suibhne (formerly University of Notre Dame), Breandán Ó Buachalla (University of Notre Dame), Éamonn Ó Ciardha (University of Notre Dame), Niall Ó Ciosáin (UCG), Gearoid Ó Crualaioch (UCC), Diarmaid Ó Giolláin (UCC), Cormac Ó Gráda (UCD), Eunan O'Halpin (TCD), Margaret Ó hÓgartaigh (formerly St. Patrick's College, Drumcondra), Timothy O'Neill (UCD), Garry Owens (Huron College, University of Western Ontario), Martin Sauter (Dublin City University), Paul Thompson (University of Essex), Elizabeth Tonkin (formerly QUB), Efrat Tseëlon (UCD), Fionnuala Williams (Linen Hall Library), and Christopher J. Woods (RIA). Several anonymous readers who read through the entire manuscript presented constructive commentary.

Intellectual stimulation was offered through invitations to present research seminar papers and conference lectures at prestigious forums, where embryonic arguments were tested through exposure to critical audiences. In addition to some of the above, organizers of these events included Helen Brocklehurst and the late Robert Phillips (University of Wales, Swansea), Dominic Bryan (Institute of Irish Studies, QUB), Richard Caldicott and Anne Fuchs (UCD), David Cannadine (Institute of Historical Research), Edward Coleman (UCD), Enda Delaney (QUB) and Sean Patrick O'Connell (formerly University of Ulster), Louis Cullen (TCD), Mary Daly (UCD), Dr. Phyllis Gaffney (UCD), Roddy Hegarty (Ulster Federation of Local History), Hiram Morgan (UCC), David Hopkins (formerly University of Glasgow), Catherine Kelly and Mark McCarthy (Galway-Mayo Institute of Technology), Edna Longley (formerly QUB), P. J. Mathews (St. Patrick's College, Drumcondra), Linda Connolly and Clíona Ó Gallchoir (UCC), Michael O'Neill (UCD), and Noel O'Neill (Mayo Archaeological and Historical Society).

I am also grateful for the counsel received from Kenneth Dawson (RTÉ), Theo Dorgan (formerly Poetry Ireland), Michael Garvey (formerly RTÉ), Mary Gibbons (Westport House), Louis Lentin (formerly RTÉ), Jonathan Mason (Heritage Planning and Design Services), Méadhbh Ní Chonmhidhe Pisorski (Folklore of Ireland Society), and Brian Quinn (Ireland-Israel Friendship League). A number of budding postgraduate scholars selflessly extended assistance and shared ideas; in particular Anna Bryson (TCD), Marella Buckley (Cambridge), Giulia Ceccere (UCD), Coleman Dennehy (UCD), Noreen

Giffney (UCD), Ultan Gillen (Exeter College, Oxford) Anat Inbar (Tel Aviv University), Keiko Inoue (TCD), Aki Kalliomäki (UC Santa Cruz), Owen McGee (UCD), Tadhg O'Sullivan (Trinity College, Oxford), Richard Mac Mahon (UCG), Carlo Pellizzi (University of Pisa), Ronen Steinberg (University of Chicago), Yaron Toren (St. John's College, Oxford), Joanna Susan Wydenbach (QUB), and Veronika Zangl (University of Vienna). Matthew Stout (St. Patrick's College, Drumcondra) kindly extended cartographic services and provided maps to my specifications.

The staff of the Department of Irish Folklore at UCD (currently the Delargy Centre for Irish Folklore and the National Folklore Collection) offered considerable support. Besides those already mentioned, thanks are due to Bo Almqvist, Anna Bale, Deirdre Hennigan, Críostóir Mac Cárthaigh, Bairbre Ní Fhloinn, Micheál Ó Curraoin, Tom Munnelly, and Ríonach uí Ógáin. I am particularly grateful to the head of the department for permission to consult and publish material drawn from the Irish Folklore Collections. The administrative staff of the Combined Departments of History at UCD and the School of History at TCD were always ready to lend a helping hand and thanks are due to Maeve Bradley, Catriona Ogston, Eiriol Townsend, Louise Kidney, and Jill Northridge. Work with Irish language material was rendered possible thanks to the patient tuition and dedicated guidance of Ailín Ni Chonchúir, Nóirín Ní Ghallachóir, Dónall Ó Braonáin, Dáithí Ó hÓgáin; the teachers of Bord na Gaeilge at UCD, Áras Mháirtín Uí Chadhain (An Cheathrú Rua, Conamara, Co. Galway), and Oideas Gael (Glen Cholm Cille, Co. Donegal); and, above all, the indefatigable Éamonn Ó Dónaill (formerly UCD).

My searches for source material were greatly assisted by the librarians and archivists of the National Library of Ireland, National Archives of Ireland, Trinity College Dublin (in particular the History librarian Anne Walsh), University College Dublin (in particular the Humanities librarian Maureen Cassidy), Royal Irish Academy, Roinn an Taoisigh Library, Dublin Corporation Libraries, Mayo County Library (in particular Ivar Hamrock and Austin Vaughan), Public Records Office of Northern Ireland, Belfast Central Library (in particular the Ulster and Irish Studies librarian Patricia Walker), Linen Hall Library in Belfast, Queen's University Belfast (in particular the Special Collections Librarian Deirdre Wildy), Public Records Office (currently the National Archives) at Kew Gardens in London, National Army Museum in London, Warburg Library in London, Bodleian Library in Oxford, the CARAN at the Archives Nationales in Paris, and Archives de la Guerre at the Château de Vincennes in Paris. I am in debt to Marie Boran (Special Collections librarian, UCG) for sending me material; to Michael Webb (Department of Special Collections and Western Manuscripts, Bodleian Library) for calling my attention to a manuscript source; to Philip and Anna O'Malley Dunlop of Hawthorn Lodge, Castlebar, county Mayo for showing me family papers; and to Alice Kearney and Stephen Lalor for allowing me access to files on the 1798 Bicentennial in the library of the Department of the Taoiseach.

As an exercise of engaging with "democratic history," this study refers to numerous people, some of whom are alive while others are recalled in living memory. I am indebted to each and every one of them and can only hope that those concerned (and their relatives) will not take offence at being subject to dispassionate historical inquiry and analysis. A meaningful acquaintance with the localities in question was attained with the help of many people who patiently answered my questions during repeated visits. I would particularly like to acknowledge the assistance of local historians and commemoration organizers. These include John Banks (Collooney, Co. Sligo), Jimmy Breslin (Ballinamuck, Co. Longford), Attracta Brownlee (Research Officer, Collooney), Sean Burke (Poolathomas, Erris, Co. Mayo), Tom Collins (Castlebar, Co. Mayo), John Cooney (Director of the Humbert Summer School), Betty Creegan (Ballinamuck), Gerry Cribben (Ballyhaunis, Co. Mayo), Fr. Owen Devaney (Mullahoran, Co. Cavan), Tony Donohue (Lahardane, Co. Mayo), Patricia Fitzgerald (Killala, Co. Mayo), Jude Flynn (Longford), John Garavan (Castlebar), Joe Gilmartin (Castlebar), Jimmy Gilvary (Crossmolina, Co. Mayo), Colm Harte (Longford), Brian Hoban (Castlebar), Olive Kennedy (Killala), Tom Kettrick (Castlebar), Sean Lavin (Lacken, Co. Mayo), Kenneth Lyons (Castlebar), Wendy Lyons (Collooney), Michael McEvilly (Dublin, formerly from Castlebar), Tony McGarry (Chairman of the Humbert Summer School, Killala), Terry McKenna (Ballinamuck), Cathleen MacLoughlin (Castlebar), Mary MacNamara (formerly in Ballinamuck Visitor Centre), Sean Maguire (Castlebar), Sheila Mulloy (Westport Historical Society), Jack Munnelly (Killala), Michael Murphy (Killasser, Co. Mayo), Sean Murphy (Castlebar), Clára Ní Ghiolla (currently in Belfast), Seán Ó Brádaigh (Dublin, formerly from Longford), the late Dennis [Donncha] Ó Gallachoir (Currain, Achill Island), Bríd O'hEslin (Cloone, Co. Leitrim and NUI Maynooth), Seamus Ó Mongain Sr. (Dohooma, Erris, Co. Mayo), Padraig Rehill (formerly from Ballinamuck), and Ernie Sweeney (Castlebar). Special thanks are due to Stephen Dunford (Killala, Co. Mayo), whose forthcoming book on the Year of the French will undoubtedly make a major contribution to the field. Monsignor Joseph Spelman (Collooney, Co. Sligo) kindly went out of his way to provide a photograph to replace one of my own that was damaged.

Acknowledgments

The decision to head off for Ireland was encouraged by David Katz, Zvi Razi, and David Wasserstein of Tel Aviv University. My initial stay in Dublin was facilitated thanks to the support of the ambassador of Israel Zvi Gabay and his successor Mark Sofer. At an early stage, the research benefited from a UCD Open Postgraduate Scholarship and was completed thanks to the financial support of a Government of Ireland doctoral scholarship and postdoctoral fellowship, awarded by the Irish Research Council for the Humanities and Social Sciences. I apologize to the many other individuals who helped along the way but have not been mentioned by name.

This paperback edition has benefitted from corrections suggested by Mícheál Briody, who kindly read through the original hardcover edition and identified errata. His book on the history, ideology, and methodology of the Irish Folklore Commission, published in 2007, includes detailed information and incisive analysis, which I regret was not available to me when writing this book.

Abbreviations

ADG	Archives de la Guerre, Château de Vincennes, Paris
A. Nat	Archives Nationales, Paris
AT	Antii Aarne and Stith Thompson, *The Types of the Folktale* (Helsinki, 1961)
BL	British Library
BOD	Bodleian Library, Oxford
H.C.	House of Commons Parliamentary Papers
IFC	Irish Folklore Collection, Department of Irish Folklore, UCD (renamed in 2005 the National Folklore Collection, UCD Delargy Centre for Irish Folklore): the Main Manuscript Collection (IFC) and the Schools' Manuscript Collection (IFC S); the numbers on either side of the colon in citations represent the volume and the page numbers respectively
NAI	National Archives of Ireland
N.S.	National School
NUI	National University of Ireland
NLI	National Library of Ireland
PRO HO	Public Record Office (renamed the National Archives), Home Office Files, London
PRO NI	Public Record Office of Northern Ireland
QUB	Queen's University, Belfast
RIA	Royal Irish Academy
RTÉ	Radio Telefís Éireann (Irish Radio and Television)
TCD	Trinity College Dublin (The University of Dublin)
UCC	University College Cork (NUI, Cork)
UCD	University College Dublin (NUI, Dublin)
UCG	University College Galway (NUI, Galway)

Phonetic Note

The terms *Bliain na bhFrancach* (the Year of the French) and *seanchas* (historical folklore traditions), which appear throughout the text, are pronounced phonetically as blɪ:ən na fra:ˉkəx (in approximate transliteration, "bleeyen na frankuch"), and ʃæ:nəxəs ("shanachus"), respectively. For pronunciation of Irish (Gaelic) words in Connacht dialects see Tomás de Bhaldraithe, *The Irish of Cois Fhairrge, Co. Galway: a phonetic study* (Dublin: Dublin Institute for Advanced Studies, 1945), Éamonn Mhac an Fhailigh, *The Irish of Erris, Co. Mayo: a phonemic study* (Dublin: Dublin Institute for Advanced Studies, 1968), and Mícheál Ó Siadhail, *Learning Irish* (New Haven: Yale University Press, 1995; orig. ed. Dublin, 1980), 208–17.

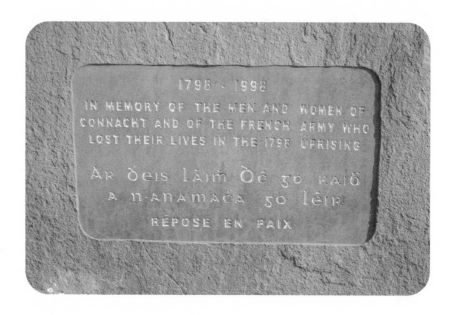

FIGURE 1. 1798 bicentennial monument in Killala, county Mayo
(unveiled 1998). The simplicity of design (a plaque on a rock), in contrast to the more imposing nationalist figures of the 1798 centenary, is
typical of bicentennial iconography. Photo by the author.

Remembering the Year of the French

Introduction

Recycling the Dustbin of History

To Speak of Ninety-Eight

The past is dead. Nothing, for good or ill, can change it;
nothing can revive it. Yet there is a sense in which the past
lives on: in works of human hands and minds, in beliefs, institutions, and values, and in us all, who are its living extension.

T. W. Moody, "Irish History and Irish Mythology"

G O WHERE YOU OUGHT TO GO, into the dustbin of history!"[1] Within a few
years, the man who said these famous words was himself airbrushed out
of official history books. The "dustbin of history" is a treasure trove that has
amassed a wealth of neglected historical wonders and curiosities waiting to be
retrieved.

The selectivity of history writing is founded on distinctions between what is
considered central and peripheral. In contemporary times, folklore has largely
been disregarded in professional historiography, yet folklore sources prove
invaluable for historical studies of popular culture and *mentalité*. Likewise,
provincial experiences, which are not always in the limelight of national history,
can challenge and even overturn the understanding of historical events and their
popular reception. By interrogating the ways by which provincial communities
narrated, interpreted, reconstructed, and commemorated their pasts, it is possible to uncover traces of vernacular historiographies and discover practices of
popular remembrance, which are distinct, though not entirely independent of
national historiography and commemoration. Such a study of traditions of
"remembrance in the village," undertaken through an exploration of folk history, can facilitate a recalibration of the burgeoning and diffused field of social
(or collective) memory studies, which may serve to refocus its contribution to
the understanding of history. Ireland, renowned for its vibrant oral traditions, is
a particularly suitable location for a case study of the relationship of folklore,
memory and history. Accordingly, this book examines how members of

communities in a region of Ireland remembered and commemorated into the mid-twentieth century an episode that took place in the late eighteenth century.

In the summer of 1798 a series of uprisings, headed ostensibly by the secret society of the United Irishmen, shook large areas of Ireland in what is currently known as the "Great Irish Rebellion of 1798." Following the suppression of large-scale insurrections in the eastern province of Leinster (particularly around county Wexford) and northeast Ulster (counties Antrim and Down), the belated arrival of a French military expedition sparked an additional rebellion in the western province of Connacht. On 22 August 1798, three French frigates (*Concorde, Médée,* and *Franchise*) commanded by Chef de Division Daniel Savary sailed into Killala Bay in northwest county Mayo. On board was a small French expeditionary force of, according to the embarkation dockets, only 1,019 soldiers (80 officers and 939 soldiers) armed with 2,520 muskets, under the command of General Jean Joseph Amable Humbert.[2] The invading troops disembarked near the village of Kilcummin, proceeded to the small diocesan town of Killala, and the following day secured the neighboring town of Ballina (23 August). Although United Irish organization was particularly underdeveloped in the area, they were joined by hundreds of Irish recruits. Within five days of landing, the French army and its Irish auxiliaries defeated a much larger government force stationed in Castlebar, the principal town of Mayo, at a battle that was to be popularized as the celebrated "Races of Castlebar" (27 August).[3] In the wake of the victory, a "Republic of Connaught" was proclaimed, emulating French satellite republics established on the Continent, and a young local radical, citizen John Moore of Moore Hall, was appointed president.

Expecting the arrival of further shipments of troops from France, the invaders waited in Castlebar for several days. When the much-needed reinforcements failed to arrive, on 4 September Humbert launched a daring military campaign, leaving behind a small garrison of about two hundred French troops backed up by Irish rebels from the locality. Initially heading north, the strategy soon developed into a desperate attempt to team up with United Irish forces reported to be mobilizing in the midlands, with the probable intention of continuing from there on to Dublin. The insurgent army marched through north county Mayo and into south county Sligo, where they engaged in a small-scale battle at Carricknagat, near the town of Collooney (5 September). They then headed eastward, crossing county Leitrim, only to be ultimately defeated in north county Longford at the village of Ballinamuck (8 September). Two weeks later, the remaining French force and rebel grouping in Killala were overwhelmed (23 September), putting an end to the attempted French invasion and the local uprising. At Ballinamuck, and again at Killala, the French surrendered and were recognized as prisoners of war, yet their Irish allies were massacred *en masse*. The insurrection was not completely over, in the following months (and years) surviving rebels maintained a type of guerrilla resistance in the more rugged areas of west Connacht, mainly in the hills of Erris and Tyrawley (northwest county Mayo) and Connemara (northwest county Galway).

Overall, the main narrative of the French invasion and the Rebellion in the West of Ireland[4] is fairly well known, though several key issues remain unstudied, and comparison between different studies of this episode reveals noticeable discrepancies. For example, the number of French troops is frequently cited inaccurately, and many accounts falsely claim that the French landed on 23 August, when they actually disembarked and entered Killala on the evening of the previous day. Such carelessness, apparent in erroneous citations of seemingly minor details, typifies dismissive treatment of topics that are relegated to "footnotes" in national historiography.[5] The extent of popular participation in

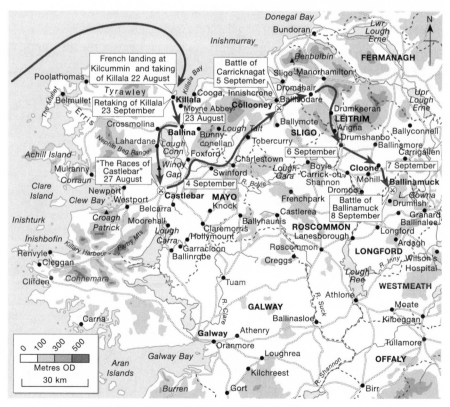

MAP 1. Franco-Irish Campaign, 1798. Courtesy of Matthew Stout.

this arena of the Rebellion is also unclear. Contemporary sources show the confusion of the authorities at the time. Writing on 31 August 1798, the senior government advisor John Beresford cautioned that

> We cannot depend upon a word we hear, little intelligence is sent up to us from the scene of the action and reports are all contradictory, some say 30,000 rebels have joined, others 10,000, others 3,000, some say not as many as a hundred, all is uncertain.

To this he added on 3 September: "We do not know, if any, or how many of the country people have joined, some say 700, some say 10,000."[6] Figures floated by different historians range from 1,000 to 10,000, a disparity that stems from crude estimates generally based on unsophisticated use of sources.[7]

Many factors discouraged mass rallying to the rebel cause, in particular the weakness of the United Irish organization in Connacht, the deterring example of the brutal suppression of the insurrections earlier that summer and the conspicuously inadequate number of French troops, as opposed to the sizeable armed forces of the Crown assembled against them. Considering these unfavorable conditions, the extent of popular Rebellion was surprisingly substantial. Moreover, the invasion triggered large-scale local risings in the Irish midlands (particularly in county Westmeath), while the suppression of the Rebellion involved massive mobilization of militia and yeomanry units, which engaged in extensive counterinsurgency measures against local civilians. Yet, although the Rebellion in the West had an impact on large populations spread across over a quarter of Ireland, Irish historiography has allocated little space to this historical episode, characteristically depicting it as a sideshow of the 1798 Rebellion, at best an anecdotal incident in the grand narrative of modern Ireland. In the words of Roy Foster, "the strange episode of the Republic of Connacht is a footnote to Irish history."[8]

The main works of professional Irish history have mostly been written from a metropolitan perspective, showing a preference for political and administrative history. In contrast, the following chapters examine how provincial communities directly affected by the French invasion remembered historical events. The discussion oscillates between the study of an actual past and interpretative representations of the past in the changing context of an ethnographic present. Teasing out the dissonance between these conceptualizations, a duality that is shared by history and memory, serves to demonstrate how social memory offers new perspectives for the study of the past. There can be no engagement in history without historiography. Historical understanding is founded on an accumulative chain of self-referential interpretative reconstructions produced by skilled practitioners. The bicentenary of 1798 spurred a "mighty wave" of academic preoccupation with the Rebellion, which a critic labeled "Ninety-Eight Studies."[9] One of the fresh features of the many new publications is a heightened historiographical awareness, perhaps best typified in an essay by Kevin Whelan on "The Politics of Memory,"[10] which the author subsequently described as a "precise calibration of the remarkably sinuous historiography of '98 after '98."[11] Yet historiographical inquiry has mostly been directed to the prominent works of notable historians, inadvertently complying with the incisive critique of the American historian Peter Novick, who noted that: "if when dealing with the outside world, historians have repudiated the 'great men theory of history,' there appears to be a residual great men theory of historiography."[12] The inevitable outcome of this elitist approach is that vernacular histories have been overlooked. The few references historians made to "folk-memory" of 1798 were mostly characterized by sweeping generalizations and seldom grounded in substantial evidence.[13]

Historians have often displayed unease toward popular traditions. The author of a study on the function of traditions in modern times noted:

> Not all nineteenth- and twentieth-century history, but a good portion of it, falsely reconstructed the traditions of the past, and thereby fundamentally misrepresented them. By this I mean that the narratives many historians related did not focus on the traditions considered essential by the people who lived within them. Rather, the historians focused on the traditions that seemed most crucial to them as historians—and in deciding what was crucial they were, of course decisively shaped by their class, social position, and intellectual training. Consequently, the details of the traditions they recounted or the continuities they described were generally only those that the historians believed were worth remembering, and too often these had little or nothing to do with the communal traditions that the people *inside* of them would have wanted to preserve.[14]

Over five days in May 1998, thirty-six leading experts offered a showcase of contemporary historiography at the official "1798 Bicentenary Conference" held in Belfast and Dublin. Remarkably, bar one noteworthy exception,[15] the presentations did not consider oral traditions.[16] The quintessential nineteenth-century ballad "The Memory of the Dead" provocatively asks: "Who fears to Speak of Ninety-Eight? Who blushes at the name?"[17] It appears that, in 1998, scholars did not "fear to speak of Ninety-Eight" and yet, as a rule, were not particularly concerned with the narratives of "common" people who had spoken about 1798 in the past. In a high-profile bicentennial television documentary, a prominent authority on the French connections of the United Irishmen brazenly announced that "the oral history of 1798 was almost nil."[18]

In striking contrast to this academic disregard, there is an extremely rich and voluminous body of available sources for the folk history of 1798, including numerous traditions that have been documented.[19] With regards to the French landing and the Rebellion in the West of Ireland, folklore accounts have been collected not only in the four counties through which the Franco-Irish army campaigned (Mayo, Sligo, Leitrim, and Longford) but also in a much wider area including the other counties of Connacht that were also deeply affected—Galway and Roscommon—and down into the bordering Munster county of Clare. Upon crossing the Shannon, the rebel army moved in to the province of Leinster, and strong memories remained of the local uprising in Westmeath. The agitation in the north midlands spread to the bordering Ulster counties of Cavan and Monaghan, and additional traditions traveled north along the western coastline to county Donegal. Folklore accounts reveal that communities throughout this large area of distribution remembered *Bliain na bhFrancach*, as it was commonly referred to in Irish-speaking communities, or the "Year of the French" (often pronounced "Frinch"), as it was known in English, as a central episode in their historical identity and a major landmark in the chronology of the relatively recent past. Historical traditions of 1798 persevered into the twentieth century and, even though by then they were no longer expressions of "living memory" proper (in terms of recollections of people that actually witnessed the events themselves), these accounts were often expressed realistically and vividly. For the people of Connacht and beyond, the Rebellion was generally considered the most significant historical event in the pre-Famine period.[20] In order to distinguish between popular and academic perceptions of 1798, the names the "Year of the French" and *Bliain na bhFrancach* are used here to signify the historical episode as it featured in provincial folk history and social memory. Similarly, the term "Ninety-Eight" is used to signify the 1798 Rebellion as an evocative category in Irish national historical consciousness, which is analogous to the kind of connotations induced by the "Forty-Five" (1745) in Scotland.

It has been acknowledged that "'1798' provides a classic example of an Irish *Lieu de Mémoire*—a site of collective memory—transmitted and transmuted through song, story, stone and commemoration."[21] Whereas southeast Leinster and northeast Ulster are recognized as battlegrounds of memory in which the legacies of Ninety-Eight have been publicly contested and subjected to overt political manipulations, by contrast, it may seem that the social memory of 1798 in the West was less exposed to politicization. This distinction is founded on the privileging of high "Politics." Yet, the social memory of the Year of the French was reshaped through social and political contestations conducted at local levels. While a multitude of traditions coexisted and also competed against each other for primacy and recognition, there were repeated attempts from the metropolitan centers to influence provincial social memory of Ninety-Eight. Moreover, "center" and "periphery" are not fixed categories. As shown in a chapter below on commemorative ceremonies, by the end of the nineteenth century, during the centennial commemorations in 1898, Connacht and in particular Mayo were considered central political arenas on account of the nationalist agrarian reform politics of the "Land War." An extraordinary example of an attempt to manipulate the memory of the Year of the French can be found in a local World War I recruitment poster that called upon the people of Connacht to "Remember how the French helped us in Killala Bay in 1798. Remember Castlebar and ask yourselves: shall we desert the French people now?"[22] This cynical use of history (considering that in 1798 Irish rebels and their French allies were engaged in a struggle against Britain) suggests that the memory of 1798 was recognized as a strong component of regional and national identity.

Pointing out the tension in Irish academic debate between a political national history and fissiparous regional histories, where social, economic, and cultural perspectives are at the fore, Whelan has argued for a dialogue between "the meta-narratives by which intellectuals structure their thoughts" and "the micro-narratives by which people understand their lives."[23] Folklore accounts, which reflect how historical events were interpreted locally, are not only apposite sources for such analysis but can also, by exhibiting indications of instances when "official" versions of history filtered into popular discourses, accommodate a history of reception. Folklorists have often strived to eliminate "contaminating" influences of literacy in order to extract vestiges of "pure" oral tradition. In contrast, historical inquiry demands consideration of the interactions between the various agencies and media through which folk history was negotiated and expressed. The study of the Year of the French offers a provincial context in which traditions can be traced over a limited time and within a limited geographical area.

The field of Irish folk history is largely unknown in historical studies. By identifying and examining some of its main features, this book offers a case study for historical use of folklore sources. Folk histories do not adhere to the criteria of professional historiography. This does not mean that they are one-dimensional or unsophisticated. As close examination clearly shows, folklore is in fact extremely complex and fluid. Each historical tradition can operate on several levels and carry various meanings in different contexts. Consequently, folk history does not lend itself readily to narration in the chronological-linear format in which academic history is generally ordered. Rather than imposing a linear timeline, which would presume to precisely chart the evolution of social memory over two centuries, a thematic approach proves be more useful for an exploration of the mechanics of remembrance. The result is a multilayered structure, which reflects to some extent the complexity of the subject matter.

Part 1 (Collecting Memory) provides a methodological background, which critically discusses the fields of oral history and social memory, and presents overviews of sources for the study Irish folk history. The field of folk history is then delineated in part 2 (Folk History), with reference to its genres of performance, practitioners, and kaleidoscopic temporal frameworks. Part 3 (Democratic History) demonstrates how folk histories facilitated democratic, though not egalitarian, engagements with the past. The largest section, part 4 (Commemorating History), explores various forms and contexts of remembrance, and devotes particular attention to the "negotiations" of social memory, which were intensified at times of high-profile public commemoration and mediated through influences of popular print and education. The conclusion (Alternative History) outlines a model for an "Archaeology of Social Memory," which suggestively proposes to turn the study of history on its head. Perhaps, the nature of oral culture could have been better represented in hypertext, allowing readers to move back and forth and pursue various threads and directions according to their own interests. For practical reasons, the kaleidoscopic world of vernacular historiography has been reluctantly committed here to the confines of a textual straitjacket. Occasional cross-references in the text indicate that it is also possible to order the sources of folk history in different patterns, according to the questions that are examined. The methodology applied in the analyses, which may appear original in an Irish context, was informed by insightful scholarship from a wide range of disciplines, spanning the humanities and social sciences. In turn, a provincial Irish experience has proved useful for identifying inadequacies in some of the prevailing paradigms on the relationship of history and memory.

Overall, the study of the remembrance of the Year of the French calls attention to the often-neglected alternative vernacular histories found outside the domains of mainstream professional historiography. These were generated by a wide range of dedicated and talented practitioners, who over time created and transmitted reconstructions of the past, collected source material, and even studied it. Such popular versions of history were anathema to the founders of the "New Irish History." Theodore William Moody, a central figure in the professionalization of Irish historiography, drew a clear line between popular and professional history, which he maintained was "a matter of facing the facts of the Irish past" in order to debunk the harmful fallacies embedded in popular "mythology."[24] Such derogatory use of the term "mythology" is ignorant of the emergence of folklore as an academic discipline that specializes in the study of myths and legends.[25] Despite the prominence of Irish folklore studies, this dichotomy continued into the debate over "Irish revisionism," with prominent historians contrasting the study of history to the "accumulation of folklore" and defining history in opposition to "mythology."[26] Consequently, "a continuous compulsion to confront myth and mythology" has been identified as "a striking characteristic of modern Irish historiography."[27] If not faux-naif, this stance exhibits a lack of critical reflexivity, and it has been noted that "many Irish historians who proudly espouse the need to attack myths are unconscious of the ideological implications of their position."[28]

Admittedly, traditions have been subjects of historical interest but their interpretation was often skewed by antagonistic perceptions, which framed them as a fictional maze of populist quasi-historical myths. Though largely unacknowledged and even berated, popular historical discourses can be of greater social and cultural significance than those proliferated by the academy. Communities throughout Ireland recalled their pasts in ways that did not passively comply with the agenda of professional historiography. Folk history is therefore a field of study in its own right and cannot be consigned to the margins of historiography. In a study of academic traditions of footnoting, Anthony Grafton commented:

> In the end, the production of footnotes sometimes resembles less the skilled work of a professional carrying out a precise function to a higher end than the offhand production and disposal of waste products. Historians however cannot afford to ignore waste products and their disposal.[29]

Indeed, the traditions recalled in folk history cannot be simply discounted as insignificant "footnotes" in the metanarratives that authoritatively claim to represent *History*.

Though the majority of the hundreds of folklore accounts in this study have long been available for inspection, with a few exceptions (most notably the work of Richard Hayes), they have not previously attracted scholarly attention. In a different context, the nineteenth-century English historian Thomas Babington Macaulay mischievously recounted a parable:

> At Lincoln Cathedral there is a beautiful painted window, which was made by an apprentice out of the pieces of glass which had been rejected by his master. It is so far superior to every other in the church, that according to tradition, the vanquished artist killed himself from mortification.[30]

Recognizing that practitioners of history are increasingly showing more willingness to engage with alternative ways of crafting the past, this study sets out to rummage in what has been undeservedly relegated to the dustbin of history in order to retrieve and explore some of the fascinating patterns of remembrance recalled in folk history.

Part 1

Collecting Memory

1

Oral History and Social Memory

All history was at first oral.

Samuel Johnson
in *Journal of a Tour of the Hebrides*

Coming to Terms With Oral History

SINCE FOLKLORE is by and large gathered through oral interviews, it follows that historical study of folklore sources requires an understanding of oral history. Though Ireland is renowned for its vibrant oral culture, surprisingly, the field of oral history has not been at the fore of Irish historical studies. A preliminary report on oral archives in Ireland compiled in 1997 concluded that "although certain positive trends are in evidence there still seems to be a reluctance to view oral archival material as essential and valuable source material."[1] Innovative oral history research takes place in Ireland, but it is often advanced through a disparate assortment of projects that are spread across a variety of disciplines and seldom attain wide recognition in mainstream historiography.[2] It is therefore worth locating the field of oral history within a broader context.

To an extent, orality is an intrinsic, though often unacknowledged, feature of most historical sources, which generally describe events in the past that were witnessed, most likely discussed, and only then documented. Therefore, textual archival sources are almost invariably products of primary oral verbalization. Historians and chroniclers from antiquity to early modern times willingly used oral sources.[3] The professionalization of the discipline of history in the nineteenth century, and in particular the influential school of historicism promoted by the adherents of the German historian Leopold von Ranke, confined the scholarly study of history to written documents found in archives and excluded oral evidence, which was delegitimized and deemed untrustworthy. One of the noticeable historiographical developments in the second half of the twentieth century has been the emergence of oral history as a distinct field. It has taken root all over the world and received recognition throughout the humanities and social sciences, although some prominent historians remain obstinate in expressing their disapproval.[4] Oral history studies distinguish between two main categories of sources: oral *history* proper, defined as recollections of contemporary events, and oral *tradition*, referring to knowledge from the past that was transmitted orally over several generations and is generally considered the collective property of a community. The academic study of each of these fields has developed separately.

Beginning in the 1920s, oral history in the first sense, that is information compiled by researchers through interviews with informants about events that took place in their lifetime, was acknowledged as an indispensable tool by social scientists and anthropologists. Around the middle of the century it was reintroduced to historical studies. A precursor of what would later develop into a new social oral history can be found in the Federal Writers' Project of the Works Progress Administration (WPA) in the United States. Funded federally between 1935 and 1939 as part of the New Deal policy to combat the Great Depression, and continued under state sponsorship until 1943, oral history interviews targeted the rural poor (also recording oral traditions of slave narratives). The collections were deposited in the U.S. National Archives but until the 1960s were largely neglected by scholars. With the increasing availability of affordable tape recorders, oral history fieldwork flourished after World War II. A noteworthy landmark in the development of oral history was the establishment of an Oral History Research Office at Columbia University in 1948 under Allan Nevins. Nevins and his protégé Louis Starr institutionalized oral history in North America, founding a specifically dedicated archive and setting standards for interviews and documentation.[5] By staking out a distinct field on the periphery of "mainstream" historiography, they directed the focus of oral history research in the 1940s and '50s toward the biography of prominent individuals associated with political and administrative history.

Under the inspiration of the socially radical Zeitgeist of the 1960s and '70s, oral history was redirected toward the study of nonliterate and historically disenfranchised communities. Grassroots activists utilized oral history projects to address socialist, feminist, ethnic, local, and other "minority" agendas, thus contributing to the rewriting of history "from below."[6] Whereas Edward

Said's postcolonial critique famously accused Western academic elites of silencing "the colonised"[7] and neo-Marxist Indian scholars, seeking to reclaim "lost voices" of oppressed groups, developed the field of "subaltern" history,[8] the study of oral history preceded these progressive trends. It spearheaded efforts to democratize history by lending an ear to the alternative histories of the vanquished and disinherited, whose experiences were often excluded from official records.[9]

As long as oral history was mainly concerned with interviewing and collecting testimonies, criticism was generally limited to questioning the eclectic tendency of such projects, which was condescendingly dismissed as a "multiplication of rubbish."[10] Since the 1980s, oral history underwent a third major shift, as researchers transcended the imperative of collecting oral testimonies and explored methods of interpretation. Oral historians consequently suggested new ways of presenting history and demanded acknowledgment, beyond their own circles, for their contributions. The qualitative progression from "oral archivists" to "oral historians" sharpened and intensified conflicts between oral history studies and dominant trends in the discipline of history. To a large extent, oral history has been professionalized, and practitioners now have handbooks at their disposal,[11] while an increasing number of third-level institutions offer training programs. Oral history plays a key role in popular history presentations, multimedia exhibitions, radio broadcasts, and most noticeably on television, where historical documentaries regularly features interviews with participants and witnesses who recall historical events. Yet publications of academic-"conventional" history have often been slower in elevating oral history to a front stage.

Distinguished from oral history, the study of oral tradition was incorporated throughout the nineteenth century into the emerging academic discipline of folklore.[12] In a historiographical survey, Peter Burke shows that the relationship between the disciplines of folklore and history has changed over time. Even though it started off harmoniously (prior to World War I), for most of the twentieth century it was characterized by suspicion, which partly abated since the 1970s but fell short of open cooperation.[13] Since the mid-twentieth century, historians have examined oral traditions in an attempt to write precolonial history outside Europe.[14] Alex Haley's reconstruction of a model microhistory of African American slavery, which was presented to the general public in his bestseller *Roots* (1976), compellingly demonstrated how oral tradition may offer access to the historical experiences of those who did not leave written records.[15] Yet reappraisals of this work exposed the sensitivity of oral tradition to the demands of its audience and external influences of the written word.[16] In 1961, with the publication of the book *De la tradition orale,* the Belgian anthropologist Jan Vansina made a major methodological contribution to the study of oral tradition, which was later developed in his seminal work *Oral Tradition as History.*

Based on the findings of his African fieldwork, Vansina demonstrated how oral sources could be examined using techniques similar to those applied to written documents, thus making oral tradition more accessible to historians.[17] This approach, however, has come under criticism. Most notably, the anthropologist Elizabeth Tonkin denounced Vansina's conceptualization of orality as a "talking book fallacy," which ignores the flux of performances. Rejecting analogies between oral accounts and written documents on the grounds that every telling is a re-creation of tradition, she suggested that multiple transmissions of oral tradition over several generations are essentially similar to multiple performances of oral history over the course of a lifetime. Hence, the standard distinction between oral history and oral tradition can be challenged.[18]

Generally speaking, it is possible to discern two schools in the study of oral history and tradition: positivist and interpretative. The positivist approach is characterized by an aspiration to identify "hard facts," which incurs reservations concerning the trustworthiness of oral sources. For the most part, oral testimonies are retrospective accounts that are recorded at a later date. The documentation is not contemporaneous to the historical event, and questions can arise pertaining to its reliability and validity.[19] To a certain extent, such issues can be addressed by checking the consistency with which individuals retell a story on different occasions and collecting, if possible, accounts from several people on one event. A well-thought-out selection of informants combined with reference to sociological data can validate the representativeness of oral history and test whether individual testimonies are indeed typical of wider social trends.[20] Paul Thompson, for example, utilized archival records to generate a sampling procedure for some five hundred interviews with men and women born between 1872 and 1906 in order to portray the various socioeconomic strata of Edwardian Britain through recollections of twelve carefully selected individuals.[21]

The American folklorist Richard M. Dorson laid out useful criteria for assessing positivist oral history: the possibility of corroborating oral testimony with other primary sources; the measure of support from mnemonic devices;[22] the presence of professional narrators; continuities in the locus of transmission (in terms of sociodemographic stability as opposed to migration); and the prevalence of individualistic versus folkloristic elements in the narrative.[23] With these considerations in mind, oral sources can be integrated into a comprehensive historical investigation, which ideally pools together all available data. From a positivist perspective, oral sources can be categorized as retrospective "memory claims," highly susceptible to bias and therefore to be treated with particular caution.[24]

On the other hand, the interpretative school of oral history calls attention to some of the unique characteristics of oral sources and their particular value for the study of mentalities.[25] Its adherents contest the viability of empirical attempts to overcome "bias" in oral testimonies. Tonkin, for instance, persuasively argued that all speakers "have to take a point of view on an event and its relation to themselves and to their interlocutors. 'Bias,' therefore, is an essential part of any communication, and is not a flaw to which oral tellers are particularly prone."[26] In a review of oral history studies, John Tosh concluded:

> oral research is less important as *histoire vérité* or as an expression of community politics than as precious evidence of how popular historical consciousness is constructed. . . . The very subjectivity of the speaker may be the most important thing about his or her testimony.[27]

In this light, oral historians have pioneered discussions on the possibilities that "subjectivity" opens for the study of history. Alessandro Portelli, for example, asserted that

> oral sources had a "different" form of reliability that lay precisely in their subjectivity. By including error, imagination, and desire, oral sources reveal not only the history of what happened, but the history of what it meant; meaning (as revealed by narrative and linguistic form) rather than "fact" is what makes oral history different, and a necessary tool for the history of subjectivity.[28]

Luisa Passerini found subjectivity to be the ground for subordination, manipulation, integration, and formation of stereotypes. Rejecting the viability of separating manifestations of objectivity and subjectivity (as the presence of these notions "divides the individual himself "), she outlined three main topics for oral history research in which "subjectivity may become object and source of scientific procedures": (1) historical influences of beliefs and myths; (2) patterns of behavior and decision making strategies (which are both individual and collective, and also conscious and unconscious); and (3) understanding social groupings (where the public-political and private-personal spheres intertwine).[29] Contrary to what may be expected, accommodation of subjectivity does not necessarily render history irrational, personal, or irregular. In practice, social patterns and mechanisms can be identified, analyzed, and compared in order to draw general conclusions.[30]

Though the positivist and interpretative approaches have been positioned in opposition to each other, they are not necessarily mutually exclusive. Oral history informs about events in the past and about how they were perceived. In turn, these two dimensions of history can be juxtaposed to offer a better understanding of the past. Thompson argued that "oral evidence, by transforming the 'objects' of study into 'subjects,' makes for a history which is not just richer, more vivid and heart rending, but *truer*."[31] Oral history, as another of its practitioners noted, can offer "a key to the narrator's perceptions of the past and thus a means for researchers to see the past through an insider's point of view."[32] This empathetic quality is grounded in human experiences, which counterbalances quantitative abstracts and generalizing categories that are often imposed by researchers.[33] Gwyn Prins credited oral history with providing the professional historian access to biographical detail, humanity, emotion, and a "well developed skepticism about the entire historiographic undertaking," thus enabling the study of the past to look beyond the historian's own culture so as to reveal "what it was like to have been there."[34]

The inherent subjectivity of oral history may therefore, somewhat surprisingly, be advantageous even for "positivist" historical enquiry. Vansina admitted that subjectivity of oral recollections is:

> part and parcel of that very past and once taken into account gives the historian's reconstruction of it a little more authenticity. It helps us to understand the past much better. So here is the paradox: the more subjective the source, the better it reflects a reality of the past!

Pace the French historian Henri-Irénée Marrou, who perceptively observed that historical accounts are the product of a ratio of subjectivities—that of the witness and that of the historian, Vansina pointed out that "oral traditions are sources of exceptional value since they convey not only the interpretation of the witnesses to an event but those of the minds who have transmitted it."[35] Paradoxically, in some ways, oral tradition may be considered more "authentic" than professional history, for it takes into account a multitude of voices from the past, which balance the centrality of the contemporary voice of the historian. This is of course a highly contentious argument considering that the historian's claim to impartial objectivity, as Peter Novick demonstrated in a North-American context, can be perceived as the "founding myth" of professionalized history and any questioning of its validity is "an enormously charged issue."[36] The usefulness of insisting on a clear-cut distinction between positivist and interpretative investigation of oral history is evidently limited, and this study deliberately integrates both approaches in its analysis of oral traditions, which are considered both as recollections of events in the past (in this case late-eighteenth-century Ireland) and as representations of the ways these recollections were subsequently narrated in local communities. Ultimately, the study of oral history and tradition cannot be confined only to the past but, like E. H. Carr's succinct definition of history, it is in effect "an unending dialogue between the present and the past."[37]

Through source criticism, oral historians developed an understanding of variability in forms of oral sources, which can be subjected to literary-"textual" and folklore analysis in order to reveal levels of discourse and hidden meanings.[38] However orality is expressed through performances, which are conditioned by narrators and audiences. Therefore, oral sources are social products, and text cannot be meaningfully separated from context.[39] By collecting testimonies from individuals, oral history may appear to privilege biographical experiences. Yet, transmission, performance, and reception ground personal accounts in a collective, community-based experience, which is often implicit in the way narrators tend to alternate unconsciously between the usage of first person singular (I) and plural (We).[40] At its best, oral history ranges between the personal uniqueness of biographical history and the representativeness of social history.[41] As noted by the folklorist and oral historian Charles Joyner, "an oral history interview is a communicative event, not comprehensible apart from the social interaction, and intimately bound with the changing values and institutions of a changing society."[42] This is clearly the case for oral tradition, which by definition is a communal discourse. Paradoxically, the study of oral history entails an unconscious shift from performance to text. The original *orality* is often lost in research, which tends to be based on transcripts of oral interviews. Ultimately the findings of oral history are published in textual-printed form. Therefore, distinctions between *oral* and written or printed sources should not be reified or overstated.[43]

From Oral History to Social Memory

Oral history, like the interpretation of oral tradition, inevitably faces the issue of the role of memory in its work

David Henige
Oral Historiography

The study of oral history—and arguably all history—is essentially the collection and analysis of memory accounts. Accordingly, oral tradition may be regarded as a compilation of "memories of memories."[44] Therefore, the study of folklore and oral tradition clearly requires an understanding of memory.

The discussion above argued that oral history, and even more so oral tradition, has a strong social dimension. Reviewing corpora of oral traditions in Africa, Vansina concluded that "the structure and social dynamics behind the corpus vary, but it is always a communal social pool of information and the memory is communal."[45] Elsewhere he stated that "to a very large extent the oral tradition is a collective thought because the mnemonic code it reveals is a collective enterprise."[46] Evidently, the type of memory referred to in the study of oral tradition is primarily a social construction. All consciousness is mediated through memory, and memory is far from being a homogenous entity. Different types of memory relate to several senses and perform diverse tasks in various capacities that are not necessarily connected. Hence, any brief analysis of memory is doomed to be partial and limited. The following discussion, which is less concerned with the neurobiological faculty of memory and the collection of mental abilities scientists attribute to it, is restricted to general observations on social memory that may serve as a theoretical background for historical analysis in subsequent chapters.

Scholarly preoccupation with issues of memory has a long history with an ancient pedigree, which can be traced through classical antiquity, the Middle Ages, the Renaissance, and the Enlightenment.[47] The scientific study of memory was launched in 1885 with the publication of an influential monograph by Hermann Ebbinghaus, which led to the endorsement of an experimental approach in psychological studies of memory phenomena.[48] For the next fifty years, research was based mainly on experiments with meaningless syllables until the British experimental psychologist Sir Frederic C. Bartlett argued that memory is an "effort after meaning" and redirected memory studies to focus on "everyday memory" in a social context. Bartlett, who was particularly interested in the oral transmission of stories, concluded that memory is not "fixed and lifeless" but constructed through processes that involve blending, condensing, omission, invention, and a tendency to reduplicate detail.[49] In his opinion, recall was similar to such constructed processes as imagination and thought (all these activities being mental exercises that transcend the constrictions of present time and space),[50] and therefore memory can be understood as a form of interpretation. Though he suggested that processes of "individual recall" may have parallels in social conventionalization, he did not find positive evidence for "group memory."[51] Deconstructing Bartlett's work through scrutiny of his main sources of influence, the anthropologist Mary Douglas later showed that the dominant paradigms in contemporary psychology limited the scope of his study of memory to individual cognitive psychology, preventing him from pursuing his initial interest in social aspects of memory.[52]

At the end of the nineteenth and early twentieth century, vigorous intellectual debates on memory spanned across disciplines, most notably Sigmund Freud's psychoanalysis, Henri Bergson's antiempiricist philosophy, and the fiction of modernist writers (such as Proust and Joyce), reflecting a perceived "memory crisis."[53] This pervasive preoccupation with memory typically focused on individual remembrance, though it was propelled by an anxiety that the survival of collective traditional knowledge was imperiled by the sweeping changes ushered in by modernity and that the emergence of mass society would perpetuate widespread forgetting. The founding father of the concept of collective memory was the French sociologist Maurice Halbwachs, who furthered ideas raised by his illustrious mentor Émile Durkheim[54] to argue against the validity of individual psychology[55] and to claim that memory is fundamentally a collective function.[56]

According to Halbwachs, the past is not preserved in recollections of individuals, but rather "it is language, and the whole system of social conventions attached to it, that allows us at every moment to construct the past." Rejecting the Freudian concept that the entire record of an individual's memory is stored in an unconscious psyche, he asserted that memory is a social construct and that members of a society constantly rearrange their recollections in accordance with variable conditions in the present. Consequently, "only those recollections subsist that in every period society, working within its present-day frameworks, can reconstruct."[57] However, he did not see a homogenous collective memory playing a uniform role in society. Allowing for diversity, he asserted that there are as many collective memories as there are groups and institutions in a society, specifically identifying collective memory in the contexts of family, religion and class.[58] Halbwachs even insisted that all memory is collective, insofar as individual recollections are structured by group identities and conditioned by social consciousness,[59] so that "no memory is possible outside frameworks used by people living in society to determine and retrieve their recollections."[60]

The sociological study of collective memory pioneered by Durkheim and Halbwachs was complemented by the work of the social anthropologist Edwards Evans-Prichard[61] and the social-behaviorist George Herbert Mead,[62] both of whom contributed to the study of collective thought with reference to the past. More recently, social scientists have argued that memory cannot be accounted for by reference to mental processes alone, but must be understood in the wider contexts of ideology, social action, culture, and the everyday pragmatics of communication.[63] Contemporary research in the humanities has also enhanced the understanding of memory with contributions from various disciplines showing memory to be a multiauthored, both textual (in terms of generating narrative) and contextual, function.[64]

The writings of Halbwachs on collective memory inspired his colleague, the eminent historian Marc Bloch.[65] Both Halbwachs and Bloch perished at the hands of the Nazis in World War II,[66] and the historical study of memory appears to have been dormant in immediate postwar historiography. Following a prolonged lull, in the 1980s historical interest in collective memory reemerged and rapidly developed since into a burgeoning interdisciplinary field.[67] National commemoration, and in particular monumental commemoration of wars, has attracted considerable attention in contemporary studies of collective memory.[68] In particular, the legacy of World War I stirred critical debates on remembrance of the dead.[69] Similarly, the traumatic experiences of World War II, and more specifically scholarly recognition of the imperative to preserve recollections of Holocaust survivors, also contributed to renewed interest in collective memory.[70] More recently, Holocaust scholarship has begun studying "second generation memory" (i.e., children of survivors) and introduced the term *postmemory*, which is "distinguished from memory by generational distance" and "characterizes the experience of those who grew up dominated by narratives that preceded their birth."[71] The usefulness of this term in the context of this study, as opposed to oral tradition or social memory, is questionable.

New research shows discomfort with vacuous definitions of *collective memory*, which has been critically labeled a "term in search of a meaning,"[72] and several alternative terms have been proposed in its stead. The search for a more appropriate substitution is not merely an issue of semantic nuances but is indicative of conceptual differences. In the early 1980s a group of scholars in the Centre for Contemporary Cultural Studies in Birmingham developed the term *popular memory* to advance a neo-Marxist model of two sets of dialectic relations between "popular" and "dominant" memory, and between "public" and "private" memories.[73] A complementary study chose to use the term *public memory* to signify the "battleground" where hegemonic and dominant social group memories confront subordinate and oppositional group memories[74] and similarly a study of commemoration in twentieth century United States located *public memory* at the contested "intersection of official and vernacular cultural expressions."[75] Paul Connerton wrote an innovative monograph outlining practices by which *societies remember*, while David Middleton and Derek Edwards edited a collection of essays on *collective remembering*. These studies shifted the emphasis from examination of a supposedly static entity of "memory" to the dynamic processes that produce, convey, sustain, and reconstruct collective memory.[76] Elizabeth Tonkin suggested replacing the term *collective memory* with *social memory*, so as to accommodate inequalities and changing affiliations while acknowledging the role of socializing processes.[77] Striking a balance between the social dimensions of an individual's life and individual consciousness (which was largely neglected by Durkheim and Halbwachs), a critical study by the anthropologist James Fentress and the historian Chris Wickham also endorsed the term *social memory*. Moreover, the rejection of "collective" also served to disassociate their work from a Jungian notion of "collective unconscious."[78]

Another term currently in vogue is *cultural memory*.[79] A concept of collective-cultural memory was already put forward in the 1920s by the art historian Aby Warburg, who considered art works as visual expressions of memory that facilitate the transmission of symbols and motifs over time.[80] Academic discourse that adopted this term is often typified by conceptual vagueness. It has proved instrumental in identifying representations of the past as a critical category in interdisciplinary cultural studies, yet the term has frequently been employed ahistorically, with analyses focusing on texts and often ignoring the sociohistorical contexts of cultural production and reception.[81] The folklorist Dan Ben-Amos noted that the prevalence of expressions of memory in popular culture and everyday life "calls for a shift in the perception of collective memory from the monumental to the mundane."[82] The German Egyptologist and cultural critic Jan Assman argued that before cultural memory is codified in its fixed form, it is initially generated in casual, primarily oral, social interaction, which he labeled *communicative memory*.[83]

The surge of interest in group remembrance, expressed through such divergent terms as collective, popular, public, social, cultural, and communicative memory, triggered disapproving reactions. Critics objected to what they perceived as misleading anthropomorphic and metaphorical conceptualizations, pointing out that memory is fundamentally an individual psychobiological function. This argument was phrased forcefully by Amos Funkelstein: "just as a nation cannot eat or dance, neither can it speak or remember. Remembering is a mental act, and therefore it is absolutely and completely personal."[84] However, orthodox reliance on a supposedly objective conception of memory as a faculty of an "isolated brain," and therefore an exclusively individual experience, has been contested by social psychology. Combining psychoanalysis with sociology, Jeffery Prager argued that an individual's recollection is dependent on social and cultural contexts, with memory "actively symbolizing the self's relation to its own body and its social world." [85] Elsewhere, a discourse-analysis approach concluded that remembering was an "organized social action," primarily constructed (and not merely reproduced) through conversations.[86]

Such definitions of individual memory are amenable to conceptions of social memory.

Considering the array of available terminology and the arguments that have been put forward by contributors to the debate, this study of memory and Irish history prefers the term *social memory* when referring to representations of traditional bodies of knowledge, and *social remembering* (or simply *remembrance*) in reference to dynamic processes of reproduction. The broader scope implied in the term *social* reflects the intention to go beyond the standard use of *collective memory*, which has tended to limit itself to political history of national "mythologies." Although it may be unfeasible to pinpoint social memory as referring to a single clearly defined subject, nonetheless it is possible to positively identify expressions of social memory and moments of social remembering in action. Individual recollections are normally shared through social interaction, creating discourses of social memory, which in themselves function as reflexive agents that influence individual memories. Peter Burke pertinently commented:

> If we use terms like "social memory" we do risk reifying concepts. On the other hand, if we refuse to use such a term, we are in danger of failing to notice the different ways in which the ideas of individuals are influenced by the groups to which they belong.[87]

Without binding the term to a restrictive definition, social remembrance can be roughly described as a process by which members of a community negotiate the identity of the society with which they are affiliated in relation to its past; the "past," in social-cultural terms, being a selective collection of interpretative constructions based on both authentic and fabricated sources.

Social memory is collective insofar as it is neither the exclusive property nor the faculty of one individual, but commonly shared by a community. It is a discursive reconstruction of the past performed and promulgated by multiple agents and relating to numerous participants. Members of a society draw and contribute to a communal body of cultural knowledge relating to the past. An attempt to understand social remembering involves questions of multiple authorship, as different people construct and influence social memory, and also concerns issues of multiple receptions, as there are conceivably at least as many interpretations of social memory as there are group members. Social memory is an organic and dynamic synthesis rather than an eclectic compilation. It does not merely reflect the total sum of individual memories in a community at any given time, but is grounded in a set of frames of reference by which individuals can locate and reinterpret their own recollections. As a metaconstruct, social memory assumes collective characteristics, which may come in conflict with individual memories. At the same time, it is in itself a heterogeneous battleground, subject to struggles and contestations. Since social memory is extremely complex and multifaceted, generic reference to the term cannot be definitive or precise. Moreover, the fluid nature of social memory, which is apparent as perceptions of the past change over time, defies static atemporal examination. For these reasons it is probably best to speak of "social," rather than "collective," locating remembrance within processes that are intrinsic to the normal functions of a society. Before proceeding to examine a case study of social memory in modern Irish history, the relationship between this concept and the wider discipline of history needs to be clarified.

Mnemohistory and Mythistory: Synthesizing History and Social Memory

> Our memory truly rests not on learned history but on lived history.
>
> Maurice Halbwachs
> *The Collective Memory*

Both history and memory appear to be primarily preoccupied with the past, yet in practice their fundamental concern is the relationship between past and present. Generally speaking, it is possible to discern two scholarly approaches to the study of collective memory, which have been labeled by the cultural sociologist Barry Schwartz "cultural revision" and "cultural continuity."[88] The school of cultural revision, subscribed to by the likes of Maurice Halbwachs, George Herbert Mead, and David Lowenthal, advocates that events from the past are remembered solely in the context of the present, i.e., the beliefs, interests, aspirations, and fears of the here and now.[89] On the other hand, upholders of cultural continuity maintain that each generation preserves and passes on traditions from the past. To quote, for example, Vansina: "Traditions in memory are only distinguished from other more recent information by the conviction that they stemmed from previous generations, just as memory itself is only distinguished from other information by the conviction that the item is remembered, not dreamt or fantasized. The convictions can on occasion be erroneous, but by and large they hold up well."[90]

In a way, the debate on the essential nature of social memory echoes the controversy outlined above between interpretative and positivist approaches to oral tradition, which is also founded on divergence of present-centered versus past-centered approaches to the study of narratives on the past. Though seemingly incompatible, both arguments on the nature of memory are valid to an extent. Just as history is based on dynamics of continuity and change, which are not necessarily mutually exclusive, it is most rewarding to consider social memory in dialectical terms involving both continuity and reconstruction.

Communal traditions practically transform a society into a "community of memory," constituted partly by recalling a shared past.[91] In this way, the past influences the present just as much as the present reconstructs the past. Throughout this book, "folklore" and "folk history" are treated as vernacular discourses and sets of traditional practices associated with local and regional "communities of memory." These have been recognized by folklorists as representative of widely shared communal knowledge and attitudes, and so are not merely narratives generated by individuals that concern only an immediate personal-family social circle. By and large, they are worthy of consideration as representations of social memory, while accounts recited by maverick storytellers, which are unrepresentative of more vocal-mainstream traditions, may express recalcitrant traditions that reflect alternative memories. In subsequent chapters, numerous examples demonstrate that although such folklore accounts are essentially expressions of historical consciousness, which was subject to renegotiations of social memory and transformed over time, they can also contribute toward a better understanding of events in the past.

Commenting on the current boom in historical studies of memory, the American historian Kerwin Lee Klein remarked that "memory can come to the fore in an age of historiographic crisis precisely because it figures as a therapeutic alternative to historical discourse."[92] Influential studies of memory and history have typically insisted on a division between the two fields. Halbwachs, whose concept of history was strongly influenced by Auguste Comte's positivism,[93] contrasted self-conscious "historical memory," defined in positivist terms as a "record of events," with spontaneous "collective memory," defined as a "depository of tradition," arguing that the two were diametrically opposed.[94] The French historian Jacques Le Goff accepted this irreconcilable opposition, adding that memory is subservient to history: "just as the past is not history but the object of history, so memory is not history, but one of its objects and an elementary level of its argument."[95] Pierre Nora furthered this argument maintaining that history is inherently in conflict with memory since "at the heart of history is a criticism destructive of spontaneous memory. Memory is always suspect in the eyes of history, whose true mission is to demolish it, to repress it." According to Nora, from the end of the nineteenth century, history has consummated its divorce from memory and entered a "historiographic age," characterized by an ongoing attempt to influence collective memory, so that "every major revision of historical method has been intended to broaden the base of collective memory." Accordingly, the innovative historiographical school *Les Lieux de Mémoire,* associated with Nora, maintains that history is now irrevocably separated from memory.[96]

The usefulness and validity of this stringent differentiation is questionable. Suggestively, in ancient Greek tradition, Mnemosyne, the goddess of wisdom and memory, was the mother of Clio, the muse of history. It may be enlightening to think of history as symbolically, and perhaps even practically, originating from memory. Though such an assumption raises the question of when, and how, does memory become history? Edwin Ardener argued that "structural oppositions are built into history as it happens. There are, indeed, plenty of grounds for saying that 'memory' of history begins when it is registered. It is encoded 'structurally.'"[97] Rather than opposed, history and memory can be perceived as structurally linked from the outset and therefore virtually inseparable. Tonkin denounced Nora's concept of memory as reductionist, observing that it does not properly allow for repeated revisions of memory that occur when representations of the past are reinterpreted in oral transmission, and also that it deceptively depicts memory (*pace* Halbwachs) as entirely unconscious.[98] The historian Raphael Samuel presented memory as "dialectically related to historical thought, rather than being some kind of negative other to it."[99] He asserted that reciprocal relations exist between "popular memory" and written history, so that memory is not simply dominated by history.

Jan Assman (whose studies on the memory of ancient Egypt offer a long historical perspective) maintained that "memory and history are different but inextricably related," describing them as "poles of the same range of activities." He introduced the term *mnemohistory* for investigations of "the history of cultural memory," which are concerned with "the past as it is remembered."[100] Such examinations of social memory pose problems that suggest a need to rethink the study of the past. To begin with, they indicate that history, like memory, invariably involves a subtle subtext of anachronism, as the past is remembered, portrayed, and interpreted from a contemporary point of view. Awareness of the often-transparent imposition of anachronistic perspectives on the past requires critical vigilance in order to distinguish its influences. Another issue worthy of consideration is the subjective selectivity inherent in the definition of memory (*pace* F. C. Bartlett) as an interpretative construction (rather than a library or archive of retrievable information). Selectivity is of course an inevitable feature of all forms of representation, and like the study of history, memory cannot attempt to retain all knowledge from the past. This apparently self-evident truism calls attention to the important realization that memory necessarily involves forgetting. In fact, as put succinctly by David Lowenthal, "for memory to have meaning we must forget most of what we have seen."[101] This point is wittily illustrated in the story "Funes, the Memorious" by the celebrated Latin American author Jorge Luis Borges, who concluded that "to think is to forget a difference, to generalize, to abstract."[102]

It follows that any comprehensive examination of memory cannot restrict itself to what has been preserved from the past but must also be aware, to some extent, of forgotten information, which can sometimes be traced by identifying silences and pauses in sources that conceal omissions.[103] Researchers of social memory face the challenge of explaining why certain information was remembered and other information forgotten. Loss of memory can occur as an unconscious process, but it may also be the outcome of intentional acts of censorship and suppression. Further investigation, however, may uncover "countermemories" that persistently recall supposedly erased memories. Observing that both the past and the present can be desegregated into numerous, often conflicting components, the Irish historian Ian McBride astutely remarked that "although remembrance is always selective, the selections depend upon a complex interaction between the materials available and the dominant modes of political and social organisation."[104] Selectivity cannot be simply taken as given and needs to be historicized.

Another problematic issue for the researcher in search of reliable information on the past is the apparent inaccuracy of memory. Yet psychological research has shown that careful analysis can qualify levels of accuracy in recollected testimonies, although one must be weary of rhetorical devices that supposedly assert competence and truthfulness of memory.[105] Distortion of historical events in memory does not originate in a singular event, but is a dynamic process, changing over time. It follows that an evaluation of accuracy in memory requires a historical dimension that charts the collected data on a time axis. Inaccuracy also has an important social dimension. Tracing developments through which social memory was preserved or reshaped can accentuate the changing historical circumstances that exercised social constraints on memory. Consequently, once identified, occurrences of consistency or of change shed light on the social, cultural, and often political contexts, which facilitate usages and manipulations of the past.

Appreciation of social memory also suggests a need for a radical reassessment of chronology in order to accommodate subjective perceptions of time. Just as Salvador Dali's surreal painting *The Persistence of Memory* (1931) symbolically portrays melting clocks, memory does not appear to conform to the linear-chronological paradigm of historical time and therefore challenges standard historical periodization. Halbwachs's work on collective memory influenced Fernand Braudel, a prominent member of the *Annales* historiographical school, who proposed substituting standardized homogeneity of historical time with awareness to the different *durées* by which historical change can be perceived.[106] Though Braudel suggested that different time spans are required for the evaluation of historical events, he remained faithful to a linear concept of the progression of time. However, as Bill Schwarz pointed out, "memory undoubtedly, disrupts any uni-directional movement from past to present to future."[107] In an essay on time and history, Siegfried Kracauer challenged historians with a concept of time inspired by Marcel Proust's celebrated literary exploration of memory in *À la recherche du temps perdu* (*Remembrance of Things Past*), which in turn was influenced by the writings of his cousin by marriage, the philosopher Henri Bergson, on the subjectivity of memory and time.[108] Contemplating the perplexities of time as perceived in memory, Kracauer provocatively proposed replacing chronological delineations of historical processes with a model of kaleidoscopic changes.[109] Acknowledging the influence of Proust, Nora's innovative historiographical project *Les Lieux de Mémoire* rejected "linear temporality" and advocated a history based on multiple kinds of time as experienced "at the levels where the individual takes root in the social and collective."[110]

Oral tradition and folk history reflect a synthesis between memory and history that constitutes a *mythistory*,[111] which defies the viability of a dichotomy between "myth" and "fact." The juxtaposition of history with social memory allows historians to take into account views and opinions founded on recollections that reflect both real and imagined perceptions, which helped determine historical events. Undoubtedly, this is a tricky undertaking. A cautionary observation made by a pioneering scholar of Jewish memory, Yosef Hayim Yerushalmi, is pertinent: "memory is always problematic, usually deceptive, sometimes treacherous."[112] By examining social memory expressed in oral traditions and folk histories of the Year of the French, the following chapters present a case study that discusses the practicalities of the theoretical issues raised in this chapter and demonstrates some of the possibilities and insights that a "mnemohistory" of Irish "mythistory" may offer.[113] Before delving into such a study, there is a need to review the available sources and consider the precepts and circumstances through which they were compiled in order to identify particular strengths, weaknesses and prejudices.

2

Irish Folklore Collections

In our own day folk tradition has ceased to be a living force;
it survives only if it is fossilised in some form of permanent
record.

Kevin Danaher
"History and Oral Tradition"

Institutionalizing the Collecting of Irish Folklore

THE STUDY OF FOLKLORE in Ireland and its use as a historical source has a long history that dates at least as far back as *Foras Feasa ar Éirinn*, the monumental work of seventeenth-century Gaelic historiography written by Geoffery Keating ([Seathrún Céitinn], ca. 1570–ca. 1644), who referred to "béaloideas na sean"—oral instruction of the ancients—as a primary source.[1] Antiquarians in the late eighteenth and early nineteenth century, who were renowned for their study of old Irish manuscripts, were also fascinated with oral traditions.[2] Their ethnographic work paved the way for early-nineteenth-century Anglo-Irish writers who enthusiastically collected oral traditions, which they presented in a literary form to the general public,[3] an endeavor that was advanced from the mid- to late nineteenth century by a new generation of distinguished writers.[4] In the north of Ireland, Edward Bunting (1773–1843) began collecting traditional Irish music at the end of the eighteenth century and continued this preoccupation well into the following century,[5] when other notable music collectors, such as George Petrie (1789–1866), continued this task.[6] From the mid-nineteenth century, a group of northern antiquarians mostly based in Belfast showed a keen interest in oral traditions as valuable sources for historical information and found the *Ulster Journal of Archaeology* as a platform for their work, with a first series (1853–62) edited by the pioneering folklore collector Robert S. McAdam ([Roibeárd McÁdhaimh], 1809–95).[7] By the end of the nineteenth century, Irish folklore scholarship had established a distinguished pedigree.

The eminent scholar and cultural revivalist, Douglas Hyde (1860–1949) was largely responsible for advancing folklore work in Ireland from an amateur pursuit of devoted individuals to a recognized academic study.[8] His collection of tales *Beside the Fire* (1890) is recognized as the first anthology of Irish folklore to identify the names and localities of the storytellers and reliably reproduce their speech.[9] Hyde was the first president of the Irish language revival organization the Gaelic League (founded 1893), whose members were enthusiastic collectors of folklore in Irish, though their professed agenda was driven by a programmatic initiative to preserve living language resources rather than historical interest. In the beginning of the twentieth century, Irish folklore achieved wide international acclaim after highly esteemed scholars visited the Blasket Islands off the west coast of county Kerry, noting oral traditions in Irish,[10] while also encouraging talented storytellers to commit autobiographical accounts to writing.[11] Though folklorists primarily collected oral traditions as literary artifacts, without necessarily acknowledging their historical value, numerous historical traditions were nonetheless documented and made available for future scholarship.

The central figure in institutionalizing Irish folklore as a professional field of study was James Hamilton Delargy ([Séamus Ó Duilearga], 1899–1980), a native of Cushendall, county Antrim. Appointed in 1923 as assistant to Douglas Hyde, who was then

FIGURE 2. James Hamilton Delargy ([Séamus Ó Duilearga], photographed by the Welsh Folk Museum). As the Honorary Director of the Irish Folklore Commission, Delargy sought recognition for the historical and cultural value of "the lore of the people, the traditional oral teaching to which each generation has added its share, all that rich treasure of song and story, of saga and legend, of wisdom and nonsense, which we inherit from a remote past" (*Béaloideas*, 1932). Courtesy of the Department of Irish Folklore, University College Dublin.

professor of Modern Irish at University College Dublin (UCD), he went on to study with several renowned Scandinavian folklorists, most notably, Carl Wilhelm von Sydow of the University of Lund. Delargy was involved in founding the Folklore Society of Ireland [An Cumann le Béaloideas Éireann] in 1926 and served as the editor of the society's journal *Béaloideas* for the next forty-five years. In 1930 he was appointed director of the state-sponsored Irish Folklore Institute [Institiúid Bhéaloideas Éireann], which was replaced five years later by the Irish Folklore Commission [Coimisiún Béaloideasa Éireann]. He held a post in Irish folklore at UCD (as a statutory lecturer from 1934 and a professor from 1947).[12] Following Delargy's retirement (1970), a Department of Irish Folklore was established in UCD. It hosts the Irish Folklore Collection (IFC), which was founded on the legacy of the Irish Folklore Commission (1935–70).[13] In the sheer volume of source material, the broad scope of issues covered, and the high quality of preserved documentation, it is among the finest archival collections of oral tradition in the world. Although the holdings are evidently an invaluable resource for social and cultural historical research, they have hitherto been underutilized in the study of modern Irish history. As of yet no comprehensive history has been written of the work of the commission, and so there is a need to briefly outline how the sources of its archive were compiled and thus identify its key strengths and weaknesses from an historian's point of view.[14]

Across Europe, the emerging field of folklore was predisposed toward notions of romantic-nationalism and strongly influenced by the writings of the late-eighteenth-century philosopher Johann Gottfried von Herder (1744–1803), who attributed great importance to folklore.[15] Mary Helen Thuente argued that in Ireland "folklore was central to the evolution of cultural nationalism during the nineteenth century when nationalists tried to reflect as well as to create the oral traditions of the people."[16] By the turn of the nineteenth century and early twentieth century, a dominant branch of Irish folklore studies was closely affiliated with nationalism, an association exemplified in the career of Douglas Hyde, who went on to become an Irish Free State Senator (1925–26), and following constitutional change in 1937, was elected first president of Ireland (1938–45).[17] From the outset, academic folklore scholarship and the Irish Folklore Commission were inextricably linked to UCD, an academic institution that originated in the Catholic University (established by the hierarchy in 1854 under the rectorship of Cardinal John Henry Newman), which was renamed University College (1882) and later reconstituted as part of the National University of Ireland (1908). In its formative years, the college, sometimes inadvertently, fostered Catholic nationalism,[18] and served as an intellectual powerhouse for the nationalist movement, with many staff and alumni going on to become prominent figures in the struggle for independence.[19]

Folklore has often been used to advance the nationalist claims of ethnic communities,[20] and in the newly independent Ireland folklore was recognized as a cultural resource for national identity. In particular, the rhetoric of Eamon de Valera (1882–1975), the long-serving prime minister (1932–48, 1951–54 and 1957–59) and later president (1959–73), was imbued with explicit folkloristic references.[21] This was conspicuously evident in the radio broadcast of his famous 1943 St. Patrick's Day speech, which referred to images of peasantry in a land "whose firesides would be the forums of wisdom of serene old age."[22] Reference to firesides and old age (also used in contemporary radio broadcasts by the British Prime Minister Stanley Baldwin and American president Franklin Roosevelt) carried evocative folkloric associations.[23] The Irish Folklore Commission was founded with the support of de Valera's government, which symbolically allocated an annual budget of one hundred Irish pounds for each of the thirty-two counties in the greater Ireland. State support, however, was not limited to de Valera's Fianna Fáil party.

The commission's precursor, the Irish Folklore Institute, was originally sponsored by W. T. Cosgrave's Cumann na nGaedheal government (1930), and despite political changes the commission benefited from continuous state support, with postwar increases in public funding resulting in a significant budget raise allocated by the Fine Gael-led coalition government of J. A. Costello (1950). Folklore collecting was endorsed across the board and identified as a national concern, often associated with Irish-language policy. After prolonged delays, by 1966 the commission's staff members were recognized as professional civil servants, receiving increments, severance pay, and pension rights from the state.[24]

In a contemporary European context, the introduction of a state-supported national folklore project in the 1930s has alarming connotations. Under the Nazi regime, German folklore scholarship (*Volkskunde*), which was influential throughout Europe, fell prey to race theorists who found folkloristic notions of nationalism, primitivism, and the idealization of peasantry to be particularly appealing for their base ideology.[25] The repercussions of this "betrayal of the intellectuals," to use a term coined by a French critic,[26] were apparent in other countries under Fascist rule, such as Italy and Vichy France. Fortunately, Irish folklore scholarship did not follow such a perverted direction. Moreover, as Delargy aptly pointed out, "folklore is both national and international."[27] Studies of Irish folklore have characteristically steered away from national insularity by exploring connections with folklore of other countries, in particular with

FIGURE 3. Seán Ó Súilleabháin, Carl Wilhelm von Sydow, and Caoimhín Ó Danachair
(1949). An advocate of comparative folklore, Professor von Sydow of the University
of Lund (*center*), encouraged the development of folklore studies in Ireland, inspiring
Delargy and other key figures, such as the Irish Folklore Commission's archivist Seán
Ó Súilleabháin (*left*) and full-time ethnographer Caoimhín Ó Danachair ([Kevin Danaher],
right). Courtesy of the Department of Irish Folklore, University College Dublin.

European regions that have shared common experiences in the past, whether
Celtic, Scandinavian, and albeit more reluctantly, English traditions.[28]

While Delargy served as Honorary Director, other principal members of
the Irish Folklore Commission's original staff included the archivist Seán
Ó Súilleabháin, ethnographer Caoimhín Ó Danachair [Kevin Danaher], and
secretary and administrative manager Máire MacNeill. Fieldwork was undertaken by designated "collectors," who were either employed full-time, part-
time, or contracted for specific projects. Charged with documenting oral narratives and "folk-life" practices, they were provided with notebooks and, when
possible, were equipped with wax-coated cylinder phonographs known as Ediphones.[29] Once the information was transcribed, the cylinders were reused and
consequently the original sound recordings were lost. Following the introduction of rural electrification and the growing availability of portable battery-
powered tape recorders, from the early 1960s the technology available to collectors was progressively upgraded and since then, all magnetic audio and video

recordings (and more recently digital minidisk and MP3) have been preserved in the IFC archive. In contrast to the image of early Irish folklorists, who mostly hailed from a metropolitan elite, the commission's collectors were considered "insiders," familiar with local customs and dialect. It was believed that "people had confidence in them and willingly shared what they knew with them."[30] Yet, it is also probable that storytelling performances were influenced by the exceptional circumstance of a visit by a representative of a state agency who was entrusted with a mission of national importance and was evidently perceived as a figure who commanded authority and prestige.

Initial instruction manuals offered collectors only cursory guidance,[31] but from 1942 they could consult Seán Ó Súilleabháin's *A Handbook of Irish Folklore*, which was the instrumental text in standardizing folklore collecting in Ireland. The *Handbook* set rigorous standards for precise documentation of oral traditions:

> Even very small or seemingly trivial items or information should be recorded. . . .
> Record the information in the exact words of the speaker, if possible. . . .

FIGURE 4. Collecting folklore, photographed by Kevin Danaher (1948). Though ediphones provided verbatim transcripts, certain collectors (such as Tadhg Ó Murchú, shown recording Paddy Óg Liath Ó Súilleabháin in county Kerry) preferred handwritten documentation of historical traditions. Courtesy of the Department of Irish Folklore, University College Dublin.

The collector should state clearly (either on a slip affixed at the head of each item or else as a note at the end) the name, age, and full address of the person from whom he recorded the information. It is most important that the source of information be given correctly.[32]

Ó Súilleabháin had studied the classification of folklore at the Landsmaalsarkiv [Dialect and Folklore Archive] in the University of Uppsala in Sweden, under the direction of well-known folklorists (such as Åke Campbell and Fröken Ella Odsedt), and the *Handbook*, which follows the "Uppsala System," includes a chapter specifically dedicated to "Historical Tradition" (chapter 11). The *Handbook* encouraged the collecting of local history, and Ó Súilleabháin later noted that "a large body of information of this kind has now been written, and it remains for future researchers to assess the historical and social value of what has been recorded."[33] Yet there was distinct preference for legendary hero tales (such as those relating to the Ulster and Fenian mythological cycles) and only an approximate 9 percent of the vast material collected was recognized as "Historical Tradition" (i.e., stories about historical episodes), adding up in 1970 to about 16,500 accounts out of a total 180,000.[34] However, other folklore sources often include indirect references of historical value. Overall, by the time the commission was disbanded (1970), its "Main Manuscript Collection" held 1,746 volumes (of 200–600 typically A4-size pages each), of which 102 volumes had been collected before 1935 by the Irish Folklore Institute and the Folklore of Ireland Society. Continuing to grow, the collection currently holds over 2,300 manuscript volumes. The writings of the collectors are supplemented by acquired collections of private papers and replies to questionnaires issued by the commission.[35] These occasionally incorporate historical subjects—most notably the celebrated 1945 questionnaire on "The Great Famine of 1847,"[36] which has been consulted in several studies on the memory of the Famine.[37] In addition, diaries of full-time collectors provide illuminating commentary on the context and conditions of their fieldwork.[38]

Delargy, who described himself as "the eleventh hour chronicler of an older world,"[39] impressed on his colleagues and staff the need to preserve Irish traditions on the verge of their disappearance. Consequently the imperative of collecting and cataloging folklore was often upheld at the expense of research and publication.[40] Folklore has generally been construed as a study of a vanishing subject, which salvages last traces of a passing world. This characteristic mourning for the passing of traditional society, which an American folklorist aptly labeled "Poetics of Disappearance,"[41] echoes a familiar sentiment expressed already by one of the founders of social anthropology Bronislaw Malinowski.[42] It is a trope that masks the complicity of ethnographers, who often inadvertently introduce influences of "modernity" while purporting to objectively observe "traditional" life.[43]

The nebulous concept of the final hour of "authentic" folklore already underlies the work of early-nineteenth-century Irish folklore collectors. Toward the middle of the century, writing on the "Habits and Characters of the Peasantry," the patriotic poet and writer Thomas Osborne Davis (1814–45) noted that the popular practices of his time "are vanishing into history, and unless this generation paints them no other will know what they were." Unwittingly he also demonstrated the inability of a contemporary observer to accurately identify what traditions will decline, as some of the examples he cited to illustrate his argument (such as Orange Lodges) continued to survive.[44] The conviction that folk traditions were passing away was expressed more forcefully in the aftermath of the Great Famine. The novelist William Carleton wrote in 1854:

> The old armorial bearings of society which were empanelled upon the ancient manners of our country, now hang like tattered escutcheons over the tombs of customs and usages which sleep beneath them; and, unless rescued from the obliterating hand of time, scarcely a vestige of them will be left even to tradition itself.[45]

A hundred years later, Irish folklorists looked back at Carleton's period as one of vibrancy and voiced in similar terms their concerns of the transience of tradition in their time.[46]

In the preface of a collection of folklore published in 1852, the surgeon and antiquarian William Robert Wills Wilde candidly admitted that "Nothing contributes more to uproot superstitious rites and forms than to print them."[47] In modern times, the ethnographer James Clifford has argued that written description may have destructive repercussions for a culture's oral life.[48] The work of the Irish Folklore Commission had its contemporary critics. The poet and novelist Patrick Kavanagh (1909–67) argued that efforts should be directed toward cultivating the transmission of traditional knowledge as a living culture rather than documenting it. Reacting to congratulatory newspaper coverage of the volume of folklore collected in a project run by the commission (described as "weighing over 20 tons"),[49] he acerbically remarked that "one phrase on the lips of an old woman is better than a ton of collected stuff" and cautioned "tell it [to the collector] and it dies."[50] The novelist Máirtín Ó Cadhain (1906–70), himself an independent collector of oral tradition, insisted that Irish folklore could only be fully appreciated when located in the sociopolitical context of *Gaeltacht* (native Irish-speaking areas) culture.[51] Nonetheless, the Irish Folklore Commission deserves recognition for its extensive documentation of community-shared oral traditions at a time when popular culture in rural Ireland was rapidly changing through exposure to processes of modernization.[52]

The compilation of the IFC archive was a product of its time and embodied ideological premises that influenced the nature of the collected folklore material. Even though the *Handbook* instructs collectors to "make no 'corrections' or changes" to oral accounts,[53] the clear and confident handwriting in most IFC manuscripts (which in itself follows an instruction to "write as neatly and legibly as possible") suggests that the interviews were indeed carefully transcribed. There is a possibility that this process may have entailed subtle, perhaps unconscious, mechanisms of editing and even censorship, as the collectors, who were inevitably affected by the highly charged political and social climate of the newly independent Irish state, were aware that they were contributing to a national project.

In accordance with contemporary trends in European folklore scholarship, the Irish Folklore Commission focused on traditions associated with what was considered the indigenous-peasant population. Though this was folklore's raison d'être, it excluded traditions of groups that did not appear to correspond with an overly romantic notion of "folk." Corresponding to a wider postcolonial pattern, characteristic of newly liberated countries that promoted the cultural heritage of the dominant emancipated population and rejected traditions associated with previous hegemonies,[54] oral traditions of Protestant minorities and of populations that had been loyal to the Crown—though undeniably an integral part of Irish history—were not subject to extensive documentation and study. At a time when the southern Irish Protestant and unionist community suffered from decline,[55] and its authors struggled for appropriate recognition in the culturally hostile environment of the newly independent Ireland,[56] it was believed that views associated with the "Ascendancy" were extensively covered in standard archives and in prolific Anglo-Irish literature. Championing demotic classes, the IFC aimed to preserve the voices of dispossessed populations, which were excluded from the cultural canons of literate elites. However, even though it offers a unique record of the traditions and practices of predominantly Catholic communities in rural Ireland, its subaltern nature need not be overstated. As a whole, the popular culture represented by folklore was indeed distinct and expressed an alternative worldview, but it was also permeated with the influences of official and unofficial interactions with metropolitan culture.[57]

At the time of its inception, the academic study of Irish folklore was strongly associated with the study of the Irish language and from the outset favored material in Irish. Although Delargy cautioned against exclusion of folklore in English[58] and the *Handbook* specifically advised collectors of the need to document folklore in English-speaking areas,[59] the overwhelming majority of the accounts collected are in Irish, amounting in 1970 to roughly 80 percent of the Main Manuscript Collection. The collectors' fieldwork spanned all thirty-two counties of Ireland but focused primarily on *Gaeltacht* areas, privileging "Gaelic" over "Anglicized" traditions. Collected less rigorously, Irish folklore in English from outside the *Gaeltacht* received less scholarly attention.[60] This reflected a larger cultural bias, founded on a policy of affirmative action that addressed several needs. It prioritized areas that were most exposed to the cultural change, as the number of native Irish speakers was in decline, and the *Gaeltacht* areas were rapidly diminishing. It recognized the value of vernacular "oral literature" and of customs preserved and cultivated in the Irish language. It also provided ample sources for cultural-revivalist doctrines, whose manifesto was defined in Hyde's inaugural lecture as president of the National Literary Society (25 November 1892) as "The Necessity for De-Anglicising Ireland,"[61] an ideal championed by the likes of the journalist D. P. Moran (1871–1936), the historian and politician Eoin MacNeill (1867–1945), and the writer and literary critic Daniel Corkery (1878–1964).[62]

The focus on Irish-speaking areas did not accommodate the sociolinguistic process of language shift, whereby from the late eighteenth century English rapidly replaced Irish as the primary vernacular,[63] though inadvertent echoes of language change can be found in the collected folklore.[64] The "Census of Ireland for the year 1851" registered only 4.9 percent of the total population of Ireland as monoglot Irish speakers and noted that 23.3 percent of the population could speak Irish; these figures were significantly higher in the province of Connacht, with 13.6 percent monoglots and 50.8 percent Irish speakers.[65] There is reason to suspect, however, that this was an understatement and that many Irish speakers refrained at the time from declaring to the authorities their competency in the language, as the contemporary antiquarian-folklorist Robert McAdam observed, "either from a false shame, or from a secret dread that the Government, in making this inquiry (for the first time), had some concealed motive, which could only be for their good."[66] Subsequent census surveys, conducted every decade, trace the continuous decline over the second half of the nineteenth century. By 1936, at the time the Irish Folklore Commission was launched, the percentage of people in Ireland over three years of age who could speak Irish had partly recovered and was registered as 23.7 percent, but in Connacht it had decreased to 36.7 percent, of which only 35.8 percent resided in *Gaeltacht* areas.[67]

While urban folklore was duly acknowledged in the instructions for the collectors, partiality was delicately expressed toward collecting in rural areas.[68] This lacuna was only addressed later through the Urban Folklore Project in Dublin (1980–81),[69] and the ongoing North City Folklore Project in Dublin (running since the early 1990s)[70] and Northside Folklore Project in Cork (established in 1996).[71] Although the Irish economy (excluding Belfast and its hinterland) did not undergo an industrial revolution on a similar scale to mainland Britain, nonetheless, from the late eighteenth century, sweeping socioeconomic changes and developments took place,[72] effectively transforming Irish popular culture.[73] Modern infrastructures penetrated even remote areas through the spread of railroads, telegraphs, provincial press, banking, and retail networks. By disregarding such historical processes of modernization and cultural discontinuity, folklore studies tended to portray a static image of a supposedly timeless "peasant" culture. The Harvard Irish Social Anthropology Survey, carried out by Conrad Maynadier Arensberg (1910–97) and Solon Toothaker Kimball (1909–82) in County Clare in 1932–34, located contemporary Irish society in a transitional phase between tradition and modernity, and commented on "the paradox of seeming timelessness and unceasing change."[74]

The somewhat illusory image of stability upheld by folklorists was partially sustained by overlooking the full impact of the major demographic trends of emigration and migration throughout modern Irish history. Official returns for numbers of emigrants from each county (available from 1852) show that emigration was acute in the West of Ireland from the mid-nineteenth century onward.[75] By the mid-twentieth century, at the very time when the Irish Folklore Commission's work was under way, the western and northwestern counties (from which the bulk of the folklore of the Year of the French was collected) were particularly affected by emigration.[76] Contrary to the working assumptions of contemporary ethnographic studies, folklore and social memory was primarily attached to people, rather than places. Moreover, traditions associated with certain places often traveled and complicated the task of folklore collecting. To take an example relevant to this study, there is ample evidence that traditions relating to the 1798 Rebellion "migrated" abroad, though they have not been collected systematically. Writing his memoirs at the end of the nineteenth century, the veteran Fenian Jeremiah O'Donovan Rossa (1831–1915) recalled meeting in New York an elderly man named Thomas Crimmins, who had personally known United Irishmen who had emigrated there and who would tell stories "regarding the men of '98."[77] A great loss in this respect is the continuing absence of a comprehensive folklore collection project in the Irish diasporas, an endeavor that could complement the project of the Irish Folklore Commission and perhaps even identify reflexive influences, since letters from abroad and stories told by returning emigrants conceivably influenced local traditions in Ireland.[78]

Continuous high rates of emigration among young adults in conjunction with customary delayed farm inheritance, which deferred succession to a late age, resulted in a disproportionately elderly population throughout rural Ireland. In 1946 it was estimated that the average age of farmers was fifty-five and that about one fifth of all farmers were over sixty-five.[79] Commenting that "the country people live long and die often very old indeed," Arensberg and Kimball noticed that old men commanded considerable authority within rural communities and that they would regularly gather among themselves and engage in storytelling.[80] Folklore collectors showed a distinct preference in approaching elderly informants. The figures for this study show that an overwhelming majority of those interviewed on traditions of Ninety-Eight in the West were over the age of sixty (88 percent in the Main Manuscript Collection and 77 percent in the Schools' Manuscript Collection), though ages of informants are often approximate.[81] Historically, in "so-called traditional societies," old people were recognized as custodians of collective memory.[82] Like other projects of recording oral history and oral tradition, Irish folklore collectors generally assumed that older people in the community were less exposed to influences of modernity and offered better access to "authentic" traditional knowledge. The old age of many of the informants raises questions concerning the condition of their memory, though clinical research on the decline of memory abilities with advancing age shows a large degree of variability, and discrepancies in the existing literature defy conclusive verdicts on this issue.[83] Occasionally, collectors provided comments on the mental condition of aged informants, but it is plausible that in some cases lucidity was overstated.

For the study of modern history, longevity may give the impression of bridging between generations and bringing the oral historian closer to the original event. This can be demonstrated through examples relating to folklore of Ninety-Eight. Less than one hundred and fifty years passed between the events of the French invasion and the bulk of the folklore collecting undertaken in the 1930s. There are records from some sixty years before the Irish Folklore Commission was established of individuals who could still recall the events of 1798 in Connacht from first hand experience. In 1876 it was reported that an allegedly 114-year-old man from near Westport in county Mayo (Michael O'Malley of Slogger) "recollects the history of his life vividly, and relates many of the incidents in connection with the rebellion of '98."[84] As late as 1902, the death of allegedly 113-year-old Eibhlín Ní Aodhagáin was reported, noting that she "had a good memory of the time the French came to Killala, and when they were on the road to Ballinamuck to give battle, herself and nine or ten other girls slipped away from the village in order to see the soldiers."[85]

By the early twentieth century actual eyewitnesses were no longer alive, and recollections of the 1798 Rebellion had been transmitted as family traditions over two or three generations. In 1927 a local newspaper reported the death of 106-year-old Michael Hughes of Bofeenaun, county Mayo, who was reputedly the oldest man in Ireland at the time. Both his grandfather (who had died at the age of 108) and also his father were known to have "seen the French journeying through the Windy Gap to the attack on Castlebar in 1798 and subsequently witnessed the arrest and execution of the patriot priest, Father Conroy."[86] Numerous elderly people who were interviewed in the 1930s could recall hearing accounts of the events from their grandparents who had participated in the Rebellion, and as late as the 1950s Dan Sheridan of Corrinagh, county Longford (three kilometers from Ballinamuck), who lived to the age of 113, recounted stories of how his father could remember hearing as a boy the roar of cannon fire and the sight of French soldiers in 1798.[87]

In 1933 the collector Pádraig Mac Gréine interviewed Patrick Gill ("Grey Pat"), approximately ninety-five years old, of Edenmore, a townland near Ballinamuck in county Longford. Gill recounted stories he had heard of the battle of Ballinamuck from his grandmother (a Cassidy of Fardromin), who had been there alongside his grandfather (Michael Gill) and granduncle (the celebrated local hero Robin Gill). Mac Gréine described him as "a tall, spare, well-built old man, looking twenty years younger than he really is" and noted that: "Pat is a very intelligent old man and can read and write. His memory is good, but as he said himself: 'There's times when I'm in better humour than others.'"[88] At the time when this book was written, the indefatigable Pádraig Mac Gréine (b. 1900), who joined the Irish Folklore Commission the year it was founded (1935) and has been aptly described

FIGURE 5. Pádraig Mac Gréine, photographed by Bairbre Ní Fhloinn (1995). When presenting a seminar paper at the Department of Irish Folklore in UCD, the distinguished ninety-eight-year-old collector Mac Gréine (b. 1900) vividly recalled collecting traditions of the Year of the French in 1933 from ninety-five-year-old Patrick Gill of Edenmore, who had heard firsthand accounts of the Battle of Ballinamuck from his grandmother. Courtesy of the Department of Irish Folklore, University College Dublin.

as "an authority on the folklore and traditions of the County Longford,"[89] had himself passed the ripe old age of one hundred. When presenting a seminar paper at the Department of Irish Folklore at UCD in 1998, he could clearly recall his meetings with Patrick Gill sixty-five years earlier.[90] In the absence of authoritative documentation, stated figures for old age are not necessarily reliable. They were frequently based on estimations and, in some circumstances, may even stem from fraudulent attempts to claim entitlements for old age pensions in the early twentieth century.[91] Nonetheless, through reference to longevity, historical traditions profess a direct link to the past. By covering the life spans of just two or three individuals, aged storytellers appear to bridge between the present generation and the recollections of those who had actually experienced events in the late eighteenth century, thus adding a sense of relevance and immediacy to history.

The commission collectors were instructed to inquire of their informants the source of information and to note down where the tradition had been acquired. This annotation moves the time and location of the performance from the first half of twentieth century (when the folklore was collected) to the second half of the nineteenth century (when the tradition was allegedly first heard). Since reference to years and age is imprecise, it is unfeasible to calculate the exact date when an account was originally told. Transmission cannot be traced with accuracy as oral narratives have changed over time and, through multiple performances, folk history was repeatedly reconstructed. Furthermore, source information was often not provided. Less than half of the accounts examined here from the IFC Main Manuscript Collection include references to the original source from whence the account had reputedly derived, among them one-third referred generically to "the old people" (*na seandaoine*) of the locality. This is a familiar formula that calls attention to the communal nature of oral tradition, while on the other hand it is also a cliché that masks subtle mechanisms of legitimization and appropriation of social memory, which endorsed specific accounts told by certain individuals.

The use of the term "the old people" presumed to imply communication of folklore through "traditional," largely illiterate, and therefore primarily oral social interaction. This connotation is misleading, as influences of popular print were widespread in popular culture.[92] Throughout the second half of the nineteenth century, illiteracy was progressively on the wane, even in Connacht, which had the highest rate of illiteracy in Ireland.[93] A casual observation made by the nationalist writer A. M. Sullivan (1830–84) is particularly illuminating: "There is now scarcely a farmhouse or working man's home in all the land in which the boy or girl of fifteen, or the young man or woman of twenty-five, cannot read the newspaper for 'the old people.'"[94] Accordingly, any idealization of "the old people" as the last remaining conveyors of "pure" oral culture needs to be questioned.

It has been shown that, in the nineteenth century, "collecting the tales and legends of Ireland was the pursuit of men, while women featured only rarely as their informants" and this prejudice was continued by the Irish Folklore Commission, which unconsciously sustained a patriarchal attitude that relegated women to gender specific roles.[95] Consequently, the volume and range of material collected from women was relatively limited. The folklorist Fionnula Nic Suibhne claimed that

> not more than one-eighth of the thousands of part-time collectors who contributed material to the commission were women, and no woman was employed as a full-time collector. With male collectors outnumbering female ones, it is not surprising to find that only one-sixth, or 6,000, of the 40,000 informants were female, and that the material compromising the archive reflects a particularly male perspective.[96]

This issue is discussed in depth in relation to 1798 folklore in chapter 10. Thus, the ratios of male/female collectors and informants of sources in the IFC Main Manuscript Collection used in this study support Nic Suibhne's argument and demonstrate the overwhelming male dominance in folklore collecting.

Overall, the limitations of the IFC do not invalidate its value as an archive of oral tradition. The folklorist Diarmuid Ó Giolláin perceptively observed that "the positivistic élan behind most folklore collection has, in many ways, benefited research. Free of overtly theoretical constructs (though based on theoretical premises), new analysis can depart from the same rich data on which old analysis was based."[97]

The Main Manuscript Collection and Bliain na bhFrancach

Scholars can now study in depth oral traditions and folk history in Connacht and the north midlands thanks to the dedicated collectors who worked in the region, both in full-time[98] and part-time[99] capacities. The vast amount of historical folklore they documented and compiled includes numerous references to *Bliain na bhFrancach*—the Year of the French. Moreover, executive members of the Irish Folklore Commission also engaged in collecting folklore. A notable example can be found in the commission's founding member Seán Mac Giollarnáth (1880–1970), whose grandfather (Seán Mór Mac Giollarnáth from Carrafareen, county Galway) had witnessed in 1798 (at the age of twelve) local

FIGURE 6. Michael Corduff, photographed by James Hamilton Delargy (ca. 1939). An outstanding part-time collector, Corduff (d. 1962) repeatedly encountered local traditions of *Bliain na bhFrancach* in his home area of Erris in northwest county Mayo. Courtesy of the Department of Irish Folklore, University College Dublin.

men heading to Mayo to join the French.[100] Mac Giollarnáth, a republican revolutionary who had taken part in the struggle for independence and a former
editor of the Gaelic League's organ *An Claidheamh Soluis* (1909–16), began
collecting folklore independently at a young age and joined the Folklore of Ireland Society in 1926, shortly after its foundation. As district justice for Galway
(1925–50), he traveled around Connemara collecting oral traditions that were
subsequently published in several books, one of which includes a chapter on
traditions of *Bliain na bhFrancach*.[101]

The collectors received limited guidance for this particular task. The chapter on "Historical Tradition" in their *Handbook* includes a concise section on
"The Rebellion of 1798":

> Was your district actively connected with this rebellion? In what way? Tradi-
> tions about the men who fought should be sought along the following lines: local
> leaders; strength of the fighting men; equipment (detailed accounts of pikes,
> guns, and other weapons); preparations for the struggle; detailed accounts of
> fights, battles, sieges; smaller encounters and incidents; individual heroism;
> shootings, burnings, and other atrocities (pitchcaps, picketing, half-hanging);
> fate of captured men (death by hanging, shooting, transportation); fugitives;
> end of the rising. Detailed accounts of the activities of Croppies, Yeomen, Fen-

FIGURE 7. James Delaney (*right*), photographed by Leo Corduff (1956). James G.
Delaney (1916–2000), who worked as a full-time collector from 1954 to 1986, collected
numerous traditions of the Year of the French in county Longford. Courtesy of the
Department of Irish Folklore, University College Dublin.

cibles, Militia, Redcoats, and other bodies during the campaign. Parts played by the people and priests in struggle. Stories about individual leaders . . . Songs and ballads about the rising.[102]

Of fifteen "individual leaders" mentioned by name, three relate to 1798 in the West, including a senior British commander (Lake), the French commander-in-chief (Humbert), and an Irish rebel commander (Blake). Overall, these instructions set a predetermined agenda, privileging "traditions about the men who fought," while overlooking other people affected by the Rebellion. Although the list may appear to be comprehensive, in practice certain assumptions did not comply with the way Ninety-Eight was remembered in local folklore. For example, upon instructing collectors to inquire of the fate of captured men it was implied that all prisoners were subjected to corporal punishment ("death by hanging, shooting, transportation"). However, the historical reality was more complex. A proclamation issued by Lord Lieutenant Cornwallis following the defeat of the rebels at Ballinamuck promised "His Majesty's Pardon to any man who joined the Enemy, providing he surrenders himself to any of His Majesty's Justices of Peace, or to any of His Majesty's officers and delivers a French firelock and providing he has not served in any higher capacity that that of private."[103] Such writs of pardon were popularly named "Cornies" in recognition of Cornwallis's liberal conciliatory policy.[104] In some cases rebel officers, who could not benefit from this amnesty, succeeded in escaping. This was reflected in folklore accounts, which include numerous narratives of escape and refer to death sentences that were stayed,[105] although several traditions also tell of rebels who were executed by vindictive loyalists with a "reprieve in sight."[106]

The *Handbook*'s passage on 1798 is preceded by a separate entry on "Foreign expeditions to Ireland," which explicitly encouraged collectors to document local traditions referring to the French arrival in Killala, alongside other contemporary French expeditions to Bantry Bay (December 1796) and Lough Swilly (October 1798). Folklore collectors were asked to bear in mind several key issues:

Which year was referred to as *Bliain na bhFrancach*? How did the people receive the French soldiers? Write down traditional accounts of the expectation and arrival of the various expeditions; appearance of the ships and soldiers; the landing of the troops; marches; fights and battles in which they were engaged; accounts of individual incidents; end of the campaign. . . . Did any of the French soldiers settle down to live in Ireland? Do their descendants still flourish? Give names. Songs and ballads about these expeditions.

It was assumed that "accounts will be most readily forthcoming in the districts directly affected by the expeditions or in adjoining ones, and enquiry in those areas should be as detailed and as full as possible." Yet, in reality, relevant folklore was not confined to the route of the French army and it was also recalled how rebels traveled from afar to join the French and how later outlaws fled to remote areas. In the years following the Rebellion, people traveled away from their homes, taking their recollections and traditions with them. Furthermore, since folklore is migratory by nature, stories traveled outside of their place of origin. Aware of these pitfalls, the *Handbook* alerted collectors that "stray traditions about these events are, however, to be obtained in other districts also."[107]

In total, the IFC Main Manuscript Collection hosts about one hundred separate folklore accounts that refer to the Year of the French. Approximately three-quarters of the relevant sources were collected in counties Galway and Mayo, with further significant contributions collected in Leitrim, Longford, Sligo, and Roscommon, and additional folklore collected in the Ulster counties

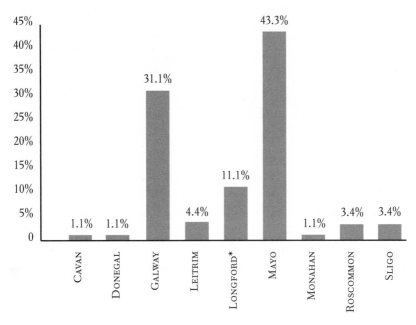

CHART 1. Locations where 1798 traditions were collected (by county). IFC Main Manuscript Collection.

Note. These figures are based on ninety separate folklore sources and do not include other relevant traditions collected in counties Cork, Waterford, and Wexford.

* The sources from Longford were all collected by the folklore collector James Delaney and these statistics do not include the numerous additional traditions documented in volume IFC 1858 (collected by Maureen O'Rourke in the mid-1960s).

of Cavan, Monaghan, and Donegal, and even farther afield (see chart 1). In addition, an entire volume of relevant material (IFC 1858) was collected in the mid-1960s by the American folklore student Maureen O'Rourke of the University of Indiana, now Professor Maureen Murphy of Hofstra University. O'Rourke interviewed locals in her family's ancestral area of Ballinamuck, county Longford, and numerous references to 1798 can be found in the 123 typed pages of her transcripts.[108] More than half of the sources from the Main Manuscript Collection are in Irish (56 percent), and most of these accounts are from counties Mayo and Galway.[109] The overwhelming majority of the sources were documented by male collectors (nearly 90 percent). O'Rourke's outstanding work is also exceptional insofar as she was one of only seven women who collected folklore on 1798 in Connacht and Longford. Most of the informants were male (ca. 80 percent), and similarly, most of the interviewees who identified a specific source for the tradition cited a male as the original informant (ca. 80 percent) (see chart 2).

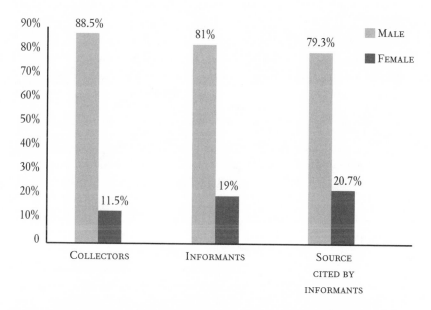

CHART 2. Gender (collectors, informants, cited sources). IFC Main MSS Collection.

Note. These figures are based on eighty-eight accounts of which eighty-four informants are identified, while only twenty-nine informants cited their source of information.

The Schools' Manuscript Collection
and the Year of the French

In 1934 a largely unsuccessful attempt was made to collect folklore in schools. The following year, with the foundation of the Irish Folklore Commission, efforts were made to resuscitate this initiative through cooperation with the Department of Education [An Roinn Oideachais] and the Irish National Teachers' Organisation (INTO). To this effect, Delargy presented a paper at the INTO Congress in Dublin on 23 February 1935, which was widely publicized in the national press[110] and in local papers.[111] The overwhelmingly enthusiastic response of teachers nationwide resulted in the immensely successful Schools' Scheme of 1937–38, which involved fifth and sixth form pupils (ages 11–14) from some 5,000 participating national primary schools and ultimately produced the Schools' Manuscript Collection [Bailiúchán na Scol] in the IFC archive.[112]

For guidance, Seán Ó Súilleabháin penned *Irish Folklore and Tradition* (which appeared in Irish as *Béaloideas Éireann*), a concise manual issued in 1937 by the Department of Education and distributed to principals and teachers in national schools. As a general working assumption, it noted:

> The children should remember that very little is known about the traditions of their district and they should record everything which throws a light on these traditions. It does not matter for the carrying out of this scheme whether similar traditions have been written down already. Even if it is believed that certain people have recorded them before, the only safe standpoint for teachers and pupils to take is to proceed as if nothing has been recorded in the district, and to remember that if they do not record the material it will die and be forgotten as if it had never been.

The instructions required that, at the end of each "composition," the collector (pupil) and informant (storyteller) should be identified.[113] Blank copybooks were sent out to participating schools. A circular on "Collection and Preservation of Folklore and Oral Traditions" (CMT 9/37), issued by the Department of Education to principals and teachers of national schools, distinguished between the original copybooks, where the pupils wrote their compositions, and designated notebooks ("Manuscript Books"). To avoid repetition, selected material from the copybooks was to be transcribed into the school's official notebook. A following circular (CMT 17/38) required that all collected material—including both copybooks and notebooks—should be sent to the Department of Education and then forwarded to the Irish Folklore Commission.[114] The success of the 1937–38 Schools' Scheme can be measured in the enthusiastic response, which yielded by March 1939 an impressive return of 4,575 notebooks (drawing on an estimated 40,000 copybooks).[115]

Within its territorial remit of the twenty-six counties of independent Ireland, the Schools' Manuscript Collection covers areas that were untouched by the collectors of the Irish Folklore Commission. The archival organization of the collection allows for examination of folklore from specific schools and parishes. Contributions vary from school to school, with the quality depending on individual pupils and teacher supervision. The preservation of original copybooks alongside the manuscript volumes enables critical evaluation of the selective compilation process, which can uncover information excluded from the official notebooks and reveal circumstances when teachers edited original compositions. At least in relation to Ninety-Eight folklore, comparison between manuscript volumes and the original copybook versions reveals, for the most part, only minor alterations of style and wording, which are either the result of corrections marked by the teacher or an outcome of omissions that occurred when the pupil copied the text. It therefore appears that the extent of editing by teachers was limited. On the other hand, examination of copybooks reveals that there was extensive selection of submissions. Numerous relevant sources did not make the cut, possibly because they repeated information already covered by other pupils or because they were considered to be of inferior quality. In addition, pupil attendance in the national school system was overwhelmingly Catholic (96.3 percent),[116] and since participating pupils principally collected folklore from family members, there was a pronounced partiality toward traditions of Catholics.

Assessing the value of the Schools' Scheme, Ó Súilleabháin subsequently noted that

> it covered all areas in the Republic, which the full-time or part-time collectors could never hope to do; it brought the parents and neighbours close to the school-work; it gave the children an interest in their own districts and the lore to be found in them; and it provided future research workers with a large body of lore (varying, naturally, in quality) which could not have been amassed in any other way.[117]

The IFC Schools' Manuscript Collection proves to be a repository of oral traditions that is indispensable for any local study of folk history.

Of the fifty-five separate topics in the guidebook for the Schools' Scheme, one section was dedicated specifically to "Historical Tradition" and informed pupils that "your district has been connected in some way with one movement or another in Irish history." While it noted that historical traditions may relate to "an account of a battle," 1798 was not mentioned.[118] Other sections that indirectly encouraged the collection of Ninety-Eight folklore referred to Local Heroes, Local Happenings, Local Monuments, Emblems and Objects of Value, The Old Graveyards, and The Local Forge. In total, approximately twice as many accounts relating to the Year of the French (the English rather than the Irish name was generally preferred in submissions to the Schools' Scheme) appear in the bound volumes of the IFC Schools' Manuscript Collection in comparison to the Main Manuscript Collection. More than two hundred sources from official notebooks are examined in this study, in addition to numerous other sources in the original pupil copybooks. Although they were not specifi- cally prompted to focus on this topic, the eagerness teachers and pupils dis- played in collecting numerous traditions of 1798 in the West demonstrates the pervasiveness of this historical episode in social memory. The Schools' Scheme facilitated systematic folklore collecting all along the route of the Franco-Irish rebel army and beyond, covering localities that had not been exhaustively mined by the commission's collectors. In fact, in some of these localities folk- lore had hitherto never been collected.

Even before the Schools' Scheme, many teachers were drawn toward col- lecting and studying folklore. Seán Ó Súilleabháin (b. 1903) was originally a primary schoolteacher and so were some of the outstanding collectors of the Irish Folklore Commission, such as the afore-mentioned Pádraig Mac Gréine of Ballinalee, county Longford, or Pádraig Ó Mórain of Callowbrack, New- port, county Mayo (b. 1886). The Schools' Scheme opened the way for further involvement in folklore fieldwork. Some six hundred primary teachers, who expressed special interest in folklore, were identified as correspondents and local liaisons for questionnaires intermittently issued by the commission.[119] Several teachers were also local folk historians in their own right and had engaged in independent-spontaneous study of folklore. The Schools' Scheme acknowledged their work and provided a larger framework in which it could be incorporated. They not only presided over folklore collecting undertaken by their pupils but included also in the submitted notebooks of their schools accounts of oral traditions that they had personally collected, sometimes more than two decades earlier. Schoolteachers around Ballinamuck were particularly motivated in collecting Ninety-Eight folklore.

A considerable body of folklore on the Year of the French was collected in counties Mayo, Leitrim, and Longford (see chart 3), with a noticeable concen- tration in the area of Ballinamuck. Just under a fifth of the sources were col- lected in the immediate vicinity of the village (18 percent), while more than half of all the accounts (65 percent) were collected in the general area of Ballina- muck (including adjacent areas in counties Longford, Leitrim, Westmeath,

Cavan, and Roscommon). This concentration corresponds with the findings of the contemporary historian and collector of 1798 traditions Richard Hayes (whose work is discussed in chapter 3). Around that time, Hayes also commented on the particular wealth of historical traditions in the north midlands, noting "in Ballinamuck and its neighbourhood I heard more stories of local events in 1798 than in any other part of my travels, and most of them were from descendants of insurgents who joined Humbert."[120] The reasons why the area of Ballinamuck generated so many traditions of Ninety-Eight in comparison to other areas that were also deeply affected by the French invasion and the Rebellion poses a puzzle. Although the number of people from the area who joined the rebel army on the eve of its impending defeat would have been limited, the wholesale massacres of Irish insurgents following the French surrender at Ballinamuck together with the reign of terror inflicted on the locality in the aftermath of the Rebellion evidently left a strong impression on local social memory. Additional relevant historical traditions were collected in areas on the periphery of the Franco-Irish expedition, including counties Cavan, Clare, Donegal, Galway, Roscommon, and Westmeath.

Unlike folklore of 1798 documented by the collectors of the Irish Folklore Commission, the traditions collected for the Schools' Scheme were almost entirely in the English language (less than 2 percent was submitted in Irish). Another salient difference is the better-maintained gender balance of the young collectors, which shows an advantage of girls over boys. Females collected 58 percent of the relevant sources, though this ratio is moderated when taking into consideration that there were slightly more girl than boy pupils in the participating classes (see chapter 10). Nonetheless, the interviewed storytellers were primarily male (see chart 4). In accordance with the Folklore Commission's reverence for the venerable, pupils were instructed, to approach their grandparents and other respectable elderly people in the community, and in most cases they appear to have followed this guideline. Yet, the substantial figure of almost a quarter of the informants aged under sixty (23 percent) suggests that quite often parents and people of younger age were interviewed.

Assigning the task of collecting folklore to pupils did not always result in independent fieldwork. As can be expected, in some cases, individual pupils did not actually do the work themselves but rather copied accounts from others. More significantly, the original copybooks of the Schools' Scheme note the exact dates when compositions were written. This information reveals that in many cases entire classes wrote compositions on oral traditions of the local 1798 experience on certain dates, most probably following specific assignments issued by teachers. As this historical episode was of particular interest to those teachers in Connacht and the north midlands who wanted to instill in their pupils a pride in local heritage, in some schools every pupil was required to collect folklore on the Year of the French. It is possible to identify recurring themes and motifs in the written accounts and to notice, in comparison, unique contributions that stand out from the general patterns. As classroom influence can often be detected in repetitive accounts, the Schools' Manuscript Collection has particular value for the study of reception of history lessons, a point discussed and demonstrated in chapter 15 in a section on historical consciousness and education. On the whole, the quantity and the quality of regional Ninety-

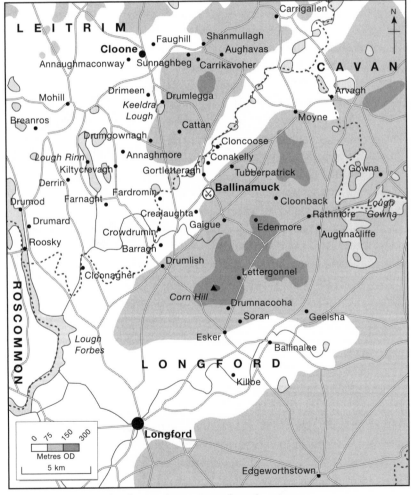

MAP 2. Greater Area of Ballinamuck. Courtesy of Matthew Stout.

Eight traditions collected by pupils for the Schools' Scheme are remarkably high. Spurred on by committed teachers, it appears that the young collectors were motivated by genuine interest as they undertook a systematic documentation of folklore in their communities, uncovering numerous recollections of the Rebellion that were maintained through oral traditions.

Writing in relation to the Great Famine, Cathal Póirtéir observed that the major obstacle preventing the use of folklore sources by historians has been the absence of an "acceptable methodology."[121] Reviewing Famine scholarship, the novelist Colm Tóibín reiterated this point and commented that although the IFC archive is undoubtedly "an invaluable treasure trove," it can "be anything you want it to be."[122] This book sets out to address the prevalent confusion and demonstrate how folklore sources can be used in the study of modern history. Oral traditions have been classified and cataloged in ways that are not necessarily ideal for historical research. The Main Manuscript Collection is indexed by collectors, informants, districts, and also by subjects, which generally follow the chapter headings of Ó Súilleabháin's *Handbook*. An interim catalog covers

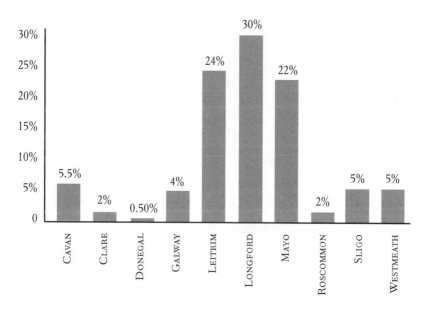

CHART 3. Locations where 1798 traditions were collected (by county). IFC S.

Note. These figures are based on 218 traditions found in the main volumes of the Schools' Manuscript Collection and do not reflect additional sources in the pupils' original copybooks.

the Schools' Manuscript Collection, but the original copybooks remain un-indexed. Much of the IFC holdings remain uncataloged. The historian Niall Ó Ciosáin suggested a preliminary typology for a multilayered study of Famine narratives in the IFC archive. He distinguished between three structural levels: on one side there is "local memory," which is by nature concrete and grounded solely on local knowledge so that it corresponds "roughly to the conception of folklore as a recollection"; at the other extreme is "global memory," typically abstract, usually national, and generally derived from written accounts; and in the middle there is "popular memory," defined as cultural representations that draw on a repertoire of images, motifs, and short narratives characteristic of a predominantly oral culture. In this model, popular memory functions as a mediator for the formulation and wider reception of local and global memories.[123] Predominantly preoccupied with local traditions, but heavily influenced by popular and national notions of rebellion and foreign aid, the social memory of the Year of the French operated on all of these levels, and this study demonstrates some of the "negotiations of memory" that took place as these categories interacted with each other at times of high-profile public commemoration or through influences of popular print and national school education.

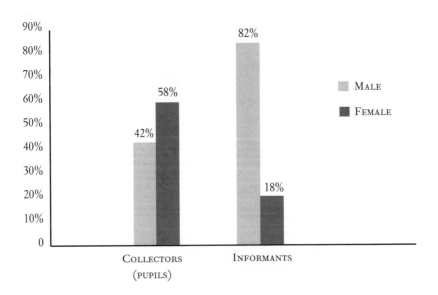

CHART 4. Gender (collectors and informants). IFC S.

Though they may reflect facets of *collective* or social memory, folklore sources primarily embody *collected* memory in the form of "fossilized" records of living-oral traditions. The folklorist Lauri Honko presented an innovative model for the "folklore process," which he divided into "two lives of folklore." The "first life" relates to traditions in a genuine living environment and follows their documentation through collection, conservation, and initial scholarly analysis. Folklore archives are the ultimate outcome of this endeavor. The "second life" in this model "denotes the resurrection of folklore from the depths of the archive."[124] It is in this context that historical research such as that undertaken in this study takes place. At the same time, public access to the IFC archive allows for "recycling mechanisms," which may result in folklore returning to the original community in new cultural contexts, for example through heritage projects and exhibitions. As a result, the IFC is not only a unique resource for historical research but it also facilitates the regeneration of folklore traditions in new forms, thus contributing to reformulations of social memory. Moreover, folklore archives not only store collected oral traditions but, as James Fentress and Chris Wickham pointed out, "archives are often themselves *acts* of commemoration, monuments to the past, as well as (or, sometimes, rather than) the complex historical sources that they can be when they are critically analysed."[125] As such, the IFC archive is a testimony to the importance of folklore in the heritage and history of Ireland. It does not, however, have a monopoly over folk history, and abundant sources for the study of the Year of the French can also be found elsewhere.

3

Richard Hayes and
The Last Invasion of Ireland

The tradition has lived on, for all that, just long enough to
allow a man of great patience, great reverence, and great
simplicity of word, to put it together again in a story of
epic stature.

Sean O'Faolain
Irish Press, 11 August 1937

I N THE SUMMERS OF 1935 and '36, around the same time as the Irish Folklore
Commission began to send out collectors to document oral traditions in
rural Ireland, and while preparations were underway for collecting folklore in
national schools, the maverick historian Dr. Richard Hayes was also engaged in
collecting traditions of Ninety-Eight:

> Setting out from Humbert's landing place on the shore of Killala Bay, I followed
> his line of march through four counties to the scene of his surrender at Ballina-
> muck. I gathered as I went what varied lore could be found bearing on the event.
> Though *bliadhain na bhFranncach* (the Year of the French) is still among the liv-
> ing traditions of the west, I had not proceeded far till the realisation came that
> I was a little late. And I could not help often thinking of the rich harvest that
> might have been garnered a generation or two ago when men were still alive who
> saw the soldiers of France march through Connacht and heard their drums beat-
> ing along its roads.[1]

Despite his concern that he was too late for recording oral history, Hayes collected an extensive volume of oral traditions from people he interviewed en
route, many of them descendants of those who participated in the Rebellion.
This information was incorporated into his book *The Last Invasion of Ireland:
When Connacht Rose*, which was originally published in 1937, with an enhanced

edition issued shortly after (1939).[2] It is widely regarded as the most significant historical examination to date of the French invasion and the 1798 Rebellion in the West.

Richard Francis Hayes (1882–1958)—not to be confused with his notable contemporary namesake Richard James Hayes (1902–76), the director of the National Library of Ireland and Celtic Studies bibliographer—was an Irish revolutionary, medical practitioner, historian, theater director, and film censor.[3] Born in Bruree, county Limerick, he was a boyhood friend of Eamon de Valera. After graduating from the Catholic University Medical School in Dublin in 1906, he was stationed in several hospitals and then appointed dispensary doctor in Lusk, county Dublin, for the duration of World War I. Committed to the national struggle for independence, he joined the Irish Volunteers and commanded the Fingal Battalion. In 1916 he served under Thomas Ashe and Richard Mulcahy at the engagement at Ashbourne, county Meath, where he attended to the wounded of the only military success of the Easter Rising. In the aftermath of the ill-fated insurrection, he was arrested, court-martialed, and condemned to death; his sentence was later commuted to twenty years imprisonment. Released in June 1917 under a general amnesty, only to be rearrested in 1918, he was elected MP for Limerick while in Reading Jail and soon after elected TD (Teachta Dála—member of parliament), representing East Limerick in the First Dáil (independent Irish parliament). During the Irish Civil War of 1921–22, Hayes sided with the pro-treaty camp. Nevertheless, in later years he did not sever ties with anti-treaty activists.

Resigning from the Dáil in 1924, Hayes assumed the arduous position of a Dublin dispensary doctor, first as medical officer for No. 1 South Dublin Union and later at the Donnybrook No. 2 Dispensary.[4] From 1930 on, he increasingly devoted his time to the pursuit of historical scholarship, receiving an honorary DLitt from the National University of Ireland (NUI) and later the prestigious NUI Historical Research Prize (1934), a rare accolade considering that he was not trained as a professional historian.[5] In 1934 Hayes was appointed a director of the national Abbey Theatre. Between 1940 and 1954 he served as the official Film Censor and was responsible for implementing the Emergency Powers Order of 1939, which facilitated extensive wartime censorship of feature films and newsreels.[6] His other affiliations included vice president of the Military History Society and membership of the Royal Irish Academy, the Irish Academy of Letters, and the Royal Academy of Medicine.

Though he never entirely stopped practicing medicine and was also involved in many other cultural and scholarly activities, as a historian Richard Hayes was extremely prolific.[7] He became a leading authority on Irish connections with

IRISH REBELLION, MAY, 1916.

DR. RICHARD F. HAYES,
(Medical Officer, Lusk, Co. Dublin).
Sentenced to 20 Years' Penal Servitude.

FIGURE 8. Richard Hayes (postcard issued after the Easter Rising). As a revolutionary nationalist, Hayes tended to agree with the claim "that an authentic history of Ireland remains to be written" and saw in the French invasion and the 1798 Rebellion in the West a story of "high adventure, with not a few epic qualities," which deserved greater recognition (Introduction to *The Last Invasion of Ireland*). Courtesy of the manuscripts collections of the National Library of Ireland.

France in the seventeenth to the nineteenth centuries, with a particular interest in Irish mercenary soldiers abroad (the "Wild Geese"). In recognition for his contribution to French history he received the distinction of the Legion of Honour (*Légion d'honneur*) in 1951. To supplement his study of 1798 in Connacht with later findings, he wrote an updated narrative of the Battle of Castlebar[8] and an essay on the involvement of priests in the Rebellion.[9] He also published an English translation of a memoir of one of the principal French officers who participated in the expedition to Ireland.[10]

Like his illustrious French contemporary, the leading *Annales* historian Marc Bloch, Hayes believed in the importance of enlivening the findings of research in archives and libraries with field trips. He reverently chose to refer to his travels in the West as a "pilgrimage."[11] With an outstanding number of some 155 references to oral traditions published in *The Last Invasion of Ireland*, the impressive extent of this collection surpasses the number of relevant sources relating to 1798 in the West in the Main Manuscript Collection of the folklore archives.[12] A revealing illustration of Hayes's methodological approach is offered in the remarks that preface the description of the battle of Ballinamuck:

Many accounts are available of that fateful day which ended in capitulation of Humbert and the massacre of his Irish allies. These, coming from contemporary French and English authorities, with local tradition as well, are naturally enough often tinged with bias. They are, accordingly, so conflicting, and some so fantastic, that it is difficult to obtain from them anything like a true picture. After several visits to the battlefield and after a comparative study of all the material, printed and documentary, I have made an effort to present here such a picture; and in doing so due regard is paid to the traditions that have survived locally.[13]

In pursuit of a "true picture," Hayes utilized available archival sources from all participating sides (Irish, English, and French) alongside folklore. His historiographical approach was evidently positivist, as he set out to overcome "bias," echoing Leopold von Ranke's famous maxim of reconstructing the past "as it really was" (*wie es eigentich gewessen*).[14] Accordingly, his analysis of oral traditions was limited to the identification of what appeared to be kernels of historical facts and, because he was not particularly interested in subjectivity or popular historical consciousness, did not consciously incorporate an interpretative approach.

The Richard Hayes Papers, stored in the National Library of Ireland, consist of three boxes packed with the notebooks, papers, and letters written during the course of his historical research in France and Ireland.[15] Spreading over hundreds of pages, they provide further evidence of the vast amount of information he compiled and uncover accounts of additional, unpublished oral traditions. Unlike collectors of the Irish Folklore Commission, Hayes did not have a recording device and so could only jot down rough draft notes, which were later used to reproduce an account of the conversation. Though this technique may appear unfaithful to the spoken dialogue of the original interview, it was acceptable by contemporary folklore standards[16] and certain collectors of the commission consciously preferred using pencil and notebook to the use of an Ediphone when collecting historical traditions.[17] Describing his use of oral traditions, Hayes noted:

> From my gatherings I have selected what seemed to be the most interesting of the stories which I heard bearing on incidents of the Insurrection. Told from generation to generation, they often throw a vivid light on the time; and they are set down here in the narrator's own words even when, in some of their details, they seem now and then not to be quite in accord with fact.[18]

Comparison between the original fieldwork notes and the published text reveals that oral narratives were consistently subjected to editing, which produced polished and sanitized versions of the cruder and often cluttered original testimonies. As a historian he was able to identify stories that were ahistorical (in a positivist sense) and, despite his professed intentions, in practice he suppressed certain information deemed fanciful. As a result of selection, the corpus of folk history traditions that is made readily accessible to the general public through the book is partial.

Although there is no record of his receiving guidance and training from the Irish Folklore Commission, Hayes was in contact with the director Delargy (who forwarded him folklore accounts collected in Leitrim)[19] and the archivist Ó Súilleabháin (who, following the publication of his book, sent him an account from Mayo).[20] The format in which Hayes chose to publish the historical traditions he collected did not comply with the standards set by the commission, as he often neglected to note details concerning the informant's identity, the original source of information, and the context of the interview. Nevertheless, Hayes was a competent collector of folk history, whose historical knowledge extended beyond that of the average collector, while his fieldwork benefited from scholarly analytical methods. Hayes was also known for his amiable character, which was particularly suited for collecting oral history. His close friend, the celebrated writer Frank O'Connor ([pseudonym of Michael O'Donovan], 1903–66) was, in the words of his biographer, "impressed by the readiness with which people of all kinds offered information and documents to Hayes."[21] Over the course of his travels, Hayes identified local folk historians, who were mostly unnoticed by other collectors of folklore, and established with them a rapport that proved beneficial in getting access to a fund of historical traditions.

Hayes's communications with local folk historians were not limited to interviews conducted during his fieldwork, and after returning to Dublin he maintained cordial contacts. For example, many letters were subsequently exchanged with his primary informant in Mayo—the folk historian Patrick O'Donnell of Newport, who continued to send Hayes traditions after the publication of the book.[22] The respect and admiration with which Hayes was regarded by his informants is typified in a letter in which O'Donnell wrote "I only wish I could in any way help to make your Book, and your patriotic labours greater in every way," adding that "Connacht is for ever indebted to you for your great work."[23] The section on folk historians in chapter 6 discusses the special relationship Hayes fostered with O'Donnell, yet this friendship was not exceptional, as Hayes collected traditions through correspondence with several other local folk historians. Numerous letters from informants such as J. P. Donnelan of Killeany in the Aran Islands, county Galway, and Father R. Morris of Donapatrick, county Galway, date from the mid-1930s through the 1940s.[24]

Upon publication, *The Last Invasion of Ireland* was highly acclaimed and received glowing reviews. One enthusiastic reviewer even suggested that: "an abridged edition of this book [be] made available for use in Irish schools."[25] Particular praise was heaped on the collecting and study of folklore traditions.[26] Two years later, further commendations followed the publication of the second edition.[27] The historian Nuala Costello, who at the time was also examining archival documents on the French invasion, wrote an overall favorable review for the first issue of *Irish Historical Studies*—the leading periodical of the "New Irish History."[28] Costello made a valid point of criticism, noting that "the value of the book would be immeasurably increased were the author to have indicated the exact sources of his manuscript material."[29] The deficiency in indexing of references goes beyond manuscript sources and is also a major problem in relation to Hayes's work with folk history. Although most of the sources in the chapter that focuses exclusively on "Traditions of the Insurrection" are identified, throughout the book numerous references are attributed anonymously to "local tradition," without annotation. There is a likely possibility that much of the information in the book draws on additional folklore sources that are not pointed out and so cannot be definitely recognized as such. The Richard Hayes Papers offer resources for redressing this problem and therefore deserve systematic editorial work in order to provide, whenever possible, source references for cited folklore traditions and to supplement the book with unpublished folk-history traditions.

Imbued with the principles of the recently professionalized academic discipline of Irish history that aspired to write value-free history, a positivist credo espoused by the likes of the influential historians T. W. Moody (1907–84) and Robert Dudley Edwards (1909–88),[30] Costello made another salient point of criticism. Referring to Hayes's overt sympathy with the rebel cause, she observed that he had "not always succeeded in preserving the strict detachment of the impartial historian." Since Hayes was an unashamed nationalist, there is a need to determine to what extent his partisan sympathies influenced his work. There are circumstantial grounds to suspect that his political views may have introduced subtle self-censorship into his historical work. For example, his objection to Frank O'Connor's critical study of Michael Collins suggests that he preferred not to question the dominant nationalist trends of his time.[31] Further suspicions arise from his involvement with state censorship, though he apparently maintained that censorship was required to protect children and should not be applied with the same rigor for adults.[32] Hayes was outspoken in his caustic critique of post-1798 loyalist historiography, which he deemed "unreliable." He objected to the publication by the Irish Manuscripts Commission of a valuable primary source written by the loyalist Anglican clergyman Rev. James Little on the grounds that "this vulgar diatribe" was a "travesty on our country."[33] This patriotic attitude did not deter him from utilizing the source and begrudgingly acknowledging that "the truth shines here and there through the prejudice enveloping it."[34] In regard to folklore sources, even though Hayes referred to traditions associated with sectors that opposed the Rebellion and wrote a short section on loyalist songs,[35] such traditions were evidently not collected with as much fervor as those associated with the rebels.

One reviewer observed that "for those who belong to the household of the National Faith, the book will carry with it something that is re-vivifying."[36] The classicist and politician Michael Tierney (1894–1975), who was originally from county Galway in Connacht, described Hayes as "a sympathiser with the republican tradition" whose writings show "warmth, colour, and sympathy" for the Irish rebels.[37] Historians have been repeatedly cautioned not to cross an imaginary fine line between empathy and sympathy, yet a clear distinction cannot be made. Hayes's sympathetic collecting of folklore traditions enabled him to write with empathy about the experiences of participants in the 1798 Rebellion. To his credit it should be acknowledged that he made no secret of his own stance so that readers are alerted to the author's perspective and can recognize its limitations. All considered, his innovative use of oral traditions as sources alongside archival documents offer historians an inspiring exemplar of how to use folklore sources. More particularly, Hayes took first steps toward collecting and examining the folk history of the Year of the French, a project this book attempts to readdress.

4

Ancillary Folk History Sources

It is in these ideological traditionalizings, inscribed in appropriate genres such as police reports, sermons, magazine articles, tourist brochures, memoirs and local histories, that
local memories reach the center.

Dorothy Noyes and Roger D. Abrahams
"From Calendar Custom to National Memory"

T HE MAIN COLLECTIONS of folklore of the Year of the French were
mostly compiled in the first half of the twentieth century: the bulk of 1798
traditions documented by the collectors of the Irish Folklore Commission was
taken down in the 1930s–'50s, the Schools' Scheme took place in 1937/38, and
Richard Hayes's fieldwork was conducted in 1935/36. Collectively they offer
a "snapshot" of how this episode was discussed and remembered locally at that
time. By surveying Irish popular culture over the past two hundred years, it is
possible to identify numerous additional sources for the remembrance of
Ninety-Eight in Connacht and the north midlands. These have not been assembled in specific collections but are scattered throughout miscellaneous locations, where they appear in a variety of formats. Dating from the events themselves to the present day, such sources are useful for charting noticeable
developments and reconstructions of social memory.

Polemical contestations over the representation of 1798 have continuously
featured in historical works and political tracts, as put succinctly by Kevin
Whelan: "The rebellion never passed into history, because it never passed out
of politics."[1] Following the Rebellion, a proliferation of pamphlets reflected
political debates between those who sought to censure the rebel cause and those
who attempted to rehabilitate the memory of the United Irishmen. Even

though they sometimes purported to reflect popular attitudes and occasionally described experiences of participants in the events, as in the case of a loyalist pamphlet phrased as the testimony of a rebel supposedly executed at Ballina-muck,[2] these tracts were not naïve representations of genuine oral traditions but attempts to influence public opinion. Shortly after the Rebellion, Walter ("Watty") Cox (ca. 1760–1837), who had been both a United Irishman and an informer, published colorful accounts of the events. According to the Chief Secretary Robert Peel (1788–1850), Cox's antigovernmental *Irish Magazine and Monthly Asylum for Neglected Biography* (1807–15) "was distributed occasion-ally gratis and generally sold at a price which could not defray the expense of printing." Peel noted that it was "greatly admired by the common people," and corroborating evidence confirms that it was read aloud in public and received with enthusiasm.[3] Such popular publications, which straddle oral and written transmission, clearly affected folk history.

Partisan treatises and histories cannot be sweepingly dismissed as fabrica-tions. Although Patrick Kennedy (1801–73), a nineteenth-century collector of Wexford Ninety-Eight folklore, derisively considered the ultraloyalist Sir Richard Musgrave (ca. 1755–1818) to be the "author of the least trustworthy history of the Insurrection of '98 ever published,"[4] in compiling his highly influential history of 1798, *Memoirs of the Different Rebellions in Ireland* (orig-inally published in 1801), Musgrave made a conscious, albeit biased, effort to collect testimonies of loyalists.[5] Three decades after the Rebellion, surviving Ulster rebels were interviewed by local historians in county Antrim, both by the Rev. Classon Porter of Larne (1814–85), who was sympathetic to the rebel cause,[6] and by Samuel McSkimin of Carrickfergus (1775–1843), who was antagonistic.[7] In the following decade, the Carmelite monk Brother Luke Cullen (1793–1859) sympathetically collected rebel testimonies in Wexford and Wicklow.[8] A half century after the Rebellion, Richard Robert Madden (1798–1886) tracked down surviving former rebels and their relatives, associ-ates, and friends and deferentially incorporated their recollections in his monu-mental biographical history of the United Irishmen.[9] Regrettably, oral history was not collected with such rigor in the West at the time; however, evidence of early folklore accounts can also be found in other popular styles of writing.

The passage of the Act of Union (1800) promoted a plethora of social reports and geographical surveys, which aimed to explain Ireland to English and Anglo-Irish readers and to propose reforms and improvement schemes. This scholarly administrative literature occasionally included passing refer-ences to traditions of 1798. Listing historical places, a *Statistical Survey of the County of Mayo* commissioned by the Dublin Society in 1802 noted that

Castlebar, Killala and Barnagee-gap [*Bearna na Gaoithe*—the Windy Gap] will, during any vestige of the history of Ireland, remain conspicuous for the landing of the French under General Humbert in Mayo, their progress through those places, and the events consequent thereof.[10]

Sixteen years later, a guidebook addressed to "The Scientific Tourist" acknowledged that Castlebar and Killala were recognized as "memorable" places because of their association with the French invasion.[11] Such writing developed into a popular sociological tradition from which ethnographic data can be gathered. The author of a late-nineteenth-century study on "The Irish Peasant," for example, observed that recollections of 1798 were still strong in a Mayo *Gaeltacht* and that locals continued to cultivate expectations of another French invasion.[12]

The Ordnance Survey of Ireland (1824–46), which produced a detailed six-inch map, also had a topographical department (closed in 1842), which compiled supplementary information on local history and folklore.[13] As a rule, recollections of 1798 were considered too recent and contentious, yet sporadic references appear in the Ordnance Survey's letters and memoirs. For instance, writing about Granard in county Longford, the renowned Gaelic scholar John O'Donovan (who was employed as a fieldworker from 1830) identified a Mr. Major as "a fine intelligent Presbyterian who headed the rebels in '98." In the neighboring area of Sliabh Cairbre, O'Donovan observed how recollections of the Rebellion were intertwined with folklore of an ancient malediction, so that Ninety-Eight was remembered as a desperate struggle to "shake off the curse of St. Patrick and the English yoke." He was also told of a condemned rebel who impertinently taunted his executioners by exclaiming: "I

FIGURE 9. Richard Robert Madden (engraved by S. Allen in 1858 after an original painting by George Francis Mulvany). A polymathic physician, reformist and emancipist colonial administrator, foreign correspondent, and travel writer, Madden was also a historian with a passionate interest in the United Irishmen and appreciation of oral history. Courtesy of the National Library of Ireland.

can't help but laugh when I think of what a fine trouncing (driving) we gave the rascals into the river; it was the happiest day of my life."[14]

The team of luminary scholars employed by the Ordnance Survey rejuvenated Irish antiquarian folklore studies.[15] Associating early-nineteenth-century folklore writing with Protestant conservative and unionist politics, Joep Leerssen claimed that by focusing on the fairy world, antiquarians de-politicized peasant culture.[16] This echoed a romantic response to modernization, which was typical of elites throughout Europe.[17] However, the scope of his argument that after 1798 Anglo-Irish elites deliberately distanced themselves from popular history of recent events can be called into question. Literary journals of antiquarian scholars, namely the *Dublin Penny Journal* (founded in

FIGURE 10. Thomas Crofton Croker (etched in 1849). Recognized internationally for his writings on Irish fairy lore and popular traditions, Crofton Croker was an Admiralty clerk and antiquarian with an avid interest in the history and folklore of the 1798 Rebellion. Courtesy of the National Library of Ireland.

1832) and the *Dublin University Magazine* (1833–77), presented occasional references to folklore of Ninety-Eight. The pioneering folklorist Thomas Crofton Croker (1798–1854) was particularly interested in oral traditions of the 1798 Rebellion. His *Researches in the South of Ireland* (1824) contains several notes on the Rebellion in Wexford, including an appendix with a "Private Narrative of the Rebellion of 1798." He also compiled a collection of *Popular Songs Illustrative of the French Invasions of Ireland* (1847) with a section devoted to the expedition that arrived in Killala (parts 3 and 4). Crofton Croker's ardent loyalism undermined his claim to lack of prejudice in collecting and presenting information on 1798, and it is possible to discern instances where bias impaired his writings, most notably in his editing of the *Memoirs of Joseph Holt* (London, 1838). Comparison to the original version has exposed his fraudulent claim to be an "impartial editor" who purportedly "adhered in the text closely to the original manuscript," by revealing disingenuous revisions designed to cast the protagonist (a prominent United Irish general in counties Wexford and Wicklow) in a negative light.[18]

Antiquarians also partook in a style of travel literature that incorporated detailed descriptions of local traditions and customs.[19] Typical examples are the travel books of Rev. Caesar Otway ([also known by the pseudonym "Terence O'Toole"], 1780–1842), founding co-editor of the *Dublin Penny Journal*, whose *Tour in Connaught* (1839) and *Sketches in Erris and Tyrawley* (1841) mentioned local traditions of Ninety-Eight.[20] Though often written by authors who were unsympathetic to the popular culture of the Catholic rural populace, such works were inspired by a keen interest in the landscape and its past, and were peppered with revealing observations on historical traditions. The polymathic scope of antiquarian studies also encouraged the writing of histories that utilized sources from popular culture. An example that illustrates the broad cultural interests of this nineteenth-century intellectual milieu can be found in the writings of the novelist and historian Rev. William Hamilton Maxwell (1792–1850), who was the Anglican prebendary at Balla, county Mayo. Although a self-professed political conservative and unsympathetic to the rebel cause,[21] his travelogues and historical fiction referred to oral traditions of 1798 that he encountered in Mayo and Connemara and these reappeared in his history of 1798.[22]

Throughout the nineteenth century, numerous travel books offered descriptions of Connacht that referred to the events of 1798.[23] By the turn of the century, the travel genre was reclaimed by nationalist writers,[24] most notably the often-prejudiced William Bulfin ("Che Buono," 1864–1910), author of the highly popular *Rambles in Eirinn* (1907). Such travel writing proves to be a useful source for tracing developments in commemorative practices associated with the landscape. Bulfin's description of the area of Collooney in county Sligo, for example, commented on the impressive sight of the monument erected in 1898 in honor of the bravery of the United Irishman Bartholomew Teeling in 1798.[25] Throughout the twentieth century and into the present time, travel literature has flourished in Ireland and has included occasional, mostly incidental, references to oral traditions of 1798.

More directly, folklore has featured in the literature of heritage tourism and commemorative events, which has typically favored colorful narratives that were selected from a broad range of available accounts and endorsed as representative of "local tradition" while leaving out much local folk history information. Moreover, in presenting traditional accounts, the wider regional, national, and international dimensions of folklore are generally overlooked.[26] Commemorative initiatives seeking to celebrate Ninety-Eight organized exhibitions open to the general public, demonstrating that popular representations of history are not necessarily textual and may include various visual artistic forms, such as illustrations, paintings, and caricatures, and also material objects. Accompanying descriptive notes can inform visitors of traditional narratives by which these relics were perceived and interpreted locally. Curators, however, have not always applied the standard requirements of annotation with the same rigor to folklore exhibits, which are often presented as anecdotal asides, without adequate contextual information on precisely where and when the tradition was documented, the identity of the collector, provenance of the tradition, and so forth. In 1998 high-profile bicentenary exhibitions on 1798 were held at the Ulster Museum in Belfast (3 April–31 August 1998), the National Museum of Ireland at Collins Barracks Dublin (24 May–31 December 1998), and the National 1798 Centre in Enniscorthy, county Wexford.[27] Reflecting a larger historiographical oversight, folklore did not feature prominently in any of these. In contrast, a bicentenary exhibition in the James Hardiman Library at University College Galway included a designated section on "folk memory,"[28] and numerous local community events also showcased information drawn from folk history.

Local historians, from the late nineteenth century onward, have been instrumental in uncovering and publishing folk history. Numerous sources from the folklore of the Franco-Irish campaign can be found in the works of Archdeacon Terence O'Rorke on Sligo (1878 and 1889), James Farrell on Longford (1886), James Woods on Westmeath (1907), T. M. O'Flynn on Leitrim (1937), and J. F. Quinn on Mayo (1930s).[29] The late-twentieth-century boom in local studies has greatly contributed to the publication of local traditions. Journals of local history societies, in particular *Bliainiris* (North Mayo), *Cathair na Mart* (Westport), and the *Journal of the Galway Archaeological and Historical Society*, and also the less-frequent *Back the Road* (Newport), *Swinford Echoes* (Swinford) and *Teathbha* (Longford), periodically include articles on 1798, which often refer to folklore accounts.

The emergence of Irish folklore studies as an academic discipline has encouraged the publication of historical folklore. Contributions to *Béaloideas*, the journal of the Folklore of Ireland Society, reproduced sources from the IFC archive that relate to *Bliain na bhFrancach*.[30] Repertoires of storytellers have appeared in print and folklore of the Year of the French can be found, for example, in an edited collection of tales told by the Connemara storyteller James Berry (1842–1914)[31] and in a book by the Mayo storyteller Seán Henry ([John Edward Henry], b. 1906).[32] Traditional music and songs have also been recognized as vital sources for historical folklore and have been collected by antiquarians, folklorists, and cultural revivalists.[33] Immediately after the 1798 Rebellion, Edward Bunting employed Patrick Lynch ([Pádraig Ó Loingsigh], 1757–ca. 1820) to collect folk songs in Connacht (1802).[34] Throughout the nineteenth century, songs and ballads of Ninety-Eight were published in copious popular anthologies, though these often overlooked songs that were prevalent in local oral tradition.[35]

Newspapers and popular journals sought to inform and entertain their readers with excerpts of folklore and in this context traditions of Ninety-Eight were reproduced in the national and local press. Journals associated with Irish language revival, namely *Irisleabhar na Gaedhilge*, *Fáinne an Lae*, and *An Claidheamh Soluis*, were committed to the publication of traditions in Irish. Accounts of folk history can also be found in private collections of correspondence and personal papers, and thanks to the devotion of local historians, several such manuscripts have been published. Relevant examples include traditional accounts of the battle of Ballinamuck by Michael Connell of Soran (reproduced by Fr. Owen Devaney)[36] and by James O'Neill of Crowdrummin (published posthumously by Seán Ó Brádaigh).[37] Additional family traditions frequently surfaced in memoirs and biographies.

It is often claimed that modernization struck a deathblow to "traditional" oral culture. Yet, developments in communication and information technologies also provided new media for the transmission and documentation of folklore.[38] Folklore has been collected over the telephone (in the Faeroe Islands for example), and new possibilities are currently available for folklore collecting by e-mail. In the 1980s local historians in Mayo and north Longford began recording local commemorative events and traditions of the Year of the

French on video.[39] Radio programs have hosted storytellers, ballad singers, local historians, and folklorists. Several television documentaries on the 1798 Rebellion were prepared for the bicentennial year, though they mostly ignored folklore traditions.[40] The Internet is increasingly becoming a popular forum for sharing information and several websites display traditions of 1798.[41] Technological developments present methodological and conceptual challenges for historians since, as the anthropologist and oral historian Gwyn Prins remarked, "the move to a post-literate, newly global, electronically oral and visual culture deflates the professional self-esteem of traditional document-driven historiography."[42]

The wide range of miscellaneous sources for folk history reiterates a point made earlier that, at least throughout modern Irish history, oral historical traditions have been in constant interaction with influences of literacy.[43] Therefore, it is impossible to impose a clear-cut dichotomy between oral and literate cultures similar to that introduced in other studies of oral tradition, for example by Africanists.[44] As a form of communication, oral tradition was reshaped by multiple agencies and is therefore best considered within the larger parameters of popular culture.[45] Print and other mass media reconfigured oral tradition, making it presentable to a larger public. At the same time, transitions from oral performances of history-telling (addressed to intimate audiences) to publication or broadcasting of excerpts from folk history created new historical contexts for remembrance of the past.

A cultural history based on such hybrid sources requires a rethinking of the assumptions behind standard historiographical terminology. In his study of literate culture, Wlad Godzich commented on the nineteenth- and early-twentieth-century European and North American professionalization of the humanities within academic disciplines, observing:

> There arose then with respect to literature and other fields of inquiry, notably philosophy and history, a generic distinction between primary and secondary texts previously restricted to the relation of sacred text and commentary, the impact of which is still very much with us.[46]

The study of folk history inevitably questions the fundamental methodological distinction between primary and secondary sources. In social memory, history and historiography—the past and its representations—are intrinsically tied. Traditions of the Year of the French collected in the nineteenth and twentieth centuries may be considered "secondary" sources for a positivist history of 1798, even though they are firsthand sources for the ways by which the Rebellion was subsequently remembered and commemorated, and this duality in the nature of the sources needs to be taken into account.

One of the main problems in identifying sources that are not deposited in a designated collection is that they are scattered in diverse locations, which are mostly not cataloged or indexed. Consequently, trawling for miscellaneous sources of folk history inevitably involves an element of "hit and miss." Nonetheless, there is clearly a wide array of sources for the study of remembrance of the Year of the French. A preliminary requisite for such an undertaking is a better understanding of the unique nature of Irish folk history, its forms of performance, and its practitioners.

Part 2

Folk History

5

History-Telling

> It was through folk tradition that the ordinary people
> learned the story of their own past, and folk tradition
> remembered those things which seemed important.
>
> Kevin Danaher
> "History and Oral Tradition"

O UTSIDE THE ACADEMY, the historical past has always been a topic of conversation and remembrance. In his mid-nineteenth-century voluminous history of the French Revolution, Jules Michelet (1798–1874) advocated the importance of "popular belief" (*croyance populaire*), maintaining that legends constituted an alternative history of "the heart of the people and their imagination" (*l'histoire de cœur de peuple et de son imagination*). He insisted that in addition to use of standard sources found in books and manuscripts, it is important to study oral tradition, which "generally remained scattered in the mouths of the people, which everybody said and repeated, the peasants, the townsfolk, the old people, the mature men, the women and even the children."[1] Similarly, the history of the 1798 Rebellion in Ireland can benefit from an examination of oral traditions, which need to be located within a larger context of Irish folk history.

Folk history in Ireland was commonly known by the name *seanchas* (pronounced "shanachus"), which derived from reference to antiquity—*sean* (old),[2] and has been succinctly described as "orally preserved social-historical tradition."[3] The term has been used with a variety of meanings: "history, lore, ancient law, a record or register, a minute description, a pedigree, an ancient tale; [an] act of storytelling, gossiping; inquiring (about one's condition, health etc.)"[4] In comparison to *scéalaíocht*, which derives from the Irish for story (*scéal*) and refers to structurally complex long tales that were often local versions of international folktales (similar to the German *Märchen*) or indigenous hero tales (*scéalta gaisce*) from the Irish mythological cycles, *seanchas* referred to shorter realistic accounts (though their content could be fanciful).[5] Irish storytellers tended to specialize in one or the other of these narrative categories, and folklore scholars have shown greater interest in narrators of the longer tales (*scéalaithe*). However, *seanchas*, which regularly discussed and remembered the past, is of particular interest to historians. The American folklorist Henry Glassie, who studied oral traditions in the townland of Ballymenone in county Fermanagh, observed that "history is a topic for conversation"[6] and that "hundreds of discrete tales represent a limited set of categories that interlock into a unity."[7]

In a different context, the historian of Holocaust remembrance James E. Young introduced the term *history-telling* to signify a medium that "works through" the dissonance between impersonal historical narrative and personal "deep memory." Young argued that incorporating the voices of the participants into historical narratives allows for a presentation of history that combines events and their representations.[8] This concept can be extended beyond biographical oral history accounts, to incorporate oral traditions as recollections of historical events retold over several generations. Such history-telling, manifested though repeated remembering and narrating of the past, was a central activity in the *seanchas* storytelling and singing of communities in Ireland. Obviously, the vernacular narratives that it generated did not adhere to the dispassionate approach, which scholarly history has aspired to uphold since its professionalization. Folklore was designed first and foremost as a form of popular entertainment and social interaction, vividly evoking events from the past in an animated fashion. Consequently, history-telling promoted an intimate relationship with the past that may be described as "living history," where past interacted with present, subjectivity supplemented and often overrode objectivity, and the tangibility of physical reality was perforated and complemented by the elusiveness of imagination.

Folklore has been concisely defined as "artistic communication in small groups,"[9] and traditional Irish storytelling was associated with the custom of night visiting (*ar cuairt/cuaird*) and evening gatherings in *céilí* (visiting) houses.[10] These social meetings, which were described by anthropologists in the 1930s as "the seat of traditional lore and entertainment,"[11] have been recognized as the primary forum for a variety of folkloristic activities, not only storytelling but also music sessions, singing, dancing, card-playing, discussing local news, and exchanging gossip.[12] At the same time, there were many other opportunities in everyday life that allowed for recital and performance of historical folklore. However, the bulk of documented folklore accounts originated at a remove from the original social context, in artificially induced interviews between folklore collectors and selected informants. New trends in folklore studies have attempted to accommodate this duality and to bridge the distance by advising folklore collectors "to view the informant as a co-researcher, as a producer of research information in principle enjoying equal status."[13] Overall, folklore proves to be both organic, insofar as it is an integral part of a culture, and superorganic, since its continued existence is not dependent on whether it remains in its indigenous environment.[14]

In its form and content, history-telling is culture-specific and therefore, as Vansina noted, historians should be "interested in the constraints, models and directions that mold a message in a given culture and these are given in that culture's specification of genre."[15] In Ireland, the folk history of Ninety-Eight was propagated through various genres, including stories, songs and ballads, poems, rhymes, toasts, prophecies, proverbs and sayings, place-names, and a variety of commemorative ritual practices. Each of these modes of expression needs to be examined on its own terms and placed within a wider historical context.

Tales and Mini-Histories

And in Connaught around the turf fires,
The "gossoons" with hands beating high,
Do list to the "céilidheóir" telling,
The stories that never will die.

Ballinamuck ballad
"The Connaught Rising"[16]

The majority of collected sources on the Year of the French are in prose narrative and generally shorter than one thousand words, although occasional stories exceeded double that length. Folklorists have classified *seanchas* stories into several types: folk legends (*eachtraí*) set in the recent historical past and believed (or fancifully believed) to be true; anecdotes that sum up to brief narratives that tell of unusual people, events, or objects; and local legends, which are grounded in particular places.[17] Stories of Ninety-Eight appeared in all these forms, and most stories focused on experiences of local heroes.

Many of the stories referred to outlaws, who were rebels that were forced to go "on their keeping" following the defeat. In Irish folk history, "resistance fighters" (i.e., rebels) normally turn into "brigands" (i.e., outlaws) when they are on the run.[18] The 1798 setting corresponds to a general European scenario, as the eighteenth century has been described as the "golden age of bandit heroes."[19] Recollections of the adventures and dramatic escapes of outlaws in the Year of the French were reshaped into narratives that incorporated familiar storytelling motifs; these could assume the form of a-historical folktales about heroes with remarkable physical strength, who were depicted as exceptional duelists and athletes.[20] In one story, Pádraig Liath ("Grey Patrick") Ó Lochlainn of Lacken, county Mayo, a steward in the service of a landlord in Tyrawley who joined the rebels in Castlebar, escapes from a party of "peelers" (an anachronistic reference to law enforcers) after overcoming their daunting leader—a Judge Kirkwood, who was reputed to be the strongest man in Killala at the time.[21] In a long story told in the parish of Ross in county Galway, a former British officer of noble birth named Captain Loughrey joins the rebels and later defeats a group of Orangemen in an athletic contest. Loughrey then travels to London incognito and, thanks to the intervention of a sympathetic queen, wins a pardon from a reluctant king.[22] The adventures of Éamonn Ó Treasaí, a Connemara 1798 outlaw hero who was described by an eighty-eight-year-old storyteller as "the man who most helped Ireland ever," were narrated as a long folktale, which incorporated traditional motifs of chivalry and bravery.[23]

History-telling of Ninety-Eight also appeared as concise and simplified historical narratives, which combined oral tradition with information derived from literary sources. Such accounts can be labeled *mini-histories*. They offer insight into how an entire historical episode was perceived in folk history. A pupil near Ballinamuck collected a typical mini-history of the Rebellion from his forty-one-year-old father:

> In the year seventeen of 1798 [*sic*] the Irish people were looking for foreign help, long before that the Irish people were persecuted by the English. A lot of men from the county Longford fought at Ballinamuck. An army of French men landed at Killala and marched to Ballinamuck, where they were joined by an Irish army. The Irish were defeated, and when they were flying they had to leave arms everywhere. At Ballinamuck the gonner [gunner] Mcgee was shot dead and his gun was captured.[24]

Narrating the entire Franco-Irish campaign in less than ninety words, this account, which features historical inaccuracies, presents a synopsis of history as perceived from a locality, without adhering to an ordered chronological scheme. The greater historical events serve as a background for the local experience and its heroes. Mini-histories could appear as introductions to detailed stories, providing a general context for the recollection of local traditions. A pupil from near Ballinalee in county Longford heard from his seventy-three-year-old uncle:

> In the year 1798 there came to Killala Bay an army of French Soldiers who were under General Blake and shortly after landing they fought the English at Castlebar. The English were beaten and they fled across the country until they reached Ballinamuck. They [*sic*] English soldiers were too strong for the other army and so they beat the Irish in two hours. The Irish soldiers were chased through the bogs and over the hills.

This Ballinamuck-centered account, which mistakenly identifies the Irish hero General Blake as commander of the French, was followed by references to sites of death and popular commemoration of rebels who died in the locality.[25]

An illustration of how such mini-histories reduced the complexity of historical events can be found in the story of "One shot took Castlebar" (*Urchair amháin a thóig Caisleán a Bharra*), recounted in 1941 in northwest Mayo. Repeating an account that he heard from his great-grandfather, a sixty-seven-year-old storyteller explained that the small rebel force attained victory at Castlebar against an army of superior numbers thanks to a well-aimed cannon shot fired by a French officer.[26] Though clearly an attempt to rationalize the unexpected outcome of the battle, the motif of a single decisive shot is an old trope already in circulation at the time of the Rebellion. At a court-martial in Castlebar in December 1800, a prosecution witness (David Hodgin) testified that an accused rebel (Thomas Rigney) had opposed the release of a loyalist prisoner held by the French in Killala by claiming: "Ireland was lost by one shot before and he would take care it should not be so again."[27] Evidently, popular culture generated traditions of simplified explanatory narratives that were recycled in folk history and used repeatedly for historical interpretations.

Apart from storytelling, more than sixty songs and poems relate to the French presence in Connacht. As David D. Buchan showed in a study of narrative songs from northeast Scotland, historical ballads "can be much nearer to the truth than is normally realized. They can contain factual truths that are found in the often-scanty records, and they can contain emotional truths, the attitudes and reactions of the ballad-singing folk to the world around them."[28] Despite the publication of numerous popular collections of "songs of 1798," many songs collected as local oral traditions have not appeared in print. These forms of lyrical *seanchas* appeared both in English and Irish, reflecting distinct cultural traditions. Although English and Irish songs influenced each other, it is instructive to examine the development of each tradition separately, while bearing in mind the conditions of diglossia resulting from performers and audiences who were bilingual to some extent, at least in the case of songs in Irish.[29]

Amhráin na ndaoine: *Songs and Poetry in Irish*

Is cinnte go dtaispeántar sa traidisiún béil go raibh tionchar
ag imeachtaí Éirí Amach 1798 ar shaol, ar sheanchas, agus ar
amhráin an phobail thiar.

[Oral tradition positively demonstrates the influence of
the events of the 1798 Rebellion on the life, the *seanchas,* and
the songs of the people of the West.]

Ríonach uí Ógáin
"Béaloideas 1798 Thiar"

Oral poetry that referred to 1798 reflects both earlier and subsequent influences.
Tom Dunne pointed out that

> between the rebellions of 1798 and 1848 a significant corpus of political songs
> and poems in Irish illustrates the continuing strength of the seventeenth-century
> anti-colonial tradition, but also how it was adapted to meet the profound cultural
> and social changes of the period. Some of the material, often called "amhráin na
> ndaoine" (songs of the people), survived in the oral tradition.[30]

The poetic conventions that produced folk poetry and songs in Irish about
Bliain na bhFrancach may have their roots in long-standing Gaelic literary traditions, as there are abundant examples of remnants of earlier poetry that
vibrantly survived in oral tradition and were documented in the twentieth
century.[31] Exponents of *gesunkene Kulturgut,* an approach that maintains that
literary works of high culture diffuse into oral popular culture,[32] have suggested that traditions of folk poetry originated in the classic poetry of the
early-modern period, a time when the imminent collapse of the Gaelic order
precipitated an intense poetic prolificacy.[33] However, the popular impact of
elite bardic poetry, which explicitly denigrated the demotic poetry of *filí
pobail* (community poets),[34] is questionable and a seminal thesis put forward
by Daniel Corkery, asserting that Irish peasant culture was founded on aristocratic origins, has been critically challenged.[35] The political relevance of six-
teenth- and seventeenth-century Gaelic poetry is moot, with scholars arguing
that it expressed coherent political commentary (namely Brendan Bradshaw,
Breandán Ó Buachalla, and Marc Caball) confronting those who claimed that
it was essentially apolitical (namely Tom Dunne, Nicholas Canny, Bernadette
Cunningham, Joep Leerssen, and Michelle O Riordan).[36] In contrast, scholars have increasingly acknowledged the value of late-eighteenth-century vernacular poetry as an indispensable source for the study of popular political
opinion.[37]

Scholarship has convincingly demonstrated that eighteenth-century Irish poetry was immersed in Jacobite ideology, which championed the cause of the exiled Stuart monarch James II and his descendents, constituting a rebellious discourse expressed though millenarian and sectarian rhetoric.[38] A predominant theme in Irish Jacobite poetry was the expectation of foreign military aid that would fulfill ancient prophecies and overturn the existing political and social order, reinstating disposed Catholics. Songs hailing the imminent arrival of French troops on vessels[39] prepared the ground for reception of radical ideologies influenced by the French Revolution[40] and anticipated poetic descriptions in Irish of the French invasion attempts in 1796 and 1798.[41] While Jacobite poetry may have set the tone for popular responses to the French arrival in Mayo, it did not dictate a set reaction from the local poets of the time.

The celebrated Mayo poets Richard Barrett ([Riocard Bairéad], ca. 1746–1819) and Michael Sweeney ([Micheál Mac Suibhne], ca. 1760–1820) were both United Irishmen and implicated in the 1798 Rebellion; moreover Barrett was subsequently imprisoned in Castlebar. Verses of their poetry that survived in oral tradition do not include explicit references to *Bliain na bhFrancach*.[42] Similarly, the works of contemporary minor Irish language poets who were active in northwest county Mayo also neglect to refer to the French invasion. In the early twentieth century, Michael O'Gallaher ([Micheál Ó Gallchobhair], 1860–1938) of Chicago, who was originally from Erris in county Mayo, collected oral poetry attributed to the Erris folk poets Séamus MacCosgair, Doimnic Beag MacCosgair, and Cathaoir Bán Ó Gallchobhair. Although these poets were alive and active in 1798, O'Gallaher was surprised to discover that "none of them seemed to have tried to compose anything regarding the most momentous occurrences of their own time."[43] Poetic references deemed to be subversive may indeed have been suppressed: in the early nineteenth century, association with the 1798 Rebellion still carried harmful ramifications.

In 1802 the Gaelic scholar Patrick Lynch was employed by the traditional music collector Edward Bunting to collect folk songs in Connacht and was instructed to communicate regularly with the McCrackens of Belfast, a family known for its United Irish connections. He initially traveled through counties Leitrim and Sligo, yet most of his impressive compilation of 193 songs was collected in northwest county Mayo, where he resolved to apply himself to "the lower classes." As a conspicuous outsider, who liased with northern radicals and encouraged people in the countryside to perform songs in Irish, Lynch soon aroused suspicions among loyalists. Accosted by the postmaster in Westport,[44] Lynch was accused of engaging in seditious activities and consequently people were afraid to be seen in his company. Though he took down several versions of songs from the Jacobite tradition, in his collections there are no explicit

references to the recent events of the French invasion.[45] Some three decades later, biographical notes on Richard Barrett, Michael Sweeney and their renowned contemporary Anthony Raftery ([Antoine Raiftearaí], 1779–1835), penciled sometime between 1828 and 1835 probably by the Leitrim poet Theophilus (Teige) O'Flynn, conspicuously avoided mentioning their involvement in the Rebellion.[46]

In contrast, a popular folk poem generally attributed to Raftery and collected orally one hundred years later includes specific references to 1798 in Connacht and was occasionally referred to as "Amhrán na bhFranncach" (The Song of the French), though it has also been associated with eighteenth-century agrarian protest and has accordingly been referred to as "Na Buachaillí Bána" (The Whiteboys). It mentions John Gibbons of Westport, the treasurer of the local United Irish organization, who was transported to Germany for his involvement in the Rebellion ("Oh Johnny Gibbons, my five hundred healths to you / You are long away from me in Germany"). Other verses refer to his outlawed son Johnny Gibbons and kinsman Fr. Myles Prendergast, who went into hiding together and continued to resist the authorities after the Rebellion was quelled ("Johnny Gibbons and our Father Myles / Are being guarded out on the bog"). Such tributes, set on the background of an abundance of oral traditions about "Johnny the outlaw,"[47] contradict the early-nineteenth-century Protestant historian Maxwell, who claimed that "Gibbons was a detestable scoundrel—malignant and sanguinary, without a single trait of 'savage virtue' in his character. He robbed rich and poor alike, and hence he died without exciting the pity of the peasantry."[48]

The poem angrily castigates Denis Browne, a prominent Mayo landlord and member of parliament who partook in the terror that accompanied the suppression of the Rebellion. This policy earned him the derogatory nicknames "Donnchadh an Rópa" (Denis of the [Hangman's] Rope), "Soap the Rope,"[49] and "Buinneachaí Buí" (yellow diarrhea or scourbag) and his notoriety was repeatedly recalled in folk history.[50] This livid antipathy was encapsulated in a stanza of the poem attributed to Raftery:

A Dhonncha Brún chraithfinn láimh leat
Ní le grá dhuit é ach le fonn thú a
   ghábhail,
Chrochfainn suas [thu] le róipín cnáibhe
Agus chuirfinn mo spiar i do bholg mór.

[Denis Browne I should shake hands
   with you
it is not with love for you but with desire
   to capture you,
I would hang you up with a little hemp
   rope
and I would shove my spear in your big
   belly.]

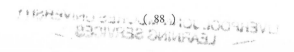

Verses from this poem featured prominently in folk memory and appeared in numerous accounts collected in counties Mayo and Galway.[51]

Several other relevant poems in Irish appear to have originated around the time of the historical events of 1798 and to have subsequently entered into the folklore repertoire. They include "Cúl na Binne" referring to the United Irish Captain Peter Jordan of Coolnabinna near Lahardane, county Mayo (and also mentioning the outlaw Anthony Daly);[52] "An Caiptín Máilleach" about the United Irish Captain James O'Malley ("Séamus Bán"—fair-haired James) of Edenpark, Knock, county Mayo;[53] "Na Francaigh Bhána" (The Fair-haired French) also known as "Teacht na bhFrancach go Cill Alaidh" (The Arrival of the French in Killala);[54] and a Connacht version of the well-known song "An Spailpín Fánach" (The Migratory Laborer) that refers to the French in Killala and Castlebar.[55] In addition, miscellaneous references to this episode appear in contemporary Irish-language poetry, such as the compositions of the former United Irishman Mícheál Óg Ó Longáin of county Cork, who mentioned Connacht rebels in his poem "Maidin Luain Chincíse."[56] The song "An Róipín Caol Cnáibe" (The Little Thin Hempen Rope) laments the execution of Captain George Chambers [Seorsa Sémbers], a son of a Mayo landowner who fought on the rebel side. A version, which was recognized as "a great favorite of the old people of the neighborhood of where the event transpired," was collected in 1885 from an eighty-year-old woman who was related to Chambers.[57] Poetic folklore of Ninety-Eight in Connacht also included several other songs styled as laments for fallen local heroes, most notably Affy ("Austin") Gibbons [Aifí Mac Giobúin] and Fr. Manus Sweeney [An tAthair Mánus Mac Suibhne], and these are discussed as an expression of commemoration in chapter 11.

Composition of popular poetry with references to the Year of the French continued throughout the nineteenth and into the twentieth century. In 1959 the collector Michael Corduff described folk poetry attributed to Michael McGrath of Glengad, a nineteenth-century Erris poet locally known as Micheál na nAmhrán ("Michael of the Songs"). McGrath, who was illiterate and without any formal education, composed patriotic songs of Catholic-nationalist senti-ment; he died around the middle of the century. Among the compositions ascribed to him was a popular song in Irish about the arrival of the French in Kil-lala and the recruitment of local rebels by Fr. Henry O'Kane[58] and also a poem with a verse about the aforementioned United Irish leader Captain O'Malley issuing a report on the condition of the rebels under his command, who are "standing firm" (*ar sheasamh go buan*).[59] Such poets enjoyed great popularity in their locality, as demonstrated in an amusing anecdote set in a bar at City Quay in Dublin around 1910, when Mayo men poked fun at a condescending scholarly stranger by claiming that in Erris Micheál na nAmhrán, "the bard of Glengad," was better known than Shakespeare, "the bard of Avon."[60]

While retaining the more stylized compositions of acknowledged poets, the song repertoire of oral tradition also featured popular poetry that was composed spontaneously. Such poetry was not linked to a particular individual and was considered a communal production. An example of this genre is the popular love song "Is óra a mhíle grá," which belonged to a women's tradition of extempore composition of verses to pass the time while engaged in spinning.[61] In 1936 a version of this song was collected from a woman in the village of Devlin [Deibhleán] in Erris, who claimed to have heard it performed by an eighty-five-year-old woman thirty years earlier (ca. 1906). This version incorporated an explicit reference to the French presence in Mayo, which was perceived as a distinct event in the historical calendar of the community:

Is óra, óra, agus óra, a mhíle grá,	[No young woman left Devlin since the
Níor fhág aon bhean óg Deibhleán	French were in Ballina.][62]
Ó bhí na Francaigh i mBéal an Átha.	

There are no records of other versions of this song with this specific verse,[63] so it is likely that this particular tradition reflects a casual, perhaps one-off, poetic expression recalling the local 1798 experience. This utterance apparently made a significant impression on the audience and was preserved in social memory only to be repeated decades later to a collector from the Irish Folklore Commission.

The children's song "Mise agus Tusa," which probably originated in Mayo but remained popular into recent times in *Gaeltacht* areas in Donegal, includes explicit references to 1798:

An raibh tú i gCill Ala'	[Were you in Killala
Nó i gCaisleán an Bharraigh,	or in Castlebar,
Nó an bhfaca tú an campa	Did you see the camp
a bhí aige na Francaigh?	of the French?][64]

The form of the song is reminiscent of a template of 1798 songs in English popular in the 1840s.[65] In this particular case, it is phrased as a humorous song with a lively tune in a jig dance rhythm (triple meter), which demonstrates that *seanchas* of 1798 was not restricted to solemn tunes. It also shows how historical lore can be remembered inadvertently in children's rhymes, a subject that has been studied in depth by Iona and Peter Opie[66] and a point discussed in a following section on rhymes. In some versions of this song *Cill Alaidh* [Killala] was substituted with *Cill Dara* [Kildare].[67] This may well originate in the song migrating to Leinster and then being readapted to the new locality. However, it is worth noting that following the French landing in Mayo insurgency spread throughout county Kildare and neighboring areas,[68] where it was reported that "the mass of the people in them showed suddenly a strong sensation and a spirit of combination."[69]

In modern times there have been several attempts, influenced by folklore, to write poetry in Irish about Ninety-Eight. As a young man, pioneering-folk-lorist-to-be Douglas Hyde was fascinated with the memory of 1798 and wrote in 1879–80 a series of "Ballads of '98" under his pseudonym "An Craoibhín Aoibhinn."[70] His recitation "Bás an Chroipí" (The Death of the Croppy), which was originally circulated in 1898, reflects an attempt to write in a style reminiscent of oral tradition.[71] Another, more recent, composition is the recitation "An Gunnadóir Mac Aoidh" (Gunner Magee [McGee]) by the Galway poet and novelist Eoghan Ó Tuairisc (first published in 1949).[72] Both these poems are written in a romantic-nationalist style that appears to emulate nineteenth-century sentimental political balladry in English in the tradition of Thomas Davis and the Young Ireland movement, rather than long-standing traditions of songs and poetry in Irish.[73]

Rebel Songs and Ballads in English

Those in power write history, those who suffer write the songs.

Frank Harte, accompanying notes to the CD
1798: The First Year of Liberty

Alongside poetry in Irish, folk history of the Year of the French includes numerous local ballads in English that correspond with traditional patterns of oral narrative singing,[74] while also reflecting literary influences.[75] In the years immediately following the Rebellion, there was no attempt to collect such songs and ballads in the region. Fifty years later R. R. Madden compiled an outstanding anthology of Ninety-Eight ballads (to which he added his own poetic compositions), but it did not include references to Connacht and the north midlands.[76] Yet, some of the folklore sources collected in later periods appear to stem from political balladry that was in circulation at the time of the original historical events. An example is the fragmented survival in Mayo of the chorus "Viva la," which had been popularized by the United Irishmen and was known to have been sung in the autumn of 1798.[77]

Inspired by the radical ideologies of the Scottish Enlightenment and the

French Revolution, in the 1790s the United Irishmen launched a multifaceted attempt to mold public opinion.[78] In addition to utilizing popular print ("literary mischief"), they introduced, as Kevin Whelan has demonstrated, "a series of genres designed to be permeable across the reading/speech divide."[79] Just as political songs were central to the French revolutionary program,[80] the United Irishmen spread seditious ideas and rhetoric through songs and ballads.[81] Among their first publications was a collection of six songs that had been composed for a commemorative celebration in Belfast, which marked the third anniversary of the storming of the Bastille (14 July 1792).[82] Additional songs appeared in their organ *Northern Star* (1792–97), but the primary vehicle for publication of rebellious songs was the anthology *Paddy's Resource*, which was reissued in several editions.[83] Songs from this collection were continuously republished throughout the nineteenth century.

Whelan maintained that United Irish propaganda penetrated oral culture creating a "communal store of knowledge, accessible to all."[84] Tom Dunne, however, questioned the effectiveness of the indoctrination of enlightenment ideas and argued that attempts by the United Irishmen to promulgate egalitarian ideology did not filter into contemporary oral tradition.[85] Popular culture could not simply be shaped from above through processes of cultural colonization, since propaganda emanating from the political centers was subject to popular reception. The balladry in English reflects cross-fertilization of revolutionary Jacobin-inspired songs with older Jacobite songs in Irish, which were central in eighteenth-century Catholic popular culture.[86]

This cultural fusion is perhaps best typified in the immensely popular song "The Shan Van Vocht," which first appeared in print in the early 1840s,[87] but by that time a song collector had already noted that "the versions of this song are numberless."[88] Its English form originated from a song in Irish, which was sung in Mayo, about a young man who regrets his marriage to an old woman ("An tSeanbhean Bhocht").[89] The politicized song in English refers to a French fleet sailing to Ireland ("The French are on the sea!"). This would suggest that it is probably a late eighteenth-century composition about General Hoche's expedition to Bantry Bay in 1796 or General Humbert's expedition to Killala in 1798. In the song, the expected arrival of French aid and the imminent victory over loyalist-Protestant forces ("And the Orange will decay") is proclaimed by the *Shan Van Vocht* (Poor Old Woman), a variation of a traditional personification of Ireland as a woman. This carrier of a prophetic message was taken from the Jacobite *aisling* (vision/dream) poetic genre, which centered on a legendary female character—the *spéirbhean* (sky-woman), who originally assumed a royal persona (associated with the names Éire or Eriú, Banba, and

Fodla) but was oftentimes known by names of fictional commoners (Síle Ní Ghadhra, Siobhán Ní Mheadhra, Meidhbhín Ní Shúilleabháin, Síle Bhán Ní Shléibhín, Móirín Ní Chuileannáin, or Caitlín Ní Uallacháin). She was usually portrayed as a young beautiful woman, but could also appear as an old wizened woman, reminiscent of the ancient mythological *Cailleach Bhéarra* (Hag of Béarra). Similarly, Whiteboy and Defender acts of agrarian violent protest ("outrages") were often carried out in the names of symbolic females (Siobhán, Sadhbh Olltach, Joan Meskel, or Caitlín).[90]

Songs of such hybrid nature were espoused by those who joined the rebel ranks and persevered as expressions of sedition long after the Rebellion was suppressed and the threat of French intervention had passed away. An indication of their lingering relevance can be deduced from the fact that they were deliberately omitted from early-nineteenth-century popular collections of Gaelic political poetry in translation. The Connacht historian and antiquarian James Hardiman (1782–1855), who was born in Mayo and lived in Galway, was undoubtedly familiar with songs and folklore of the French invasion but chose not to commit such information to writing, and his history of Galway prudently restricts itself to passing references to local displays of loyalism in 1798.[91] He included an extensive section on "Jacobite Relics" in his celebrated anthology of edited Gaelic poetry and songs *Irish Minstrelsy,* which were controversially restyled in a romantic nationalist fashion,[92] but conspicuously refrained from referring to songs about Ninety-Eight.[93] Similarly, a collection of Irish poems translated by the poet Edward Walsh (1805–50) also ignored songs on the Rebellion, though his *Reliques of Irish Jacobite Poetry* enjoyed popular circulation as sixteen penny-weekly issues (1844) prior to its release as a book.[94] Traces of Jacobitism continued to linger in popular culture but, following the death of "the old pretender," James Francis Edward Stuart (1766), and his son, "the young pretender"—Charles Edward Stewart (1788), were no longer perceived as a political threat[95] and were therefore conducive to early romantic revivals of folk poetry. In contrast, songs associated with 1798 were deemed too subversive for publication in the early decades of the nineteenth century and so were preserved mainly as oral traditions.

The longevity of popular tunes of rebellion is illustrated in a story that Richard Hayes heard in the village of Lahardane, county Mayo (on the route the rebel army took from Killala to Castlebar):

> There was a lot from here joined the French. There was a poor labouring man— "Paidin a' choga" [*Páidín an Chogaidh*—Paddy of the War] he was called— went from here to Killala when he heard they were landed. He lived over in Rawkell. He fought well with them through all the battles and came back after

the troubles were over. And when he was dying long after, he sent for Liam Pleimoinn [Pléimeann], whose own father was with the French, and he told Pleimoinn that he had sixteen shillings left in his pockets and to get a piper to play "The White Cockade" over his grave when he was dead.[96]

Apparently, at some indefinite time in the nineteenth century, the playing of the Jacobite anthem "The White Cockade" was considered a fitting tribute to the memory of a veteran rebel of Ninety-Eight in a village in west Mayo. Though usually associated with Scottish Jacobitism and the failed rebellion of 1745, Irish versions of the song, known as "An Cnota Bán," were composed in the eighteenth century by the poets Seán Ó Tuama (ca. 1705–75) and Seán Clárach Mac Dómhnaill (1691–1754).[97] There is written evidence that corroborates that the tune was performed in Ireland in the beginning of the nineteenth century[98] and, in the absence of further literary sources, folklore proves to of particular value for tracing transformations in popular reception of such rebel songs. Several versions of the nineteenth-century local Ninety-Eight ballad "Tom Gilheany," which remained extremely popular in counties Leitrim and Longford into the first half of the twentieth century, refer to the playing of "The White Cockade."[99]

Songs associated with 1798 underwent revisions as oral tradition changed over time and incorporated reflections of later influences. Georges Denis Zimmermann, the author of a comprehensive study of Irish broadsides, maintained that the political balladry, which flourished in popular print from the late eighteenth century, can be perceived as "a nearly collective expression of commonly held beliefs or prejudices and of popular aspirations, and we may regard them as a running commentary on Irish political life seen 'from below.'"[100] The example of "The Shan Van Vocht" is, once again, illuminating. In its original form the song presumably referred to the events of 1796/98, but it was continuously revised throughout the nineteenth century so as to address changing political contexts.[101] A. M. Sullivan observed that: "In every election the street ballad-singer is as important a power as the platform orator or the village band, and I never knew an Irish election poet that did not invoke the 'Shan Van Vocht.'" Indeed, versions of the song appeared in the 1860s in election campaigns in Connacht (1865) and county Longford (1869).[102]

Maura Cronin (née Murphy) noted that "many of the most seditious ballads were never printed, but were passed on orally." Nineteenth-century government reports, which monitored ballad singing, shed light on the historical contexts within which ballads were produced and performed. They call attention to the role of professional ballad singers—men and women who traveled around the country, purchasing ballads from local printers and performing at fairs.[103] A statement extracted in 1841 from the ballad singer Denis Sheehan revealed that over the course of a year he had traveled through the provinces of Munster (counties Limerick, Tipperary, Clare, Kerry, and Cork), Leinster (King's County), and Connacht (counties Galway and Roscommon) singing various "seditious ballads," including "The Brave Spalpeen Fanouch" (an English version of "An Spailpín Fánach"), which referred to 1798. This remarkable route demonstrates the wide circulation of ballads, which may have appeared originally in print but were then passed on through oral performances.[104] As Delargy remarked, "the student of the social and the literary history of Ireland must bear all these wandering people in mind."[105]

With the readaptation of traditional songs and the continuous addition of new songs and ballads to the burgeoning Ninety-Eight song repertoire, the Rebellion became a principal source of inspiration for Irish balladry in English.[106] Mid-nineteenth-century cultural nationalism promoted by the Young Ireland movement encouraged the composition of political songs, many of which referred to 1798. Young Ireland's popular ballad anthology *Spirit of The Nation* (first published in 1843), which allegedly sold more copies than any book published in Ireland after the Act of Union (1800),[107] initiated the publication of cheap patriotic songbooks (in order to circumvent government intervention and censorship, the books were often published in Scotland or the United States). The *Oxford Companion to Irish Literature* notes that these collections of songs and ballads in English "formed the greatest bulk of Irish literary publishing throughout the second part of the nineteenth century."[108] Many of these songs were absorbed into oral traditions and subsequently collected in the 1930s as bona fide folklore.[109]

An illuminating example of the readaptation of literary ballads in oral tradition relates to "The Rising of the Moon" by John Keegan Casey (1846–70), who was popularly known by the pseudonym Leo. Though it was officially first published in Casey's first collection *Wreath of Shamrocks* (1866), as locals later recalled, the ballad was available in manuscript form "long before it appeared in print."[110] In 1865 one thousand copies of "The Rising of the Moon" were distributed in "neat form" (printed slips) in counties Longford, Cavan, and Westmeath.[111] By 1867 the song was reported to be "well known in some of our Midland counties and admired, except by the authorities."[112] Initially circulated on broadsides, the ballad soon appeared in newspapers and songbooks, and rapidly gained national recognition. Its popularity was partly due to its catchy air. It was set to the tune of the United Irish songs "Green Upon My Cape" and "The Wearing of the Green," which, in turn, originated from an eighteenth-century Scottish march ("The Tulip").[113] "The Wearing of the Green" was sung continuously from the time of the Rebellion through the first half of the nineteenth century[114] and enjoyed a popular revival when adapted into the nationalist melodrama *Arrah-na-Pogue* (first performed in 1864) by Dion Boucicault (1820–90), a rendition described by a contemporary as the "finest street ballad ever."[115]

"The Rising of the Moon" was popular in areas associated with the 1798 Rebellion in county Longford. It inspired a local nationalist ballad about the battle of Granard ("Down by the Sheelin's Vale at sunset"), which was preserved in oral tradition.[116] A version of this ballad ("A place called Sheila's Valley") could still be recited for the benefit of the folklore collector James Delaney as late as 1977. The collector immediately recognized the source of influence, yet his eighty-nine-year-old informant emphatically insisted that the ballad did not derive from Leo's composition (even though family tradition recalled the poet visiting the area and meeting his father). He clearly remembered all nine verses of the local ballad but could only recite a fragment of "The Rising of the Moon."[117] This would suggest that in a regional context, the local oral ballad might have been more popular than the original, supposedly better-known, literary ballad that served as its inspiration. Moreover, in 1956 Delaney collected a fragment of what appears to be an older song about the battle of Granard, which may even stem back to the time of the Rebellion.[118] However, it appears that, thanks to the memorable tune popularized by Leo (among others), the nineteenth-century local ballad was remembered in its entirety, whereas the verses of the older song were largely forgotten.

The case of "The Rising of the Moon" demonstrates a characteristic feature of folk songs, which consist mostly of new verses sung to familiar tunes of older airs. As Cronin perceptively observed "memory of the rebellion could be preserved not only by detailed narrative but also by "the *shape* of a song—its title, rhythm, refrain and the air to which it may have been sung."[119] A collection of airs from Connacht and the north midlands (focusing on county Leitrim and adjacent areas in Sligo, Galway, Mayo, and Roscommon) taken down by the Cork musician and outstanding traditional music collector William Forde in the mid-nineteenth century (ca. 1840–50), preserved the musical score of several early songs referring to local 1798 experiences, though by then the verses had been forgotten.[120] One of them, "At Cloone Church gate [the fight began]," was clearly about the battle of Ballinamuck. According to Forde, another air— "The John[ny] Gibbons March"—was performed to the tune of an earlier song titled "Captain McGreal of Connemara." Both these titles refer to 1798 insurgent leaders who continued to maintain resistance in Connemara and were remembered as popular outlaw heroes.[121] In county Leitrim, Forde met the exceptional fiddler Hugh O'Beirne of Ballinamore from whom he collected in 1846 eighty-seven airs. Among them, O'Beirne identified "The Yeomen of Ballinamore" as referring to a local 1798 skirmish, explaining that "the yeomen ran away from the French at Fenagh."[122] In the 1930s Cyril Knox of Palmerstown, county Mayo collected in his locality tunes of marches, which reputedly had been sung by French troops in 1798 and were remembered locally.[123]

Cronin distinguished between two forms of nineteenth-century public singing:

> The street ballad was sung by one individual to an audience who cheered and encouraged the singer, but did not join in the song. The songs of the public house, on the other hand were for communal singing. One man might lead the song, but the others joined in the refrain and a spirit of camaraderie was fostered by this participation, even the gestures of the singers pointed to this camaraderie.[124]

Both these styles of performance merged in the rural *céilí* gatherings, which hosted "singers, and those who, while they could not sing themselves, knew the words of a large number of songs."[125] The folk song collector Tom Munnelly pertinently pointed out that "the ballad singer documented the events of '98 at the time and through the looking glass of later years."[126] Comparative analysis of different versions of songs collected mainly in the twentieth century can offer insight into the scope of variation. However, the fluidity of *seanchas* renders it impossible to trace back every performance and identify the "original" versions as they were sung in the nineteenth century and, in some cases, possibly as far back as the end of eighteenth century. Often, what appears to be older material survived as folklore in fragmented form and therefore does not lend itself to reconstruction, so that original complete versions remain unknown.

Occasionally, it is possible to identify moments of transition, through which a history of developments in local song traditions can be provisionally reconstructed. A ballad from the Ballinamuck area known as "The Connaught Rising" tells the story of the French campaign, with particular detail devoted to the battle of Ballinamuck and its aftermath. It was known to have been printed in the centennial year of 1898 and was attributed to a former national schoolteacher in Cloone named Anthony Curran.[127] By the 1930s it was considered an "old ballad"[128] and the author could no longer be identified.[129] In 1965 a collector noted:

> I haven't a notion who is the author or where it came from or who made it. I don't know. I must have heard it going on with some of . . . indeed the man I used to hear sing it, Red McCastle, he's in America somewhere now.[130]

Songs that appeared in print could enter seamlessly into oral tradition, and while noteworthy performers of the song were often remembered, the original author was readily forgotten.

Communities in the north midlands preserved a rich body of 1798 song traditions in English. These songs mostly commemorated local "pike-men" heroes who were not recognized among the national heroes of Ninety-Eight lauded in canonical nationalist balladry. Many songs were preserved in family traditions. For example, a fragment of the song "Willie O'Keefe and the Old Grey Mare," about a local rebel leader from Ballinalough who fought in 1798 at Granard and Ballinamuck, was recalled by his descendants into the end of the twentieth century.[131] The most popular Ninety-Eight songs in the Leitrim-Longford area were attributed to a folk poet named Patrick Higgins of Cloncoose, county Leitrim (three kilometers north of Ballinamuck), who died around 1900 and was locally esteemed as "a great poet." He was still remembered in the locality more than thirty years after his death, when pupils from Drumgownagh National School (N.S.) in county Leitrim were told by their parents that "people liked him very well because of the nice poems and songs that he sung"[132] and "that the people from the district used to gather into his house almost every night to hear him composing poetry and rhymes, and telling about olden times."[133] Higgins's ballad "Tom Gilheany" (also spelled "Kilheany") appears to have been the most well-known song in English about the Year of the French.

Despite the length of the ballad, which runs to thirty-three stanzas or a staggering 222 lines, numerous versions of "Tom Gilheany" have been collected.[134] This commendable feat of memory, assisted no doubt by the ballad's flowing poetic structure and simple rhymes does not appear to have been extraordinary or associated with select individuals.[135] The Leitrim historian T. M. O'Flynn observed in 1937 that knowledge of the poem was common and "preserved among the peasantry."[136] Traditions of Tom Gilheany also demonstrate the codependency and fluidity between the different genres of *seanchas*. The narrative recalled in the ballad appeared also in several prose versions as a tale,[137] but it apparently bore more currency in verse.[138] Although most of the poetry attributed to Higgins of Cloncoose expressed patriotic-nationalist sentiments,[139] "Tom Gilheany" does not correspond with the dominant nationalist tone of late-nineteenth-century official 1798 commemoration, which was often structured along partisan sectarian lines. The ballad and stories present a reconciliatory narrative about a fugitive rebel (Gilheany) who is betrayed by an informer ("Shuffling Shawn")[140] but saved by an honest Protestant yeoman (Bob Ferguson), who in turn is repaid years later, when the grateful hero saves him from a lynch mob at a local fair.[141]

"Jack O'Hara," a popular local 1798 ballad also attributed to the poet Higgins, tells the tale of yet another Ballinamuck fugitive. In this ballad, the protagonist (O'Hara) is brought to a Protestant household, whose owners (Nichols) had a reputation for saving Catholics. Although kind hospitality is offered to the starving prisoner by the woman of the house, a bloodthirsty yeoman commander (Isaac Clements) insists on executing him. In compliance with a familiar storytelling motif, the persecutor is mistakenly killed by the firing squad while the hero masterfully succeeds in escaping.[142] Elements of this story were transferred to another local hero—Paddy Reilly, known as "Paddy Shan Bawn" ("Sean Bán," or old fair-headed Paddy).[143] As in the case of Tom Gilheany, this north midlands' tradition also incorporated references to fugitive rebels who encountered assistance and kindness from Protestants. Such examples demonstrate how popular ballads in regional oral tradition maintained a measure of independence from the dominant characteristics of the political balladry written in Dublin and circulated through popular print, differentiating them from Ninety-Eight songs in other areas. Though nineteenth-century folk poets, like Patrick Higgins, were clearly influenced by the romantic-nationalist balladry of their time, they readapted these influences in accordance with the particular character of local folk historiography.

Many songs remained anonymous and were not attributed to a particular poet or songwriter. Noteworthy Ninety-Eight examples from the song traditions of the north midlands refer to the local Leitrim heroes Myles Cullen of Drumshanbo ("Milie of the Spear")[144] and Billy Connell.[145] The anonymity of folk songs is indicative of the most basic dynamic of *seanchas,* which invariably originates in the creative initiative of a talented individual but, upon gaining wider popularity, attains a communal identity and is ultimately incorporated in local oral tradition.[146] James C. Scott argued that the collective anonymity of folklore allows it to express subversive messages in defiance of dominant culture.[147]

Whereas the assimilation of *seanchas* into communal tradition is an unconscious and largely unnoticed hidden process, nineteenth-century cultural revivalists attempted to emulate and influence folklore by actively engaging in a similar form of cultural production. Nationalist writers deliberately assumed a collective voice. The popularity of writing under pseudonyms, which were typically nationalist names for Ireland or names of mythic heroes, alongside the fascination with anonymity and the vogue of populist soubriquets such as the "peasant poet" (John Keegan) or "fear na muinntire" ("The Man of the People," William Rooney), reflected an aspiration to revoke the notion of the professionalization of the author in favor of a more abstract concept of literature as "the soul of the nation."[148] Yet, the impact of such literary imitations of folk-lore was moderated by popular reception. As a rule, regional popular culture promoted folk histories that were distinct from the versions of national history propagated from the political center.

Loyalist Songs

They [Irish Protestants] are a very song-making nation.

Stewart Blacker
testimony before the Select Committee
appointed to inquire in the Nature, Character, Extent,
and Tendency of Orange Lodges, Associations
or Societies in Ireland, 1835

The very notion of "popular culture," which is often founded on a questionable distinction between an allegedly inclusive "common" people's culture in contrast to what is perceived as an exclusive elite culture, tends to overlook the folk traditions of "unpopular" groups. Such is the case of loyalism and its folklore, which have been overshadowed in many studies of modern Irish history by the vibrant popular culture of Catholic nationalism. In a discussion on "Insurrection Ballads and Songs," Richard Hayes included a brief section on songs that opposed the French invasion and the Rebellion in Connacht, noting that these were composed by "paid writers" as part of a "campaign of calumny" promoted by "the government faction in Ireland."[149]

Such propaganda was proliferated in songbooks, pamphlets, and broadsheets. Loyalist songs lampooned the rebels' cause, gloating over the defeat and pouring scorn on the leaders. Originally published after Ballinamuck, the ballad "Humbert's Mistake" (set to the tune "Moggy Lawder") declares: "The traitor Blake / Submits to Lake / With Ninety-three poor peasants; / Teeling and Roche / (Their isle's reproach) / Are now convicted felons."[150] The rebel general George Blake was hanged at Ballinamuck and the Franco-Irish officers Bartholomew Teeling and Roche (also known as La Roche) were court-martialed in Dublin, where the former was executed and the latter allowed to leave the country.[151] The burlesque broadsheet "Erin go bray" (set to the tune of "Marlbrook"), composed by Dr. Law—the Protestant bishop of Elphin, was presented as if it had been found in the pocket of a French officer, who was ungraciously depicted in a woodcut as a hussar mounted on a donkey. It featured the chorus "And Erin may go bray," which parodies the rebel rallying cry "Erin go bragh."[152]

Widely feared and despised by Catholics, the Protestant ultraloyalist Orange Order (instituted in 1795), which actively participated in the repression of the Rebellion through sectarian acts of violence, had a limited presence in Connacht in 1798. Only a handful of lodges were established in counties Leitrim (10), Roscommon (3), Sligo (2) and Galway (2),[153] yet Orangemen also infiltrated yeomanry and army units stationed in the locality. Overcoming various governmental bans and prohibitions, Orangeism transformed and mutated through the nineteenth and twentieth centuries while cultivating loyalist traditions, some of which explicitly referred to the events of the Rebellion. The first Orange songbooks were published in 1798 and were continuously recycled, often in unchanged form, throughout the nineteenth century.[154] The most popular of these songs was "Croppies Lie Down," which explicitly called for opposition to a insurrection supported by a French invasion: "We soldiers of Erin, so proud of the name, / Will raise upon rebels and Frenchmen our fame." After the victory over the rebels, it was sung triumphantly at loyalist celebrations[155] and was already known in multiple versions in 1798.[156]

Zimmermann perceptively observed that, though it may seem paradoxical, "both streams of Irish political verse flowed in a parallel direction" and consequently "'Green' and 'Orange' Irishmen have more in common than their mutual hatred."[157] Several Orange songs were written as parodies of well-known United Irish songs and, at a later period, of popular nationalist balladry. An early example is the Orange song "British Lion, or the New Viva La,"[158] written in response to the United Irish song "Rouse, Hibernians," popularly known as "Vive La." The loyalist song "We've a Law," which lauded the virtues of the British constitution in contrast to the violent anarchy of Revolutionary France, was set to the tune of "Vive La."[159] These compositions were primarily poetic forms of literary propaganda and, as the folksong scholar Terry Moylan soberly noted, in many cases "it is impossible to say if the songs were ever sung."[160]

Orange-broadside ballads, which were performed, have been classified as "half-way between oral tradition and song books." Zimmermann also acknowledged that

> as was the case of nationalist ballads, booklets were only one of the ways of circulating Orange songs. Ballads were also transmitted by oral tradition; a number of them are still to be heard in the countryside, sung in the same way as the traditional nationalist ballad in other parts of the country, with perhaps more vigour or aggressiveness and less frequent *melismata* and *portamenti*.[161]

Oral traditions of Protestants and parties that were loyal to the Crown in 1798 were not collected systematically, neither by the Irish Folklore Commission nor by Richard Hayes. Triumphalist by nature, loyalist songs and ballads were generally considered offensive by collectors of folklore in a newly independent Ireland. Consequently, the source material available for studies of oral expressions of popular loyalism and its song traditions was impoverished. This lacuna is discussed further in chapter 16, "Memory and Oblivion."

Rhymes

> Jingles and other sayings in rhyme or rhythm, even when unmeaning to those who repeat them, sometimes have considerable significance for the scientific observer.
>
> Charlotte Sophia Burne
> *The Handbook of Folklore*

Other than songs, there was also a more basic genre of poetic expression in the form of rhymes, which were either independent couplets or fragmented verses of forgotten ballads. These were particularly popular among children.[162] In 1937 two siblings from Mohill, county Leitrim, attending Drumgoisnagh N.S, noted in their copybooks that "there were a lot of rhymes about the battle of Ballinamuck." As an example, they recited:

> Croppy get up for you are long enough down
> until we banish the Orangemen out of the town[163]

This rhyme appears to be a response to the aforementioned Orange song "Croppies Lie Down," which in itself (like another loyalist song, "Down in reply to up") may have been composed in reaction to the United Irish ballad "Up."[164] The folk rhyme from the Ballinamuck area is therefore an indication of popular "poetic dialectics" in oral tradition, which mirrored the partisan paraphrasing and mocking of songs in political pamphlets.

Other rhymes were less explicit in their reference to Ninety-Eight. The epigraph of Hayes's *The Last Invasion of Ireland* quotes a rhyme "from a ballad popular in the South":

> Be a good boy and I'll buy you a book
> And I'll send you to school at Ballinamuck

The folklorist Bairbre Ní Fhloinn remembered from her childhood that her aunt in county Roscommon would recite a couplet with a similar rhythm:

> Anthony Duck, Anthony Duck
> Follow the Leader to Ballinamuck

Ní Fhloinn recalled that "the recital of the rhyme was always accompanied by her [the aunt] beating out the rhythm of the words with her knuckles on a hard surface, in a very distinctive and quite difficult way."[165] The unwitting recital of these rhymes called attention to the site of the infamous battlefield of Ballinamuck and inadvertently promoted interest in historical folklore of Ninety-Eight.

Proverbs and Sayings

An Seanchas gearr, an Seanchas is fearr.
[Short *Seanchas* is the best *Seanchas*.]
Connacht proverb

Proverbs have been defined as "short and witty traditional expressions that arise as part of everyday discourse as well as in the more highly structured situations of education and judicial proceedings."[166] Their two essential characteristics are didacticism of contents and conciseness of form.[167] As pithy idiomatic summaries of values, attitudes, and communal knowledge, proverbs and sayings encapsulate "folk wisdom" and offer insight into a community's overall outlook, or *mentalité*. Mostly they appear to be timeless, yet occasional historical references can serve as indications of how events in the past were called upon to draw lasting lessons with continued relevance that lingered long after the original sociopolitical context changed. Therefore, from an historian's point of view, Irish proverbs and sayings (*seanfhocail*) can incorporate inadvertent reflections of vernacular attitudes to the past.

Only a few sayings have been recorded that relate specifically to the events of the Year of the French. In his pioneering study of Hiberno-English in the early twentieth century, Patrick Weston Joyce notes that "In and around Ballina in Mayo, a great strong fellow is called an *allay-foozee*, which represents the sound of the French *Allez-fusil* (musket or musketry forward), preserving the memory of the landing of the French at Killala (near Ballina) in 1798."[168] There are several other records of French expressions, which obliquely filtered into local parlance in Mayo.[169] In 1940 the collector Michael Corduff heard in Kilcummin, county Mayo, about "an incident of 1798," which referred to the engagement at Carricknagat, county Sligo. According to this tradition, the Irish rebels could not comprehend the French command to advance till one of their officers exclaimed: "Beigh Éire go deo agun [againn] agus Carraic a Chat," to which the Irish responded by attacking and defeating the enemy cavalry. This was supposed to be the origin of a common saying in Erris—"Éire go deo agus Carraic a Chat" (Ireland forever and *Carrick a Chat*), which was used as an exclamation to celebrate success.[170] Through such sayings, peripheral events that do not appear in official historical accounts, such as a skirmish within a small-scale battle, were inadvertently remembered in local folk history.

Interviewed in 1965, the sixty-one-year-old Ballinamuck schoolteacher Peter Duignan of Gaigue observed that locals often referred to a large person as a "Mahussian" and that it was commonly said: "Oh! he's a big Hussian of a fellow. She's a big Hussian of a girl."[171] The name "Hussian" is a colloquial pronunciation of "Hessian,"[172] a term that was commonly used in reference to Baron de Hompesch's dragoons. According to the Muster Masters General's records, this regiment of continental mercenaries (mostly German) in the service of the British army was recruited in January 1798 and was stationed in Ireland till 1802.[173] In 1798 "Hompesch's Dragoon Riflemen" took part in General Gerard Lake's campaign against the French in Connacht. They left a strong impression on social memory and were commonly associated with traditions of terror and atrocities in the area of Ballinamuck.[174] A cavalry column of Hessians under the command of Colonel Robert Crauford pursued the Franco-Irish army from Castlebar to Ballinamuck. Although their green and red uniform did not resemble the silver-gray attire of the French hussars,[175] the

FIGURE 11. *Hessian dragoons in the Irish Rebellion of* 1798 by William Sadler (ca. 1868–80). Folk history recalled the Hessian mercenaries (Baron de Hompesch's dragoons) as hefty foreigners who were responsible for widespread brutalities and atrocities in Ninety-Eight. Courtesy of the National Library of Ireland.

appearance of foreign soldiers in the service of the Crown caused much confusion among the local population. Lord Carleton, the Chief Justice of Common Pleas, later wrote that "the Irish, deceived by their dress and foreign language, took them for the French and came to join them in great numbers, but were immediately cut down and their pockets rifled by their supposed friends."[176] To combat this situation, French officers were placed in the rear guard in order to identify the "Hessians" by pointing at them and calling out "George's mana!" (i.e., King George's Men).[177] Several traditions from the area of Ballinamuck tell of rebels making the fatal error of mistaking Hessians for French troops,[178] and one account even suggested that a wily English officer had purposely disguised his soldiers in French uniform.[179]

In retrospect, Hessians were remembered as extremely large and brutal foreigners. Writing in 1839, Rev. Caesar Otway recalled how in the summer of 1799 he was assaulted in Kilbeggan, county Westmeath, by Hessians who mistook him for a rebel. He described them as "a set of outlandish soldiers— gigantic looking fellows with terrible *moustaches* and other marks denoting them to be foreigners."[180] In popular parlance "Hushian" was used to describe any "rough or cruel person."[181] Many traditions told of rebels killing Hessians, yet in reality the official medical report lists only four Hessians killed and three others injured from gunshot wounds at Ballinamuck.[182] Stories of local resistance were evidently readapted so that, at least in some versions, the enemy soldiers were identified specifically as Hessians, a detail that emphasized the bravery of the protagonist.[183]

References to Hessians in the north midlands relate to 1798 lore in Wexford, where their mostly fictional reputation for cruelty and molesting women[184] generated the popular saying: "You'll have to kill a Hussian for yourself."[185] Like other narratives in folk-history, stories about Hessians incorporated historical folklore motifs. For example, a tale from Ballinamuck recounted how Manus Devaney of Kilmahon (Ballinamuck) killed in self-defense a Hessian and then attempted to remove his tightly fitted boots, but had to resort to pulling the legs off the corpse.[186] This is a version of a familiar international folklore motif, classified as AT 1281A and AT 1537. It is often told as part of the popular Irish folktale "The Cow That Ate the Piper"[187] and several other variants relating to 1798 have been collected, both as tales and ballads.[188]

Following the circulation of numerous popular histories during the centenary commemorations of 1898, by the early-twentieth-century local traditions of Hessian atrocities in 1798 enjoyed general recognition among Irish nationalists. They were so widespread that British World War I propaganda attempted to utilize these emotive images in the pro-war campaign. A recruitment poster circulated toward the end of the war evoked the memory of Hessians and unashamedly claimed: "The Germans are the same in 1918 as in 1798."[189] As the example of Hessians demonstrates, although uttered casually, a local saying can serve as an index referring to a larger body of historical folklore.

Prophecies

> Prophecy is a political grammar into which highly subversive ideas can be inserted and which is accessible to a very wide range of actors.
>
> Bertrand Taithe and Tim Thornton
> *Prophecy*

Folklore could invoke the past in future tense, as traditions of prophecy were often associated with rebellion and foreign invasion. Although prophecies featured in various *seanchas* accounts, they have not been recognized as a distinct genre in Irish folklore studies. Divination has been classified by folklorists under the category of "popular belief and practice," while prophecy has also been associated with blessings and curses.[190] Irish manuscripts reveal numerous expressions of vaticination that were attributed to mythological Celtic figures such as Conn Cétchathach, Fionn Mac Cumhaill, and various Christian holy men, in particular the sixth-century saint Colum Cille.[191] These traditions stem back to medieval times, though the authenticity of modern collections of prophecy was occasionally subject to scholarly controversy.[192] Keith Thomas demonstrated how prophecies of supposedly ancient origin appeared as a "validating charter" (originally orally and, from the mid-seventeenth century, also in popular print) in practically every English early-modern rebellion. While prophecy "brought authority and conviction to those staking all on a desperate step," it also "gave a sort of moral justification to those engaged in the gambler's throw of rebellion; and it kept up the spirits of the defeated by assuring them that time was on their side."[193]

Although Ireland did not share the decline in prophecy noticeable in England from the seventeenth century, in both isles there was extensive prophetic preaching and writing during the French Revolutionary and Napoleonic period.[194] In the 1790s there was a flourish of Irish millenarian prophecies, driven by sectarian and agrarian unrest. A prime example were the widely circulated apocalyptic "Pastorini prophecies,"[195] which continued to play a subversive role into the early 1820s, when they were manipulated by the agrarian

Rockite movement.[196] According to the novelist William Carleton, the failure of these prophecies to fulfill themselves by their promised dates (1821 or 1825) "nearly demolished the political seers as a class, or compelled them to fall back upon the more antiquated revelations ascribed to St. Columkill, St. Bridget and others."[197] Despite this setback, as folklore sources show, traditions of prophecy continued to circulate in popular culture.

The United Irishmen used prophecies and apocalyptic literature as a tool for popular politicization.[198] Musgrave observed that seditious prophecies (supposedly "delivered by the ancient Irish bards and prophets") were particularly developed in Ulster and traveled to Mayo and Sligo with the migration of Catholics escaping persecution at the hands of Orangemen just prior to 1798.[199] He maintained that sectarian prophecies had "a very great effect on the minds of the lower class of people" and spread fears among credulous Catholics of impending massacres.[200] Agitations during the war with France also contributed to sporadic outbursts of millennial-driven mass-hysteria. The Longford historian J. P. Farrell noted that at the time red skies provoked widespread consternation:

> A great many people thereupon declared that this phenomenon, which was nothing more or less than a phase of the *aurora borealis*, was prophesied by St. Columbkille to be the forerunner of dire misfortune to the Irish race; and so alarmed did some people become over it, that the clergy had to intervene to allay the general clamour.[201]

Set on this volatile background, prophecies generated expectations of an impending French landing. The Wexford United Irishman Miles Byrne (1780–1862) later recalled that when hiding in the Wicklow mountains around the time of the French invasion his band of fugitive rebels was joined by deserters from the Antrim militia that was stationed in the area. Their leader, a sergeant commonly known as Antrim John, claimed that:

> according to a prophecy they had in the north, Ireland could not be free before the autumn of 98, when the French were to land, and then the English yoke was to be shook off for ever, and Ireland once more become a nation, governing herself, and trading with all the world as a free country is entitled to do.[202]

When the French actually arrived, popular perceptions of their campaign were influenced by such prophecies.

Rev. James Little, the Anglican rector of Lacken, county Mayo (in the area where the French landed), and an eyewitness of the invasion, quoted a local account whereby "an old woman (as true a prophetess as Cassandra) had predicted that since French blood had been shed in Killala on their first arrival there their enterprise would not succeed." Rev. Little questioned the veracity of French casualty reports, which only listed a wounded soldier, and claimed that French corpses were buried covertly in Killala:

> I believe that the story I heard was true and that the French thro' policy concealed the death of their men and endeavoured to stifle the story of the prophecy, lest is should make a discouraging impression on the rebels, whose superstition they had become so well acquainted with from the instruction of their Irish associates, the coinage of false prophecies was one of the principal arts employed for their seduction.[203]

Memory of this prophecy survived in local oral tradition. One hundred and forty years later, George Monnelly, "an old man of splendid physique and fine intelligence" in the village of Kilcummin, repeated to Richard Hayes stories of the French landing that he had heard from his grandfather (who had been around in 1798), noting: "there was an old woman prophesied that they wouldn't win because French blood was spilt in the streets of Killala when they first went into it."[204] As this example illustrates, although some prophecies were circulated through pamphlets and chapbooks, they were primarily transmitted through oral communication and subsequently survived in folklore.

Individual prophets were remembered as popular heroes, and their visions were repeated as proof of their foresight or (when they remained unfulfilled) as warnings of events yet to come.[205] Mayo folklore, for example, cherished its own legendary heroes, such as the seventeenth-century prophet Red Brian Carabine of Erris.[206] The ability to predict the future was a recognizable sign of distinct greatness often associated with folk heroes. Stories from Mayo about Fr. Manus Sweeney [An tAthair Mánus Mac Suibhne], a local Ninety-Eight hero, mentioned that already at birth there were signs of the tragic fate that awaited him. In addition to his other magical powers (which were extolled in stories of potent blessings and curses), Fr. Sweeney allegedly foresaw his own death.[207]

A rich body of traditions relating to prophecy associated with the Year of the French was collected in county Galway. Incorporating a recurring theme of a local "prophecy man" who foretold the arrival of the French (often with the help of a book attributed to Colum Cille), these narratives tell how he is at first admonished and proscribed by a local landlord or military officer but then is vindicated when the alarmed figure of authority turns to him seeking reassurance that the invasion is only a passing event. This structure of a confrontation between a prophet and a skeptic in which the balance of power shifts is a readaptation of a familiar motif reminiscent of the biblical story of King Saul and the "witch" (or to be more precise, the soothsayer) of Ein Dor.[208] The names of the local protagonists associated with the Ninety-Eight legend change in the different versions: the prophet was identified either as Seán 'ac an Iomaire and his rival as Captain O'Flaherty,[209] Conroy and Captain Pearse,[210] or Seán 'ac an Eith and Colonel Martin.[211] In some versions, the outlawed prophet is a blacksmith by trade[212] and is thereby implicitly associated with abundant folklore referring to preparations of pikes for rebels in 1798.[213]

In a story collected in the parish of Clare, county Galway, Páraic of Ciolla Chealla, who prophesies the exact day and time of the landing of the French (described as noon on the day of the fair of Turlogh Mor), is confronted by skeptical neighbors only to be eventually proved right.[214] A similar motif featured in traditions associated with the French arrival in Bantry Bay, county Cork, in 1796, where a common story told of local prophets who predicted the arrival of the French on Christmas Day but were confronted by a priest who opposed the French venture.[215] In contrast, Galway Ninety-Eight folklore does not reflect this kind of internal Catholic struggle. The tumultuous events of the the Year of the French in Connacht were used as a setting to portray a more general conflict between upholders of native-traditional culture and representatives of government authority, who are reluctantly obliged to acknowledge the validity of popular belief. Other prophecies from Connemara linked the Year of the French with the proscription of popular Catholic practices. In 1933 a sixty-six-year-old woman from Cleggan recalled hearing at the beginning of the century the prophetic verses "beidh áthrú creidimh ann, ó bhliain na bhFrancach / agus teampall gallda ar an Áltóir Mhóir" (There will be a change of religion there, from the Year of the French / and there will be an Anglican church on the Great Altar).[216] The "Great Altar" is a dolmen in Connemara popularly known as the "Altar of the Druids" (*Altóir na Droidhthe*). At a similar site in the area, known as *Geata na h-Altóra* (the Altar's Gate), a local tradition maintained that "Mass was said at it [in] the time the French came to Ireland."[217] Prophetic references to the arrival of the French recall eighteenth-century Jacobite culture, which proliferated prophecies of French ships carrying troops that would champion the cause of oppressed Irish Catholics.

It has been suggested that popular perceptions of the calamity at Ballinamuck may have been amplified by a "Prophecy of Columbkille," which referred to an apocalypse in the "Valley of the Black Pig," a mythical place associated with the locality, as the Anglicized place-name Ballinamuck derives from the Irish *Béal Átha na Muice* (the Mouth of the Ford of the Pigs).[218] Despite the setback, the French surrender at Ballinamuck did not put an end to prophesies of French forces bringing salvation. Folklore collected for the Schools' Scheme in the area of Cooga, in northwest county Sligo, recalled that

Irish recruits mobilized for the last rebel stand at Killala were promised that another French expedition would soon arrive.[219] These hopes were bolstered by several additional French expeditions that arrived on the northwest coast in following weeks. On 16 September 1798 the United Irishman James Napper Tandy landed with 270 French troops and a large supply of weapons and ammunition on Rutland Island, off the west coast of county Donegal. After a night of drinking with the local postman, he issued a proclamation in English, phrased in a high-flown style that bore little relevance for the mainly Irish-speaking populace, and sailed away.[220] Nevertheless, this short-lived debacle was remembered in local folklore, and the flagstone on which Tandy first stepped upon landing was later pointed out.[221]

One month later, on 12 October 1798, a more substantial French invasion force of 2,800 men under General Hardy arrived in Donegal Bay in a fleet of ten ships commanded by Admiral Jean Baptise Françoise Bompard and was defeated by a British fleet under Sir John Warren in a naval victory that was widely celebrated in loyalist pamphlets.[222] Subsequently, the illustrious United Irishman Theobald Wolfe Tone was captured aboard the flagship *Hoche* in Lough Swilly. This episode entered into nationalist mythology, and Wolfe Tone later became the most prominent icon of Irish republicanism. Donegal folklore vividly recalled *Lá an Bhriste Mhóir ar an Fharraige* (the day of the great sea battle) and the time "when there was a great sea-battle out beyond Tory between the French and the English."[223] In 1936 an eighty-two-year-old Donegal shoemaker recounted that his aunt, who was an infant in 1798, would tell of the anxieties that spread throughout the locality when the French sailed into Lough Swilly.[224] Finally, on 27 October 1798, the three frigates that had brought Humbert's expedition to Ireland returned to Killala Bay with another corvette carrying a reinforcement army of 1,090 under Adjutant-General Cortez but turned back upon realizing that they had arrived too late.[225] Even though the local insurrection had only recently been brutally quelled, the arrival of this squadron aroused local disaffection, and the loyalist population of Killala was evacuated as "panic became universal."[226]

Throughout the Revolutionary and Napoleonic wars, numerous plans were drawn for further French landings in Ireland. Humbert himself continued to propose invasion plans from 1799 to 1801 (and in 1810 suggested invading England).[227] Intercepted intelligence of French invasion plans,[228] in conjunction with reports of local preparations for a landing in Connacht,[229] continued to trouble the British authorities after 1798. Although Britain secured naval superiority following the decisive victory at Trafalgar (1805), as a precautionary measure against the threat of a French invasion, Martello towers and battery fortifications were constructed around the British and Irish coasts (1804–12).[230] Local fears and expectations of French troops returning to the west coast did not subside and were probably exacerbated by military preparations, such as the establishment of a military post in Bishop Stock's residence in Killala,[231] which unintentionally transmitted to the population the imminent possibility of another invasion.

Expectations for the return of the French were fortified by the messianic reverence accorded to Napoleon Bonaparte in popular traditions, which continued to reverberate even after his defeat.[232] A scholarly writer traveling through Ireland at the end of the nineteenth century noted that in an Irish-speaking area in county Mayo "a man who spoke some English asked me if I thought that the French were likely to come again to free Ireland."[233] These seemingly naive sentiments were deeply embedded in popular culture and occasionally resurfaced in unrelated *seanchas*. For example, a Wexford folksong collected in 1935 about the use of seaweed as fertilizer referred to popular belief that the French would "surely come."[234] In such ways, prophecies of a French invasion persisted as a subversive reminder of an unfulfilled promise and survived into the twentieth century to be collected by folklorists.

Toasts and Other Genres

In Ireland, history and politics can be evoked over a casual drink. *A Handbook of Irish Folklore* refers to healths and toasts made during everyday social intercourse and, in particular, at times of recreation when imbibing alcoholic drinks,[235] though blessings uttered at times of drinking could also have a religious nature.[236] In the late seventeenth and eighteenth centuries, Irish Catholics espoused toasting as a popular medium for rebellious expressions of Jacobitism.[237] United Irishmen regularly met in taverns in the 1790s and encouraged seditious toasting as a lively form of "propaganda by deed." Whereas the leadership toasted to the radical and enlightened aspirations of the republican cause, on a ground level toasts often carried sectarian messages that were commonly associated with the violent activities of the Catholic Defender secret society. These popular toasts were often unashamedly vivid in their graphic descriptions of macabre retributions wished on political opponents. Drinking in public rendered the movement susceptible to observation by informers, and so the United Irish leadership attempted to put an end to this practice by advocating abstinence in the period immediately before the outbreak of the Rebellion.[238]

To date there has been no comprehensive study of the remembrance of political toasts in folklore. In some cases, toasts were recalled inadvertently. A striking example from county Galway was documented in a letter to the Lord Lieutenant, written soon after the Rebellion in Connacht, that informed on a man in the village of Oranmore who "has been taken up for drinking the toast, "That the King's skin may be converted into boats for Bonaparte," which wish was inserted in a song that was sung in ale-houses and whiskey shops." Richard Hayes regretted that "that song is lost for ever."[239] However, in February 1965, folklore collectors recorded an eighty-five-year-old man in a nearby area of county Clare performing a version of the popular folk song "Ó, a bhean an tí," which included the unusual verses: "Go bhfeicfimid Seoirse a chrochadh le corda / agus a chraicean mar bhróga ar Bhonaparte!" (May we see George hanged by rope and his skin used to make boots for Bonaparte). Despite the singer's claim to have composed these verses himself, they appear to be a rendition of the original subversive song from 1798. The oral version calls attention to the more plausible allusion to "boots," rather than "boats," and the corruption may stem back to an incorrect translation or a mishearing by the spy who submitted the report to the government authorities.[240] This is yet another illustration of how, thanks to structured verse, song traditions can preserve fragments of historical information in their original form over long periods of time.

Nonetheless, this example is untypical. Difficulties in finding traces of the survival of seditious toasts in *seanchas* traditions appear to question the impact of the United Irish attempts to reshape popular culture. Political toasts were integral to esoteric cultural practices of secret societies but apparently did not have a larger, everyday social context. Therefore, they had a short life span, rapidly losing relevance with the changing of political events. As a rule, such toasts were not preserved as lasting elements of folklore and did not figure prominently in folk history-telling.

Stair-sheanchas (history-*seanchas*) is a useful term to denote explicit historical information in folklore, such as stories and narrative songs about past events,[241] but historical information was evidently dispersed throughout oral tradition and expressed through a miscellany of less obvious genres of *seanchas*. The sections above do not offer an exhaustive typology of Irish historical folklore, and even in the context of the Year of the French other genres can be discerned. Genealogies, for example, offered a lineage of respect through which descent could be traced back to local heroes, who were often rebels. Nationalists in the late-nineteenth and twentieth centuries took pride in reclaiming the memory of their ancestors who had participated in the 1798 Rebellion. The prominent local political activist and journalist James Daly of Castlebar, who played a central role in the centenary commemorations of 1798 in Connacht, was widely known to be a descendant of the local United Irish leader Anthony Daly of Coolnabinna (near Lahardane), county Mayo.[242] The Longford County Councilor James O'Neill (1855–1946) of Crowdrummin, who was a recognized authority on traditions of Ballinamuck, was proud of the bravery in 1798 of his rebel granduncle Bryan O'Neill of Drumderg and boasted that all of Brian's five grandnephews had participated "in fighting the black and tans in the war of Independence."[243] Similar examples of patriotic genealogies linked to Ninety-Eight were common in the West, and descendents of rebels were acclaimed as "the most upright and respected people in the countryside."[244] The bona fide nationalist credentials of Lord Ashbourne, the president of the Gaelic League from 1928 to 1933, were corroborated locally by tracing his ancestry to the Presbyterian United Irishman John Gibson of Drumlin county Cavan, who was a local hero in folk history.[245]

On the other hand, evocations of 1798 ancestry were also used for defamation of individuals who were pointed out as descendents of people who had allegedly committed treachery or atrocities against rebels, thus sustaining non-patriotic genealogies.[246] In consequence of a story told in Arigna, on the border of county Roscommon and Leitrim, which identified a man named D'Arcy as a traitor, it was noted that "the D'Arcy's got no life in the County after that" and, following continuous harassment, "had to change their name to Doherty."[247] Vilification was often handled discreetly, without explicitly mentioning names but rather relying on local familiarity with folk history narratives that generated odium. A folklore collector in Longford observed that in the event that "descendants of the person whom the story concerned are still in the area," storytellers would announce, "I won't mention any names, because the breed of them is still there." Similarly, a common local expression used to profess one's integrity stated "I was never an informer, nor the breed o' me."[248] Descendents of informers were subject to retribution by vigilantes and it was recalled that the family of an informer in Drumshanbo, county Leitrim, was forced to leave the district and immigrate to Australia and that even then "the name followed them."[249] Indeed, emigration was no guarantee of reprieve from the vindictive persistence of vilification in social memory, which could continue to reverberate in Irish diaspora communities over several generations. In 1937 the Irish scholar Michael O'Gallaher recalled hearing in Chicago how a Mayo man named Conway was "cast up" (castigated) for being an ancestor of an informer whose testimony had supposedly led to the conviction and execution of the popular Ninety-Eight folk hero Fr. Manus Sweeney.[250]

Historical pedigree was not only associated with people but also with places. The vital connection between the present and the past, which is characteristic of folk history, was strengthened through identification of current proprietors of sites of historical importance. Writing in 1939, a Castlebar pupil considered it important to note down the present owners (Mrs. Haughey) of the French headquarters where the "Republic of Connacht" [*sic*] was declared, commonly known as "Humbert's House."[251] Similarly, Ballinamuck traditions collected in the 1930s did not fail to note the present residents of the houses where the rebel General Blake had been executed (at Mrs. Devine of Kiltycrevagh) and where his corpse was waked (at the house of James McKenna).[252] The genealogy of heritage sites calls attention to another extremely rewarding way of uncovering history-telling and practices of folk-commemoration, which can be studied through microtoponymic research of commemorative place-names. This issue is explored in detail in chapter 12, which discusses the concept of "vernacular landscape."

All in all, classification of various expressions of historical folklore according to distinct genres is an artificial methodological exercise undertaken by the modern-day scholar. In their natural environment, these genres cross-fertilized as already noted through examples of stories and songs that fed on each other. It is therefore more beneficial to regard *seanchas* as a communal historical discourse performed through various interdependent and correlated genres. The ability to perform these genres required expertise. Observing that local storytellers "not only tell history, they 'rehearse' it, turning it over in thought to keep it fresh," Glassie concluded that "history lives in performance and beyond."[253] With this in mind, the performers and social contexts of performance of folk history need to be considered.

6

Practitioners of Folk History

Folklore is folklore only when performed.

Roger D. Abrahams
"Personal Power and Social Restraint
in the Definition of Folklore"

Performances of History-Telling

PERCEPTIONS OF STORYTELLERS change over time and the passing away of the revered *seanchaí*, defined either as a custodian of tradition or as a traditional storyteller,[1] is a trope that echoes the lament for the death of folklore.[2] Despite the demise of the Gaelic Order, in the late eighteenth century the Munster poet Eoghan Rua Ó Súilleabháin (1748–84) alluded to the prevalence of "éigse is suadha an tseanchais"—learned men (poets) versed in *seanchas*.[3] By the mid-nineteenth century, the author William Carleton (1794–1869) claimed that "the regular senachie—the herald and historian of individual families, the faithful genealogist of his long descended patron—has not been in existence for at least a century and a half, perhaps two." In his place, Carleton described the archetypal storyteller of his time as a semiprofessional elderly itinerant who "feeling himself gifted with a strong memory for genealogical history, old family anecdotes and legendary lore in general, passes a happy life in going from family to family, comfortably dressed and much respected."[4] Writing about north Connacht in the late nineteenth century, the Sligo historian Archdeacon Terence O'Rorke (1819–1907) proclaimed that "the Irish *seanachie* is dead and gone" and dated the last traditional reciters of historical tradition to the previous generation.[5] Nonetheless, in the mid-twentieth century, the collectors of the Irish Folklore Commission were able to find storytellers who recited *seanchas* and were regularly described as the last of their kind.

A schoolteacher of the proselytizing "Irish Society for Promoting the Education of the Native Irish through the Medium of their own Language," described in 1821 the "general practice in Connaught and Munster" for residents of rural localities to "assemble in some cabin to play cards, or to hear some of their old fabulous stories," noting that at these forums the "historian" would regularly address his audience ("either by heart, or out of an old manuscript").[6] Recitals of folk history were not confined to these evening gatherings of traditional storytelling (*céilithe*), which continued into the early twentieth century, and were not only performed and transmitted by acknowledged storytellers, but were integrated into daily life through countless utterances and rituals. Like other aspects of folklore, the theaters of history-telling were both private and public and could take place within the intimacy of the family or at communal gatherings.[7] Though recited by individuals, *seanchas* constituted a communal discourse, through which personal recollections and family traditions were shared and thus became social memory.

The Irish Folklore Commission did not recognize an exclusive historiographical folklore activity independent from other aspects of folk life and so did not train designated collectors to focus on historical traditions. It is worth considering the possibility that history-telling may have been a distinct practice and that the absence of a separate branch of folklore studies dedicated to folk history may be indicative of an academic oversight. Reflecting on a visit to Ireland in 1934, the eminent Swedish folklorist C. W. von Sydow recalled being taken by Delargy to county Wicklow, where he was introduced to an eighty-four-year-old woman, who recounted stories of her family's participation in the 1798 Rebellion two generations earlier. He noted that the woman's repertoire included only historical traditions, showing no interest whatsoever in other types of folklore.[8] Although it is possible that if the storyteller had been cajoled, she may also have displayed knowledge of other topics, such cases call attention to the existence of "history-tellers" who consciously specialized in historical lore. "Staireolach," defined by Dinneen as somebody "skilled in history or story-telling,"[9] may be a fitting term to denote this proficiency.

Specific historical episodes featured prominently in the repertoire of certain storytellers, who in turn were renowned particularly for their performances of history-telling. Mrs. Bridget Corduff of Rossport, a ninety-year-old storyteller from northwest Erris in county Mayo, who was commonly known as "Biddy Rooney," was described by a local collector in 1946:

> She, it was, who could tell the stories and she delighted in telling them. She was born shortly after the year of the French landing in Killala and it was most inter-

esting to hear her tales as she heard them from people who were eyewitnesses of the invasion—the ships coming into Kilcummin Bay, the march of the French army into Killala and on to Ballina, men who went from Erris to join up with the French forces, and such incidents of that memorable year in Irish history.[10]

This is an example of a storyteller with a reputation for recounting stories of *Bliain na bhFrancach*. Nevertheless, folklore of Ninety-Eight was normally disseminated through history-telling that covered related topics, such as narratives of outlaws and other rebellions, and incorporated themes from cognate areas of *seanchas*.

Issues of reception are central to any discussion of folklore performance and history-telling is by definition a communicative activity, involving both performers and auditors. The folklorist Richard Bauman argued that:

> A true understanding of the social base of folklore must be based upon investigations which focus upon those social identities which are relevant to the performance of folklore within the context of particular situations and events for it is only here that we will find the true locus of the inter-relationship between folklore and its bearers.[11]

Paradoxically, by documenting oral traditions, folklore collectors removed "living traditions" from their natural environment. Even the use of sound recording could not prevent the uprooting and transplanting of oral performances as, in effect, it introduced "schizophonia," a term coined by R. Murray Shaffer to define "packaging and storing techniques for sound and the splitting of sounds from their original contexts."[12] The researcher of folk history is therefore required to recontextualize accounts in folklore sources in order to reimagine how they may have originally functioned within a community. It is practically impossible, however, to reconstruct each and every performance of history-telling. The particular circumstances in which audiences gathered to hear folk history remain largely unknown. What can be more readily ascertained is the ethnographic-historical context in which accounts were collected (by following the date, place, and the circumstances of the interview), and from there it is sometimes possible to tentatively trace previous transmissions.

Folk Historians and Seanchas Collectors

Local history is too important to be left to the professionals.

Raymond Gillespie and Gerald Moran
"A Various Country": *Essays in Mayo History, 1500–1900*

Apart from the history-tellers who specialized in reciting historical traditions, there were also "folk historians" who were steeped in the historical folklore of the locality and whose expertise was often called upon as an authoritative source when information from the past was required for consultation. They engaged in a spontaneous form of grassroots folklore collecting and processing, which was not sanctioned by an official body. In his insightful analysis of the "folklore process," Honko identified a stage of "folklore from within," which is driven by "tradition specialists."[13] The activities of folk historians relate to this phase of emerging awareness among members of a community toward the value of their local oral traditions. Honko pointed out that internal recognition was often stimulated by "external discoverers of folklore" and in Ireland these include the antiquarians and pioneering folklorists of the eighteenth and nineteenth centuries, whose respectability and scholarly interest encouraged local preoccupation with folk history. The term "historian" is appropriate because folk historians were not merely knowledgeable of the past but, like professional historians, they also retrieved and studied historical evidence. Ideally, folk historians collected and processed sources, attempted to reconstruct a coherent picture from fragmented information and then tried to make sense of the acquired knowledge by offering interpretations.

Folk historians commanded a degree of authority within the community. They usually had respected occupations, most notably as teachers. This is particularly true of national schoolteachers in the early twentieth century, though there is some evidence of teachers who were preoccupied with folk history in the previous century. An early example relating to Ninety-Eight in Connacht is the case of the schoolteacher and author Matthew Archdeacon of Castlebar (d. 1853). In the early nineteenth century, Archdeacon interviewed locals on their experiences in the Rebellion. Although he was a liberal loyalist, he was not hostile to the accounts of former rebels and thus incorporated their narratives into his writings.[14] This example of an established author calls attention to another distinctive characteristic of folk historians: whereas history-tellers were not necessarily literate, folk historians could commit their findings to writing. Examples from the area of Ballinamuck are manuscripts of traditional accounts of the battle by James O'Neill of Crowdrummin and Michael Connell of

Soran.[15] In many cases, their work remained unpublished and did not receive wide recognition. Folk historians also had access to written sources. For example, in the 1930s the schoolteacher Seán Ó hEslin of Ballinamore, county Leitrim, supplemented the accounts he collected orally with information from newspaper clippings and a recently published local history book.[16] The distinction between history-tellers and folk historians is often obscure and literacy alone cannot be a definitive criteria. Indeed, many folk historians were also renowned history-tellers.

As mentioned earlier, the 1937–38 Schools' Scheme offered a vehicle for teachers to engage in folklore collecting and to receive recognition for their work as folk historians. For example, the national schoolteacher Pádhraic Maguidhir of Carrigallen, county Leitrim, submitted to the Schools' Scheme traditions of the Year of the French that he had personally collected from elderly people in the area. He apparently had a long-standing interest in historical traditions and mentioned that more than twenty-five years earlier a local man named Thomas Kiernan of Cloughla (b. ca. 1831) had provided him with "many vivid descriptions of the '98 period which he had from his father." After interviewing several informants and comparing the different versions, Maguidhir added commentary to their accounts, annotated a folk ballad, and provided a diagram of a local site associated with remembrance of acts of yeomen terror in 1798. He not only documented oral traditions but also applied analysis and drew conclusions.[17] Similarly, upon attempting to identify the exact route the English commander-in-chief Lord Cornwallis took on the way to Ballinamuck, James McKenna of Mohill, county Leitrim, challenged local belief with a contrary account that he had heard more than twenty-five years earlier from his mother (Mrs. B. McKenna of Lear, who died at the age of sixty-four in 1912) and also consulted the parish priest Fr. Conefry, who was well known for his knowledge of local 1798 traditions.[18] It is this reflexive and even critical approach that sets apart the folk historian from the folk history-teller.

FIGURE 12. Michael Timoney [Micheál Ó Tiománaidhe]. In 1894, having made his fortune in Australia, Timoney returned to his native area near Crossmolina in county Mayo and began collecting local folk history in Irish, including traditions of *Bliain na bhFrancach*. Courtesy of the Department of Irish Folklore, University College Dublin.

Folk historians were first and foremost spontaneous collectors of historical folklore. A noteworthy case of a Gaelic scholar and folk historian, who anticipated the Irish Folklore Commission by independently collecting folklore in Mayo around the turn of the nineteenth century, can be found in the work of Michael Timoney ([Micheál Ó Tiománaidhe], 1853–1940) of Cartron, county Mayo (near Crossmolina).[19] His main informant, Liam Pléimeann of Lahardane (from whom he collected about eighty stories), was familiar with traditions of Ninety-Eight.[20] Timoney was knowledgeable of both scholarly historiography and folk history of the 1798 Rebellion. He collected numerous traditions about *Bliain na bhFrancach* and wrote down a detailed account of the French campaign, which combined information from written historical sources with oral tradition.[21] As can be expected, folk historians did not comply with the thorough academic standards of professional historiography. Sources were often not identified and therefore folk historians were instrumental in introducing literary influences into oral tradition. Consequently, the writing down of oral traditions by folk historians cannot be seen as a simple act of verbatim transcription. Dorothy Noyes and Roger D. Abrahams pointed out the role of local elites as mediators between metropolitan and local culture,[22] and similarly Jim Mac Laughlin observed that "far from disproving myths and dispensing with tradition, local nationalists and intelligentsia nourished the political imagination with myths and folk history and introduced a strong element of tradition into the political consciousness"[23] Folk historians were influential in reshaping oral traditions and presenting them to a general public. One of Timoney's popular books, for example, includes several references to Ninety-Eight folklore (in particular, traditional songs in Irish).[24]

As noted earlier, the historian Richard Hayes, who was also familiar with Timoney's work,[25] was an accomplished collector of *seanchas* and had a keen awareness of the value of the information that could be acquired from the contributions of local folk historians. The publication of *The Last Invasion of Ireland* accorded wide recognition to the historical traditions that the folk historians strove to preserve. A prime example of his fruitful contacts with local folk historians is the case of Patrick O'Donnell (b. 1867), a shopkeeper from Newport in county Mayo, who was devoted to the cause of the Irish language and the preservation of the folk history of his locality.[26] Described by Hayes as an "indefatigable collector of Mayo traditions,"[27] O'Donnell's reputation was widely recognized in his locality, and a contemporary local historian observed that O'Donnell "more than any other man in Mayo knew his history."[28] The folklore collector Pádraig Ó Moghráin described him posthumously as "fear a chuir an-tsuim san nGaeilg, agus i stair agus i seanchas agus i mbéaloideas na hÉireann" (a man who took great interest in the language, history, traditions, and folklore of Ireland), which is perhaps a suitable definition for folk historians in general.[29]

In recognition of O'Donnell's contribution, Hayes wrote: "his wide knowledge of the history of his native county of Mayo, its lore and traditions, was always at my disposal."[30] Among the many historical traditions Hayes received from him were stories about Fr. Manus Sweeney, the rebels of the McGuire family of Derryloughlan and Colonel Austin O'Malley.[31] In addition, Hayes's draft papers show that he often based his research on notes furnished by O'Donnell.[32] The title folk *historian* is especially suitable for O'Donnell, who was not only able to recite tales of the Rebellion but his special interest in local history led him to collect historical traditions from people in the locality. In scholarly fashion, he took notes of these interviews and then attempted to corroborate the information. Inspired by the Irish proverb "Is mór í an fhírinne agus buafaidh sí" (truth is powerful and shall prevail),[33] his quest for historical knowledge was not restricted to oral tradition but was also directly influenced from reading historical literature and engaging in research of accessible documented sources. Upon examining folklore about members of the loyalist O'Donel family of Newport House (Sir Neal O'Donel and his sons, who were commanders in yeomanry units in 1798) and their involvement in the execution of the rebel priest Fr. Manus Sweeney, O'Donnell declared that "tradition is indeed most valuable" since "every scene and incident is still recalled." Inspired by the critical approach to tradition of Eoin MacNeill, the professor of early and medieval history at UCD, he confronted local folklore with the primary historical accounts of Bishop Joseph Stock (1740–1813), Sir Richard Musgrave, and, more surprisingly, with the records of a court-martial that had been published in a rare pamphlet dating back to 1801 (*Proceedings of a Court of Inquiry held at Castlebar, the 1st of December, 1800*). He also consulted early-nineteenth-century newspapers and referred to the colorful contemporary accounts of Sir Jonah Barrington (1760–1834).[34]

O'Donnell's particular interest in 1798 was long-standing and recognized in the centenary commemorations of 1898 in Castlebar, when he was called upon to read an address to distinguished guests at the Imperial Hotel.[35] He was also involved that year in launching a campaign to erect a monument in memory of Fr. Manus Sweeney,[36] an endeavor that finally came to fruition in 1912 with the unveiling of a Celtic cross on the rebel priest's grave in Burrishoole Abbey, county Mayo. In 1901 he submitted to *An Claidheamh Soluis* a poem in Irish, which he had collected locally, about the O'Malleys of Burrishoole, who had fought at Castlebar and Ballinamuck.[37] In 1904 he collected a version of

Fr. Sweeney's lament on Achill Island,[38] and some years later he provided Timoney with traditions of Fr. Sweeney.[39]

In 1936, when presenting Hayes with notes on 1798 traditions that he had collected more than ten years earlier (from Paddy Walsh of Burrishoole), O'Donnell also informed him of traditions he collected "many years ago" from another local folk historian (the national schoolteacher William Flynn) concerning an army officer named Arbuthnott, who allegedly assisted rebels in getting reprieves. To corroborate this tradition, O'Donnell not only looked up biographical information on Arbuthnott in the *Concise Dictionary of Irish Biography* but also located his gravestone in the local Protestant cemetery.[40] For the second edition of *The Last Invasion of Ireland*, O'Donnell was able to furnish Hayes with a copy of a letter, which had been written in 1798 by an outlawed rebel who had escaped to America (John Gibbons of Newport).[41] Furthermore, his relentless pursuit for Ninety-Eight folklore led him to track down informants of Mayo descent in the Irish diaspora, as in the case of his correspondence with Micheál Ó Gallchobhair of Chicago (d. 1937), whose grandfather, Cathaoir Ó Gallchobhair of Tawnagh—known locally as Cathaoir Bán (d. 1845), had been present at the French landing and joined the rebels on their way to Castlebar.[42] He forwarded these traditions to Hayes, observing that "there is more real Irish tradition of Ireland's past history in America (family traditions) than we have at home,"[43] and subsequently they were published in an appendix to the revised edition of Hayes's book.[44]

The energetic activities of Patrick O'Donnell illustrate the potential of considering folk history as a specific sphere of activity within the larger study of folklore. Although he was recognized in his lifetime as "an authority on the local history of his native county,"[45] the collectors of the Irish Folklore Commission in Mayo missed Patrick O'Donnell and failed to benefit from his invaluable knowledge of historical traditions.[46] For unknown reasons, in 1939 he refused to be interviewed for the Schools' Scheme by pupils of St. Joseph's Convent N.S. Newport.[47] Following the publication of *The Last Invasion of Ireland*, further attempts were made to interview O'Donnell, but once again the opportunity was missed.[48] Subsequently, the holdings of the IFC archive do not include historical traditions collected from O'Donnell in his lifetime.[49] After his death, O'Donnell was referred to locally as a source for historical information,[50] and more than sixty years later he was still remembered as a "well known scholar."[51]

The Haitian anthropologist Michel-Rolph Trouillot remarked that "the fact that history is also produced outside of academia has largely been ignored in theories of history."[52] In this regard, the late radical historian Raphael Samuel noted that "If history was thought of as an activity rather than a profession, then the number of its practitioners would be legion."[53] History-tellers, folk historians, and *seanchas* collectors were, to borrow again from Samuel, "the invisible hands" that perpetuated vernacular historiographies. Thanks to their often-undervalued work, folk histories of the Year of the French were propagated and preserved throughout Connacht and the north midlands. Though their names are largely unacknowledged in professional historiography, by uncovering their work, researchers of social and cultural history can gain access to the rich sources of folk history. In turn, such a pursuit can contribute toward developing an awareness of the vernacular historical discourses that appear to have always played a central role in the life of communities throughout Ireland.

7

Time and Calendar

Is maith an scéalaí an aimsir.
[Time is a good storyteller.]
Irish proverb[1]

MODERN HISTORIANS, who are particularly concerned with time—"the date being regarded by us not as an accidental property of an event but as an essential feature,"[2]—have been baffled by the way perceptions of time in folk history do not comply with standard historical conventions. The American historian Richard White was confounded by the storytelling of his Irish-born mother (Sara Walsh from Ahanagran, county Kerry), remarking:

> I expect people to move through time together; the clock ticks and they will all move forward. I do not expect people to drop out of time. I expect a single category of time with the same uniform minutes, hours and days. But in Sara's stories the past is not a single frame.[3]

While academic historiography is, by and large, grounded in the concept of linear-chronological time, social memory integrates various frameworks and rhythms of time.[4] In scholarly histories, the chronology of the French invasion of Connacht in 1798 is straightforward: it begins with the arrival of the French ships in Killala Bay (22 August), leads to the surrender and defeat at Ballina-muck (8 September), and concludes with the rout and massacre of the remaining rebels in Killala (23 September). In contrast, folklore of the Year of the French involved more complex notions of time.

Repeated events tend to merge in oral tradition.[5] Periods could be condensed, often omitting recollection of troublesome episodes, and, in compensation, other periods could be artificially lengthened.[6] Such telescoping may give the impression that memory creates a "flat" time, which is in essence ahistorical, but this hasty conclusion would be an oversimplification. The elusive nature of time in folk history is not beyond the scope of scholarly investigation, and its various temporal frameworks can indeed be traced. In this context, Françoise Zonabend's seven-year-long ethnological study of the village of Minot in Burgundy proves instructive as an exercise in gauging the functions of time in local social memory. Zonabend realized that "time in a village breaks up and fragments, as it were, into a series of parallel times that fuse with one another." In general, she noted that "the collective memory functions in accordance with a cyclical movement which constantly tends to seek permanence," thus creating a "stable time" that is essentially static ("a time outside the reach of Time"), although critics have pointed out that her argument for the predominance of cyclical time may have been overstated.[7] In addition, she identified habitual use of other temporal frameworks, including standard chronological time, "time of daily life" (referring to mundane occurrences that are linked to daily and seasonal routines), "time of life" (organized around the key moments of an individual's life cycle), and "time of the family" (based on genealogy, so that "computation is provided by descent; memory is supported by biographical axis"). She also maintained that each community developed its own notion of "Unique Time," which is specific to the heritage of the locality. Moreover, oral tradition encourages idealized notions of a communal past, since "by concealing the written and relying on the spoken word, the community invents a time without blemish or interruption and adorns it with every virtue." In terms of the passing of time, she argued that the various durations observed by historians (particularly the French *Annales* school, which introduced the concept of *longue durée*) are not segregated but in practice are linked and constantly blend through cross-references.[8]

Calendars are encoded embodiments of social and cultural values that are specific to a community.[9] Acknowledging that "the calendar is indeed one of the most codified aspects of social existence," the sociologist-anthropologist Pierre Bourdieu used a hypothetical Algerian agrarian calendar to demonstrate how

> identical periods are given different names, and still more often, identical names cover periods varying considerably in length and situated at different times in the year, depending on the region, the tribe, the village, and even the informant. Moreover, at two different points in the same conversation, an informant may offer two different names (e.g., one Berber, one drawn from the Islamic tradition) for the same moment in the year.[10]

Similarly, the French landing in Mayo was perceived through the convergence of several, seemingly incompatible, calendars.

In historical literature, the arrival of the French is dated by the standard Gregorian calendar month of August 1798. Yet from their own perspective, according to the republican calendar established by the French Revolutionary Convention in 1793 (and backdated to commence on 22 September 1792), it was the month of *Fructidor* in the sixth year of the French Republic.[11] The French officers who wrote accounts of the campaign in Ireland referred to this calendar, which was purposely designed to disrupt the chronology of the so-called *Ancien Régime* and to symbolically reflect the principal ideologies espoused by the French Revolution (i.e., secularism, rationalism, naturalism, and nationalism).[12] According to Nora, the ultimate failure of this calendar system (which was abolished by the Napoleonic regime on 1 January 1806) has turned it into a *lieu de mémoire*.[13] In 1798 these two competing official calendars collided with the calendar of folk custom, which, although largely unacknowledged by the authorities, was exceedingly rich in its rituals and traditions, and exerted considerable influence on the daily life of the rural population.[14] Shortly before the French arrived, the folk calendar marked the ancient Celtic festival of *Lúnasa*, traditions of which, as Máire MacNeill has demonstrated, were still celebrated (albeit sometimes unwittingly) into the twentieth century.[15] Moreover, observing the Catholic calendar, Lady's Day—the feast of the Assumption of the Virgin Mary—was celebrated on 15 August, a week before the French landing. In more recent times, from the late nineteenth century on, this became the parade day of the Catholic-nationalist organization the Ancient Order of Hibernians (AOH) and was used for commemorations of Ninety-Eight.

According to traditional custom, the festival of the Assumption was considered the day that marked the passing of the year,[16] so that the French invasion ushered in the new year. The scholar of mythology and religion Mircea Eliade observed that in traditional ("primitive") societies "the New Year is equivalent to the raising of the taboo on the new harvest," which expresses "the need of archaic societies to regenerate themselves periodically through the annulment of time."[17] Indeed, in the agricultural calendar, the invasion coincided with the harvest season. It was remembered that the French came into Killala "on a fine harvest day"[18] and that "Bliain na bhFranncaigh—bhí 'n foghmhar go luath, bliain bhréagh a bhi inti" (in the Year of the French the harvest was early and the weather was fine).[19] In 1798 the harvest benefited from a spell of prolonged sunshine, but the weather later changed for the worse and the Franco-Irish campaign from Castlebar into the north midlands suffered from adverse weather conditions.[20]

Many indirect references were made to the agricultural season. Collecting for the Schools' Scheme, a pupil in county Roscommon heard from his sixty-five-year-old father, whose own father had known participants in the Rebellion, that among the rebels were local agricultural laborers who were employed in harvest work away from home but opted to return and take part in the fighting.[21] Stories from the north midlands about rebels escaping the calamity at Ballina-muck mention fugitives seeking refuge in fields that were being reaped or hiding in haycocks and stooks of oats.[22] A tradition from the area of Mohill, county Leitrim, which told of a rebel hiding under a "hand-shaken" (haystack), also referred to a newly wed woman. Indeed, in the folk calendar the harvest season was generally considered to be the preferred time for marriages.[23] A nineteenth-century manuscript describing the escape of the Mayo United Irish leader James Joseph McDonnell, who fled from Ballinamuck and took refuge in Connemara, notes that on his way he met Irish speakers making haystacks and later avoided capture by pretending to be a laborer forking hay in Frenchpark, county Roscommon.[24] Such details date the stories within a more specific agricultural calendar that broke the harvest time into shorter periods of "small seasons" asso-ciated with particular farming activities, such as the "saving" (stacking and stor-ing) of hay and oats. This did not pinpoint a precise time; the numerous subdi-visions of agricultural seasons created overlapping temporal frameworks so that, as Glassie argued, "set in one cycle, you are set in several unsynchronized."[25]

For communities in Ireland, Ninety-Eight also represented a "Unique Time." In this sense, it resembles other major historical episodes, which were embedded in mythic time. Writing about the 1916 Easter Rising, the folklorist Gearóid Ó Crualaoich claimed that its memory "cannot be made subject to any brute chronological fixation in some objective calendar" or reduced to "a fixed point of time."[26] Memorable names were often assigned to significant dates that assumed legendary proportions in folklore. A noteworthy example is the "Night of the Big Wind" (*Oíche na Gaoithe Móire*), which referred to a violent storm that swept through Ireland on 6 January 1839.[27] With the passing of the Pension Act of 1909, personal recollection of the Big Wind was at first accepted in lieu of a birth certificate, but this naïve attempt to incorporate the folk calendar of social memory was annulled when the authorities discovered that it was widely abused.[28] The prevalence of several special names in folklore for the period of the 1798 Rebellion signifies the magnitude of this historical episode, which carved out its own mythic time in social memory.

An account collected for the Schools' Scheme referred to the local experience of 1798 as "the time of the trouble."[29] This term appears to have been already in popular use in the early nineteenth century. The indefatigable travel writers Samuel Carter Hall (1800–89) and his wife, Anna Maria Hall née Fielding (1800–81), mentioned the return from France in 1836 of the veteran rebel Colonel

Austin O'Malley and his failed attempt to recover by lawsuit his confiscated property in Burrishoole, county Mayo. The Halls observed that O'Malley "was treated with marked courtesy by court, jury and counsel; and no single word was uttered having reference to his connection with the 'time of the troubles.'"[30] A scholarly debate in the beginning of the twentieth century published in the Gaelic League's newspaper *An Claidheamh Soluis* noted earlier use of Irish equivalents—*Bliain na Buairte* (the Year of the Troubles) or *Bliain an Bhuartha* (the Year of the Trouble)[31]—and these were still remembered in the 1930s.[32]

Just as in folklore the term *Aimsir an Drochshaoil* (the Bad Time) commonly denoted the Great Famine period but could also refer to memories of other famines and even allude to other dark periods remembered in communal history, such as seventeenth- and eighteenth-century discrimination under Penal legislation[33] and even Viking raids,[34] the "time of the troubles" evoked associations with other periods of civil strife and rebellion. In this way, traditions of 1798 in the West of Ireland could be mixed with earlier epochs in Irish history.[35] Similarly, local traditions of the "troubles" of 1798 could be linked with more-recent recollections of the Easter Rising and the War of Independence (1916–22), which were either mentioned explicitly[36] or surfaced indirectly in anachronistic references (such as "flying columns") that inadvertently appeared in 1798 folklore.[37] A old man from county Cavan who recounted for the Schools' Scheme a story of a yeomanry unit known as "the Black Horse" from "Northern Ireland" that massacred a party of pikemen in 1798 with "machine guns,"[38] apparently mixed a Ninety-Eight tradition with impressions of more recent acts of violence by Ulster loyalist paramilitaries.[39] Since the late 1960s, the "Troubles" in the North of Ireland have generated their own folklore, adding new layers of meaning to the term the "Time of the Troubles."[40]

Several other names were used in folklore to mark the period of the Rebellion. In the early nineteenth century, the novelist, painter, and folklore collector Samuel Lover (1797–1868) wrote down a folktale of 1798, which mentioned "the time of the ruction," a name that, in all probability, derived from the word insurrection.[41] In 1930 the folklorist Seán Mac Giollarnáth described a sixty-seven-year-old man in Connemara who was knowledgeable of *seanchas* pertaining to *bliain na Speir* (the year of the houghing), which was an adjunct to *Bliain na bhFrancach*.[42] This name places the remembrance of the Rebellion within a larger context of contemporary agrarian violence typified by the practice of maiming cattle (houghing, or hamstringing) belonging to local landlords, which was instigated by secret societies (notably the Whiteboys and Defenders). An "epidemic of cattle houghing" swept through the West of Ireland in the late 1790s[43] and recollections of "Whiteboyism" were often mixed with traditions of 1798 insurgency.[44] From complaints of landlords, it is apparent that, in the chaotic disorder that followed the Rebellion, "the maiming of cattle in the most cruel manner" continued to be rife in the West of Ireland (in particular in counties Galway and Mayo).[45] In 1806 the authorities clamped down on a secret society known as the "Threshers," who were active all along the former route of the Franco-Irish campaign. Although they carried pikes and were described as "rebellious," they were chiefly concerned with revoking payment of tithes, and their implication with the "the troublesome times" of the Rebellion remained circumstantial and unproven.[46]

By far the most prevalent calendar names referred explicitly to the French presence in Ireland, as in *Bliain na bhFrancach* (the Year of the French) and *Aimsir na bhFrancach* (the Time of the French). Though seemingly interchangeable, the latter term was more vague in its time reference, whereas the former alluded to a specific year. The *Handbook of Irish Folklore* reminds collectors that there were several French expeditions to Ireland and asks them to clarify "which year was referred to as *Bliain na bhFrancach*."[47] In the southern province of Munster the term was generally used in reference to the failed expedition to Bantry Bay in 1796, whereas in Connacht and the north midlands it was associated with 1798. The writings of the Castlebar schoolteacher Matthew Archdeacon show that the "time o' the Frinch" [*sic*] was already in popular usage in the years immediately following the Rebellion.[48]

The local uprising and the French invasion were considered to be of such major significance in the social memory of Connacht that 1798 soon became a landmark in local calendars. Describing a sojourn in Erris, county Mayo, in the early nineteenth century, Rev. W. H. Maxwell observed that "the landing of the French is a common epoch among the inhabitants of Ballycroy. Ask a peasant his age, and he will probably tell you, 'he was born two or three years before or after *the French*.'" Local happenings were dated in relation to this point of reference, as in the example of a sighting of a legendary leprechaun in the area of Achill, which supposedly occurred "the year before the French."[49] This popular way of measuring time continued into the twentieth century. In 1946 the collector Michael Corduff noted that it was said of the ninety-year-old storyteller Mrs. Bridget Corduff ("Biddy Rooney") of northwest Erris that "she was born shortly after the year of the French landing in Killala."[50] This statement not only provides further testimony to the prevalence of the practice of calculating ages and dates in reference to the Year of the French but also demonstrates the liberal way in which this was applied in reference to a woman born ca. 1855. Though more than half a century had passed since 1798, in retrospect this date was still considered to be in proximity to the Rebellion, possibly because at the time there were still people alive who had participated in the events and had actually seen the French. However, the Year of the French may not have been universally used throughout the West and the north midlands. In the 1960s, Maureen O'Rourke discovered that although the old people in the area of Ballinamuck told numerous stories about Ninety-Eight, they did not have any special name for the Rebellion.[51]

In addition to using general calendar systems, each community maintained its own calendar, which cross-referenced dates of larger historical significance with events of local importance. For example, a tradition collected in 1938 recalled that "on the morning the French landed in Killala the church built in the graveyard at the end of the town was slated" and that "a man named 'Chalk' was the plasterer of the said church."[52] Recollections of this episode persevered in the locality. Some fifty years later, the writer Desmond Fennell was traveling in the area, and on visiting the site of the old deanery in Killala, he was informed that workmen first spotted the French ships in 1798 from the roof.[53] In this way, oral tradition recalled how the arrival of the French had been perceived locally. Such cross-references also appeared in family traditions, where anecdotal events of private significance were remembered through reference to 1798. For example, the Killeen family in Kilcummin recalled that at the time of the French landing robbers had attempted to break into their house.[54] By juxtaposing recollections of everyday life with the larger historical narrative, local events were dated according to historical events and vice versa, each system of calendar validating the other in social memory.

Knowledge of the Rebellion was so widespread that it functioned as a milestone in the chronology of folk history, around which the events of the eighteenth and nineteenth centuries could be structured. It facilitated orderly remembrance of events in local history, such as a struggle at Friar's Ford in county Leitrim, which was said to have happened "about twenty years before the Insurrection of 1798,"[55] or agrarian agitation in county Galway associated with the secret society of Ribbonmen, which occurred several years after 1798.[56] The dating of events in the folk calendar was typically crude and often grossly inaccurate, as the passing of time in social memory did not necessarily conform to standard measurements, but rather to more subjective temporal modes. For example, in 1935, for one seventy-one-year-old man in county Galway, the Rebellion appeared to have occurred two hundred and fifty years back,[57] whereas around the same time (1938), an eighty-four-year-old in Mayo believed the events took place "almost a hundred years ago."[58] Subjective perceptions of time vary, so that for some (particularly the young pupils collecting for the Schools' Scheme), the Rebellion happened in the distant past—before the time of the Famine (another major landmark in the calendar of recent folk history). Yet, from the deeper perspective of the full scope of folk history (which reached back to early antiquity), it belonged to a relatively recent period. In the early 1990s members of the Crossmolina Genealogical Society interviewed an elderly woman from Lacken, in the vicinity of the site of the French landing. When asked about the 1798 Rebellion, to their surprise, she answered that she could not recall anything about this episode but that she was familiar with traditions about the Spanish Armada, implying that 1798 was too recent to register in folk history.[59]

Competing notions of various "depths" of time were colorfully expressed in a vibrant discussion in 1958 between the collector Michael Corduff and a ninety-year-old storyteller from Erris, who came from a well-known family of *seanchaithe*. As a boy, the storyteller had heard stories of *Bliain na bhFrancach* from his grandmother and from the first national schoolteacher in the area ("old Master Doherty"):

> "Sure, it is not two hundred years since the French landing," (turning to me, for verification).
> "No" I said, "it is just one hundred and sixty years ago."
> "Ah! I was thinking it was not the two hundred, and sure that is not so long ago," he replied.
> "Bedad, then!" said a young fellow who was smoking a cigarette, rather quizzically. "I would say one hundred and sixty years is quite a very long time."
> "Well! There are a good many days in it" said another listener.
> "Ah!" replied the old nonagenarian (almost) "one hundred and sixty years is not a long time, nor one thousand and sixty years in point of time, compared with all the time that has passed, and is yet to come."[60]

The passing of historical time was often measured in generations. Many of the informants interviewed in the 1930s to the 1950s could draw a direct lineage between their accounts of Ninety-Eight and the recollections of actual participants. Often storytellers claimed that they received traditions from their own grandparents, who in turn had heard it from their parents or grandparents, who had taken part in the Rebellion. This can be criticized as a validating formula that contracts time and also functions as a rhetorical device that appears to create an illusion of unbroken contact with the original historical events. Nevertheless, it is worth taking into account that the period was relatively recent and by focusing on elderly storytellers the collectors could indeed hear folklore that had been transmitted over only three or four generations.[61]

Despite ubiquitous references to a titular year in the popular names *Bliain na bhFrancach* and the Year of the French, in reality the French campaign in

Ireland lasted merely a single month, with eighteen days passing from the initial French landing to the surrender of the main force at Ballinamuck, and another lapse of fifteen days till the final defeat of the garrison in Killala. The brevity of the Rebellion was not lost on folk historical consciousness. The phrase "The Hurry" was used in Connacht to denote this short-lived episode,[62] and its usage continued until recent times.[63] This name apparently has an older pedigree and enjoyed a wider distribution. Writing in the late nineteenth century the Ulster historian Robert M. Young noted, "For a long time after the Rebellion a witty question was asked of ladies who wished to be thought young—What age were you at the 'Hurries'?"[64] The term was popularized in the early twentieth century in a verse of the well-known Ninety-Eight recitation about the United Irishman Thomas Russell, "The Man From God-Knows Where" (first published 1918), composed by the Ulster poet Florence Mary Wilson (1874–1946) and including the reference "in the time o' the Hurry."[65]

The elapsing of time in the historical past was often assigned symbolic figures that fit into familiar folkloristic patterns. For example, a Connemara tradition, about a local military commander who received news of the arrival of the French and feared being called up to Mayo to face them, noted that the Rebellion lasted only twenty-four hours.[66] In this local tradition, the noticeably brief period of the French campaign was symbolically condensed even more so as to comply with the recognizable storytelling motif of a day and a night. An intriguing case relates to numerous stories about the aftermath of the Rebellion, which allude to some sort of sabbatical amnesty. According to these traditions, after an interval of *seven years*, outlaws on the run returned to their home community, and following a policy of reconciliation, relations improved between landlords and tenants.[67] The marking of the passage of time with the figure seven makes use of a popular typological number, which commonly appears in folklore.[68] Nonetheless, these narratives should not be too hastily dismissed as ahistorical. Oral traditions recalled that peaceful life was not restored immediately and explained the gradual processes of normalization and reconciliation, through which areas that had been strongly affected by the Rebellion and traumatized by the terror with which it was suppressed eventually settled down. Together with the many stories of outlaw activities in the wake of the Rebellion, they provide insight into the guerrilla warfare that continued (particularly in the hills of Connemara, Erris, and Tyrawley) after the French defeat, a feature of 1798 that has been studied elsewhere but has not yet been adequately addressed for the Rebellion the West.[69] Reports of sustained resistance by former Mayo rebels in anticipation of another French landing were continuously sent to the authorities in Dublin in the aftermath of the Rebellion but remarkably peter out by 1805—exactly *seven years* after 1798![70] Normalization varied in each locality. For example, by 1803 former rebel leaders were once again employed on many estates in Connacht, much to the chagrin of Lord Sligo.[71] This variability is reflected in folklore, as reconciliatory traditions did not necessarily insist on a lapse of seven years.[72]

Apart from recalling the actual past, folk history was also preoccupied with imaginary frameworks of time that contemplated what could have happened and speculated on what may yet happen in the future. By pointing at preventable shortcomings in the rebel campaign, namely instances of faulty planning or alleged acts of French treachery, storytellers encouraged a "refusal of existing history," which corresponds with a common feature of oral history that has been named "uchronic dreams" by the Italian historian Alessandro Portelli.[73] Distinct from the trend in academic historiography of experimenting with counterfactual narratives,[74] the uchronic motif in vernacular histories singles out a specific (often trivial) event among the actions of the losing camp, which is identified as a wrong turn in history. This has a double function of reinforcing the group's sense of its central role in history and of providing hope for future success, at a time when mistakes from the past will not be repeated.

For example, in south county Leitrim and north county Longford, copious oral traditions explained the traumatic defeat at Ballinamuck through reference to the theft of chains used to draw the rebel artillery during a stopover at the village of Cloone on the eve of the fatal battle.[75] It was widely believed that had the advance of the Franco-Irish army not been impeded in this way, the insurgents may have succeeded in teaming up with United Irish reinforcements in Granard, county Longford (which was less than twenty kilometers from Ballinamuck), then may have continued into neighboring country Westmeath to join additional rebel forces, and ultimately would have attained victory, for "if they'd got as far as Granard they'd win."[76] This apocryphal tale takes place in a counterfactual timeframe, which inflated the local community's role in the larger narrative of events. As Tonkin observed, such "'uchronic dreams' bear witness to the depth of the conflicts involved, the problem which lay behind a final action which we have to call 'history' because that, ultimately, was the road chosen."[77] By planting doubts and suggesting alternative possibilities, the imaginary time frame of "uchronia" allowed folk history to imagine parallel histories, which reflect present hopes and expectations.

Moreover, folklore defiantly rejected the nineteenth-century rationalist "reform of time," which sought to marginalize the popularity of prophecy by introducing general use of personal clocks and calendars as tools to manage the future.[78] In his essay "The Concept of History" (1940), Walter Benjamin critiqued historicist adherence to standard chronology, which he summed up as "telling the sequence of events like the beads of a rosary." In its place, he argued for a "conception of the present as the 'time of the now' which is shot through with chips of Messianic time." Recognizing the intrinsic historical connections between past, present, and future, he commented that "soothsayers who found out from time what it had in store certainly did not experience time as either homogeneous or empty. Anyone who keeps this in mind will perhaps get an idea of how past times were experienced in remembrance."[79] In Ireland, the copious millenarian references associated with the 1798 Rebellion in particular and with expectations of delivery at the hand of foreign saviors in general, created a futurist time.[80] A prophecy collected by the Irish Folklore Commission in county Waterford proclaimed:

Tiocfaidh an samhradh gan teas gan ghrian	[The summer will come with neither warmth nor sun
Is tiocfaidh an [na] Franncaigh is teach[t] an bliadhan na dhiaidh.[81]	And the French will arrive the following year.]

At an eschatological level, the Year of the French was yet to take place.

Collectively, the multiple temporal perspectives in folk history present cubist portrayals of the past.[82] However, in the transition from orality to textual representation, collectors only captured the temporal references that appeared in specific tellings and so the documentation of folklore detracted from the original complexity and fluidity. The act of storytelling in itself creates a mental time frame, which Glassie aptly refers to as "passing the time."[83] Portelli observed that "the remembering and the telling are themselves *events*, not only descriptions of events," and since oral history accounts are collected in an interview scenario, "all aspects of time in the collected text are thus the result between two interacting subjects."[84] Ninety-Eight in folk history can be defined as the time of the Rebellion recalled through the filter of the time when the traditions were documented, which was itself a multilayered concept that incorporated temporal references from earlier history-tellings. The kaleidoscopic nature of time and calendar in social memory poses a challenge to standard historical periodization, which presumes to authoritatively date events along a set linear sequence. It also undermines attempts to locate the 1798 Rebellion within a quasi-"Whiggish" teleology of late-eighteenth-century radicalism.[85] Ultimately, folk history, to quote Raphael Samuel, "refuses to be safely boxed away in card indexes or computer programmes: which instead pivots on the *active* relationship between past and present, subjective and objective, poetic and political."[86] To paraphrase Karl Marx, in social memory "all that is solid melts into air,"[87] and the remembrance of the Year of the French was not merely a straightforward chronology of the events that happened in Connacht over a month in the late summer of 1798. Overall, the field of Irish folk history evidently had distinct characteristics, both in its variety of form, contexts of performances, practitioners, and modes of temporality. All this should be kept in mind when examining the content of collected folklore sources, a task that may illustrate more specifically how the Year of the French was remembered.

Part 3

Democratic History

8

Who Were the Men of the West?

I give you the gallant old West, boys,
Where rallied our bravest and best
When Ireland lay broken and bleeding;
Hurrah for the men of the West!

William Rooney
"The Men of the West"

A T A CEREMONY to unveil a Ninety-Eight memorial in Castlebar, Richard Hayes lauded the anonymous heroes of the Rebellion: "Most of them were simple men of the towns and countrysides whose names are largely unknown, but known their courage and daring."[1] Surprisingly, the thousands of Irish rebels who flocked to join the French army have not taken the center stage in histories of the Rebellion in Connacht, which (with the notable exception of the work of Hayes) have focused on a select leadership and portrayed "General Humbert's Campaign" in narrow military terms as a clear-cut case of an inevitable failure.[2] The rebel rank and file were depicted collectively and marginalized. In loyalist historiography they were denigrated as a mob and in nationalist historiography they were idealized, but in both cases they mostly remained anonymous. R. R. Madden's monumental biographies of leading United Irishmen, which were instrumental in forming a national Ninety-Eight pantheon of heroes, by and large overlooked the 1798 experience in the West.[3] In contrast, folk history-telling presented democratic history—a "people's history" par excellence, insofar as they were narrated by "the people," about "the people," and for "the people."

Historians who choose to ignore folklore sources limit their choice of sources for local participation in the Rebellion. Lists of prisoners and wanted outlaws issued by Dublin Castle provide numerous names, yet scarce information is provided on the roles these individuals actually played. These are supplemented by records of courts-martial, which offer skewed descriptions of rebellious activities given by prosecutors and hostile witnesses.[4] While rebels in Connacht did not leave firsthand written testimonies, there is a sizeable volume of contemporary accounts written by French invaders and by loyal supporters of the Crown's government in Ireland. In addition to miscellaneous references in archival naval documents,[5] accounts of French officers include the logbook of Chef de Division Daniel Savary (who did not disembark in Ireland),[6] General Humbert's reports to the Directory,[7] and memoirs written by adjutant-General Jean Sarrazin,[8] adjutant-General Louis-Octave Fontaine,[9] Captain Jean-Louis Jobit,[10] Sergeant-Major Jean-Baptiste Thomas,[11] and Second-Master Gunner Moreau de Jonnès.[12] Numerous Irish rebels appear in Sir Richard Musgrave's chapters on the Rebellion in the West in his *Memoirs of the Different Rebellions in Ireland* (1801), though all the information about them is filtered through the author's ultraconservative eyes.[13] The standard eyewitness account of the events in Mayo is the anonymously published *Narrative* of Dr. Joseph Stock, the Anglican bishop of Killala and Achonry, who documented his interactions with the rebel forces in Killala.[14] This is complemented by the diary of Rev. James Little, the Protestant rector of Lacken.[15] Other loyalist accounts were written by the Sligo gentleman Humphrey Thomson[16] and by Rev. Edward Mangin, who accompanied a unit of the British army.[17] The authors of all these accounts did not speak Irish, and in consequence, both the extent of their communications with rebels and the depth of their observations on popular attitudes were limited. Personal comments by Rev. Little, who candidly described himself noting "I have led a recluse life, am unacquainted with business, incurious in my temper, and inattentive to common reports," are instructive as he openly admitted: "I understand not the Irish language which is the common dialect here used among the peasantry and without which no one can know the country."[18] The fact that these standard historical sources were written and compiled at a remove from the experience of the local population clearly has implications for social and cultural histories, which have been consequently eclipsed by political and military histories.

The democratization of the historical subject in folk histories generally occurred through two main processes: transformation and inclusion. In the first instance, the image of historical heroes of national fame was readapted in order to reflect popular perceptions of their character. Examples from folk drama may serve to illustrate this dynamic, which can transpire within a relatively short period. A description of mummers in Cork city from 1685 reveals that lasting attributes of Oliver Cromwell's caricatural depiction in Irish folk history (namely his association with the devil and his having a brass or copper nose) had already been formulated in the forty-year period following the Cromwellian campaign in Ireland (1649–50).[19] Transformations of historical figures into folk heroes were not devoid of subtle political influences. In the late nineteenth century, traditional mummers' rhymes in Wexford were rewritten by a local schoolmaster (a Sinott from Bree) so as to portray the pantheon of Ninety-Eight heroes as they were represented in Fr. Patrick Kavanagh's influential *Popular History of the Insurrection of 1798*, which was the founding text of the Catholic-nationalist ("Faith and Fatherland") school of 1798 historiography.[20] The revised rhymes, which were circulated by a local printer (an Evoy from Adamstown), rapidly gained popularity and soon became the standard version in folk performances.[21] From such comparative examples, it may be expected that leading historical personages involved in the Rebellion and its suppression became the heroes and villains of folk histories of the Year of the French. But, in practice, this proves not to be the case. Although Ninety-Eight in its politicized republican form has been associated nationally with the illustrious United Irishman Theobald Wolfe Tone (1763–98), neither himself nor other major United Irishmen featured prominently in local folklore. More surprisingly, as the following section shows, General Humbert, who is at the center of all scholarly narratives of the Rebellion in Connacht, did not become the main folk hero of provincial social memory.

Another way in which folk histories broadened the scope of the historical agenda was through the inclusion of local heroes. Like the transformation of well-known personages into more accessible and familiar characters, this process also reflects the ways in which people who participated in historical events were perceived, talked about, remembered, and sometimes even commemorated by members of local communities. The subaltern construction and narration of folk histories promoted a "history from below," which was fundamentally democratic. In order to demonstrate this point, the sections in this chapter examine traditions concerning a sample of likely candidates for primacy in folk historiography and refute their preeminence. Examinations of folklore accounts that refer to the French Commander-in-Chief (General Humbert), a senior Franco-Irish officer and interpreter (Colonel O'Kane), and a leading Irish insurgent commander (General Blake) reveal that there were no overarching heroes in the folk historiography of the Year of the French.

By charting oral traditions associated with various folk heroes it is possible to identify separate constituencies of memory that interacted with each other, thus presenting a dynamic and composite picture of social memory. Considering traditions associated with the memory of a typical "pikeman" hero from the vicinity of Ballinamuck (Robin Gill of Edenmore) and other examples of local heroes and villains, the discussion proceeds to explore the nature of decentralized historiography that was propagated through folk history-telling. The concept of democratic history is further developed through an investigation of the representation of women in local Ninety-Eight folk history, which stands out in comparison to the predominantly male canon of official historiography. Overall, the discussion aims to illustrate how social memory facilitated a democratic, albeit not egalitarian, approach of retelling the past, which promoted alternative historiographies that complement and, at the same time, challenge academic historiography. Through analysis of folklore accounts, the examples demonstrate the value of folk history for an understanding of how the Year of the French was remembered at the time the sources were collected and also in offering new perspectives on the events of 1798.

The French General: Humbert

> Yes, his grandfather had told him all about the French invasion of 1798 under General Humbert—u'ber Grandfather used to call it.
>
> Frank O'Connor
> *Leinster, Munster and Connaught*[22]

General Jean Joseph Amable Humbert (1767–1823) arrived at the shores of Mayo on 22 August 1798. He had enlisted in the French republican army only six years earlier but already had a meteoric career behind him, having made brigadier general by 1794. After seeing action in several campaigns, he distinguished himself in suppressing the counterrevolutionary uprising in the Vendée as a protégé of one of the revolution's rising young stars, General Lazare Hoche (1768–97), and, in 1796, sailed to Ireland with Hoche in the unfortunate expedition to Bantry Bay.[23] In Irish folklore, *Général Humbert* (ymbɛr) became *Humbert* (hʌmbəːt). The difference in pronunciation is not merely a semantic detail but indicates that the French general was transformed into quite a different character, reflecting the way his persona was perceived by locals and subsequently reconstructed in storytelling traditions.

Humbert left a distinct impression on the people of Kilcummin, where he landed. In particular, recollections of his despair of local recruits who joined his army lingered for at least two generations. In 1935 George Monnelly of Kilcummin, whose grandfather had witnessed the French landing, told Hayes:

A lot of the fishermen here got guns and joined them. And 'twas one of the Kil-cummin fisherman, a man named Hegarty that nearly shot General Humbert by accident when they got into Killala. But Humbert didn't blame him; he blamed them that gave a gun to a man that didn't rightly know how to use it.[24]

Dominick McDonnell of nearby Muingrevagh (whose memory was "failing owing to his advanced age, but he seemed to have a clear recollection of some names and certain details"), repeated fragments of stories that he heard from his grandfather:

Humbert was watching the guns when they were giving them out to the Irish. "Ah," says he after a while, "I'm lost among ye," when he saw they weren't able to use the guns he brought. "My curse on ye," says he, for he was looking at them catching the muzzle and using the gun as a hammer against the rocks and wall.[25]

Humbert's dismay at the abuse of guns by new recruits is a reflection of a historical reality described by Bishop Stock, whose *Narrative* also confirms that a misfire by an undisciplined recruit (who was "instantly punished with an unmerciful caning") almost hit the general and that consequently restrictions were put on the issue of ammunition to Irish rebels.[26]

Prior to leaving France, Humbert sequestered from the storehouses in La Rochelle "a large quantity of helmets and odd clothing of various colours" in order to dress local recruits. Matthew Tone (the brother of Theobald Wolfe Tone), who was on the expedition, expressed the concern that "Pat will look droll in a helmet without any corresponding article of dress."[27] Bishop Stock mockingly described the poverty of the Irishmen who enlisted in Killala and the awkward situations that arose from the issue of quality French military equipment: "The coxcombry of the young clowns in their new dress; the mixture of good humour and contempt in the countenances of the French, employed in making puppies of them."[28] Mayo folklore also acknowledged the dearth of local rebels, but showed more empathy toward their plight. A tradition claimed that more than half of the Mayo recruits arrived barefoot and that many of them deserted upon receiving boots.[29] In folk history, the derisive attitude of French soldiers was personalized and attributed specifically to Humbert. This image did not necessarily correspond to the historical Humbert, who sympathetically remarked to the bishop: "Look at those poor fellows, they are made of the same stuff with ourselves."[30] A French officer recalled that in public Humbert concealed his disappointed with the poor quality of the recruits and "received them very kindly."[31] The dismissive attitude attributed from the beginning to Humbert in folklore anticipated the disparagement openly voiced by disillusioned French officers after their surrender.[32]

Frictions within the rebel camp were personified in a Leitrim tradition from the area of Drumshanbo that told of a duel on the eve of the battle of Ballina-muck between Humbert and the Irish rebel leader General George Blake.[33] An argument between the two concerning the placing of Irish pikemen was also said to have taken place on the battlefield itself:

> Blake wanted them on the hillside of Shanmullagh, and Humbert wanted them round the Black Fort. "Don't think," says Humbert, "that I'm going to lose my men for a lot of savages." Some of the Irish then were marched up the hill with Humbert and some stayed on the road with Blake.[34]

These narratives from the north midlands reflect the growing tensions between the French and the Irish as the situation of the insurgent army became increas-ingly more desperate. They also resonate with the knowledge of hindsight that Humbert was to abandon his Irish allies on the battlefield by surrendering and negotiating a truce that protected only the French soldiers. Following a folk narrative structure defined by the folklorist Axel Olrik as an "epic law" of "two to a scene," whereby the plot focuses on a confrontation between two leading characters,[35] the French commander (Humbert) was juxtaposed in folk mem-ory against a well-known Irish commander (Blake), each representing his respective camp. The method of transforming a remote military commander into a more personal folk character who represents his entire army is typical of folk history. For example, numerous traditions about the Cromwellian land set-tlement presented Oliver Cromwell as a villain who personally confronted locals and conducted evictions.[36] However, the character of Humbert was not adapted and integrated into folk history to such an extent.

Social memory often attributed the Rebellion's failure and the traumatic calamity of Ballinamuck to French disloyal behavior. When interviewed by a local schoolteacher, the eighty-seven-year-old storyteller John Clancy (d. 1936) of Faughill in county Leitrim recalled that he had "often heard that the French didn't act well to the Irish after the battle. It is said that they pointed out the Irish to the English when they were separating them after the battle."[37] Stories of French soldiers betraying Irish rebels were in popular circulation already at the time of the events.[38] Allegations of treachery also spread to high political circles, so that in 1811 Humbert's former deputy—General Sarrazin, an anti-Bona-partist who defected to England, had to defend the reputation of his actions in Ireland by insisting that he was "a soldier of honour" who "might be beaten, but could not be bought."[39] In several oral traditions, the generic accusation of French treachery was directed personally against Humbert. Such narratives developed at an early stage of folk historiography and persisted into the twentieth century. Three decades after the Rebellion a historical novel (published anonymously in 1830) based on testimonies of former rebels and Mayo peasantry mentioned that "the insurgents themselves (at least a great portion of them) have always ignorantly accused Humbert of treachery and alleged that he was bribed to surrender."[40] More than a hundred years later, an account collected in 1935 from an eighty-year-old blind man in Granard, county Longford, mentioned that "'twas thought by some that General Humbert was a bit treacherous. He didn't care whether Ireland won her freedom or not."[41]

The most prominent example of the transformation of a modern historical figure into a folk hero is the remembrance of Daniel O'Connell (1775–1847), who probably generated more folklore than any other person in Irish history. In oral tradition, O'Connell became a folk hero par excellence, he was commonly known as "The Counsellor" or "The Liberator" and was virtually canonized into a "king without a crown."[42] In contrast, the most striking realization when evaluating the character of Humbert in folklore is the scarcity of narratives about him. Although the *Handbook,* which guided the collectors of the Irish Folklore Commission, specifically asked for stories about Humbert,[43] relatively few stories were collected. It is not that his image was not suitable for a hero's role. After the surrender at Ballinamuck, he impressed Dublin salon circles with his striking good looks.[44] Even Bishop Stock, who as a prisoner of the French was prone to be hostile to Humbert, described him as "extraordinary" and maintained that he purposely projected a daunting persona "with the view of extorting by terror a ready compliance with his commands."[45] The adventures of Humbert's youth spurned oral traditions in the villages of his native area in Lorraine.[46] Yet, Irish oral traditions had little to say about his appearance and personality. In this respect, folk historiography differed drastically from conventional historiography, which placed Humbert in the center of all historical narratives of the 1798 Rebellion in Connacht.

It has been erroneously claimed that Humbert was not only the principal folk hero of Ninety-Eight in the West but was even regarded as a second Napoleon by his Irish partisans.[47] However, there is no comparing the lingering messianic reverence accorded to Napoleon Bonaparte in Irish folklore, which was manifested particularly in song and ballad traditions, to the passing references made to Humbert. Mention of Bonaparte in popular culture can be traced back to the French expedition to Bantry Bay in 1796, with the song "Ó, a bhean an tí" referring to General Hoche clearing the way for Bonaparte.[48] In popular imagination there appears to have been a degree of association between Humbert's campaign in 1798 and Napoleon. In a Connacht version of the Munster song "An Spailpín Fánach," Bonaparte was substituted for Humbert:

Tá na Francaigh anois istigh i gCill Ala	[The French are now inside Killala
Agus beimid go leathan láidir;	And we'll be broad and strong;
Tá Bonaparte i gCaisleán an Bharraigh,	Bonaparte is in Castlebar
Ag iarraidh an dlí a cheap Sáirséal.	Seeking Sarsfield's law.][49]

The present tense in which the song is phrased suggests that this reference may reflect the confusion of the first few days following the French landing. Rumors of Napoleon planning to arrive in Ireland were rampant in the summer of 1798, and in a rash moment of wishful thinking, Lieutenant-General Sir James Stewart even announced his capture off the coast of Cork (27 July).[50]

Seeking to enhance their reputation, French troops in Mayo claimed to be part of Napoleon's army. The Franco-Irish officer Henry O'Kane, who was responsible for recruiting Irish locals, was heard to have declared "that the sword he had in his hand was given to him by General *Bonaparte*,"[51] and a variation of a popular recruitment song generally associated with O'Kane (discussed in the following section) linked Bonaparte to the French invasion of Mayo:

Tá na Franncaigh i gCill Átha(r)	[The French are in Killala
cuidiú acu [leo] i mBéal an Átha	helping them in Ballina.
Togaigí bhur gcroidhe agus bhur	Raise your hearts and your courage
misneach	and steal away with Bonaparte.][52]
agus éalóigí le Bonapairte.	

The Mayo storyteller and folk historian Seán Henry recounted a local tradition, which recalled that in 1798 the Ballina town crier announced that Napoleon had landed in Killala.[53]

Several other Ninety-Eight songs in Irish, some of which have been dated to the time of the Rebellion, refer to Bonaparte.[54] A popular lament for the beloved rebel priest Fr. Manus Sweeney includes the verse: "Dá mhairfeadh sé agus grásta, is Bónapart theacht thar sáile" (If he were still alive, and Bonaparte sailing across the sea),[55] while another version added the verse: "acht a dtigidh Bónapáirtí buainfeam sásadh amach go fóill" (if Bonaparte comes we will get satisfaction yet!).[56] Though the French expedition to Ireland may have been perceived locally as a realization of deep-rooted Jacobite aspirations,[57] paradoxically it was Bonaparte, who in 1798 chose to sail to Egypt rather than Ireland, and not Humbert, who actually arrived in Ireland, who was accorded the veneration worthy of an awaited Jacobite deliverer.[58] Humbert countermanded popular expectations of a monarchist restoration by unequivocally pointing out the republican nature of his mission to Ireland and announcing that his cause "is no longer the contest between the houses of Hanover and Stuart."[59] After his campaign was crushed, political poetry in Irish reflected intensified hopes that Napoleon would now come to the rescue.

The song "Na Francaigh Bána," which gives an account of the French campaign in Connacht (without mentioning Humbert by name), concludes by stating that, after the defeat, Irish expectations were redirected toward providential aid to be delivered by Bonaparte:

> Ach tá dúil mhór agam as Rí na Grásta
> Is as Bonapartaí nach ndearn ariamh feall,
> Go dtiocfaidh ár gcaraid i measc na námhad
> Is go mbainfidh siad sásamh as Clann na nGall.[60]

This has been poetically translated to:

> But I have great hope in the King of Glory
> And in Bonaparte who never did wrong
> That our friends will come and rewrite our story
> And take revenge on the English throng.[61]

Similarly, a lament in Irish for three Leitrim priests who were persecuted in 1798 (Fathers Ford, O'Reilly, and Ambrose Cassidy) duly acknowledges Humbert's aid but refers to future expectations from Bonaparte.[62] In the early 1830s William Carleton observed that "Scarcely had the public mind subsided after the Rebellion of Ninety-eight when the success of Bonaparte directed their eyes and the hopes of the Irish people towards *him,* as the person designed to be their deliverer."[63] Napoleon's downfall did not put an end to this reverence, and Carleton observed elsewhere that there were people

> who will not hesitate to assure you, with a look of much mystery, that the real "Bonnyparty" is still alive and well, and will make his appearance, *when the time comes;* he who surrendered himself to the English being but an accomplice of the true one.[64]

The aggrandizement of Napoleon in poetry peaked during his imperial triumphs on the Continent, a time when he was depicted as a messianic savior in the song "Bónaigh ó'n bhFrainnc."[65] Numerous nineteenth-century popular political street ballads and broadsheets in English lauded Bonaparte, including: "Bonny Bunch of Roses," "The Green Linnet," "The Royal Eagle," "The New Granuwale," "Young Bony's Freedom," "Napoleon the Brave," "Napoleon's Farewell to Paris," "Boney's Exile," "Napoleon Crossing the Rhine," "Napoleon's Retreat," "I am Napoleon Bonaparte," "Napoleon Bonaparte's Farewell to Paris," "Napoleon's Lamentation," "The Grand Conversation on Napoleon," "The Grand Conversation Under the Rose," "Ye Sons of Old Ireland," "Napoleon is the Boy for Kicking up a Row," "The Wheels of the World," "Fallen Boney," "Bonaparte's Defeat," "Napoleon Bonaparte," "Napoleon's Dream," "Bonaparte's Farewell," "The Isle of Saint Helena," and a version of "The Wearing of the Green" where the "poor distressed Croppy" sails to Paris to meet "young Boney."[66] This long list of titles attests to Napoleon's centrality in Irish popular culture.

In contrast, the only explicit messianic reference to Humbert appeared in a version of the aforementioned lament for Fr. Sweeney, which states that "The French are now equipped and harnessed and Humbert is again sailing across the sea."[67] The disparity between the respect accorded to the two French generals was commented upon by ninety-one-year-old Michael Lyons, who was the oldest man in Killala when Hayes visited the town in 1935. As a boy he had heard the old people of the town, among them pilots who had helped land the French, talk about Humbert:

> A fine well-set-up man I heard them say he was. He was friendly to the Irish and the Irish thought well of him. But I never heard any songs praising him. He wasn't as great a man as Napoleon or Wellington.[68]

Irish popular opinion, which recognized Napoleon's superiority over Humbert, was vindicated by Bonaparte's rise to grandeur in contrast to Humbert's relatively unspectacular subsequent career.[69]

References to Humbert in folk history could be appropriated by parties with an invested interest. An apocryphal anecdote noted that Humbert complimented Colonel Charles Vereker, the commander of the garrison at Sligo town that confronted the Franco-Irish army at Collooney, by remarking: "I have met many generals in Ireland, but the only soldier amongst them was Colonel Vereker."[70] This tradition was documented in numerous variations in the early nineteenth century, with Humbert reported to have said that Vereker was "the only British officer he had faced fit to command fifty men," "the only British officer he had encountered who was capable of commanding a hundred men," or "I met many generals in Ireland—but the only general I met after all—was Colonel Vereker."[71] It most probably originated in propaganda promulgated by supporters of Vereker, who was a formidable Limerick landowner. Despite the fact that the minor engagement near Collooney was indecisive and contemporary evaluations of the outcome were ambiguous,[72] prestigious honors were heaped on Vereker: a congratulatory address was issued by the High Sheriff and County Sligo Grand Jury;[73] the Irish parliament offered him a vote of thanks; Dublin Corporation conferred on him the Freedom of the City; he was raised to the peerage as Viscount Gort, and the King awarded him the privilege of adopting "Colloney" as his motto; the city of Limerick presented him with a sword of honor and minted medals with the inscription "To the heroes of

Collooney";[74] moreover, a main thoroughfare in Limerick city was renamed "Collooney Street" to commemorate the victory.[75] All this proved to be beneficial for Vereker's political career as a Tory MP, whose reputation as a war hero was flaunted during the conservative campaign against the Act of Union in 1800, and it subsequently assisted him in repeated re-elections to parliament till 1817.[76] The story of Humbert's esteem for Vereker, which was "a legend, unsupported by any evidence,"[77] may well have been fabricated for political purposes and then subsequently filtered into social memory.

Folk history concerning Humbert also appeared in non-narrative forms, and several sites in Mayo were associated with his memory. In Ballina, the house in Pearse Street, which briefly served as his headquarters, was pointed out[78] and in Castlebar, the building in Main Street, where the Republic of Connaught was declared, was later referred to as "Humbert House" (currently the Humbert Inn).[79] To the north of Castlebar, the hill of Slievenagark (*Sliabh na gCearc*), where Humbert located his troops before attacking the town, was for years afterwards known as "Mount Humbert."[80] The folk monument locally known as "Humbert's Stone," which commemorated Humbert's landing in Kilcummin, is discussed in chapter 13.

Throughout all folklore accounts, the Franco-Irish insurgent army was commonly referred to as "Humbert's army" so that Irish recruits joined "Humbert." In this metonymic sense, Humbert's name functioned mainly as a contextual reference. He served as a "peg" to which social memory was attached. While his name was synonymous to the French army, the insurgent leadership, the rebel camp, or even the experience of the Rebellion, his character was not developed. The historian Peter Burke raised the apposite question of "why some people are, shall we say, more 'mythogenic' than others" and suggested that

> the central element in the explanation of this mythogenesis is the perception (conscious or unconscious) of a "fit" in some respect or respects between a particular individual and a current stereotype of a hero or a villain—ruler, saint, bandit, witch, or whatever. This "fit" strikes people's imagination and stories about the individual begin to circulate, orally in the first instance. In the course of this oral circulation, the ordinary mechanisms of distortion studied by social psychologists, such as "levelling" and "sharpening," come into play. These mechanisms assist the assimilation of the life of the particular individual to a particular stenotype from the repertoire of stereotypes present in the social memory in a given culture.[81]

This tentative hypothesis falls short of explaining why certain historical personages evoke associations with familiar heroic folklore motifs while other seemingly suitable candidates do not.

Scarcity of specific folklore about Humbert can be attributed to the general's remoteness and lack of direct personal contact with Irish rebels and local bystanders. He did not speak their language and spent most of his time consulting with his officers and adjutants, so he failed to leave a strong personal impression on the local inhabitants. Folk history does not necessitate direct contact between a folk hero and the public, but distance has to be bridged in some form. For example, Daniel O'Connell did not personally meet the tens of thousands who attended his "monster meetings," yet the sophisticated mechanisms of his political activism personalized his image, making it accessible to a mass public.[82] Humbert, however, was inaccessible and consequently his character was not central in folk history. If not Humbert, then who was the main hero of the Year of the French in folk historiography?

A Franco-Irish Officer: Henry O'Kane

Colonel Kane was a brave soldier; he was great talker, too, and the people used to say [that] there was no one [who] could handle a crowd like him. There was a song about him I heard my grandfather sing . . .

Dominick McDonnell of Muingrevagh
in *The Last Invasion of Ireland*

While Humbert does not feature in the rich corpus of Ninety-Eight songs and ballads, a song in Irish that stands out in the repertoire of local traditional singing repeatedly refers to a Franco-Irish officer named Kane. Though it has eluded the numerous printed collections of 1798 songs, it was particularly common in north Mayo, and there is evidence that suggests that it may have been sung throughout the county and in other areas of Connacht.[83] By the mid-twentieth century, only fragments of a stanza could be collected in the countryside, yet reminisces of the song left a poignant imprint on local social memory.

The only surviving complete version of the song was dictated by Micheál Mag Ruaidhrí (1860–1936) of Lacken in county Mayo, a gardener at St. Enda's (the celebrated secondary school founded by the writer and revolutionary Patrick Pearse) who was widely acknowledged in Irish-language revival circles for his oratory and storytelling skills. Eoin MacNeill described him as "the greatest seanchaí of our time," and Douglas Hyde nicknamed him "The Mayo Poet" on account of "the musical quality of his Irish."[84] Mag Ruaidhrí claimed that his great-grandfather Donncha Cúipéar [Dennis Cooper] had composed the song in 1798 and that it had been preserved in Tyrawley as a work song, which was hummed by women weavers. Once spinning wheels were no longer in use, the tradition of chanting the song passed away, and Mag Ruaidhrí, who had learned the song from women engaged in weaving, believed that he was the last person alive to remember it in full. The text, according to him, was:

Tá na Francaigh i gCill Ala	The French are in Killala
B'fhada cabhair ó Chlanna Gael	Long have they been needed by *Clanna*
Tógai' suas bhur gcroí is bhur misneach	*Gael* [Irish tribes]
Siúlai' amach le Coirnéal Kane.	Raise up your heart and your spirit
	And step out with Colonel Kane.

Go feirc gach airm in bhur námhaid	Bury every weapon in your foe
'tá a' marú sagairt na bhfíor Ghael	Who are killing priests of the *fíor Ghael*
Nach mór an sólas a bhronn Dia orainn	[true Irish]
Ár ndeoraí álainn Coirnéal Kane?	Did not God bestow upon us a great
	solace
	In our handsome exile Colonel Kane?

In éineacht libh, a Ghaela fíora	Along with ye, o *Gael fíor* [true Irish]
Bhur phící in airde faoi faobhar géar	Your pikes aloft with edges sharp
Bíodh gach amas fíochmhar fuilteach	Let every attack be fierce and bloody
Sin í comhairle Choirnéal Kane.	That is the counsel of Colonel Kane.

Tá ár saoirse i mbéal a' dorais	Our freedom is at the door
Má throideann gach ball de shliocht na	If every member of *sliocht na nGael* [the
nGael	Irish seed] fight along
I gcomhair leis na Francaigh bríomhar'	With the strong and vigorous French
láidir	Under the command and care of
Faoi spraic is cúram Choirnéal Kane.	Colonel Kane.

Anois nó go brách a ghaiscígh bríomhar'	Now or never, o vigorous warriors
Tá Dia ins na Flaithis in aghaidh an Pale	God in the Heavens is against the *Pale*
Beidh Íosa Críost in aingeal	[English heartland]
choimhdeachta	Jesus Christ will be a guardian angel
Cos ar chois le Coirnéal Kane.[85]	Step by step with Colonel Kane.

The graphic lyrics employ loaded terms from the imagery of eighteenth-century Irish Jacobite poetry,[86] some of which reappeared in Anglicized nineteenth-century nationalist poetry.[87]

All other collected fragments of the song are variations on the first stanza.[88] On a slip of paper tucked away among his fieldwork notes, Hayes jotted down what appears to be a reconstructed text, perhaps based on a performance that he

had heard, though the source is unidentified. In this version, the song has three stanzas, which are variants of the familiar stanza, and also a chorus:

> *fí fá la* the French is coming
> *fí fá la* they'll soon be here
> *fí fá la* the French is coming
> Everyman must volunteer[89]

The refrain *fí fá la*, which is confirmed as the chorus in other versions, is a transliteration of the French *vive la*. Intriguingly, "Viva la, United heroes" is the chorus of the song "Rouse, Hibernians," the text of which was allegedly found on the mother of a Wicklow rebel killed in autumn 1798 and was then reproduced by Musgrave. This song refers to the French presence in Mayo: "From Killala they are marching / To the Tune of Viva la."[90] The notes for the tune "Viva la! The French are coming" were recorded by the antiquarian and folk music collector George Petrie in the middle of the nineteenth century.[91] Inadvertent references to this tune being sung by rebels in Connacht crop up in historical fiction.[92] In all probability, this "rebel march song" (set to the time of $\frac{2}{4}$) is the air to which the words of the Mayo song were sung, though there are a couple of other tunes known as "Captain O'Kane" (set to the time of $\frac{6}{8}$), which offer less likely possibilities.[93]

The recurring phrase *fí fá la* reflects a late-eighteenth-century revolutionary expression as it was received and preserved in social memory. Cries such as *Vive la République* and *Vive la Liberté*, which appeared in United Irish propaganda,[94] were probably among the few French expressions that local Irish rebels picked up, just as *Éirinn go brách* (Ireland for ever) in its popularized form *Erin-go-bragh* was adopted by the French as a slogan and rallying cry (equivalent to *Vive l'Irlande*) through which they attempted to communicate with their Irish allies.[95] Taking the chorus and tune into account, the Mayo song appears to have originated as a local adaptation of a contemporary United Irish song with new verses drawn from the political vocabulary of Gaelic popular culture. This fusion illustrates a point made earlier (see chapter 5), demonstrating how a song produced in the political center was transformed in the periphery and blended influences of Jacobitism and Jacobinism.

In a version of the song collected by Hayes, a verse reads "B'fhada codladh Chloinne Gaedheal" (*Clanna Gael* have long been asleep) and the people are called upon to "shake up" (*crothaidh suas*) their courage. This phrasing echoes a nationalist literary trope, which transformed the traditional motif of "the resurrection of the Irish warrior" into a politicized concept of awakening the nation.[96] It is conceivable that this particular rendition of the local Ninety-

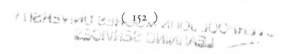

Eight song reflects the influence of the immensely popular ballad "The West's Asleep" by the early-nineteenth-century cultural nationalist Thomas Davis, which was originally published in the *Nation* and then popularized widely through the many editions of the *Spirit of the Nation*.[97] The original source of influence is unclear, however, as Davis toured Connacht in the autumn of 1843 and collected "scraps of local songs," which inspired his ballad compositions.[98]

In different versions of the song, Kane's rank varies—he appears either as a corporal, captain, or colonel. In Irish peasant culture such titles were honorary. Bishop Stock referred to O'Keon (the spelling preferred also by Musgrave) as both major and captain since "he was called indifferently by both names."[99] There is also variation in the location of the French, who are referred to either as "coming over the sea" (*teacht thar saile*), entering (*siúd isteach*), situated "in Killala" (*i gCill Alaidh*), or "helping them in Ballina" (*cuidiú acu [leo] i mBeál an Átha*). These references appear to reflect different stages of the first days of the campaign. In a verse repeated in most versions, after being called upon to show their courage, the people are then invited to "step forth with" (*siúil amach le*) Kane. This phrase may well be the key to recontextualizing the surviving fragments of the folk song, which are probably remnants of a rallying song voiced throughout Mayo and beyond to persuade local Irishmen to join the ranks of the rebel army. They appear to echo the recruitment campaign undertaken by the Franco-Irish officer Captain Henry O'Kane in the northwest Mayo baronies of Tyrawley and Erris immediately after the French landing.[100] The popular appeal of music and song as recruitment aids were recalled in folklore. Stephen McKenna of Arigna, county Roscommon, recounted how, according to family tradition, his great-grandfather Terry McKenna, "then a mere boy followed the French to Ballinamuck, attracted by the music."[101]

Who was this heroic Kane (also referred to as O'Kane, O'Keon, O'Keaon, and Keane), who was still lauded in folk song in the middle of the twentieth century, and how central was his memory in folk historiography? Born in 1768 to a family residing in the vicinity of Ballina, who were "heartily affected to the French,"[102] Fr. Henry O'Kane [Ó Catháin] was a priest in the Mayo barony of Tyrawley. It was later recalled locally that in his youth he had been involved in seditious Whiteboy activities,[103] which may have influenced his decision to immigrate to France, where he became the *curé* of Saint Hermand, near Nantes in Brittany (1788). Evidently a radical, he was member of a freemason lodge known as Les Irlandaise du soleil levant (the Irish of the Rising Sun) and enlisted in the French army with the outbreak of the Revolution.[104] In preparation of the attempted invasion of Ireland in 1796, O'Kane (listed in military files as O'Keane) was appointed captain by General Hoche.[105] In the summer of 1798, when General Humbert was eager to sign on Irish speakers, O'Kane (listed in the maritime files as MacKeon) was the only such officer to be found and was thus commissioned as a staff officer and interpreter for the expedition to Ireland.[106] Throughout the Connacht campaign he stayed in Mayo and was appointed "Colonel de la légion des habitants Irlandais" by Humbert, who subsequently commended "le Citoyen Henry O'Keane" for showing the "utmost of bravura, intelligence and action."[107] He was captured with the fall of Killala and court-martialed in Castlebar on a charge of high treason. A death sentence was reprieved following favorable loyalist testimonies made on his behalf and he was returned to France,[108] where he resumed his military career as a captain in the Sixty-fifth Regiment and several years later was reassigned at his request to the Irish Legion.[109] Serving on the Continent in campaigns throughout the Republican and Napoleonic Wars, he ultimately received the Legion of Honour, before retiring during the second Bourbon Restoration in 1815.[110]

O'Kane was described by Bishop Stock as "a fat, jolly looking man, with a ruddy countenance that carried nothing forbidding in it except that his thick black eye-brows ran into each other, as they often do in aboriginal faces."[111] The United Irishman Miles Byrne, who later met O'Keon in Paris, described him as "good humoured and generous to a degree." Byrne also mentioned that O'Kane had written a detailed multilingual account of the expedition to Ireland ("the notes were sometimes written in Latin, sometimes in English and sometimes in Irish"), alluding to a lost primary historical source, which evidently would have been of great value for the study of the 1798 Rebellion in the West.[112] His familiarity with the locality of north Mayo and his command of the required languages (i.e., French, the local Connacht dialect of Irish, and a sufficient level of English) made him indispensable to the French staff. In addition, complements were heaped on O'Kane by contemporary loyalist commentators. Bishop Stock claimed that "his language breathed nothing but mildness and liberality" and that he exerted himself to protect loyalists.[113] Even Musgrave, who as a rule presented Catholic priests as ruthless fanatics, noted that O'Keon "was humane, having on all occasions opposed the bloodthirsty disposition of the popish multitude," that he was "free from the sanguinary spirit which actuated the common herd," and that "more than once he prevented the rebels from murdering the Protestant prisoners."[114] Humphrey Thomson maintained that O'Keon was responsible for countermanding the "sanguinary measures" proposed by desperate rebels in the last days before the fall of Killala.[115]

It is therefore not surprising that this widely respected local man, who traveled the countryside to recruit locals and exhibited valor on the battlefield, would leave a lasting imprint on social memory. According to a west Mayo tradition, O'Kane was popularly known as the "Green Horseman"[116] a nickname that reflects an authentic recollection documented by an eyewitness of the French landing, who noted:

> They were preceded by a single horseman, a robust middle-aged man, dressed in a long green hunting frock, and high conical fur cap; stopping for a moment he saluted us in the Leinster patois of Irish, with "Go de mu ha tu" (how do ye do?)[117]

Mag Ruaidhrí, who claimed that his great-grandfather had attended school with O'Kane in Castlebar, recounted a vivid narrative of O'Kane's arrival on the shores of Kilcummin, as it was remembered locally. In this account, O'Kane made use of his Irish to reassure the terrified locals that the strangers were not English soldiers (a misconception brought on by the fact that the French ships deceptively displayed British flags). He then sent messengers, symbolically depicted as twelve men (in imitation of the apostles), around Tyrawley and into Erris to announce the arrival of the French through use of the song "Tá na Francaigh i gCill Ala" (discussed on 151–53).[118] Reports from Mayo that arrived in Dublin shortly after the French landing described O'Kane as second-in-command of the French invasion force, which would suggest that at the time his recruitment campaign made a strong impression.[119]

History records notable cases where an interpreter to a foreign invasion force was popularly remembered as being a main figure in historical events. Most strikingly, Doña Marina (Malinche), the interpreter of Hernán Cortés, appears in every important scene of the sixteenth-century Amerindian pictorial history *Lienzo de Tlaxcala* (ca. 1550), and her figure is typically depicted larger than that of Cortés.[120] Folklore recalled that, during the French invasion of Ireland, Catholic priests who had been trained in seminaries on the Continent mediated between the invaders and the local population.[121] Several such priests enthusiastically joined the rebels, such as Fr. Michael Gannon of Louisburgh in west Mayo, a former chaplain to the Duke of Crillon in France, who was appointed a commissary to the Franco-Irish army in Castlebar and proved to be a valuable intermediary.[122] As a local Catholic priest, a senior Franco-Irish officer and an officially designated interpreter who constantly interacted with locals, O'Kane appears to have had the makings of a major folk hero. However, further examination puts the scope of this assumption into question. Although the resilient survival of fragments of the song about O'Kane—through several generations in spite of the decline of the Irish language—suggests that it may well have been one of the most popular local Ninety-Eight songs in the West, he was far from being the main hero of the Year of the French.

Knowledge of O'Kane was not universal in social memory. Recounting a tradition from Cooga in Inishcrone, county Sligo (northeast of Ballina), which noted the bravery displayed by Keane in rescuing local rebels before the last stand in Killala, the storyteller felt obliged to clarify the protagonist's identity as "a rebel leader."[123] Overall, remarkably few stories were collected about O'Kane, and among them several narratives are ambiguous. An account collected in the north Mayo parish of Kilbride (some seven kilometers from the French landing site) told of terrified locals who went into hiding to avoid O'Kane's recruitment efforts, which apparently involved intimidation. At the same time, it was also recalled that he was courteous and praised a woman who served him a griddle cake,[124] an act of hospitality that stands out in contrast to a popular Ninety-Eight legend of a lone woman who deceptively offered a visiting government soldier a drink of milk before killing him.[125] A family tradition collected for the Schools' Scheme in Ballina told of a confrontation with a local man who refused to dig a grave for three rebel officers on the grounds that O'Kane "would not take the first three bits out of it."[126] Apparently O'Kane, who proudly presented himself as a Catholic priest,[127] did not respect traditional burial rites, which required that a priest dig the first three shovels of earth and place them on the coffin.[128] Through such stories, folk history preserved subversive narratives that recalled that the recruitment of Irish rebels was also a coercive endeavor that met with resistance—an aspect of the French invasion that has been neglected in conventional historiography. On the whole, Henry O'Kane was a local hero primarily in the vicinity of north Mayo and even there his memory was tinged with ambivalence. This may be partly because he was an insider/outsider who did not participate in the campaign into the north midlands. It is therefore worth inspecting the folklore of a local rebel leader who marched from Mayo to Ballinamuck.

An Insurgent General: George Blake

Young Blake is the name of the hero who sleeps,
In the dear little spot where the peasant still weeps.

Ballinamuck ballad—"Blake's Grave"

The insurgent commander George Blake of Garracloon in south county Mayo is yet another likely candidate for primacy as a major hero in folk historiography. He was depicted in contemporary loyalist reports, as "the only man of any name who has joined the French"[129] and has since been described as "the most notable of all the patriot leaders" involved in the 1798 Rebellion in Connacht.[130] Blake came from a distinguished family; his father's Anglo-Norman lineage stemmed back to Richard Cadell, who received a grant of land from Edward I in Connacht (1278) and adopted the family name Niger [Blake]. His mother, Eliza O'Donnell, claimed aristocratic Gaelic lineage back to the famous rebel heroes Shane "the Proud" O'Neill ([Seán an Díomais], ca. 1530–67) and Owen Roe O'Neill (ca. 1590–1649).[131] Through Eliza he was also related to the Mayo magnate Sir Neal O'Donnell of Newport, who was active in suppressing the 1798 Rebellion. Blake was a veteran officer of the British army and had served in the West Indies as a cornet (second lieutenant) in the Twentieth Regiment of the Light Dragoons but had apparently been discharged in consequence of a dueling affair.[132] An eyewitness described him at the time of the Rebellion:

> He was twenty seven or twenty eight years old; a tall well-made man, with a clear skin, large blue eyes, fair hair, a long hooked nose, and a very short upper lip.[133]

His appearance was portrayed more affectionately in folklore. In 1935 an eighty-year-old woman in the area of Ballinamuck recalled "a handsome good-looking man, I heard them say, General Blake was."[134] He joined the French army in Ballina shortly after their arrival (26 August) and was subsequently appointed commander-in-chief of the Irish rebels. After distinguishing himself at Castlebar, he led a party of rebels in securing the area of Ballinrobe in south county Mayo and then rejoined the main body of the Franco-Irish army for the campaign to Ballinamuck, where he was captured and executed.[135]

Blake's rank of general in folk history is confirmed in a report issued by the British commander Lieutenant-General Gerard Lake, which noted that he was among three rebel leaders "called general officer."[136] Though several other notable Irish "chieftains" also joined the rebels in Connacht, only Blake was mentioned by name in the list of leaders of the 1798 Rebellion provided to collectors of the Irish Folklore Commission.[137] A relatively large number of historical traditions about Blake have been documented, yet most of these were taken down by Hayes and by the young collectors for the Schools' Scheme (who were not using the Commission's *Handbook*). The bulk of the accounts relating to Blake were collected in the vicinity of Ballinamuck, an area that was deeply traumatized and subsequently became a hotbed of Ninety-Eight folklore. They tell of his heroic performance on the battlefield, how he at first escaped but was then captured and executed, and of a clandestine wake and the burial of his corpse. Blake's popular reputation overstated his actual role so that several contributions submitted to the Schools' Scheme identified him as the overall commander of the Franco-Irish army, speciously contending that he was also in charge of the French troops.[138]

Only few traditions about Blake appear to have originated in his native area in south Mayo. A local tradition from his home locality of Garracloon and Cong told how Blake discouraged local United Irishmen from joining the French by saying: "There is no use in bringing any more, for none of us will return."[139] In contrast to mainstream narratives, which emphasize the insurgents' enthusiasm, this somewhat subversive story reflects ambivalence toward the Rebellion. The portrayal of a disillusioned Blake soberly turning back volunteers is corroborated in the way he was portrayed by the contemporary pro-government press. Dublin's primary loyalist-conservative newspaper described him as "a man of profligate character and desperate fortune" and alleged that he had offered to surrender to the authorities in exchange for a sentence of exile,[140] a rumor that circulated in government circles and was repeated by Lord Shannon.[141] After the Rebellion, the *Freeman's Journal* reported that:

> the Rebel Chief, Blake, when thousands were flocking to his standard (in disappointment of his hopes from Humbert's conduct) urged them to depart to their homes—at the same time observing that the die was cast respecting himself, and many of his companions; and that therefore they, though entirely despairing of accomplishing their purpose, were obliged to go on and meet certain death.[142]

All the same, such stories of supporters of the Rebellion discouraging enlistment are common in the folk historiography of 1798. Fr. O'Flanagan of Granard was reported to have said: "Go back and don't get yourselves butchered, you're a hundred years too soon." A similar statement was attributed in the area of Ballinamuck to a Protestant farmer who sympathized with the rebel cause but cautioned: "It's no use; ye will be beaten this time; ye are a hundred years too soon. This time a hundred years ye'll win."[143] This is a traveling motif in Ninety-Eight folklore and was also told in relation to Fr. Blanchfield of Hacketstown, county Carlow.[144] These traditions, which often display clear signs of anachronism, appear to express a tone of regret in the way social memory looked back at the unfortunate fate of the doomed rebels. In contrast, other traditions recalled names of locals around south Mayo who did join Blake.[145]

A tradition in Blake's home village told of a "false hanging" and of "Master George" escaping to the continent. This apocryphal story was told to Hayes by an old man near Garracloon whose grandmother had allegedly heard it from Blake's wife. Hayes suggested that it may have originated in confusion with Blake's kinsman, General Joachim Blake of Furlough—a distinguished Irish officer in the Spanish army.[146] The question of General Blake's fate sparked a controversy among authorities on folk history, which was brought to public attention in the 1930s by the local historian and journalist Joseph F. Quinn in his "History of Mayo" series, published in the Ballina paper *Western People*. Dr. Marley Blake of Ravensdale, county Louth, a descendant of George Blake and who was familiar with family folklore, repeatedly refuted this legend, and this position was reiterated by the Blake family historian, Martin J. Blake. In response, the folk historian Patrick O'Donnell of Newport forcefully insisted that their arguments "were unsupported by a particle of documentary evidence or tradition," and the issue remained unresolved.[147]

The Garracloon tradition relates to what the historian Eric Hobsbawm defined as the ultimate accolade of the bandit hero: popular refusal to believe in his death.[148] Oral tradition habitually discredited news of execution of local resistance heroes and generated alternative narratives of secret escape and continued life in exile. A noteworthy comparable example from the folk history of the Year of the French relates to the fate of the nominal president of the Connacht Republic, John Moore of Moore Hall.[149] Moore's death sentence was commuted to transportation to New Geneva, but he died en route to Duncannon Fort (6 December 1799). Hayes noted that "a legend grew up in the west that he escaped to Spain from Castlebar jail and lived to a good old age." In 1935 John's grandnephew, the statesman Colonel Maurice Moore (b. 1854), testified that family tradition had embraced and further embellished this story.[150] Since the details of Moore's death in prison were not in the public domain until Hayes uncovered the documentation in the British Museum, uncertainty encouraged the development of "many romantic tales" about him in social memory.[151] In 1937 Hayes pointed out that Moore was buried in an unmarked grave in Ballygunner cemetery in Waterford,[152] and traditions of secret escape to the continent were ultimately deflated in 1961, when the remains of John Moore's corpse were reinterred with a state funeral in Castlebar.[153]

In the case of Blake, numerous contemporary testimonies of English soldiers irrefutably confirm that he was indeed executed.[154] The alternative narrative of Blake's escape may have drawn support from a misreading of Musgrave's account of the Rebellion, published only two years after the events. Writing about the rebels after Ballinamuck, Musgrave observed: "Three of their leaders were taken, among who was Mr. Blake, a popish gentleman, who was hanged."[155] Yet elsewhere, in reference to the fate of the Mayo rebel leader Colonel James Joseph McDonnell of Carnacon, he wrote:

> He [McDonnell] and colonel Blake concealed themselves in a bog. Blake was taken prisoner, but he [McDonnell] had the good fortune to escape and made his way from thence into the wild mountains of Connemara, and from thence embarked for Spain or France, with some other fugitives of his own description.[156]

The wording of this passage is slightly confusing and may be interpreted to mean that Blake escaped from captivity, though it intends to state that Blake was captured while McDonnell escaped.[157] Indeed several readers were misled, including Madden[158] and the Mayo historian Quinn, who concluded that Musgrave produced an inconsistent and "chaotic narrative" and that therefore the story of Blake's escape to Spain was "apparently, a better authenticated tradition" than the records of his execution at Ballinamuck.[159]

The martyrdom of Blake was a central theme of history-telling in the Ballinamuck area. Local folklore traditions included numerous narratives of Blake's execution in Ballinamuck, his wake in a house in Kiltycrevagh, and the burial of his corpse in the graveyard of Tubberpatrick. However, this martyrology was not an integral part of local tradition in his home area. It appears that in social memory around Garracloon, Blake was venerated as a celebrated personage, and news of his distant death was even rejected by some. Therefore, the distribution of Blake's folklore suggests that he was less a national hero of Ninety-Eight but rather a regional hero, with two distinct constituencies that preserved his memory: South Mayo and the Ballinamuck area in south Leitrim—north Longford.

Hayes noted a "saying in the west," without specifying its origin and distribution: "Is cosmhail le Blácaigh na Gearra-Chluana iad, ceann aca i n-arm Shasana, ceann eile i n-arm na hÉireann!" (They are like the Blakes of Garracloon, one in the English army and another in the Irish army).[160] Indeed, while George Blake was a senior insurgent leader, one of his younger brothers served as an officer in the British army. This caused some confusion about Blake's identity and allegiance, which was already an issue of contention in the immediate aftermath of the Rebellion. The loyalist *Dublin Journal* accused the radical English newspaper *The Star* of confusing the rebel leader with a "very loyal and worthy Gentleman of the County of Galway," father of a "gallant son who serves his King, with honour and fidelity in the Royal Irish Artillery."[161] In its everyday usage, the saying marked quarrels between brothers or relatives. Inadvertently, it also highlighted a largely overlooked aspect of the Rebellion, which at times involved elements of civil war, pitting relatives and friends against each other. This theme, which has several records in folk history, has not been properly addressed in scholarly historiography.[162]

Oral traditions about Blake can serve to elucidate some key points on the function of variation in local folk history, which could simultaneously recall different, even contradictory, traditions that interacted with each other. An example of such cultural dialogue can be found in the folklore of the betrayal of General Blake. A tradition from around Ballinamuck recalled how Blake was handed in to the authorities by a yeoman named Leslie and his servant Hugh McDermott.[163] A verse from a popular ballad recounts this narrative:

> General Blake, he lay in the bog
> While Hughie and Leslie were making their prog;
> Twenty-five guineas he gave to the two
> To spare him his life, but all wouldn't do.[164]

Another song from the locality, which recalls the seditious act of planting a "Tree of Liberty," also refers to McDermott:

> If you plant the Tree of Liberty,
> Plant it on the hill of Kilglass,
> For fear that MacDermott the traitor
> Himself or his stagers would pass.[165]

Local interpretation of this song explained that McDermott benefited materially from his denunciation of Blake and acquired stagecoaches and retainers of his own. The appreciation of this point evidently depended on the audience's familiarity with the story of McDermott's treachery. The correlation and cross-referencing between these two songs demonstrates the communal nature of social memory, which refers to a shared reconstruction of history.

In another version of the story, Blake unsuccessfully tries to bribe the informer by offering his "watch and chain," a motif that appeared also in Ulster Ninety-Eight balladry about Henry Munro, the leader of the rebels in county Down at the fatal battle of Ballynahinch (13 June 1798).[166] In this north Longford account, the traitor was called McGlynn,[167] a name that may have been drawn from another local folk history discourse about betrayal, since it was also attributed to a villain who sabotaged the advance of the rebel army, after they rested at the Leitrim village of Cloone on the eve of the Battle of Ballinamuck, by stealing the chains used to draw the artillery.[168] The association between the two traditions may have occurred as a result of the use of the word "chain." Alternatively, the accusation of betraying Blake may be the common denominator—as the popular legend of the cannon chains was referred to in a Ballinamuck ballad as "The Betrayal of Blake at Cloone."[169] In another version of the story, the traitors who informed on Blake's whereabouts are identified as Latley and McGrinn.[170] While these variations may appear to illustrate the versatility of folklore, they also demonstrate the unreliability of reference to names in folk historiography. Whereas a basic narrative could remain intact in oral tradition, multiple transmissions commonly corrupted names, as in the case of "Leslie" and "Latley" or "McGlynn" and "McGrinn." This issue is discussed further in "Local Heroes and Their Constituencies" in chapter 9.

Since variation does not entail irreconcilable splintering of a narrative, diversity in folk historiography did not necessitate the balkanization of social memory. In the area of Ballinamuck many traditions told of Blake's execution, and though local storytellers acknowledged the variety of available traditions,[171] the basic story remained constant. Almost all accounts mentioned that Blake was hanged on the spokes of a cartwheel (noting that the loyalist landlord and local yeoman commander Dukey Crofton of Mohill, county Leitrim, was involved in the execution) and that his body was reclaimed by locals, waked in the McKenna household in Kiltycrevagh, and buried in Tubberpatrick graveyard.[172] Other versions insisted that Blake was hanged on a "boultree" (elder bush),[173] and the exact location of his execution was disputed.[174] Even though

FIGURE 13. 1798 memorial in Ballinamuck, county Longford. Dedicated to the Ballinamuck heroes General George Blake and Gunner James Magee [McGee], the wrought-iron cross was originally placed by the National Graves Association on Blake's Grave in Tubberpatrick in 1933 and relocated to the "Croppies Graves" on Shanmullagh Hill in 1948. Photo by the author.

FIGURE 14. 1798 monument to General Blake in Tubberpatrick, Ballinamuck, county Longford (erected 1948). Recalled in folk stories and poetry, the "green grave" of General Blake was originally marked by ash trees and later adorned by various small memorials. The Celtic cross has been maintained by the republican National Graves Association. Photo by the author.

such minute details may appear trivial to an outsider, they cannot be dismissed; in certain contexts they had particular significance for locals.

As befits a folk hero, Blake's grave in Tubberpatrick became a local site of commemoration.[175] It was originally marked by four ash trees,[176] which were replaced around 1910 by a small, carved stone decorated with Celtic art designs, financed by Rev. Lawrence Cosgrove of Rosemount, Minnesota.[177] In 1933 the Longford branch of the republican National Graves Association (NGA) placed on the site an iron cross dedicated both to General Blake and to Gunner Magee, another well-known Ballinamuck hero (see fig. 13). This simple memorial was relocated in 1948 to the "Croppies Graves" on the battlefield of Ballinamuck and in its place a more impressive Celtic cross was erected (see fig. 14).[178] The site was the subject of a local ballad titled "Blake's Grave" that emulates Thomas Davis's celebrated ballad "Tone's Grave" and even lifts its opening verse: "In Bodenstown churchyard there is a green grave," which reappears as: "In Tubberpatrick graveyard, there lies a green grave." Like in Davis's composition, the narrator in "Blake's Grave" visits the gravesite and is approached by a venerable man who calls for "a more fitting tomb" to be raised in honor of the martyr.[179] In such ways canonical nineteenth-century nationalist martyrology was readapted and integrated into local tradition.

Blake's heroic status was not without blemish. Though folk historiography did not aspire to examine the past dispassionately, it was capable of exercising self-criticism. Indeed, some of the traditions relating to Blake's heroic performance on the battlefield of Ballinamuck expressed restrained disapproval. A storyteller put a strategic error down to Blake's zeal, commenting that his "heart was better than his head. If he had a little patience and [did] not allow the pikemen over so soon, there wouldn't be so many of them killed."[180] Similarly, a Ballinamuck ballad, which lauds "Intrepid Blake," gingerly concedes that "faults he had some."[181] Undoubtedly, Blake was a folk hero but, despite the voluminous body of folklore about him, he was not the overall hero of the Year of the French. Even in Ballinamuck, the core area of his remembrance, he was but one of a plethora of Ninety-Eight heroes, many of them "pikemen"—the rank and file of the rebel army. An understanding of the democratic character of folk history requires further examination of these traditions.

An Irish Pikeman: Robin Gill of Edenmore

Yes, he would have been a pikeman. He would have fought
in the battle all right. And he escaped, lived afterwards . . .

Peter Duignan of Gaigue, IFC 1858:11–12

In 1928 a monument was erected in Ballinamuck. It is not a statue of Humbert, Blake, or any of the other leaders in the Rebellion, but in the tradition of nationalist Ninety-Eight centenary monuments, it is a statue of a pikeman—a generic representation of an Irish rebel. A transcript of a conversation recorded in 1968 by a folklore collector in Ballinamuck shows that this collective anonymous representation was not lost on people in the locality:

> BERNARD THOMPSON: That wasn't General Blake that's in Ballinamuck, you know, that's only to represent the soldiers that fell. That man, they say, [is] the pikeman, he's nobody.
>
> PATRICK JOE REILLY: He's an unknown warrior.
>
> MARGARET (REILLY) THOMPSON: Yeah. He's only just to represent those that fell . . .
>
> BERNARD THOMPSON: On the battle fields of Ballinamuck.[182]

The formation of national collective memory through monuments of anonymous soldiers is a familiar phenomenon in modern European history and has

been extensively researched, specifically in the context of World War I.[183] David Thelen argued, through the example of the Vietnam Veterans Memorial in the United States, that while such memorials set out to legitimize elite policy by consolidating national myths that promote uniformity and stability, they also provide space for nurturing private recollections.[184] Oral history is a vital tool for tapping into such unofficial discourses of remembrance. More specifically, folk history narratives reclaim the archetypal pike-

FIGURE 15. 1798 monument in Ballinamuck, county Longford (unveiled 1928). The pikeman, an image popularized by the monumental iconography of the 1798 centenary, was generally recognized as a familiar collective representation of an anonymous rebel, yet others maintained that it was a memorial to the insurgent leader General Blake. Photo by the author.

man from his anonymity and move beyond a history of leaders, offering a more democratic historical outlook.

Whereas the historical record of the engagement at Ballinamuck notes that the French troops laid down their arms after a perfunctory exchange of fire, folk history focused on the events from the perspective of the Irish rebels, who were left to fend for themselves. In social memory, the debacle at Ballinamuck became a major battle, which featured numerous acts of reckless bravery. In order to understand how combatants were elevated to local folk heroes it is necessary to probe the grassroots construction of social memory. This can be demonstrated by considering the case of an exemplar hero in Ballinamuck folk history—Robin Gill of Edenmore, a local man who according to oral tradition joined the rebel army on the fatal day. He reputedly lived to the age of eighty-five and in his latter years would defiantly exclaim: "Boys, keep your pikes well sharpened, they may serve another day!"[185]

Many stories were told about Gill's valor on the battlefield and about his subsequent escape. Through close examination of the documented folklore sources it is possible to trace the origin of these traditions to the storytelling of his grandnephew Patrick Gill of Edenmore ("Grey Pat," ca. 1840–1936), who was renowned locally for his knowledge of Ballinamuck folklore. Both the collector Pádraig Mac Gréine (1933) and Hayes (1935) interviewed Grey Pat in his midnineties and collected from him tales of his granduncle's bravery.[186] After his death, his son Patrick repeated his stories for the benefit of the Schools' Scheme and also recited a ballad of twenty-four quatrains about Robin Gill's escapades, which was known to have been "one of Grey Pat's favorites."[187] Grey Pat was also named as the direct source of information in other accounts,[188] and he most probably influenced stories of Robin Gill told by other storytellers of similar age, who lived in neighboring townlands, including accounts collected in 1935 from eighty-year-old James O'Neill of Crowdromin[189] and in 1938 from eighty-six-year-old Michael Grimes of Kiltycrevagh.[190] Further evidence of his influence is apparent in a farrago in the copybook of a pupil, who collected "A '98 Tale" that mistakenly identified the pikeman hero as *Patrick* Gill of Edenmore, confusing the source of the account with its subject.[191] Some thirty years later, the collector Maureen O'Rourke discovered that Grey Pat's stories about Robin Gill were still remembered around Ballinamuck.[192] More recently, a descendent of the Gills of Ballinamuck raised in Dublin, Clára Ní Ghiolla ([Gill], b. 1930), recalled that her uncle Mick Gill (b. 1880) would recite the lengthy ballad and that as a child she would often hear family traditions of Robin Gill's bravery, noting that Grey Pat was also mentioned.[193]

Individuals traced their heroic ancestors through patriotic genealogies, and these family traditions were integrated into a community tradition of folk history-telling. The impact of Patrick Gill's storytelling demonstrates the agency of individual storytellers who inculcated *seanchas* traditions, which were then awarded external recognition by folklore collectors. Accounts collected from Grey Pat were exposed to a wider public in scholarly publications and were then quoted in popular print. Shortly after appearing in *Béaloideas,* the journal of the Folklore Society of Ireland (1934/35), excerpts of the account collected by Mac Gréine were republished by the popular columnist "Roddy the Rover" [Aodh de Blácam] in the *Irish Press,*[194] and some forty years later they reappeared in the *Longford News.*[195] In the bicentennial year of the Rebellion (1998), the centrality in local folk history of Patrick Gill stories about Robin Gill received official endorsement when they were incorporated into a permanent exhibition of 1798 heritage in the newly opened Ballinamuck Visitor Centre.[196]

The mass slaughter of Irish rebels is acknowledged in all scholarly histories of the battle of Ballinamuck; however, this shattering experience is usually covered through reference to crude estimated statistics, which do not meaningfully qualify the carnage. In contrast, folk histories focused on the experience of local rebels. Traditions about Robin Gill recount how he was wounded but succeeded to escape from a party of soldiers, though the comrades who accompanied him were less fortunate.

In different variations of a similar narrative, the fugitive Robin Gill is credited with killing a pursuing soldier on horseback. The story of a pikeman on foot defeating a cavalryman is a common motif in Ninety-Eight folklore. It recurs in numerous accounts about unnamed pikemen in the Year of the French[197] and appeared in a romantic-nationalist literary style already in mid-nineteenth-century popular print.[198] It was also found farther afield in the folk history of the 1798 Rebellion in Leinster.[199] In Ballinamuck traditions, this motif was not only associated with Robin Gill but was also told about other local heroes, namely Bryan O'Neill of Drumderg[200] and Art McQuaide of Gaigue.[201] Their authenticity, in positivist terms, has been disputed, since a medical report of casualties and injuries sustained by Crown forces lists only two puncture wounds (of the kind that would be caused by a pike) throughout the whole campaign, both of which occurred in Ballinamuck.[202] They cannot be altogether discredited, as the report did not cover yeomanry units, who were engaged in the hunting down of rebels, and also the military had an interest in downplaying the damages incurred from Irish rebels.[203] More significantly, from an interpretative point of view, formulaic folklore narratives of single-handed combat provided a familiar framework to which episodes of distinguished bravery by individuals could be attached and remembered.

Robin Gill is but one example of a Ballinamuck Ninety-Eight hero. Foremost among the many rebels recalled in the folk history of the battle was Gunner James Magee [McGee], a former Longford militiaman who changed sides and joining the rebel army at Castlebar. In folklore, Magee's valor on the battlefield assumed legendary proportions. The most dramatic imagery in Ballinamuck traditions relates to graphic descriptions of Magee fearlessly manning the rebel cannon and, thanks to the self-sacrifice of his devoted crew, continuing to discharge makeshift shells even when ammunition had run out and defeat was imminent.[204] Magee's heroic status received national recognition with the opening of the Magee Barracks in Kildare (1938), which hosted the Depot and School of Artillery of the Defense Forces. It was promoted further by the introduction of the Magee Gun Trophy (1944), awarded annually to a field artillery regiment that wins an all-army competition.[205] Though other individuals did not receive such exposure, the inhabitants of the townlands around Ballinamuck devotedly remembered their local heroes, just as other localities also recalled the names and experiences of people from their area who had participated in the Rebellion. In this way, the Year of the French produced a panoply of local heroes. It is this breaking up of the historical metanarrative and its relation to the larger picture, which needs to be conceptualized in order to appreciate the character of folk history.

9

Multiple Heroes in Folk Historiographies

How many heroes can one history accommodate?

Brian Friel, *Making History*

Local Heroes and Their Constituencies

I N THE EARLY 1930s, James P. Donnelan, a national schoolteacher on the Aran Islands off the coast of Galway and a native of Knock in county Mayo, wrote to J. F. Quinn's local history column in the Mayo newspaper the *Western People.*

> It seems to me that an effort should be made to compile a list of the names, with biographical particulars as far as possible, of all the Mayo men who lost their lives or took a prominent part in the Rebellion. Mayo's "Roll of Honour" has never been published. In almost every parish there are traditions of local people who suffered in one way or another that year. It is a pity that these should be allowed to die without an effort being made to preserve them.[1]

A couple of years later, this plea was addressed to some extent in the work of Hayes, to whom Donnelan willingly sent folklore traditions.[2] It articulates the reality that information on the local heroes of the Year of the French was scattered in folk historiography throughout communities in the West and was mostly not collated.

As shown in the previous chapters, provincial folk history-telling did not simply broaden the limited pantheon of national historiography by adding a number of additional figures who had left a mark on social memory. The truly democratic nature of folk historiography was manifested in the ways each locality remembered its own heroes. By accommodating numerous narratives, which referred to multiple heroes and were told in different versions, a corpus

(168)

of historical folk traditions is more a case of multiple *histories* than of a uniform history. Moreover, the notion of "folk" itself is not homogenous, as Dorson pointed out: "more than one folk exists, and each folk group records events and personalities of the past through its own particular lens."[3] Folk history, therefore, presents a complex and decentralized historiographical model. Though scholarly historiography, which offered a platform for lively controversies, is not monolithic, it consistently failed to acknowledge the central narratives and local variants of folk histories. This disparity is particularly noticeable in the case of events that were regarded minor "footnotes" in national history, which were generally considered unworthy of serious study by professional historians, but were often central episodes in folk histories.

Folk historiography was not insular. Although folklore flourished in local communities, it was subject to influences from national discourses. Judging by local reception, national history did not enforce a uniform metanarrative to which regional folk histories were subjugated, but instead provided a kind of porous metanarrative, which facilitated a patchwork of variegated micronarratives. In effect, "history" served as a loose framework, in relation to which local communities could narrate an array of vernacular histories presented from provincial perspectives, thus relocating the focus of historical attention away from the metropolitan center.

Because folk history-telling was, as a rule, locally oriented, each locality affected by the Franco-Irish insurrection and its repression generated its own heroes of the Year of the French. The pikemen heroes of Ballinamuck were not central to folklore elsewhere. Just twenty kilometers southeast of Ballinamuck, in the neighboring area of Granard, a voluminous body of oral traditions recalled the events of the local uprising, which was crushed on 5 September. Fugitives from Granard went on to join the Franco-Irish army at Cloone and to fight at Ballinamuck, and this caused elision in local folk history, which often mixed the two engagements, so that history-tellers were incapable of sorting out the correct sequence of events. Even an account collected for the Schools' Scheme in nearby Ballinalee, county Longford (some ten kilometers from both Ballinamuck and Granard), which insisted in noting "the truth" in face of the "many mistakes given about this battle in history," was riddled with inaccuracies.[4]

Though passing references were made to Ballinamuck heroes such as Gunner Magee and Robin Gill, Ninety-Eight traditions from Granard recalled a long list of local heroes, most distinguished among them were Patrick O'Farrell of Ballinree, Willie O'Keefe of Ballinlough, the O'Connells of Cranary (Paddy, Nicholas, and Harry), the Dennistons of Clonbroney (Alexander and Hans), the O'Reillys (Phil Dubh and Miles), and Captain Mulligan of Aghakine (who headed a contingent of rebels from the parish of Colmcille).[5] A vivid account of the insurrection in Granard as told in 1935 by blind eighty-year Patrick Mulligan, who had learned traditions from "the old people" and from his grandmother (Rose MacIntyre, an eyewitness of the events), was branded by Hayes "picturesque but rather fantastic."[6] Nevertheless, its references to the participation of local rebels are more insightful than a contemporary account by the French adjutant-general Fontaine, who quixotically described a rebel leader from Granard as "bearing a striking resemblance to a valiant knight of the thirteenth century."[7] Local traditions continued to recount detailed descriptions of the Rebellion in Granard late into the twentieth century, as in two versions of an account collected from relatives of the Ninety-Eight rebel hero Willie O'Keefe in 1956[8] and in 1998.[9]

Folk history not only extolled popular heroes but also portrayed notorious villains. A well-known example in traditions from Granard and neighboring parishes in Westmeath was "Hempenstall," infamously labeled "the Walking Gallows."[10] In 1797 Lieutenant Edward Hempenstall of the Wicklow Militia was stationed in Westmeath and Edenderry, King's County, and engaged in violent acts of "counter-insurgency."[11] An immensely tall man, he was notorious for the use of the sadistic technique of "half-hanging"—suspending victims by the neck from his shoulder. Prior to the Rebellion, concerned loyalists referred to his abhorrent nickname when denouncing his excessive brutality.[12] After the Rebellion, a graphic image of "Hempenstall the Walking Gallows" was popularized in a cartoon by the painter Henry Brocas (1762–1837), which was originally published in Watty Cox's *Irish Magazine* in January 1810 and then republished in numerous publications on 1798. Cox, a former United Irishman, was originally from Westmeath and may have personally been aware of Hempenstall's reputation.

Folklore about Hempenstall was formulated immediately after his death in 1801 (mistakenly cited by Madden as "about 1813"), when a priest by the name of Barrett composed a sarcastic epitaph:

> Here lie the bones of Hempenstall
> Judge, jury, gallows, rope and all.[13]

The rhyme was repeated more than a hundred years later for the Schools' Scheme in Ballymore, county Westmeath.[14] The source for this account may be literary, as the couplet, alongside details of Hempenstall's cruelty against suspected rebels, was published originally in the mid-nineteenth century in Madden's *The United Irishmen* and was reproduced by the biographer W. J.

Fitzpatrick (1830–95) in his popular book *The Sham Squire*, which was widely sold in chapbook reprints.[15]

Hempenstall's reputation for persecuting rebels was widespread in the folk history of the Year of the French throughout the north midlands and beyond,[16] and some accounts went so far as to claim that he was the commander of the government army forces at the engagement in Granard. In oral traditions he was named "Dopin(g) (or Doppil) Hempenstall"—an anachronism deriving from a family alliance in the mid-nineteenth century, when Ralph Anthony Dopping of Derrycassan, county Longford, married Diane Margaret, heir of Rev. Lambert Watson Hepenstal of Altidore, county Wicklow, and adopted the name Dopping-Hepenstal (1859).[17] A curious testimony to the persistence of local recollections into the twentieth century can be deduced from nationalist interparty political propaganda during a South Longford by-election in May 1917. At the time, the campaign of the Sinn Féin candidate Joseph Mac Guinness attempted to capitalize on fears that support for the opponent Irish Parliamentary party might result in the introduction of conscription in Ireland for the remainder of the Great War. The party's leader John Dillon (1851–1927) was crudely depicted in a defamatory leaflet as "Worse than Heppenstall [*sic*], the Walking Gallows."[18] Such manipulation of folklore obviously relied on popular recognition.

Though traditions of local heroes and villains were dispersed throughout Connacht and the north midlands, a fragmented notion of autonomous folk histories preoccupied solely with heroes from the locality is misleading. Folklore accounts indicate that remembrance of the Franco-Irish campaign, which crossed four counties and brought rebels from Mayo into Longford, facilitated regional discourses that brought together local constituencies of social memory. In addition to people from their own locality that participated in the Rebellion, communities also recalled contacts with rebels from other areas. For example, the O'Briens of Curlough, Drumshanbo, county Leitrim, recalled how in 1798 their ancestor (Jemmy O'Brien) concealed a Mayo rebel, who escaped from Ballinamuck but was prevented from crossing the Shannon River and making his way home on account of military surveillance.[19] Similarly, it was remembered in Ballinamuck how a farmer from the neighboring townland of Aughavass, sheltered a mortally wounded rebel named Jack Leonard and traveled to Mayo to bring the fugitive's brother to his deathbed.[20] Through such narratives, folk historiography formulated a broad overarching storyline of the French invasion, which was shared by communities throughout the West of Ireland. From a bird's-eye view, provincial folk historiographies wove a rich tapestry, which stitched together the numerous folk histories that were generated by local communities.

To some extent this regional folk history was part of a larger folk history of Ninety-Eight. An account collected for the Schools' Scheme in Kilconry, county Clare, told of an engineer named O'Byrne who had fought at the fatal battle of Vinegar Hill in county Wexford (21 June 1798) and had fled to the West.[21] "The Lamentations of Patrick Brady," a ballad sung in Ballinamuck, tells of a rebel who fought in Wexford, went on to fight in the battles of Castlebar and Ballinamuck, and then sustained armed resistance in the Wicklow hills, where he was arrested and sentenced to death.[22] It appeared under the title "Heroes of '98" in Madden's mid-nineteenth-century collection of 1798 songs and was circulated in print as a broadside.[23] Although Hayes believed that it was a contemporary ballad ("in the plain Irish rhythm") and reflected the experiences of an insurgent from the East who traveled to Connacht,[24] it has been pointed out that it is "one of the class of narrative ballads . . . which try to include as much information as possible" and is therefore most probably an attempt to phrase the entire history of 1798 in song (omitting the Rebellion in northeast Ulster).[25] Such songs and stories located the Year of the French in a national narrative of the 1798 Rebellion.

To complicate the picture, folk histories of Ninety-Eight were also recalled in Irish communities abroad. On the odd occasion, folklore collectors in Ireland heard references to traditions of the Year of the French that had emigrated. For example, Michael Corduff noted that rebel songs from Erris in county Mayo, including a poem about the Mayo United Irishman Captain O'Malley, "were sung in the mining villages of Pennsylvania" and were regularly performed at "social reunions in foreign countries."[26] Scattered references to 1798 can also be found in letters, private papers, and personal testimonies of emigrants from Connacht and the north midlands who moved to such diverse places in the United States as Brooklyn,[27] Chicago,[28] Nebraska,[29] West Virginia,[30] Ohio, and New Hampshire.[31] The international appeal of Ninety-Eight remembrance can also be inferred from the way fund-raising campaigns for memorials in the late-nineteenth and twentieth centuries often targeted emigrants. For example, the committee in Knock, county Mayo, sent out an appeal to the United States and Australia.[32] The most significant contributor to the Father Manus Sweeney Memorial Hall in Newport, county Mayo, was Martin J. Berry of Chicago, who was originally from Newport.[33] There are numerous accounts that testify that folklore was remembered in Irish diasporas up to recent times, in such places as England,[34] Australia,[35] and Canada.[36]

The democratic nature of folk historiography is twofold in its numerous practitioners and in its content, which refers to numerous subjects, who are primarily "common" people. However, it is not an egalitarian historical discourse, as inevitably not everybody from the past is remembered. Collectively, across its widespread constituencies, the social memory of the Year of the French recalled the names of several hundred individuals who were involved and affected by 1798 Rebellion in Connacht and the north midlands. Impressive as it may seem, this figure is a fraction of all those who had participated or witnessed the events first hand. The survival of certain names was dependent primarily on history-tellers (the storytellers and ballad-singers that performed historical traditions) and their audiences, and subsequently on the work of folk historians and folklore collectors. The activities of these practitioners of folk historiography involved (sometimes unconsciously) processes of selection. Furthermore, not everybody became a hero in social memory, and among the many names cited in folk histories only the characters of certain people were developed. As shown in the case of Robin Gill, family traditions had an invested interest in the preservation and aggrandizement of the names of their ancestors, thus insuring that particular names and narratives were not forgotten. When the relation was less personal, the accurate transmission of names could be extremely problematic and was often prone to erosion.

A comical take on the lack of precision in the recollection of names of "common people" appeared in a bicentennial humorous television parody by the Northern-Irish comedy troupe "The Hole in the Wall Gang" facetiously titled "1798: The Comedy." The program ended with the execution of a fictional rebel named Barry Simpson, who takes comfort in the knowledge that his name will be immortalized, yet immediately it is forgotten and referred to erroneously (as Garry, Harry, Larry, etc.).[37] Indeed, over the course of multiple transmissions, names were often distorted and discrepancies appeared in variant folklore accounts. The Leitrim outlaw *Jack* O'Hara, who was the hero of a popular ballad in the area of Ballinamuck, was mistakenly named in a story *Pat* O'Hara.[38] *Seamus* Dov ([Dubh], black haired) Horkan of Rathscanlon in the area of Swinford, a United Irishman who distinguished himself in several engagements in Mayo, was referred to in some accounts as *Máirtín* Dov Horkan.[39] One of the reasons for such confusion is that in the countryside people were often known by several first names (referring to their parents and grandparents). Folk historians and *seanchas* collectors would sometimes attempt to redress misnomers, though unintentionally they could also introduce errors through careless transcriptions of oral accounts. Hayes edited folklore accounts and corrected references to names. For example, he collected a story about a Mayo rebel who was detained in Ballina on his return from Ballinamuck but escaped prison and fled to France with his wife's help, and corrected the name from *Danny* to *Larry* Gillespie.[40] From a historiographical perspective, such editorial cleansing, which was based on familiarity with other historical sources, is misleading because it erases traces of distortions that are part and parcel of transmission of folk histories.

Depictions of Religious and Class Conflict

Throughout modern history, Irish society has been polarized across partially overlapping religious and class divides, and this condition obviously impinged on the portrayal of heroes and villains in predominantly rural Catholic folk histories. Quite a few descriptions of the Year of the French were couched in overt sectarian terms. For example, an account collected in Irish from a storyteller in west county Sligo (near where the Franco-Irish army had passed) emphasized that "the Catholics helped the French but the Protestants helped the English" ("Thug na Caitlicigh cunamh dos na Francaigh acht thug na Protastúnaigh cabhar dos na Sasanaigh").[41] A pupil collecting folklore for the Schools' Scheme in county Leitrim heard from his mother (b. ca. 1890) that the Catholics who joined the French on the way to Ballinamuck were killed on their return by their Protestant neighbors.[42] Some thirty years later, in 1966, Maureen O'Rourke heard in Ballinamuck that "the croppies, they killed every Protestant."[43] Skirmishes in Cavan in the aftermath of Ballinamuck were interpreted locally through explicitly sectarian narratives.[44] These narratives appear to express long-standing local animosities, which went far beyond the memory of 1798.

At the same time, folk history also acknowledged the involvement of Protestant United Irishmen. In 1956 an eighty-four-year-old man in north Longford informed a folklore collector that "the Protestants around Killoe went out and fought with the Rebels in 1798."[45] Local traditions recalled that one of the main rebel leaders at the battle of Granard was the Protestant landowner Alexander Denniston of Clonbroney in county Longford, who was later sheltered by "his own Presbyterian friends."[46] The inclusion of such heroes in folk historiography undermined simplistic portrayals of the Rebellion in the West as a sectarian jacquerie by crossing religious and class boundaries. Moreover, nuanced narratives challenged stereotypes of sectarian conflict. A story collected in the area of Cloone, county Leitrim, which told of a Protestant yeoman in nearby Drumhallow killing his Catholic rebel neighbor, was presented as an exception to a modus vivendi by which "around this part (Cloone) in '98 some of the Protestants and Catholics, that were friendly with each other, agreed that they would not have a hand, act or part in the Rising."[47]

Traditions told of loyalist Protestants who compassionately concealed fugitive rebels that fled persecution at Ballinamuck.[48] Ballads and stories about the outlawed Leitrim heroes Tom Gilheany and Jack O'Hara state that they were sheltered by local Protestant loyalists—a yeoman named Bob Ferguson and a Nichols of Rossan.[49] A tradition in Killala credited a Protestant named Arthur Wallace with attempting to save Catholic youths during the bloodbath that followed the final defeat of the rebels,[50] and upon collecting local folklore for the Schools' Scheme, a pupil from Killala National School was told that "the people were grateful to him for many years afterwards."[51]

Folklore accounts also referred to Catholics who protected Protestants from reprisals. Such traditions were in circulation already in the generation after the Rebellion. Writing about his travels in Erris around 1840, Caesar Otway described a promontory where a Protestant gentleman and his family took refuge for six weeks during the French occupation of the area and were supported by a "poor Roman Catholic schoolmaster."[52] However, narratives of people providing shelter are not necessarily as straightforward as they initially seem and, under further investigation, can prove to be misleading. They supposedly exemplify aid across the sectarian divide, but in practice were regularly used to make a polemical point by way of demonstrating ingratitude once the tables were reversed. For example, an eighty-year-old man from near Carrick-on-Shannon in county Leitrim told a Schools' Scheme collector that

> a protestant was known to be very hostile to the French in their march through this district. If the French got him they would certainly shoot him. He hid himself for a few days in a Catholic house. No one told where he was. On the English Regiment appearing however the [man] ran out of the house and joined them saying "The morning was yours but the evening is mine."[53]

Didactic stories of this kind subtly reinforced sectarian preconceptions in local remembrance of Ninety-Eight.

Whereas a heated academic debate has raged over the role of sectarianism in the 1798 Rebellion in county Wexford,[54] it is generally agreed that excesses committed by the rebels in Connacht were irregular and that they paled in comparison to the unrestrained brutality shown by yeomen in suppressing insurgency. This consensus among historians has not always been the case. Writing immediately after the events of 1798, Musgrave vehemently argued that it was a Rebellion of "popish banditti" and went to great pains in order to assure readers that his uncompromising vilification of "the errors of popery" in Connacht was not exaggerated. He approached Protestant landowners for information on sectarian discord,[55] scrupulously documented any rumor of "plans to butcher

Protestants" following the French invasion,[56] compiled testimonies from the depositions submitted to a "Commission for the Relief of Suffering Loyalists,"[57] and composed a tirade against Catholic priests that linked the consequences of their seditious activities to the "amount of the losses sustained by the loyalists."[58] Though probably exaggerated, compensation claims show that considerable damage was caused to property of predominantly Protestant loyalists during the three weeks of the insurrection in Connacht, with 722 claims submitted in county Mayo (for a total sum of £93,744, 16s. 9d.)[59] and a further 197 claims in county Sligo (of which 175 claimants received compensation to a total of £3,881, 5s. 3½d.).[60]

During the Rebellion, fears circulated to a limited extent among Protestants in Connacht and the midlands of intended sectarian massacres,[61] and seeking French protection, terrified families of Protestant clergymen took refuge in Bishop Stock's "palace" in Killala.[62] It has been suggested that Bishop Stock's career may have suffered in consequence of the liberal tone of his anonymously published *Narrative*, which met with disapproval in conservative Ascendancy circles.[63] All the same, Stock harbored little sympathy for the "zealous papist" rebels whom, he believed, were driven by "bigotry and rapacity."[64] He blamed Catholic priests for "treasonable enterprise" that resulted in acts of "religious intolerance" against Protestant churches.[65] Moreover, unpublished lists of civilian casualties by Anglicans in the Church of Ireland parishes around Killala suggest that Protestant civilians may have been targeted.[66] On the other hand, Rev. Little maintained that assaults on Protestants were instigated by undisciplined rebels and were not sanctioned by the rebel leadership, "two or three malignant priests excepted," so that overall "the mildness of spirit in the county of Mayo" prevailed.[67]

From standard historical sources, at least eighteen Catholic priests were known to have supported the rebels in Connacht.[68] These are all recalled in folk historiography, which also lists several other names that have eluded official historical records.[69] Three Mayo priests stand out among the folk heroes of the Year of the French. Fr. James Conroy of Addergoole (also spelled Adragoole) was remembered for contributing to the victory at Castlebar by guiding the Franco-Irish army through the back road known as "the Windy Gap" (*Bearna na Gaoithe*).[70] Oral traditions portrayed Fr. Myles Prendergast of Murrisk Abbey—popularly known as "our Fr. Myles" ("ár n-athair Maolra"), an Augustinian friar who joined the rebels at Castlebar and continued guerrilla resistance in the Connemara hills till 1805[71]—as a popular outlaw hero.[72] Arguably, the most acclaimed of the priest heroes in the folk historiographies of *Bliain na bhFrancach* was Fr. Manus Sweeney [An tAthair Mánus Mac Suibhne] of Newport, who was remembered through numerous stories and a widely sung lament.[73] The many legends about Fr. Sweeney typify the heroic image of outlaw priests in Irish historical folklore.[74] They tell of his thaumaturgical powers and the admiration of his followers. Narratives of his execution imitate the passions of Christ, who is the ultimate archetype of a Christian martyr, and use motifs borrowed from traditions of Irish Catholic martyrology, which originated in the Counter-Reformation struggles of the sixteenth and seventeenth centuries and enjoyed a popular revival in the late nineteenth and early twentieth centuries.[75]

The prominence of Catholic priests among the folk heroes of Ninety-Eight in the West appears to strengthen the image of the Rebellion as a religious conflict. But at the same time, folk history also recalled Catholic priests who had advocated loyalty to the Crown. A tale that was recounted in 1937 by an eighty-three-year-old storyteller in Erris described a struggle between Fr. Sweeney and his nemesis, a Fr. *Hugh* Conway [Aodh Ó Conmhacháin]. In this story, recollections of the historical Fr. *Michael* Conway,[76] the parish priest of Ardagh in county Mayo who opposed the Rebellion and collaborated in the apprehension and conviction of Fr. Manus Sweeney, were reworked into a familiar folklore structure of a conflict between a wicked and a righteous priest.[77] In addition to mentioning a loyalist priest, the account subverted standard sectarian roles by noting that Protestant ministers in Newport and Killala helped Fr. Sweeney escape.[78] Loyalist priests were generally considered unpopular, and a local tradition recalled that when Fr. Bernard Grady, the parish priest of Kilfian and Rathgreath in county Mayo, publicly denounced the rebels, he was dragged from the altar by infuriated parishioners.[79] However, these narratives often show ambiguity in depictions of priests who opposed the Rebellion.

Folklore insisted that Fr. Flanagan, the loyalist parish priest of Kilbride (near the French landing place in Kilcummin) who had defiantly confronted the rebel General Matthew Bellew,[80] did not turn his back on his parishioners. An old man in the parish was repeatedly told by his grandfather that in 1798 the priest had courageously protected him from persecution at the hands of a notorious Protestant zealot (William Burke of Lacken).[81] Folk history told of other Catholic priests who alerted their parishioners to the futility of the Rebellion and at the same time expressed sympathy with the popular cause. Such ambivalent behavior is particularly noticeable in traditions from the greater area of Ballinamuck. In the village of Cloone, local traditions told how Fr. Charles Redehan welcomed the Franco-Irish army during their overnight stay but discouraged local recruits from joining them by pointing out that the rebels were outnumbered and would soon be defeated.[82] Even though his curate,

Fr. Anthony Gregory Dunne, openly supported the rebels, a local tradition maintained that he informed Humbert that "he hadn't a chance in a thousand of winning."[83] These attitudes may stem from recollections of a common dilemma in 1798, a time when the hierarchy openly opposed the Rebellion while on a ground level a number of parish priests identified with the plight of their community. Yet, by defending the reputation of untrustworthy priests, they also fulfill an apologetic function.[84] Although there is reason to suspect that a Catholic priest in Cloone provided the British army with information,[85] such allegations of treachery did not explicitly appear in local folklore, which preferred to point an accusing finger at the more recognizable target of a local Protestant farmer (William West).[86]

From the range of complexities in folklore narratives it would appear that overt sectarianism was not a stable overriding theme in the remembrance of the Year of the French, and yet sectarian imagery was readily available to individual storytellers. Interfaith relations changed over time, and sectarian overtones could enter into vernacular historiography through specific performances of *seanchas*, which catered to particular political and social pressures. Such contingent circumstances were influenced by the demographic trend of a sharp decrease in non-Catholics in Connacht and the north midlands over the second half of the nineteenth century, which stands out in the general pattern of continuous depopulation in post-Famine Ireland. Precise census figures broken up by denomination were only compiled from 1871, but a pre-Famine estimate can be calculated by transferring data collected by the Commissioners of Public Instruction in Ireland (organized by diocese and parish) in 1834 onto a secular-administrative map (see tables 1 and 2).[87]

Non-Catholics were mostly Church of Ireland Episcopalians, with Presbyterians constituting the next largest minority group. In both Connacht and county Longford, demographic decline was more pronounced among Presbyterians (approximately by two thirds) than among Episcopalians (approximately by half). The reasons for Protestant attrition are varied and partly unknown, though explanations advanced for county Longford, which identified the significance of local sectarian political aggression, suggest that recollections of the 1798 catastrophe at Ballinamuck provided ideological coherence to militant mass mobilization of Catholics already in the first half of the nineteenth century.[88] Since sectarian motifs could be introduced into specific performances of traditions, it is conceivable that folk history was exploited to fuel local animosities that encouraged migration of Protestant loyalists. The problem is that it is difficult to pinpoint such occurrences, because it is practically impossible to definitively trace all past performances of oral historiography.

TABLE 1. Connacht population by religious affiliation*

Year	Total population	Catholics	Non-Catholics	Percentage of non-Catholics in total population
1834	1,326,295	1,265,085	61,210	4.6%
1871	846,213	803,849	42,364	5.0%
1881	821,657	783,116	38,541	4.7%
1891	724,774	692,369	32,405	4.5%
1901	646,932	619,815	27,117	4.2%
1911	610,984	588,004	22,980	3.9%
1926	552,907	538,277	14,630	2.6%
1936	525,468	513,232	12,236	2.3%

TABLE 2. Longford population by religious affiliation*

Year	Total population	Catholics	Non-Catholics	Percentage of non-Catholics in total population
1834	112,102	101,490	10,612	9.5%
1871	64,501	58,138	6,363	9.9%
1881	61,009	55,501	5,508	9%
1891	52,647	48,071	4,576	8.7%
1901	46,672	42,742	3,930	8.4%
1911	43,820	40,297	3,523	8%
1926	39,847	37,555	2,292	5.8%
1936	37,847	36,005	1,842	4.9%

*Source for 1871–1936: *Census of Population, 1936*. Parliamentary Report, compiled by the Department of Industry and Commerce (statistics branch), Saorstát Éireann (Dublin, 1936).

Sectarian tensions also had a class dimension. This was symbolically addressed in a curious account collected for the Schools' Scheme near Carrick-on-Shannon, which claimed that General Humbert obliged a reluctant local Protestant landlord (Minor St. George) to allocate a site for a Catholic church.[89] Class conflict in the Irish countryside was inextricably linked to land agitation of Catholic peasants and farmers against a predominantly Protestant gentry. A substantial proportion (12 percent) of the numerous documented traditions about landlords in Irish folk history refer to violent reprisals made against them by secret societies or individual outlaws though, as a rule, these accounts did not "project an obvious sectarianism."[90] Many traditions of Ninety-Eight folk history rebuked landlords. Names such as Bingham of Erris,[91] Sir Neal O'Donnel of Newport,[92] Denis Browne, the MP for Mayo (and brother of the Earl of Altamont, who in 1800 became the first Marquess of Sligo),[93] Dukey Crofton of Mohill,[94] Stritten of Drumkeeran,[95] and numerous other landlords who were commanders of yeomen units were depicting as villains on account of their involvement in suppressing the insurrection and prosecuting suspected rebels. As chapter 14 shows, many local activists involved in late-nineteenth- and early-twentieth-century "Land War" campaigns were also organizers of local Ninety-Eight centennial commemorations and were instrumental in reformulating the social memory of the Rebellion. But despite this circumstantial connection, there is scant documented evidence that oral traditions of the Year of the French were explicitly invoked to serve politicized agrarian agitation.

Folklore accounts collected in the 1930s do not show distinct recollections of such manipulation, and it appears that defamatory references in this context were mostly articulated incidentally. For example, in the early twentieth century, traditions of the villainous Hempenstall were purposely conjured up in order to discredit Diana Dopping-Hepenstal, the last scion of a Longford gentry family. In 1929 a member of the Longford Board of Health, named Monaghan, castigated the Dopping-Hepenstals by remarking that "one of them was known as The Walking Gallows" and suggesting that the family kept a hanging noose as a triumphalist heirloom ("I suppose she had the old relic of '98").[96]

A particularly noticeable drop in the local Protestant population occurred during the Irish War of Independence and Civil War (1919–23), though the accusations of a "campaign of loyalist extermination," which were originally put forward to the Irish Grants Committee (1926–30), are debatable.[97] Over this period, at least 210 country homes of Irish landlords were deliberately destroyed in the twenty-six counties that formed the Irish Free State.[98] These "Big Houses" were identified as symbolic bastions of Ascendancy and were popularly perceived as "monuments" of domination. Coincidentally, at that time nationalists imaginatively used references to 1798 as a source of inspiration. An IRA "flying column" in west Mayo was evocatively named "The Men of the West" (1916–21), a title taken from William Rooney's celebrated Ninety-Eight ballad.[99] Several militant nationalist activists in Connacht and the north midlands took particular pride in their ancestors who had been active in the 1798 Rebellion (see chapter 5, 112–13), and family traditions recalling patriotic genealogies may even have spurred volunteers to join the IRA.[100] But it is unclear whether folk history narratives were used to exacerbate sectarian and class animosities directed against loyalists in these turbulent years.

In January 1923 Moore Hall by Lough Carra in Ballyglass (southwest county Mayo), the nonresidential family home of Colonel Maurice Moore (1854–1939)—a founder of the Irish Volunteers and an Irish Free State senator—was burned down during a series of attacks on houses of senators authorized by Liam Lynch (1893–1923), the chief-of-staff of the Anti-Treaty IRA forces.[101] Untypical of landed families, the Moores were Catholic, and Maurice Moore's father, George Henry Moore (1810–70), had been a nationalist member of parliament.[102] Various rumors have speculated on the reasons behind the house's destruction, suggesting that it had been disgracefully looted and also that neighboring farmers wished to possess land on the estate.[103] The outrage was committed despite the fact that this was the ancestral home of John Moore, who in 1798 was proclaimed president of the Republic of Connaught, a heritage claim that should have been respected by devotees of nationalist-republican traditions. Evidently, folk history could also be conveniently forgotten and disregarded in times of conflict.[104]

Recalcitrant Traditions

Certain narratives emerged to the fore of social memory, but although dominant trends can be identified within the regional folk history of 1798, the diversity of folk historiography allowed for the persistence of alternative oral traditions, which did not conform to prevalent orthodoxies. In 1941 a sixty-seven-year-old Irish-speaking farmer in Erris contrasted traditions that he had heard from "the old people of the place" (*seandaoine na h-áite*) with stories that he had heard at home about the local response to the coming of the French:

> Some of the people would say that a party that was in these townlands went to Killala at the time that the French came there. But I heard my grandfather saying that they didn't go as he had always heard it. Of course the people who were here were so backward that they didn't know properly how anything was. Their

attention was mostly not on fighting and struggle, no more than anything else, but trying to provide a bite [of food] for themselves. They had enough to do in getting that food for themselves half the time. But I think that none of them had any great hand in the business of Killala or Castlebar.[105]

Mainstream folk histories of the Year of the French tended to formulate stories of collective patriotism, and these traditions were endorsed and embellished in late-nineteenth-century nationalist historiography and commemoration. Through this process, communities in the West of Ireland reconstructed their social memory to recall universal mobilization and mass rallying to the rebel cause. Taking pride in local participation in the Rebellion, practically every townland remembered those who had gone forth from their midst to join the French. These accounts were authoritatively attributed to "the old people," a traditional formula that represented the dominant voice of local folk history. But an instance when a storyteller heard from his grandfather that local reaction to the French was not as enthusiastic as it was later made out to be is an example of traditions that subvert the prevailing narratives and "tell otherwise."

Such accounts recalled, for example, the apprehensions and uncertainties with which local communities perceived the arrival of the French. A witness of the landing later told his grandson:

> 'Twas over at Pollaclogher in Kilcummin that Humbert landed. He came unaware, and the people didn't show where they stood. A lot of them ran from the shore to the mountain when the French landed, for they were afraid they'd mow them down.

He also remembered that when the French called for recruits "a lot of people hid themselves away for there was terror on them."[106] In an account of the rebel armies' passage through the village of Lahardane in county Mayo, Hayes was told

> They came to free Ireland, but a lot of people at the time were afraid and didn't rightly understand. The people gathered around them in the green but they couldn't understand the French language.[107]

In 1938 an eighty-year-old man from near Bangor in Erris recalled hearing from his mother that

> when the report spread that the French of 1798 were spreading around the townlands, the people were frightened and terrified. They were afraid that not a bite of food would be left to them if the Frenchmen came their way. People were careful of them [the French] for a long time but they never came to Gleann Chuilinn [Glencullin] all the same. During that time the people were on the lookout for the French.

The storyteller added: "The French caused great consternation to people around here. They upset them greatly, they were afraid of the English army and of the French army."[108]

A number of local traditions even mentioned armed resistance against the French. A peculiar version of a popular Erris folk tale about a local hero known as "The Fool of Barr Rúscaí" (*Amadán Bharr Rúscaí*) relocated the setting from an earlier period of Gaelic Ireland to 1798 and recounted how a steward of a local landlord courageously resisted the invaders with improvised wooden arrows.[109] A story from Corrofin in county Galway, which told of a man named Patrick O'Connor setting out to fight the French in Killala, may reflect a corruption of a tradition about a pikeman traveling to join the rebels, but since the account was accepted for the Schools' Scheme, such a scenario was not considered improbable.[110] Indeed, traditions from the same Galway parish recalled that local men were recruited to the yeomanry and sent out to oppose the French in Killala.[111] Some narratives even challenged the popularity of the insurrection by recalling confrontation between rebels and the local population. An eighty-year-old man near the border of counties Clare and Galway recalled from his youth (ca. 1880) that his uncle would tell how his father, a Maughan (*Mochán*) of the townland of Kilchreest (*Cill Chríosta*), was accosted by a party of local pikemen on their way northward to join the rebels in Mayo and their horses were confiscated.[112]

Though most of the documented traditions of Ninety-Eight collected in the 1930s and '40s chime with the contemporary nationalist ideology of early independent Ireland, nonconforming references to incidents of local opposition to the rebel army recall expressions of popular loyalism and hint at the less studied "civil war" aspects of 1798. They served as a subversive reminder that the Rebellion, which pitted Irishmen against each other, was not simply a nationalist struggle of native Irish against colonial British. The example of the insurgent General George Blake of Garracloon whose brother was an officer in the British army has already been noted (chapter 8, "An Insurgent General"). Similarly, the executed rebel George Chambers of Kilboyne House in county Mayo had a brother who was a captain in the British army.[113] Family tradition recalled that both the father and brothers of the insurgent colonel James Joseph McDonnell of Carnacon in county Mayo, who was described by Hayes as "the best known of the United Irish chiefs of the west," served as yeomen officers.[114] There are several examples in the folk history of the Year of the French that recall deep personal dilemmas arising from situations of conflicting loyalties. A noteworthy case relates to Alexander O'Malley, a Catholic magistrate of Edenpark, near Knock in county Mayo, who allegedly approved the execution of his own son, the United Irishman Captain James O'Malley.[115] Stories in south Leitrim mentioned that Captain Crofton of Lurragoe, an officer in the British army, recognized at Ballinamuck the corpse of his rebel friend Terence McGlavin and permitted a rebel officer (Thomas O'Cahan of Cloone) to remove the body for burial.[116] These recalcitrant traditions, which broaden the range of experiences that are covered and even suggest alternative notions of heroism, challenge some of the simplifications and generalizations implicit in mainstream traditions, and thus bolster the complexity of folk history. However, the discussion so far has neglected the inclusion of women in traditional narratives, which is another democratic feature of folk history.

10

Who Were the Women of the West?

My grandmother, who told me all I know of the battle, was
there too. She was then a young woman and carried a child
two years old on her back. She went over to Drumshanbo
till the troubles were over.

Patrick Gill of Edenmore
in *The Last Invasion of Ireland*

LORD CARLETON (1739–1826) recalled that "at Ballinamuck, one of the
most beautiful Irish girls ever seen, who had ventured probably into fire
to repost a brother or lover, was found shot through the heart."[1] Despite the
availability of such fitting candidates, folk histories in Connacht and the north
midlands did not laud legendary women heroines similar to the familiar
Ninety-Eight Joans of Arc in Leinster and Ulster, whose memory was romantically valorized, politicized, and effectively reconstructed in nationalist balladry and popular print.[2] The folklore of women's involvement in the Rebellion in the West is fragmentary, and though it provides a rich assortment of
narratives, its study requires concerted effort. Moreover, if women had a
propensity to cultivate remembrance of women's experiences, the compilation
of their testimonies was conditioned by the predominance of men in the institutionalized collecting of Irish folklore.

The gender composition of the Irish Folklore Commission was far from ideal
for collecting women's folklore. Its leading staff members were all men; even
though the acclaimed folklorist Máire MacNeill (1904–87) played a significant
role, she was officially designated an administrative manager so that her academic
career was launched only after she married the Irish-American scholar Jack
Sweeney and emigrated to Boston.[3] The scholarly ambitions of her replacement,

Bríd Mahon, were curtailed by the Commission's requirement that clerical staff focus on their office duties in order to facilitate the work of the collectors.[4] Other female staff of the Commission included several clerical assistants and typists, whose career options were limited by the convention that women retire on marriage. There were several part-time and specially assigned female collectors, but women were not appointed as full-time collectors. Consequently, more than 85 percent of the sources from the Main Manuscript Collection of the IFC examined in this study were written down by male collectors.[5] The implications of this bias for collecting oral traditions from women cannot be underestimated. The psychologist Michael Gorkin, who collected women's oral narratives alongside female researchers, asserted that "a man is at a distinct disadvantage in interviewing women. Even when social conventions allow him access to them, women almost invariably talk less freely, and differently, to him than they do with female interviewers."[6]

The local coordinators of folklore collecting for the Schools' Scheme were individual schoolteachers who opted to participate in the project. At the time, 68 percent of teachers in the national schools were women,[7] but most of the teachers who supervised the documentation of Ninety-Eight traditions from the West were male. This tendency mainly reflects the personal interests of individual teachers who were devoted to folk history. For example, a large volume of local traditions was collected about the battle of Ballinamuck thanks to the enthusiasm and dedication of Peter Duignan of Gaigue N.S. and James McKenna of Kiltycreevagh N.S. The fifteen-page booklet issued in preparation for this project by *An Roinn Oideachais* [the Department of Education] and signed by the Permanent Secretary for Education Seosamh Ó Néill (1885–1953), a philologist and an accredited novelist with a Connacht background (born in Tuam and raised on the Aran Islands), professed the expectation that "especially the boys, will take an enthusiastic interest."[8] In practice, the 1937–38 Schools' Scheme proved this assumption to be wrong. While 52.3 percent of registered fifth- and sixth-standard (grade) pupils in Connacht and 54.8 percent in Longford were female, 58 percent of the relevant folklore accounts on Ninety-Eight were collected by girls.[9] Moreover, it has been subsequently acknowledged that contributions submitted by girls were often of higher quality.[10]

Although the collectors purportedly approached elderly people of both sexes, significantly more men than women were interviewed. More than 80 percent of the sources on the Year of the French in the Main Manuscript Collection and a similar ratio in the Schools' Manuscript Collection were collected from male informants. Similarly, Hayes, who harbored an austere attitude to women,[11] cited only three women among the seventeen informants identified in his chapter on "Traditions of the Insurrection."[12] It has been pointed out that women in the Irish countryside "who ran after stories and gossip and hawked them had a bad reputation, not only as silly rumourmongers but also as women who did not fulfil their real duties."[13] Acknowledging that various genres of *seanchas* were "as a rule, associated with women; at any rate they excelled the men in these branches of tradition," Delargy commented on their unassuming role in traditional evening social gatherings (*céilithe*):

> While women do not take part in the story-telling, not a word of the tale escapes them, and if their relatives or close friends make any slip or hesitate in their recital, it is no uncommon experience of mine to hear the listening woman interrupt and correct the speaker.[14]

Whereas the participation of women in such male-dominated public forums was reserved, they generally played a more dominant role in domestic and private recitals of *seanchas* within family circles.[15] The gender dynamics embedded in social customs of hospitality limited the access of male folklore collectors to the everyday situations in which women could exchange stories in an intimate environment. Even when the female researcher Maureen O'Rourke deliberately interviewed couples in the area of Ballinamuck in 1964, the wives were typically soft-spoken and the discussions were dominated by their husbands' contributions.[16]

An introduction to a collection of essays on women and folklore notes that "folklorists have long paid lip service to the importance of women's expressive behavior, though usually that behavior was recognized and accorded legitimacy only when it occurred in predetermined genres that fit the prevailing image of women."[17] Recognized Irish women storytellers were desexualized and, usually, elderly widows. The iconic Irish woman storyteller was Peig Sayers of Dunquin, county Kerry (1873–1958), who told hundreds of tales to folklore collectors but was not known for telling historical traditions.[18] In contrast, the examples of Bridget Corduff of Erris and Mrs. O'Toole of Wicklow (see chapter 6) show that some women storytellers did have an interest in folk history and recited traditions of Ninety-Eight. Regrettably, historical traditions recounted by women were often overlooked in favor of the more collective and public forms of history-telling, which gained public recognition as "local tradition."

At the same time, the pivotal role of women in the chain of transmission of folklore is generally unacknowledged. Observing that oral traditions often pass from grandparents directly to grandchildren, the historian Marc Bloch

maintained that this habit of skipping a generation "is the source of that tradi-
tionalism inherent in so many peasant societies."[19] Examination of documented
folklore accounts reveals that, in many cases, male storytellers cited a female
relative, usually a grandmother, as the original source of information. Indeed,
grandmothers were valued storytellers who bequeathed to their grandchildren
(and sometimes great-grandchildren) lively descriptions of their remembered
experiences in 1798. For example, at the age of ninety-five Patrick Gill of
Edenmore could still vividly recall stories told by his grandmother—a Cassidy
of Fardromin in county Longford—about her participation in the Battle of
Ballinamuck. She had told him that she brought food to the starving French
soldiers, while carrying a two-year-old baby on her back, then participated in
the battle and went into hiding "till the troubles were over."[20]

Seventy-six-year-old Patrick O'Reilly, who was born and raised in Enaghan
(ten kilometers northeast of Ballinamuck), county Longford, repeated to a
folklore collector his great-grandmother's compelling account of how she had
personally witnessed the atrocities and slaughter in Ballinamuck after the
rebels' defeat, where "the corpses were lyin' like sh'aves of oats in a harvest
field." Her story told how she pleaded for her husband's life and appeased a
party of plundering soldiers by offering money and then cooking for them her
only two hens.[21] These narratives of genuine feminine courage are distinct
from the romantic ways women were presented in nineteenth-century nationalist literature. They demonstrate that male descendents could provide male
folklore collectors with second-hand accounts of how women remembered and
chose to narrate their personal experiences in 1798, thus rescuing from oblivion
sources for women's history which otherwise would have been left unrecorded.

References to women are scattered throughout the folklore of the Year of
the French. Mayo traditions recalled names of women who joined the rebel
ranks as combatants. According to local tradition, Bessy Sweeney of Fun-
chona, who was reputed to be an expert shot, was among the recruits who
joined General Blake at Ballinrobe.[22] Another tradition listed three young
Swinford women—Larkin, Ryan, and Brennan—in a party of United Irishmen who prevented reinforcements from reaching Castlebar on the eve of the
decisive battle.[23] More generally, Ballinamuck traditions noted the "undaunted"
and "heroic" women who "came out to help their brothers, husbands, fathers
and sons."[24]

Female supporters of the Rebellion also appeared in folk history in sub-
sidiary capacities. There are many accounts of women feeding the starving
rebel forces as they passed through their locality.[25] Several accounts also refer
to camp followers. A storyteller in county Leitrim noted that "there was a

power of girls and women at the battle. Some of them went to carry food, and others went out of anxiety for their friends that were in the battle." Among them was an O'Rourke of Garadice (near Ballinamore) in county Leitrim who accompanied her father and brother to Ballinamuck, and following the death of the former, "they say the girl carried her father home in a creel and buried him."[26] Similarly, an eighty-year-old woman from a townland between Cloone and Ballinamuck told Hayes of two girls from Cloone who followed their father to Ballinamuck, where he died and "they wheeled him home along this road in a turf barrow."[27] It was remembered that women identified the rebel dead. For example, members of the Collum family of Barragh (five kilometers southwest of Ballinamuck) repeated the tales of their grandmother (Jane Anne McLoughlin of Mill House, Crealaughta), who had lost several of her brothers at Ballinamuck and later recounted how, on the evening after the battle, women recognized the dead by the socks on their feet.[28] It was also recalled that when men went into hiding to avoid persecution, women were left the responsibility of burying dead rebels. For instance, traditions from the area of Granard told of a local woman burying a man named O'Reilly, "the men being out on the hill sides."[29]

Though they probably were reworked in memory over time, the accounts of women filling such auxiliary roles bear the marks of reminiscences that stem back to authentic female experiences in 1798 and can partly be corroborated by passing references in contemporary sources. The French General Sarrazin noted: "wherever we halted we were immediately surrounded by the local inhabitants who brought us milk, meat, potatoes etc. The women showed towards us the care which they have for children, brothers and friends."[30] Commenting on the corpses that littered the streets of Killala after it was retaken from the rebels, the wife of the Anglican dean described "the unfortunate female relatives trying to inter them in great holes dug for the purpose."[31] Even when the description of such experiences was colored with fanciful folktale motifs, the core information was presented realistically. A schoolteacher from the area of Cloone recalled hearing in his youth (sometime in the early twentieth century) a great-aunt tell of a woman named Murray from Catten (near Ballinamuck), who fed two starving rebels and in return they disclosed to her the secret whereabouts of "the French gold." Stories of heroes who help a stranger in need and are rewarded with a treasure follow a familiar folklore motif.[32] Nonetheless, this narrative was considered a plausible explanation for the improvement in the family's fortunes, so that "people began to whisper that the money didn't come right to them, and in a short time they sold their place and went to Canada and were never heard of again."[33]

Family traditions remembered the plight of women and children who had to flee their homes and seek refuge for fear of soldier and yeomen repression. For example, children in the townland of Kiltycreevagh (near Ballinamuck) were told about the distressing experiences of their great-grandmothers in 1798. Collecting folklore for the Schools' Scheme, one pupil heard that his fair-haired great-grandmother took to the bogs and hid in a local "fairy fort," where she was warned to "keep down or they will see your white head."[34] This story remained in the family and was repeated to a folklore collector thirty years later (1965).[35] In 1956 a seventy-five-year-old man recounted how his great-grandmother, a Carty of Geelsha (ten kilometers southeast of Ballinamuck), had escaped to the bogs when she was merely seven years old.[36]

By including traditions about women, folk history widened the circle of recognized victims affected by the Rebellion. A story noted that the wife of a proscribed rebel—Rogers of Derrycassan (near Granard)—was in confinement when her husband took refuge in the house and that "she took fright and died in a few days."[37] It was recalled locally that the wife of an Erris rebel, Dáithí Sweeney of Ballycroy, was overwhelmed with grief when her brother-in-law was arrested, and drowned herself.[38] Overall, narratives that recalled the experiences of civilian women during the Rebellion served to broaden concepts of heroism in folk history beyond the narrow gauge of raising arms in combat, so as to include more mundane acts of courage. For example, a Mrs. O'Neill from south Leitrim was remembered as a "local heroine" for sheltering a fugitive rebel.[39] Other stories in the area recalled how a Mrs. Duignan of Lear (seven kilometers west of Ballinamuck) risked the five-kilometer walk back to her parents' home in Mohill at a time when yeomen were terrorizing the local population.[40]

Folklore accounts about women are of particular historical value since contemporary sources offer scant information on the involvement of women in 1798. Reminiscing about his encounters with women, French General Sarrazin wrote:

> Irishwomen are tall, handsome and well proportioned, and, like all women everywhere, are tender hearted and generous. But they have a passionate regard for those immortal principles which overcome prejudice of all sorts and which give to humanity all its rights. Worthy rivals of Roman women, they desire an Irish Republic, and I do not doubt that their wishes will soon be realized.[41]

Explaining why he refrained from detailing the experiences of his wife and sister-in-law during the Franco-Irish occupation of Killala and ultimately censored all references to women in his *Narrative*, Bishop Stock noted:

Female heroism shrinks away from the need of human praise; because it most commonly inherits the temper of its natural parent, piety; that chaste though ardent piety, which would gladly hide itself from the notice of every being except the Supreme.[42]

United Irish propaganda portrayed women as generic symbols of Ireland or virtuous maidens who were grieved by the brutality of the King's soldiers.[43] Radical political literature in the aftermath of 1798 employed gender typecasting in its reflections on the Rebellion. This attitude is illustrated in a poem by the United Irishman William Drennan (1754–1820):

> To men, who gave for us their blood;
> Ah! what can woman give but tears![44]

Nineteenth- and early-twentieth-century historical writing continued to portray women through sentimental tropes that, as Anna Kinsella pointed out, "reinforced the relegating of women to 'Kinder, Kuchen und Kirche' roles."[45] These moralistic images of women were reinforced in contemporary historical fiction, which informally supplemented competing historiographical interpretations of 1798.[46] With these limitations in mind, it has been argued that insight on the roles of women in the Rebellion should rely on "folk memory."[47] However, oral accounts do not always allow for simple straightforward readings. Family traditions were reconstructed in compliance with familiar folklore types, and women in folk history could be assigned stereotypical roles that were often influenced by the literary imagery of romantic nationalism.

Certain oral accounts were clearly fitted to a narrative structure, such as a widely popular Ninety-Eight legend about a lone woman who killed a soldier or yeoman. Typically, it told of a trooper who approached a woman in her house and asked for refreshments; he was then treated to a noggin of milk or buttermilk, but while he partook of the drink, she killed him by striking a blow at his head with a kitchen utensil and then hid the corpse. Oral traditions collected in the 1930s in Wexford, which associated this story with the bravery of Anne Flood,[48] may have been influenced by Fr. Patrick Kavanagh's seminal *Popular History of the Insurrection of 1798*, which included an appendix with the story of "How a Wexford woman slew a Hessian Captain."[49] Numerous versions of this story were also collected in the area of Ballinamuck.[50] Maureen Murphy linked this legend to the Old Testament story of Jael and Sisra[51] and the apocryphal book of Judith,[52] an association already made by Fr. Kavanagh, who alluded to "the heroic Judith of Scriptural renown" and praised the Ninety-Eight heroine as "our Wexford Judith."

In the regional folk history of the West this was a migratory legend, which was not confined to the north midlands, and additional versions were collected in north Mayo.[53] In each case the name of the female protagonist and the particulars of the incident change, so that a south Leitrim version, for example, told of the red-haired wife of a man named Blake from Currycamp near Gortletteragh (ten kilometers west of Ballinamuck), who killed a Scotch soldier known as "the Highlander."[54] This narrative structure provided folk history with a recognizable framework for local recollections of women's resistance in situations when households were violated by the intrusion of undisciplined soldiers. Murphy argued that the narrative could have been used didactically as an inspiring tale that presented young women with role models for showing individual courage in the service of the national struggle, or in taking the more personal choice of leaving home and emigrating.[55] Its function as a storytelling device could also be used more generally, however, since the protagonist in several variations collected near Ballinamuck is a man.[56] Two Mayo variations collected by the Schools' Scheme demonstrate further the flexibility of this motif by turning the tale on its head and, instead of an act of aggression, refer to women who offered hospitality to French soldiers in need.[57]

Explicit typecasting of women was part and parcel of certain themes in Ninety-Eight folk history. In the many outlaw stories of the Year of the French, women generally appeared as faithful sympathizers who assist the hero in his escape,[58] or as treacherous informers who betray him to the authorities. In these accounts, women fill stereotypical roles as side characters in a familiar scenario. Such narratives thrive on drama, and consequently women were not identified as historical figures and usually remained unnamed, although certain references stand out. For example, an untypical tradition mentioned that the Erris outlaw Dáithí na Miodóige ("of the dagger") Sweeney was accompanied by his sister.[59] Relatives generally had fixed roles in escape narratives, which often told of wives or female associates paying a visit to an imprisoned rebel and then helping him escape in women's garb. This scenario is a recognized international folktale motif,[60] which proved to be a useful way to recall stories of escapes that, according to the historical record, were generally carried out by other means.[61] In some cases the event was completely fictional, as in an account of the escape of Patrick Farrell of Ballinree,[62] who in fact died on the battlefield of Granard, a fate that is acknowledged in several traditions.[63] Readaptations or inventions of such escape narratives express a general belief that women were treated more leniently by the authorities, a perception that is grounded in a historical reality, as "few (if any) women were tried by court-martial."[64] The images of women in these accounts reflect nineteenth-century representations of passive feminine patriotism and occasionally can be traced to a romantic literary source. For example, the story of how Larry Gillespie's wife helped her husband escape from Ballina prison was told orally to Hayes but had appeared in popular print in 1858.[65]

A patent example of a romantic nationalist female caricature is the reworking of the enduring image of the "patriot mother," who unflinchingly faces tyrannical persecution at the hands of foreign soldiers and sacrifices her child in the service of the nation. In 1936 Hayes heard an account in Drumshanbo, county Leitrim, that had originally been recounted "many years ago from an old woman, Peggy Waugh, who was a ten-year old girl in 1798," which told of how "Redcoats" responded to a local ambush:

> The main body of them soon came on and, when they saw their dead comrades, they were furious and caught hold of a little boy and tried to make him tell who did the deed. His mother spoke to him in Irish and told him on his life not to tell anything. They took him into Drumsna and the mother followed. They got a barrel there and spiked it with nails, and when he again refused they put him into it and rolled it down the hill of Drumsna. But he kept his secret.[66]

This horrific tale of torture is a version of an age-old universal motif that is not recognized in the standard index of folklore motifs, which dismissively relegated narratives of patriotism to a general category.[67] It originally appeared in the ancient Jewish tale of a mother whose seven sons were executed in the Hellenic-Maccabean period, an era that provided founding myths for Judeo-Christian martyrdom.[68] Variations on this motif can be found in numerous popular legends in Irish folk history, such as references to the undaunted wife of the Limerick outlaw "Staker" Wallace [Wallis].[69] Popular print was instrumental in styling 1798 narratives of the "patriot mother," and an early literary example appeared in the decade following the Rebellion.[70] This image was promulgated in nineteenth-century balladry.[71] An anonymous "Ballad of '98" titled "The Patriot Mother," which Madden related to "personal reminiscences of the tortures inflicted upon the Irish people of those days,"[72] appeared in Charles Gaven Duffy's (1816–1903) immensely popular song anthology *The Ballad Poetry of Ireland*, which was originally published in 1845 and by 1866 was in its fortieth edition.[73] The ballad, later featured in Ninety-Eight centennial songbooks,[74] was in fact a mid-nineteenth-century composition by the romantic nationalist poetess Mary Eva Kelly (1825–1910) of Headford, county Galway, who wrote under the pseudonym "Eva of *The Nation*" (and was otherwise known by her married name, Mrs. Kevin Izod O'Doherty).[75] Such influences filtered into local oral traditions. A Mayo Ninety-Eight ballad about a patriotic mother was preserved by an Irish emigrant family in Canada and can be traced back to Bridget Lillian Clifford (b. 1865).[76]

Quixotic descriptions of maternal suffering could be utilized to heighten dramatic effect. In a version of a story told around Ballinamuck, a soldier on horseback hunts down a woman fleeing the battlefield with a child on her back and savagely cuts off the infant's head. The woman remained anonymous and was intentionally portrayed as a helpless grieving mother in order to accentuate the chivalry of the rebel men who avenge the horrific killing.[77] The legend focused on the memory of the Ballinamuck hero Art McQuaide, and the role of the woman "heroine" is superfluous, as is revealed in another version that omitted her altogether by telling how McQuaide "took his first born young son tied him up with a sheet on his back" and, despite this handicap, skillfully defended the child and defeated the assailant.[78]

In contrast, to the few firsthand accounts left by loyalist women who documented their experiences during the French invasion, namely the letters of Mrs. Brigit Thompson of Castlebar (the wife of Dean Thomas Thompson) and the writings of women in the Edgeworth family in Longford,[79] Protestant women were relentlessly subject to stereotyping in predominantly Catholic folk histories. Though an exceptional local tradition in Ballygilcash (just north of Dromore West), county Sligo, remembered that the Protestant Mrs. Meddleton Walker sheltered Catholic children,[80] loyalist women were generally not identified by name and appeared as representatives of supposed typical sectarian responses to the Rebellion. In the Leitrim town of Mohill, an old man repeated to Hayes stories that he had heard from his grandfather, Owen Clyne of Dromard (twelve kilometers west of Ballinamuck), who had joined the rebels in 1798:

> When the French come into Cloone, there were two Protestant women come running for safety to my grandfather's house at Dromard. They stayed in it for two days and nights, and he gave them food and everything the best he could. And then the English marched into Dromard, eighteen thousand of them. The women come out and joined them. "Come, Owen," they said to my grandfather, "are you coming to Mohill?" "Oh, no," says my grandfather, "I have no business there." "Oh, come," says they, "come and dance on the croppies' graves." And wasn't that a nice thing for ladies to say and they after getting food and shelter for two days?[81]

As the irony in this rhetorical question indicates, the ungratefulness of women in such stories served to illustrate the insensitivity of the Protestant community in general, as it was perceived and remembered in local traditions cultivated by Catholic families associated with the Rebellion.

Loyalist women were incriminated in narratives that recalled acts of violent punishment. A tradition from Granard about the public flogging of a Bob

Fitzsimmons, who was arrested and interrogated in order to extract information on his rebel brother, noted that "it was a woman who flogged him."[82] Female relatives of Protestant loyalists were crudely vilified. Traditions from the area of Carrigallen (thirteen kilometers north of Ballinamuck) in county Leitrim can serve to illustrate this point. Recollections of yeomen terror recounted that "a wife of one of the officers seems to have been more like a demon than a woman" and took delight in the torture of victims.[83] An apocryphal etymological explanation for the Ninety-Eight rebel nickname "Croppy" claimed that the daughter of a Protestant landlord in Carrigallen partook in the execution of rebels by unashamedly cutting off their hair.[84] These traditions appear to reflect entrenched resentment of Protestant women of property. They may have originated in recollections of what has been described as a "zeal for the prosecution of former rebels which in a number of instances quickly developed into a lust for persecution," an attitude that was characteristic of the testimonies of female approvers, who "were often the preferred instrument of loyalist retribution" in the courts-martial that followed the suppression of the Rebellion.[85]

At least some of the folklore about women was clearly the product of popular imagination, and an intriguing example of implicit fantasy can be found in recurring traditions that tell of female French soldiers. An elderly Irish speaker from Kilcummin claimed to have witnessed a French woman in uniform paying the troops upon landing.[86] In 1936 an old man in Kilcummin informed Hayes that his grandfather had told him that

> There was a woman [who] came with the French. After they landed they were all paying attention to her and went down to the rocks and brought up dilisk [seaweed] and limpets to her . . . when they were going up to the encampment the Frenchwoman marched up with the soldiers and was keeping step with them.[87]

In 1938 a local schoolteacher was told by her seventy-eight-year-old grandmother that "it was believed locally that with the French were ladies riding on horseback and dressed in French uniforms. We are told that the ladies spoke the Irish language fluently."[88] Sligo folklore mentioned a "handsome French woman who had come with the expedition from France and had fought in the various engagements up to this with much bravery. From her belt hung pistols, while in her hand she carried a sword."[89] The revolutionary activist Countess Constance Markievicz (1866–1927) recalled hearing as a young girl in Lissadell in northwest county Sligo "a tale of a mysterious woman who rode into battle with the French army" told by "Mickey Oge" [Óg], who was recognized as "the oldest man in the district." The storyteller, whose father had witnessed the 1798 engagement in Collooney, described the woman as "dressed in a green habit, with the tricolour and red plume in her hat" and claimed that "she rode in the front ranks of the French troops."[90] A local history published in 1878, written by the Collooney-born Terence O'Rorke, described the female soldier as

> a French amazon, armed cap-a-pie, and seated on a magnificent and superbly caparisoned charger. Two richly-mounted pistols shone in the housing of her saddle; in her hand she carried a glittering sword, which she brandished from time to time; and from under her helmet streamed over her shoulders, down to the horse's back, a profusion of jet black hair, that excited the wonder of the spectators, and gave some a superstitious idea of her prowess.[91]

Twenty years later, this description was reproduced verbatim in the short story "A Fair Insurgent" by J. J. Moran, who embellished the folklore account and transformed the woman into a tragic and crazed fictional character named Leonie Guiscard.[92]

The commander of the squadron that brought the French expeditionary force to Ireland noted in his journal that six or eight servants boarded the frigates and two of them were females in disguise.[93] These unregistered female camp followers may have accompanied the French troops after they disembarked but would not have fulfilled the combatant roles assigned to them in folklore. The only French officer to touch on a related issue was Moreau de Jonnès, whose memoirs were written some forty years after the events and have been criticized for incorporating elements of "haute fantaisie."[94] He mentioned a young woman named Henrietta de la Tour who participated in the campaign disguised as a man, but de Jonnès insisted that her female identity was unknown to anybody and that he himself was later "completely dumbfounded" by "this strange metamorphosis."[95] Folklore accounts of exotic French female soldiers appear to reflect the fascination entailed in the local encounter with foreign troops. They may originate in stereotypes of female licentiousness associated with French women and, in particular, representations of iconic female radicals in late-eighteenth-century conservative propaganda emanating from England and Dublin.[96] Folk history emboldened such images into romantic stories of "French amazons."

Altogether, the numerous references to women in folk history stand out in comparison to the prolonged neglect of women in professional historiography. General interest in the topic of women in 1798 was aroused around the centenary commemorations, when the writers Alice Milligan (1866–1953) and Ethna Carbery [pen name of Anna MacManus, née Johnson (1866–1902)], both former editors of the *Northern Patriot* (1895), founded the short-lived monthly journal the *Shan Van Vocht* (1896–99), which intentionally called attention to the involvement of women in the Rebellion.[97] The first attempt to produce a study on the subject, a long essay titled "The Women of '98" by Countess Markievicz, was serialized in 1915 in a radical feminist newspaper,[98] but the author's intention to develop this pioneering work into a monograph did not come to fruition.[99] Shortly thereafter, at the time of the Irish War of Independence, *Women of 'Ninety Eight* by Helena Concannon (1878–1952) was published. It featured nationalist, virtually hagiographical accounts of women related to United Irishmen (mothers, sisters, wives, and sweethearts), alongside "some obscure heroines."[100] Scholarly interest then subsided for the next eighty years, until bicentennial scholarship introduced fresh perspectives to the field.[101]

Just as women's history of 1798 promises to broaden the scope of scholarly historiography "from concentration on a relatively small number of male leaders to include the scale of the contribution at every level by the men and the women of all classes who are not seen as 'leaders,'"[102] oral traditions of women in the Year of the French prove to be an invaluable resource in qualifying the democratic nature of folk history. Although gender conceptions in folk history were clearly not egalitarian, references to women's experiences in the Rebellion often served to fill in gaps in official historical narratives that focused on the actions of men. By presenting recollections of the actual involvement of women in the Rebellion, of the archetypal roles women were assigned in traditional narratives, and of the imaginary roles that women were associated with, folklore accounts can offer more gender-balanced insight into the ways communities remembered their pasts.

The examination of folklore accounts in part 3, "Democratic History," demonstrates the plurality of folk histories. The complexity is further complicated by the intrinsic fluidity of social memory, which is not an atemporal reconstruction of the past passed on unchanged from one generation to the next. Traditions could be transmitted over time with remarkable accuracy, yet dialectical pressures of continuity and change were exerted on the remembrance and performance of each history-telling. Even seemingly stable narratives that were repeatedly recounted, without showing noticeable signs of change, appeared in different variations, and the contrasting details between these competing versions reflect the contingent malleability of traditions. Consequently, folk history is not merely the sum of residues of surviving historical information but is rather an organic entity regenerated through discursive acts of remembrance. It follows that folk *history* has a *historiography* that developed over time. The seemingly oxymoronic term *oral* historiography (given the etymology of the term historiography, which denotes the *writing* of history) is apposite since oral histories in modern Ireland were invariably permeated with literary influences. Moreover, the collecting and documentation of folklore inevitably involved the representation of oral accounts as written texts. Therefore, *oral historiography* intertwined expressions of orality and literacy.[103]

In sum, the ways in which communities recalled their pasts reveal a composite bricolage of vernacular historiographies.[104] Each instance of history-telling has an oral historiography of its own, which ideally follows the social and cultural processes through which it was constructed, repeatedly recalled, and transformed over time. The possibility of reconstructing these elusive historiographies is limited, as folklore was not systematically collected on a continuous periodic basis. In light of the dearth of references to "common people" in general, and to women in particular, the information provided in standard historical sources often proves to be inadequate for fully recontextualizing folk history accounts. Moreover, historical traditions were subject to local, regional, national, and even international influences and so did not develop in isolation. The mechanics of remembrance in the village can be further elucidated by exploring the contexts in which social memory was generated and reworked in order to identify the spheres and mediums of remembrance through which folk history was reformulated.

Part 4

Commemorating History

11

Spheres and Mediums of Remembrance

All—all are gone—but still lives on
The fame of those who died;
All true men, like you men,
Remember them with pride.

John Kells Ingram
"The Memory of the Dead"

THE RECITAL OF FOLK HISTORY is a rudimentary form of commemoration. As long as the past is talked about, it is in effect commemorated, a truism lucidly encapsulated in a Swahili tradition by which the dead continue to "live" in the community and only perish once the last descendant who recalls them has passed away.[1] Through mourning and memory, death—the most individual of human experiences—becomes a social event. In an essay called "Collective Representation of Death," the Durkheimian anthropologist Robert Hertz distinguished between a "first burial," which includes mortuary rituals of waking and mourning, and a "second burial," in which the deceased is interred and symbolically sent on to a communal afterlife.[2] An appreciation of social memory suggests that even then, a community's relationship with its dead is not terminated by funerary rites but persists through remembrance until it is unconsciously severed in a muted "third burial" of oblivion.

Traditional cults of ancestors are inherently selective, and as Halbwachs noted, "each family has at its command a store of a limited number of names among which it must choose the names of its members."[3] Longevity of remembrance is a privilege accorded to certain individuals, who are chosen as subjects of folklore. In this sense, oral traditions are essentially abstract monuments, as phrased in verse by Madden:

Save those which pass from sire to son
Traditions that are bred
In the heart's core and make their own
Memorial of the dead.[4]

Though history-telling was a prevalent medium of remembrance, vernacular patterns of commemoration extended beyond recitals of oral narratives. They encompassed various ritual performances, which Paul Connerton (*pace* Henri Bergson) labeled "bodily social memory,"[5] adding that "if there is such a thing as social memory, we are likely to find it in commemorative ceremonies."[6]

Adhering to the presumption that the modern state is a self-appointed "curator of the national memory,"[7] commemorative ceremonies have been studied as coded representations of collective memory, whereby changes in public rituals are considered to be indices of manipulation from above.[8] The production of ceremonies and the erection of monuments, however, are part of a much larger scope of social remembrance. As Jay Winter masterfully demonstrated in the case of European remembrance of World War I, authorized "sites of memory" coexist with more spontaneous "sites of mourning."[9] Troublesome private memories, such as those of embittered war veterans, can contradict official polices that aspire to orchestrate public memory for the sake of uniformity and stability.[10] Official commemorative programs are therefore subject to reception and modification by individuals who need to recognize their own past in the group's shared memory (or reorganize their memories accordingly). Though scholarship has shown a preference for well-documented national commemorations, studies of remembrance also need to take into account the many different spheres of social interaction in which the past was reenacted as well as the various cultural mediums, which allowed such performances to take place. Commemoration may appear initially in private spheres, where personal acts of remembrance are practiced within family circles. It can also take place in the intimate public spheres of local communities. On a larger scale, acts of commemoration can be performed within greater sociopolitical frameworks, which sanction official ceremonies and commission monuments. These spheres are interdependent so that commemorative practices are effectively dialogic cultural processes, which create and modify social memory through negotiations that take place both within each sphere and between various spheres of remembrance.

The vernacular traditions of "folk commemoration" recalled in folk history were generally more spontaneous and less regulated, offering an alternative to official commemoration. Historically, they have also been more democratic, insofar as official commemoration of individuals is a relatively recent custom.

In nineteenth-century Europe, war memorials did not attempt to name the dead of a specific campaign and confined their reference to an elite selection of heroic individuals or to collective-anonymous representations.[11] In contrast, though influenced by official commemoration, traditions of folk commemoration allowed local communities to remember and honor *their* dead, often in personalized form.

This can be demonstrated through the case of laments for the dead. Traditions of lamentation, primarily associated with women, were observed by numerous travelers and visitors to Ireland and date back to the Middle Ages and Early Modern period, but they were only committed to writing in the nineteenth century.[12] Crofton Croker noted the value of traditional keening (*caoineadh*) as a representation of folk history.[13] Enthralled by the passion of mourning expressed in folk poetry, W.B. Yeats and Lady Gregory memorably adapted selections from the traditional lament "Donncha Bán" (Fair-haired Denis), which is attributed to the sister of the deceased and was preserved in Erris oral tradition, into their play on the French landing in Mayo, *Cathleen Ní Houlihan* (1902). Despite common association with 1798, the lament relates to a man wrongly hanged for horse theft.[14] Laments in Irish for beloved rebels who died in 1798 were remembered in folklore and served as a vernacular commemorative medium. Such poetic oral traditions of the Year of the French eloquently recalled the anguish that deaths wreaked on the families and friends of the deceased. The philosopher Paul Ricoeur compared Freud's celebrated analysis of the healing function of memory, or "memory as work" (*Erinnerungsarbeit*) as discussed in the essay "Remembering, Repetition and Working Through" (1914), with his famous analysis of "Mourning and Melancholia" (1917) and concluded that "it is quite possible that the work of memory is a kind of mourning and also that mourning is a painful exercise in memory." He pointed out that in Freudian terms both memory and mourning are forms of reconciliation that facilitate a therapeutic process of "working through" (*Durcharbeiten*), which is in essence a struggle for "the acceptability of memories."[15] Indeed, innovative research on folklore of the Finnish Civil War (1918) has shown that, when public weeping and mourning was proscribed for the vanquished of a violent conflict, folklore of lament could express a social memory that fulfilled a commemorative-psychotherapeutical function.[16]

A beautifully styled lament for the schoolteacher Affy ("Austin") Gibbons [Aifí Mac Giobúin] was collected in several versions along the western coast of north Galway and south Mayo.[17] Affy participated in the Rebellion and then took refuge on the island of Inishbofin, off the shores of Connemara, where he was later betrayed and murdered. He came from a prominent Mayo family, which was heavily involved in the 1798 Rebellion and many of its members suffered the consequences. John Gibbons, the head of the clan, was sentenced to deportation, escaped to France, and became an officer in the Irish Legion; his elder son Edmund was also sentenced to deportation to Australia, escaped to France, and became an officer; his younger son "Johnny the Outlaw" was eventually apprehended and executed; an uncle named Thomas was deported, escaped, and returned to become an outlaw; Affy's namesake—Austin Gibbons—escaped to France and also became an officer; Peter Gibbons of Newport was sentenced to death in Castlebar (although a tradition tells of his escape to America); and Peter's brother Richard was deported and imprisoned in England. The Connemara storyteller James Berry recalled meeting an acquaintance of Affy Gibbons who described him as a "capital poet" and a "poet laureate," but this account probably confused the subject of the popular poetic lament with its author.[18] Angela Bourke noted that "laments composed in the eighteenth and nineteenth century were usually written down only after they had become famous within oral tradition."[19] Due to multiple transmissions and variations, it is difficult to positively determine the authorship of folk poetry, and various claims were made concerning this particular lament. In 1933 the Connemara storyteller Séamus Ó Ceannabháin (b. 1857) claimed that Affy's brother Seán (probably referring to "Johnny the Outlaw") composed the lament upon paying a visit to the grave on Innishbofin.[20] In 1937 Hayes maintained that the elegy was written by Affy's uncle from Crump Island near Renvyle in county Galway,[21] and in 1942 an eighty-two-year-old man on Clare Island in county Mayo attributed the lament to a local poet named Nicholas Dugan and dated its composition to 1815.[22]

It is likely that a skilled poet was commissioned by the family to compose the lament, which was then phrased as if spoken directly by a kinsman of the deceased.[23] Yet even though it is written in traditional poetic tropes, the lament appears to reflect the deep grief of a relation or close friend. In one version, it specifically mentions "an buartha [buaidhreadh] atá ar do ghaoltaí" (the sorrow of your relations) and includes a blessing for the Gibbons family (*Sonas agus séan, cion agus meas dhá réir ar chlann Chiobúin go deo, mar 'sé a thuill siad*). In another version, the lament touchingly speaks of Affy's demise as: "cuireadh fuair an peárla go flaithis Dé ina fhéasta" (the pearl got an invitation to the heaven of god and to his feast). Mourning was extended with the entry of the lament into the repertoire of local oral tradition, as the folklore of communities in a peripheral area of west Connacht co-opted personal grief that originated in an intimate circle. Studies of traditional lament have realized that "the messages conveyed could make political points under the guise of personal grief."[24]

The lament for Affy Gibbons commemorates the death of an individual while, at the same time, the verses also expressed a tone of communal bitterness directed against the coming of the French:

Ba as Cíll Alaidh a ghluais an dian-smál [It was from Killala the catastrophe
a dhíbir muid ó chéile.   originated
Ná Frannca' theacht go hEirinn   that scattered us from each other.
mo chreach is mo chráidh.   It was the coming of the French to
                                                            Ireland,
                                                            my woe and my sorrow.]

Since such popular embittered sentiments were stifled and censured in official commemorative celebrations of Ninety-Eight, evidently laments embodied grassroots commemoration, which represented a subaltern *mentalité*.

Likewise, an elegy for Fr. Manus Sweeney [An tAthair Mánus Mac Suibhne] reflects both private and communal remembrance. The lament voices deep personal sorrow ("it is my bitter grief that he is lying in the grave") and in one version refers to the dejected condition of three individuals (Andí, Séamus, and Éamonn) who were probably kinsmen of the deceased. But the poem also mentions widespread popular participation in the mourning of the rebel priest: "there is lamentation far and wide since the death of Father Manus, and the poor heart-broken Gaels are shedding tears with the coming of every day."[25] The folk historian Micheál Ó Gallchobhair of Chicago (d. 1937), whose great-grandmother claimed she was present at Fr. Sweeney's execution, maintained that the poem was composed by a man named Éamonn Ó Maolmhaodhóg [Mulloy], about whom nothing is known. A hermeneutical reading of the collected folklore accounts suggests that the stylized lament may have originated in the spontaneous keening of Fr. Sweeney's sister at his gallows. Oral tradition recalled that Fr. Sweeney responded to her cries of grief by calling out: "grian árd os cionn duibheagáin, a dheirbhshiúr ó!" (high sun over darkness, dear sister). These profoundly altruistic words of solace appear to answer a verse in a version of the lament: "darkness is in the sky, a mist obscures all the stars."[26] Scholarship of Irish laments has been criticized for its reliance on textual analysis and neglect of oral performance,[27] and Bourke has called attention to the theatrical nature in which women publicly performed poetic laments.[28] Through such performances private grief entered the public sphere and was shared as a communal experience.

The remembrance of Fr. Sweeney's execution was not only lamented in song but also recalled in numerous folk narratives.[29] It eventually received official public acknowledgment in the twentieth century, when Mayo communities in Achill (his place of birth), Newport (his place of death), and Burrishoole (the site of his grave) erected commemorative memorials in his honor. It would appear that private and personal rituals of remembrance instigated by those who were directly related to the deceased were maintained through family traditions and then publicly shared within a sympathizing community through theaters of social memory, such as storytelling and ballad singing. Perpetuated as local traditions, these commemorative practices eventually received official recognition. However, a schematic model of grassroots folk commemoration growing out of personal mourning and gradually turning into official commemoration underestimates the many agents that intervene and influence the choice of subject, the content, and form of remembrance. The memorials in honor of Fr. Sweeney clearly reflect the popularity of the nationalist practice of erecting monuments, which was promoted by the 1798 centenary celebrations in 1898.

The impact of national commemorative ceremonies on patterns of folk commemoration is discussed in depth in chapter 14 (in "Ceremonies, Monuments, and Negotiations of Memory"). Yet, it is worth looking beyond the obvious and briefly mentioning another influential factor—religious devotion. The hagiography of Fr. Sweeney in folk narrative depicted the description of the events leading to Fr. Sweeney's execution with themes echoing the passion of Christ. This construction of martyrdom utilized evocative motifs drawn from deep layers of Christian consciousness. Associations of spiritual devotion were especially appealing, beginning in the second half of the nineteenth century. The historian Emmet Larkin suggested that the dramatic changes in popular religious practices in post-Famine Ireland constituted a "devotional revolution" and that the recently reformed clergy made a concerted effort to increase the zeal and piety of the laity during the late nineteenth century. Their attention centered on the sacraments of Penance and the Eucharist, and consequently attendance of mass rapidly increased. Another facet of this transformation in Irish Catholicism was the introduction of Roman devotional exercises, among them the cult of the Sacred Heart and the Immaculate Conception, jubilees, triduums, pilgrimages, shrines, processions, and retreats.[30] In the West of Ireland, Knock emerged as a center for Marian pilgrimage following the reported apparition of the Virgin Mary there in August 1879,[31] an event that could be interpreted as a traditionalist reaction to religious innovations (and so was initially greeted with suspicion by the church authorities).[32] These popular spiritual rituals all share an underlying theme of commemoration. Halbwachs perceptively noted that: "if we survey the different components of the Christian cult, we realize that each one of them is essentially the commemoration of a period or an event in the life of Christ."[33] With its focus on ahamnesis, the ritual of mass is a daily act of commemorating Christ, which is practiced on an individual, family, and community level. In popular Catholicism, where commemoration of Christ was supplemented by the cults of the Virgin Mary and patron saints, pilgrimages to local holy sites and reverence of relics were effectively acts of communal commemoration.

The iconography of Ninety-Eight memorials and their official ceremonies of dedication frequently utilized religious symbolism and ritual in order to present monuments as sacred icons.[34] Alongside national commemorative ceremonies, religious zeal encouraged and influenced various practices of folk commemoration discussed throughout this book, such as martyrology of local heroes and the designation of sanctified sites associated with the memory of the dead. The connection between devotion and commemoration was illustrated in a tradition from Castlebar, which recalled that in 1798 a local woman (from Ansboro house on Main Street) married a wounded French soldier and ended up going with him to France. As the story goes, they had two daughters who became nuns, and one of them later sent back her rosary beads, which were treasured locally as a memento of Ninety-Eight.[35] The veneration of objects imaginatively identified as relics associated with the Rebellion, such as these commemorative rosary beads, is yet another medium of folk commemoration that encompassed private and public spheres and emulated Catholic devotional practices.

With such demotic commemorative traditions in mind, the examination of various spheres of remembrance in the following chapters demonstrates that, contrary to a common misconception, commemoration of Ninety-Eight in Connacht and the north midlands did *not* begin with the centenary celebrations of 1898. Unofficial commemoration is first examined through a discussion of folklore traditions embedded in the cultural geography of the Year of the French. This is followed by a discussion of private and communal commemorative traditions that relate to material artifacts. The impact of political metropolitan culture on the reshaping of provincial social memory is then explored at length through a critique of official commemorative ceremonies and an examination of the cultural interactions between oral tradition, popular print, and education. Overall, remembrance is shown to be multilayered and complex, rather than a straightforward construction allegedly orchestrated from above by ostensibly hegemonic political elites, which is how commemoration has often been misrepresented. The section concludes with a discussion on the limitations of folk commemoration within the larger contexts of the selectivity of social memory in general and the debates on uses and abuses of commemoration.

12

Topographies of Folk Commemoration

The history of Ireland must be based on a study of the
relationship between the land and the people.
J. C. Beckett
The Study of Irish History

Folk history was associated with localities, and the traditions of folk commemoration that it recalled were embedded in the landscape, which, as Vansina noted, could serve as a "powerful mnemonic device."[1] In the 1930s there were people all along the route of the Franco-Irish insurgent army, from Kilcummin to Ballinamuck, who could point out to folklore collectors exactly where they believed the rebel army had passed and could identify sites of local military encounters. For the people of Connacht and the north midlands, the French invasion was not an abstract episode in a remote past but a vital part of the heritage of their district. In some cases, communities that were not on the officially recognized map of the campaign felt excluded and claimed that side-forces passed through their locality. A pupil near Kiltimagh in county Mayo wrote for the Schools' Scheme the textbook version of the army's route, which "every schoolboy knows," but he also insisted that "some of them must have passed through Kiltymagh," though he was aware that "the authorities" did not mention his neighborhood.[2]

Just as natives of the Columbian Andes "will interpret the past as they pass by those topographic sites in which historical referents are encoded,"[3] Glassie showed that an Irish community's historical consciousness was grounded in references to the landscape so that "in place the person is part of history."[4] Yet the topography of remembrance did not simply chart spatial coordinates in a physical reality. By setting experiences in the landscape, traditional narratives reflected a "sense of place." As Kent Ryden observed in a North American context: "regional folklore encapsulates and transmits the intimate and otherwise unrecorded history of a place; it reveals the meaning of a place to be in large part a deeply known and felt awareness of things that happened there."[5]

Halbwachs recognized the importance of literary representations of landscape as reflections of "collective memory,"[6] and Simon Schama has shown how mythic meanings have been attached to landscapes throughout history.[7] Irish traditions pertaining to landscape have an ancient pedigree. *Dindshenchas Érenn* (commonly known as *dinnseanchas*), the large body of medieval toponymic lore written in metrical verse and in prose, constituted, in the words of the Gaelic scholar Robin Flower, a "kind of Dictionary of National Topography."[8] The *Oxford Companion to Irish Literature* notes that this corpus "reflects a mentality in which the land of Ireland is perceived as being completely translated into story: each place has a history which is continuously retold."[9] It has been pointed out that oral traditions of places were often distinct from those found in written sources.[10]

The geographer and archaeologist Emyr Estyn Evans advocated that the "personality of Ireland" could best be understood through an interdisciplinary "trilogy of regional studies," which would examine "the total physical environment" (*habitat*), "the written record of the past" (*history*) and "the unwritten segment of human history" (*heritage*).[11] Raphael Samuel described the built environment as a "palimpsest on which an alternative view of the national or local past is inscribed."[12] Similarly, Kevin Whelan, echoing the *géographie humaine* of the French *Annales* school, described landscapes as "communal archives, palimpsests created by the sedimentation of cultural experiences through time." He suggested that a landscape can be seen "through the eyes of those who made it" and interpreted as "a democratic document from which can be recuperated the history of the undocumented."[13]

The geographer J. B. Jackson coined the term "vernacular landscape" in reference to "territory of an impoverished and illiterate population with no written history, no written laws or records, and no documented title to the lands it occupies," as opposed to the "political landscape" of ruling classes (crown, aristocracy, clergy, etc.).[14] An exploration of vernacular landscape in Ireland can offer insight into the mental geographies that were vividly evoked in folklore accounts and illustrate the vital relationship between local communities and their surroundings. However, this term, which was conceptualized with an English and German experience in mind (referring specifically to *Deutsche Rechtsalertümer*, Jacob Grimm's 1828 collection of local law and customs), needs to be adapted to accommodate local conditions. Looking at Irish poetic and narrative traditions about places, the cultural critic Pat Sheeran and the sociologist Nina Witoszek pointed out that "as a result of colonization, two kinds of landscape emerged in the seventeenth and eighteenth century. One was political and Ascendancy, the other vernacular and Gaelic."[15] This distinction should not be over-reified, as over the course of modern history cultural negotiations took place between these two landscapes and the vernacular landscape served as a commemorative platform that did not remain purely Gaelic.

Irish vernacular landscape can be mapped through a microtoponymic study of place-names, which together with the folk history narratives associated with them, served as an everyday medium of commemorating past events of local significance. Place-names, as Whelan noted, "must represent communal values if they are to take root as an intrinsic part of the indigenous mind" and can therefore "act as a very powerful summation of large aspects of one's own biography, the history of one's family, the history of one's community and the history of one's nation."[16] In a study of folklore in northwest Erris, Séamas Ó Catháin and Patrick O'Flanagan uncovered a rich repository of traditional narratives and customs through which members of a rural community demarcated and explained the "living landscape" around them. With almost eight hundred place-names documented in the parish of Kilgalligan alone, the enormous range of toponymic folklore in just one locality proves to be overwhelming. Popular engagement with the landscape was intense, and people attached names to practically every distinct site in their area.[17] Naming was not limited to prominent landmarks and was extended to plots of land, as noted by the geographer Patrick Duffy: "One distinctive mark of the local is the intimate baptism of the fields with individual familiar names."[18] When suggesting a typology for this variety of myriad place-names, Ó Catháin and O'Flanagan included a category of "commemorative names," which explicitly embodied the relationship of a community in the ethnographic present with the historical past.[19]

In 1801 Killala and Castlebar were already listed as places of historical interest on account of their association with the 1798 Rebellion.[20] Samuel Lewis's *Topographical Dictionary of Ireland* (1837) shows that from the early nineteenth century, the French invasion was acknowledged as a significant historical episode in the geographical identity of the West; this is confirmed in numerous contemporary travel books, most of which were addressed to an English or Ascendancy readership.[21] However, external recognition of the heritage of the Year of the French was largely restricted to the main towns and sites associated with the campaign (Killala, Ballina, Castlebar, and Ballinamuck) and did not incorporate the vernacular landscape, which was by and large an unofficial geography. Place-names were typically anchored in oral tradition and thus impenetrable to those who did not have access to an insider's knowledge of local folklore. Therefore, the *seanchaithe* and *staireolaithe*, the storytellers who were authorities on local folk history, were invaluable interpreters of the vernacular landscape.

An early attempt to facilitate a comprehensive study of Irish vernacular landscape was undertaken by the topographical department of the nineteenth-century Ordnance Survey, which, in the words of Joep Leerssen, "turned the entire countryside of Ireland into one vast *lieu de mémoire*."[22] Under the direction of the musicologist, archaeologist, and landscape painter George Petrie, outstanding scholars, such as John O'Donovan (1809–61) and Eugene O'Curry (1796–1862), joined military surveyors in conducting ethnographic fieldwork on topography and local history. Their research was documented in letters and historical memoirs. The first toponymic fieldworker was employed in 1830, and by 1839 the topographical department's staff had grown to eleven. But due to continuous criticism, the authorities terminated their work in 1842.[23]

Maura Cronin's observation (based on the case of letters for counties in the eastern province of Leinster) that "the dearth of references to 1798-related sites and memories is striking"[24] corresponds with the Ordnance Survey letters from counties in the West and north midlands of Ireland, which only rarely mention Ninety-Eight.[25] The illusion of a "collective amnesia" given by this lacuna contrasts with the prevalence of references to places associated with the Rebellion in popular songs and contemporary oral accounts, which include a "stream of names of smaller places unknown to most outsiders."[26] It appears that subversive recollections of Ninety-Eight were generally considered out of bounds for a government-initiated project conducted in the turbulent context of the early nineteenth century. Locals were evidently conscious of the sensitivity of remembering the Rebellion and, as Gillian Doherty (née Smith) noted in relation to the surveyor's fieldwork in Ulster, "people in neighbouring regions refused to give information about the location of hiding places used in the 1798 rebellion."[27] As a result, the Ordnance left precious few records from pre-Famine Ireland of commemorative traditions associated with the vernacular landscape of the Year of the French.

In his speech to mark the establishment of the Irish Folklore Commission in 1935, the Mayo-born Minister of Education Tomás Ó Deirg (1897–1956), who had served in the War of Independence as the commanding officer of the IRA West Mayo Brigade and was a former headmaster of the Ballina Technical School, described the collecting of folklore as a continuation of "work abandoned 100 years ago" by the Ordnance Survey.[28] In their natural environment, toponymic traditions marked *loci memoriae* proper, not in the sense of classical discourses on rhetoric preoccupied with mnemonics[29] but places to which "living" social memory was attached, as opposed to Pierre Nora's concept of multilayered *lieux de mémoire* that are repositories of "dead" memory.[30] Removed from local communities and stored in an archive, the traditions loose their vitality and, as Richard White perceptively remarked, "in Dublin these stories are out of place."[31] Therefore, the documented commemorative place-names of Ninety-Eight need to be relocated and recontextualized within the provincial folk history and social memory of the Year of the French.

Mapping Commemorative Microtoponymy

Dan Ben-Amos pointed out that "place names engrave on the land the people's memory of the past,"[32] and indeed the French invasion left a string of place-names in its wake through which the events of 1798 were remembered. The place where the French camped after disembarking was known as *Baile an Champa* (Place of the Camp),[33] and a nearby well (*Tobair Choir*) was pointed out as where the troops drew their water.[34] Similarly, the spot where the rebel army breakfasted before the engagement at Collooney was remembered as "Camp Hill,"[35] and the encampment at Cloone, where they rested on the eve of the Battle of Ballinamuck, was known locally as "Camp Field."[36] Place-names track the rebel army's journey from Mayo to the site of their defeat in north county Longford. Thoroughfares along the route were popularly named "French roads," most notably between Killala and Castlebar in county Mayo[37] and between Cloone and Ballinamuck in the north midlands.[38] Similarly, the path the rebel army took through Drumshanbo in county Leitrim was known as the "French Lane."[39] Actual naming was often superfluous, as it was general knowledge in a locality that the French had marched on certain roads.[40] Some names were more obscure and assumed a familiarity with local folk history. The path through the Belleek demesne by which the French vanguard approached Ballina was known as *bóthar na sop* (the road of straw). This name supposedly recalled how sympathizing locals set aflame straw in order to illuminate the way for the French,[41] though it may have actually derived from market-day traffic, which would regularly leave the road covered with straw.[42] The presence of United Irishmen alongside the French troops was recalled through use of the familiar sobriquet *croppy* in place-names such as "Croppy's Gap" (a field on Kiltycreevagh Hill near Ballinamuck)[43] or "Croppy's Bud" (a bush on the Ballinamuck battlefield).[44] As late as the 1980s, Tom Reilly, whose family lived on the battlefield of Ballinamuck, recalled that the field where the horses were stabled after the battle was known locally as "cavalry field."[45]

Place-names recalled the locations of engagements. Fighting was supposed to have taken place at Barnaderrig (*bearna dhearg*)—"the Red Gap" near Ballina.[46] Memory of "the Races of Castlebar" was cemented through several place-names. North of Castlebar, the hill of Slievenagark (*Sliabh na gCearc*), where the rebel forces positioned themselves before attacking the town, was afterwards known as "Mount Humbert."[47] Similarly, a strategic position at Sion Hill (on the northern outskirts of the town), where the British forces were stationed before the battle, was popularly referred to as "Lookout Hill."[48] The street through which the rebel forces entered the town was known by the name "Staball," supposedly recalling the battle cry of an English officer[49] or, as children in the 1950s were told, it recalled "the women who came to their doors calling on the French to 'stab them all.'"[50] The location of the French headquarters in Castlebar was referred to as "Humbert's House."[51] The place-name "French Hill" (*Cnoc na bhFrancach*), a hill four kilometers south of Castlebar, marked the site where a party of French dragoons under Bartholomew Teeling was killed by troops under Lord Roden.[52] This name was in popular use in the first half of the nineteenth century[53] and by the end of the century was officially recognized in commemorative ceremonies.

The map of the Year of the French in social memory went beyond the footsteps of the rebel army and also charted sites associated with popular agitation and local uprisings, routes Irish recruits took on their way to join the French, local skirmishes between smaller forces separated from the main body of the army, the flight of fugitives after the defeat at Ballinamuck, pockets of guerrilla warfare and outlaw banditry after the French surrender, and the punitive actions of regular military and yeomen who repressed the local population. The geographical delineations associated with this range of activities do not necessarily correspond with fastidious studies of military historians. Nevertheless, for the people of Connacht and the north midlands, remembrance of the French invasion and its aftermath was an integral part of their vernacular landscape, and the ahistoricity of oral traditions is of lesser relevance to understanding the influence on popular imagination. For example, it was told locally that Lord Edward Fitzgerald (1763–98), the intended leader of the United Irish insurrection, had visited a house on Aran Street in Ballina in order to secretly plot the Rebellion in the West. This story is apocryphal and has strong anachronistic undertones, since it probably originated in an attempt to rationalize the French landing in an area where United Irish organization was underdeveloped and to find a connection between the Connacht experience and the national narrative of the 1798 Rebellion. Although there is no corroborating evidence, folk history identified a site and grounded the tradition in the locality.[54]

Many place-names marked features of the landscape associated with outlaws on the run. In 1956 a ninety-two-year-old man in northwest Mayo recalled that eighty years earlier (ca. 1875) his father had told him of a place named *Poll na bhFrancach* (the Hole of the French), which was believed to be the hiding place of fugitive French soldiers.[55] Other place-names related to specific individuals. In Mayo, "Carraig Tony" was a cave in the Nephin mountains where Anthony Daly of Coolnabinna sheltered,[56] and "Rory's Cave" in Glenree was the hide-out of Rory Dubh, a survivor of Ballinamuck who became a highwayman.[57] Several caves in Connemara were associated with the legendary outlaws Fr. Myles Prendergast and his kinsman Johnny Gibbons Jr. ("Johnny the Out-law"). Gibbons, who armed his followers with French cannons and guns, was described by the Mayo magnate Denis Browne as "the captain and leader of all mischief in this province." Government reports noted that Fr. Prendergast was constantly on the run, yet was "looked up to by the disaffected" and "concealed by all the inhabitants who love him,"[58] while a Presbyterian missionary remarked that he was the captain of a hundred men who would exercise in broad daylight on Rosshill in Connemara.[59] The two sustained rebellious activities in the hills of Connemara till 1805.[60] Among the places of refuge remembered in oral tradition were "Scailp an Athar Maoilre," "Pluais an Athar Maoilre," and "Scailp Johnny."[61] The outlawed priest was also associated with Fr. Myles's Mass Rock (*Carraig an Athar Maoilre*), Fr. Myles's Well (*Tobar an Athar Maoilre*),[62] Fr. Myles's Bed, and Fr. Myles's Den.[63] Another reputed place of refuge of Fr. Prendergast was "Aill an Phíobaire" (Cave of the Piper), which supposedly recalled the priest's skills as a bagpipe player.[64] Although the Connemara storyteller James Berry (b. 1842) mentioned that he had heard from a survivor of the Rebellion that Fr. Myles played bagpipes in social gatherings,[65] the place-name relates to an ancient folklore motif of a musician who enchants a monster in a cave, and the connection to Fr. Prendergast is probably a recent commemorative tradition attached to an already familiar site.[66]

Place-names kept alive the memory of local agitation and unrest on the periphery of the major events and recalled episodes that were largely overlooked in scholarly historiography. Folklore from Brackla, an area between counties Galway and Roscommon from where locals went to join the rebel ranks, demonstrates this point. A "wide sod fence" was believed to have been built as a fortification by United Irishmen under the leadership of the local Ninety-Eight hero Mick Tobin, who successfully confronted Denis Browne after the final defeat at Killala.[67] It was claimed locally that the Tobinstown estate in Brackla was named after Mick Tobin, although it was most probably in use prior to his involvement in the Rebellion.[68] County Cavan does not appear on official maps of the 1798 Rebellion in the West, yet United Irishmen from the south Ulster area flocked to join the Franco-Irish army,[69] and several place-names recall local acts of Rebellion, such as "Rebel Hill" beside the Lisgar Demesne near Balieborough,[70] the nearby "Bloody Bridge" at Cornanaff,[71] and also "Soldier's Bray" near Snugboro, where allegedly Catholic locals attacked "the Protestant soldiers" returning from "the Ballinamuck."[72] In Bruskey near Ballintemple in county Cavan, a field was named "Ballinamuck" supposedly by yeomen who returned from the battle and divided their loot there.[73] Though place-names are associated with specific sites, oral traditions can migrate with people who continue to commemorate historic events in a new location. There is even a likely possibility that place-names of 1798 were recalled in Irish diasporas by deported and exiled United Irishmen and later by emigrants, who wished to preserve the folk history of their native area.[74]

Place-names, which served as verbal monuments to remembered injustices and grievances, recalled prolonged resentment of punitive reprisals against rebels. A field near Granard was locally known as the "Farm of the Burnt House" in memory of the destruction of the house of the Dennistons of Clonbroney.[75] The brothers Alexander and Hans Denniston were Protestant landowners and members of the Mostrim yeomanry who joined the United Irishmen and fought at Granard. Folklore frequently merged them into a single heroic character named "Denniston."[76] Even though the farm passed into the hands of a loyalist family, the name of the house that had stood there (Prospect) was preserved in social memory.[77] In such ways, folk history subversively commemorated the devastation of a remembered landscape. Alongside the valor of resistance, communities also recalled the suffering and terror caused by the Rebellion and its suppression. Folk history identified places of hiding in which local inhabitants took refuge, such as "forts" (prehistoric settlement remains associated with fairy lore) in Drumkirk and Drumgibra in south Leitrim[78] or in Clonback near Ballinamuck.[79] By far the most prevalent commemorative place-names of Ninety-Eight relate to places of death and burial, and these turned the vernacular landscape into a "weeping landscape" of remembered grief.

Sites of Death, Burial, and Supernatural Encounters

The high mortality of the Year of the French was commemorated ubiquitously in the vernacular landscape. The battlefield at Ballinamuck was remembered for the merciless massacre of hundreds of Irish rebels, which was acknowledged in government sources.[80] Similarly, the route by which the Mayo rebels retreated toward their last stand in Killala, where a contemporary account reported "considerable slaughter" and "dreadful carnage"[81] and an eyewitness observed "such terrible slaughter as took place is impossible for me to describe,"[82] was remembered as *casán an áir* (the pathway of slaughter).[83] Local traditions recalled sites of communal tragedy inflicted on the civilian population. Stories about Pollnashanthana (*Poll na Sean-Teine*)[84] at Down-patrick Head in Laggan, county Mayo, recounted that in 1798 the men of the village were let down the cliffs by rope and took refuge at low tide on a con-cealed ledge by the sea in order to avoid military repression. The fugitives sub-sequently drowned after the womenfolk were prevented from rescuing them in time.[85] Visiting the area fifty years later, Rev. Caesar Otway noted that "a gen-eration of the males of that poor hamlet was swept away, and at this day not an old man is to be found there."[86] This story, which was recounted locally in the 1930s and '40s, appeared in several variations.[87]

Folk history identified numerous locations where apprehended insurgents were executed. Several sites were subsequently known as "Gallows Hill," includ-ing one by Rathduff Castle, near Ballina,[88] another at Belcarra (Ballycarra), near Castlebar,[89] and a particularly infamous site at Carrick-on-Shannon,[90] where on the direction of Major-General George Hewitt nineteen prisoners taken at Ballinamuck were selected for execution by lottery.[91] A field in county West-meath, where rebels were hanged after an engagement at Wilson's Hospital, was known locally as "the hanging field."[92] In the early twentieth century, the dramatist and folklorist Lady Gregory was told that "there is a tree near Denis Browne's house that used to be used for hanging men in the time of '98."[93] In the 1930s, "hangman's trees" were pointed out to folklore collectors all along the trail of the Rebellion. In county Leitrim alone the sites of such trees were identified in Drumshanbo,[94] Lakefield Hill near Farnaught,[95] Breanros near Mohill,[96] and at Roosky on the border with county Roscommon.[97] Around Ballinamuck, great importance was attributed to trees (or elder bushes) in the townland of Kiltycreevagh on which it was believed that many of the rebels captured after the battle (including the famous General Blake) were hanged.[98] Even when the trees were cut down, they continued to survive in the imaginary landscape of social memory. In the Longford townland of Cavan (one kilo-meter west of Ballinalee) it was remembered that "the trees on which they [Croppies] were hanged stood there up to a short time ago, the track of the rope being visible."[99] In recent times, the local historian Rev. Owen Devaney met an old man in Cavan who claimed that he remembered seeing the irons on a par-ticular tree from which hanging ropes had been suspended in 1798.[100]

The impact that a "Gallows Hill" had on local social memory was vividly expressed in an account collected in 1938 from an eighty-four-year-old man from Ballycarra in county Mayo (seven kilometers southwest of Castlebar), whose father at age ninety could personally recall the executions:

> Local people especially the aged tell the awful deeds that took place here almost a hundred years ago. In about 1798 a Gallows was set up here by the English soldiers to put to death the Irish fools who had any hand, act or part in the rising of that awful time. My father said that a doshen [*sic*] at the least was put to death in his day and threw inside the walls like (dogs) and buried like dogs. Today inside the walls at this spot you can see the hillockiens where they were berried [*sic*]. The stone wall also the small gardeneens on which they lived. From '98 down the people who owned the land never stirred a stick or stone at this place.

The account also told of sightings of ghosts who haunted the site (a guilt-ridden ghost of an executioner and an agonized ghost of a victim's relative) and concluded by noting: "They say it is not right to pass this spot without saying a prayer for the dead."[101] In this way the narratives and rituals associated with place-names turned places of execution into local sites of commemoration. Indeed, in Irish folklore, it was generally believed that a corpse bequeathed supernatural properties to the ground at the place of death (*fód an bháis*), allowing the living to make contact with the dead.

Sites of execution of popular heroes became venerated sites of commemoration. A notable example is the case of Fr. Conroy of Addergoole, who was publicly hanged on the Mall in Castlebar (opposite the Imperial Hotel). The execution and funeral left a strong impression on local residents. The distinguished nineteenth-century Catholic Archbishop of Tuam, John Mac Hale (1791–1881), was a seven-year-old boy at the time, and local tradition recalled that he dispatched messages for Fr. Conroy (his parish priest), who called upon families in the area to join the rebels.[102] He himself later described

FIGURE 16. Plaque marking the execution site of Fr. Conroy at the Mall in Castlebar (erected 1998 as part of a bicentennial 1798 heritage trail). The location was remembered with reverence even after the notorious hanging tree was uprooted by a storm in 1918. Photo by the author.

witnessing the execution as a life-changing experience, having "then and there resolved, that if given life, ability and position, he would expose the misdeeds of those who ruled Ireland."[103] The hanging tree was an object of local reverence until it was uprooted by a storm in 1918, on the eve of a visit by Eamon de Valera, and then the tree's remains were invested with symbolic capital. When de Valera visited Castlebar as President in 1961, it was recalled that over forty years earlier "when the blasted oak tree was shown to Mr. De Valera, legend has it that he said this tree was the symbol of tyranny and its destruction was the portend of the downfall and end of tyranny."[104] Celtic crosses were made from the timber of the tree by a local woodcarver (Sam McCormick of Knockthomas on Thomas Street), whose father and uncle had been active Fenians in 1867, and these souvenirs were preserved locally.[105] Their status as nationalist relics was publicly confirmed at a civic reception in Castlebar in 1924, when one of the commemorative crosses was presented to the venerable Irish-American Fenian leader John Devoy (1842–1928),[106] who used the opportunity to deliver a speech in support of the Irish Free State and associated the Anglo-Irish Treaty with the sacrifices of Fr. Conroy and the patriots of 1798. One of the crosses remained with the McCormick family (bequeathed to Frank McCormick of Dublin, a chairman of the Mayo society Muintir Mhaigh Eo) and was put on public display in 1948 for the Ninety-Eight commemoration in Castlebar (see fig. 17).[107] Another cross was bestowed on Fr. MacEvilly, a distinguished republican priest who had taken part in the War of Independence, and was put on public display in 1937 for the unveiling of a memorial in honor of Fr. Conroy in Lahardane.[108]

Commemorative landscape does not require tangible-physical markings but may rely solely on remembered places, which no longer exist. The site of Fr. Conroy's uprooted hanging tree was remembered in folk history and was identified as a "site of '98 historical interest" during the sesquicentennial commemoration celebrations.[109] A photograph of the tree is on permanent display in the reception of Daly's Hotel (the

FIGURE 17. Celtic cross carved from Fr. Conroy's hanging tree. Crafted by Sam McCormick of Knockthomas, Castlebar, these 1798 commemorative crosses were recognized locally as nationalist relics. Photo by the author. Displayed courtesy of Gearóidín Ní Ghrúineíl, Principal of St. Angela's N.S., Castlebar, county Mayo.

Imperial Hotel) in Castlebar. Similarly, the execution site of "Johnny the Out-law" (John Gibbons Jr.) at the top of Peter Street in Westport was remembered locally.[110] In the 1930s people around Ballinamuck would point out the site of a barn on the top of the hill in Kiltycreevagh in which rebels had been incarcerated and executed, even though the building was no longer standing.[111]

In addition to sites where rebels were killed, the vernacular landscape of the Year of the French was littered with graves. In particular, social memory was fascinated by places of burial of French troops. An old bridge outside Drumsheen in northeast county Mayo was named "the French Bridge" (*Droichead an Fhrancaigh*), as bodies of French soldiers were supposedly interred nearby.[112] An account for the Schools' Scheme near the neighboring town of Bunnyconnelan noted a commemorative tradition whereby "as people pass by they throw in a stone over the bridge."[113] Untypically, "Frenchman's Bridge" was recognized by surveyors and appears in the Ordnance survey map. From local folk history accounts it appears that this site was confused with a nearby "Frenchman's Grave," where a French soldier collapsed on the march from Mayo to Sligo.[114]

Graves associated with French soldiers, which were normally marked by a big stone or mound, were widespread in the vernacular landscape of the Year of the French. As the local historian Seán Ó Brádaigh observed, the area of the battlefield of Castlebar was "dotted with soldier's graves,"[115] and "French graves" were pointed out in the neighboring townlands of Cornmacinc (near Burren),[116] Boradruma,[117] Derrylahan,[118] Knockaskibbole (*Cnoc na Scioból*),[119] and at the Windy Gap (north of the town).[120] Around Mayo, such sites were also found in Lacken (at a place known as "Garraí Francach" [French Garden]),[121] Garryroe near Kiltimagh,[122] and in the parish of Meelick just west of Swinford.[123] The owner of a field in the Mayo parish of Killasser, in which a big stone was said to mark the grave of a French soldier who was fatally injured from a horse's kick (at the present location of Carramore N.S.), dug up the site in 1923 and uncovered a skeleton. The local physician, Dr McCarthy, was asked to inspect the remains, and his verdict that they belonged to a youth aged under twenty-five appeared to support local tradition.[124] A Frenchman's grave, which was shown to Hayes in 1935, half a mile east of Lough Talt in county Sligo, was still remembered sixty years later.[125] In county Leitrim, Frenchman's graves were pointed out by Ardnarney N.S. in Dromahair[126] and along the road to Drumkeeran.[127]

Traditions recounted by the Reilly family of Enaghan in county Longford (ten kilometers northeast of Ballinamuck) told of three mortally wounded French soldiers who were sheltered by locals and then buried facing France on the shore of Lough Gowna.[128] Although one member of the family (James Reilly) claimed that the site had been dug up and found to be empty, another (Joey Reilly) still pointed out the graves in 1998.[129] Quite different traditions relate to a hill near Charlestown in county Mayo known as "Cnoc Rua" (Red Hill), where it was said that local villains killed, robbed, and buried a French soldier who had gone astray from his unit.[130] This scandalous story tarnished the reputation of the locality, and a later version of the narrative justified the deed by claiming that the Frenchman was suspected of espionage.[131]

A tradition from the area of Ballina recalled that a teacher named Barrett buried two French soldiers (who had allegedly preferred to shoot each other rather than be captured) at Gallows Hill in Rathduff and marked the grave with a big stone. Barrett's family immigrated to South Africa but preserved the tradition so that his grandchildren later returned to visit the grave and took back mortar and moss as souvenirs.[132] In the area of Castlebar, locals placed small iron crosses on graves of French officers. Three officer graves (two marked with crosses) were discovered in 1905,[133] and in 1948 the site received official recognition when the French ambassador placed wooden crosses and laid wreaths on the graves.[134] Originally, such local acts of remembrance were non-

FIGURE 18. "French grave" at Derrylahan, Castlebar, county Mayo. In the photograph, local historian Ernie Sweeney identifies a site, which, like many other "French graves" and "Croppies' Graves" once preserved in the vernacular landscape of folk history, is now derelict. Photo by the author.

FIGURE 19. Lyden family grave, Castlebar, county Mayo. The iron cross by
the graveside was originally used by
the Castlebar blacksmith John Lyden to
mark the grave of French staff officer
Colonel Guignon. Photo by the author.

institutional. They were undertaken
spontaneously by individuals and
could decline with the passing away
of those involved, though they did
not necessarily pass into oblivion. It
was remembered locally that a
Castlebar blacksmith named John
Lyden (1799–1855) tended in the
early nineteenth century the grave
of Humbert's chief-of-staff,
Colonel Guignon, who was shot
dead by an English marksman during the battle for Castlebar, and
marked the site with an iron cross.[135]
Even though by the 1930s the location of the site was forgotten, two
generations later the grandson,
Martin Lyden (1905–93)—a fish-
monger from Staball Hill who was commonly known as "Darkey Leydon"—
recalled family traditions of tending to the grave and decorating it with
flowers.[136] In fact, the original iron cross is currently located on the Lyden family grave in Castlebar graveyard.[137]

The remembrance of French graves stirred controversy in Castlebar in the
1950s when the Urban District Council authorized the widening of roads to
provide access for large turf cutting machines. "Yankie Mangan" and Martín
McGowan, two relatives of the Mayo United Irish captain William Mangan,[138]
objected to construction at Rathbaun Road on Sion Hill by claiming that
French soldiers were buried there. McGowan, who had played a major role in
organizing a battle reenactment for the 1948 commemorations, was recognized
locally for his knowledge of Ninety-Eight traditions.[139] Indeed, upon excavat-
ing the place, the workmen allegedly discovered remains of bodies in French
uniform.[140]

Popular remembrance was of course not restricted to graves of French soldiers. Immediately after the Rebellion, families of the deceased turned the graves of Irish rebels into private sites of commemoration. Though written in a romanticized literary style, Archdeacon's short story "The Rebels' Grave" (1839), which tells of a Castlebar mother (Agatha Sweeny, aided by her daughter Eliza) frequently visiting the grave of her two executed sons, is based on oral history sources, including an interview with the proprietor of the local graveyard.[141] "Croppies' graves," the common denotation for the burial places of the insurgents of 1798, were widespread throughout the West.

A concentration of these graves was found in the vicinity of Ballinamuck.[142] Rebels who were captured after the battle, court-martialed, and sentenced to death were buried collectively in the "Bully's Acre" in Ballinalee.[143] But apart from this designated site of burial, as a folklore collector was authoritatively informed in 1964, "there's graves that are dotted around the whole district."[144] In 1938 a pupil from nearby Soran (nine kilometers south of Ballinamuck) was told by his seventy-three-year-old uncle that "the battlefield is full of graves all of which are still to be seen covered with large mounds of clay and stones."[145] These croppies' graves were lyrically described in a local ballad:

> For miles over fields and by road sides,
> And up by the lonely boreens,
> Each marking a croppy's sepulchre,
> Stout crosses and mounds may be seen.
> May God bless the brave boys who perished,
> On the side of that old rocky hill;
> No stone marks the spot where they're buried,
> But their memory lives with us still.[146]

A writer who visited the "field of the massacre" shortly after the Rebellion was shown "the large pits, into which heaps of Irish carcasses were thrown, without the ordinary rites of Christian internment."[147] The locations of these mass graves were remembered locally, and when Hayes visited the battlefield, he was directed to a field known as the "grave meadow," where "the Irish are buried in heaps."[148] Sixty-five years later, a field named "Garraí Cam" (Crooked Field), owned by the Breslin family, was still pointed out as a site of mass burial.[149] From the wide distribution of graves around Ballinamuck, one particular site on the battlefield (located by a knocked-down embankment on land belonging to the Reilly family) was privileged with the title "The Croppies' Graves" and from 1898 became a designated locus for public commemoration.

Rebels who unsuccessfully attempted to escape the carnage at Ballinamuck left a trail of graves. According to a local folk historian a place known simply as the "Graveyard" in east county Leitrim was believed to be a croppies' grave.[150] Farther afield, a mound in Tullinloughlan (north of Belhavel Loch) in northwest county Leitrim was said to be the grave of a fugitive rebel named Mulvey.[151] Pikemen from Cavan were buried at "the Roilig" (*reilig*, graveyard) near Tobar in northwest Cavan and beside a nearby rock in the townland of Carricknabrennan.[152] A mass grave of executed rebels from Kilbeggan in county Westmeath was known locally as a "Croppies' Grave."[153] The graves of Longford rebels who died trying to escape after the engagement at Granard were identified in the neighboring townlands of Ballinagall, Gallid, Clough, and Carrickduff.[154] It was believed locally that most of the rebels who died at Granard, including their leader Patrick O'Farrell, were buried in the "Croppies' Hole," at the site of what is presently St. Mary's Catholic church.[155] A great quantity of bones was found when the foundations for the church were laid in 1860, and these were placed in a box and reburied a short distance away, at an unmarked site.[156] Local traditions often refused to accept that revered heroes were not given a proper burial. It was told in Ardagh, county Longford, that O'Farrell's body was secretly reclaimed and laid to rest in the family plot at the old graveyard (by the ruined church).[157] Similarly, the family of the Mayo rebel leader James O'Dowda of Bonniconlon, who was executed at Ballinamuck, maintained that his corpse was secretly brought back to his ancestral home and lies buried in the cemetery of Kilgarvin.[158]

Social taboo ensured that sites identified as graves of rebels were respected. This reverence was poetically depicted by the Young Ireland writer Thomas D'Arcy McGee (1825–68): "Peace be round the Croppies' grave, let none approach but pilgrims brave."[159] Describing a field where rebels were buried, eighty-two-year-old James O'Neill of Crowdrummin (near Ballinamuck), noted in 1938 that "the place is treated as holy ground being not tilled."[160] When asked how people recognize unmarked graves, the schoolteacher Peter Duignan told a folklore collector: "people just don't . . . they don't dig it up or interfere with it."[161] The corner of a meadow in Corlislea, Crosserlough, county Cavan, where three fugitive rebels from Ballinamuck died of their wounds and were buried, was not mown in respect to their memory.[162] In the 1970s an old woman in Castlebar showed Seán Ó Brádaigh the grave of a French soldier in her back garden at the bottom of Sion Hill and declared that "his feet are here and his head there and we'd never build on it."[163] Indeed, when two sheds were later put up on the property, they were located carefully and a large gap was left between them so as to avoid damaging the grave.[164]

Many graves were unmarked mounds, and their identification relied solely on social memory. Others were marked with piles of stones, which were known by several names in Irish: *carn, leacht, meascán,* or *clochán.* Such tokens of respect were the product of traditional acts of spontaneous commemoration.[165] A vivid description of such a practice appears in a work of early-twentieth-century historical fiction, which refers to the remembrance of rebels in county Roscommon:

> You see the pile of stones there beyond. These indicate the very spot of a "Croppie's grave." The people have been piling up stones there now for a century or more. When they pass through this pasture going after the cows in the evening or going along the road to the market or fair day, every person picks up a stone and throws it on that heap and says "Lord have mercy on his soul for he died for Ireland." You may listen to tales like this every day from the peasantry of Ireland as you walk over these old fields where heroes died for faith and fatherland.[166]

Piles of stones that marked the graves of rebels that were massacred after fleeing Killala stood above the shore in Cortoon (two kilometers northwest of Killala) until 1934.[167] In other cases, cairns were associated with specific names. Maughan's Field in the townland of Lissadrone East, near Kilcummin, was given its name from a small mound of stones, which according to local tradition marked the grave of a rebel named Maughan who was armed with a sword when apprehended and killed by soldiers after the fall of Killala.[168] Near Killoe in county Longford, a heap of stones was said to have been placed on the grave of a rebel called O'Farrell, who was shot dead when fleeing Ballinamuck and buried on top of "Cairn Hill."[169] Variant narratives facilitated competing traditions on the identity of the commemorated subject. According to an alternative tradition, the heap of stones on top of Cairn Hill was known as the "Meascone" (*Meascán*) and believed to mark not just O'Farrell's burial place but also a mass grave for thirty-six rebels.[170] People of the locality paid homage to this site with a yearly visit on the first Sunday of June.[171] Cairns were recognized folk monuments, which were neither particular to 1798 nor associated only with popular heroes. The cairn known as "Leacht Little" (pronounced locally as "Lyghtel"), a prominent landmark on *Cnoc Ceathrún* (Cortoon Hill) on the road to Achill Island, marked the death spot of an infamous villain who disrespectfully mocked the execution of the beloved Mayo priest Fr. Manus Sweeney.[172]

Other vernacular graves were marked in a distinct way. For example, a stone was placed on both ends of the "Killala Man's Grave" in Gaigue (near Ballinamuck).[173] Standing stones at nearby Lettergonnel were locally known to mark a "common croppy's grave."[174] A grave of three rebel officers in Knockanillaun, between Ballina and Crossmolina in county Mayo, was marked with a solitary stone.[175] Croppies' graves in county Leitrim were decorated with flowers planted in the shape of a cross or a coffin. In 1938 flowers were still blooming on two such graves, one on the banks of the canal below Aughoo in the parish of Ballinamore, and another on Aughawilliam Hill in the parish of Lower Drumreely.[176] Local tradition in Rathowen, county Westmeath, maintained that an ash tree in Russagh churchyard was planted by a Miss Katie Daly of the Mill (Russagh) over the grave of her sweetheart, an O'Brien of Rath, who died at Granard.[177]

In some cases a proper gravestone was erected. A memorial was put up by the roadside at Slatta in county Roscommon (near Rooskey) for Roger ("Ratchie") Farrell of Clondra in county Longford, who was killed by yeomen after escaping Ballinamuck.[178] The inscription on the O'Dowda family tombstone in the Kilgarvin cemetery in county Mayo mentions "Col. James Vipplar O'Dowda who was executed by the English on the 10th September 1798 for his part in the Mayo Rising."[179] In the old Crossmolina graveyard, a stone with an inscription in Irish was placed on what was believed to be the grave of the United Irishman Patrick Gill-Walsh, who was executed on the eve of the French arrival to Ballina (though according to another tradition his skeleton was discovered in Ballina).[180] Fr. Manus Sweeney was buried in his parent's grave in Burrishoole cemetery, and his name, age, and date of birth were cut on the grave-slab. In 1912 a Celtic cross was erected on the grave, and the gravesite was publicly recognized as a commemorative site.[181] In 1939 the national press reported the chance discovery of the remains of a memorial for a local United Irish leader on the border of county Roscommon and county Galway:

> A sculptured stone, bearing a hand and dagger and the inscription "Lambert 1798" was unearthed during the removal of the foundation of a wall at Creggs, Roscommon. The stone was, evidently, intended as a memorial to Capt. Lambert, Milford House, Creggs, who, with his company from North Galway, took part in the rout of the English at the "Races of Castlebar."[182]

At the time of the discovery, Captain Lambert was still remembered locally, and oral traditions about him had been collected for the Schools' Scheme the previous year.[183]

In some cases, folk history appears to expose deliberate efforts to conceal participation of individuals in the Rebellion through falsification of dates inscribed on gravestones. The gravestone of James O'Connor, a Protestant from Lanesborough in county Longford, notes that he died on the twenty-fifth of August (two weeks before the Franco-Irish army arrived in the area), whereas local tradition tells of his death at Ballinamuck.[184] An inscription on a grave in Moyne Abbey reads: "Pray for the soul of Matthew Bellew Esq. who departed this life on 3rd March 1797." Bellew was a veteran of the Austrian army who was appointed an insurgent general, though Stock and Musgrave claimed that in practice he was constantly drunk and was of little use to the rebel cause. He was apprehended following the final defeat at Killala, then court-martialed and hanged on 24 September 1798. Efforts to conceal his involvement in the Rebellion were instigated to counter contemporary anti-Catholic propaganda that tried to implicate his brother Dominick Bellew, the Catholic bishop of Killala, with support of the rebel cause.[185]

Folk commemoration was typically devoted to the memory of local rebel heroes, yet several narratives noted the graves of soldiers of the Crown. A schoolteacher was told in 1938 that the "Croppy's Bud" in Ballinamuck "is a misnomer: it was an English Yeoman Captain that was shot and buried there by the French."[186] A pupil in Crowdromin (near Ballinamuck) was told that a mercenary soldier killed by his great-great-grandmother was buried in the "Hessians' Field,"[187] and a local tradition in Drumconney, county Leitrim, identified a field where a yeoman captain was killed.[188] Similarly, "the Soldier's Gap" in Ballyharney, county Westmeath, marked the spot where reputedly two soldiers had been killed during the local insurrection on the eve of the battle of Ballinamuck.[189] These traditions, which identify a precise gravesite without naming the victim, relate more to the commemoration of local bravery and resistance to brutal repression than to remembrance of the dead. A more subversive case of recalcitrant remembrance can be found in a narrative that recalled that local residents who fell victim to arbitrary acts of violence by French troops were interred in fields near Cloone.[190]

In addition to identifying graves of rebels, folk history also remembered burials, which are, as Ben-Amos observed, "an elementary form of transforming the Earth into a vessel that contains collective memory."[191] Numerous stories about secret burial recall how interment was a problematic act, which implied sedition and resistance at a time of widespread terror. Returning from Granard, the O'Connells of Cranary [Cranally] died in a skirmish at Clogh and their corpses were initially buried on the spot, and only several months later were relocated to their native area (Inch).[192] Patrick O'Reilly of Enaghan in county Longford, recalled how his grand-uncle, who "was only a gossun [dialect: young boy] at that time," was shot dead by Cavan loyalists (identified as Orangemen), but the relatives

> were afraid to bury him in Columcille [graveyard] and they had to take him out and bury him near a mill dam. They had to leave him there for a fortnight before they could take him up and bury him in the churchyard.[193]

It was remembered locally that a brother and friend reclaimed from Ballinamuck the body of an O'Connor from Lanesboro in county Longford and had to hide from patrolling soldiers before they were able to bury the corpse.[194] Local tradition told how Honor Daly, the sister of the rebel hero Anthony Daly of Culnabinna, furtively prepared for burial the corpse of John McGuire of Derryloughan, who was hanged in Castlebar following a failed prison escape.[195]

The stealth required to bury executed rebels is best exemplified in the vivid accounts from around Ballinamuck about the rebel leader General Blake. Patrick Dolan of Kiltycreevagh Cross repeated the recollections of his grandfather:

> After he was hung, my grandfather and Jimmy McKenna and others of the neighbours about brought his body that night to McKenna's barn. They kept the body there and got a coffin made, and when it was dark they buried him in Tubberpatrick.[196]

The story of how Blake's corpse was taken at night to McKenna's barn in Kiltycreevagh "so that the English wouldn't get his body" was reiterated in nearby Edenmore by Patrick Gill[197] and by seventy-four-year-old James McNerney (who repeated the stories of his father, Chas McNerney, who lived to the age of ninety-six).[198] A more detailed account was collected from James McKenna, whose grandfather (b. 1784) recalled his own father's involvement in the events:

> General Blake was waked in our barn where you are now standing. My great-grandfather and the McManuses went over to Jack Griffin's place, where Devines live now, the evening he was hung there. They dragged his body across the fields through the gripes [*sic*]. Grandfather minded well of it and 'tis his words I have for the whole of it. The following night they buried him in Tubberpatrick. And when daylight came the morning after, the Stakeums of Tubberpatrick came and sodded the grave. When my great grandfather and the McManuses went over to Griffins for the body, there was ne'er a body there but his own. He was taken all alone and hung. Old robbers, horsedealers and the scum of the country that was about him when they hung him. I heard it as an upcast [dialect: reproach] to the Croftons of Mohill that they were at the hanging. They did not hang him the day they came at all, but the next day when the battle was over.[199]

Other names of locals who assisted in reclaiming the remains of Blake's corpse (including Terence Grimes, Paddy MacAliney, Paddy Skally, and Lennon) were remembered by Michael Grimes of Kiltycreevagh, who added that: "it was too dark for burial, so they hid the bag [with the remains] in a ditch and returned next day to bury it."[200] Local tradition even recalled that Blake's coffin was made from an oak dresser belonging to James McNamee of Corglass.[201] Blake's grave at Tubberpatrick subsequently became a memorial site and a designated focal point for commemoration of Irish rebels who died in Ballinamuck (see "An Insurgent General" in chapter 8).

The haphazard burials under conditions of threat resulted in the uncovering of skeletons and bones in following years. The *Ballina Herald* of August 1892 reported the discovery of two skeletons, which were believed to belong to rebels executed on the eve of the French entry to the town, and one of them was believed to be Patrick Walsh.[202] A skeleton was reputedly discovered by an ash tree in Killala known locally as a site of execution in 1798.[203] Bones of rebels were said to have been found in a quarry in Cortoon near Killala[204] and near Ballintra Bridge on the border of counties Leitrim and Roscommon.[205] A resident of Ballinamuck recalled that around 1895 he discovered skeletons with exceptionally long bones, which he coffined and reburied.[206] Skulls and bones can function as mnemonic aids for recalling the past,[207] and skeletons that resurfaced in the "living landscape" of Ninety-Eight called attention to the memory of the dead. Reburials of these skeletons by people of the locality also constituted acts of remembrance, which were recalled in folk history.

Ó Catháin and O'Flanagan demonstrated in their study of Kilgalligan, Erris, that the "living landscape" does not involve only "real"—earthly places—but also includes a rich body of folklore pertaining to the supernatural. Fairy lore, which was central to Irish oral tradition, presented a parallel world that may appear fantastic but nevertheless played a real and concrete role in the life of rural communities.[208] *A Handbook of Irish Folklore* notes: "in Irish tradition the dead and the fairies appear to be inextricably mingled. People who tell stories about them are not always quite clear as to whether the fairies or the dead are being spoken of."[209] Such traditions pose problems for historians and cannot be simply integrated into positivist studies.[210] Angela Bourke, who has written about the "virtual reality of Irish fairy legend,"[211] has marvelously demonstrated how stories of fairies provide essential insight for deciphering the mental world of communities on the periphery of modernization.[212]

At times, the vernacular landscape that commemorated the Year of the French also embraced the supernatural. An enigmatic story of a mystical act of commemoration associated with the United Irishman Francis French was remembered in a family tradition from Knock in county Mayo. James P. Donnellan, a native of Knock, recalled:

> My cousin, Mrs. Nora Walsh (née Donnelan), told me that James Donnellan (my great-great-grandfather) was a neighbour and a special friend of Francis French. He was present at the execution of poor Frank. It was late in the evening

when my ancestor set out on his horse from Castlebar for his home at Rockfield, a distance of some fifteen miles. Night overtook him on his journey. At that time there was a little chapel at Barnycarrol, two miles from Claremorris on the road to Knock (it was there the people of Kilcoleman, which included Rockfield, attended Mass). When James Donnellan reached the chapel he was surprised to see the door open and the interior illuminated. He got off his horse and looked in. A strange sight met his eyes. His friend's execution was being reenacted within the chapel exactly as he had witnessed it on that sad day at Castlebar.[213]

Another case refers to Ballintra Bridge by Lough Allen, an area on the border of Leitrim and Roscommon that saw disturbances throughout the 1790s.[214] At this place the Franco-Irish army crossed the Shannon River, and folklore recalled their passage through the locality and the punitive actions of the "Redcoats" that ensued.[215] In 1935 a seventy-year-old woman told a folklore collector that a skirmish at Ballintra Bridge was reenacted periodically by supernatural forces: "ivery 7th year on New Year's night that same battle is fought all over again as frish as iver [*sic*]." She added with conviction:

I often seen the lights on Lough Allen meself goin' in an' out through other for hours an' hours of a New Year's night. Every one in Glan'll tell you that. They're to be seen plain. Loch Allen be's pure glitterin' with lights man [*sic*].[216]

In this tradition, the fairy world provided for the local community a periodic commemorative display of an engagement in 1798. Fairies could also mourn the deceased. An account from Droughill in county Cavan recalled that on the death of a Ballinamuck veteran named John Sheridan, sounds of marching soldiers and horses were heard throughout the night, and the house was later visited by fairies.[217] Ninety-Eight fairy lore also expressed collective trauma. A north Connacht legend told of a mysterious glen named *Átha na gCeann* (Ford of the Heads) where fairy women lamented the dead of the battles in 1798. Although people supposedly heard the tortured cries, this was an imaginary valley, which, like death itself, functioned as another world from which visitors did not return.[218]

Horrific scenes from the past were recalled through traditions of supernatural visitations. A tree in the townland of Lanour near Drumshanbo in county Leitrim was known as "the Spy Bush" in memory of an act of reprisal in which "a man who sold a priest to the redcoats" was killed and his body was left out to rot as a public spectacle. According to "several old people of the district," every year on the night of the sixteenth of October (the anniversary of the killing), the "strange drama" was reenacted and the odor of corpse could be sensed "just as it decayed there in the dark days of '98."[219] While in reality skeletons and bones reappeared and served as a concrete link with the past, folk narratives tell of the dead reappearing as ghosts and impinging on the living.[220] A story from the parish of Granard in county Longford told how the ghost of a Leitrim rebel who died in the locality haunted a local (a Kiernan of Clough). Once the body was reinterred in Leitrim among "his people," the ghost was appeased and "the image was never seen there."[221] Ghost stories offered a medium for remembering grievances. It was remembered that a man who refused to divulge information about rebels was unjustly tortured and executed by yeomen at the Cross at Quinn in county Clare and that "ever since, the place is haunted and it is reported that a soldier has often been seen at the Cross."[222] Through such narratives, folk commemoration tapped into a readily available reservoir of fairy lore and folk tradition about the other world, which was enhanced by ritual traditions of blessings, charms and curses. Respect for the dead mingled with belief in the supernatural in forming the basis for private commemorative rituals. For example, up until the late 1950s, the Flynns of Gortletteragh in county Leitrim faithfully preserved the sanctity of the "High- lander's Grave" on their property, which was supposedly a burial site of a Scot- tish soldier killed in 1798 that was guarded by the fairies. Once a year at harvest time, the time of the Rebellion, a cock (a small pile) of hay was respectfully placed by the grave.[223]

Considered as a whole, the many aspects associated with the vernacular landscape of the Year of the French, including the imagined map of the Rebel- lion, sites of death, stories of burial, and traditions of the other world, reveal patterns of popular commemoration that were mostly practiced without official recognition. Local familiarity with this folklore provided storytellers with a myriad of commemorative place-names that could be injected into narratives to add context and relevance. References made in passing to the vernacular landscape provided color and narrative depth to a storytelling performance and, at the same time, inadvertently functioned as a subtle form of commem- oration. In this way, place-names and graves provided communities with ubiq- uitous folk monuments. The vernacular landscape may appear static, but over time traditions were subject to changes, while certain practices were forgotten and new rituals were introduced. Since this is an unofficial commemorative topography, which by and large remained undocumented till the 1930s, these developments cannot be definitively traced. It is with this in mind that the inter- actions between official and unofficial spheres of remembrance need to be crit- ically examined in order to identify the conditions that may have influenced changes in folk commemoration.

13

Souvenirs

> To an imaginative person, an inherited possession . . . is not
> just an object, an antique, an item, on an inventory; rather it
> becomes a point of entry into a common emotional ground
> of memory and belonging.
>
> Seamus Heaney
> "The Sense of the Past"

IN 1962 A NONAGENARIAN veteran of the Mashona and Matabele risings
against the South African Company's rule in Southern Rhodesia (1896–97)
presented an axe to Joshua Nkomo, the leader of the Zimbabwe African Peoples
Union. This symbolic act, which implied an imaginary apostolic succession of
resistance to colonial domination, used a relic of a rebellion to recontextualize
social memory in light of contemporary nationalist politics.[1] It was also a transitional moment when private remembrance fed into public commemoration.
Similarly, weapons and relics from the 1798 Rebellion were later produced to
reawaken recollections of the historical events, though in the West of Ireland
this would usually take place in more mundane situations that were not so
overtly politicized.

The weapon most associated in popular imagination with Ninety-Eight was
the pike, which was considered the standard armament of the "common" Irish
rebel.[2] An eyewitness observed that following the landing of the French, "on
the next day the manufacture of pikes commenced at almost every Smith's
Forge" and that "those who had not musquets [*sic*] were supplying themselves
with pikes as fast as the smiths could forge them."[3] An apocryphal local tradition even claimed that pikes were being manufactured in Killala prior to the
French arrival.[4] By the mid-nineteenth century, pikes were considered curiosities and in 1852 were included in an exhibition of antiquities sponsored by the

Belfast Natural History and Philosophical Society.[5] They were also among the mementos collected by Irish nationalist separatists and sent to the Fenian Brotherhood fair in Chicago in 1864 (though there was a noticeably poor response from Connacht).[6] Pikes, or to be more precise iron pike-heads (since the wooden shafts decayed), were treasured by locals as souvenirs of the Rebellion. Several of these were found in the bogs around Ballinamuck, and at least one was found as late as the mid-1970s in the townland of Gaigue Cross. The rarity of pikes was attributed to a tradition that Lord Farnham, the commander of the Cavan Militia, had triumphantly collected pikes from the battlefield to decorate the gateway to his demesne.[7]

The folklore of pikes recalled how blacksmiths forged pike-heads and how they were then mounted, sharpened, and prepared for battle.[8] Drills and the ways in which pikes were wielded in combat were also remembered.[9] The recital "The Rake Up Near the Rafters," which was described by a local authority on folk history in Ballinamuck as a "fenian ballad or poem," recalled how pikes were concealed.[10] The theme of a pike hidden up in the thatch of a roof to be used again at a later date is prevalent in nationalist popular culture. The association with Fenians is not incidental, as pikes belonged to a long tradition of rebellious activities. After 1798 they were used again in Robert Emmet's rising in 1803, by the Young Ireland insurgents in 1848, the Fenians in 1867, and albeit symbolically, by Volunteers in 1916. Indeed, the military historian G. A. Hayes-McCoy observed that "it is not possible to date any Irish pike which does not bear a maker's mark," and recently manufactured pikes (such as those used, by the Carnmore Volunteers in county Galway) could be easily mistaken for relics of Ninety-Eight.[11] Moreover, newly made pikes were used for reenactments in commemorative ceremonies and subsequently became souvenirs.[12]

The National Monuments Act of 1930 broadly defined "archaeological objects" as "all ancient movable things" and required that any discovery of such items should be reported to the appropriate authorities. This law was brought to public attention by the Irish Department of Education [An Roinn Oideachais] through the circulation of a bilingual *Guide for Finders* in 1942.[13] Even though folklife was mentioned, the emphasis was clearly on prehistoric and early-Christian artifacts.[14] Consequently, in the eyes of the public in rural Ireland, the right of ownership of objects from modern periods of Irish history remained somewhat vague. In 1939 Richard Hayes donated to the National Museum a French musket that he had acquired during his travels in the West.[15] It was recalled in Ballinamuck that a pike had been sent to Dublin for display in the Municipal Art Gallery,[16] but generally such findings remained in private possession. A pupil collecting for the Schools' Scheme was told of pikes, "battle axes" and "pikel-pitch-forks" from 1798 that were kept by local residents in the townlands of Cloonart and Clooneen in county Longford (thirteen kilometers southwest of Ballinamuck).[17]

Other weaponry and ammunition found around Ballinamuck were also kept as relics of the battle. The schoolteacher Peter Duignan of Gaigue knew of numerous musket balls that were dug up on the battlefield and kept by locals.[18] Around 1895 a helmet, sword, and cannonballs were found in potato furrows at Kiltycreevagh Cross near Ballinamuck, and musket balls "the size of marbles" were found when tilling a field at the "Croppy Gap."[19] The Shannon River was apparently a rich source for findings of 1798 relics. It was remembered that workers had found swords there and that, sometime around 1898, a local man from Arigna in county Roscommon (Philip "Paddy" McManus of Seltinaveeney) found two cannonballs, which he kept at home.[20] Such relics were still being discovered near the battlefield up until recent times.[21] They are mostly uncataloged and are only incidentally brought to public attention. For example, when two Mayo men, Gerry Ryan and Pat Donohue, embarked on a commemorative walk in the footsteps of the Franco-Irish army from Kilcummin to Ballinamuck in 1998, they met a Leitrim couple who claimed ancestry to Ballinamuck rebels and showed them a cannonball, which they had unearthed a couple of years earlier.[22]

Select items were put on public display at different commemorative events. In 1938 twelve "relics of 1798," including projectiles, swords, and bayonets found on the Ballinamuck battlefield, were exhibited at St. Mel's College Diocesan Museum in Longford.[23] The Longford History Society kept a cannonball from the area of Ballinamuck, which in the late 1970s was exhibited in various towns in the county at an annual traveling "summer museum."[24] Another cannonball found in a quarry near Ballinamuck was placed at the nearby Gaigue schoolhouse, where it was fancifully maintained that it had been fired by none other than the legendary folk hero Gunner Magee [McGee].[25] This claim evidently left a lasting impression, as many years later former pupils could still recall the cannonball.[26] The 1798 Memorial Hall at the bicentennial Ballinamuck Visitor Centre displays a pistol found by the proprietors of the local '98 Bar, musket balls, and a cannonball that was found near Athlone,[27] which probably dates back to Battle of Aughrim, fought at nearby Kilcommodon in 1691.

A considerable cache of armament was also found on the 1798 battlefields in Mayo. During renovation works on the Linen Hall in Castlebar in 1899, a solid cast-iron bullet was found and referred to as a "relic of '98."[28] The discovery of

French officers' graves in 1905 also yielded a broken and rusted sword.[29] A decorative tip of a military pennant was dug up on the battlefield at Castlebar (on the McDonald property),[30] and in the 1970s a cannon shell and musket balls were unearthed in the locality.[31] A sword was found in field at the "Red Gap" (Barnaderrig) in Ballina, and it was recalled that a local farmer had found pikes and the remains of French uniforms when plowing his field.[32] Souvenirs were often mislaid. It was remembered locally that sometime in the 1950s a cannonball found near the reservoir at Castlebar was lost (or stolen). It was also recalled that Br. Cassian, a schoolteacher from the De La Salle order who taught at St. Patrick's N.S. in Castlebar from 1950 to 1957, dedicated one day a year to teaching the history and folklore of 1798 and that during the lesson he would produce a "cannon shell" and French medal. These relics were lost after the old schoolhouse on Chapel Street burned down.[33]

In a companion volume to a bicentennial exhibition on 1798 in the National Museum, Whelan maintained that unlike historical narratives, physical objects "retain the perfect memory of materiality."[34] However, even if unchanged in form, artifacts that survive through time are displaced from their original historical context and the meanings associated with them are rarely self-evident. Use of material culture is part and parcel of social interaction, and as ethnological "folklife" studies show, a rich repository of folklore was attached to objects and tools in traditional societies.[35] Old items can therefore be re-contextualized by talking with elder members of a community and evoking recollections of their past usages.[36] In practice, artifacts provide the basis for an argumentative encounter in the present with the past. Relics can be appropriated to support oral traditions and, despite the fact that the authenticity of the interpretations attached to them may be dubious, their status is enhanced with the passing of time.

An old British six-pounder cannon in Ballina was believed locally to be the famous cannon manned by Gunner Magee [McGee] at Ballinamuck though, as the Mayo journalist-historian Terry Reilly soberly commented: "the history of the cannon and how it came to be with the French at Ballinamuck is open to interpretation." The cannon had been mounted at Palmerstown House by Killala Bay until it was acquired by a local schoolteacher (Hugh Nolan of the Ballina Vocational School). After passing through the hands of a local garage owner (Jack White), it was finally owned by another resident of Ballina (Jack McHale of Clare Street), who gave it on loan in 1983 to the Ballinamuck Community Association for a local commemorative event. The cannon was received enthusiastically by the people of Ballinamuck and consequently was donated to them in 1985.[37] It was placed on permanent display in the center of the village, next to the Ninety-Eight monument, even though skeptical local historians questioned the validity of the cannon's association with Gunner Magee.[38] Shortly after the cannon's relocation, a group from the North Mayo History Society borrowed what was believed to be a French cannonball from 1798 kept by Mrs. Melvin, the proprietor of Ballybrooney House (four kilometers south of Killala), and brought it over to Ballinamuck to test the compatibility of the two relics.[39] Although the caliber did not match, popular opinion did not dismiss the cannon's credentials, and the gun became part of Ballinamuck's Ninety-Eight folk-history heritage.

The social scientist Alan Radley argued that artifacts, which are functional, concrete and apparently trivial, "play a central role in the memories of cultures and individuals." Outliving their makers and original owners, they become "indices of the past" and facilitate remembrance by providing tangible evidence that is open to interpretation.[40] Artifacts are not only *aides-mémoire*—mnemonic devices that evoke recollections—but also portable *lieux de mémoire*—symbolic entities that represent constructions of social memory. A pupil from Cloonagher in county Longford (thirteen kilometers southwest of

FIGURE 20. "The Cannon used by Gunner McGee at the Battle of Ballinamuck in 1798," Ballinamuck, county Longford. Although there is no evidence that this was indeed the artillery piece manned by the legendary folk hero Gunner James Magee [McGee], the British six-pounder donated in 1985 by Jack McHale of Ballina to the Ballinamuck Community Association was placed beside the 1798 pikeman monument. Photo by the author.

Ballinamuck) was told by her sixty-six-year-old grandfather that he kept as "an emblem of Ballinamuck" a long musket barrel (with a bayonet attached to it), which he found on the battlefield of Ballinamuck. He apparently had mixed feelings for this souvenir and, "for some reason" buried it for a few years. But after he accidentally rediscovered the barrel when plowing, he resolved this time to preserve it, declaring that "he would not like to see anything happen to it." Another resident of Cloonagher (George Woods) uncovered a similar rifle barrel beside the remains of soldier and kept it at home.[41] In an entry on "emblems and objects of value," a pupil from Inishcrone in county Sligo (across the bay from Killala), reported how her father acquired a French anchor found by fishermen in Killala Bay and treasured it for "the past forty years."[42] As Radley pointed out, symbolic artifacts can invoke national myths.[43] Though serving as a private medium of remembrance, relics of Ninety-Eight located folk history within regional historical narratives. Concurrently, rituals of national commemoration influenced attitudes toward these relics. The "French anchor," like some of the 1798 weapons around Ballinamuck and Mayo, was found in 1898. The date is indicative of the influence of centennial commemorations (see chapter 14).

Specifically manufactured commemorative souvenirs were sold and widely circulated during the centennial year.[44] In 1898 the Belfast jewelers Whiteman and Co. ran a series of advertisements in the local press announcing the sale of Erin-go-Bragh brooches and '98 centenary pins (in a range of gold and silver).[45] The profitable sales of fabricated souvenirs encouraged local communities to recognize the value of what they perceived as authentic relics from the time of the Rebellion, and consequently relics in private possession surfaced and received wider recognition at times of public commemoration. In 1948, at the sesquicentennial commemoration celebrations in Castlebar, an assortment of Ninety-Eight souvenirs was presented to the Castlebar commemoration committee. These included a wooden cross, two period artillery field pieces with cannonballs, a bayonet, a pike-head, and "Humbert's Flag."[46] This list of items reflects the variety of material culture preserved by devotees of folk history, which, among other things, included relics invested with folk belief and also erroneously labeled historical artifacts. The cross was one of the commemorative relics carved thirty years earlier from the tree on which the local hero Fr. Conroy of Addergoole was hanged (see chapters 9 and 12). The heavy armament could not be definitely dated to 1798 and the pike head, which is currently in the possession of St. Patrick Boys N.S. in Castlebar (where it is displayed alongside a period pistol), is marked "D. Sargent" and is not a rebel weapon but a half pike used by a British army "color sergeant" (a noncommissioned officer responsible for protecting the unit's colors).[47] The flag is currently held at Westport House, where it is displayed in a bog oak frame made in 1928 and labeled with a caption:

> This standard was made in France by order of the *Directoire* in 1798 and was presented by General Humbert at Killala, in August 1798, to the Mayo Legion when he raised that force. When the French surrendered in September 1798, the Mayo Legion was disbanded and this standard was handed over to the Earl of Altamont who, as the Lord Lieutenant of the county Mayo, was the representative of Great Britain and Ireland. It has remained in the family ever since.

According to the guides in the house, local tradition recalls that dedicated French women sewed the flag in preparation for the expedition to Ireland. However, this small green pennant, which sports the title "The Mayo Legion" and professes in its Latin motto allegiance to King and Country (*Pro Rege Saepe, Pro Patria Semper*) evidently belonged to the local volunteer corps commanded by Lord Altamont and not to a French republican army unit.[48] Social memory invested souvenirs with an authority that was clearly not grounded in reliable historical claims (in a positivist sense) but based primarily on belief and imagination.

In absence of official memorials, revered souvenirs could serve as vernacular monuments, which facilitated traditions of popular commemoration. A

FIGURE 21. Humbert's Stone in Kilcummin, county Mayo. Believed to be the first stone on which General Humbert set foot upon landing, it was relocated at the time of the 1798 centennial and appropriated by a local publican who hoped to cash in on its status as a folk monument. Photo by the author.

prime example of how an artifact became a medium of folk commemoration is the case of "Humbert's Stone" in Kilcummin, county Mayo. It was remembered locally that the invaders landed at Clogher [Clocher], some eight hundred meters southeast of Kilcummin Head (also known as Benwee).[49] This was acknowledged on the original Ordnance Survey map, which marked the site with the caption "French landed in 1798." Local tradition distinguished between two stages in the landing, with a vanguard under Humbert coming ashore at a site locally known as *Béal a' Dá Chnuic* (the Mouth of the Two Hills) and the rest of the expeditionary force disembarking at *Leac a' Bháid* (the Flat Shore-Rock of the Boat).[50] In 1938 a seventy-eight-year-old woman in the adjacent townland of Banagher (two kilometers south of Kilcummin) recounted:

> General Humbert was French and the first stone he left his foot on when coming ashore, can be seen to day in Banagher where the Robinsons once lived. It was brought there by Peter Nealon who afterwards owned the place, and it was at once intended to send it to Dublin to be used as a base for Parnell's statue. The stone was pointed out by Walter Coultry, who said his grandfather showed it to him as the first stone Humbert left his foot on when coming ashore. A writing to testify to the above is held in Banagher still by Mrs. Loftus. The stone is of a considerable weight and was brought by a horse and float, across a green field, below Saint Cummin's Well, and afterwards brought to Banagher on a cart.[51]

Forty years earlier, when an English lady of Irish descent visited Killala in 1897 and asked to see sights associated with the Rebellion, she was taken to the shore where the stone was still in its original location. At the time, it was anticipated that in the following centennial year many visitors would flock to the site.[52] By 1903 however, as the folk historian Michael Timoney observed, the stone had been removed and was in the possession of the Nealon [Ó Nialáin] family.[53]

It follows that Humbert's Stone was rediscovered, or—to use a term borrowed from the medieval cult of relics—"invented" (*inventio*),[54] at the turn of the nineteenth century. It was identified on the basis of oral tradition through a chain of transmission that could allegedly be traced back to the original historical event, though mention of a written certificate suggests that oral testimony was not considered sufficient to authenticate the relic. With considerable effort it was then transported, or to use again the medieval terminology—"translated" (*translat-*; also *transferre*), from its original place. The timing of the resurgence of interest in the stone suggests that it was a folk reflex to the centenary celebrations in 1898, when nationalists erected monuments to Ninety-Eight around Ireland. Though seemingly a spontaneous initiative, it may have been driven by commercial interest. It was later recalled that the local resident who moved the relic, a local publican named Nealon, appropriated the stone because he assumed that he could gain profit by offering it to the Ballina Ninety-Eight centenary club for their commemorative celebration.[55] Nealon ultimately placed the stone outside his licensed premises, apparently with the intention of benefiting from the relic's reputation by turning it into a local heritage attraction.[56] When Hayes was shown the celebrated stone in 1935, he commented on its commemorative importance as a monument of the French landing but expressed regret that "some more fitting memorial should not mark the spot."[57] Just over a decade later, during the Ninety-Eight sesquicentennial commemorations in 1948, a busload of people from Ballina, who came to attend the celebrations in Killala, went on to Kilcummin to visit Humbert's Stone in a pilgrimage that consolidated the commemorative status of the relic.[58]

Curiously, local tradition recalled an association between the relocation of the stone and the dedication of the Dublin monument in honor of the preeminent late-nineteenth-century nationalist leader Charles Stewart Parnell (1899).[59] This reference, made in passing, is in itself symptomatic of a popular attitude at the time of the Ninety-Eight centenary, which maintained that "when monuments could not be placed on sacred spots, parts of sacred spots could sometimes be brought to monuments, and a symbolic link forged in the process."[60] Foundation stones for several Ninety-Eight monuments were brought over from sites of historical relevance including the intended Wolfe Tone monument in Dublin (from McArt's Fort in Cave Hill outside Belfast), Enniscorthy (from Vinegar Hill), Wexford (from Three Rocks), and New Ross (from "Three Bullet Gate"). The actual foundation stone of Parnell's statue was quarried on land belonging to his family in county Wicklow.[61] The unveiling of Parnell's monument (1911) concluded a concentrated period of nationalist statue building. In the area of Kilcummin, Humbert's Stone was evidently considered a sacred relic within the larger framework of nationalist interpretations of the 1798 Rebellion and, as such, was perceived locally to be worthy of being enshrined in a memorial dedicated to a revered national icon, even though it bore no relevance to Parnell.

A Connemara tradition recalled a fugitive from Wexford who referred sentimentally to his gun as "mo chomrádaidhe bocht" (my poor comrade).[62] Mementos from the Rebellion were surreptitiously cherished by the participants and bequeathed to their heirs. They subsequently served as a medium of remembrance for deceased loved ones. An American folklorist observed in a different context that "because mementos tend to signify particular events, people, and experiences, they are more highly focused stimuli for reminiscence."[63] A stocking with a bullet hole in it, which had belonged to a Mayo rebel named Gill-Walsh of Crossmolina, who was shot in the ankle when attempting to escape captivity, was known to have been kept by a local woman (Biddy Flynn) until she died.[64] A family in the parish of Dromard in county Longford held on to an apron stained in 1798 with the blood of a young child, who was shot dead by Cavan Orangemen returning from Ballinamuck. By preserving the apron over several generations, private-maternal grief developed into a tradition of family remembrance.[65]

In 1935 an old woman in the outskirts of Ballina repeated the account of her grandfather, who had witnessing the passing of the French vanguard through the neighborhood:

> And the children pulled at the shiny buttons in the sogers' [dialect: soldiers] coats and began crying to get them. The sogers with their bayonets cut off the buttons and gave them to the children. And the buttons were kept in some of the houses here till a few years ago, but I haven't seen one now for a long time.[66]

There are several other known instances of French buttons preserved as souvenirs. In 1876 brass tunic buttons were dug up on French Hill in Castlebar and kept by the Daly family as relics of Ninety-Eight.[67] Several decades later, sometime in the early twentieth century, "buttons of the French uniforms" were dug up on the eastern side of Lough Gowna at Derrycassan near Granard in county Longford.[68] Such buttons served as mementoes of the local encounter with the French. Some of them were later lost; others were given as treasured keepsakes to relatives that chose to immigrate to the United States.[69]

Perhaps the most peculiar Ninety-Eight souvenirs were commemorative horses. The most famous of these had supposedly belonged to the rebel commander General George Blake of Garracloon, whose servant Patrick Nevin allegedly failed to deliver a horse to an appointed place in Ballinamuck.[70] According to one account, this "Frenchman's horse" was stolen by Protestants from Drumkeeran in county Leitrim and kept by a local loyalist family (Porteous). The horse's fame spread throughout the locality, and he was even exhibited in Dublin. Although crippled and hobbling in his latter years, the family provocatively held on to this symbolic trophy of loyalist commemoration until its death. Perhaps in response to the triumphalist parading of the horse, a violent act of reprisal was directed against another local family (Dorsy) associated with the loss of the horse.[71] Indeed, in Ireland's polarized society one community's trophy represents defeat and maltreatment for another community. Such resentment is subtly worked into another version of this tradition in which General Blake's mare frustrated the family of the yeoman who were its new unlawful owners (identified this time as the

Pattersons) by displaying animosity toward "redcoats" and charging women who happened to wear a red cloak.[72] Despite the peculiarity of this narrative, by the 1960s recollections of the theft of General Blake's horse had become obscure.[73]

Writing some forty years after the Rebellion, Otway recalled popular responses to the widespread plunder of horses by the forces of the Crown: "When, however, matters were subsided into peace, many who lost their horses and had information of where they were to be had, took short and not very legal ways to get back what they considered their own."[74] It was recalled in Sligo that a woman (Mrs. Lougheed of Rockbrook House) near Coola (eight kilometers southeast of Collooney) preserved for fifteen years the "gallant grey" of the United Irishman Bartholomew Teeling. According to local tradition, she coaxed the soldier who seized the horse after Teeling's capture at Ballinamuck to leave her the animal by warning him that parading the horse of the beloved local hero would set him up as a target of violent retribution.[75] In another version, the story was adapted to a familiar folklore narrative whereby the protagonist ("a woman from around Riverstown") outwitted the soldier by exchanging the fine horse for her old nag.[76] In a Mayo tradition of a stolen "souvenir horse," members of the Jordan family of Derryhillagh (three kilometers north of Newport) who joined the rebel army had a row with a cavalry officer in Castlebar, whom they killed. They allegedly took his horse back home with them. and as recently as the 1980s, their descendant Tommy Jordan could point out the place where the horse took shelter in times of bad weather.[77] Other Ninety-Eight arenas also had traditions of commemorative horses. For example, traditions in county Meath told of a horse fondly known as "the Croppy Boy," which had supposedly belonged to the local heroine Molly West.[78] This fascination with "souvenir horses" hints at a larger context in which relics of 1798 were located—the early-nineteenth-century popular interest throughout the British Isles in souvenirs of the Republican and Napoleonic Wars (and in particular relics of the Battle of Waterloo).[79] Marengo, Napoleon Bonaparte's famous horse, stirred a sensation when displayed publicly in London in 1823, and commemorative snuffboxes were later made from his hooves (1832).[80]

Not all loyalist mementos were exhibited. Gentry preserved historical souvenirs of 1798, which were mostly kept away from the view of the general public. Once property changed ownership, such private items were offhandedly misplaced or sold and, in absence of records, were often lost. Sometime around 1908, a mahogany box with a silver plate that bore the inscription "Presented by General Humbert and the officers of the troops of the French Republic to the

Lord Bishop of Killala, in remembrance of his kindness to them when confined in his palace as prisoners of war on parole, 1798" was sold in an auction in county Cork. Like many other relics from 1798, the subsequent whereabouts of this relic are unknown.[81]

Souvenirs of Ninety-Eight were often produced as evidence to confirm local folk-history narratives. The discovery of artifacts attributed to 1798 in locations associated with the memory of the Rebellion appeared to validate the authenticity of the vernacular landscape of the Year of the French. As in the case of the landscape, interpretation of relics required a familiarity with local traditions. Objects do not intrinsically retain memory. Rather, memory was generated through the meaning and interpretations that were attached to objects. Therefore, the folklore associated with relics, and not the relics themselves, functioned as a medium of remembrance. Edward Shils maintained that "the inherent durability of material objects . . . enables the past to live into the present."[82] Despite their apparent durability, material objects do not survive through time intact. They are subject to erosion and eventually cease to physically exist, while changes in appearance affect the ways in which they are perceived.[83] Social memory can secure an afterlife for artifacts that are still recollected in oral tradition even when they are no longer present. Relics prove to be a most appropriate source for an *archaeology* of social memory (a concept outlined in my conclusion). The historian Stuart Semmel observed:

> The relic is fragmentary by its very nature; if not actually (as so often) an incomplete scrap, then fragmentary in the sense that, in representing a historical or mythic scene, it holds within itself the synecdochic capacity of articulating a much fuller tableau. The de-articulation and decomposition that are detected in the relic can themselves, moreover, serve as subjects for meditation.[84]

The study of the folklore of souvenirs can reveal some of the mechanisms of popular remembrance, while a reconstruction of the history and social function of relics can expose influences of official commemoration on practices of folk commemoration. In order to understand the nature of these influences it is necessary to examine high profile commemorative ceremonies, which reached their zenith during the centenary of the 1798 Rebellion.

14

Ceremonies, Monuments, and Negotiations of Memory

Sure we give processions in honour of the dead who died for
Ireland as freely as Mr. Carnegie gives out libraries.

D. P. Moran
in the *Leader*, 3 October 1903

T HE PROPRIETOR OF Daly's Bar in Mulrany in west county Mayo (by the
gateway to Achill Island) keeps two treasured souvenirs from the Year of
the French: a coin and a bayonet that were found in remarkable circumstances
in which his great-grandfather, James Daly, had been involved.[1] Back in 1876
Castlebar residents formed a committee to erect a monument on French Hill,
a Ninety-Eight place-name outside the town. Folk history recalled that in 1798
a party of Lord Roden's cavalry killed four French dragoons there, and the precise location where locals had buried the soldiers was identified in oral tradition
over several generations. When preparing the ground for the monument's
foundations, the site of the "French Grave" was excavated and the remains of
corpses still clothed in fading blue uniform were allegedly discovered, but once
exposed to daylight and fresh air, the cloth crumbled. Several artifacts were
found, including brass tunic buttons, a bayonet, and three eighteenth-century
silver coins; James Daly, a key member of the committee,[2] assumed custody of
these items.[3] Several months later, the monument was unveiled (July 1876), and
the site of memory became a locus for provincial commemorations in 1898,
1948, 1953, and 1998. The commemorative spheres and mediums of history-
telling, vernacular landscape, souvenirs, monuments, and ceremonies con-
verged in facilitating public commemoration of Ninety-Eight, which evidently
began before the centennial.

The Centennial of Ninety-Eight

In the nineteenth century, a wave of "statuemania" (*statuomanie*), to use a term coined by Maurice Agulhon,[4] engulfed Europe and America.[5] Statues were ubiquitously erected to honor iconic representations of nations and patriotic heroes, whose memory was also fêted in countless ceremonies that were steeped in commemorative rituals. The Irish manifestation of a nationalist culture of commemoration emerged in competition with imperial and Ascendancy-unionist public sculpture.[6] It commenced with the unveiling of monuments for "the Liberator" Daniel O'Connell in Limerick (1857) and Ennis, county Clare (1865).[7] Fundraising for an O'Connell monument on Sackville Street (currently O'Connell Street) in Dublin began in 1862. Eighteen years after the foundation stone was laid, the impressive statue was unveiled in 1882 at a ceremony reputedly attended by half a million people, probably the century's largest gathering in the city.[8] Unveiled in 1870 the Dublin statue of William Smith O'Brien, the leader of the failed Young Ireland insurrection in 1848, was the first memorial associated with violent resistance to British rule.[9] Other early nationalist monuments honored the patriotic orator Henry Grattan in Dublin (1880), and the Jacobite general Patrick Sarsfield in Limerick (1881), while numerous memorials throughout Ireland paid tribute to the "Manchester Martyrs"—William Philip Allen, Michael Larkin, and Michael O'Brien (three Fenians executed on 23 November 1867).[10] Like in other European countries,

FIGURE 22. Bayonet and coin found on French Hill (1876). The French bayonet and coin were discovered in 1876 alongside other French military artifacts in a grave on French Hill and are currently held at Daly's Bar in Mulrany, county Mayo. The five-franc coin minted in Year 6 of the French Republic (1798) and inscribed "Union et Force" was worn as a medallion by James Daly at an inaugural centennial event on French Hill, outside Castlebar, county Mayo (9 January 1898). Photo by the author. Displayed courtesy of John Daly.

rituals of commemorative demonstrations were also formulated in mass funeral processions for distinguished nationalists, whose coffins were paraded through the streets of Dublin to Glasnevin cemetery.[11] The most spectacular of these was the meticulously orchestrated funerary procession of Charles Stewart Parnell (11 October 1891), which was attended by over 100,000 spectators, and subsequently the death of "The Chief" was commemorated annually on "Ivy Day" (6 October).[12]

Nationalist commemoration reached its apex in the centennial celebrations of the 1798 Rebellion, which were planned as a separatist counterdemonstration to Queen Victoria's Diamond Jubilee (1897). On the face of it, the centennial of Ninety-Eight appears to show all the trappings of what Hobsbawm labeled mass-produced "invention of tradition." Yet the impression of top-down manipulation of popular culture "largely undertaken by institutions with political purposes in mind"[13] is predicated on an unawareness of provincial grassroots agency and its reliance on folk history. The reality was more complicated, since there were contestations both in the metropolitan and provincial arenas in which commemorative ceremonies were organized.

The promoters of commemoration were not unified, and aspirations to control the national centennial program proved to be highly contentious. In a bid for primacy, the Irish Republican Brotherhood (IRB) established a committee to organize centennial celebrations and appointed the veteran Fenian John O'Leary (1830–1907) president and Fred Allen, the IRB Supreme Council's secretary, as coordinator of events. Rival nationalist factions formed competing committees, and in its initial stages, centennial organization was driven by squabbling and political intrigue. Only halfway through the centennial, in May 1898, was an amalgamated committee finally formed.[14] Republicans, home-rulers, socialists, Irish language revivalists, Catholic devotees and Gaelic sports enthusiasts consented to share a platform.[15] This ad hoc cooperation between the various camps of Irish nationalism served to heal some of the divisions left by the "Parnell split," which had shattered the broad coalition supporting the Home Rule movement several years earlier (1890–91). It has been argued that the centennial signaled the rise to prominence of a militant "New Nationalism,"[16] but this claim has been challenged.[17] Nevertheless, the radical Cumann na nGaedheal movement (a precursor of Sinn Féin) was launched two years later, and its ideology was promoted in the pages of the weekly *United Irishman* (founded in 1899). Like its precursor the Belfast monthly *Shan Van Vocht*, the newspaper's editor, prominent politician Arthur Griffith (1871–1922), deliberately chose a title that evoked the memory of 1798, while also paying tribute to one of his role models—the Young Irelander John Mitchel, who fifty years earlier had remembered Ninety-Eight by choosing that very name for a separatist newspaper.[18]

Central centennial organizations extended their influence around Ireland through centennial clubs chaired by local prominent nationalists. Shortly after the original centennial committee elected its executive in Dublin City Hall (4 March 1897),[19] a statement was circulated in the provincial press:

> It is desirable [that] Local Committees shall be formed in very town and parish in Ireland, and in every district out of Ireland where Irishmen are resident; and we call upon our countrymen in sympathy with the Centenary movement to take the necessary steps for the purpose of establishing such committees.[20]

This initiative was received enthusiastically, and it is therefore tempting to interpret the centennial as a "spider's web" extending from the political centers out to the peripheries. But ground-level commemoration deserves closer attention, as it did not simply replicate a pre-determined national agenda.

A month after the Dublin call was issued, nationalists in Mayo formed the "Castlebar Central and Barony of Carra '98 Centenary Association" (27 May 1897) and initiated the establishment of Ninety-Eight committees throughout Connacht.[21] By the end of December 1897, police reports counted nine such committees in the province, including one in East Galway (30 members), two in West Galway (100 members), three in Mayo (295 members) and three in Sligo (47 members).[22] Additional clubs were formed during the centennial year, and membership rapidly increased. Once founded, the committees immediately commenced activities, meeting regularly to plan events for the centennial celebration.[23] In the West, there was a strong connection between commemoration and popular political organization on agrarian issues. This was particularly apparent in Mayo, which at the time was "the cauldron in which a major land agitation was brewed."[24]

The essay "Who Fears to Speak of '98?" by the nationalist politician William O'Brien (1852–1928), who was resident in Mayo since 1895, was widely distributed as a penny pamphlet.[25] The disillusionment with parliamentary politics expressed in the text reflected the mind-set behind the foundation of the United Irish League (UIL) at Westport in county Mayo (January 1898). Though it was an agrarian organization dedicated to upholding the rights of smallholders, its name explicitly commemorated the rebels of 1798 and O'Brien committed its support to the centennial.[26] Contemporary newspaper accounts show a direct correlation between the founding of UIL branches in Connacht and the organization of Ninety-Eight commemorations.[27] Under the presidency of the energetic nationalist labor leader Michael Davitt (1846–1906), in the years following the centennial the UIL rapidly gathered popular support spreading its power base from Mayo throughout Connacht.[28] According to police reports, by 1901 it boasted 1,150 branches with 121,443 members nationwide, of which 44,919 were in Connacht (301 branches).[29]

Former leaders of local agrarian protest movements assumed key roles in centennial commemoration. James Daly (1838–1910), who in his lifetime was noted for his "inexhaustible fund of knowledge of the people"[30] and has since been described by the historian Joe Lee as "the most undeservedly forgotten man in Irish history," was appointed president of the Connaught '98 Centenary Council.[31] Daly was a central figure in Connacht tenant rights agitation, having twenty years earlier co-founded with Davitt the Land League of Mayo (1879), which developed under the presidency of Parnell into the immensely influential Irish National Land League.[32] He was also the editor and former proprietor of the provincial newspaper the *Connaught Telegraph*, which was instrumental in promoting the Land League's activities.[33] The chairman of the centennial program in Ballinamuck was the parish priest Fr. Thomas Conefry (1837–1917), who had been pivotal in Land War agitation in county Longford nearly two decades earlier (1881).[34] In general, the key players behind provincial

Inauguration du monument du général Humbert à Ballina, en Irlande. — [Voir l'article, page 341.]

FIGURE 23. Unveiling of the 1798 centennial monument in Ballina, county Mayo (engraving by Charaire and published in *l'illustration journal universel*, 27 May 1899). Construction was completed within nine months of the dedication ceremony marking the centenary of the French landing (21 August 1898) at which the monument's foundation stone was laid in the presence of Maud Gonne. Courtesy of the National Library of Ireland.

FIGURE 24. 1798 centennial monument in Ballina, county Mayo (unveiled 1899). Although widely referred to as the "General Humbert monument," the predominantly republican local '98 centennial committee opted for a statue of Erin armed with a sword (alongside the familiar harp and wolfhound) and standing triumphantly above two flags perched on pikes. Urban development later necessitated its relocation. Photo by the author.

commemoration were local dignitaries, many of them Poor Law Guardians, town commissioners, and county councilors, whose popular mandate stemmed from their local activism and not from a Dublin committee.

The national highlight of the centennial was the great celebration in Dublin on 15 August 1898, which was attended by an estimated 100,000 people. A procession culminated in a punctiliously staged ceremony at the top of Grafton Street, where John O'Leary dedicated the foundation stone of a proposed monument for Wolfe Tone. The fifth section of the pageant was composed of representatives from the centennial clubs of Connacht, including Galway, Castlebar, Sligo, and Balinasloe.[35] Ceremonies in Connacht and the north midlands followed over the next few weeks. On 21 August the foundation stone was ceremoniously laid for a statue in Ballina, which was commonly referred to as the "General Humbert monument" although it was actually cast in the form of Erin (the female representation of Ireland). A week later a ceremony took place at French Hill near Castlebar (28 August). The following week a ceremony was held in Ballinamuck (4 September), and the "Bartholomew Teeling Monument" was dedicated outside Collooney (5 September). This sequence of events might give the mistaken impression that Dublin set the tone and local commemorations followed suit.

However, the major ceremonies in the late summer of 1898 were preceded by numerous spontaneous local centennial events, which had generated interest and excitement. At the beginning of the year, it was reported that 10,000 people from around Mayo attended an inaugural commemorative ceremony in Castlebar (9 January 1898). This "national demonstration," which had been planned for several months in advance,[36] anticipated many of the features of the Castlebar ceremony in August: it took place on French Hill; James Daly presided over the ceremony; the celebrity guest was the colorful revolutionary activist Maud Gonne (1866–1953), and among the honorary speakers was the poet, journalist, and language revival enthusiast William Rooney (1873–1901); the day's proceedings enjoyed a festive atmosphere thanks to the playing of patriotic songs by fife and drum bands from around Mayo.[37]

On New Year's Eve, midnight celebrations to usher in the centennial were held in Sligo town and nearby Ballymote.[38] January also featured a "Great Meeting" at Collooney where, despite bad weather, thousands of nationalists assembled from all over county Sligo.[39] In March 1898 a "Monster Public Meeting" was organized in Ballina to which numerous dignitaries were invited, and participants arrived from Mayo and Sligo.[40] On the night of 23 May 1898, torchlight processions were held and bonfires were lit at various locations throughout county Sligo, with a particularly large bonfire on "Gunner's Hill" at Collooney (a site associated with the bravery of Bartholomew Teeling).[41] This popular act of commemoration, reminiscent of the signal fires that had been lit on hills in Wexford to mark the outbreak of the Rebellion (26 May 1798) and of the bonfires that were lit in Mayo to celebrate the Franco-Irish victory at Castlebar (27 August 1798),[42] drew on popular familiarity with the annual folk ritual of lighting midsummer bonfires on 23 June to celebrate St. John's Eve (*oíche an teine chnáimh* or *teine fhéile' Eóin*).[43]

Similarly, a series of events in the area of Ballinamuck lead up to the major centennial ceremony in the village. In February 1898 a crowd headed by the Longford Fife and Drum Band marched to the site of the battlefield and heard an oration by Fr. Conefry. In June the local bishop Dr. Hoare brought boys from St. Mel's College in Longford to the battle site, and on 7 August a thousand Leitrim residents from the villages of Cloone, Carrigallen, and Aughavas, led by fifes and drums, visited the Croppies' Graves.[44] Overall, the proliferation of local celebrations shows that in practice the centennial was an accumulation of grassroots events, which culminated in large-scale official ceremonies.

Commemorative celebrations were organized despite the bitter political rifts and acrimonious arguments within local Ninety-Eight committees, which were indicative of the fervent temperament of contemporary nationalist politics. The founding members of the umbrella committee for the province of Connacht had unanimously agreed that "this Irish movement must be non-sectarian, non political (from the standpoint of the wretched politics of to-day) and altogether aloof from the paltriness of modern 'isms.'"[45] Local committees throughout the province echoed this lofty sentiment. The Claremorris '98 Club, for example, professed at its foundation meeting the aspiration that

> no partisan or illiberal spirit shall be observed in the centennial celebrations this year, and that all Irishmen, no matter of what shades of national opinion to

whom the memories of '98 are a common heritage shall be welcomed to participate in the control and guidance of the celebrations, as only a spirit foreign to
the Celtic nature could suggest any attempt to invest with secure prejudices a
movement so eminently calculated to obliterate them.[46]

Differences and rivalries, however, were soon distinguishable in the political
composition of local committees.

The Ballina '98 Club, whose militant chairman vehemently proclaimed that
the commemoration honored "men whose life blood sprinkled our streets and
whose bodies dangled from the tree stumps along the roadside,"[47] was dominated by republicans, who adamantly rejected constitutionalist and clerical
involvement.[48] In contrast, Castlebar hosted prominent parliamentarian dignitaries. Foremost among them were John Dillon (whose father, the Young Irelander John Blake Dillon, was born and raised in Ballaghaderreen, on the border of Mayo and Roscommon) and William O'Brien, who took the opportunity
to promote agrarian issues by protesting against a local eviction.[49] Infighting
was covered up in reportage, which only alluded to it in passing. When describing the formation of the Longford '98 Centenary Celebration Association, a
local newspaper tactfully noted that it was a "noisy meeting" in which "some
rough expressions were hurled."[50]

Provincial centennial celebrations left a strong impression, which was
amplified in nationalist newspapers. Coverage of commemorations in the local
and national press was colored by the characteristic hyperbole of centennial
rhetoric. Each event was described as "magnificent" and "memorable," and
was predictably deemed to be one of the largest and most successful public
demonstrations ever to take place in the locality, in the region, or even in the
whole of Ireland. Reporting on the ceremonies in Mayo, the *Connaught Telegraph* noted: "Not on any occasion for many years past has such a vast assemblage of people been seen in Ballina."[51] An event at Castlebar was compared
to the great gatherings of the mass movement to repeal the Act of Union in the
pre-Famine era, which were still recalled in living memory:

> It was undoubtedly the most grandly superb display that has been witnessed in
> Castlebar for fully a half century, and many persons, whose memory extends
> over that lengthy period, have assured us that it was not very much inferior in
> dimensions to the great monster meeting which in the middle of the Forties
> gathered round O'Connell on that same eminence of French Hill.[52]

The nationalist press had an invested interest in magnifying the centennial so
that it is difficult to estimate the actual numbers of participation. Just as the editor of the *Connaught Telegraph* was personally involved in organizing com-

memoration, other local papers were also committed to applaud the success of the events. Nonetheless, it appears that provincial centennial celebrations indeed enjoyed mass-popular attendance, drawing people from beyond the immediate locality.

As Timothy O'Keefe observed, "the actual historical events commemorated received a wide variety of interpretations from orators, pamphleteers and propagandists."[53] Republicans commemorated United Irish leaders and centered their attention in particular on the remembrance of Wolfe Tone. Starting in 1891, Tone's grave at Bodenstown in county Kildare was the locus for IRB annual commemorations that built-up toward a centennial ceremony in June 1898.[54] In the beginning of 1898 the republican-dominated centennial Executive Council and local centennial clubs organized a pilgrimage to the grave of the eminent historian Richard Robert Madden, in the suburb of Donnybrook in Dublin.[55] Madden's *The United Irishmen,* originally issued in three series and seven volumes (1842–46) that were later followed by a "second edition" of an additional four volumes (1857–60),[56] was considered a canonical centennial text, though by the 1890s it had become a collector's item and was out of print.[57] At the time, the predominant historical interpretation of 1798 was formulated in Fr. Patrick Kavanagh's immensely successful *A Popular History of the Insurrection of 1798* (first published as *The Wexford Rebellion* in 1870).[58] A centennial fourth edition issued in 1898 received acclamation in the nationalist press.[59] Focusing on Wexford, this book portrayed the Rebellion as a Catholic insurrection and downplayed the role of the United Irishmen, who were presented as a susceptible and even corrupt secret society. This "Faith and Fatherland" approach put forward a polemic that fuelled the conflict between Catholic nationalism and revolutionary Fenianism.

These ideological tensions are visible in the choice of centennial commemorative representation, with statues of the Wexford rebel priest hero Fr. Murphy competing against secular images of lone pikemen.[60] Though conflicting historical interpretations determined the design of Ninety-Eight monuments,[61] across the board there was a shared imagery. The rich ritual of the ceremonies and figurative detail of the monuments projected a cultural nationalism that combined influences of popular Catholic rites together with militaristic symbolism, which reappeared in the defiant rhetoric of ceremonial speeches and the exultant newspaper coverage of commemorative demonstrations.[62]

Centennial ceremonies were an elaborate undertaking that required months of planning and organization. In general, erection of monuments was marked by two ceremonies: first a dedication to lay the foundation stone and finally an unveiling of the completed statue. The extent of the interval between these events depended on the commitment and resourcefulness of the sponsors. The centennial monuments in Connacht were constructed within a remarkably short period. Dedicated in the end of the summer of the centennial, they were unveiled within a year. The Ballina statue was already completed by May 1899.[63] The location of centennial monuments was carefully chosen. As a rule, in order to attain maximum exposure, central areas were preferred, though in some cases statues were later relocated in order to accommodate urban development.[64] For example, traffic of heavy vehicles required that the centennial monument in Ballina be moved from its original place to a less prominent location nearby. Because nationalist commemoration explicitly confronted unionist and loyalist public culture, the desire to cause a political provocation was also a primary factor in selecting a location.[65] Both these considerations could be countered by the intention to erect monuments in the proximity of the historical site.

The Sligo '98 club, in which the mayor of Sligo town P. A. McHugh, was "the leading spirit," argued that a memorial should be erected in the provincial center.[66] Even though the town of Sligo had not fallen to the Franco-Irish army and so had not been directly affected by the Rebellion, the committee that coordinated commemorations throughout the county endorsed this initiative. However, the president of the Collooney '98 Club, Fr. P. J. O'Grady, obstinately opposed this proposal and insisted that a monument should be inconveniently located on the outskirts of Collooney at the battlefield of Carricknagat.[67] The uncompromising rivalry between the two locations resulted in the erection of two centennial monuments in county Sligo. A foundation stone was laid in Sligo town in early October 1898[68] and the monument was unveiled eleven months later (3 September 1899).[69] Permission was granted to locate the Bartholomew Teeling monument on private property outside Collooney, and the landowner, Owen Phibbs of Seafield House, even contributed an entrance gate (see fig. 25).[70] Dedicated on 5 September 1898, at a "magnificent demonstration" sketched by the budding artist Jack Butler Yeats (1871–1957),[71] it was unveiled on 2 July 1899.[72] Although Fr. O'Grady was transferred to the diocese of Achonry prior to the unveiling, his contribution to the Teeling memorial was widely recognized in Collooney.[73] Local tradition maintains that the statue's features (which do not appear to match the portrait of Bartholomew Teeling) were modeled on Fr. O'Grady, who was commonly regarded as possessing a heroic countenance.[74] In this way the statue not only recalls the bravery of Teeling in 1798 but is also a subtle tribute to the dynamism of Fr. O'Grady in 1898. Indeed, it is often overlooked that monuments have a double commemorative function. They not only commemorate the historical subject but also pay homage to the organizers and sponsors of the commemoration, who are generally acknowledged on a plaque.

Memory of the French invasion was symbolically fortified through the prominent presence of French representatives at centennial ceremonies. Maud Gonne, who was a member of the London centennial organization chaired by W. B. Yeats,[75] had adopted France as her second homeland and had previously promoted relations between Irish and French nationalists by assisting in the editing of *La Patrie* and founding the journal *l'Irlande Libre* (1897). When attending commemoration ceremonies in Mayo, she assumed responsibility for entertaining the French delegations and liaising with the French press.[76] Gonne, who had corresponded with the Castlebar committee since its foundation in May 1897, was the main celebrity at the first commemoration event at French Hill (January 1898).[77] Invited to Ballina to give a public lecture on 12 March,[78] five months later she also attended the town's main centennial event and performed there what was described as an "interesting ceremony" at the center of the "enthusiastic proceedings" to dedicate the Ballina centennial monument.[79]

At the time, the nationalist press lauded Gonne as the Irish "Joan of Arc," an adulatory title that was enthusiastically adopted by Mayo newspapers.[80] Her visits to the locality left a strong and lasting impression. A reporter (using the pseudonym "A Boy from Connaught") listened in on a conversation of "country folk" from the area of Belcarra (seven kilometers southeast of Castlebar), and commented on the significance of Gonne's presence at the January demonstration, reproducing their dialogue:

FIGURE 25. 1798 centennial monument outside Collooney, county Sligo (unveiled 1899). Completed within ten months (dedicated on 5 September 1898 and unveiled on 2 July 1899), the statue of the United Irishman Bartholomew Teeling on Parker's Hill ("Gunner's Hill") commemorates the Battle of Carricknagat. Local tradition maintains that the portrait was modeled on the enthusiastic president of the Collooney '98 Club, Fr. P. J. O'Grady. Photo by Monsignor Joseph Spelman.

"Columbkilla's prophecy is comin' thrue at lasht."
"How do you mane?"
"He said Ireland would be freed by a woman and he was never wrong yet."
"Thrue, but wasn't it a red-haired woman he sed?"
"Yis" (a big pause). "But what kind of a color is it they call auburn, too?"
[*sic*][81]

On 22 August, Gonne visited the village of Kilcummin and unveiled a plaque at the pier "in order to commemorate the landing of my countrymen here one hundred years ago,"[82] which explicitly associating her with the French soldiers of 1798. Forty years later, a pupil from the area of Kilcummin who wrote an account of the landing based on family tradition mentioned Gonne's visit. By then, her French connection had achieved legendary proportions, and she was described as Humbert's granddaughter.[83]

Representing the Celtic Literary Society and the Gaelic League at ceremonies in Ballina and Castlebar, William Rooney delivered addresses in Irish. Rooney was considered to be "the Thomas Davis of the 1890s"[84] and his nationalist ballad writing was extremely influential in reshaping the social memory of 1798. His centennial ode "Ninety-Eight" devoted a stanza to Mayo:

Killala still her weary watch maintaining
Beside the ocean's boom
And Castlebar in faithful guard remaining
Around the Frenchmen's tomb.[85]

His highly popular ballad "The Men of the West" called attention specifically to the Rebellion in Connacht.[86] By the 1930s these compositions had filtered into the repertoire of folk ballads. An account written in 1938 by a Leitrim schoolteacher referred to the battle of Castlebar noting that "this victory is commemorated in the well known song by William Rooney" and quoted a verse. Though the poem derived from a literary source, the Irish Folklore Commission accepted the contribution without question.[87]

At the main ceremony in Castlebar, James Daly pointed out that the centennial was both about remembering dead patriots and undertaking to "abide by the principles of the men of '98 until their country was free again and took its place among the nations of the earth."[88] In staging popular representations of history, public commemorations are generally organized to serve two seemingly contradictory purposes: creating a sense of continuity with the past and changing the presentation of the past to suit the present.[89] Indeed, centennial programs in Connacht and the north midlands commandeered the memory of the "sufferings and sacrifices of the United Irish patriots, aided by the gallant soldiers of France" in order to promote a nationalist commitment to "resolve never to cease our efforts until the full and complete acknowledgement of Ireland's claim to be a nation."[90] Commemoration not only recalled 1798, but also reshaped the ways in which the events were remembered so that the centennial, which promoted historical revision, became an exercise in nationalist mass-politicization of historical consciousness. Once again, this was not simply imposed from above. On a local level, social memory nourished the content of centennial commemoration just as much it fed from it.

A striking example of reinterpretation is the reclaiming of the engagement near Collooney. Even though it had been an indecisive skirmish, which bore little consequence on the final outcome of the French campaign and in the aftermath of the Rebellion was even claimed as a victory for the Crown forces, the memory of the "Battle at Carricknagat" was reconstructed for the centennial as a major rebel triumph. This revision was promoted by newspaper articles, which described "a decisive victory for the United Irish and French forces."[91] The dedication of the Ninety-Eight monument on the battlefield was a significant event for the region[92] and was described in the provincial press as "the greatest popular demonstration ever witnessed in the West and one which will be remembered for many years to come."[93] Its importance was recognized by the national press, which reported that a "magnificent demonstration" had assembled "the largest gathering of people which had been seen in the West of Ireland for many years."[94]

A key promoter of this glorification was the nationalist politician and poet John O'Dowd of Bunninaddan (1856–1937), who at the time was Chairman of the Tubbercurry Board of Guardians and was later a Home Rule MP for South Sligo (1900–1918). O'Dowd, who had formerly been involved in the Land League and was currently active in the UIL, was an enthusiastic organizer of centennial celebrations throughout county Sligo. He addressed meetings in Ballymote, Tubbercurry, Collooney, and Sligo, and headed the subscription lists to raise funds for local Ninety-Eight monuments.[95] He also composed nationalist political poetry under the pseudonyms "Adonis" and "A Sligo Suspect," and was a regular contributor to the *Weekly News, Shamrock,* and the *Nation.*[96] In 1898 the provincial press published his poem the "Battle of Carricknagat," which encapsulated the new nationalist version of the battle:

A cheer for Ireland and for France,
    And one for Liberty!
No more the scarlet lines advance,
    They turn and break and flee.
They leave their wounded and their slain
    The battle plain upon—

> The Green in triumph waves again
> and Carricknagat is won.[97]

Forty years later, this composition was accepted as bona fide folklore when a pupil interviewed the poet and submitted the poem to the Schools' Scheme.[98]

The centennial interpretation was grounded on the story of a remarkable display of bravery by the Franco-Irish officer Bartholomew Teeling. He reputedly rode out and shot from close range with his pistol an artillery gunner named Whittier, silencing the cannon that had wreaked havoc on the rebel ranks. As a tribute to this act of valor, the centennial monument was purposely erected on Parker's Hill (nicknamed "Gunner's Hill"), where the cannon had been stationed. The statue depicts Teeling in uniform, triumphantly raising an arm and holding a flag at his side (see fig. 25). He is mounted on an obelisk pedestal, over seven and a half meters (twenty-five feet) in height and just under three square meters (nine feet six inches) at its base, which is perched on a rocky outcrop that further enhances its imposing appearance. All the same, the story of Teeling's bravery is apocryphal. Although he was a commissioned French officer (known as "Biron"), Teeling is not mentioned in French accounts of the engagement,[99] and the incident does not appear in his personal papers.[100] Contemporary loyalist accounts, which commend the conduct of a Captain Whistler of the Twenty-fourth Light Dragoons in checking the advance of the French, acknowledge the loss of artillery pieces but put this down to the death of transport horses.[101]

The nationalist interpretation, however, was not an entirely innovative creation. Rather than imposing a new narrative, nationalist commemoration was strengthening the voice of local tradition. The Collooney-born local historian Archdeacon Terence O'Rorke noted in 1889:

> Teeling's disposal of Whitters [the gunner] is almost the only incident of the engagement now remembered in the neighbourhood. Even the names of Vereker and Humbert have slipped from people's memories but Teeling and his famous grey are still as vivid in the traditions of the Ox mountains as they were in the morrow of Carricknagat.[102]

Thirty years after the Rebellion, the former United Irishman Charles Hamilton Teeling (1778–1850) wrote that his brother Bartholomew's "romantic courage and humanity" had "been alike conspicuous throughout the whole campaign and proverbial in every quarter of the province, where, to this hour, his memory is cherished and his fate lamented."[103] But this claim is exaggerated. Even though he appeared in traditions in his home area of Lisburn in county Antrim,[104] outside of county Sligo, Bartholomew Teeling's reputation was limited and memory of him was often muddled in Ballinamuck folk-lore.[105] Originally, oral traditions of his act of bravery were particular to the folk history of Collooney and only later spread through commemorative popular print.[106]

Organizers of centennial commemoration were arriving on a scene that carried strong oral traditions of the events of 1798. These indigenous voices had an impact on centennial clubs, where local politicians could not simply follow directions from the political center in Dublin without satisfying the demands of their constituency and endorsing folk history. Consequently, Hayes found that Ninety-Eight Clubs (particularly the clubs of Dromod in county Leitrim and Tobercurry in county Sligo) were a fruitful source for local folk history.[107] Rather than perceiving local politicians merely as agents who enforced hegemonic-nationalist culture, it proves more rewarding to consider their role as "cultural brokers" who mediated between provincial social memory, grounded in traditions of folk history, and a national agenda, which attempted to reshape collective memory through officially sanctioned commemorative ceremonies.[108]

A prime example is the case of James P. Farrell (1865–1921)—political activist, historian, journalist, and founder of the influential local newspaper the *Longford Leader* (1897). His grandfather (Robert Farrell) had been an insurgent leader in 1798,[109] and his profound knowledge of local folklore was exhibited in his history of county Longford, which included several references to traditions of Ninety-Eight in the area of Ballinamuck.[110] Later, as MP for county Longford, he was involved in organization of centennial commemoration. A founding member of the national centennial committee,[111] he brought to Dublin knowledge of local traditions and an awareness of their importance for his electorate.

The centennial celebrations generated new folklore and eventually entered into social memory as notable historical events in their own right. Although the dignitaries were mainly local, the main event at Ballinamuck (described contemporaneously as a "meeting" and subsequently referred to as a "monster meeting") attracted nationalists from the larger area of Leitrim, Cavan, and Longford.[112] Forty years later, the song "The Meeting of Ballinamuck" composed by a young local woman (Miss Byrne of Cornakelly) who attended the celebration before immigrating to America, was still remembered in the area.[113] It described the commemoration in 1898 rather than the 1798 Rebellion itself:

> I saw the flags of green and gold, unfurled to display
> The feelings of both young and old, assembled there that day,
> From far and near to celebrate, their bands and banners took,
> In memory of the ninety eights, who fought at Ballinamuck.[114]

One hundred years later, when performed at a bicentennial ceremony, the song reportedly struck a "poignant note."[115] Similarly, a song collected in 1937 about a centennial event in south Sligo ("The '98 Demonstration at Ballyrush") is written in a style that strongly echoes the rhetoric of the centennial celebrations and can be traced at least thirty years back.[116]

Altogether, it is difficult to assess the precise impact of the centennial on provincial social memory. In absence of amplification, the prolific oratory of public addresses did not reach many ears. Speeches however were reproduced and circulated by the press, and these texts were influential. In comparison to other theaters of 1798 commemoration (particularly county Wexford), Connacht traditions were less subject to overt politicization. Centennial organizations vigorously promoted popular education of patriotic history,[117] exposing nationalist sympathizers to historical reinterpretations. Among them were many schoolteachers and local folk historians, who were instrumental in collecting folklore several decades later. In addition, information derived from commemorative literature was integrated into folk history.

Positively tracing the spread of information into folklore may prove elusive, yet it is often evident and can occasionally even be pinpointed. For example, excerpts of a Ninety-Eight story published in the Cavan newspaper the *Anglo-Celt* shortly after the centennial were submitted forty years later to the Schools' Scheme in Balieborough, county Cavan, and accepted as folklore.[118] The impact of popular print and formal education on social memory is discussed in detail in following chapters, but the influence of nonverbal and nontextual sources is even more complicated to measure. Ceremonial ritual and creative use of symbols in the design of monuments clearly impressed the public and established new commemorative practices. Moreover, the official ceremonies at the French Hill monument outside Castlebar and the erection of centennial monuments in Ballina and Collooney acknowledged local experiences of Ninety-Eight, which were accepted as valuable components of a larger narrative of struggle for national liberation. The immediate effect of this external recognition was a surge of confidence in the value of local traditions.

Consequently, other communities along the route of the French invasion wished to demonstrate their patriotic contribution in 1798 and sought recognition for local traditions of their involvement in the Rebellion. This instigated a process of transition from vernacular practices of remembrance to more official public commemoration. In east county Mayo, a local campaign was launched to construct a monument to the "Knock heroes and martyrs of '98," honoring a list of names recalled hitherto only in folk history: Captain Richard Jordan of Rooskey, his brothers Patrick and Thomas and his niece Jane Taaffe,

FIGURE 26. 1798 monument to Fr. Manus Sweeney in Burrishoole Abbey, Mayo (unveiled 1912). Fulfilling an initiative launched during the 1798 centennial, commemoration of Fr. Sweeney was largely based on folk history. Photo by the author.

James O'Malley of Edenpark ("Séamus Bán"), Geoffrey Cunniffe of Carramore, and Tom Flatley.[119] The main activist behind this grassroots initiative was Henry Taaffe of Edenpark, who used the pseudonym "Senex." Taaffe was raised in a household that boasted a strong connection to the Rebellion and could personally recall his father hosting surviving rebels in their old age.[120] Though the centennial campaign set out to publicize the memory of the local heroes, it also reconstructed their biographies in order to comply with contemporary conventions of nationalist martyrology.[121]

A "'98 Knock Martyr's Monument Committee" was formed in May 1899 and received the blessing of the parish priest, Rev. John Fallon. The officers, who were described as "influential men of unquestionable integrity," included several members of the district and county councils, and a poet of local renown, William Cunnane.[122] The committee met frequently and collected subscriptions through appeals to "fellow-countrymen and women at home, in the antipodes, and in the greater Ireland beyond the Atlantic." It enjoyed much publicity in the local and national press and, thanks to Patrick Ford's *Irish World*, also among Irish communities abroad.[123] Emulating centennial hype, each meeting was repetitively reported as "one of the largest yet."

The monument was finally erected in the main street of Knock in 1904. It was designed as a large Celtic cross, the centennial being a time when such "Celtic crosses came out of the graveyards and into the main thoroughfares." This commemorative trend, which imitated Catholic ritual, was inspired by popular republican remembrance of the Manchester Martyrs,[124] although none of the seventeen monuments for the martyred Fenian trio erected between 1867 and 1906 were located in Connacht.[125] The legend inscribed on the Knock memorial presents the heroes of Ninety-Eight as patriotic role models: "May their actions tend to stimulate us to do something to throw off the yoke of the stranger."[126] Thirty years later, a folklore account of these local heroes cited the monument as a source for information and drew an analogy between the 1798 Rebellion and the 1916 Rising.[127] It even showed a misreading of the inscription, which states that Geoffrey Cunniffe "paid the penalty of devotion to Ireland." The storyteller assumed that the rebel hero had been executed after Ballinamuck, but he actually lived to an old age.[128]

During the centennial, key figures from the community of Burrishoole in county Mayo initiated a campaign to commemorate the local Ninety-Eight hero Fr. Manus Sweeney. Among them were Seán McHale (a relative of the famous Archbishop of Tuam, John McHale), who was active in local tenant agitation, and the folk historian Patrick O'Donnell. Two commemorative outcomes ensued. The "Father Manus Sweeney Memorial Hall," funded with contributions from Ireland and abroad, was built in Newport, where the rebel priest had been executed.[129] Following a prolonged fund-raising campaign, a Celtic cross monument was erected on Fr. Sweeney's grave in Burrishoole Friary.[130] On 9 June 1912 a crowd of five thousand marched in procession from Newport to the grave, where Rev. Ambrose Coleman delivered an oration, and the Newport parish priest, Rev. MacDonald, unveiled the monument.[131] An additional ceremony with guest dignitaries was held in Newport, where the Burrishoole parish priest Fr. Martin O'Donnell, who was also professor of Irish at St. Jarlath's College in Tuam (and a brother of Patrick O'Donnell), delivered a lecture on Fr. Sweeney based on "well-founded tradition."[132] Though these local ceremonies and monuments were inspired by official-metropolitan culture, in absence of sympathetic written or archival sources, the contents of provincial commemoration were founded on oral traditions. In effect, folk history was not so much "invented" as reconstructed through centennial commemoration, and this process of regeneration continued into the twentieth century.

Commemoration into the Mid-Twentieth Century

The popular demand for monuments commemorating Ninety-Eight did not subside at the close of the centennial. A survey of Irish public sculpture shows that the "majority of the monuments erected in the years immediately succeeding the centennial year were the '98 memorials that had been conceived in the enthusiasm of that year."[133] As the examples of Knock and Burrishoole demonstrate, financing of local monuments required sustained fund-raising, both in Ireland and abroad. Several years could pass from the original commitments undertaken in 1898 (signified by the dedication ceremony) to their ultimate fruition (celebrated in the unveiling).[134] In some cases commemorative initiatives never materialized. Despite initial enthusiasm at the time of the centennial, due to organizational incompetence and lack of funding, the grandiose plans to erect an impressive monument for Wolfe Tone were reluctantly aborted, leaving a lingering "presence of absence" in Dublin city center.[135] In other cases, proposals gestated for several decades. The Ballinamuck monument originated in a suggestion that was floated ten years after the centennial at a commemorative march of the Ancient Order of Hibernians (August 1908).[136] It then took twenty years of fund-raising till the pikeman statue was unveiled at a "monster meeting" to mark the one-hundred-and-thirtieth anniversary of the battle (9 September 1928).[137]

Several years after the centennial, communities on the periphery of the map of the French invasion (who had largely been overlooked by centennial commemoration) were still awaiting official recognition for their folk heroes. In August 1937 a Celtic cross monument for the rebel priest Fr. Conroy of Addergoole was erected in the Mayo village of Lahardane (see fig. 27); it was later recalled that the parish priest "was not too pleased at the time as he thought the presentation of a bell would have been more suitable."[138] The monument was financed by the local folk historian Michael Timoney [Micheál Ó Tiománaidhe],[139] who as a pioneering collector was knowledgeable of traditions of the Year of the French and was aware of the important role attributed to Fr. Conroy in guiding the Franco-Irish army from Ballina through the Windy Gap on to Castlebar.[140] Whereas scholarly historiography generally

listed Fr. Conroy's Christian name as James, folklore from his home townland maintained that he was actually called Andrew,[141] and Timoney guaranteed that this local tradition would be recognized in the monument's inscription (dedicated to "An athair Aindréis Ó Conaire"). Hence, folklore played a key role in the design of the monument.

By that stage, folklore was impregnated with centennial influences. During the centennial, memory of Fr. Conroy had been widely publicized by Rooney's popular ballad "The Priest of Adergool," which was awarded in 1898 a prize for the best poem on 1798 in a competition organized by the *Weekly Freeman*.[142] The ballad was soon recited orally in Connacht and

FIGURE 27. 1798 monument to Fr. Conroy in Lahardane, county Mayo (unveiled 1937). Financed by the local folk historian Michael Timoney, the content of commemoration was deeply informed by folk history. Photo by the author.

entered into local folklore shortly after its publication.[143] In the late twentieth century, a version of this ballad was collected as part of the singing repertoire of the area of Nephin Mountain in county Mayo. Comparison with the original text shows that the ballad had been slightly altered in oral tradition and was also missing a stanza.[144]

Official commemoration did not obliterate vernacular commemorative traditions. With the drive for erecting monuments in the early twentieth century moving away from the provincial centers to the periphery, the impetus of official commemoration decreased in Castlebar after the centennial celebrations. Though stories of Father Conroy were common throughout Mayo, especially in Castlebar where he was executed,[145] plans to erect a memorial at the site of his execution did not materialize.[146] In absence of a monument, social remembrance in Castlebar continued to focus on the tree on which Fr. Conroy was hanged until the early twentieth century, when the tree was uprooted.[147]

Even when monuments were erected, the relation between official and vernacular remembrance was not straightforward. Memorials were given a form of "patriotic license," which allowed them to take liberties with historical and even traditional knowledge. Recollections of young men from Achill Island, setting out to join the French and not returning, were noted already in the early nineteenth century,[148] but were not commemorated during the centennial. Seeking acknowledgement for their involvement in the Rebellion, in 1944 residents of Achill unveiled in the presence of the Archbishop of Tuam a memorial at the supposed birthplace of the local Ninety-Eight hero Fr. Manus Sweeney in Dookinella.[149] Shortly afterward, the folklore collector Pádraig Ó Moghráin pointed out that this was not the authentic place of birth of the rebel priest, but accepted that "anything that helps to preserve for ever the names and deeds of our patriot dead in the public memory is worthy of praise."[150] At the same time, the misplacing of a monument fostered recalcitrant notions of "collective deception," with knowledgeable locals bemused at the sight of visiting misinformed "outsiders," among whom were eminent historians. Noncompliant local narratives sustained "hidden transcripts," to use a term coined by James C. Scott, which subversively undermined confidence in authoritative rhetoric.[151]

Moreover, official commemoration could not replicate the flexibility and diversity of folklore traditions. Statues are literally made in stone, placed in a specific location and labeled with a concise inscription. When erecting monuments, local communities privileged select versions of traditions and sanctioned certain locations, unconsciously codifying folk history. This process of "petrifying" oral tradition could not represent the plurality and dynamism of vernacular historiographies, and inevitably disregarded the orchestra of alternative voices in social memory along the commemorative route of the French invasion. To give a recent example, oral traditions mentioned several possible sites for the execution of General George Blake at Ballinamuck. However, when in 1982 a local initiative set up a 1798 heritage trail, only one site was selected to be marked by a sign reading "General Blake was hanged here," while other possibilities were ignored.[152]

After their inauguration, monuments became landmarks that continued to operate as agents of commemoration, which silently and almost inconspicuously continued to uphold the memory of the Rebellion in public, giving the centennial a prolonged afterlife. As Gary Owens observed, "once monuments were raised, they became reference points in the physical and mental landscape of the communities that built them. They occupied 'sacred spaces'—locations that were effectively nationalist territory."[153] A story collected by the Irish Folklore Commission in Wexford in the 1930s inadvertently referred to the Ninety-Eight monument as a landmark in the town's market place, confirming also its significance in local historical consciousness.[154] The commemorative function of statues can diminish with time, as put provocatively by the historian Peter Novick: "They attract more attention from pigeons than they do from human passers-by."[155] Therefore, references to monuments in folklore are valuable for gauging popular attitudes.

FIGURE 28. 1798 signpost in Ballinamuck, county Longford (erected 1982). Signposts put up by the Ballinamuck Community Association in 1982 identified local sites that had previously been remembered in the vernacular landscape of oral tradition. Photo by the author.

Although the form of a statue does not change, observers can subjectively attach to it different meanings and interpretations. In a penetrating study of a monument for the Warsaw Ghetto, James E. Young observed that "we might ask not only how the monument reflects past history but, most important, what role it now plays in current history." Instead of a standard analysis, which unimaginatively debates the historical accuracy of monumental representation, he posed a series of questions for a more innovative line of investigation:

> How have monuments like this organized historical memory? What are the social, political, and aesthetic dimensions compromising the monument's public life? What is our role in it all? and finally, What are the consequences for our current lives in light of the ways our past is memorialized?

Young defined "memorialization" as a three-part process: first between events and the memorials, then between memorials and the viewers, and finally between viewers and their lives in light of this memorialized past. He concluded that the efficacy of remembrance through monuments "depends not on some measured distance between history and its monumental representation but in the conflation of private and public memory, in the memorial activity by which minds reflecting on the past inevitably precipitate in the present moment."[156] Indeed, monuments facilitated different, sometimes competing, forms of commemoration. Even though the monument in Ballinamuck was cast in the image of a wounded pikeman and was supposed to generically represent Irish rebels, several folklore accounts indicate that it was perceived locally as a personalized memorial dedicated to the local hero General Blake.[157] Official acts of remembrance were subject to interpretations that were conditioned by local oral traditions, and commemoration proved most meaningful when it related to familiar narratives recalled in folk history.

Although nationalist commemorative practices formulated in the late nineteenth century persisted into the twentieth century, the founding of an independent Irish state marked a significant change. With government officials endorsing commemoration of Ninety-Eight, bureaucratic and military apparatus were put at the disposal of organizers of public commemorative ceremonies. Consequently, mainstream commemoration lost its oppositional edge, and expressions of militant republicanism were no longer acceptable in commemorative programs backed by the establishment. At the 1928 celebrations in Ballinamuck, the achievements of the Irish Free State were lauded by Fr. John Keville, the parish priest of Drumlish (who chaired the proceedings), and Canon Joseph Guinan, the parish priest of Ardagh. When J. J. Killane, the Fianna Fáil TD (member of the Irish parliament) for Longford-Westmeath who had taken the anti-treaty side in the Civil War, attempted to deliver a republican speech, he was abruptly interrupted by the chair.[158]

In response, nonconforming republicans developed alternative commemorative programs, which appropriated sites in the vernacular landscape of the Year of the French. During the centennial, the "Croppies' Graves" at Ballinamuck had been visited by residents of neighboring Leitrim villages (7 August 1898), but plans to incorporate a visit to the site during the commemorations of 1928 were aborted for lack of time. In May 1938 a wreath was defiantly laid on the "Croppies' Graves" at a republican ceremony organized by the Longford Easter Commemoration Committee and attended by some 1,000 people.[159] The National Graves Association (NGA), a republican organization formed in 1926 to upkeep patriot graves and monuments, assumed responsibility for the care of several prominent Ninety-Eight commemorative sites, including General Blake's grave at Tubberpatrick and Bartholomew Teeling's monument outside Collooney.[160]

A county Longford committee with a local Ballinamuck subcommittee organized the official 140th anniversary at Ballinamuck (11 September 1938). The program included speeches, songs, marching bands, and processions to commemorative sites, including Tubberpatrick and Michael Devine's field, a place where local folk history recalled that rebels were hanged. Thanks to the introduction of amplification, for the first time many of the 4,000 people attending the event were able to hear the speeches.[161] School copybooks show that the celebrations made a strong impression on pupils from the neighboring villages in county Leitrim.[162]

Ten years later, the sesquicentennial of the Battle of Ballinamuck was once again planned by a countywide committee with subcommittees from around Longford. On 19 September 1948 the ceremonies were attended by a reported crowd of 10,000 and hosted many prestigious guests, among them President Seán T. O'Kelly, Seán MacBride (Minister for External Affairs), and Seán MacEoin (Minister for Justice).[163] Scenes from the day's festivities, including a photograph of the dignitaries standing by the pikeman statue and another of the procession, were reproduced by the Valentine company as souvenir postcards. It was later recalled that the official program acknowledged the vernacular landscape by placing white crosses on the Croppies' Graves scattered around Shanmullagh Hill.[164] That year, a Celtic cross memorial was also erected in the neighboring Longford town of Granard to commemorate the failed local insurrection attempt in 1798.[165]

At the 1948 celebrations in Sligo six pipe bands and contingents from all over the county, headed by twenty pikemen and forty horsemen, marched in two processions from Ballisodare and Collooney up to the Teeling monument (3 October 1948). Among the dignitaries were several TDs and Cahir Healy, the nationalist MP for Fermanagh. The Taoiseach (prime minister) John Costello had recently announced that Ireland was to be declared a republic (7 September 1948). Consequently, the speeches, which were preoccupied with contemporary politics, repeatedly remonstrated against Partition, which separated the six counties of Northern Ireland from the independent Irish state. Another honored guest was the Conservative MP for Brighton, Captain William Teeling, a descendent of Bartholomew Teeling. By then, the centennial was considered a memorable historical event in its own right. A local newspaper reprinted the centennial poem "The Battle of Carricknagat" by John O'Dowd, centennial banners were paraded, and places of honor were given to surviving participants from the commemorations of 1898.[166] In turn, the events of 1948 also entered into social memory and for the bicentennial year, fifty years later, an oral history project undertaken by a local FÁS (government sponsored training and development) scheme collected reminiscences from participants.[167]

In the early decades of the twentieth century, there were no large-scale celebrations to commemorate 1798 in Mayo. Following in the footsteps of a centennial initiative in county Sligo,[168] in 1936 two streets in Ballina were renamed

FIGURE 29. Sesquicentennial of the Battle of Ballinamuck (19 September 1948). Though adhering to nationalist commemorative practices formulated during the centennial, such as processions lead by local fife and drum bands, the attendance of prestigious state dignitaries and the participation of the army signified that official commemoration of Ninety-Eight had relinquished its oppositional republican character. Courtesy of the National Photograph Archive, National Library of Ireland.

after the United Irish heroes Bartholomew Teeling and Patrick Walsh.[169] Urban architecture and place-names, which are more permanent than periodic commemorative ceremonies, can also fulfill commemorative functions.[170] As Raphael Samuel observed, "street-names serve in some sort as almanacs, registering those personalities and events—mythic or real—which have imprinted themselves on popular consciousness."[171] Street-names are transparent agents of commemoration in town landscapes, which "merge the past they commemorate into ordinary settings of human life."[172] Like monuments, they can mark political initiatives to disseminate and consolidate official versions of history,[173] but they are also subject to contestations and the extent of their efficacy is dependent on popular reception.[174] Nationalist renaming of urban spaces did not always succeed, as the public sometimes preferred to keep using the previous, more familiar, names.[175] In 1920 the Castlebar Urban District Council instigated a patriotic renaming of streets. Several proposed street-names referred to the Year of the French, including Humbert Street (Main/Market Street), '98 Street (Thomas Street) and Fr. Conroy's Green (the Mall), but the new names did not enter popular use.[176] More than fifteen years after the failure of this commemorative proposal, Hayes complained that "walking through Castlebar, one cannot help observing that its streets are named after representatives of the English ascendancy."[177]

In 1938 a Castlebar resident complained that the Minister of Defense Frank Aiken, when speaking in Wexford, had ignored "those who fought at Killala, Castlebar, Collooney and Ballinamuck."[178] No official commemoration was held in Castlebar that year, and although local newspapers paid homage to the Rebellion in Mayo,[179] a reader (using the pseudonym "Gael") inquired: "what on earth has become of the '98 enthusiasts?"[180] Hayes lamented that "it is almost an anomaly that there is nothing in the town to commemorate the brilliant victory, and only one can hope that a resurgent Ireland will soon raise a fitting memorial there."[181] A decade later, commemorative fervor was reaffirmed in Castlebar when sesquicentennial celebrations were reportedly attended by 20,000 people (1 August 1948). Distinguished guests included President O'Kelly, the Taoiseach John Costello, the head of the opposition Eamon de Valera, the president of the Supreme Court Chief Justice Maguire, the Archbishop of Tuam, and the French Minister Count Stanislas Ostrorog. Public addresses stressed "the cause for which the men of '98 died and not to lose sight of the fact that the final freedom for the whole of Ireland had yet to be achieved."[182] Following a reconstruction of the battle and a military pageant, wreaths were laid at the monument on French Hill.[183] Three weeks later, thousands attended celebrations at Killala (21 August) and were entertained by bands playing music.[184]

That year, a set of two commemorative stamps was issued, featuring a ship sailing on a stormy sea and a pikeman. These iconic images of the French expeditions and the Rebellion were overshadowed by the profile of Wolfe Tone so that the national hero—and not the local experience recalled in social memory—was at the center of official attention. Nevertheless, the Taoiseach's speech at Castlebar acknowledged the vital importance of folk history:

> For 150 years the memories of the last French invasion of Ireland and the victory of Castlebar have been recorded with pride in the folklore of our people. They have informed part of our national consciousness and survived the malevolence of partial and prejudiced historians who by ridicule and slander tried to expunge "Bliain na bhFrancaigh" from the annals of our history.[185]

By this time, Richard Hayes was recognized as a leading authority on the French invasion of Connacht and was among the dignitaries at the ceremonies in Castlebar and Ballinamuck. A commemorative booklet produced for the Castlebar celebrations included extensive quotations from his monumental book, *The Last Invasion of Ireland,* and also reproduced the entire text of a lecture on "Castlebar and the Rising of 1798," which Hayes had delivered in the town a decade earlier (17 March 1938).[186] The historian, who previously had traveled through the area and listened to people recount traditions of Ninety-Eight was now informing them authoritatively about their past.

At the 1948 commemorations, the "County Mayo '98 Commemoration Committee" finally resolved to erect a monument in Castlebar. Six years later, President Seán T. O'Kelly unveiled a monument located at the Mall of Castlebar (5 September 1953). This time the commemoration committee had a strong clerical presence. Its president was Rev. G. J. Prendergast, the parish priest of Ballyhaunis, and its patrons were the Archbishop of Tuam Rev. Dr. Walsh and the Bishop of Achonry Rev. James Fergus. Reflecting the contemporary prominence of Catholicism in Irish public life, the monument, which was blessed by the Archbishop of Tuam, displayed a bronze engraving of a pikeman receiving a blessing from a priest (see fig. 30). On its reverse side it showed the Virgin Mary,[187] reflecting the Marian cult that reached its apogee in Ireland in the mid-twentieth century (ca. 1930–60).[188] Following the declaration of a Marian Year by Pope Pius XII, at the end of 1953, numerous Marian shrines were dedicated around Ireland, and this devotion had an impact on commemoration of Ninety-Eight.

The 1953 celebrations included an impressive parade lead by a party of the old IRA, under the direction of General Michael Kilroy. Accompanied by James Daly Jr., the French ambassador Lucien Felix laid a wreath at the monument on French Hill, which Daly's father had been involved in constructing seventy-seven years earlier.[189] As in previous commemorations, the local press enthusiastically reported the events and also served as a platform for copious articles on the French landing and the Rebellion in Connacht.[190] Once again, Hayes was welcomed in Castlebar as an honored guest, and his outstanding contribution to advancing the history of 1798 was publicly acknowledged. The influence of his book on perceptions of social memory was greater than people realized.

In the customary introduction in Irish, President O'Kelly's speech made reference to the continued prevalence of story and song traditions of *Bliain na bhFrancach*. He then recited two verses from traditional songs of Ninety-

FIGURE 30. 1798 monument in Castlebar, county Mayo (unveiled 1953). Reflecting the clerical influence and prevalence of popular piety of the time, the monument, which features bronze engravings of a pikeman receiving a blessing from a priest and (on the other side) of the Virgin Mary, was unveiled on the eve of a Marian Year. Photo by the author.

FIGURE 31. Grave of John Moore on the Mall in Castlebar, county Mayo (unveiled 12 August 1961). Following the discovery of his grave at Ballygunner Cemetery in Waterford, the one-time president of the short-lived Republic of Connaught was reinterred in Castlebar with a state funeral at which President Eamon de Valera delivered a graveside oration. Photo by the author.

Eight.[191] This performance was a recycling of folk history. Both quotations were taken from folk songs reproduced by Hayes in *The Last Invasion of Ireland*.[192] The songs were originally part of living social memory but, once collected and published, now reappeared in an entirely new context. The president assumed that the local crowd was familiar with the verses. In reality, it is doubtful if more than a handful of people in the audience had actually heard the songs performed as living oral traditions, though there were definitely people who, thanks to Hayes, had encountered them in print.

In the years following the celebrations of 1948 and 1953, the only major commemorative ceremony of the Rebellion in Connacht was a result of the discovery in 1960 of John Moore's grave in Ballygunner Cemetery in Waterford. A year later, the remains of the corpse were exhumed and brought into Waterford city in a ceremonious procession attended by an estimated 20,000 people (11 August 1961). Commemorative plaques were placed at the site of Moore's final internment (on George's Street in Waterford)[193] and his supposed place of death at what had been the Royal Oak Tavern in Muinebheag (Bagenalstown), county Carlow.[194] "Ireland's First President" was then ceremoniously dispatched to Castlebar and reinterred in the Mall "with all honours of church and state."[195] The funeral, complete with a guard of honor and army bands, hosted many dignitaries, including President Eamon de Valera, the Taoiseach Sean Lemass, several TDs, the ambassadors of Spain and France, and Moore's living descendants. In accordance with republican tradition, the venerable head of state, de Valera, delivered a graveside oration.[196] At the time, several local people raised objections concerning the choice of location for the burial in the town of Castlebar, as opposed to the derelict ancestral home at Moorehall.[197] This left a latent resentment, which was rekindled thirty-seven years later when a Mayo county councilor controversially proposed re-exhuming Moore's remains and moving them to the family estate.[198] Following the outbreak of the "Troubles" in Northern Ireland, the Irish Government, which had enthusiastically engaged in large-scale commemorations to mark the golden jubilee of the 1916 Rising (1966), succumbed to a prolonged state of "commemoration embarrassment."[199] State-endorsed commemoration of Ninety-Eight was discontinued and only reemerged in the 1798 bicentennial four decades later.

The numerous official commemorative celebrations of 1798, from the late nineteenth century into the mid-twentieth century, attempted to reshape social memory, accumulatively adding new connotations to public remembrance of the Year of the French. By the mid-twentieth century, folklore collectors and interviewed informants were inculcated by influences of public commemorations, but remembrance in the periphery was not completely constructed from the political centers. Simplistic explanations that misleadingly chart the influence of official commemoration on folklore through a one-way (top-down) flow of information prove to be inadequate. In practice, the interaction of social memory with external stimuli was far more complex and involved dynamics of continuity and change. Studies of commemoration are characteristically steeped in iconoclasm and tend to discredit "traditions" as fabrications.[200] However, attempts to reconstruct representations of the past according to present needs are ultimately limited by the malleability of traditions.[201] Many so-called "invented traditions" are susceptible to popular reception because they are based on an historical core that links them to the older traditions and allows them to be perceived as authentic.[202] So-called invention entails assemblage, supplementation, and rearrangement of cultural practices so that in effect traditions can be preserved, invented, and reconstructed. Rather than a fixed event, the more accurate term "reinvention of tradition" signifies a creative process involving renewal, reinterpretation and revision.[203]

Social memory was not a passive recipient of official commemorative discourse. Folklore could reject external versions of history that did not correspond with the way the past was remembered locally. A spirit of rapprochement and cordiality toward the French engulfed official commemorative ceremonies in 1898 and 1948 (and again in Castlebar in 1953). Yet locals frequently regarded the inclusion of French representatives among the honored guests with cynicism. Acknowledging the victorious "Races of Castlebar" and the declaration of the "Republic of Connaught," folk history in Castlebar was generally favorable toward the French. But in other areas this was not the case. In the north midlands, in particular, attempts from above to express appreciation of the French were undermined by indignant recollections of inequality during the joint campaign and met with stubborn refusal to forgive the French for surrendering and deserting their Irish allies. Addressing the Ballinamuck Society in 1969, the local schoolteacher Peter Duignan of Gaigue (b. 1904) recalled his dismay when tribute was paid to "our gallant French allies" at the unveiling of the Ballinamuck monument in 1928 and at the 1948 ceremony.[204] People in the area of Crossmolina in north county Mayo would direct pejorative remarks toward the centennial monument in Ballina and derisively claim that a statue should not have been erected in honor of the French.[205]

A curious example of the sensitivity of provincial commemoration appears in a plaque adjacent to the 1798 monument at Collooney. When erected, the monument had been criticized by Irish language enthusiasts for having an inscription only in English.[206] A trilingual plaque sponsored by the NGA later addressed this shortcoming. Validating provincial social memory, the texts in Irish and English recall the calamity at Ballinamuck and acknowledge that "after the battle the French were granted prisoner-of-war status, but over 500 Irish soldiers were slaughtered." The French text, however, diplomatically neglects to cite this troubling information and instead salutes the French sacrifice of two hundred French soldiers who perished during the campaign.

As a rule, the agenda of official commemoration, which practically canonized a select pantheon of national heroes and referred to a constricted range of subjects, has been extremely limited. In contrast, the democratic nature of vernacular historiography encompassed a much richer variety of historical preoccupation with the people and events of 1798. Therefore, the traditions of folk history were not always directly affected by the propaganda of official public commemoration. Rather than imagining a model of popular culture colonized from above through pageantry and rhetoric, it is more beneficial to construe the interaction between official commemoration and folklore in terms of cultural dialogues and negotiations of memory. Subjected to popular reception, the ideological messages projected by official commemoration were either rejected or accepted, and even then they were usually readapted and transformed. Apart from instances when commemorative songs and poems, which were specifically composed with anniversaries in mind, were memorized by rote, information stemming from official celebrations rarely entered folklore unchanged. The popular impact of official commemoration was often manifested indirectly. As the discussion in chapter 13 on "Humbert's Stone" demonstrated, to a large extent the designation of folk monuments and the discovery of relics in the vernacular landscape was a reflection on a local community level of the national trend to commemorate the heroes of Ninety-Eight.

It is occasionally possible to retrace chains of transmission by which oral traditions were passed from generation to generation, and these clearly show that folk history-telling was in existence long before public nationalist commemoration came into vogue. More than anything else, the centennial and subsequent commemorations reaffirmed traditions of folk history and remembrance that were already in existence. These traditions were then recharged, as communities adopted patterns of official commemoration and constructed monuments for their local heroes. Like national history, national commemoration offered a porous metanarrative, providing a heterogeneous historical framework to which local traditions could relate. Transformations in social memory often occurred through subtle modifications by which folk-history narratives were retold in ways that corresponded with the way 1798 was presented at commemorative ceremonies and on monuments.

When James Daly and his colleagues set out to erect the monument on French Hill in 1876 (three years before the founding of the Land League), they anticipated centennial commemoration by more than two decades. This act of public commemoration originated in a firm belief in folklore tradition and focused on an act of local history that was peripheral to the greater events of the Franco-Irish campaign. It did not pay direct tribute to "The Races of Castlebar," a victory that was lauded extensively during the centennial, but called attention to an incident that was anecdotal and overlooked in scholarly histories. The French Hill monument unveiled in 1876 is in the form of a cross on top of a nine-meter (thirty-foot) granite pyramidal base (see fig. 32).[207] This

FIGURE 32. 1798 monument on French Hill outside Castlebar, county Mayo (erected 1876). Grounded on validation of folk history, this local commemorative initiative preceded centennial commemoration. Photograph by the author.

choice of representation preceded the popularity of Celtic crosses as Ninety-Eight centennial monuments first introduced in 1898. Similarly, in county Wexford, a Celtic cross memorial was erected in 1875 in St. Mary's cemetery in Newtownbarry near Bunclody to mark the reinternment of skeletons that were identified locally as belonging to rebels from 1798.[208] Unlike the contemporary Fenian commemorative crosses for the Manchester Martyrs, which were typically inscribed with the legend "God Save Ireland," the inscription on French Hill reads: "In grateful remembrance of the brave French soldiers who were killed here in 1798 fighting for Ireland's freedom."

Twenty-two years later, when nominated president of the Connaught '98 Centenary Council, Daly brought with him a strong conviction in the historical value of folklore. Speaking at the ceremony on French Hill that inaugurated the centennial commemorations (9 January 1898), he authenticated a detailed account of the Battle of Castlebar by stating "I have that from a man named Walsh, who was an eyewitness to the whole thing." His respect for oral tradition was backed up by reverence of relics. Daly wore one of the French coins found in 1876 as a medal and exhibited this five-franc piece, inscribed "Union et Force" and minted in Year 6 of the French Republic (1798), at a centennial ceremony, declaring that it "lay for seventy-seven years with the bones of one of the French officers that fell here."[209] This souvenir was then respectfully preserved and displayed locally as a cherished medium of remembrance. In the early twentieth century it was shown to the visiting historian Rev. E. A. D'Alton,[210] and in 1935 Daly's son showed Hayes the other coins and buttons that had been found in the grave.[211]

Clearly, the content of public remembrance was not simply dictated from above by a central nationalist agenda that enforced hegemonic dominance. It was rooted in local nationalist initiatives and based on vernacular commemorative traditions with an older pedigree. Accordingly, the formation of provincial social memory can be understood as a two-way commemorative process that facilitated negotiations between the metropolitan agenda of high-politics and local traditions embedded in folk history. With initiatives to inculcate nationalist history and the dissemination of historical literature peaking during periods of high profile commemoration, the influence of popular print produced by literate elites on a predominantly oral folk history needs to be teased out further.

15

Mediations of Remembrance

Endless and conflicting images and interpretations of 1798
have been transmitted by novelists, poets, artists, journalists,
and cultural entrepreneurs, as well as by scholars and teachers, in contested efforts to shape the collective memory of
Ireland's past in order to influence its present and determine
its future.

Kerby A. Miller
in *Eighteenth Century Life* 22, no. 3

Remembrance and Popular Print

SOCIAL MEMORY of the Year of the French was constructed and regenerated
in a larger context of the spread of popular literacy in Ireland.[1] Literacy
rates in English consistently rose over the nineteenth century, a trend that accelerated after the Great Famine (see table 3). By the early twentieth century, with
84.8 percent of the population of Connacht and 90.5 percent in Longford listed
in 1911 as able to read, the influence of print was pervasive.[2] Yet the once orthodox historical model that considered modernization in Ireland to be a linear
progression from a "primitive" traditional society—allegedly oral, mostly
Irish speaking and illiterate, based on economic subsistence, and believing in
folk religion—toward a "modern" capitalist society—typically English speaking, subsumed in print culture, commercialized, and devoted to an official form
of Catholicism—does not hold water when taking into account interactions in
popular culture.[3] Diffusion and reading of literature precipitated interfaces
between traditional and modern practices. Popular print did not supersede oral
culture though it clearly influenced it, so that chapbook romances, for example,
were retold as oral narratives.[4]

TABLE 3. English literacy rates in Connacht
(percentage of the population claiming knowledge of reading)*

Year	1841	1851	1861	1871	1881	1891	1901
Ability to read	28%	34%	43%	51%	62%	73%	78%

*H.C. 1902, vol. 129, 57. Figures combine the rates of literacy for over-five-year-olds who were listed as only able to read and as able to both read and write.

Nineteenth-century literature in the so-called Celtic peripheries of Britain championed literacy and showed ambivalence toward orality, which was paradoxically both romantically idealized and denigrated. To use terms coined by Penny Fielding in a comparable Scottish context, literature introduced "rites of speech," which attempted to contain oral culture, and in response agency and self-determination of subaltern classes challenged the marginalization of orality and claimed "rights of speech" for vernacular traditions.[5] Even through the reading public was exposed to an abundance of texts on the 1798 Rebellion, the formidable aspirations of historical literature to reshape perceptions of the past were conditioned by the persistence (often through mutations) of traditions embedded in social memory. The already tenuous boundaries between elite and popular culture were debilitated further as supposedly highbrow literature enjoyed popular consumption when issued in inexpensive editions. 1798 being a topic of great popular interest, primary and secondary historical sources on the Rebellion were reproduced and circulated, either through republication or, indirectly, when quoted in new publications. Moreover, historical fiction also propagated representations of Ninety-Eight. Although the information promulgated by print fed into oral traditions, folk history was not merely a passive recipient. Folklore accounts were mostly preoccupied with traditions that were overlooked in written works. Once collected, these traditions could reappear in printed form, allowing for reflexive interactions between remembrance and popular print.

Leerssen claimed that the memory of 1798 went through fifty years of "embarrassed and confused" incubation only to erupt in a proliferation of literary representations around the late 1840s, which was spearheaded by Young Ireland and then reshaped through Fenian influence.[6] However, the validity of the argument for an initial period of silence is limited. A heated political debate over the historical interpretation of the events began immediately after the Rebellion, and in following years numerous polemical tracts appeared in historical books, pamphlets, newspapers, and journals.[7] A prominent example can be found in Watty Cox's immensely popular *Irish Magazine* (1807–15), which was launched less than a decade after the Rebellion and unashamedly stirred public debate over the grievances of 1798.

In one of his acclaimed *Peter Plymley's Letters* (1807), the English wit Sydney Smith (1771–1845) alerted the general public to the significance of the French expedition in Ireland, offering a "precis of its exploits."[8] Nonetheless, even though Ninety-Eight was considered a major event in Irish historiography, for most of the nineteenth century scant scholarly attention was paid to the Rebellion in the West. The French invasion, described as "the most desperate attempt which is, perhaps, recorded in history," was covered in John Mitchel's polemical *History of Ireland* (1868). This immensely popular book, which was reissued in numerous editions and enjoyed large sales, selectively repeated information found in early historical accounts written by Bishop Stock, the Catholic cleric Francis Plowden (1749–1829), and the Anglo-Irish historian-cum-raconteur Sir Jonah Barrington.[9] The two eminent Victorian historians of Ireland, James Anthony Froude (1818–94) and William Edward Harpole Lecky (1838–1903) presented conflicting interpretations of 1798. Froude, who devoted a whole volume to the United Irishmen and the Rebellion in Wexford, mentioned Connacht only in passing.[10] In contrast, Lecky accorded the West considerable attention and consulted numerous primary sources, though he offhandedly remarked that "the story is one which would have more of the elements of comedy than of tragedy, if it were not for the dark spectre of a bloody retribution that was behind."[11] The depth of his archival research made sure that Lecky's influence would be long-lasting.

During the centennial, a couple of articles on the topic were published in periodicals. An essay that utilized sources available in print appeared in the *Dublin Review*.[12] A more substantial essay was written by the historian and member of the Royal Irish Academy Caesar Litton Falkiner (1863–1908), who complained that "the story of the French invasion of Mayo, which lies outside the general history of the Rebellion, has been written with rather less elaboration than the rest of the narrative"[13] and that this episode "has scarcely received its meed [deserved share] of attention."[14] For his study "The French Invasion of Ireland" (originally published in 1898 and reissued in a second version in 1902), Falkiner consulted archival documents and unpublished correspondence, and even visited the scene of the events, though he did not attempt to incorporate folklore traditions.

Several years earlier, the Russian émigré Valerian Gribayédoff (1858–1908), who was a pioneering journalistic illustrator and photographer hailed as "the originator of newspaper illustration in New York,"[15] wrote *The French Invasion of Ireland in '98* (1890), which was published in New York. Gribayédoff did not have access to local folklore sources and was not particularly preoccupied with the personal experiences of Irish rebels. He made an exception when portraying the martyrdom of the United Irishman Patrick Walsh, who was executed in Ballina immediately prior to the taking of the town by the French. The circumstances of his death were amplified in an emotive description and graphically portrayed in a striking illustration that inspired a lithograph in a popular nationalist newspaper (see fig. 34).[16] A year after its original publication, extensive excerpts from Gribayédoff's book were reprinted in the *Western People* (a Parnellite newspaper in Ballina that competed with Castlebar's *Connaught Telegraph*), which praised the work as a "wonderfully clear and sympathetic history."[17] Later, chapters from the book were serialized in a national newspaper—the *Weekly Independent* (1894).[18]

By then, following a period of intense growth, daily and weekly newspapers played a significant role in Irish life. Whereas prior to 1830, Connacht had thirteen newspapers (eight of them in county Galway); over the following seventy years, fifty-four new newspapers were established in the province, some of which were short lived. Sixteen newspapers were founded in county Mayo and six of them survived into the twentieth century.[19] Before 1830, county Longford did not produce any newspapers, but in following years five newspapers were established in Longford town,[20] and the county was also served by papers from neighboring areas.[21] By the end of the nineteenth century, influential newspapers were formidably established throughout Connacht and the north midlands.

Developments in transportation networks and a flourish of local newsagents enabled mass circulation of provincial and national press.[22] Police surveillance of national newspapers observed that in 1898 the *Weekly Freeman* sold approximately 36,000 copies, the *Weekly Independent* 18,000, the *Weekly Nation* 17,000, and *United Ireland* 2,000. In 1900 it was estimated that the *Freeman's Journal* sold between 24,000 to 30,000 copies, the *Independent* 13,000, and the *Nation* 13,500 (the latter two were to merge and run 19,000 copies).[23] Bolstered by the spread of nationalist reading rooms,[24] pervasive readership of newspapers allowed large segments of the public to engage with topical affairs and to combine interest in national matters with local concerns.[25] Newspapers not only called attention to historical issues but also allowed general access to specific information that had hitherto been in the domain of specialists. Even though in the early twentieth century Bishop Stock's *Narrative* was said to be available in Mayo "from any book-seller who stocks Irish literature,"[26] its local readership was restricted. But in the autumn of 1927 the *Ballina Herald* serialized an edited version of this key historical text, which had appeared earlier that year in the republican paper *An Phoblacht*.[27] Lesser-known historical sources were also brought to the public eye. In 1931 the *Western People* reprinted excerpts from the memoirs of the French officer Moreau de Jonnès.[28]

Direct influence of historical publications on folk history is occasionally apparent in references to precise dates and names of military commanders. This is, however, mostly tangential and does not seem to have completely transformed oral tradition. Though there is scant evidence that details from Gribayédoff's study filtered into folklore accounts, the book did not pass unnoticed by those who wished to politicize popular history. The offhand claim that Irish rebels did not display bravery at the Battle of Castlebar prompted Joseph McGarrity (1874–1940), an activist in the Irish-American republican organization Clan-na-Gael who was in constant contact with IRB members in Ireland, to write in 1914 an essay called "The French at Killala in '98," which was circulated not only as a pamphlet in 35,000 copies[29] but also delivered as a lecture to the Mayo Society in Philadelphia (1916).[30] Stressing the valor of the Irish rebels, this overtly nationalist text exaggerated British losses and placed the Rebellion in Mayo within a familiar nationalist framework of successive republican insurrections (including 1803, 1848, 1867, and 1916). Such populist reinterpretations of the Rebellion were rife in the aftermath of the centennial celebrations, and though they did not subsume the democratic micronarratives of folk history, they exerted pressures on local traditions to conform to an imposing national metanarrative.

In addition, the influences of flowery cultural-nationalist writing on popular culture cannot be underestimated. Romantic myth-making was initiated by the distinguished writer Thomas Moore (1779–1852), who as a young man had lived through the events of 1798 and then commemorated the Rebellion in his celebrated poetry and prose.[31] Inspired by Moore, the writers of Young Ireland enthusiastically produced romantic nationalist writing. The success of their weekly organ, the *Nation*, was phenomenal. Launched on 15 October 1842, within a year it had become Ireland's leading newspaper, running 10,300 copies per issue. Its editor boasted a readership of 405,000, based on an inflated calculation, by which 300 copies went to newspaper reading rooms and were each read by 100 readers (30,000), 1,100 went to officers in the Repeal movement who would read the paper out aloud to average audiences of 150 (165,000), 300 went to six-penny subscriptions typically collected from groupings of a dozen workmen (3,600), and each of the remaining 8,600 copies allegedly passed through two dozen hands (206,400)[32] Making allowances for exaggerations, an impressive readership of 250,000 would seem a more realistic estimate.

When defining the newspaper's goals, Thomas Davis paraphrased Wolfe Tone and the United Irishmen by calling for the realization of a national identity "which would embrace Protestant, Catholic and Dissenter."[33] However, the attitudes toward 1798 expressed in the paper were not straightforward. Contributors, who were threatened by repressive incrimination, stressed "the romance of violent resistance to England, so long as it was safely in the past."[34] Sean Ryder observed:

> On the occasions when Young Ireland did remember 1798, it clearly aimed at desectarianizing and de-republicanizing the memory of the rebellion and casting it in a more romantic, heroic, mythic mode that was politically flexible and more amenable to O'Connellite constitutionalism.[35]

There were also more militant writers like John Mitchel (1815–75), who briefly edited the *Nation* in 1847 and founded in February 1848 the republican newspaper *United Irishman*, which sold 5,000 copies on its first day of issue but was soon suppressed. This newspaper sported a title specifically chosen to commemorate 1798 and endorsed a violent strain of nationalist politics.

The pages of the *Nation* regularly included polemic commentary on the Rebellion and featured reprints of earlier historical works sympathetic to the United Irish cause alongside original popular histories, which were then reissued as separate publications. The West, however, was largely neglected. The Dublin publisher James McCormick (fl. 1842–52) produced a 207-page anthology of history writing, government reports, newspaper articles, and fiction on 1798, which mentioned Connacht in fewer than two pages.[36] McCormick also published the "National Library for Ireland" history series, which included the four-penny booklet *The Rising of '98* that did not deliver on its promise to provide an account of the "French Alliances, Invasions, etc.," as it ignored the French landing in Mayo. Absence of explicit references to Connacht and the north midlands limited the direct impact of literary productions on folk history of the Year of the French. This disregard of the provincial experience did not pass without comment. When planning was going ahead toward the centennial, a resident of Castlebar complained that "Irish writers have not given it [the Rebellion in the West] due attention, while the poets seem to have neglected it altogether" and provocatively asked: "When will some Irish poet give us a worthy strain in celebration of an event so deeply interesting and so pregnant with suggestion as 'The Races of Castlebar'?"[37] This lacuna was addressed shortly after in the centennial poetry of William Rooney, which (as demonstrated in chapter 14) was enthusiastically assimilated into folklore.

More subtle traces of cultural nationalism are apparent in romantically styled renditions of oral traditions, which are particularly evident in local poetic compositions that emulate the poems and ballads published in the *Nation*. Indeed, there was no shortage of inspiring literature that could offer resources for provincial remembrance. The nineteenth-century boom in political ballads openly appropriated the memory of 1798, which proved to be an effective tool for stirring public opinion.[38] This commemorative balladry was recycled in copious popular songbooks and anthologies, many of which were devoted exclusively to Ninety-Eight.[39] Cultural nationalists aspired to emulate and re-create oral traditions and in particular folksongs. As Thuente pointed out, their compositions "exemplify all the definitive characteristics of folklore: traditional oral texts subject to variation and possessing a common stock of motifs and ideas."[40]

Pride of place among the poetic compositions that trumpeted remembrance of 1798 was given to "The Memory of the Dead" by John Kells Ingram (1823–1907), first published anonymously in the *Nation* and popularly known by its opening line "Who fears to speak of Ninety-Eight?"[41] A designated tune, generally attributed to William Elliot Hudson (1796–1853), soon appeared in the first edition of *The Spirit of the Nation* (1843), turning the poem into a song,[42] which was then frequently reprinted on numerous broadsides and in nationalist songbooks. Popularized by Young Ireland's Confederate Clubs (1847–48),[43] the song achieved canonical stature within fifty years when it was labeled "The Irish Marseillaise" and performed with veneration as a national anthem of commemoration at 1798 centennial ceremonies nationwide.[44] By then it was practically a paean—when played at a ceremony in Ballina, for example, "all heads remained uncovered."[45] Verses from the ballad were reverentially engraved on the Ballina Ninety-Eight centennial monument.

Nationalist popular print and monumental commemoration worked in tandem, formulating, drawing from and promoting a common pool of patriotic imagery.[46] A prominent example is the figure of Erin, characteristically equipped with a Celtic cross, harp, wolfhound, and inscribed banner. This romantic-nationalist amalgamation of evocative symbolism was popularized in the writings of Young Ireland and featured widely in late-nineteenth-century political illustrations.[47] Through association with cemetery effigies of the Virgin Mary, centennial sculptures of Erin also tapped into Catholic funerary symbolism.[48] Erin appeared on statues in two variants, a triumphant "Liberty Erin" and a gentler "Virgin Erin,"[49] and this distinction mirrored rival political stances within Irish nationalism. The statue erected by constitutionalists in Sligo was popularly known as "Lady Erin,"[50] whereas an IRB-dominated committee in Ballina required that Erin hold a sword, and beneath her stand two pikes draped in flags (see fig. 24, chapter 14).

Nineteenth-century literature was obsessed with the memory of Ninety-Eight. Publishing with the Minerva Press shortly after the Rebellion, Charles Lucas (1769–1854) made use of contemporary loyalist sources and conservative propaganda to locate the entirely fictional plot of his anti-Jacobin novel *The Infernal Quixote* (1801) on the background of the events of 1798 and included references to the French landing at Killala and their subsequent defeat.[51] In 1806 Edward Mangin (1772–1852) inserted into a novel an account of the defeat of the Franco-Irish rebel army based on his own recollections of having witnessed the events at Ballinamuck.[52] Ascendancy literature in the years after the Rebellion featured implicit allusions to 1798,[53] which can be traced in the writings of Maria Edgeworth (1767–1849),[54] Charles Robert Maturin (1782–1824),[55] and Lady Morgan ([Sydney Owenson], ca. 1776–1859).[56] The latter two published with Henry Colburn (d. 1855), the London publisher and editor of the *New Monthly Magazine,* who discovered a profitable market for historical fiction as well as memoirs of rebels.[57] In the 1820s novels about the Rebellion were continuously churned out. Though the majority of these were set in Leinster and Ulster, some of them briefly referred to the French invasion. For example, in *O'Halloran: The Insurgent Chief* (1824), a popular novel about 1798 in county Antrim by James McHenry (who used the pen name "Solomon Secondsight,"1785–1845), which was republished in numerous editions, loyalists and rebels from the North go on to take part in the Rebellion in Connacht and its suppression (for some reason located at Tuam in county Galway instead of Ballinamuck).[58]

Several lesser-known historical novels centered on the Rebellion in the West. Matthew Archdeacon (ca. 1800–1853) was prompted to write *Connaught, A Tale of 1798* (1830) when he realized that the contemporary popularity of literature on "the insurrectionary proceedings in 1798" did not include any reference to "the invasion of our country, and the consequent rising." Archdeacon, who was a schoolteacher in Castlebar, described himself as "being from infancy in the habit of having details of the time of the Frinch [*sic*]," as he "had an opportunity of frequently hearing the insurrectionary scenes described by some of the actors themselves." He claimed to base his romantic narrative on an interview with a participating rebel, supplemented with local traditions.[59] Likewise, his short story "The Rebels' Grave" (1837) was also based on oral sources.[60] Though he was a moderate loyalist, Archdeacon's depiction of the insurrection is not entirely hostile to the rebels, and the list of subscribers to his books reveals a highly educated and distinguished readership, which included

Protestant magnates alongside Catholic priests and nationalists (among them Daniel O'Connell).

Around that time, William Hamilton Maxwell wrote *The Adventures of Captain Blake* (1838), narrated as the recollections of the son of a Protestant landowner and former soldier who lived through the French invasion and its aftermath.[61] Maxwell, who a decade earlier had written a novel on 1798 in county Down (his birthplace),[62] was knowledgeable about the written historical sources for the Rebellion[63] and was also aware of oral traditions in Mayo and Connemara, which he incorporated into his historical fiction.[64] In the mid-nineteenth century, Charles James Lever (1806–72) wrote *Maurice Tierney* (originally serialized in the *Dublin University Magazine*, 1850–51), a novel that tells the story of a French officer of Irish descent who took part in the expedition to Killala. After the victory at Castlebar, the hero is dispatched to Donegal, so that the narrative covers the events of Napper Tandy's landing and the capture of Wolfe Tone but does not follow the Franco-Irish campaign into the north midlands.[65] Lever's sources are not clear and may derive from his acquaintance with Maxwell. Apart from the major historical personages (i.e., Humbert, Tone, Teeing), one of the only Irish rebels mentioned in the novel who is actually based on a historical person is the "active chief of insurgents" Neal Kerugan [Kerrigan], a Killala United Irishman recalled in local folk history.[66] It is plausible that several references in the novel derive from oral tradition. In 1832, when treating victims of a cholera epidemic in county Clare (1832), Lever collected traditions from the West of Ireland for his colorful stories of rural life. He also became acquainted with folk history accounts as the editor of the *Dublin University Magazine* (1842–45), which published traditions collected by Caesar Otway in northwest county Mayo.[67]

Eileen Reilly observed that "the number of '98 novels produced in the years immediately surrounding the centenary mushroomed" so that "the rebellion provided the theme for more historical novels in the period 1880 to 1914 than any other subject."[68] Very few of the copious "centennial novels" refer to the French invasion. *The Shan Van Vocht* (1889) by James Murphy (1839–1921) is set on the background of the French expedition, but it focuses solely on the fleet that sailed with Wolfe Tone and only inadvertently mentions the landing at Killala.[69] Similarly, *Kathleen Mavourneen* (1898) by Randal William McDonnell (b. 1870) dedicates a chapter to Wolfe Tone's expedition but makes only passing reference to Humbert.[70] A legend of French gold from 1798 believed to be hidden in a bog in the mountains of west Connacht was the setting for *The Snake's Pass* (originally serialized in 1889), the first novel written by Bram Stoker (1847–1912).[71] Curiously, a story still remembered in Castlebar refers to a "box with a snake on the lid" left behind by a French soldier and later found at Derrynadiva by Mount Burren in county Mayo.[72] It remains a puzzle whether this oral narrative was influenced by the novel or whether a recollection of an older local tradition inspired the novelist, who incidentally was descended from the family of the local rebel leader General George Blake.[73]

A book titled *Ninety-Eight* (1897) pretended to be based on the reminisces of Cormac Cahir O'Connor Faly, a rebel who supposedly fought at Wexford and later joined the French in Mayo, was taken prisoner at Collooney and sent into exile, where he enlisted in the French army and participated in the Napoleonic campaigns. The author, Patrick C. Faly ([pseudonym of John Hill], fl. 1880s–1904), claimed that he had inherited the memoirs of his illustrious grandfather (alongside a treasured pikehead), but it is, however, a fictitious account.[74] Testimony to the enthusiastic reception and lasting influence of such historical fiction appeared forty years later, when Joseph Fowler (b. 1883) wrote a collection of pamphlets ("launched at a price and in a form that would reach the humblest of people") for the 140th anniversary of the Rebellion (1938), one of which was dedicated to "The Landing of the French at Killala" (no. 7). In his childhood, Fowler had read Faly's novel at the time of the centennial and found it to be "just the book to enthral and inspire an Irish youth."[75]

In *The Rebels* (1899) by Mathias McDonnell Bodkin (1849–1933), a rebel from Leinster participates in the Rebellion in Mayo and then escapes to America aboard a schooner.[76] Bodkin, who was a nationalist MP for North Roscommon (1892–95), was familiar with the importance attributed to Ninety-Eight in Connacht, his mother being an O'Donnell of Westport in county Mayo. *Stories of the Irish Rebellion* (1898), by the Aberdeen-based author James J. Moran, includes two sentimental stories set in Connacht. "Eily's Friend in Need" lauds the gallantry of Bartholomew Teeling and "A Fair Insurgent" dramatizes the engagement at Collooney, which in accordance with the centennial reinterpretation is portrayed as a major rebel victory and described speciously as "our first stiff fight" in comparison to which "our other engagements have been nothing." Without acknowledgment, the author lifted sections off Terence O'Rorke's *History, Antiquities and Present State of the Parishes of Ballysadare and Kilvarnet* (1878) and *History of Sligo* (1889) and imaginatively depicted historical characters with exaggeration. For example, Whittiers, the British artilleryman allegedly killed by Teeling, is presented as a "celebrated gunner" and a highly skilled adversary. Like many of the novels that drew from available secondary sources, Moran's fiction readapted information from historical studies and presented it to a general reading public at a second remove.[77]

In the early twentieth century, the Rebellion in Connacht was again the topic of several literary works. *The "Peep 'O Day Boy"* (1900) by Robert Buchanan (1841–1901), an author who was fascinated by Irish secret societies, concludes with a brief historical account of the French campaign and parenthetically notes that the novel's protagonist joined this "most desperate and determined effort." The popular novel *The Race of Castlebar* (1914), written by Emily Lawless (1845–1913) and Shan F. Bullock (1865–1935), is narrated by a fictional Englishman staying at the residence of Bishop Stock in Killala.[78] Largely based on Stock's *Narrative,* it contributed to the indirect dissemination of information drawn from primary historical sources.[79] Other literary works were more receptive to folklore sources. The language-revival organization Connradh na Gaedhilge (the Gaelic League), which also vigorously promoted Irish historical literature,[80] published Seaghán ua Ruaidhrí's novel *Bliadhain na bhFrancach* (1907). Intended primarily to serve as a language primer, the book included a vocabulary list and glossary, and so was relatively accessible to readers with basic competency in Irish. The author claimed that it was based on recollections of an oral narrative that he had heard as a child and attributed to a storyteller named Domhnall Thomáis Mhóir.[81]

Published in the United States, *Slieve Bawn and the Croppy Scout* (1914) was devoted entirely to the Rebellion in north Connacht and the north midlands. The author, Rev. James Joseph Gibbons, claimed descent from residents of Ballinamuck who had witnessed the events—his grandfather, Mick McQuaide, had concealed a wounded rebel and his uncle, Tom McQuaide, was subsequently pressed into army service. Gibbons recounted "the tale of the brave Mulcaghy and his colleen" from county Roscommon as he allegedly "learned it from the lips of his ancestors seated around the fire on winter nights." A folk historian (or history-teller) "born but a few years after the 'Risin'" is also cited as a source of information and is colorfully described as

> a man over the hundred mark, who still wore knee-breeches and carried the black thorn and let his long grey locks grow in waving ringlets down his shoulders, manifesting the culture for which he was known in the neighbourhood around as one who "knew a powerful lot of history," and possessed "a deal of knowledge of everything." . . . The stories of seventeen ninety-eight were as green and fresh in the vigorous old intellect as in the days when he was a little boy and the "Croppies" sat at his father's hearth and told of their adventures and struggles for the "freedom of Ireland."

References to oral tradition are dispersed throughout the novel, such as an anecdote told around Ballinamuck of a Mayo simpleton who was shocked by the sight of British cannon fire and called out: "Come quick and see the devil; he has broken loose and is coming up the street vomiting fire."[82]

At nationalist events, dramatic scenes from Ninety-Eight were silently reenacted as *tableaux vivants*. More formally, theaters presented audiences with melodramatic stage versions of the Rebellion, written and produced by the likes of Dion Boucicault (1820–90), P. J. Bourke (1882–1932), and J. W. Whitbread (1848–1916).[83] Like the novels, the popular plays mainly referred to the better-known 1798 arenas of Leinster and Ulster, with occasional, often erroneous, references touching on the Rebellion in Connacht. For example, in Bourke's *When Wexford Rose* (1910) Leinster rebels hear of Humbert's landing in Killala, though in reality their insurrection was crushed a couple of months prior to the arrival of the French. A bibliography of Irish plays put together by the theatrical dilettante Joseph Holloway notes a couple of less familiar melodramas from the early twentieth century, which focused on the West. The Ulster dramatist Alice Milligan (1866–1953) composed the five-act drama *The French are on the Sea* (unpublished). Joseph Malachi Muldoon wrote the three-act drama *The West's Awake*, which was produced in June 1911 by both the Sligo Dramatic Company and the Irish Theatre and National Stage Company in Dublin.[84]

Celebrated luminaries of the Irish Literary Revival were also preoccupied with the memory of 1798. W. B. Yeats (1865–1939) in collaboration with Lady Augusta Gregory (1852–1932) wrote for the Irish Literary Theatre (the predecessor of the Abbey Theatre) *Cathleen Ni Houlihan* (also spelled *Kathleen Ni Houlihan* and *Cathleen Ni Hoolihan*, 1902), described by Yeats as "the first play of our Irish School of folk-drama."[85] Produced by the National Dramatic Company, it premiered on 2 April 1902 with Maud Gonne in the lead role and was received favorably by Dublin audiences. The play is set in the "interior of a cottage close to Killala" at the time of the French landing and borrows motifs from folk tradition, though the imagery reflects the nationalist reinterpretations of the centennial celebrations, with which both Yeats and Gonne had been involved.[86] Lady Gregory, whose aged childhood nurse in Roxborough, county Galway, remembered hearing the cheering of locals at the time of the French landing in Killala,[87] was impassioned by local historical traditions. The title of her one-act play, *The Rising of the Moon* (1904), which was produced by the Irish National Theatre to popular acclaim in 1907, was inspired by John Keegan Casey's ballad of that name (composed ca. 1866), which recalled United Irish activity in the north midlands, and the play refers to seditious singing of 1798 rebel songs.[88] While these literary representations of Ninety-Eight related to nationalist popular culture, critical commentary on the 1798 centennial in the writings of James Joyce focused on Dublin and did not make an impression on provincial social memory.[89]

Popular print could also supplement text with illustration, which as Eileen Reilly commented "both amplifies and simplifies the concepts of the narrative by providing a parallel symbolic text."[90] Lawrence McBride noted that political illustrators "understood, perhaps unconsciously, the power of a large reservoir of folk memory that enabled a rising group of nationalist enthusiasts to interpret and then act upon a story of their collective past and present."[91] Drawings were mass-produced as color lithographs in nationalist newspapers and popular magazines, such as *Young Ireland,* the *Irish Fireside,* the *Irish Emerald,* and the *Shamrock.*[92] Prior to the centennial, John D. Reigh (fl. 1875–1914), the favored illustrator of the *Shamrock,* produced two illustrations of events from 1798 in Connacht: *The Castlebar Races*[93] and *"Died for Ireland": General Sarrazin, of the French Army of Invasion, Embracing the Corpse of the Peasant Patriot, Patrick Walsh, hanged by the English in Ballina, 1798.*[94] These pictures, designed to be removed and displayed in public view, were kept as treasured memorabilia by local nationalists in Connacht.[95] The latter, based on an illustration drawn by Edward Siebert that appeared in Gribayédoff's *The French Invasion in Ireland,* reinforced the heroic status of Walsh as a local martyr.[96]

Several illustrations portraying scenes from the French invasion were published in the early twentieth century in a twelve-volume enhanced edition of Madden's *The United Irishmen* (1910–16). The frontispiece of volume seven

FIGURE 33. *The Castlebar Races* by John D. Reigh (*Shamrock,* Christmas, 1887). Such nationalist color lithographs received wide exposure, beyond newspaper readership, when hung up as posters. Courtesy of the National Library of Ireland.

featured an original drawing by Seth B. Thompson titled *The Battle of Killala*, and the frontispiece of volume ten displayed a reproduction of the *March of the French Army Under General Humbert* by T. Carry (the original was in the possession of the Belfast antiquarian Rev. W. S. Smith). Elsewhere, the book also included a portrait of the French adjutant-General Sarrazin (drawn by "an unknown French artist").[97] While illustrations of 1798 reproduced in print contributed to the popular imagination of the Rebellion, many visual depictions remained for a long time out of public view in the exclusive domain of art connoisseurs and so could not influence social memory. *The French in Killala Bay, 1798*, an impressive oil painting by William Sadler (fl. 1868–80), was only recently exposed to a wide audience. Following its purchase by the National Gallery of Ireland, it was first put on display at an exhibition for the fiftieth anniversary of the 1916 Easter Rising,[98] and three decades later it was exhibited for the bicentennial of the 1798 Rebellion in the Ulster Museum in Belfast and reproduced in several history books.[99]

Although the French invasion and the Rebellion in Connacht and north midlands were not on the front stage of 1798 literature, considered in its entirety, there evidently was a voluminous corpus in print relating to this arena. These literary contributions articulated historical representations and provided evocative imagery, which permeated into the social memory of the Year of the French. Popular print sometimes ignored, but at other times embraced, folk history. Since cultural nationalism endorsed folklore as part of a new national canon, the publication of oral traditions gave recognition to local folk historians and collectors. The public was offered opportunities to participate in this process through columns such as "The Fireside Club" in the *Weekly Freeman* and equivalents in the *Irish Emerald* and the *Irish Fireside* or the Gaelic League's *Fáinne an Lae* and *An Claidheamh Soluis*, which invited contributions from their readers. These provided an outlet for local folklore. For example, in 1901 a contributor, who was most probably the folk historian Patrick O'Donnell of Newport, submitted to *An Claidheamh Soluis* a poem in Irish about the O'Malleys of Burrishoole, prominent Mayo rebels who had joined the French and fought at Castlebar and Ballinamuck. The verses, which were attributed to a Mathew Gibbons, had been collected from Hugh O'Donnell of Kilmeena in county Mayo, who was recognized locally for having a "wealth of folk-lore."[100] In such cases, publications served as a vehicle for preservation and recasting of folk history.

Through popular print a larger public read oral traditions, which had been rewritten in stylized literary form. Mass circulation of such transformed traditions exerted pressures on folk history. Oral narratives were readapted to

FIGURE 34. *Died for Ireland* by John D. Reigh (*Shamrock*, 1 August 1891).
Bringing to general public attention an illustration that had originally
appeared in a historical publication the previous year, the striking image
of a French general honoring a local rebel both bolstered and influenced
folk history. Courtesy of the National Library of Ireland.

conform to increasingly popular printed versions, while published stories were retold orally. An example is the story of the Mayo rebel Larry Gillespie, which was written down in romantic style in May 1858 and soon after published as "A Story of the French Invasion of '98."[101] The narrative includes references to local insurgents and draws heavily from folk history, yet it was written in a register and style foreign to oral storytelling. Eighty years later, Hayes collected the story of Larry Gillespie from a local man in Mayo, John McNeeley of Lahardane. The narrative had been reinstated into an oral folk history repertoire, though references to the names of the landlords who tried Gillespie and to the date when the rebel returned from exile suggest that influences of printed information had been retained.[102]

Oral traditions that were collected systematically in the mid-1930s along the route of the Year of the French reflect recollections that had been exposed to recurrent influences of print. Yet some of the publications in circulation also incorporated representations of folklore, which reinforced existing traditions. Through such cross-fertilization, the spoken and the written word were inseparably interwoven. For example, in 1930 the *Western People* serialized an article by Patrick O'Donnell, which juxtaposed oral traditions with historical sources that had previously appeared in print.[103] In following years, the newspaper published numerous articles on Ninety-Eight, which typically set oral traditions alongside information from written records.[104] It is not known how many of the storytellers in Mayo, who were subsequently interviewed by folklore collectors, read these pieces and inadvertently reshaped their narratives accordingly. This was not simply a case of "invented tradition" transmitted from above. Much of the detail in the collected folklore had not previously appeared in written form. Although studies of memory have categorically claimed that print and literacy wiped out oral culture,[105] the efficacy of popular print as an agent and medium of remembrance was subject to popular reception and did not overwhelm or replace vernacular historiography.

Historical Consciousness and Education

Schools were responsible for the spread of popular literacy in Ireland, and the influence of history lessons is conspicuous in several folk history accounts collected by national school pupils in 1937/38. A pupil from Kiltimagh in county Mayo supplemented a local tradition with information acquired in the classroom, which "every schoolboy knows."[106] A pupil in Castlebar, who wrote about the rebel priest Fr. Conroy, candidly admitted that "I got this in school, in my lessons on local history, and in conversation with people in the neighbourhood,"[107] while another, who had taken down details about "Humbert House" and the declaration of the Republic of Connaught, noted: "I got these in school and from a person who heard a former resident of the town."[108] One could even wonder to what extent the people interviewed about the Year of the French were themselves repeating what they had learned at school in their youth. Formal education purports to forge historical consciousness. Charged with imparting an understanding of history, pedagogues tend to dismiss folk history as a collection of unreliable and spurious myths that should be replaced with authoritative knowledge. In practice, however, the nature of the development of education in modern Ireland casts doubts as to whether it was able to dictate and completely dominate social memory.

In the years immediately following the 1798 Rebellion, the main source of education available to the rural masses remained the proliferation of unregulated "hedge schools," which had originated in the demand for clandestine Catholic education during the enforcement of Penal Laws from the late seventeenth century.[109] It has been estimated that, in the early nineteenth century, hedge schools educated between 300,000 to 400,000 predominantly Catholic children.[110] An independent survey of Mayo undertaken for the Dublin Society in 1801 listed, alongside establishments that benefited from patronage, several such "petty schools, kept and paid for by the poor."[111] In 1824, reports of the Commissioners of Education Inquiry counted 1,523 schools of various types in the province of Connacht, which educated a total of more than 70,000 pupils (with slight discrepancies between figures returned by Protestant and Catholic clergy), and in county Longford 180 schools taught more than 9,000 pupils. Most of these were still hedge schools, which were unaffiliated with educational societies, and the overwhelming majority of pupils were Catholic (over 80 percent).[112]

Hedge schools were a congenial environment for cultivating remembrance of Ninety-Eight. In the 1790s many hedge schoolmasters were actively involved in various secret societies, including Whiteboys,[113] Defenders[114] and United Irishmen.[115] In the early nineteenth century these schoolmasters were constantly accused of subversive teaching, and Crofton Croker portrayed the typical schoolmaster as an advocate of "the broadest republicanism" who propagated a nationalist interpretation of Irish history that lauded the United Irish struggle.[116] William Carleton, himself a former hedge school pupil and teacher, accused the schoolmasters of utilizing history lessons to promote dissident Catholic politics and circulate seditious textbooks.[117] A study of books actually used in the schools challenges these polemical observations by showing that there was a wide-range of available curriculum, though "an exact readership figure for any of these books cannot be ascertained nor can it be stated that every hedge school contained a set of standard textbooks or reading books."[118] An inventory of such books compiled by the Commissioners of Education Inquiry, who examined a representative county in each province (with Galway selected in Connacht), lists twenty-seven history titles on a broad scope of topics, including a *History of the Irish Rebellion of 1798*.[119]

Loyalist educationalists voiced concerns about the teaching of Irish history, fearing that it would inculcate anti-English sentiments and foster rebellious tendencies.[120] The authorities set out to discipline popular education by sponsoring trustworthy alternatives to hedge schools. Parliament funded schools run by Protestant proselytizing societies, such as the Association for Discountenancing Vice and Promoting the Knowledge and Practice of the Christian Religion (founded in 1792) or the London Hibernian Society (founded in 1806). These were soon surpassed by the Society for the Promotion of the Education of the Poor in Ireland, better known as the Kildare Place Society (founded in 1811), which was allocated substantial state funding from 1816. In 1827 the society was running 156 schools with more than 10,000 pupils in Connacht and 21 schools with some 1,400 pupils in Longford.[121] This influential society, which by 1831 had established 1,621 schools with 137,639 pupils across Ireland,[122] attracted increasing criticism from Catholics who preferred to endorse their own teaching congregations, such as the Irish Christian Brothers (founded by Edmund Ignatius Rice in 1802). With the establishment of the Board of Commissioners for National Education in 1831, state funding was diverted from philanthropic societies to a national school system. Notwithstanding these institutional changes, there was a large degree of continuity, and during the 1830s many parochial hedge schools transformed into national schools.[123]

The national school system was responsible for the introduction of standardized education at primary level throughout Ireland.[124] Its rapid expansion during the nineteenth century was startling. Despite a sharp decline in the population, there was a constant growth in numbers of schools and pupils (and a corresponding increase in certified schoolteachers and assistants). In 1835 there were 117 national schools in Connacht with 17,453 registered pupils.[125] By the turn of the century, there were 1,525 schools with 124,323 pupils and an average daily attendance of 71,629.[126] Regardless of the Irish Education Act of 1892, which required compulsory attendance for children between the ages of six and fourteen of at least seventy-five days in each half year, these figures did not reflect universal education.[127] In Connacht, only 70.8 percent of children at eligible age were enrolled, while the more sober figure of average daily attendance stood at 40.8 percent.[128] Numbers of schools and pupils declined from the early twentieth century, but thanks to legislation passed in 1926, attendance rates improved.[129] In 1937/38, when the Schools' Scheme for collecting folklore in national schools was in operation, Connacht had 1,212 primary schools with 89,115 pupils and an average daily attendance of 72,041 (about 80 percent).[130] This pattern of development (with slight local variations) applied to the principal counties from which most of the folklore sources on the Year of the French were collected (see tables 4 and 5).

Although national schools also provided manual instruction,[131] their main purpose was teaching literacy in English, which was considered essential for productive citizenship in a modern state.[132] Even so, on a ground level education was not necessarily perceived as a vehicle for modernization and Anglicization and, as John Logan observed, "for some parents the school may have been regarded as the means of observing traditional forms of communication and custom."[133] The teaching of Irish history was deliberately excised from the curriculum by the Anglican archbishop of Dublin Dr. Richard Whately

TABLE 4. Number of national schools (in principal counties)*

Year	Galway	Mayo	Leitrim	Longford
1835	31	47	13	6
1840	43	38	24	21
1850	136	146	99	61
1860	194	232	147	84
1870	287	273	188	96
1880	314	307	198	106
1890	403	396	195	110
1900	428	423	207	114
1910/11	411	416	196	104
1920/21	400	408	181	95
1930/31	372	377	162	83
1937/38	355	362	155	78

*Tables 4 and 5 are compiled from the annual *Report for the Commissioners of National Education in Ireland,* see H.C. 1835, vol. 35; 1842, vol. 23; 1851, vol. 24, pt. 1; 1861, vol. 20; 1871, vol. 23; 1881, vol. 34; 1890–91, vol. 24; 1901, vol. 21; 1911, vol. 21. Data for independent Ireland appears in "Statistics Relating to National Education for the Year 1921–22" and the annual Reports of the Department of Education; for relevant volumes see 1930–31, 1937–38.

(1787–1863), who was a prominent commissioner of national education. Despite vocal criticism from cultural nationalist circles, this policy continued throughout the nineteenth century.[134] Therefore, although some aspects of the rise of modern Irish nationalism conform to a larger European pattern, the case of education in Ireland is not comparable to sovereign states, which used national schooling to instill patriotic history, and is more akin to the condition of politically marginalized ethnic groups.[135]

In 1868/69, Catholic educationalists interviewed by a Royal Commission of Inquiry into Primary Education (commonly known as the Powis Commission) challenged the Board of Education's control over textbooks and forcefully argued that the teaching of Irish history should be permitted. Rev. John McMenamin, the parish priest of Stranorlar in county Donegal, cautioned that the current program "shuts out from every kind of history" and therefore "pupils grow up ignorant until they begin with reading newspaper periodicals, and very often violent articles, and they adopt these isolated views without due

TABLE 5. National School attendance (in principal counties)*

	GALWAY		MAYO		LEITRIM		LONGFORD	
Year	Number of pupils on rolls	Average daily attendance	Number of pupils on rolls	Average daily attendance	Number of pupils on rolls	Average daily attendance	Number of pupils on rolls	Average daily attendance
1835	6,242	N/A	5,789	N/A	1,495	N/A	872	N/A
1840	6,758	N/A	3,703	N/A	3,054	N/A	2,567	N/A
1850	17,270	N/A	15,913	N/A	10,648	N/A	6,742	N/A
1860	28,258	9,191	32,014	9,197	19,022	5,832	10,536	3,369
1870	42,581	13,701	46,529	13,455	23,729	7,796	13,018	4,278
1880	48,601	19,154	57,473	21,701	24,392	9,942	14,095	5,305
1890	51,229	21,821	55,537	24,399	20,558	9,503	12,254	5,251
1900	36,285	21,110	37,402	21,015	14,153	8,363	7,941	4,702
1910–11	33,079	21,650	34,037	21,667	11,327	7,078	7,221	4,908
1930–31	30,875	25,309	31,752	25,948	9,906	7,837	6,524	5,189
1937–38	29,025	23,841	27,302	22,360	8,419	6,794	5,907	4,686

*Attendance is unavailable prior to 1852. When statistics were calculated on a term basis, the average daily attendance cited is for the second term (which in the nineteenth century, ended on 30 September). From 1877, reported pupil enrollment and attendance was generally slightly lower than the actual figures, since returns were not received from all schools. Until 1900 the figures of pupils on rolls show the total number, whereas later years show the average number (which was lower). Attendance by county is unavailable for 1919–21 (the transition from British rule).

reflection." Remonstrating against the "anti-national monopoly" on school-books, Cardinal Paul Cullen (1803–78) sardonically remarked that "if all the books printed by the National Board were sent to the middle of the Atlantic and cast out into the ocean, Ireland and her literature would suffer no great loss." Pressures arising from deep-rooted political and religious divides practically guaranteed that the censure on history classes was not removed, but the commissioners recommended that "any schoolbook should be allowed without privilege" and decided to "leave free the use of suitable books to managers and teachers," though the National Board retained the right to veto "any objectionable works previously to their use."[136]

Unapproved Irish history textbooks were widely available, and some of them even included questions to be used in the classroom in order to ascertain comprehension of the lessons. Although these books reviewed 1798, their treatment of the Rebellion in the West was cursory and often dismissive. Martin Haverty's *History of Ireland, Ancient and Modern, for the use of Schools and Colleges* (1860) briefly referred to "Humbert's quixotic enterprise."[137] Townsend Young's *The History of Ireland, from the earliest records to the present time for the use of schools* (1863), which aspired to be "candid and conciliating—honest and inoffensive—fit for youth and age—for the school, the study, and the drawing room—and undefiled by a single trait of religious asperity," labeled the Connacht rebels "misguided peasantry." Those who fought at Ballinamuck were a "naked, uncomfortable, desponding multitude" and those who remained in Killala were "unresisting and defenceless wretches."[138] The two thousand copies of the first edition of *An Illustrated History of Ireland* by Mary Frances Cusack, "The Nun of Kenmare" (1829–99), were enthusiastically circulated by clergy and sold out within three months. The book devotes one sentence to the "worse than useless" French landing.[139] William Francis Collier's popular *History of Ireland for Schools* (1885) covered the episode in four short sentences.[140]

The Commissioners of National Education had no control over independent schools. Most notably, the influential Christian Brothers, who in 1836 had opted to secede from the national system, saw themselves as a Catholic educational avant-garde. Even though their numbers were relatively small, they acquired a reputation as superior educators who put a particular emphasis on teaching Irish history,[141] and from the end of the nineteenth century on, their lessons increasingly inculcated militant nationalism.[142] Nonetheless, *Historical Class-Book* (1859), which remained their main history textbook into the early twentieth century, only assigned one sentence (backed up by a sketchy footnote) to 1798, ignoring completely the French invasion.[143]

Secondary schooling was introduced in 1878 through the intermediate education system.[144] From its inception, its success in Connacht was dismal. In its first year, only 273 pupils in the province were presented for exams and 20 percent of those examined were incapable of answering a single question in many of the subjects.[145] By the end of the century only twenty-eight schools in Connacht (and three in Longford) had been opened, and numbers of pupils were low,[146] a situation that continued well into the twentieth century.[147] At a postprimary level, history was combined with geography as part of the English curriculum.[148] Compared to other subjects, it suffered from low esteem,[149] and in 1899 when a comprehensive report based on testimonies of teachers and principals was compiled, history did not merit special mention.[150]

Following his appointment as resident commissioner of national education (1899), Dr. William Joseph Myles Starkie (1860–1920) introduced Irish history into the national schools primary curriculum, at first as part of the study of English (1900) and a few years later as an "ordinary school subject" in its own right (1908). Yet history textbooks continued to disregard the 1798 Rebellion in Connacht and the north midlands. For example, the extremely popular *Child's History of Ireland* (1897), written by the polymath educationalist Patrick Weston Joyce (1827–1914) and approved as early as 1898, dedicates less than a paragraph to the French invasion,[151] and Mrs. Gwynn's *Stories from Irish History* (1904) devotes a mere two sentences to this affair.[152] Teachers, however, were allowed a large degree of freedom in the way they chose to deliver the lessons, and it was expected that readers for fourth and higher standards would be supplemented by "oral instruction."[153] The Commissioners of National Education issued *Notes for Teachers* (1908), which recommended that historical facts should not merely be memorized by rote. They advised stimulating the students by reading in the classroom poems and ballads and arranging excursions in the locality from the fifth standard (grade) up.[154]

Unionists were alarmed by this new educational liberalism and, on the background of the struggle for Irish independence, a heated debate ensued on the teaching of nationalist history.[155] The combative Ulster Presbyterian educationalist Rev. William Corkey (1877–1964) insisted that textbooks used in Catholic schools glorified political violence. He claimed that "the children in the vast majority of Irish schools are being sedulously taught the most dangerous political doctrine" and "a good illustration of this false attitude in these history primers towards rebellion is found in the accounts they give of the rebellion of 1798." In particular he identified the *Irish History Reader*, introduced by the Christian Brothers in the early twentieth century, as "by far the most seditious" of nationalist textbooks.[156] However, the short section in this book on the western arena of 1798, which comes as a conclusion to lengthy chapters on the Rebellion and a prelude to a section on the death of Wolfe Tone, is not overtly politicized.[157]

After independence, the teaching of history in the Irish Free State was recognized as a valuable method for inculcating the ideal of a national Gaelic ethos and heritage. At this time, the Christian Brothers' schools were integrated into the national school system and their influence grew considerably with state funding.[158] The "First National Programme for Primary Schools" (1922), which required that from the third standard (grade) up history should be taught through the Irish language, proved to be unrealistic and was modified within a few years (1926). Beginning in 1932, Fianna Fáil governments charged history education with the responsibility of instilling Gaelic-Irish patriotism.[159] The Department of Education's *Notes for Teachers*, issued in 1933 and in effect up to 1971, prescribed teaching history through "stories of the heroic or romantic exploits of the national heroes of legend and semi-history."[160]

Though Irish history was on the curriculum in national schools from the beginning of the century, the effectiveness of teaching is debatable. Examining inspectors' reports both before and after independence, the historian David Fitzpatrick noted that forty-eight out of seventy reports for the period of 1902–14 were entirely negative and that reports submitted during 1925–30 were largely unfavorable, repeatedly complaining that history was taught by rote and that local history was being neglected. These figures seem to suggest that, by and large, history lessons "left a hasty scrawl rather than indelible imprint" on the minds of pupils.[161] The 1798 Rebellion was identified as an important topic, and teachers were instructed to put an emphasis on local history in the broadest sense—from the neighborhood to the parish, diocese, county, and province. Therefore, evaluation of how the provincial experience of 1798 was taught can serve to better qualify the impact of education.

The *Notes for Teachers* only mention the risings in Antrim, Down, and Wexford, while Wexford alone was recognized as having traditions of Ninety-Eight that are "still valid."[162] Accordingly, the textbooks in use, which were often revised versions of earlier books, focused on the insurrection in Wexford and only briefly mentioned Connacht, without offering details on the Franco-Irish campaign from Mayo to the north midlands. For example, *A School History of Ireland* by the Trinity College historian Constantia Maxwell, who also compiled a bibliography of Irish history for schoolteachers, allocates a short paragraph to the French invasion, which notes that the "poor and ignorant" Irish rebels "could render very little effective assistance."[163] Puzzlingly, a recommended history reading list for teachers set in 1933 included "The Rebellion of 1798— Hayes" (alongside Richard Hayes's *Ireland and Irishmen in the French Revolu-*

tion),[164] yet at the time there was no such book in print. This reference probably derived from common knowledge that Hayes was intending to write a book on the topic, which eventually was published as *The Last Invasion of Ireland*.

While the Year of the French was considered an important aspect of local and regional heritage, evidently teachers in Connacht and the north midlands who wished to address this topic in the classroom could not have based their lessons on information found in textbooks. The Department of Education indeed assumed that "earnest teachers will endeavour to procure, either by purchase or loan, books that deal with local history" and that they would compile newspaper clippings of historical interest that appeared in the local press. Moreover, it was considered "desirable that a number of teachers in a locality should form among themselves study groups to search out all the historical lore obtainable regarding this particular area."[165] Teachers had to independently find ways to enhance their history classes, and for this purpose extracurricular resources, especially folk history, were of great value.

Some thirty-five copybooks from Drumgownagh N.S. in Annaghmore [Eanach Mór], county Leitrim, show that in the course of the summer of 1938 pupils were repeatedly assigned compositions on local 1798 encounters, initially in early May and twice more in July (when essays written around the fifth focused on the insurgents' stopover at Cloone and a week later, around the twelfth, essays described the Battle of Ballinamuck). Although several pupils insisted that their essays were based on oral interviews, most of the accounts are repetitive and follow a constant formula, which reflects the unmistakable reception of lessons learned at school.[166] Aware of these duplications, the teachers chose not to include the bulk of these essays in the official contribution submitted to the Department of Education and subsequently entered into the Schools' Manuscript Collection compiled by the Irish Folklore Commission.[167] Nonetheless, a comparison between the essays exposes variations and identifies unique accounts, which had indeed been collected firsthand by pupils. In this case, history lessons proved effective, though they did not entirely obfuscate folk history.

Knowledge of history was not only acquired in classrooms. Educationalists have come to realize that "'unofficial' educational histories have also always existed, independent of formal schooling and rooted in popular culture."[168] In the words of an anthropologist: "We all need histories that no history book can tell, but they are not in the classroom—not the history classroom anyway. They are in the lessons we learn at home, in poetry and childhood games, in what is left of history when we close the history books with their verifiable facts."[169] In Ireland this was particularly the case, as Patrick Callan noted: "the lack of Irish history meant that pupils had to rely on the resources of their society, on the home, the ballad and the poem."[170] Lawrence McBride observed that "there was in Ireland from the 1870s, if not earlier, a massive de facto history education industry at work that served thousands of individuals whom contemporaries called 'nationalist enthusiasts.'"[171] The popular histories, newspapers, periodicals, songbooks, novels, and dramas discussed in the previous section, "Remembrance and Popular Culture," served this informal "education industry."

Above all, A. M. Sullivan's immensely popular *The Story of Ireland* (originally published in 1867), which was reissued in more than thirty editions, has been labeled "the bible of popular nationalism."[172] It was used as a supplementary reader by teachers and pupils in the intermediate classes of Christian Brothers' schools[173] and became a "family history book" in many Irish homes.[174] Roy Foster asserted that this best seller virtually constructed national memory by defining the metanarrative of Irish history,[175] though Luke Gibbons questioned whether it could totally "co-opt and control the more unruly and refractory narratives of vernacular history."[176] The short paragraph that deals with the arrival of the French in 1798 rehearses the standard formula that "they came too late, or the rising was too soon." Inferring that the momentary victory at Castlebar was representative of the whole campaign, Sullivan made the preposterous claim that "Humbert literally chased the government troops before him across the island." Remarkably, he chose not to refer to the massacres of Irish rebels following the French surrender, which was typically mentioned in popular nationalist histories.[177] It would seem that this influential national text did not determine the way the provincial experience was remembered.

Juvenile historical literature, which offered "an *ad hoc* alternative reading curriculum for young learners,"[178] included several Ninety-Eight novels written to ignite youthful imagination. One of these, *The Round Tower* (1904) by Florence Mary Seymour Scott and Alma Hodge (fl. 1896–1904), tells the story of two English boys who witness the French landing in Mayo.[179] Though they were not textbooks per se, these books could be found in school libraries. Several nationalist magazines catered to young readers; beginning in September 1914 the Christian Brothers produced *Our Boys*, which had a strong historical content that was often conveyed in comic strips.[180] These comics proved very effective in sparking interest in the past and could leave a lasting impression. Fr. Owen Devaney from Mullahoran in county Cavan, an authority on local folk history of Ninety-Eight who was raised in Esker near Ballinamuck, attributed his lifelong interest in history and oral traditions to a cartoon of swordsmen in 1798 published in *Our Boys*, which he had seen at the age of five.[181] Literary representations of Ninety-Eight in popular print could be perceived by young readers as local tradition, and this was especially the case for centennial publications, which a generation later had acquired an aura of antiquity. A pupil from Balieboro in county Cavan submitted to the Schools' Scheme extracts from a highly stylized story about 1798 published in the *Anglo-Celt* newspaper in 1899—his essay was accepted by the teacher as bona fide folklore.[182]

Commemorative ceremonies were also an important part of this mass exercise in nationalist informal education, with monuments functioning as semiotic didactic aides.[183] A Sinn Féin activist in Dublin remarked that "in absence of the systematic teaching of our country's history in the schools, these monuments would be to the child the illustrations of a portion of our National story."[184] John O'Dowd's poetic composition for the unveiling of the centennial monument for Bartholomew Teeling outside Collooney triumphantly declares:

> And here upon hallowed ground, where Teeling turned the day,
> A monument of stone is found, to honour deeds of clay!
> It will stimulate our Irish youth, heroic deeds to do.
> When next for freedom and for truth, the combat they renew.[185]

As already demonstrated (in chapter 14), essays of pupils on local Ninety-Eight folklore show that these memorials indeed made a strong impression.

Participation of youth was often purposely incorporated into commemorative programs. At the 1948 celebrations in Killala, for example, "a much appreciated feature was the recital of numerous ballads and patriotic songs by Killala National Schools' Choir."[186] James Joyce mordantly suggested that such events were not necessarily remembered favorably by the youth who attended them. In *Portrait of the Artist as a Young Man* (1916), when the protagonist Stephen Dedalus recalls his childhood experience of attending the centennial celebration in Dublin, he "remembered with bitterness that scene of tawdry tribute. There were four French delegates in a break and one, a plump smiling young man held, wedged on a stick, a card on which were printed the words: *Vive l'Irlande!*"[187] However, perhaps touched-up by nostalgia, impressions left by provincial commemorations of Ninety-Eight were remembered affectionately many years later and even entered into oral tradition. In 1998 Pat Noone of Collooney recalled that his grandfather would repeat the recollections of his father (Pat's great-grandfather) who attended as a schoolboy the local centennial celebration.[188] Pat Joe McLoughlin recalled how as a boy of seven, he had been brought to the 1948 commemoration in Ballinamuck, where he "heard the president of Ireland—Sean T. O'Kelly address the huge crowd, and had a sense of a place where history was made."[189] Fifty years on, residents of Castlebar, who had been young children at the time, could vividly recall the horses that rode through the streets of the town during the battle reenactment of "the Races of Castlebar" in 1948[190] or the parade in 1953.[191]

The notion of a distinction between formal and informal education proves nebulous, particularly in light of teachers' involvement in organizing commemorative programs. The schoolteacher John Bohan of Bornacoola (a south Leitrim parish adjacent to Longford) spoke at the 1938 ceremony at Ballinamuck,[192] and his speech was still remembered by locals interviewed thirty years later.[193] The congratulatory rhetoric of commemoration gave schoolteachers (many of whom were active folk historians) a sense of pride in their locality and reaffirmed for them the value of local traditions of Ninety-Eight. At the time of the Schools' Scheme, the legacy of this incentive was especially noticeable in the area of Ballinamuck, where the teacher Peter Duignan of Gaigue N.S. and James McKenna, the principal of Kiltycreevagh N.S., not only encouraged their pupils to collect a large body of folklore accounts on the battle of Ballinamuck but also collected numerous oral traditions themselves.[194]

Teachers documenting folklore inadvertently combined oral tradition with information that they had acquired from written historical and literary sources. These syntheses between traditional and educated knowledge are often apparent in the injection of precise dates and figures into folklore accounts. For example, a national schoolteacher in Cloone, county Leitrim, supplemented an oral narrative with the exact date of the arrival of the Franco-Irish army in the village.[195] Although teachers did not set out to consciously undermine or reconstruct oral traditions, revised folk-history accounts were then taught at school. In this way classrooms were a medium for both the transmission and the transformation of folk history.

Long before modern research confirmed the value of teaching history through stories,[196] teachers were encouraged to emulate *seanchaithe* (storytellers) by recounting "stories vividly and dramatically" and performing poems and ballads in the class, while "giving preference to those of local interest." It was stipulated that "any local song or poem in Irish or English, which commemorates some event in local history should be learnt by heart, and the allusions it contains explained even when it is of little literary merit."[197] Such learning by rote has been discredited and is not even mentioned in recent pedagogical studies,[198] for fear perhaps that it might discourage independent thought and stifle imagination, but its alleged lack of value is hardly self-evident. Poetic renditions from folk history that were acquired in class were remembered and could later be repeated. A pupil in county Galway, who had learned a pike drill in Irish from his schoolmaster Seán Ó Gairbhín, submitted this piece of *seanchas* to the Schools' Scheme.[199] Although it derived from schooling, this was a traditional recitation; earlier in the century other versions had been collected orally in the locality by Dr Thomas B. Costello and farther afield in county Offaly by the renowned folklorist Douglas Hyde.[200] Instead of replacing folklore, literacy and education found uses for it and could even contribute to its preservation in new forms.

Countless studies of commemoration have simplistically maintained that "collective memory" is embodied in the erection of a monument, the writing of a text, or the teaching of a lesson, and then assumed that such vehicles in the service of a modern nation went on to replace traditional "folk memory." Rather than supplanting folk history, public commemoration, popular print, and state education offered spheres and mediums for remembrance in which oral traditions were recycled. National and metropolitan discourses met provincial and vernacular discourses of remembrance through the mediation of, to use a term employed by Jim Mac Laughlin, the "'unsung heroes' of nation-building," such as journalists, local historians, and national schoolteachers.[201] The traditions of folk history were reproduced, and at the same modified, in a process that regenerated social memory so that *seanchas* of the Year of the French survived into the twentieth century.

16

Memory and Oblivion

Commemorations are as selective as sympathies. They
honour *our* dead, not *your* dead.

Edna Longley
"The Rising, the Somme and Irish Memory"

I T IS OFTEN SAID that history was written by the victors, but by whom was it
remembered, and what was remembered? To phrase the question in another
way, who preferred not to remember and what was not remembered? The historian Peter Burke incisively suggested:

> It might be said that history is forgotten by the victors. They can afford to for-
> get, while the losers are unable to accept what has happened and are condemned
> to brood over it, relive it, and reflect how different it might have been.[1]

In the seminal lecture "Qu'est-ce qu'une nation?" delivered at the Sorbonne in
1882, French historian and critic Ernest Renan argued that forgetting "is a cru-
cial factor in the creation of a nation," which invariably suppresses recollections of acts of violence and coercion.[2] Remembrance of problematic episodes
in the collective past challenges national metanarratives and poses a threat to
the dominant power structures. Memory proves to be subversive so that, in the
famous words of Milan Kundera, "the struggle of man against power is the
struggle of memory against forgetting."[3]

The social thinker William Graham Sumner remarked that "monuments,
festivals, mottoes, oratory, and poetry may enter largely into the mores. They
never help history; they obscure it. They protect errors and sanctify prejudices."[4] As expressions of social memory, Irish folk history and the vernacular commemorative practices it cultivated had a particular ethical value. Drawing on the resources of oral tradition, they acknowledged suffering and

humiliation that were mostly ignored in official commemoration, and allowed local communities to express empathy and sympathy with the traumatic experiences of their ancestors. To use terms introduced by Paul Ricoeur, folk history was a medium for "telling otherwise." By "letting others tell their own history" it countermanded the "abuse of commemorative festivals," which was effectively an "abuse of memory."[5] Through commemoration, metropolitan centers attempted to manipulate perceptions of the past in the periphery. National monuments were professedly erected as acts of remembrance, but they also functioned as acts of forgetting, appropriating, and attempting to "flatten," even bury, social memory by reducing it to superficial images that validate those in power. For example, memorials of the United States Civil War de-politicized ideological conflict and marginalized the issues of racial inequality over which it had been fought.[6] On the other hand, the popular reception of commemorative programs and monuments was subject to contestations from grassroots traditions of remembrance.

At the time of the 1798 Rebellion, the state set out to purge recollections of dissent. The Fifth Royal Irish Guards, for example, were disbanded for showing insubordination in 1797, and the regiment was struck off military rolls and only reassembled from scratch some fifty years later.[7] Rebels, who were mostly buried in mass graves without monuments, could not be commemorated in public. However, the ability of the state to proscribe nonconforming memories was limited. Innovative classical scholars have shown that policies of *damnatio memoriae,* exercised by imperial authorities in ancient Rome against alleged enemies of the state, did not achieve *obolitio memoriae* but in practice amounted to "a highly symbolic, universal display of pantomime forgetfulness," which "served to *dishonour* the record of the person and so, in an oblique way, to confirm memory."[8] In France, commemorative celebrations of the Revolution censured the memory of victims of revolutionary state terror.[9] Yet for all its power, official commemoration was not able to totally wipe out the deviant narratives of remembrance, which Michel Foucault labeled "counter-memories."[10] Philippe Joutard's studies of French Protestant social memory demonstrated that local oral traditions maintained alternative recollections, which had been written out of official history and national commemoration.[11]

Provincial Irish folk history was preoccupied with experiences of local communities that, by and large, did not appear in official history. Accordingly, folklore of the Year of the French focused on those who fought and lost the Rebellion. James C. Scott described underground traditions of resistance as "hidden transcripts," which could reformulate after an unsuccessful uprising, when rebels were "likely to be noted, admired, and even mythologized in stories of bravery, social banditry, and noble sacrifice. They become themselves part of the hidden transcript."[12] With Irish nationalism in the nineteenth century asserting itself as an "emergent culture" of "counter-hegemony," to use the neo-Marxist terminology of Raymond Williams,[13] the centennial commemorations of the 1798 Rebellion constituted a "public transcript," which aspired to counterbalance, if not surpass, the ostensibly hegemonic culture of contemporary imperial and unionist commemoration.[14] While these "public transcripts" were carefully monitored by government intelligence agencies,[15] the "hidden transcripts" of folk history and vernacular commemorative traditions (such as laments or place-names) remained largely unnoticed by the state.

Influences of nationalist commemoration permeated folk history, but the negotiations that reconstructed social memory did not result in its obliteration, and despite an excess of celebrations, monuments, publications, and educational programs, local oral traditions persisted into the twentieth century. The porous metanarrative promulgated by national commemorations accommodated certain micronarratives but marginalized others. Emerging out of cataclysmic conflicts and riveted by deep divisions, the independent Irish state founded in the early twentieth century suffered from "commemorative paralysis" and was practically incapable in its formative years of utilizing commemoration to promote solidarity.[16] A conservative political culture co-opted official commemoration of 1798, and alternative voices in social memory, which did not comply with the prevailing trends, were muffled. The "Irish Revolution" that gave birth to the Irish Free State, had its winners and losers, and even though it created a stable democracy (which was declared a republic on the sesquicentennial of 1798), oral traditions of marginalized social groups were excluded from public spheres and rarely allowed to transcend private and family spheres.

Leerssen distinguished between two modes of collective remembrance in modern Ireland and related them to the memory of Ninety-Eight: monumental "society remembrancing," which is typically manifested through state-sanctioned public commemoration, as opposed to traumatic "community remembrancing," which is characteristically subelite and demotic.[17] Commemoration initiated by Ascendancy circles would appear to be an expression of elite commemoration par excellence. Indeed, it was often founded on triumphalism. Following the Battle of Ballinamuck, the Eighth Armagh Militia Regiment, which had participated in the slaughter of Irish rebels, brought back the flag of the Second battalion of the French Seventieth Demi-Brigade to Gosford Castle in county Armagh and displayed it as a commemorative trophy. The colors were relocated in 1891 to the local Church of Ireland Cathedral and later exhibited at the Armagh Public Library (formerly Archbishop Robinson's Library).[18] But loyalist acts of remembrance were not necessarily triumphalist. Following the Rebellion in the West, a fund-raising campaign was launched in Dublin to collect "subscriptions for the widows and orphans of our brave soldiery who have fallen in battle and such of the Military as have been wounded in opposing the late invasion."[19] Such charitable initiatives also had a commemorative nature, recalling the suffering of those who fought on the government side.

The distinction between monumental and traumatic commemoration should not be reified, as the two are interdependent and practically define each other.[20] Although support of the Crown served the interests of political and social elites, it was part of a loyalist popular culture that generated its own oral traditions. By examining depositions submitted to the Commission for the Relief of Suffering Loyalists, Musgrave showed that loyalists had a lot to say in the wake of the Rebellion,[21] yet this early oral history project has been dismissively branded a post-Rebellion polemic.[22] The essayist Thomas de Quincey (1785–1859), famous for his "Autobiography of an English Opium Eater," visited Mayo in his youth and stayed as a guest of Lord Altamont in Westport House just two years after the Rebellion, where he constantly heard recollections of the "disastrous scenes of the rebellion" and "the Civil War of Connaught."[23]

Popular print published recollections of loyalists. As a young captain, Major-General Shortall, the commander of the Magazine Fort in Phoenix Park, had fought at Castlebar and his reminisces appeared almost fifty years later in the *Dublin University Magazine*.[24] Several years earlier, Shortall's bravery in 1798 was worked into a historical novel by Maxwell.[25] Nineteenth-century antiquarians and travel writers, like Maxwell, noted in their travels various recollections of the Rebellion among Protestants. In northwest Mayo, a Colonel Dwyer told Maxwell of a raconteur who captivated an audience at a dinner party with stories of his escapades at Castlebar in 1798. Although the "memories" of heroism in this case turned out to be fabricated, it is apparent that in certain Protestant circles there was great interest in loyalist recollections and traditions of the Rebellion.[26] A Protestant curate in the Mayo parish of Ballycastle recalled the "Connaught rebellion of 1798" when conversing with Caesar Otway (who, like Maxwell, was also an Anglican clergyman), and elsewhere Otway collected a Ninety-Eight tradition of a Protestant gentleman who took refuge in Erris.[27]

A number of loyalist women left narratives of their experiences during the French invasion, some of which appeared in print. An account by the celebrated author Maria Edgeworth, which was originally published in the second volume of her father's memoirs,[28] is complemented by her correspondence and the recollections of her stepmother (formerly Miss Beaufort)[29] and half-sister,

Elizabeth ("Bess") Edgeworth.[30] During the centennial, a letter written in 1798 by Mrs. Brigit Thompson, the wife of the Protestant dean of Castlebar, documenting her traumatic experiences in Killala under French occupation, was published in the *Cornhill Magazine*.[31]

These traditions did not sit well with a predominantly Catholic folk history and so were not collected systematically in the early twentieth century. However, social memory was heterogeneous and accounts documented by folklore collectors also recalled Catholics in Connacht who refused to join the rebels and even actively opposed the Rebellion. Although not explicitly proscribed, recalcitrant traditions of popular loyalism were frowned upon and left unacknowledged. This omission has been compounded by historiographical disregard. Critics of recent historical studies of 1798 have pointed out that "the conservatives and moderates who opposed the insurrection have attracted remarkably little attention" so that the study of the popular culture of loyalism and Orangeism "remains surprisingly neglected,"[32] while at the same time loyalist and Protestant accounts of the Rebellion have been dismissed as formulaic and "*simply* sectarian."[33]

As Irish public culture became increasingly dominated by Catholic nationalism in the late-nineteenth and early-twentieth centuries, the memory of events associated with loyalism, such as the participation of Irish soldiers in the British army in World War I, "evoked embarrassment and resentment"[34] and was "forgetfully remembered."[35] In this reversal of tables, many sites of loyalist commemoration, like the equestrian statues in Dublin, were purposely vandalized in displays of what the cultural geographer Yvonne Whelan labeled "de-commemoration."[36] Other public sites became derelict, and consequently loyalist remembrance was confined to private spheres. In Castlebar, loyalists recalled the valor of Scottish soldiers in Colonel Simon Fraser of Lovat's fencible regiment, who died defending the town from the French invaders.[37] A traveler passing through Mayo in 1801 was told of the "truly Spartan bravery" with which the outnumbered soldiers "fell at their post, victims to bravery and truth." Even then, the story was considered part of an oral history, which had not been "hitherto recorded in any account of the invasion or rebellion."[38] At the time only two soldiers were mentioned, but when Fraser erected a memorial it named six individuals. A large stone slab was placed in the eastern wall of Christchurch (Church of Ireland) in Castlebar and, describing the site, a contemporary wrote: "I saw, with strong emotion, the ground were these soldiers fell, like Spartans of old."[39] Yet only two decades later, when a larger edifice replaced the wall, the memorial plaque was discarded and left by the main gate of the church's graveyard[40] and in subsequent years was not restored or relocated to a more respectable location.[41] Nonetheless, local Protestant oral traditions continued to recall the burial of the Fencibles into the twentieth century.[42]

Many oral traditions of rebellion mention women, but even within folk commemoration they were excluded from public remembrance. They did not appear in the numerous place-names associated with the Year of the French; poetic laments, which may have originated in the keening of women, were not composed in memory of women. At the time of the centenary, the only Ninety-Eight monument dedicated to a woman was the memorial for Betsy Gray near Ballynahinch in county Down, which soon became a contested site, sparking controversies between nationalist and unionists that resulted in the memorial's violent destruction.[43] The centennial monuments in the female form of Erin do not recall the experiences of women in 1798 and do not relate to the ways in which women featured in folk history. Instead, they correspond to a wider pattern of national commemorations in which women served as "symbols of a 'lost' past, nostalgically perceived and romantically constructed, but their actual lives are most readily forgotten."[44]

An initiative in 1897 to form an Irish Women's Centenary Union (emulating the Ladies' Land League), "in which the women of Ireland will unite to do their part in honoring the martyr's of '98," stipulated that female volunteers restrict themselves to the gender-specific activities of promoting literature and education. Beside Maud Gonne, who was a prominent dignitary at centennial events, the only women on the central executive of the national centenary committee were the Belfast nationalists Alice Milligan and Ethna Carbery.[45] When folklore was endorsed, oral accounts were collected within the confines of a rigidly patriarchal society, which was not receptive to the inclusion of heroines in the pantheon of national heroes. Following independence, the only national monument dedicated to a woman was the memorial to Countess Constance Markievicz, which was unveiled in 1932 by the Taoiseach (Prime Minister) Eamon de Valera, whose speech concentrated on Markievicz's charitable work and underplayed her revolutionary activities.[46]

Through various spheres and mediums of remembrance, provincial social memory was in constant dialogue with commemoration "from above," but this was an unequal dialogue. Official commemoration typically selected and highlighted aspects of folk history that could be accommodated within prevailing historiographical and political trends, and excluded noncompliant traditions. In the second half of the twentieth century, the dominant trend in public commemoration worldwide shifted from celebration of victors to remembrance of victims, but this was not as radical a change as it may initially appear. The ability of minorities and marginalized groups to erect monuments that commemorate suffering in their pasts often depends on their economic and political affluence in the present.[47] A case in point can be found in the memorials of the Great Famine erected during the economic boom of the so-called Celtic Tiger.[48] Public commemoration is a form of cultural capital. It is typically a partisan and exclusive activity that stifles the development of more inclusive expressions of remembrance.

Despite its limitations and internal agendas, the social memory expressed in folk history fulfills a unique role. It facilitates the telling of alternative versions of history, which challenge the ways the past has been presented, packaged, and marketed by the political and cultural elites that aspire to dictate the politics of commemoration. This was not an act of individual resistance but a social activity, as performances of folk history were communal experiences that did not promote the privatization of history. Folk history was democratic but not egalitarian, it was subaltern but not necessarily radical, and like all forms of remembrance, it inevitably entailed forgetting.

Conclusion

Alternative History

Archaeologies of Social Memory

In our time history aspires to the condition of archaeology.

Michel Foucault
The Archaeology of Knowledge

PREVAILING TRENDS in European historiography maintain that, with the advent of modernity, "folk memory" underwent a fatal shock and passed away en masse. Age-old traditions of remembrance were allegedly supplanted by new constructions of "collective memory" imposed by modern states. Hobsbawm dated the extensive diffuse of "invented traditions" to 1870–1914, coinciding with the institutionalizing of national bureaucratic apparatuses.[1] Similarly, Eugen Weber's seminal study of the emergence of a modern French state and the demise of rural-peasant society outlined an almost total disappearance of folk traditions, which occurred over that same period.[2] The assumption that an antiquated but thriving "living tradition" of memory died around the turn of the nineteenth century is also at the heart of Nora's historiographical project, which takes as it starting point that "*lieux de mémoire* exist because there are no longer any *milieux de mémoire,* settings in which memory is a real part of everyday experience."[3] These dominant models of collective memory originated in Britain and France, and have been universally acclaimed and emulated.[4]

In contrast to the seemingly authoritative assertion that a sweeping modernization of *mentalité* totally transformed historical consciousness and eradicated the last vestiges of "authentic" folklore by the eve of World War I, the work of the Irish Folklore Commission demonstrated that vibrant oral traditions, which were rooted in the past, persisted well into the twentieth century—and arguably into the twenty-first century. At the same time, the folklore collectors were driven by a sense of urgency. Rural society was indeed undergoing rapid changes, and it was imperative to document oral traditions. Though many traditions were collected, inevitably countless others remained unrecorded.

When on fieldwork in 1935/36, Hayes discovered that the Year of the French was "still among the living traditions of the west," but he was also regretful that oral traditions had passed away:

> I had not proceeded far till the realisation came that I was a little late. And I could not help often thinking of the rich harvest that might have been garnered a generation or two ago when men were still alive who saw the soldiers of France march through Connacht and heard their drums beating along its roads.

He likened the traditions that he collected to "flotsam and jetsam left from the years."[5] Halbwachs, a contemporary of Hayes, chose a different maritime metaphor to illustrate the workings of social memory. He described "living memory" as a sea receding from a rocky shore and leaving behind "miniature lakes nestled amidst the rocky foundations." The rocks stand for the social frameworks (*les cadres sociaux de la mémoire*), which are the contexts in which fragmented recollections—represented by the puddles—are formed into social memory.[6] The historian, Hayes, was looking for surviving recollections of the past, while the sociologist, Halbwachs, was more interested in the contexts in which recollections of the past were reshaped.

"Living memory" is a nebulous concept. Many studies of narrative assume that memory is an organic entity, which is grounded in the personal experiences of a particular generation and can be transmitted at the very most from grandparent to grandchild. After three generations, memory is ostensibly codified and ossified. But even though vibrancy of oral traditions diminishes with time, this process of decline cannot be readily schematized. Disintegration of memory is checked by the reconstructive dynamics of remembrance that piece together fragmented reminiscences. Models of "living memory," founded on reifications of the distinction between oral history and oral tradition, tend to overlook the regeneration of recollections, which are adapted or reinvented to suit changing contexts.

Written records of oral traditions cannot capture this fluidity. To return to the allegories mentioned, not only do the tides of "living memory" ebb and flow but the rocky landscape is also transformed, and these transitions reshape the flotsam and jetsam, which is later collected on the shore. There is a dissonance between social memory and "collected memory." When collected and archived, oral accounts are effectively uprooted and relocated, so that analytical studies of folklore are generally not based as much on firsthand examination of oral traditions as on "fossilized" reproductions that have lost much of the versatility and dynamism of the originals. In a Freudian analysis of the function of archives, the philosopher Jacques Derrida argued that although they purport to preserve recollections of the past, archives paradoxically facilitate a structural breakdown of memory.[7] Studies of social memory need to find ways to address these perplexities.

Folk histories largely remained outside the domains of mainstream scholarly history and did not comply with the standards of professional historiography. As historical sources, folklore accounts prove to be multilayered and complex. While they clearly offer insight into the historical perceptions of their narrators, history-tellings claimed to provide information on the past. Moreover, in order to remain relevant and vital over several generations, traditions adapted to changing historical circumstances.[8] Embedded in them is a history of transmissions over time, involving continuities and changes. How can historians make sense of the puzzling field of vernacular historiography without falling into a dichotomy between a "positivist" approach, which searches for surviving residues from the past, and an "interpretative" approach, which focuses on the ethnographic present?

The key to this conundrum can be found in recontextualization. Social memory has been succinctly described as "the enveloping fold of a context-free meaningful past,"[9] yet the study of history requires that sources be examined within an historical context. The fragmentary state of recollections demands an exercise of restoration, in an attempt to reconstruct narratives and reimagine the history-tellings in which they were performed. The nature of these tasks suggests a comparison to nineteenth-century classical archaeology, a science preoccupied with excavation, restoration, recontextualization, and interpretation of fragments from the past. Indeed, the term "archaeology of memory" was introduced by the cultural critic Walter Benjamin, who used it in reference to the recovery of the past through recollections. Prior to that, although not referred to by name, it was also an underlining concept of the art historian Aby Warburg's multilayered spatial models of the past.[10]

As oral traditions change over time, Vansina argued that "tradition should be seen as a series of successive historical documents all lost except for the last one and usually interpreted by every link in the chain of transmission." He aphorized that "oral traditions are not just sources about the past, but a historiology (one dare not say historiography!) of the past, an account of how people have interpreted it."[11] The term "oral historiography" was discussed earlier in order to flag the need to chart changes in oral traditions. John Tosh, who maintained that "it makes more sense to regard oral tradition as a secondary source, but with the added twist that it has erased all earlier versions," likened oral tradition to the publication of a monograph "marked by the destruction of all copies of the previous work on the subject."[12] However, the introductory chapter on ancillary folk history sources questioned the usefulness of making distinctions between primary and secondary sources for the study of social memory.

It is sometimes possible to tentatively sketch the evolution of traditions. The contexts in which traditions were performed and transformed can be appreciated through the examination of "spheres and mediums of remembrance" (see chapter 11), while analysis of their content can expose marks of earlier versions and clues to when they were performed. David Gross termed such an approach "genealogical deconstruction," or more provocatively "constructive sabotage," and suggested that it should work on three levels in order to uncover the original traditions, changes that occurred during transmissions, and traditions that were "re-functioned" in a new context.[13] Ideally, each tradition needs to be subjected to its own archaeological inquiry so as to transcend present-minded discourses, "excavate" recollections of the past, and re-contextualize them.

The bulk of the sources for the folk history of the Year of the French are drawn from the collections compiled by Richard Hayes, the collectors of the Irish Folklore Commission, and the Schools' Scheme. The "ethnographic present" of these sources dates to the first half of the twentieth century, with a particular concentration in the mid-1930s. Collectively, they offer a remarkably rich body of evidence for a sociological-historical study of how the French invasion and 1798 Rebellion were remembered and commemorated at that time. Yet, the value of these sources, which derived from oral tradition, goes beyond the insight they offer on twentieth-century provincial historical consciousness. Several *seanchas* accounts, namely verses of folk songs, appear to have originated in 1798. These dates offer respectively a provisional *terminus ante quem* (ca. 1950) and a *terminus post quem* (1798)[14] for an archaeology of the social memory of the Year of the French. Between these two limits, additional "strata" of social memory delineate traditions that were introduced or reconstructed at various stages from the end of the eighteenth century and into the twentieth century. The numerous available miscellaneous sources for folk history, which include accounts taken at different dates over the period in question, are particularly useful in attempting to establish approximate dates for tracking the development of social memory. Certain dates stand out as moments of intense transition. The sections on commemorative ceremonies, popular print and education identified the centenary in 1898 as a particularly significant time for the renegotiation of the social memory of 1798. The examination of remembrance and material culture, for example, dated the discovery of many of the local Ninety-Eight relics to this landmark "stratum." Admittedly, the earlier the period in question the more erratic the sources and information on the construction of social memory in the early nineteenth century is limited.

Recontextualization of oral traditions is often speculative and inconclusive. Writing of the folk history and customs of his native *Gaeltacht* area in Ranafast, county Donegal, the Irish language novelist Séamus Ó Grianna (["Máire"], 1889–1969), observed that several French expressions had curiously filtered into local parlance, such as "cail úr a' tsíl," used to ask the time (*quelle heure est-il*), or "sláime tae geal," used as an expression of indifference (*cela m'est égal*). Local traditions traced this linguistic influence back to a local carpenter, commonly known by his trade's name as the "Jaighneoir" (joiner), who at the time of the Rebellion was an apprentice in Westport and picked up some French when in the company of the invading troops.[15] These phrases could be interpreted as fragments of social memory dating to 1798 that had been unconsciously transmitted over several generations into the mid-twentieth century. But it is impossible to verify this supposition, and there are also other plausible historical explanations. Around the late eighteenth century, the area of Westport was home to a thriving smuggling trade with France, which may also have left a cultural mark.[16]

By reversing the direction of historical inquiry, the archaeology of social memory turns historiography on its head. Setting out to retrace the origins of traditions, it starts with the period in which the sources were collected and moves backwards toward the original events. This archaeological pursuit, which works against chronology, produces surprising results. It can uncover "prehistoric" strata of social memory, as narratives evoked associations with earlier historical episodes. This does not mean that accounts were repeated unchanged from antiquity, but rather that motifs were imaginatively recycled and reappropriated as meaningful points of reference. In some instances, references to Ninety-Eight were mixed with anachronistic allusions to older periods of strife. Several accounts of the Year of the French included references to religious persecution associated with the penal laws of the late seventeenth century[17] to the popular Jacobite hero Patrick Sarsfield (who campaigned in Connacht in 1689)[18] and to Oliver Cromwell, whose campaign in Ireland (1649–50) was recalled as a lasting symbol of foreign repression.[19] In other cases, associations were more obscure. For example, the song "Amhrán na bhFranncach" (Song of the French), collected in Connemara in 1926, alluded to "bog butter," although the concealment of dairy products in bogs is commonly attributed to much earlier periods.[20] When talking about 1798, storytellers readapted earlier stories. A subversive tradition of local resistance to the French appeared as a version of a familiar story about "the Fool of Barr Rúscaí"[21]—

a popular Erris legend originally set in the background of struggles between Gaelic chieftains.[22] Through references to Saint Patrick and Colum Cille, traditions of the Rebellion could refer inadvertently to early Christian periods[23] and elsewhere they could even conjure up associations with Celtic-pagan times.[24] These examples seem to suggest that, at some level, the social memory of Ninety-Eight began long before 1798! Such a seemingly paradoxical conclusion was also reached in a study of the folklore of the Great Famine, which noted that "informants draw on a repertoire of images, motifs and short narratives, many of which predate the Famine."[25]

The proposition that memory can precede history, or more precisely that historical narratives are informed by recollections of earlier historical experiences and by traditional narratives that predate the event, was eloquently expressed by the historian Sir Lewis Bernstein Namier:

> One would expect people to remember the past and to imagine the future. But in fact, when discoursing or writing about history, they imagine it in terms of their own experience, and when trying to gauge the future they cite supposed analogies from the past: till, by a double process of repetition, they imagine the past and remember the future.[26]

It is conceivable that the long-standing Jacobite tradition that cultivated expectations of foreign invasion, in conjunction with memories of former rebellions, prepared the ground for the way the French invasion and the 1798 Rebellion were popularly perceived in 1798 and subsequently remembered. This is clearly the case of Protestant-loyalist reactions to the Rebellion, which were often based on patterns set by commemorations of atrocities committed during the rebellions in the seventeenth century.[27] Writing during the French invasion of Connacht, the moderate Sligo loyalist Humphrey Thomson rebuked chroniclers of "the bloody transactions of 1641 and 1690" for presenting accounts that generated "apprehensions of massacre" in 1798.[28] Musgrave's influential interpretation of the 1798 Rebellion, a founding text for loyalist remembrance, rehashed motifs from Sir John Temple's *The Irish Rebellion* (1646) and William King's *The State of the Protestants of Ireland Under the Late King James's Government* (1691).[29]

Just as the end date for an archaeology of social memory can move back in time, the starting date is also unfixed. In order to maintain a historical perspective, this study has focused on folk history accounts collected up to the mid-twentieth century. Since then, Irish popular culture has undergone significant changes, and developments in communication technologies have introduced new mediums for remembrance.[30] In turn, pervasive preoccupation with Ninety-

Eight during the bicentennial year has created a new "stratum" of social memory that deserves to be studied in its own right. A preliminary discussion, outlining initial observations on remembrance of the Year of the French in the late twentieth century, is briefly presented in the following epilogue.

As discussed in the previous chapter, memory also entails forgetting. Remembrance is a selective process, which privileges certain traditions and neglects others. It follows that an archaeology of social *memory* should also grapple with the chimera of an archaeology of social *amnesia*. Although it may be impossible to recover recollections that have been obliterated, by probing the editorial work of folk historians and *seanchas* collectors, traces of forgetting can be exposed and interrogated. Leads can be found in enigmatic fragments of oral tradition, which have been repeated unwittingly and preserved almost in spite of themselves. The children's song "Mise agus Tusa," which explicitly refers to the French camps in Killala and Castlebar, has a puzzling reference in its chorus to *bacaigh Shíol Aindí*. The word *bacaigh* (sing. *bacach*) translates as a lame person, a beggar, or a mean and despicable individual. The phrase can be literally read as referring to a *bacach* who is the descendant of a man named Aindí [Andy]. The lexicographer and writer Niall Ó Dómhnaill (b. 1908) maintained that *bacaigh Shíol Aindí* was a caustic reference to Irish rebels after the disaster in Ballinamuck. He cited another version of the song that refers to the Franco-Irish hybrid "bacach Irlandais" (i.e., Irish beggar), and suggested that it echoes a derogatory comment made by French soldiers on the poor condition of their Irish allies.[31]

Other scholars have suggested that it is a corrupted form of a colloquial reference to Scottish troops—"Bucky Heelanders."[32] In 1798 Scottish fencible units and regular regiments were stationed in disproportionately high numbers in Ireland and were engaged in counterinsurgency operations. In particular, Fraser's Fencibles were reported to have acted with excessive violence in Connacht and provoked local "discontent and dissatisfaction."[33] The former United Irishman Charles Hamilton Teeling, writing three decades later, noted that: "the Highland regiments were distinguished in Ireland for humane and orderly behaviour, strict discipline, and soldier-like conduct."[34] However, folk-history traditions show that "Highlanders" mostly left a strongly negative impression.[35] Notwithstanding these speculations on the interpretation of the phrase, the folk historian Patrick O'Donnell of Newport, who was extremely proficient in the folk history of Ninety-Eight, wrote to Hayes and inquired "would there be any possibility of discovering who this Aindí was?"[36] Apparently, by the 1930s, the original meaning had been forgotten in the locality and was rediscovered later, or perhaps invented, by researchers from outside.

An archaeology of social memory/amnesia may prove to be a useful method to study folk history and social memory. Yet, like all models, its practicability is limited. Unlike standard archaeological evidence, oral traditions are not concrete objects. Moreover, the validity of applying literary deconstructive analysis to oral narratives, which are not stable texts, is questionable. At some level, the archaeological analogy falters, as it aims to inspect reconstructions based on components that have not only transformed over time but were also transmogrified when they were collected. Multiple, often contradictory, narratives coexisted in folk history, and the discussion on time and calendar (chapter 7) demonstrated that oral traditions operated within different temporal frameworks. Traditions therefore cannot be simply pinned down and linked definitively to specific historical periods, classified as "memory strata."

Commenting on the emergence of coercive systems of social regulation in the eighteenth century, the radical French philosopher Michel Foucault, whose critique of the history of ideas employed the term "archaeology" in a different sense, defined disciplines as "techniques for assuring the ordering of human multiplicities."[37] Study of oral traditions from within the discipline of history necessitates a reordering of structured "multiplicities." The unique value of folk histories is that they do not conform to historical standards and therefore pose a radical challenge to historiography. Studies on the memory of Ninety-Eight have generally been limited by a restrictive notion of "collective memory," defined as a product of the major works of mainstream professional historiography and national commemoration. A seminal text in debates on the memory of 1798 asserts that the "construction of collective memory is one of the primary tasks of the historian."[38] Folklore sources shed light on the popular reception of narratives proliferated by the academy and also call attention to unofficial historiographies, which reflect the ways the past was remembered and commemorated on a ground level.

Folk history was rarely, if ever, completely independent from the pervasive influences of "official" history, yet it maintained a degree of autonomy. It not only recalled information absent in scholarly histories but also offered new perspectives on the past. At least from a local-provincial point of view, these were the historical discourses that mattered to most of the people. Whereas historians have generally downplayed the significance of the provincial experience, concluding that "in terms of numbers, if not balladry, the French-assisted Connaught rising was an epilogue,"[39] social memory insisted on telling otherwise. Communities throughout the West of Ireland (and beyond) remembered *Bliain na bhFrancach*—the Year of the French—as a central episode in their history. Evidently, prevailing notions of historical centrality and peripherality need to be rethought. What is perhaps a "footnote" in a national metanarrative is a significant landmark for a provincial constituency, which has its own ways of telling history. It follows that our understanding of *History* needs to be reconsidered in order to accommodate other available histories by which the past has been, and can be, remembered.

Epilogue

Commemorative Heritage

Remembrance in the Late Twentieth Century

> A trail of busts, plaques, monuments and commemorative
> nameplates marks the route of Humbert's short-lived and
> disastrous expedition. There has been a best-selling novel,
> a television drama, a successful annual summer school and
> even a cycling tour.
>
> Harman Murtagh
> "General Humbert's Futile Campaign"

IN THE MIDDLE of the twentieth century, remembrance of the Year of the
French fell into decline, only to be later regenerated in response to external
stimuli.[1] The waning of social memory was evident in the attitudes of a young
generation of farmers, who dismissed traditions and ignored the social taboo
that had preserved commemorative sites in the vernacular landscape. Sometime
in the mid-1970s a new owner leveled with a tractor the small mounds on the
"Graves Meadow" in Ballinamuck, which had remained untilled for generations and were respected as "Croppies' Graves."[2] In the 1980s, with the demise
of an elderly landowner, the "Highlander's Grave" in Gortletteragh, county
Leitrim (seven kilometers west of Ballinamuck), was irreverently excavated
with a mechanical digger.[3] Neglect and decay took their toll. Names of French
soldiers that had been inscribed above a fireplace on the wall of a shed in
Bohola (fifteen kilometers east of Castlebar) became practically indistinguish-
able. A small stained-glass window in Castlebar on which a French officer had
scratched his name was replaced with a modern fixture and discarded.[4] Remnants of the past were rapidly eroding. Nonetheless, interest in Ninety-Eight
did not complexly vanish. Heslins' pub in Ballinamuck had long been known as
"The '98 Bar" and Dillon's Pub at the other end of the village was renamed in
the 1970s "The Pikeman Inn," creating new commemorative place-names. In
the words of a Ballinamuck-born local historian: "there were local people who
always kept the pot stirred around this whole subject."[5] Dedicated individuals

cultivated the memory of Ninety-Eight. Jackie Clarke (1926–2000), a republican activist in Ballina, is known to have gathered an impressive collection of local memorabilia, but it was not made accessible to the general public during his lifetime.[6]

Although historical fiction on Ninety-Eight had fallen out of vogue, A remarkable novel, *l'Attaque,* was written in Irish by the Connacht-born bilingual poet and novelist Eoghan Ó Tuairisc ([pseudonym of Eugene Rutherford Watters], 1919–82).[7] Making extensive use of Hayes's research, it follows the exploits of a fictional Leitrim rebel from the landing of the French up to the victory at Castlebar.[8] A critic noted that "many Irish historical novelists celebrated the peasantry, the 'common people'; only Ó Tuairisc wrote successfully about their history in their own historical language."[9] A couple of years later, a collection of Ó Tuairisc's poetry republished his recitation "An Gunnadóir Mac Aoidh" (1949), which emotively depicted the last stand of the Ballinamuck folk hero Gunner Magee [McGee].[10] By this time, Irish had significantly declined and with only 37.6 percent of the population of Connacht professing some level of proficiency (148,708 people) in the 1961 census, the local readership of the novel was somewhat limited.[11]

Several years later, in 1979, interest in the folk history of Ninety-Eight was revived as a result of the indirect influence of another book, which was written in English. This was not the reissue of Hayes's *Last Invasion of Ireland* (in the relatively inexpensive Sackville Library series), but rather the historical novel *The Year of the French* by the Irish-American academic Thomas Flanagan (1923–2002), which entered best-seller lists and won the National Book Critics' Circle Award.[12] Praised by a distinguished critic for the way it "brings people out of the past and sets them living beside us and relevant to our present,"[13] the novel's complex narrative structure, propelled by five primary narrators and sixty-one principal characters, appears to emulate the democratic nature of folk histories. Like folklore, the novel entwines the history of the Franco-Irish campaign with mundane events. This folkloric impression is, however, misleading. The eloquent prose style of the novel is more akin to the writing of early-nineteenth-century Anglo-Irish novelists, whom the author had studied in depth, than to oral tradition;[14] and though he consulted primary historical sources, Flanagan did not explicitly use folklore accounts.[15] The rebel leader Ferdinand ("Ferdy") O'Donnell from Poolathomas in Erris, who in local folklore was a minor hero,[16] is aggrandized in the novel and destined to become the subject of a "wretched pothouse ballad," while the Franco-Irish officer Henry O'Kane, who in Mayo folklore actually was the hero of a popular song, is considered insignificant and doomed to be forgotten.[17]

When Flanagan's novel was first published, it was not particularly popular in Connacht. Three years later this changed dramatically, and Michael Keohane of Ballina, the biggest bookseller in Mayo, commented on the enthusiastic local demand, having sold four hundred hardback copies in the space of a few months.[18] The reason behind this sudden surge of interest was the adaptation of the book into a film. Allocated the largest budget up until then for the production of a drama in Ireland (1.7 million Irish pounds), the national broadcaster, Radio Telefís Éireann (RTÉ), set out to produce a television version of *The Year of the French* in collaboration with the French channel FR3 and Britain's Channel 4. It was an elaborate operation with a trilingual script (written by the dramatist Eugene McCabe in association with the French scriptwriter Pierre Lary), a multinational cast (with Irish, French, and English actors), and a production that involved consultation with museums in Dublin, Paris, and London.[19] The renowned traditional musician Paddy Moloney composed the score, and his popular group the Chieftains made a cameo appearance.[20] Broadcast as a six-part miniseries between 18 November and 23 December 1982, the film turned out to be a dud. Despite being featured as the cover story of the television guide,[21] critics found it to be of mediocre standard, film scholars noted its failure to be "critical or interpretative,"[22] and in RTÉ it was generally considered a disappointment.[23] Five years later, when RTÉ celebrated its twenty-fifth anniversary, the film was barely mentioned,[24] and it was not even rebroadcast for the bicentennial in 1998, a time when several programs were shown on the 1798 Rebellion

Ultimately, it was not the film's content, but the actual filming of many of the scenes on location in the West (from June to November 1981) that made a lasting impression. Local involvement was extensive, including five hundred extras, several among them native Irish speakers specifically recruited from Mayo *Gaeltacht* areas, and also large numbers of reserve soldiers from the Western Command of the army's reserve forces (FCÁ, An Foras Cosanta Áitiúil). For practical reasons, most scenes were not filmed in their original historical locations: the "Races of Castlebar" and the Battle of Ballinamuck were filmed in the vicinity of Ballina; the engagement in Collooney was filmed in the valley of Glenree (nine kilometers west of Bunnyconnellan in county Mayo); executions of rebels captured at Ballinamuck were filmed in Moyne Abbey (three kilometers southeast of Killala); and Humbert's headquarters in Castlebar were re-created in Multyfarnham, county Westmeath, where the filming crew was paid a visit by Flanagan, who expressed his approval of the adaptation.[25] Killala, which hosted the longest period of on-site production, was completely re-created. Shop fronts were repainted, plastic imitation-stone walling stapled to the front of houses, and turf deposited daily on the streets.[26] Modern infrastructure was concealed, so that a writer traveling through the area a few years later commented on the absence of aboveground masts and wires.[27] The RTÉ crew did not notice any local oral traditions of Ninety-Eight, and subsequently folklore did not feature in the film.[28] This may seem to be another sign of the lapse of social memory, but it is also indicative of the ineptitude of visitors from Dublin in tapping into deeper, less public, reservoirs of folk history.

By all accounts, it was a time of great enthusiasm. A local participant declared that "the filming of the event is having a greater effect than the original happening,"[29] and Killala residents formed a committee to "advise on whether the area should look two hundred years old permanently."[30] A commentator observed that the excitement "re-awakened local interest in the events of 1798, and in the society of the time."[31] In his diary, a film extra noted that "memories of '98 were evoked or revived" and people realized that "folk memories survive longer than a few generations, even if it's only in the sub-conscious."[32] The making of the film blended with traditions of folk history so that locals would subsequently confuse the events of 1798 with recollections of cinematographic re-creations. When twenty years later, primary school pupils told a local historian about a public execution in 1798, they were not referring to the hanging of the United Irishman Patrick Walsh in Ballina, which had previously been recalled in social memory,[33] but were unwittingly referring to a scene from the film, which had been shot in Killala and evidently entered into local folklore.[34] There was popular demand for historical information. An inexpensive edition of Bishop Stock's *Narrative* edited by the local historian Grattan Freyer (1915–83) of Terrybaun (near Ballina), made this key primary source readily available so that, even more than in the past, social memory of 1798 was informed by historical literature.[35] The Longford-born local historian Seán Ó Brádaigh compiled a collection of songs and ballads on Ninety-Eight,[36] and was invited by various communities to present an illustrated lecture on the French invasion.[37]

Within a few years, the Humbert Summer School was established in Mayo (1987) and has organized annual lectures and discussions in Ballina, Castlebar, Killala, and Kilcummin. Its director, the Scottish-born journalist John Cooney, who has since specialized in the history of Humbert's campaign,[38] maintained that summer schools should aspire to be an "alternative forum of Irish politics" and function as "the anvil on which attitudes to the burning issues of the day are hammered out."[39] Accordingly, the summer school's agenda was not limited to 1798 but addressed a range of topical issues, hosting over the years prominent politicians, academics, journalists, economists, army officers, priests, businessmen, diplomats, and artists.[40] The summer school's highbrow, and often iconoclastic, intellectual character did not offer a stage to oral traditions. When in 1989 the local historian Tony Donohue (b. 1918) of Creevy, near Lahardane in county Mayo, gave a talk based on traditions that he had collected many years earlier from John McNeeley of Lahardane, who had been previously interviewed by Hayes in 1935, he was rebuked by the school's director for uncritically reproducing the "Hayes tradition."[41] The summer school sponsored several Ninety-Eight memorials in Killala, including busts of the French Generals Humbert (1988) and Sarrazin (1989), and a plaque marking the remains of the outer wall of Bishop Stock's "Palace."[42] In 1986 a grassroots initiative in Lacken (near Kilcummin) erected a monument on "Garraí Francach" (believed locally to be the site of a French soldier's grave), which was unveiled by the French Ambassador Monsieur Guitton. This commemorative act did not stop the farmer who owned the field from demolishing the original heap of stones that had previously served as a vernacular memorial.[43]

If remembrance in Mayo was jolted by the filming, in Ballinamuck it was aroused by the absence of filming. Disappointed that the RTÉ crew chose not to visit their area, a recently founded Ballinamuck Community Association resolved in 1982 to mark historical sites in the neighborhood associated with 1798. Signs identified places that had hitherto been remembered only in the vernacular landscape of oral tradition: General Blake's hanging place, General Blake's burial place, the Croppies' Gap, Humbert's surrender place, Gunner Magee's last stand, and the Croppies' Graves.[44] These signs, in conjunction with a large billboard map, unveiled by the local historian Fr. Owen Devaney in 1983,[45] effectively established a local 1798 commemorative-heritage trail. Several Ninety-Eight monuments were then erected in the locality. In spite of heavy rain, crowds gathered on 9 October 1983 to see the French Ambassador Monsieur Jean Batbedat unveil, in the presence of several dignitaries, a monument on the site of Humbert's surrender.[46] Shortly after, stone memorials were erected at "Gunner Magee's Last Stand" and "the Croppies Graves."[47] Starting in 1984, mass was celebrated on the battlefield on the Saturday closest to the anniversary of the battle, thus inaugurating an annual ritual of local commemoration. As interest in Ninety-Eight spread, community activists and local historians in north Mayo and Ballinamuck met and established friendships. Consequently, "Gunner Magee's cannon" was brought over from Ballina, fitted with a new carriage and wheels, and placed permanently by the pikeman monument in Ballinamuck (1985).[48]

The numerous commemorative initiatives in Mayo and around Ballinamuck in the 1980s mark a revival in the social memory of the Year of the French and retrospectively can be seen as the beginning of a grassroots buildup toward the bicentennial celebrations in 1998. A cultural critic remarked that "the jury is still out on the 1798 bicentenary: one day to be investigated, just as the heavy-weight historiography that abounded in 1998 included studies of the 1898 com-memoration."[49] Peddling a pedestrian analysis of commemoration, early assessments of the bicentennial focused on metropolitan discourses and put an emphasis on the rhetoric of politicians, controversies between historians, and the official commemorative programs in the vicinity of county Wexford (which for all intents and purposes is a core area in 1798 debates) and in the heavily politicized commemorative theater of Northern Ireland. With provincial com-memoration and local agency largely overlooked, it would appear that this was, once again, a massive exercise of "invention of tradition" promoted by a Gov-ernment Commemoration Committee and academic historians, yet closer examination challenges this presumption.[50] The correspondence of commem-oration organizers from across Connacht and the north midlands, who applied for government funding, clearly shows that the agenda of provincial commem-oration was not dictated from above but was primarily rooted in local initiatives that were then negotiated with the powers that be.[51] A regional calendar listed

seventy-five bicentennial events in counties Mayo, Sligo, Leitrim, and Longford,[52] all of which were supple-mented by scores of unofficial cere-monies, showing an unprecedented intensity of commemorative fervor. In past anniversaries, provincial centers hosted the main official events, but the bicentennial saw a coming of age of many small communities who as-

FIGURE 35. 1798 bicentennial monument in Ballinamuck, county Longford (unveiled 1998). Dedicated to "all those who fought and died in 1798," the "Peace Monument" in the Ballinamuck Garden of Remem-brance reflects the conciliatory spirit preva-lent in 1998. Its imagery draws from local folk history, depicting relics found on the battlefield and ears of wheat that suppos-edly grew out of cereal grains stored in the pockets of dead rebels. Photo by the author.

FIGURE 36. 1798 millennium monument in Castlebar, county Mayo (unveiled 2000). Combining imagery of war and peace, the doves fluttering among a forest of pikes in the newly developed Castlebar Market Square typify the emergence of new interpretations of Ninety-Eight. Photo by the author.

sumed responsibility for organizing local commemoration. Significantly, celebrations in the small but energetic communities of Collooney[53] and Ballinamuck[54] were far grander than in the town of Castlebar.[55]

Taking into account the history of provincial Ninety-Eight commemoration, this local "statuemania" can be seen as the culmination of a long process, instigated as a reaction to the centennial, whereby local communities demanded recognition for their heroes and sites of memory.[56] In 1998 this process reached its crescendo brimming with self-confidence, which, to a large extent, was an outcome of economic affluence; it was also inspired by the breakthrough in the Northern Ireland peace process that resulted in the Good Friday Agreement and its ratification on the anniversary of the 1798 Rebellion in Wexford. Community celebrations were often driven by the commercial interests of local tourism, yet the wave of erecting bicentennial monuments could also be interpreted as a response to the erosion of the vernacular landscape from the mid-twentieth century, which had triggered efforts to revitalize social memory.

A prominent critic of the bicentennial argued that it promoted "ceiliúradh" (celebration) rather than "comóradh" (commemoration).[57] The two, however, are not mutually exclusive, as re-creation can also have an educational value. Raphael Samuel objected to the way "historians have become accustomed to thinking of commemoration as a cheat" and questioned the "unspoken and unargued-for assumption that pleasure is almost by definition mindless."[58] The issue is not clear-cut: there are many representations of popular commemoration, ranging from excessively commercialized kitsch to somber memorials and well-designed educational displays that stimulate reflection on the past. For example, two cycling events in the bicentennial demonstrated this variance. In the summer of 1998 the opening leg of the Tour de France was hosted in Ireland and officially endorsed as part of the Government 1798 Commemoration Program. Speaking in the Dáil, the Taoiseach proudly presented this sports event as "a tribute to the close Franco-Irish alliance which was reforged in the 1790s."[59] This was a patent example of shallow "commemorative spectacle." The French bicycle competition took place in the Southeast, running from Dublin to Cork through county Wexford, and did not even attempt to appropriate a meaningful commemorative gesture by tracing the route of the French army in 1798.[60] In the West, a private entrepreneur (Peadar Leonard of Mayo Leisure Cycling), supported by regional tourist boards, came up with the idea of "Tour de Humbert," a 225-kilometer signposted cycling trail, which follows the route of the Franco-Irish army from the landing spot at Killala Bay to the final battlefield at Ballinamuck. To quote the brochure: "Along the way, sites of historical interest are clearly indicated by explanatory panels."[61] These informative vignettes were, in many cases, based on select folk-history traditions that were thus given external recognition. Through such innovative projects, heritage tourism offered recreational experiences that could also facilitate a contemplative engagement with the Year of the French.

Like the centennial one hundred years earlier, the bicentennial accelerated transitions in social memory. Oral traditions were given a platform and cropped up in a proliferation of local publications, which were soon sold out, so that folk-history accounts enjoyed circulation in print more than ever before.[62] At the same time, traditions were reinterpreted and changed through cultural negotiations. The celebrations precipitated the decline of certain traditional narratives that had become redundant. A substratum of local folklore, particularly evident in the north midlands, preserved recollections of French betrayal in 1798, often expressed in defiance of official nationalist commemorative rhetoric. By 1998 such embittered sentiments seemed inappropriate in the context of Irish membership in the European Union. The main places associated with the Year of the French were twinned with provincial French partners and cultural ties developed. Ballina was twinned with Guipavas as early as 1981,[63] and in 1998 Killala was twinned with Chauvé, Castlebar with Auray, and Ballinamuck with Esset de Belfort.[64] Connections were also established with Humbert's hometown of St. Nabord, but despite an exchange of delegations in 1998, initiatives to arrange a formal twinning did not work out. French tourists were warmly welcomed at bicentennial celebrations, and old antagonisms were no longer apparent.[65]

In the beginning of the third millennium, there are still folk history-tellers to be found, among other places, in the West of Ireland. They are steeped in *seanchas* and are able to vividly recall stories about Ninety-Eight and other historical episodes, which they had originally heard performed orally more than fifty years earlier. Although their knowledge has been reinforced by historical literature and by earlier collections of folklore codified in printed form, they offer living testimony to how folk history remains a distinct discourse that underwent transformations but survived into a world of technologically enhanced and commercially popularized social memory.[66] Diarmuid Ó Giolláin asserted that "folklore and popular culture does not disappear, indeed is constantly being created, but less and less offers alternatives to modernity from an experience outside of it."[67]

Heritage projects offer new ways in which folklore can be recycled and represented for the twenty-first century. In his analysis of the "folklore process," Lauri Honko identified a "second life of folklore," in which "recycling of material in an environment that differs from its original context" is "edited according to norms other than those of the oral tradition." This generally concurs with an "emancipation of the folklore community," allowing for the "opening up of new fields of influence, the introduction of larger groups of people than normal to the lore in question."[68] On 18 July 1998, President Mary McAleese opened the "Battle of Ballinamuck Battlefield Centre."[69] It is a modest visitors center, planned with the help of a professional heritage consultant and set up in the village hall (formerly a Royal Irish Constabulary station).[70] Panels provide information on the battle and its historical context, and the visitor is invited to activate an audio device and listen to "Tales of Ballinamuck." These include several folk-history accounts, which are no longer part of a living storytelling tradition. Instead, one is treated to recordings of previously published accounts, which were collected in the area more than sixty years earlier by Richard Hayes, a national schoolteacher (Peter Kilkenny), and a collector of the Irish Folklore Commission (Pádraig Mac Gréine).[71] The stories are re-read by actors (P. J. McLoughlin and Felicity Stewart).[72] With the opening of this center, folk history of the Year of the French began a new life.

Notes

Introduction

1. Trotsky to the Mensheviks, at the Second All-Russian Congress of the Soviets, 25 October 1917; reproduced in Alexander Rabinowitch, *The Bolsheviks Come to Power* (New York: W. W. Norton, 1976), 296.

2. Including infantrymen from the Second Battalion of the Seventieth Demi-brigade, a company of grenadiers, a detachment of the Eleventh Company of the Twelfth Artillery division, a detachment of cavalry from the Third Regiment of Chasseurs à Cheval, and Humbert's personal escort, which was drawn from the Twelfth Regiment of Hussars; "Désignation des Corps," ADG B11/2. Slightly different figures appear in other naval lists. Profiles of 60 officers and 934 soldiers can be found in the troop registers; ADG 18 YC 170 and 171; 21 YC 782; XB 290.

3. In 1798 the term "races" had already been used to deplore the disorderly retreat of government troops (who fled as far as Tuam and Athlone); for example, a letter written by Mrs. B. Thompson, Castlebar, 17 October 1798; Ormsby Papers, NLI microfilm P8162; reproduced in *Cornhill Magazine* (1898), 467. Shortly after, the name "The Races of Castlebar" appears to have entered common use; see Sir Jonah Barrington, *Historic Memoirs of Ireland*, vol. 2, 280.

4. Throughout this book, "the West" is used liberally in reference to the experience of the French invasion and the Rebellion in the province of Connacht and the north midlands of Ireland. The wide spread of the map of the Year of the French in social memory ("vernacular landscape") is discussed in chap. 12.

For the geographical distribution of relevant sources in the Irish Folklore Collection, see my chart 1 (52) and chart 3 (59).

5. Similarly, a study of the memory of the controversial antipolice riot in the village of Chauri Chaura in the Gorakhpur region in India in 1922 noted that the number of victims and the date are often cited erroneously; see Shahid Amin, *Event, Memory, Metaphor: Chauri Chaura 1922–1992* (Berkeley: Univ. of California Press, 1992), 10.

6. Hardwicke Papers, BL MS 34454 ff 466, 476.

7. R. R. Madden estimated the Irish rebels at 8,000 and reckoned desertions reduced their number to 1,500; *United Irishmen*, vol. 1, 93 and 95. Valerian Gribayédoff maintained that 1,500–2,000 Irishmen left Castlebar with Humbert while a larger force stayed behind; *French Invasion of Ireland in '98*, 118. W. E. H. Lecky soberly cautioned that "the distribution of arms is no measure of the number of Irish," which he maintained did not exceed 500 when taking Castlebar and were joined there by "some hundreds of recruits"; *History of Ireland in the Eighteenth Century*, vol. 5, 47–48 and 59. Richard Hayes set the number of Irish insurgents at 1,500; *Last Invasion of Ireland*, 116. Marianne Elliott insisted that the number who joined the French "had never exceeded 3,000"; *Partners in Revolution: The United Irishmen and France*. More recently, Harman Murtagh claimed that "in all 6–700 volunteers enlisted with the French at Killala and another 3,500 at Castlebar"; see "General Humbert's Campaign in the West," in Póirtéir, *Great Irish Rebellion of 1798*, 117. Kevin Whelan has

raised this figure to 10,000; see Bartlett, Dickson, Keogh, and Whelan, *1798*, 101.

8. Foster, *Modern Ireland*, 280.

9. Ian McBride, "Reclaiming the Rebellion," 396. Overwhelmed by the growing volume of publications, the same reviewer subsequently pondered "if the time has come for a self-imposed ban on all further writings about the 1798 rebellion"; Ian McBride, "Manipulating 'Memory,'" *Irish Review* 28 (2001): 186.

10. Kevin Whelan, *Tree of Liberty*, 133–75; reproduced in Whelan, *Fellowship of Freedom*, 121–41.

11. Bartlett et al., *1798*, 98.

12. Peter Novick, *That Noble Dream: The "Objectivity Question" and the American Historical Profession* (Cambridge; Cambridge Univ. Press, 1988), 8.

13. A standard dictionary definition of "folk memory" as the "recollection of the past persisting among a people" may serve as a working definition, though the more-accurate term "social memory" is developed in chap. 1; see *Concise Oxford Dictionary of Current English*, 9th ed. (Oxford: Oxford Univ. Press, 1995), 526.

14. David Gross, *Past in Ruins*, 82.

15. For the abstracts of the lectures see the program booklet *1798 Bicentenary Conference* (Dublin: n.p., 1998); edited papers were subsequently published in Bartlett et al., *1798*. Ian McBride's contribution on "Memory and Forgetting" stood out for its reference to oral traditions.

16. "Oral traditions" can be loosely defined as knowledge that has been passed verbally through successive generations. The term is critically discussed in chap. 1, see 19–24.

17. Composed by John Kells Ingram and first published anonymously in *Nation*, 1 April 1843.

18. Marianne Elliott interviewed in "Rebellion" (RTÉ, 1998).

19. The standard defining criteria of a "tradition" is that it has been handed down over, at least, three generations; Shils, *Tradition*.

20. The "Great Famine" that devastated Ireland in 1845–52 is generally acknowledged as a major landmark in modern Irish social history.

21. Smyth, "The 1798 Rebellion in Its Eighteenth-Century Contexts," in Smyth, *Revolution, Counter-Revolution*, 17.

22. Reproduced in Robinson, *Further Memories of Irish Life*, 149.

23. K. Whelan, "The Region and the Intellectuals," 130.

24. Moody, "Irish History and Irish Mythology," 71–86.

25. See R. M. Dorson, "Mythology and Folklore: A Review Essay," *Annual Review of Anthropology* 2 (1973): 107–26 (reproduced in Dorson, *Folklore and Fakelore*, 74–100).

26. For example see Michael Laffan, "The Sacred Memory: Religion, Revisionists and the Easter Rising," in *Religion and Rebellion*, eds. Judith Devlin and Ronan Fanning (Dublin: UCD Press, 1997), 183; Michael Laffan, "Insular Attitudes: The Revisionists and their Critics," in Ní Dhonnchadha and Dorgan, *Revising the Rising*, 108. For the historiographical debate over revisionism in Ireland, see also D. G. Boyce and Alan O'Day, eds., *The Making of Modern Irish History: Revisionism and the Revisionist Controversy* (London: Taylor & Francis, 1996).

27. R. Fanning, "The Great Enchantment," 146.

28. Seán Farrell Moran, "History, Memory and Education," 216.

29. Anthony Grafton, *The Footnote: A Curious History* (London: Faber & Faber, 1967), 6.

30. T. B. Macaulay, "History," *Edinburgh Review* 47 (1828); republished in *The Miscellaneous Writings of Lord Macaulay* (London: Longman, Green, Longman, & Roberts, 1860), vol. 1, 281.

Chapter 1

1. D. Ferriter, "Archives Report," 91–95.

2. See Guy Beiner and Anne Bryson, "Listening to the Past and Talking to Each Other: Problems and Possibilities Facing Oral History in Ireland," *Irish Economic and Social History* 30 (2003): 71–78.

3. David Henige, *Oral Historiography* (London: Longman, 1982), 7–13.

4. For an overview of the contemporary "revival" of oral history and its critics see Paul Thompson, *Voice of the Past*, 62–81.

5. Allan Nevins, "Oral History: How and Why it was Born," Louis Starr, "Oral History," and R. J. Grele, "Directions for Oral History in the United States," in Dunaway and Baum, *Oral History*, 27–84.

6. For a general discussion on the radical nature of oral history studies, focusing on the contribution of local historians, see Stephen Caunce, *Oral History and the Local Historian* (London: Longman, 1994), 100–23.

7. Edward Said, *Orientalism* (London: Penguin Books, 1991; orig. ed. 1978), 21.

8. See for example R. Guha and G. C. Spivak, eds., *Selected Subaltern Studies* (New York: Oxford Univ. Press, 1988).

9. Examples can be readily found by glancing through the issues of the radical history periodical *History Workshop Journal*. For a sample of relevant studies from the late 1980s and '90s see Perks and Thompson, *Oral History Reader*, esp. 183–268.

10. See Barbara Tuchman, "Distinguishing the Significant from the Insignificant," in Dunaway and Baum, *Oral History*, 94–98.

11. For examples see Cullom Davis, *Oral History: From Tape to Type* (Chicago: American Library Association, 1977); Ken Howarth, *Oral History: A Handbook* (Stroud: Sutton Publishing, 1998); Stephen Humphries, *The Handbook of Oral History: Recording Life Stories* (London: Inter-Action, 1984); E. D. Ives, *The Tape-Recorded Interview: A Manual for Field Workers in Folklore and Oral History* (Knoxville: Univ. of Tennessee Press, 1990; orig. ed. 1974); Trevor Lummis, *Listening to History* (London: Hutchinson Education, 1987); Valerie Raleigh Yow, *Recording Oral History: A Practical Guide for Social Scientists* (Thousand Oaks: Sage Publications, 1994).

12. R. M. Dorson, "Oral Literature, Oral History and the Folklorist," in Dorson, *Folklore and Fakelore*, 127–44.

13. Peter Burke, "Folklore and History: A Historiographical Survey," *Folklore* 115, no. 2 (2004): 133–39.

14. For example see the anthology *The African Past Speaks*, ed. J. C. Miller (Folkestone: Dawson, 1980).

15. See Alex Haley, "Black History, Oral History and Genealogy," in Dunaway and Baum, *Oral History*, 252–79.

16. Tosh, *Pursuit of History*, 185–86; D. R. Wright, "Uprooting Kunte Kinte: On the Perils of Relying on Encyclopedic Informants," *History in Africa* 8 (1981).

17. Jan Vansina, *Oral Tradition: A Study in Historical Methodology* (Chicago: Aldine, 1965); Vansina, *Oral Tradition as History*.

18. Tonkin, *Narrating Our Past*, 85–90.

19. For a detailed list of criticism that has been directed against "positivist" oral history, see Anthony Seldon and Joanna Pappworth, *By Word of Mouth* (London: Methuen, 1983), 16–35. See also R. M. Dorson, "The Debate over the Trustworthiness of Oral Traditional History," 19–35 (reproduced in R. M. Dorson, *Folklore: Selected Essays* [Bloomington: Indiana Univ. Press, 1972], 199–244).

20. Alice Hoffman, "Reliability and Validity in Oral History," in Dunaway and Baum, *Oral History*, 92–103.

21. Paul Thompson, *The Edwardians: The Remaking of British Society* (London: Granada Publications, 1977, orig. ed. 1975), 97–180.

22. In *Oral Tradition as History*, Vansina listed various types of mnemonic devices, including linguistic form (14), melody and music (16, 46–47), technique and rules of performance (134–35), objects (44–45), and landscape (45–46). For poetic formulae as a mnemonic technique see A. B. Lord, *The Singer of Tales* (Cambridge, MA: Harvard Univ. Press, 1960); W. J. Ong, *Orality and Literacy: The Technologizing of the World* (London: Methuen, 1982). 34. For a psychological discussion on mnemonics, see Groeger, *Memory and Remembering*, 246–49.

23. Dorson, "Debate over the Trustworthiness," 19–35.

24. See for example Hoffman, "Reliability and Validity in Oral History," 92–103.

25. It is possible to distinguish (*pace* the French oral historian Daniel Bertaux), between two different approaches of interpretative oral history: *hermeneutic* (focusing on content, while revealing levels of discourse, hidden meanings, and ability to transmit messages) and *ethnographic* (focusing on context, while relating levels of discourse and use of language to social domains); see Louise A. Tilly and Ronald J. Grele, *International Journal of Oral History* 6, no. 1 (1985): 3–46, esp. 45–46.

26. Tonkin, *Narrating Our Pasts*, 7.

27. Tosh, *Pursuit of History*, 181.

28. Alessandro Portelli, "Oral History in Italy," in Dunaway and Baum, *Oral History*, 399.

29. See *International Journal of Oral History* 6, no. 1 (1985): 21–25.

30. For example see Luisa Passerini, *Fascism in Popular Memory: The Cultural Experience of the Turin Working Class* (Cambridge: Cambridge Univ. Press, 1987).

31. Thompson, *Voice of Our Past*, 117.

32. Barbara Allen, "In the Thick of Things: Texture in Orally Communicated History," *International Journal of Oral History* 6, no. 2 (1985): 92–103.

33. Tosh, *Pursuit of History*, 196–97. For an example of a study that challenged historiography in its field by reintroducing participants' experience to the center stage see Ronald Fraser, *Blood of Spain: An Oral History of the Spanish Civil War* (London: Pantheon, 1986; orig. ed. 1979).

34. Gwyn Prins, "Oral History," in P. Burke, *New Perspectives on Historical Writing*, 137.

35. Vansina, "Memory and Oral Tradition," in *The African Past Speaks*, 276. For Marrou's critique of positivist-empiricist conceptions of history see Henri-Irénée Marrou, *The Meaning of History* (Baltimore: Helicon, 1966; trans. by Robert J. Olsen of *De la connaissance historique* [4th. ed., Paris: Éditions du Seuil, 1959]), esp. 238.

36. Novick, *Noble Dream*, 11.

37. E. H. Carr, *What is History?* (London: Macmillan, 1961), 24.

38. For example, Ruth Finnegan, "A Note on Oral Tradition and Historical Evidence," in Dunaway and Baum, *Oral History*, 126–34; Finnegan, *Literacy and Orality*.

39. Tonkin, *Narrating Our Pasts*, 2–4. See also Richard Bauman, *Story, Performance and Event: Contextual Studies of Oral Narrative* (Cambridge: Cambridge Univ. Press, 1986).

40. Samuel Schrager, "What is Social in Oral History?" *International Journal of Oral History* 4 no. 2 (1983): 95.

41. Alessandro Portelli, "Oral History as Genre," in *Narrative and Genre*, eds. Mary Chamberlain and Paul Thompson (New York: Routledge, 1998), 26.

42. Charles Joyner, "Oral History as a Communicative Event," in Dunaway and Baum, *Oral History*, 295.

43. See Portelli, "Oral History as Genre," 25; Raphael Samuel, "Perils of the Transcript," *Oral History* 1, no. 2 (1971): 19.

44. Vansina, *Oral Tradition as History*, 160.

45. Ibid., 150, 161.

46. Vansina, "Memory and Oral Tradition," in Miller, *African Past Speaks*, 276–77.

47. See Frances Yates, *Art of Memory*; D. J. Herrmann and R. Chaffin, eds., *Memory in Perspective: The Literature Before Ebbinghaus* (New York: Springer-Verlag, 1988); D. F. Krell, *Of Memory, Reminiscence, and Writing: On the Verge* (Bloomington: Indiana Univ. Press, 1990).

48. Hermann Ebbinghaus, *Memory: A Contribution to Experimental Psychology* (New York: Dover Publications, 1964; trans. from original German, *Über däs Gedächtnis*, 1885). See Searleman and Hermann, *Memory from a Broader Perspective*, 1–21; I. M. L. Hunter, *Memory* (Harmondsworth: Penguin Books, 1964; orig. ed. 1957), 124–42.

49. F. C. Bartlett, *Remembering: a Study in Experimental Social Psychology* (Cambridge: Cambridge Univ. Press, 1932). For a description of his innovative experiments on retellings of oral narrative see Hunter, *Memory*, 143–59. Despite Bartlett's breakthrough, memory studies continued to prefer theoretical and laboratory-based work at the expense

of neglecting the study of memory in context; see for example: M. R. Banaji, and R. C. Chowder, "The Bankruptcy of Everyday Memory," *American Psychologist* 44 (1989): 1185–93. For references to current research on "everyday memory" see Groeger, *Memory and Remembering*.

50. F. C. Bartlett, *Thinking: An Experimental and Social Study* (New York: Basic Books, 1958).

51. F. C. Bartlett, *Remembering*, 291–92 and 309.

52. Mary Douglas, *How Institutions Think* (London: Routledge & Paul, 1987), 81–91, chap. 7, "A Case of Institutional Forgetting."

53. Richard Terdiman, *Present Past: Modernity and the Memory Crisis* (Ithaca: Cornell Univ. Press, 1993).

54. See Durkheim's essay "Individual and Collective Representations," in the collection *Sociology and Philosophy* (New York: Free Press, 1974; trans. by D. F. Pocock of *Sociologie et Philosophie* [Paris, 1924]), 1–34 (orig. published in *Revue de Métaphysique et de Morale*, 4 [1898]). For the way these arguments were advanced see Maurice Halbwachs, "Individual Consciousness and Collective Mind," *American Journal of Sociology* 4 (1939): 812–22, republished in Peter Hamilton, ed., *Emile Durkheim: Critical Assessments* (London: Routledge, 1995), vol. 6, 23–30.

55. Halbwachs, "Individual Psychology and Collective Psychology," *American Sociological Review* 3, no. 5 (1938): 615–23.

56. Halbwachs, *On Collective Memory*, edited by Lewis A. Coser, including edited translation of *Les Cadres sociaux de la mémoire* (Paris, 1925); Halbwachs, *The Collective Memory* (trans. of *La Mémoire collective* [Paris, 1950]). For an appraisal of Halbwach's contribution to the study of memory, see Hutton, *History as an Art of Memory*, 73–90.

57. Halbwachs, *On Collective Memory*, 183, 189.

58. Ibid., chaps. 5, 6, 7.

59. Halbwachs, *The Collective Memory*, 22–49, esp. 44–48.

60. Halbwachs, *On Collective Memory*, 43.

61. E. E. Evans-Prichard, *The Nuer* (New York: Oxford Univ. Press, 1974, orig. ed. 1940), esp. 94–138. See also Mary Douglas, *Evans-Prichard* (Glasgow: Fontana, 1980), 74–86.

62. G. H. Mead, *Mind, Self and Society* (Chicago: Univ. of Chicago Press, 1934) and *The Individual and the Social Self* (Chicago: Univ. of Chicago Press, 1982; texts of lectures on social psychology delivered orig. in 1914 and 1927).

63. See for example the multidisciplinary essays in Middleton and Edwards, *Collective Remembering*.

64. For example see Chamberlain and Thompson, *Narrative and Genre*. For the role of memory in folklore narratives see Mihály Hoppál, "Folk Narrative and Memory Processes," in *Folklore on Two Continents: Essays in Honour of Linda Dégh*, eds. Nikolai Burla and Carl Lindahl (Bloomington: Indiana Univ. Press, 1980); Anna-Leena Siikala, *Interpreting Oral Narrative* (Helsinki: Suomalainen Tiedeakatemia, 1990).

65. Marc Bloch, "Mémoire collective, tradition et coutume: A propos d'un livre récent," *Revue de Synthèse Historique* 40 (1925): 73–83 (review of Maurice Halbwachs, *Les Cadres sociaux de la mémoire* [Paris: Félix Alcan, 1925]). Bloch and Halbwachs lectured at the restructured French University of Strasbourg after World War I, and Halbwachs was appointed to the editorial board of the influential historical periodical *Les Annales*, of which Bloch was a leading light. For Halbwachs's career and intellectual milieu see Annette Becker, *Maurice Halbwachs: Un intellectuel en guerres mondiales 1914–1945* (Paris: Agnès Viénot, 2003), esp. 193–230.

66. A heartrending description of Halbwachs's death in the Buchenwald concentration camp appears in Jorge Semprun's *Literature or Life* (New York: Viking, 1997; trans. by Linda Coverdale of *L'écriture ou la vie* [Paris: Gallimard, 1994]), a memoir preoccupied with the problems of representing historical memory.

67. For critical overviews of social-collective memory studies see Olick and Robbins,

"Social Memory Studies"; Kansteiner, "Finding Meaning in Memory."

68. For example, Gillis, *Commemorations*.

69. Among the proliferation of studies on remembrance of World War I, landmark contributions include Paul Fussell, *The Great War and Modern Memory* (New York: Oxford Univ. Press, 1975); G. L. Mosse, *Fallen Soldiers: Reshaping the Memories of the World Wars* (New York: Oxford Univ. Press, 1990); Jay Winter, *Sites of Memory, Sites of Mourning: The Great War in European Cultural History* (Cambridge: Cambridge Univ. Press, 1995). For the United States see Piehler, *Remembering War the American Way* (Washington, DC: Smithsonian Institution Press, 1995).

70. The literature on memory of the Holocaust is voluminous and widespread. Seminal contributions to the debate can be partly traced through references in issues of the periodical *History and Memory*.

71. Marianne Hirsch, *Family Frames: Photography, Narrative and Postmemory* (Cambridge, MA: Harvard Univ. Press, 1997), 22.

72. James V. Wertsch, *Voices of Collective Remembering* (Cambridge: Cambridge Univ. Press, 2002), 30–66.

73. Popular Memory Group, "Popular Memory: Theory, Politics, Method," in *Making Histories: Studies in History-writing and Politics*, eds. R. Johnson, G. McLennan, and D. S. Schwartz (London: Hutchinson, 1982), 205–52; in particular 211.

74. Michael Bommes and Patrick Wright, "Charms of Residence: The Public and the Past" (ibid., 253–302).

75. John Bodnar, *Remaking America: Public Memory, Commemoration, and Patriotism in the Twentieth Century* (Princeton, NJ: Princeton Univ. Press, 1992).

76. Connerton, *How Societies Remember*; Middleton and Edwards, *Collective Remembering*.

77. Tonkin, *Narrating Our Pasts*, esp. 105–6.

78. Fentress and Wickham, *Social Memory*, ix.

79. See for example *New Formations* 30

(1996), special issue on "Cultural Memory," edited by Erica Carter and Ken Hirschkop; Ben-Amos and Weissberg, *Cultural Memory*; Richard Caldicott and Anne Fuchs, eds., *Cultural Memory: Essays on European Literature and History* (Oxford: P. Lang, 2003).

80. E. H. Gombrich, *Aby Warburg: An Intellectual Biography* (Chicago: Univ. of Chicago Press, 1986), esp. 239–59. See also chap. 17, n. 10.

81. For a critical discussion that problematizes the text-context dichotomy in cultural history studies of collective memory see Alon Confino, "Collective Memory and Cultural History: Problems of Method," *American Historical Review* 102, no. 5 (1997): 1386–403.

82. Ben-Amos, "Afterword," in Ben-Amos and Weissberg, *Cultural Memory*, 297–300.

83. Jan Assman, "Collective Memory and Cultural Identity," *New German Critique* 65 (1995), 125–33.

84. Amos Funkelstein, "Collective Memory and Historical Consciousness," *History and Memory* 1, no. 1 (1989): 6; see also Noa Gedi and Yigal Elam, "Collective Memory—What Is It?" *History and Memory* 8, no. 1 (1996): 30–50; Samuel Hynes, "Personal Narratives and Commemoration," in *War and Remembrance in the Twentieth Century*, eds. Jay Winter and Emmanuel Sivan (Cambridge: Cambridge Univ. Press, 1999), 205–21.

85. Jeffery Prager, *Presenting the Past: Psychoanalysis and Sociology of Misremembering* (Cambridge, MA: Harvard Univ. Press, 1998), 175–210.

86. Middleton and Edwards, "Conversational Remembering: A Social Psychological Approach," in Middleton and Edwards, *Collective Remembering*, 23–45.

87. Peter Burke, "History as Social Memory," 99.

88. B. Schwartz, "The Reconstruction of Abraham Lincoln," in Middleton and Edwards, *Collective Remembering*, 81–107.

89. Halbwachs's claim that the notion of the past is a social construction shaped by the present is particularly apparent in his essay "The Legendary Topography of the Gospels

in the Holy Land"; see Halbwachs, *On Collective Memory*, 193–235. See also G. H. Mead, *The Philosophy of the Present* (Chicago: Univ. of Chicago Press, 1980; ed. by A. E. Murphy from 1932 original); Lowenthal, *Past is a Foreign Country*.

90. Vansina, *Oral Tradition as History*, 147.

91. The term "community of memory" was coined by a team of social scientists conducting research on American culture; see R. N. Bellah, R. Madsen, W. M. Sullivan, A. Swidler, and S. M. Tipton, *Habits of the Heart: Individualism and Commitment in American Life* (Berkeley: Univ. of California Press, 1985), 153. The term has been developed in a study of collective memory with particular focus on Holocaust survivors; see Iwona Irwin-Zareka, *Frames of Remembrance: The Dynamics of Collective Memory* (New Brunswick, NJ: Transaction Press, 1994), 47–65.

92. K. L. Klein, "On the Emergence of *Memory* in Historical Discourse," *Representations* 69 (2000): 127–50.

93. For Comte's positivism see Harriet Martineau, ed., *The Positivist Philosophy of Auguste Comte* (London: Trübner, 1875; 2nd. ed.; select trans. of Auguste Comte, *Cours de philosophie positive* [Paris, 1836–42]); Gertrude Lenzer, ed., *Auguste Comte and Positivism: The Essential Writings* (New Brunswick, NJ: Transaction Press, 1998).

94. Halbwachs, *The Collective Memory*, 51–87.

95. Jacques Le Goff, *History and Memory* (New York: Columbia Univ. Press, 1992), 129.

96. Nora, "Between Memory and History," in Nora, *Realms of Memory*, vol. 1, 1–20, esp. 3–4.

97. Edwin Ardener, "The Construction of History: 'Vestiges of Creation,'" in *History and Ethnicity*, eds. E. Tonkin, M. McDonald, and M. Chapman (London: Routledge, 1989), 25.

98. Tonkin, *Narrating Our Pasts*, 118–21.

99. R. Samuel, *Theatres of Memory*, vol. 1, x.

100. Jan Assman, *Moses the Egyptian: The Memory of Egypt in Western Monotheism* (Cambridge, MA: Harvard Univ. Press, 1997), esp. 15 and 21.

101. Lowenthal, *Past is a Foreign Country*, 204.

102. J. L. Borges, "Funes, the Memorious," in Borges, *A Personal Anthology*, trans. Anthony Kerrigan (London: Pan Books, 1967), 35–43.

103. Luisa Passerini, "Memories Between Silence and Oblivion," in *Contested Pasts: The Politics of Memory*, eds. Katherine Hodgkin and Susannah Radstone (London: Routledge, 2003), 255–71.

104. I. McBride, "Memory and National Identity," in Ian McBride, *History and Memory*, 13.

105. See for example Ulric Neisser, "John Dean's Memory: A Case Study," *Cognition* 9 (1981), 1–22.

106. Fernand Braudel, *The Mediterranean and the Mediterranean World in the Age of Philip II*, trans. Sian Reynolds (London: Collins, 1972), esp. 17–22.

107. Bill Schwarz, "'Already in the Past': Memory and Historical Time," in *Regimes of Memory*, eds. Susannah Radstone and Katherine Hodgkin (London: Routledge, 2003), 141.

108. See Henri Bergson, *Matter and Memory* (London: S. Sonnenschein and Co., 1911; trans. by N. M. Paul and W. S. Palmer of 5th ed. [1908]; orig. ed. *Matière et mémoire: essai sur la relation du corps à l'esprit* [Paris, 1896]). Halbwachs was originally a student of Bergson though, influenced by Durkheim's empiricist approach, his theory of collective memory ultimately rejected many of Bergson's arguments; see Halbwachs, *The Collective Memory*, 90–98.

109. Siegfried Kracauer, "Time and History," *History and Theory* 5, Beiheft 6 (supplement, "History and the Concept of Time"): 75–78.

110. Nora as quoted in Le Goff, *History and Memory*, 96. Appropriately, Proust's work has been identified in its own right as a *Lieu de mémoire* of French culture; Antoine Compagnon, "Marcel Proust's Remembrance of Things Past," in Nora, *Realms of Memory*, vol. 2, 211–46.

111. The term *mythistory* was coined by the American historian William Mc Neill, without fully exploring the possibilities and challenges it presents to historians; see W. H. Mc Neill, "Mythistory, or Truth, Myth, History and Historians," *American Historical Review* 91, no. 1 (1986): 1–10. For further discussion see Peter Heehs, "Myth, History, and Theory," *History and Theory* 33, no 1 (1994): 1–19. Elsewhere, mythistory has been conceptualized as a modernist mode of writing history; Joseph Mali, *Mythistory: The Making of Modern Historiography* (Chicago: Univ. of Chicago Press, 2003).

112. Yosef Hayim Yerushalmi, *Zakhor: Jewish History and Jewish Memory* (Seattle: Univ. of Washington Press, 1982), 5.

113. For a general overview of history and memory debates grounded in modern Irish history, with particular reference to the peculiarities of Protestant and Catholic traditions, see I. McBride, "Memory and National Identity," 1–43.

Chapter 2

1. The standard bilingual edition, translated and annotated by David Comyn and Rev. P. S. Dinneen, was published by the Irish Texts Society; Geoffrey Keating, *The History of Ireland*, 4 vols. (London: n.p., 1902–8).

2. See Charlotte Brooke, *Reliques of Irish Poetry* (Dublin, 1789); Charles O'Conor the Elder, *Dissertations: An Account of the Ancient Government, Letters, Sciences, Religion, Manners and Customs of Ireland* (Dublin, 1753; 2nd ed. 1766); Charles O'Conor the Younger, *Rerum Hibernicarium Scriptores Veteres*, 4 vols. (Buckingham, 1814–28); Theophilus O'Flannagan, ed., *The Transactions of the Gaelic Society* (Dublin, 1808); Sylvester O'Halloran, *General History of Ireland* (Dublin, 1774); Charles Vallancey, ed., *Collectanea de Rebus Hibernicis* (Dublin, 1770–1804); J. C. Walker, *Historical Memoirs of the Irish Bards* (Dublin, 1786). See also Leerssen, *Mere Irish and Fíor-Ghael*; Clare O'Halloran, *Golden Ages and Barbarous Nations: Antiquarians Debate and Cultural Politics in Ireland, c. 1750–1800* (Cork:

Cork Univ. Press, 2004); Georges Denis Zimmermann, *The Irish Storyteller* (Dublin: Four Courts Press, 2001), 89–96.

3. See William Carleton, *Traits and Stories of the Irish Peasantry* (1830 and 1833); Thomas Crofton Croker, *Researches in the South of Ireland: Illustrative of the Scenery, Architectural Remains and Superstitions of the Peasantry* (London, 1824), and *Fairy Legends and Traditions of the South of Ireland* (London, 1825); Gerald Griffin, *Tales of the Munster Festivals* (1827); Samuel Lover, *Legends and Stories of Ireland* (Dublin, 1831 and 1833). See also Zimmermann, *Irish Storyteller*, 173–222.

4. See Jeremiah Curtin, *Myths and Folk-Lore of Ireland* (London, 1889), *Hero Tales of Ireland* (London, 1893), and *Tales of the Fairies and the Ghost World Collected from Oral Tradition in South-West Munster* (The Strand, 1895); Lady I. A. P. Gregory, *The Kiltartan History Book* (Dublin, 1909), *The Kiltartan Wonder Book* (London, 1910), and *Visions and Beliefs in the West of Ireland* (1914; 2 vols.); Patrick Kennedy, *Legends of Mount Leinster* (Dublin, 1855), *Legendary Fictions of the Irish Celts* (London, 1866), *The Fireside Stories of Ireland* (Dublin and London, 1870), and *The Bardic Stories of Ireland* (Dublin and London, 1871); William Larminie, *West Irish Folk-Tales and Romances* (London, 1893); Canon John O'Hanlon, *Legend Lays of Ireland* (1870) and *Irish Local Legends* (1896); Sir William R. Wilde, *Irish Popular Superstitions* (Dublin, 1852); Lady Wilde ("Speranza"), *Ancient Legends, Mystic Charms and Superstitions of Ireland* (London, 1887; 2 vols.) and *Ancient Cures, Charms and Usages of Ireland* (1890); W. B. Yeats, *Fairy and Folk Tales of the Irish Peasantry* (London, 1888) and *Irish Fairy Tales* (London, 1892). See also Zimmermann, *Irish Storyteller*, 283–317.

5. Edward Bunting, *General Collection of the Ancient Music of Ireland* (Dublin, 1796; 2nd ed. 1809); Bunting, *The Ancient Music of Ireland* (Dublin, 1840); Moloney, *Irish Music Manuscripts of Edward Bunting*. See also Ó Buachalla, *I mBéal Feirste*, 15–102.

6. David Cooper and Lillis Ó Laoire, eds.,

The *Petrie Collection of the Ancient Music of Ireland* (Cork: Cork Univ. Press, 2002; orig. pub. in 2 vols., Dublin, 1855 and 1882).

7. See Ó Buachalla, *I mBéal Feirste*, 222–68. At the turn of the century, this project was renewed with a second series of the journal (1894–1911) edited by Francis Joseph Bigger and Robert M. Young.

8. See Dorson, *British Folklorists*, 432–36.

9. Douglas Hyde, *Beside the Fire: A Collection of Gaelic Folk Stories* (London, 1890). Other collections include *Love Songs of Connacht* (1893); *Leabhar Sgéaluigheachta* (1889); *An Sgeuluidhe Gaedhealach* (1901).

10. Most notably, the linguist Carl Marstander (1883–1965), the Celtic scholar Robin Flower (1881–1946), and the classicist George Derwent Thomson (1903–87). For Flower's ethnographic observations and compilations of folklore, see *The Western Island* (Oxford: Oxford Univ. Press, 1944) and Séamus Ó Duilearga, ed., *Seanchas ón Oileán Tiar* (Dublin: Comhlucht Oideachais na hÉireann, 1956).

11. Most notably, Tomás Ó Criomthain's (1857–1937), author of *Allagar na hInse* (Dublin: Ó Fallamhain, 1928) and *An t-Oileánach* (Dublin: Clólucht an Tálbóidigh, 1929), translated as *Island Cross-Talk* (Oxford: Oxford Univ. Press, 1986), and *The Islandman* (Dublin: Talbot Press, 1934); Muiris Ó Súilleabháin (1904–50), author of *Fiche Blian ag Fás* (Dublin: Clólucht an Tálbóidigh, 1933), translated as *Twenty Years a-Growing* (London: Viking Press, 1933); and Peig Sayers (1873–1958). See chap. 10, n. 18.

12. See *Commemorative Programme for the Centenary of the Birth of James Hamilton Delargy, 26.5.1899–25.6.1980*; Diarmuid Breathnach and Máire Ní Mhurchu, *Beathaisnéis 1882–1992*, vol. 5; Bo Almqvist, "In memoriam: Séamus Ó Duilearga," *Sinsear* 3 (1981), 1–6; T. K. Whitaker, "James Hamilton Delargy, 1899–1980," *Folk Life* 20 (1982): 105–6; T. K. Whitaker, "James Hamilton Delargy," *Glynns* 10 (1982): 23–30; *Irish Times*, 26 June 1980.

13. Renamed in 2005 as the UCD Delargy

Centre for Irish Folklore and the National Folklore Collection.

14. For general overviews see Bo Almqvist, "The Irish Folklore Commission Achievement and Legacy," *Béaloideas* 45–47 (1977–79): 6–26; Séamas Ó Catháin, "The Irish Folklore Archive," *History Workshop Journal* 31 (1991): 145–48; Ó Giolláin, *Locating Irish Folklore*, 129–41; "Tuarascáil an Choimisiúin" (IFC archive: unpublished typescript report based on the quarterly and annual reports submitted to the Departments of Education and the Taoiseach).

15. F. M. Barnard, *Herder's Social and Political Thought: From Enlightenment to Nationalism* (Oxford: Oxford Univ. Press, 1965), 62. See also William A. Wilson, "Herder, Folklore and Romantic Nationalism," *Journal of Popular Culture* 6, no 4 (1973): 818–35.

16. Thuente, "The Folklore of Irish Nationalism," 42.

17. J. E. Dunleavy and G. W. Dunleavy, *Douglas Hyde: A Maker of Modern Ireland* (Berkeley: Univ. of California Press, 1991).

18. See Fathers of the Society of Jesus, ed., *A Page of Irish History: Story of University College Dublin, 1883–1909* (Dublin: Talbot Press, 1930), 473–510.

19. Donal McCartney, *UCD A National Idea: The History of University College, Dublin* (Dublin: Gill & Macmillan, 1999), esp. 98–111; T. D. Williams, "The College and the Nation," in *Struggle with Fortune: A Miscellany for the Centenary of the Catholic University,* ed. Michael Tierney (Dublin: Browne & Nolan, 1954), 166–92, esp. 176–83; F. X. Martin, ed., *The Easter Rising and University College, Dublin* (Dublin: Browne & Nolan, 1966).

20. Giuseppe Cochiara, *The History of Folklore in Europe* (Philadelphia: Institute for the Study of Human Issues, 1981; trans. by J. N. McDaniel of original from 1952), 187–374, esp. 201–19. For a broad comparative overview see R. M. Dorson, "The Question of Folklore in a New Nation," *Journal of the Folklore Institute* 3 (1966): 277–98; for useful distinctions between nationalist approaches to

folklore see Ó Giolláin, *Locating Irish Folklore*, 63–93, esp. 72.

21. Ó Crualaoich, "The Primacy of Form," 47–61.

22. *Irish Press*, 18 March 1943, 1.

23. See for example, Patrick Kennedy, *The Fireside Stories*; Douglas Hyde, *Beside the Fire*.

24. For the founding of the Irish Folklore Commission and its persistent attempts to secure government funding and adequate recognition see Gerard O'Brien, *Irish Governments and the Guardianship of Historical Records, 1922–72* (Dublin: Four Courts Press, 2004), 109–20.

25. Hannjost Lixfeld, *Folklore and Fascism: The Reich Institute for German Volkskunde* (Bloomington: Indiana Univ. Press, 1994). See also Linda Dégh, "The Study of Ethnicity in Modern European Ethnology," in *Folklore, Nationalism and Politics*, ed. F. J. Oinas (Columbus, OH: Slavica, 1978), 40; Dorson, *Folklore and Fakelore*, 67–69.

26. Julien Benda, *The Great Betrayal* (London: G. Routledge & Sons, 1928 [trans. of *La Trahison de Clercs* (Paris, 1927)].

27. Ó Duilearga (Delargy), editorial, *Béaloideas* 3 (1932): 104.

28. The international dimension of Irish folklore is apparent in parallels between Seán Ó Suilleabháin and Reider Christiansen's, *Types of the Irish Folktale* and Antti Aarne and Stith Thompson's *Types of the Folk-Tale*.

29. Introduced at the end of the nineteenth century, Ediphones were widely used by ethnologists; George List, "A Short History of the Cylinder Phonograph," *Folklore and Folk Music Archivist* 1, nos. 2 and 3 (1958).

30. Almqvist, "Irish Folklore Commission," 12.

31. See Ó Duilearga [Delargy], editorial, *Béaloideas* 1 (1928): 5–6; Seán Ó Súilleabháin, *Láimhleabhar Béaloideasa* (Dublin: Comhlucht Oideachais na hÉireann, 1937).

32. Items 2, 7, and 11 in S. Ó Súilleabháin, *Handbook of Irish Folklore*, xii–xiii.

33. S. O'Sullivan [Ó Súilleabháin], *Folktales of Ireland*, xxxvi.

34. Figures derived from an analysis of the subdivisions of an interim subject index, which correspond to the chapter headings of the *Handbook;* "Tuarascáil an Choimisiúin," 34–35.

35. See Caoimhín Ó Danachair [Danaher], "The Questionnaire System," *Béaloideas* 15 (1945): 203–5. By 1970 the replies added up to 166 volumes, and since then the Department of Irish Folklore at UCD has continued to send out questionnaires.

36. IFC 1068–75 and 1136.

37. See McHugh "The Famine in Irish Oral Tradition"; also Ó Gráda, *An Drochshaol: Béaloideas agus Amhráin*; Póirtéir, *Famine Echoes;* Póirtéir, *Glórtha ón nGorta: Béaloideas na Gaeilge agus an Gorta Mór*; Quinlan, "A Punishment from God"; Ó Gráda, *Black '47 and Beyond*, 194–225; Ó Gráda, "Famine, Trauma and Memory"; Ó Ciosáin, "Famine Memory."

38. One hundred sixty-seven such volumes were deposited in the archive by 1970. For a demonstration of the insights they may offer see Ríonach uí Ógáin, "'To tell of Murphy in Glenhull'—Some Comments on Context, Text and Subtext in Irish Folklore," in *Thick Corpus, Organic Variation and Textuality in Oral Tradition*, ed. Lauri Honko (Helsinki: Finnish Literature Society, 2000), 159–79.

39. T. K. Whitaker, "James Hamilton Delargy, 1899–1980," 105.

40. See for example: Caoimhín Ó Danachair [Danaher], "The Irish Folklore Commission," *Folklore and Folk Music Archivist* 4, no. 1 (1961): 4; Mahon, *While Green Grass Grows*, 44.

41. Barbara Kirshenblatt-Gimblett, "Folklore's Crisis," *Journal of American Folklore* 111 (1998): 289–300.

42. See Bronislaw Malinowski, *Argonauts of the Western Pacific* (New York: Dutton, 1961; orig. ed. 1922), xv.

43. See Renato Rosaldo, "Imperialist Nostalgia," *Representations* 26 (1989): 107–22.

44. *Nation*, 12 October 1844.

45. Carleton, *Tales and Sketches*, 177.

46. For example: Ó Danachair [Danaher], "History and Oral Tradition," 45.

47. Wilde, *Irish Popular Superstitions*, vi.

48. James Clifford, "On Ethnographic Allegory," in *Writing Culture: The Poetics and Politics of Ethnography*, eds. James Clifford and George Marcus (Berkeley: Univ. of California Press, 1968), 98–121.

49. See *Irish Independent*, 1 February 1939, *Irish Press*, 15 February 1939.

50. Patrick Kavanagh, "Twenty-Three Tons of Accumulated Folk-Lore: Is It of Any Use?" *Irish Times*, 18 April 1939.

51. Articles by Ó Cadhain in *Feasta*, May and September 1950; see also Ó Giolláin, *Locating Irish Folklore*, 149–53.

52. See Caoimhín Ó Danachair [Danaher], "The Death of a Tradition," *Studies* 63, no. 251 (1974): 219–30.

53. Ó Súilleabháin, *Handbook of Irish Folklore*, xii.

54. Comparative contemporary cases can be found in India and Egypt; see E. C. Kirkland, "A Projected Bibliography of the Folklore of India," in Dorson, *Folklore Research*, 127–32; R. M. Dorson, *American Folklore* (Chicago: Univ. of Chicago Press, 1959), 3.

55. R. B. McDowell, *Crisis and Decline: The Fate of Southern Unionists* (Dublin: Lilliput Press, 1997), 163–96.

56. T. Brown, *Ireland*, 106–37.

57. See Diarmuid Ó Giolláin, "An Béaloideas agus an Stát," *Béaloideas* 57 (1989): 151–63.

58. *Irish Times*, 14 January 1928.

59. Ó Súilleabháin, *Handbook of Irish Folklore*, xi.

60. See Patricia Lysaght, "A Tradition Bearer in Contemporary Ireland," in *Storytelling in Contemporary Societies*, eds. Lutz Röhrich and Sabine Wienter (Tübingen: G. Narr Verlag, 1990), 199–214.

61. C. G. Duffy, George Sigerson, and Douglas Hyde, *The Revival of Irish Literature* (London: T. F. Unwin, 1894), 115–61.

62. See D. P. Moran, *The Philosophy of Irish Ireland* (Dublin: James Duffy, 1905); Eoin MacNeill, "Irish Education Policy," *Irish Statesman*, 17 October 1925; Daniel Corkery, *The Hidden Ireland* (Dublin: M. H. Gill & Son,

1924). For the "Irish Ireland" movement and policies of "Gaelicization" in the Free State see T. Brown, *Ireland*, 45–78.

63. Garret Fitzgerald, "The Decline of the Irish Language 1771–1871," in Daly and Dickson, *Origins of Popular Literacy in Ireland*, 59–72 (for a longer version see *Proceedings of the Royal Irish Academy*, 84, C [1984], 177–55).

64. See Neville, "'He Spoke to Me in English,'" 19–32.

65. House of Commons Parliamentary Papers (hereafter H. C.), 1856, vol. 31.

66. *Ulster Journal of Archaeology*, 1st ser., 6 (1858): 172.

67. *Census of Population, 1936* (Parliamentary Report, compiled by the Department of Industry & Commerce [statistics branch], Saorstát Éireann [Dublin, 1936]).

68. Ó Súilleabháin, *Handbook of Irish Folklore*, xi. For a general discussion on the value of studying urban folklore, see Dorson, *Folklore and Fakelore*, 48–60.

69. See Éilis Ní Dhuibhne, "Dublin Modern Legends: An Intermediate Type List and Examples," *Béaloideas* 51 (1983): 55–70.

70. For sample collections edited by Terry Fagan and Ben Savage, see (all published in Dublin by North Inner City Folklore Project): *Memories from Corporation Buildings* (1992), *Those Were the Days* (1992), *All Around the Diamond* (1994), and *Down by the Dockside* (1995).

71. See the project's journal *Archive* (6 issues, 1997–2002) and its website: www.ucc.ie/research/nfp/home.htm. See also Stephen Hunter, ed., *Life Journeys: Living Folklore in Ireland Today* (Cork: Northside Folklore Project, 1999).

72. See for example Lee, *Modernisation of Irish Society 1848–1918*, esp. 1–35; Ó Gráda, *Ireland*.

73. See Donnelly and Miller, *Irish Popular Culture 1650–1850*.

74. Arensberg and Kimball, *Family and Community in Ireland*, esp. 384. For the general context of the Harvard Irish Study (1931–36) and a reappraisal of Arensberg and Kimball's work, see Anne Byrne, Ricca Edmondson, and

Tony Varley, "Introduction to the Third Edition" (ibid., i–ci).

75. See W. E. Vaughan and A. J. Fitzpatrick, eds., *Irish Historical Statistics: Population, 1821–1971* (Dublin: Royal Irish Academy, 1978), 269–353. These figures underestimated emigration from the West of Ireland to mainland Britain; see Ó Gráda, "A Note on Nineteenth-Century Irish Emigration Statistics," *Population Studies* 29 (1975): 143–49.

76. P. J. Drudy, "Irish population change and immigration since Independence," in *The Irish in America: Emigration, Assimilation and Impact*, ed. P. J. Drudy (Cambridge: Cambridge Univ. Press, 1985), 63–85; Enda Delaney, *Demography, State and Society: Irish Migration to Britain, 1921–1971* (Liverpool: Liverpool Univ. Press, 2000), 50, 131, 161, and 166; see also *Commission on Emigration and Other Population Problems 1948–1954: Reports* (Dublin: Department of Social Welfare, 1955), 5–9.

77. O'Donovan Rossa, *Rossa's Recollections 1838–1898*, 391–93.

78. For examples of folklore of the Year of the French recalled abroad see the section on local heroes and their constituencies, esp. 172.

79. *Commission on Emigration and Other Population Problems 1948–1954: Reports* (Dublin: Department of Social Welfare, 1955), 85.

80. Arensberg and Kimball, *Family and Community in Ireland*, 153–86.

81. The figures for the IFC Manuscript Collection are based on sixty-seven informants whose age is cited.

82. Le Goff, *History and Memory*, 22–23 and 73–75.

83. Searleman and Herrmann, *Memory from a Broader Perspective*, 285–94; Groeger, *Memory and Remembering*, 295–96.

84. *Mayo Examiner*, 29 May 1876 (letter to the editor, signed "Ignotus," Swinford, 26 May 1876).

85. "An Gaedhilgeóir is sine?" *An Claidheamh Soluis* 4, no. 6 (1902): 105.

86. *Mayo News*, 12 March 1927.

87. MacNerney, *From the Well of St. Patrick*, 83.

88. *Béaloideas* 4 (1933/4): 393–95; IFC 1117: 108–12.

89. Ó Suilleabháin, *Biographical Dictionary of Longford Authors*, 80.

90. Pádraig Mac Gréine, "My Seventy-five Years in the Field," seminar paper presented at the Department of Irish Folklore, UCD, 2 December 1998.

91. Ó Gráda, "'The Greatest Blessing of All': The Old Age Pension in Ireland," *Past and Present* 175 (2002), 134–42. See also chap. 7.

92. See Ó Ciosáin, *Print and Popular Culture*.

93. See table 3, 277.

94. Sullivan, *New Ireland*, 17.

95. Patricia Lysaght, "Writing Oral Traditions," in Bourke et al., *Field Day Anthology*, 1434.

96. Fionnula Nic Suibhne, "'On the Straw' and Other Aspects of Pregnancy and Childbirth from the Oral Tradition of Women in Ulster," *Ulster Folklife* 38 (1992): 12.

97. Ó Giolláin, *Locating Irish Folklore*, 183.

98. Including Liam Mac Coisdeala (Carna, county Galway, and Erris, county Mayo, 1935–39), Seán Ó hEochaidh (counties Sligo and Donegal, 1935–83), Brian Mac Lochlainn (county Galway and the coastal islands, 1936–39), Sean Ó Flannagáin (south Galway and north Clare, 1937–40); Pádraig Ó Moghráin (Achill Island, county Mayo, 1951–56), Mícheál Mac Énrí (Erris, 1954–64); Tomás a Búrc (northwest Mayo, 1940–44); Proinsias a Búrc (Connemara, county Galway, 1935–83), Ciarán Bairéad (counties Galway, Mayo, and north Clare, 1951–75), Colm Mac Gille Eathain (Connemara, 1946), Mícheál Ó Sírín (Erris, 1951–54), Séamus Mac Aonghusa, who collected traditional music (counties Galway and Mayo, 1942–47), and Michael J. Murphy (Ulster, and county Sligo, 1949–83). James Delaney was the full-time collector for the midlands, collecting, among other places, in Longford, Leitrim, Roscommon, and Westmeath, 1954–86.

99. Part-time collectors in county Mayo included Mícheál Ó Corrdhuibh [Michael Cor-

duff], Séamus Ó Piotáin (who also collected in Leitrim), Bríd Ní Chollaráin, Áine Ní Ruadháin, Pádhraic Bairéad, and Éoin Ó Súilleabháin. In other areas relevant to this study part-time collectors included Bridie Gunning (Sligo), Pádraig Mac Gréine and Philip Ledwith (Longford), P. J. Gaynor (Cavan), Séamus de Brún (Roscommon), and numerous collectors in county Galway, in particular Máirtín Ó Mainnín, Monica Ní Mhaodhbh, Seosamh Ó Flannagáin, Tomás de Paor, Kathleen Hurley, Bairbre Ní Chonaire, Tadhg Ó Coincheanainn, and Liam Ó Coincheannainn.

100. Hayes, *Last Invasion* (2nd ed.), 338.

101. Mac Giollarnáth, *Annála Beaga ó Iorrus Aithneach*, 64–84. For select translations see Hayes, *Last Invasion* (2nd ed.), 338–39 and 341–44.

102. Ó Súilleabháin, *Handbook of Irish Folklore*, 533.

103. Dropmore Papers, BL MS 71580, f. 71.

104. Edgeworth and Edgeworth, *Memoirs of Richard Lovell Edgeworth*, vol. 2, 234–35. For the policy of reprieve see Michael Durey, "Marquess Cornwallis and the Fate of Irish Rebel Prisoners in the Aftermath of the 1798 Rebellion," in Smyth, *Revolution, Counter-Revolution*, 128–45.

105. IFC 164:499–514; IFC 528:6–10; IFC 770:203–6; IFC 969:183–87; IFC 1206:364–65; IFC 1480:350–55; IFC 1512:313–18; IFC S119:518–20; IFC S141:32–34; IFC S261:129–30; IFC S758:170.

106. For example, Hayes, *Last Invasion*, 225, 274.

107. Ó Súilleabháin, *Handbook of Irish Folklore*, 532–33.

108. IFC 1858:2, 5–6, 8–10, 11–17, 24–28, 39, 41–44, 96–106, 120–23. These folklore accounts are contextualized and analyzed in Maureen O'Rourke Murphy, "The Battle of Ballinamuck: A Study in the Dynamics of Oral tradition" (PhD thesis, Indiana University, 1970).

109. Eighty-five percent of the accounts collected in Mayo and 70 percent in Galway were in Irish. Collectors of relevant folklore in Irish from these areas include Proinssias de

Burca, Liam Mac Coisdeala, Henry Corduff, Tomás a Burc, Micheál Mac Énri, and Pádhraic Bairéad.

110. *Irish Times*, 24 April 1935; *Irish Independent*, 24 April 1935.

111. For example: *Meath Chronicle*, 27 April 1935; *Limerick Leader*, 27 April 1935; *Kilkenny Journal*, 5 and 25 May 1935; *Drogheda Independent*, 25 May 1935; *Dundalk Examiner*, 4 May 1935; *Saturday Record*, 5 May 1935; *Western People*, 5 May 1935.

112. For overviews of this project see Séamas Ó Catháin, "Súil Siar ar *Scéim na Scol 1937–1938*," *Sinsear* 5 (1988): 19–30; Séamas Ó Catháin, "Scéim na Scol. The Schools' Scheme of 1937–1938," in *It's Us They're Talking About*, eds. Margaret Farren and Mag Hoken (proceedings of the McGlinchey Summer School; Clonmany, county Donegal, 1998), vol. 1 (13 pages, unnumbered).

113. Ó Súilleabháin, *Irish Folklore and Tradition*, 4–5.

114. See Ó Catháin, "Scéim na Scol" (unpaginated).

115. Official notebooks were subsequently bound as a series of 1,126 paginated volumes, arranged in sequence by province and county. Pupils' copybooks were left in their original form, unbound and unpaginated, and stored in 1,124 corresponding boxes.

116. In Connacht this ratio was even higher, with 98.5 percent Catholic pupils; *An Roinn Oideachais Turasgabháil / Report of the Department of Education 1937–38* (Dublin, n.p. 1938), 130–31.

117. Memorandum quoted in Ó Catháin, "Scéim na Scol" (unpaginated).

118. Ó Súilleabháin, *Irish Folklore and Tradition*, 36.

119. O'Sullivan [Ó Súilleabháin], *Folktales of Ireland*, xxxv.

120. Hayes, *Last Invasion*, 127.

121. Póirtéir, "Folk Memory and the Famine," 231.

122. Tóibín "The Irish Famine," 23.

123. Ó Ciosáin, "Famine memory," 95–117; Ó Ciosáin, "Approaching a Folklore Archive: The Irish Folklore Commission and

the Memory of the Great Famine," *Folklore* 115. no. 2 (2004): 222–32.

124. Lauri Honko, "The Folklore Process," *Folklore Fellows Summer School* (1991): 25–47.

125. Fentress and Wickham, *Social Memory*, 89.

Chapter 3

1. Hayes, *Last Invasion*, xxv.

2. The second edition added a translated stanza of a poem by the early-twentieth-century literary historian and novelist Aodh de Blácam (viii), an updated preface (xiii–xix), a map of the battlefield of Ballinamuck prepared by Captain Nolan of the Ordnance Survey Department (140) and an extended appendix on the aftermath of the insurrection (329–61). A third edition published in 1979 (in the Sackville Library series) was a reprint of the original 1937 edition (omitting the additions of the 1939 edition).

3. Mainchín Seoighe, *From Bruree to Corcomahide* (Bruree Co. Limerick: Bruree/Rockhill Development Association, 2000), 190–91; Boylan, *Dictionary of Irish Biography*; McRedmond, *Modern Irish Lives*; Hickey and Doherty, *Dictionary of Irish History*; tributes by Richard Mulcahy, W. T. Cosgrave, and Charles Petrie, *Irish Sword* 3 (1958): 210–12.

4. Hayes's professional posts are listed in the annual issues of the *Medical Directory* (London, 1906–45). The Dublin dispensary system was overstretched, with each doctor responsible for the treatment of some 6,220 patients; Ruth Barrington, *Health, Medicine and Politics in Ireland 1900–1970* (Dublin: Institute of Public Administration, 1987), 134.

5. See "Doctor Richard Hayes and His Work," *Catholic Bulletin* 24 (1934): 302–4.

6. See "The Bellman," "Meet Dr. Hayes or The Genial Censor," *Bell* vol. 3, no. 2 (November 1941): 106–14; Ó Drisceoil, *Censorship in Ireland 1938–1945*, 35–41.

7. Other books include *Ireland and Irishmen in the French Revolution* (1932), *Irish Swordsmen of France* (1934), *Old Irish Links with France*

(1940), and *Biographical Dictionary of Irishmen in France* (1949). He also wrote numerous articles on various historical topics; for a bibliography, see Richard J. Hayes, ed., *Sources for the History of Irish Civilisation: Articles in Irish Periodicals* (Boston: G. K. Hall & Co., 1970), vol. 2, 660–62.

8. Hayes, "The Battle of Castlebar, 1798."

9. Hayes, "Priests in the Independence Movement of '98."

10. Hayes, "An Officer's Account of the French Campaign in Ireland," trans. of adjutant-general Jean Sarrazin's "Notes sur l'Expédition d'Irlande" (orig. pub. in *L'Ami des Lois*, 8 December 1978).

11. Hayes, *Last Invasion*, inscription, xv.

12. The original edition (1937) includes ninety definite references to oral traditions in the main narrative (including footnotes); seventeen in a chapter on "Traditions of the Insurrection," with ten additional accounts of Leitrim traditions in the footnotes of this chapter (originally collected for the Irish Folklore Commission by Peter Kilkenny of Sunnaghbeg, Cloone); twenty-three references to lyrical and poetic traditions in a chapter on "Ballads and Songs of the Insurrection." An appendix added to the second edition (1939) includes approximately fifteen supplementary references to traditions (collected by District Justice Ford—Seán MacGiollarnáth, Michael O'Gallaher of Chicago, and Patrick O'Donnell of Newport).

13. Hayes, *Last Invasion*, 133–34.

14. Leopold von Ranke, *History of the Latin and Teutonic Nations from 1494 to 1514* (London, 1887; trans. of *Geschichten der Romanischen und Germanischen Völker von 1494 bis 1514* [1824]).

15. NLI MSS 13799–13801.

16. See Douglas Hyde, "Irish Folk Lore," in Ó Conaire, *Language, Lore and Lyrics. Essays and Lectures by Douglas Hyde*, 102 [text of an essay from 1889; NLI MS 17,297].

17. For example, see the description of the fieldwork of Tadhg Murphy [Ó Murchadha] in R. M. Dorson, "Collecting in County Kerry," *Journal of American Folklore* 66

(1953): 22 (republished in Dorson, *Folklore and Fakelore*, 19–42).

18. Hayes, *Last Invasion*, 216.

19. Ibid., 318.

20. On 14 July 1938, Ó Súilleabháin sent a translation of a tale collected by Liam Mac Coisdeala from seventy-five-year-old Séamus Ó Catháin of Erris, county Mayo; NLI MS 13799 (7); the original appears in IFC 507: 76–78.

21. Matthews, *Voices*, 118–19. Hayes's *Last Invasion* was written with O'Connor's help.

22. NLI MSS 13799 (3); 13800(7)

23. Letter dated 9 February 1938; NLI MS 13799 (3).

24. NLI MSS 13799 (4); 13800 (5).

25. *Irish Book Lover* 26 (July–August 1938): 18.

26. Terence O'Hanlon, "Humbert's Expedition to Ireland. Moving Story of Gambler's Throw That Almost Succeeded," *Sunday Independent*, 1 August 1937; P. S. O'Hegarty, "When Humbert Sailed into Killala: Dr. Hayes Writes the Story of a Gallant Failure," *Irish Independent*, 8 August 1937; Sean O'Faolain "When the West Rose, Dr. Richard Hayes' Thrilling Narrative," *Irish Press*, 11 August 1937; *Times Literary Supplement*, 28 August 1937; review by Séamus Ó Ceallaigh, *Ireland To-Day*, 2, no. 10 (October 1937), 79–80; review by Michael Tierney, *Studies* 26 (1937): 507–9.

27. *Irish Press*, 28 February 1939; *Irish Independent*, 7 March 1939; *Studies* 28 (June 1939): 323.

28. Costello edited two eyewitness accounts of the French invasion, which were published in *Analecta Hibernica* 11 (1941).

29. *Irish Historical Studies* 1, no. 1 (1938): 91.

30. See Moody, "New History for Ireland"; Robert Dudley Edwards, "An Agenda for Irish History, 1978–2018" (ibid., 54–67). This approach influenced the next generation of prominent Irish historians; see for example: F. S. L. Lyons, "The Burden of Our History" (ibid., 87–104).

31. Matthews, *Voices*.

32. *Bell* 3, no. 2 (November 1941): 111. Donal Ó Drisceoil suggested that "class rather than age may have been the determining factor in Hayes's differentiation"; Ó Drisceoil, *Censorship in Ireland*, 54.

33. *Studies* 30 (December 1941): 644.

34. Hayes, *Last Invasion*, xviii–xix.

35. Ibid., 251–55.

36. Séamus Ó Ceallaigh, *Ireland To-Day* 2, no. 10 (October 1937): 79.

37. *Studies* 26 (1937): 508–9.

Chapter 4

1. Whelan, *Tree of Liberty*, 133; reproduced in Whelan, *Fellowship of Freedom*, 141.

2. Anon., *The Last Speech and Dying Words of Martin McLoughlin*.

3. S. J. Connolly, "Aftermath and Adjustment," vol. 5, 18–19.

4. Patrick Kennedy, ed., *The Book of Modern Irish Anecdotes: Humour, Wit and Wisdom* (London: George Routledge & Sons, ca. 1872), 68.

5. For popular reception of Musgrave's history, which was enthusiastically adopted as a founding text of modern British and Irish conservatism, see James Kelly, "'We Were All to Have Been Massacred,'" 328–29. For its pivotal role as a "matrix of memory," which shaped Protestant memory of the Rebellion and had a seminal influence on the historiography of 1798, see Whelan, *Tree of Liberty*, 135–45.

6. Partly published in R. M. Young, *Ulster in '98*, 18–60.

7. Samuel McSkimin Papers, RIA MS 12 F 36 and MS 24 Q 22. Partly published in Young, *Ulster in '98*, 1–14 and 60–67. See also Samuel McSkimin, *The History and Antiquities of the County of the Town of Carrickfergus, From the Earliest Records to the Recent Time; Also a Statistical Survey of Said County* (Belfast: J. Smyth, 1823; orig. ed. 1811), 97–100; McSkimin, *Annals of Ulster; or, Ireland Fifty Years Ago* (Belfast: Henderson, 1849), 83–137.

8. Luke Cullen Papers, TCD MS 1472, NLI MSS 9760–9762. For published versions see M. V. Ronan, ed., *Personal Recollections of*

Wexford and Wicklow Insurgents of 1798 as Collected by the Rev. Br. Luke Cullen 1798–1859 (Enniscorthy, 1958); O'Donnell, *Insurgent Wicklow*.

9. R. R. Madden, *United Irishmen*.

10. McParlan, *Statistical Survey of the County of Mayo*.

11. Anon., "An English-Gentleman aided by the communication of several friends," *The Scientific Tourist*.

12. Anon., "A Guardian of the Poor," *The Irish Peasant*, 18.

13. See Andrews, *Paper Landscape*; Gillian Doherty, *Irish Ordnance Survey*.

14. Letters dating 15 and 17 May 1837 in John O'Donovan, *Letters Containing Information* (typescript of orig. MS in RIA).

15. Leerssen, *Remembrance and Imagination*, 100–108.

16. Ibid., 159–73.

17. Ó Giolláin, *Locating Irish Folklore*, 112.

18. See O'Donnell and Reece, "A Clean Beast"; Peter O'Shaughnessy, ed., *Rebellion in Wicklow: General Joseph Holt's Personal Account of 1798* (Dublin: Four Courts Press, 1998).

19. See Zimmermann, *Irish Storyteller*, 122–65.

20. Terence O'Toole [Caesar Otway], *Tour in Connaught*; Otway, *Sketches in Erris and Tyrawley*.

21. See W. H. Maxwell, *Irish Movements*.

22. W. H. Maxwell, *Erin-Go-Bragh*, 155–70; Maxwell, *History of the Irish Rebellion in 1798*, 251–52; Maxwell, *Wild Sports of the West*, 213–14 and 256–59 (reference to a fabricated story); Maxwell, *Adventures of Captain Blake*, 65–116. For a list of the numerous editions of Maxwell's writings see Colin McKelvie, "Notes towards a bibliography of William Hamilton Maxwell (1792–1850)," *Irish Booklore* 3, no. 1 (1976): 32–42.

23. For a bibliography of travel literature, see McVegh, *Irish Travel Writing*. For specific references see chap. 12, n. 21 (386).

24. Spurgeon Thompson, "The Politics of Photography."

25. Bulfin, *Rambles in Eirinn*, 23.

26. See Séamas Ó Catháin, "Eolas ar an Bhéaloideas," *Aimsir Óg 2000* (2001): 8.

27. See Elizabeth Crooke, "Exhibiting 1798." For publications that accompanied these exhibitions see Maguire, *Up in Arms*; Whelan, *Fellowship of Freedom*. My thanks to Bernard Browne for forwarding me a copy of "Exploring 1798," an educational pack for the exhibition in Enniscorthy. The Royal Irish Academy hosted an exhibition of contemporary sources from 1798 (1 September 1998–8 January 1999).

28. My thanks to Mrs. Marie Boran, Special Collections Librarian UCG, for forwarding me information on this exhibition.

29. O'Rorke, *History, Antiquities*; O'Rorke, *History of Sligo*; Farrell, *Historical Notes and Stories*; James Woods, *Annals of Westmeath*; O'Flynn, *History of Leitrim*; Quinn, *History of Mayo*.

30. See Mac Gréine, "Traditions of 1798, The Battle of Ballinamuck"; Ó Gallchobhair, "Amhráin ó Iorrus"; Mac Giollarnáth, "Sliocht de Sheanchas Mhicheál Bhreathnaigh"; Mac Coisdealbha, "Seanchas Ó Iorrus"; Tohall, "Some Connacht Traditions"; Séamus Ó Duilearga [Delargy], "Seanchas Phádraig Mhic Meanaman."

31. G. M. Horgan, *James Berr*, esp. 136–39.

32. Henry, *Tales From the West of Ireland*, 7–14, 42–44, 49.

33. See Leerssen, *Remembrance and Imagination*, 173–77.

34. Edward Bunting Papers, QUB MSS 4/7, 24, 25, 32, and 35 (ff 29, 30, 33). Additional items in the Bunting manuscript collection can also be attributed to Lynch on the basis of handwriting analysis; see Moloney, *Irish Music Manuscripts*, 33–34. For Lynch see Brian Mac Giolla Fhinnéin, "Pádraig Ó Loinsigh: Saol agus Saothar," *Seanchas Ardmhacha* 15, no. 2 (1993): 98–124, esp. 116–19.

35. For studies of these songs see Ríonach uí Ógáin, "Béaloideas 1798 Thiar"; Tom Munnelly, "1798 and the Balladmakers"; Moylan, ed., *Age of Revolution: 1776–1815 in the Irish Song Tradition*.

36. See Devaney, *Killoe*, 129–36.

37. Originally written down in 1938 by Ó Brádaigh's mother Máire Ní Chafraidh of Belfast; Ó Brádaigh, *Battle of Ballinamuck*.

38. See Dorson, *Folklore and Fakelore*, 61–66.

39. For example, Sean Lavin of Lackan, county Mayo, recorded on video interviews with elderly residents in the area of the French landing place in Kilcummin; interview with Sean Lavin, 22 August 2001. Some of the collected oral traditions have been published in Lavin, *History of the Civil Parish of Kilcummin*. Similarly, video tapes were made of local commemorative initiatives in Ballinamuck that celebrated events remembered in folklore; interview with Jimmy Breslin, Ballinamuck, 15 September 2001.

40. *1798 Agus Ó Shin* (Telefís na Gaeilge: 1998; director Louis Marcus); *A Patriot's Fate* (BBC Northern Ireland: 1998; director Moore Sinnerton), 2 parts; and *Rebellion* (RTÉ: 1998; producer Kevin Dawson), 3 parts.

41. For example, folklore of the Year of the French can be found on relevant sites of the Local Ireland network; see http://mayo.local.ie; http://longford.local.ie.

42. Prins, "Oral History," in Burke, *New Perspectives*, 135.

43. For interactions between literacy and orality in the context of collecting Irish folklore see Danaher, "Folk Tradition and Literature," *Journal of Irish Literature* 1, no 2 (1972): 63–76; Bo Almqvist, *An Béaloideas agus an Litríocht* (Baile an Fheirtéaraigh, Co. Kerry: Cló Dhuibhne, 1977); Seán Ó Coileáin, "Oral or Literary? Some Strands of the Argument," *Studia Hibernica* 17–18 (1978): 9–35; James Stewart, *Boccaccio in the Blaskets* (Galway: Officina Typographica, 1988); Bo Almqvist, "The Mysterious Mícheál Ó Gaothín, Boccaccio and the Blasket Tradition," *Béaloideas* 59 (1990): 75–140; L. M. Cullen, "Poetry, Culture and Politics."

44. See for example Jack Goody, "Memory in Oral Tradition," in *Memory,* eds. Patricia Fara and Karalyn Paterson (Cambridge: Cambridge Univ. Press, 1998), 73–94.

45. Finnegan, *Literacy and Orality*. For interactions between orality and literacy in traditional societies that come in contact with cultural influences of modernity see Norman Simms, *Points of Contact: A Study of the Interplay and Intersection of Traditional and Non-Traditional Literatures, Cultures, and Mentalities* (New York: Pace University Press, 1991), esp. 167–212.

46. Wlad Godzich, *The Culture of Literacy* (Cambridge, MA: Harvard Univ. Press, 1994), 147.

Chapter 5

1. Jules Michelet, *Histoire de la Révolution Française*, vol. 2 (Paris: Chamerot, 1847), 528–30.

2. Vendreys, *Lexique Étymologique de L'Irlandais Ancien*, S-84.

3. Delargy, "Gaelic Storyteller," 178.

4. Dinneen, *Foclóir Gaedhilge agus Béarla*, 1007; see also Quin, *Contributions to a Dictionary of the Irish Language*, vol. S, 177; Niall Ó Dónaill, *Foclóir Gaeilge-Béarla*, 1076.

5. See Clodagh Brennan Harvey, *Contemporary Irish Traditional Narrative*, 4–6.

6. Glassie, *Passing the Time in Ballymenone*, 109.

7. Glassie, "Folklore and History," 68–69.

8. See James E. Young, "Between History and Memory: The Uncanny Voices of Historian and Survivor," *History and Memory* 9, no. 1/2 (1997): 47–58; for "deep memory" see Lawrence Langer, *Holocaust Testimonies: The Ruins of Memory* (New Haven, CT: Yale Univ. Press, 1991), 1–38.

9. Ben-Amos, "Toward a Definition of Folklore in Context," in Paredes and Bauman, *Toward New Perspectives*, 13.

10. Other terms used for nightly visiting included *siúl, airneán, scoraíocht, bothántaíocht, ránaíocht,* and rambling. See Harvey, *Contemporary Irish Traditional Narrative*, 89–91. *Céili* was commonly used in the northern half of Ireland (down to the Boyne river).

11. Arensberg and Kimball, *Family and Community*, 186.

12. Delargy, "Gaelic Storyteller," 191–94; Séamus Ó Duilearga [Delargy], *Seán*

Ó Conaill's Book (Dublin: Comhairle Bhéaloideas Éireann, 1981; trans. by Máire MacNeill of *Leabhar Sheáin Í Chonaill*, 1948), xvii–xxi.

13. See Honko, "The Folklore Process," 26–29.

14. Ben-Amos, "Toward a Definition of Folklore in Context," 4.

15. Vansina, *Oral Tradition as History*, 82.

16. IFC S758:441. *Céilidhtheoir*, defined by P. S. Dinneen as "one who pays an evening visit," probably derives from a mix of Irish and English [i.e., *Céilí*-er]. In another version of the ballad, the term is substituted by "seanchaidhe" (storyteller); IFC S225:145.

17. Ó Súilleabháin, *Storytelling in Irish Tradition*, 48–49.

18. Ó hÓgáin, *Hero in Irish Folk History*.

19. Eric Hobsbawm, *Bandits* (Harmondsworth: Penguin, 1972), 127–28.

20. Ó hÓgáin, *Hero in Irish Folk History*, 291–98.

21. Two versions were collected by pupils from different local schools from Michael Ó Loinn of Ceapach, Ballycastle, county Mayo; IFC S140:301–2; S141:32–34.

22. Collected in 1935 from seventy-one-year-old Pádraic Ó Súilleabháin of Ballintober, on the border of counties Galway and Roscommon; IFC 164:499–514.

23. Collected in 1944 by C. I. Mac Gill-Eathain from "Big" (Senior) Mathew O'Toole [Maitiú Mhóir Uí Thuathail], who had heard a number of Ninety-Eight tales sixty years earlier (ca. 1884) from his father Martin; IFC 969:178–87, esp. 183.

24. IFC S Box 758b: copybook of Patrick Brady, Gaigue N.S., Ballinamuck, county Longford.

25. Collected by Phillip Trapp of Soran, Ballinalee from John Trapp; IFC S759:209. A similar account was collected by Kathleen Lee of Soran from her sixty-nine-year-old uncle Peter McGuire of Dernavogy, Aughnacliffe (near Granard), county Longford; IFC S759:215.

26. Collected by Tomás a Burc from Seán a Goireachtaigh [Geraghty] of Carrowteige Erris; IFC 770:203–4.

27. NAI MS 620/17/27.

28. D. D. Buchan, "History and Harlaw," *Journal of the Folklore Institute* 5, no 1 (1968): 66; see also Buchan, *The Ballad and the Folk* (London: Routledge, 1972).

29. This is best exemplified in a bilingual-dialogic genre known as macaronic songs, which featured phonetically spelled Irish verses alternating with English; Diarmaid Ó Muirithe, *An tAmhrán Macarónach* (Dublin: An Clóchomhar Tta, 1980).

30. Dunne, "Tá Gaedhil bhocht cráidhte," 94.

31. Pádraig A. Breathnach, "Oral and Written Transmission of Poetry in the Eighteenth Century," *Eighteenth Century Ireland* 2 (1987): 57–65. For examples see Thomas MacDonagh, *Literature in Ireland* (Dublin: Talbot, 1916), 164; Ó Muirgheasa, *Dhá Chéad de Cheoltaibh Uladh*; Donncha Ó Cróiní, ed., *Seanachas Phádraig Í Chrualaoi* (Dublin: Comhairle Bhéaloideas Éireann, 1982), 10–160.

32. See A. H. Krappe, *The Science of Folklore* (London: Methuen & Co., 1930), 154–55.

33. J. E. Caerwyn Williams and Patrick K. Ford, *The Irish Literary Tradition* (Cardiff: Univ. of Wales, 1992), 193–253.

34. Marc Caball, *Poets and Politics: Reaction and Continuity in Irish Poetry, 1558–1625* (Cork: Cork Univ. Press, 1998), 95; Douglas Hyde, "Gaelic Folk Songs," *Nation* (April–May 1890): 37; reprinted in Ó Conaire, *Language, Lore and Lyrics*, 104–5.

35. Daniel Corkery, *The Hidden Ireland: A Study of Gaelic Munster in the Eighteenth Century* (Dublin: Gill & Macmillan, 1967; orig. ed. 1924); L. M. Cullen, *The Hidden Ireland: Reassessment of a Concept* (Mullingar: Lilliput Press, 1988).

36. For a summary of the historiographical debate see Caball, *Poets and Politics*, 7–13.

37. Vincent Morley, "'Tá an cruatan ar Sheoirse'—Folklore or Politics?" *Eighteenth-Century Ireland* 13 (1998): 112–20; Morley, *Irish Opinion and the American Revolution, 1760–1783* (Cambridge: Harvard Univ. Press, 2002), esp. 45–7, 106–15, 177–86, 281–85.

Dunne, "Subaltern Voices"; Dunne, "Tá Gaedhil bhocht cráidhte."

38. Micheál Mac Craith, "Filíocht Sheacaibíteach na Gaeilge: ionar gan uaim?" *Eighteenth Century Ireland* 9 (1994): 57–75; Ó Buachalla, *Aisling Ghéar*; also: Ó Buachalla, "Irish Jacobite Poetry," *Irish Review* 12 (1992): 40–49; Ó Buachalla, "Irish Jacobitism and Irish Nationalism: The Literary Evidence," *Studies on Voltaire and the Eighteenth Century* 335 (1995): 103–16; Éamonn Ó Ciardha, *Ireland and the Jacobite Cause, 1685–1766: A Fatal Attachment* (Dublin: Four Courts Press, 2002).

39. See for example Georges Denis Zimmermann, *Songs of Irish Rebellion*, 31.

40. Ó Crualaoich "The French Are on the Say"; Ó Buachalla, "From Jacobite to Jacobin."

41. For example, Croker, *Popular Songs Illustrative of the French Invasions of Ireland.*

42. Hayes, *Last Invasion*, 247. For Richard Barrett, see O'Dubhthaigh, "Riocard Bairead: File Iorrais"; N. Williams, *Riocard Bairéad*, esp. 31. For Michael Sweeney, see T. Ó Máille, *Micheál Mhac Suibhne agus Filidh an tSléibhe*; Horgan, *James Berry*, 138.

43. Hayes, *Last Invasion* (2nd ed.), 348; see also Ó Gallchobhair, "Amhráin ó Iorrus."

44. At the time, the Irish post office system was used by the government for intelligence gathering; see T. Bartlett, "Informers, Informants and Information," 408–9.

45. Edward Bunting Papers, QUB MSS 4 / 24, 25, 32, and 35 ff 29, 30, 33; Robert Young Papers, PRO NI D2930/3/5/1. See also R. M. Young, "Edward Bunting's Irish Music and the McCracken Family."

46. RIA MS 240 1934, 1a.

47. For example, IFC 1318:105–7 and 111–15; Horgan, *James Berry*, 139. See also chap. 12.

48. W. H. Maxwell, *History of the Irish Rebellion*, 251; see also W. H. Maxwell, *Erin-Go-Bragh*, 162. The former position of John Gibbons Sr., who had been the agent of Lord Altamont, may have left residues of ill feeling among Westport tenantry.

49. IFC S89:434–35; Horgan, *James Berry*,

1. Although this nickname was used pejoratively, contemporary accounts testify that soap was applied to ropes as a token of mercy, as it hastened the act of execution; see Mangin, *Parlour Window*, 39; J. Sarrazin, "Notes sur l'expédition d'Irlande," in Joannon, *La Descente de Français en Irlande—1798* (trans. in Hayes, "An Officer's Account," 161).

50. For example, IFC 202:73, 485:233; IFC S94:244; IFC S138:161–62, S261:129–30; Hayes, *Last Invasion*, 183, 214, 248–49, 304–5; Lady Gregory, *Kiltartan History Book*, 60–61; M. Kelly, "The Bekan Area in 'The Year of the French.'" A more sympathetic account noted that Browne gave a reprieve to two condemned rebels; IFC S119:518–20.

51. IFC 72:31–3, IFC 202:71–73, IFC S138:161–62; Hayes, *Last Invasion*, 248–49; Henry, *Tales From the West*, 16; Hyde, *Abhráin Atá Leagtha ar an Reachtúire or Songs Ascribed to Raftery*, 192–97; S. Ó Broin, ed., *Songs of Past and People*, 33; Ó Coigligh, *Raiftearaí*, 148–50 (and notes on 8, 148–50, 163, 186–87).

52. IFC 1244:463–65. For Peter Jordan see Henry, *Tales From the West*, 8–9. See also Mag Ruaidhrí, *Le Linn M'Óige*, 8–10.

53. For a version collected by the schoolteacher, poet, and folk historian Pilib O Bhaldraithe [Philip Waldron] of Drumbaun, Ballyhaunis, see Hayes, *Last Invasion*, 250–51 and 328. See also Ó Brádaigh, *Songs of 1798*, 22; Henry, *Tales From the West*, 49. For a translation see Ó Broin, *Songs of Past and People*, 32. Traditions about James O'Malley were documented by Pádhraic Mac Thorcail of Maynooth College in 1942; IFC 1140:219–20.

54. Hayes, *Last Invasion*, 243–44; O'Rourke, "County Mayo in Gaelic Folksong," 191–92; Ó Brádaigh, *Songs of 1798*, 51.

55. Ó Muirgheasa, *Dhá Chéad de Cheoltaibh Uladh*, 26–27; Hayes, *Last Invasion*, 244–45; Ó Canainn and Ó Deaghdha, *Filíocht na nGael*, 24; O'Rourke, "County Mayo in Gaelic Folksong," 190–91; Ó Brádaigh, *Songs of 1798*, 26.

56. Ó Brádaigh, *Songs of 1798*, 56–57. "*Scéal do réab mo chroí Ionam*" (popularly

known by its opening verse: "Do Chuala Scéal") refers to the coming of the French; Rónán Ó Donnchadha, *Mícheál Óg Ó Longáin* (Dublin: Coiscéim, 1994), 89.

57. Collected from Mrs. Gibbons of Cappach Charnáin; *An Gaodhal*, June 1885, 491; reproduced in Ó Moghráin, "Gearr-Chunntas ar an Athair Mánus Mac Suibhne," 46–47. For a translation by Máire Mhac an tSaoi, see Mulloy, *Father Manus Sweeney*, 95–96.

58. IFC 1534:522–23. For a detailed discussion of this song see chap. 8, "A Franco-Irish Officer."

59. IFC 1534:530.

60. IFC 1534:534–37.

61. IFC 770:51–53. See also Séamas Ó Catháin, "Tricking the Fairy Suitor," *Béaloideas* 59 (1991): 152–53; Ó Catháin, "The Robbers and the Captive Girl," *Béaloideas* 62/3 (1994/5): 131, n. 44; Ríonach uí Ógáin and Thérèse Smith, "Cumhdachaí," *Béaloideas* 66 (1998): 199–216, esp. 212–14.

62. Collected by Pádhraic Bairéad from fifty-three-year-old Nóra Ní Ruadháin of Devlin Clogher in the parish of Kilmore, Erris, county Mayo, and attributed to eighty-five-year-old Máire Bairéad IFC 227:432.

63. uí Ógáin, "Béaloideas 1798 Thiar," 150–51.

64. Recorded in 1953 by Leo Corduff and Seán Ó hEochaidh from Róise Ní Ghrianna [Róise na nAmhrán] of Aranmore, county Donegal; IFC Tape 1188a. Éamonn Ó Dónaill, formerly of the Department of Modern Irish at UCD, informed me that his aunt recalled her grandmother—Peggy Coyle of Cnoc an Stolaire in Gaoth Dobhair, county Donegal—singing this song. A version attributed to Síle Mhicí of nearby Dobhar, Gaoth Dobhair, was recorded and released in an album by the popular band Clannad; *Crann Úll* (Tara Records, 1980). For versions in print see *An Stoc*, 19 July 1920; Hayes, *Last Invasion*, 243; O'Rourke, "County Mayo in Gaelic Folksong," 193; Ó Brádaigh, *Songs of 1798*, 15.

65. A ballad sung in South Tipperary in 1843 listed a series of questions opening with

"Were you in Ballinamuck?"; *Limerick Chronicle*, 22 November 1843. Similarly, a song by Madden poses a series of questions referring to the 1798 rebellion in Leinster, "Were you at Vinegar Hill? Or down at the battle of Tara?"; R. R. Madden, *Literary Remains*, 27. See Maura Cronin, "Memory, Story and Balladry."

66. Iona and Peter Opie, *The Lore and Language of Schoolchildren* (Oxford: Oxford Univ. Press, 1959).

67. Muireadhach Méith [Lorcán Ó Muireadhaigh], *Amhráin Chúige Uladh* (Dublin: G. Dalton, 1977), 51 and 171. Prof. Dáithí Ó hÓgáin of the Department of Irish Folklore, UCD, has informed me that he has also heard a version of the song with reference to *Cill Dara* recited in Omeath, county Louth.

68. PRO HO 100/78/230.

69. Sir Richard Musgrave, *Memoirs of the Different Rebellions in Ireland*, 578.

70. Dominic Daly, *The Young Douglas Hyde: The Dawn of the Irish Revolution and Renaissance 1874–1893* (Dublin: Irish Univ. Press, 1974), 120–21; see for example An Craoibhín Aoibhinn, "A Ballad of '98," *Irish Weekly Independent*, 22 December 1894. Hyde later published what is probably a fictional account of his grandfather's recollections of the French in Mayo; An Craoibhín Aoibhinn, "Eachtra mo Shean Athair," *Father Mathew Record* 6, no. 12 (December 1913).

71. Ó Brádaigh, *Songs of 1798*, 19; Moylan, *Age of Revolution*, 105. For an English translation see A. Griffith, *Poems and Ballads by William Rooney [Fear na Muinntire]*, 139–40. For another example see "An Sean-Chroppi agus é tinn," *Shan Van Vocht* 3, no. 11 (7 November 1898): 197.

72. See epilogue, 326.

73. For the "Davisite" tradition see George Boyce, *Nationalism in Ireland*, 2nd ed. (London: Routledge, 1991), 228–58.

74. See Shields, *Narrative Singing in Ireland*.

75. For the interrelationship between printed and oral ballad traditions see Zimmermann, *Songs of Irish Rebellion*, 12.

76. Madden, *Literary Remains of the United Irishmen*; identified in dedication as originally compiled in 1846.

77. See chap. 8, "A Franco-Irish Officer."

78. J. S. Donnelly, Jr., "Propagating the Cause of the United Irishmen"; Jim Smyth, *Men of No Property*, 161–70; N. J. Curtin, *The United Irishmen*, 174–253.

79. K. Whelan, "United Irishmen, the Enlightenment and Popular Culture," esp. 281–88; see also Whelan, *Tree of Liberty*, 59–96.

80. See Laura Mason, *Singing the French Revolution: Popular Culture and Politics 1787–1799* (Ithaca: Cornell Univ. Press, 1996).

81. Curtin, *United Irishmen*, 193–201.

82. *Songs on the French Revolution, that took place at Paris, 14th July 1789; sung at the Celebration thereof at Belfast, on Saturday 14th July, 1792* (Belfast, 1792).

83. Five editions have been identified: Belfast, 1795 (reissued in Philadelphia, 1796); Belfast, 1796; New York, 1798; Dublin, 1798; Dublin, n.d. (possibly 1803); see Thuente, *Harp Re-strung*, 234–35.

84. K. Whelan, "United Irishmen, the Enlightenment and Popular Culture," 284.

85. Dunne, "Popular Ballads, Revolutionary Rhetoric and Politicisation."

86. Ó Crualaoich, "The French are on the Say."

87. *Nation*, 29 October 1842. The editor claimed that the printed text reflected the "true version" and the "best."

88. M. J. Barry, *Songs of Ireland*, 109–11.

89. The song was collected in Mayo in 1802 by Patrick Lynch and was published in the second edition of Edward Bunting's *General Collection of the Ancient Music of Ireland* (1809); Edward Bunting Papers, QUB MS 4/7 no. 137, for a translation see MS 32; see also D. J. O'Sullivan, *Bunting Collection of Irish Folk Music and Song*, part 5, 10–21.

90. Gearóid Ó Crualaoich, *The Book of the Cailleach: Stories of the Wise-Woman Healer* (Cork: Cork Univ. Press, 2003), 55–71.

91. Hardiman, *History of the Town and County of Galway*, 191.

92. This translation provoked a scathing polemical review by the scholar and poet Sir Samuel Fergusson (1810–86); *Dublin University Magazine* 3 (1834): 465–78 and ibid. 4 (1834): 152–67, 447–67, 514–30. See also Leerssen, *Remembrance and Imagination*, 177–86.

93. Hardiman, *Irish Minstrelsy*, vol. 2, 11–159.

94. *Reliques of Irish Jacobite Poetry; with biographical sketches of the authors, interlineal literal translations and historical illustrative notes by John O'Daly; together with metrical versions by E. Walsh* (Dublin, 1866; orig. ed. 1844); *Irish Popular Songs; with English metrical translations and introductory remarks and notes by E. Walsh* (Dublin, 1883, orig. ed. 1847).

95. Ó Ciardha, *Ireland and the Jacobite Cause*, 366–72.

96. Collected from John McNeeley; Hayes, *Last Invasion*, 222.

97. Walsh, *Reliques of Irish Jacobite Poetry*, 30–38; see also Ó Buachalla, *Aisling Ghéar*, 418, 632.

98. Patrick O'Farrell's *Pocket Companion for the Irish or Union Pipes* (1804–10), vol. 3; cited also in F. O'Neill, *Irish Folk Music*, 175 (O'Neill disputed the Scottish origin of the song).

99. IFC 78:250; IFC 559:223; IFC S225:220; IFC S758:61; O'Flynn, *History of Leitrim*, 74.

100. Zimmermann, *Songs of Irish Rebellion*, 10.

101. Ibid., 133–37. Variants of the song had two distinct airs; O'Sullivan, ed., *Bunting Collection*, part 5, 16–19.

102. A. M. Sullivan, *New Ireland*, 335–36. For Connacht, see Lenihan Papers, NLI MS 5159; cited in Marie-Louise Legg, *Newspapers and Nationalism*, 98.

103. Maura Murphy, "Ballad Singer."

104. Outrage Papers, NAI MS 1841: 6/7015; reproduced in Murphy, "Ballad Singer," 88–89.

105. Delargy, "Gaelic Storyteller," 203.

106. Zimmermann, *Songs of Irish Rebellion*, 39.

107. *Nation,* 27 April 1844. By 1877 it had been issued in fifty editions in Dublin alone, with further editions published in Boston and New York; Zimmermann, *Songs of Irish Rebellion,* 80.

108. R. Welch, *Oxford Companion to Irish Literature,* 28.

109. See chap. 14, "Ceremonies, Monuments, and Negotiations of Memory."

110. Bulfin, *Rambles in Eirinn,* 300.

111. Roe, *Reliques of John K. Casey ("Leo"),* 51.

112. *Nation,* 23 February 1867.

113. Zimmermann, *Songs of Irish Rebellion,* 260, 167–70.

114. *Citizen,* January 1841, 64–66.

115. Remark made in 1887 in the *Athenaeum;* see Madden, *United Irishmen,* vol. 5, ix–xi.

116. Collected by schoolmaster Peter Duignan of Gaigue Ballinamuck from Francis Whitney of Cornakelly (a former captain in the Longford Brigade of the IRA who emigrated to America); IFC S758:174–77. Duignan later published a version of the ballad and queried whether it might have derived from the poetry of Leo; "The Battle of Granard," *Teathbha* 2, no. 2 (1971): 145.

117. Collected from Peter McDermott of Clonmucker, Moydow, county Longford; IFC 1901:259–63.

118. Collected by James Delaney from Thomas Monahan, who had heard it from his great-grandmother Mary Kiernan (1862–1940), originally from Dernafest, county Cavan (bordering with county Longford); IFC 1480:351.

119. Cronin, "Memory, Story and Balladry," 129.

120. Forde-Pigot Collection, RIA MS 24 O 24. The Forde Collection manuscripts were recovered and published by Patrick Weston Joyce; see Joyce, *Old Irish Folk Music,* part 3.

121. See Horgan, *James Berry,* 136–39. For John Gibbons Sr. and his son (popularly known as "Johnny the Outlaw"), see "Amhráin na ndaoine" in this chapter and see chapters 11 and 13. James (also called John)

McGreal of Kilgeever was known as "Shamus Rhua" ([Séamus Rua], red-haired James) and "ta Copteeine" ([an captaoin], the captain); Maxwell, *History of the Irish Rebellion,* 251–52; Maxwell, *Erin-Go-Bragh,* 155–70.

122. Joyce, *Old Irish Folk Music,* 305. Joyce, who was a leading authority on traditional music, recognized O'Beirne's "vast knowledge of Irish music, gleaned from the purest and most authentic sources." Ibid., 296–97.

123. One tune was collected (with the help of Nial McCormick of Carrowmore) from John O'Malley of Rathfran, who had learned it from his mother or grandmother, and another was collected from Vincent Ryan of Ballina, who had heard it locally from an old man named O'Hanlon; C. G. Knox, "The Knox Family in Tyrawley North Mayo," (unpublished typescript); my thanks to Jimmy Gilvary of Ballynacola, Crossmolina, county Mayo, for allowing me access to the Knox Family Papers (private possession).

124. Murphy, "Ballad Singer," 92.

125. Delargy, "Gaelic Storyteller," 193.

126. Munnelly, "1798 and the Balladmakers," 170.

127. IFC S225:144–45.

128. Hayes, *Last Invasion,* 90.

129. Collected by James McKenna, Principal of Kiltycreevagh N.S. (near Ballinamuck) from fifty-year-old P. Gorman of Drumgoo, county Longford; IFC S758:438–41.

130. Peter Duignan of Gaigue; IFC 1858:41–42.

131. Collected in 1956 from Thomas Monahan by James Delaney; IFC 1480: 351. More than forty years later a version was recited to a local journalist by Dick Monahan of Muckerstaff, Coolarty, county Longford; *Longford News,* 11 September 1998, 19.

132. IFC S Box 222a: copybook of Mary Gray (6th grade).

133. IFC S Box 222b: copybook of Michael Higgins (7th grade).

134. IFC 78:249–58; IFC 559:223–33; IFC S225:220–23 (collected ca. 1913), IFC S227:85–86, IFC S758:60–65, 68–69, 448–53;

IFC S760:443–51; IFC S Box 222a: copybooks of Mollie Brady (8th grade), Rose Brennon and Joan Costello (7th grade); O'Flynn, *History of Leitrim*, 73–79. Further references to the song, include fragments of verses; IFC S207:144; IFC S221:10a; IFC S222:618–19. My thanks also to the poet Vincent Woods for showing me another Leitrim version in a copybook from the 1930s.

135. For a psychological study of remembrance of rhythmic oral traditions see D. C. Rubin, *Memory in Oral Traditions: The Cognitive Psychology of Epic, Ballads, and Counting-out Rhymes* (Oxford: Oxford Univ. Press, 1995).

136. O'Flynn, *History of Leitrim*, 73.

137. IFC S207:144; IFC S214:417–18; IFC S221:7a–10a [reprinted in Hayes, *Last Invasion*, 325–26]; IFC 758:435; IFC S760:441–42; IFC S Box 222a: copybooks of Rose Flynn and Michael Higgins.

138. When a version of the ballad was collected from seventy-five-year-old "Micky" Creamer of Curraghmaurall (died ca. 1913), the schoolteacher Seán Ó hEslin of Ballinamore, county Leitrim, dismissively noted that the storyteller had additional *seanchas* but "it was in prose, and I did not copy and write it down"; IFC S225:223.

139. For example, S220:359–64.

140. In a note appended to a version collected by James McKenna, principal of Kiltycreevagh N.S., Ballinamuck, from sixty-year-old James Masterson of Formula, Moyne, the informer was identified by the name of Kiernan; IFC S758:449.

141. In 1998 a Mr. Bandon from Dublin, claiming to be a descendent of Tom Gilheany's brother, maintained that Gilheany came from Clogher (near Ballinamore) in county Leitrim and that he emigrated to Liverpool in 1840; *Longford News*, 11 September 1998.

142. IFC 1457:445–47; IFC S214:353–55; IFC S220:356–58; IFC S222:644–46; IFC S225:149–53. Another version referred to *Pat O'Hara*, confusing the protagonist with the poet Pat Higgins; IFC S760:439–40.

143. IFC S228:34–36a. Paddy Reilly was also associated with other historical periods including the Cromwellian campaign, the Williamite wars, or even early-nineteenth-century tithe agitation; M. Whelan, *Parish of Aughavas, Co. Leitrim*, 104–6; *Leitrim Observer*, 2 May 1936.

144. IFC 494:338–39; IFC S181:329–31. "Spear" is a colloquial allusion to a pike.

145. IFC S185:355–57; IFC S758:462–63.

146. See Ó Giolláin, *Locating Irish Folklore*, 93. For an overview of late-nineteenth- and twentieth-century controversies over the communal or individual origins of ballads, see D. K. Wilgus, *Anglo-American Folksong Scholarship Since 1898* (New Brunswick: Rutgers Univ. Press, 1959).

147. J. C. Scott, *Domination and the Arts of Resistance*, 161.

148. Seamus Deane, "Poetry and Songs 1800–1890," in Deane, *Field Day Anthology of Irish Literature*, vol. 2, 2–3.

149. Hayes, *Last Invasion*, 251–54.

150. Reprinted in A. Edwards, *A Collection of Constitutional Songs* (Cork, 1799), 118; reproduced in Croker, *Popular Songs*, 90–94.

151. Madden, *United Irishmen*, vol. 1, 95–96, 104, and 118–19. Roche persuaded Longford militiamen to "turn coat" and join the rebels in Castlebar; see *Account given by James Fullam of his desertion at Castlebar;* reproduced in Hayes, *Last Invasion*, 279–80.

152. Hayes, *Last Invasion*, 252–53; the song was republished in a loyalist song collection, which includes several songs on the danger of French invasion; *Constitutional Songs* (ca. 1798), 80–98, esp. 97–98.

153. Kevin Haddick-Flynn, *Orangeism: The Making of a Tradition* (Dublin: Wolfhound Press, 1999), 11 and 411.

154. Zimmermann, *Songs of Irish Rebellion*, 298–99.

155. For example, see the description of a march in Antrim in *The Formation of the Orange Order 1795–1798: The Edited Papers of Colonel William Blacker and Colonel Robert H. Wallace* (Belfast: Education Committee of the Grand Orange Lodge of Ireland, 1994), 161–62.

156. *A Collection of Loyal Songs, as sung at all the Orange Lodges in Ireland* (Dublin, 1798) included seventeen variant texts written to the tune; see Zimmermann, *Songs of Irish Rebellion*, 307–10.

157. Zimmermann, *Irish Political Ballads*, 305.

158. *The Patriots Vocal Miscellany or a Collection of Loyal Songs* (Dublin, 1804), 46–47.

159. NLI MS 32,487; repr. in Moylan, *Songs Composed During the Irish Rebellion*, 8–9.

160. Ibid., 4.

161. Zimmermann, *Songs of Irish Rebellion*, 299.

162. See N. J. A. Williams, *Cniogaide Cnagaide: Rainn traidisiúnta do pháistí* (Dublin: An Clóchomhar, 1988).

163. IFC S Box 222a: copybook of Mary Ann Garvey (6th grade) and IFC S Box 222b: copybook of Thomas Garvey (6th grade).

164. *Northern Star*, 17 April 1797; *Constitutional Songs* (Dublin, 1798), 66–67; see also Zimmermann, *Songs of Irish Rebellion*, 309–10.

165. Bairbre Ní Fhloinn, "Echoes of '98," *Journal of the Co. Roscommon Historical and Archaeological Society* 7 (1998): 112–13.

166. R. D. Abrahams, "Proverbs and Proverbial Expressions," in Dorson, *Folklore and Folklife*, 119.

167. Krapp, *Science of Folklore*, 143.

168. P. W. Joyce, *English as We Speak It in Ireland* (1910), 179–80.

169. See conclusion, 317.

170. IFC 1242:87, 112. The account mistakenly refers to the location as a mountain pass in county Mayo; however, this is most probably a reference to the engagement at Carricknagat, which was known in Irish both as *Carraig na gCat* (the Rock of the Cats) and *Carraig* [or *Carraic*] *an Chait* (the Rock of the Cat); see *An Claidheamh Soluis* 4, no. 27 (9 September 1902): 447.

171. Collected by Maureen O'Rourke; IFC 1858:11.

172. In a contribution to the Schools' Scheme, eighty-year-old Mathew McManus of Driney, Drumcong (near Carrick-on-Shan-non), county Longford, noted: "'Hessians' or Hussians as the old people called them"; IFC S211:393.

173. See notes by G. A. Hayes-McCoy and M. E. S. Laws in *Irish Sword* 2 (1954–6): 141, 297.

174. IFC S766:65; S758:54–55.

175. See F. Glen Thompson, *Uniforms of 1798–1803*, esp. 40–41 and 50–53.

176. Handwritten comments on pamphlet *Impartial Relation of Military Operations in Ireland* (1799), 41; Hugh Carleton Papers, NLI MS 4290.

177. Hayes, *Last Invasion*, 291.

178. IFC S211:393–95; Hayes, *Last Invasion*, 237.

179. IFC S225:147.

180. Otway, *Tour in Connaught*, 50–52.

181. This is apparent in essays for the Schools' Scheme from Drumshanbo, county Leitrim; IFC S207:110–11 and 144.

182. *A Return of Killed and Wounded in Certain Regiments from the 20th of August to 20th September inclusive;* Hardwicke Papers BL MS 35,919, f. 89.

183. IFC 1457: 656–57; IFC S758: 47; IFC 1858: 11; Hayes, *Last Invasion*, 239.

184. See Sean Cloney, "The Hessians."

185. For example, IFC 54:134–5; IFC 220:166–70. A nineteenth-century folklore collector observed a Wexford woman cursing: "You have treated me like a Hussian or a Cromwellian"; P. Kennedy, *Legendary Fictions of the Irish Celts*, 153.

186. Collected for the Schools' Scheme by Michael Dolan from John Dolan and attributed to the well-known Ballinamuck storyteller Patrick Gill of Edenmore; IFC S758:54–55.

187. It is listed as type 1281 in Ó Súilleabháin and Christiansen, *Types of the Irish Folktale*; see also Éilís Ní Dhuibhne-Almqvist, "The Cow that Ate the Pedlar in Kerry and Wyoming," *Béaloideas* 67 (1999): 125–37.

188. Lover, *Legends and Stories of Ireland*, 152; F. O'Neill, *Irish Minstrels and Musicians*, 444–47; O Lochlainn, *More Irish Street Ballads*, 74–75 and 77.

189. TCD Irish Recruitment Posters, Case 55B/50; cited in Novick, "The Advanced Nationalist Response to Atrocity Propaganda, 1914–1918," in L. W. McBride, *Images, Icons,* 145.

190. Ó Súilleabháin, *Handbook of Irish Folklore,* 377–78.

191. Eugene O'Curry, *Lectures on the Manuscript Materials of Ancient Irish History* (Dublin: Four Courts Press, 1995; orig. ed. 1861), 372–434 (esp. 399–410).

192. For example, Nicholas O'Kearney, *The Prophecies of St. Columbkille, Maeltanlacht, Ultan, Seadhna, Coireall, Bearca &c. Together with the prophetic collections of gleanings of several writers who have preserved portions of the now lost prophecies of our saints, with literal translations and notes* (Dublin, 1856).

193. Keith Thomas, *Religion and the Decline of Magic: Studies in Popular Beliefs in Sixteenth and Seventeenth Century England* (London: Weidenfeld & Nicholson, 1971), 389–432.

194. Ibid., 145.

195. Bishop Charles Walmesley's *The general history of the Christian church from her birth to her final triumphant state in heaven, chiefly deduced from the Apocalypse of St. John the apostle, by Sig[nor] Pastorini* (orig. ed. Dublin, 1790; 4th ed. Dublin, 1805). For popular circulation of this text see Maurice Colgan, "Prophecy Against Reason: Ireland and the Apocalypse," *British Journal for Eighteenth-Century Studies* 8, no. 2 (1985): 209–16.

196. J. S. Donnelly, Jr., "Pastorini and Captain Rock."

197. William Carleton, "The Irish Prophecy Man," *Irish Penny Journal* 1, no. 50 (12 June 1841): 394; republished in Carleton, *Tales and Sketches,* 208–9.

198. Curtin, *United Irishmen,* 189–90.

199. For this resettlement see Patrick Hogan, "The Migration of Ulster Catholics to Connaught, 1795–96," *Seanchas Ard Mhacha* 9, no. 2 (1979): 286–30.

200. Musgrave, *Memoirs of the Different Rebellions,* 526–27.

201. Farrell, *Historical Notes,* 102. For associations in Irish folk drama between the Northern Lights and omens of war and violence see Séamas Ó Catháin, "Midwinter's Merry Dancers," *Béaloideas* 66 (1998): 163–97.

202. Fanny Byrne, *Memoirs of Miles Byrne,* vol. 1, 304.

203. Nuala Costello, ed., "Little's Diary of the French Landing in 1798."

204. Hayes, *Last Invasion,* 216–18.

205. Ó hÓgáin, *Hero in Folk History,* 280–89.

206. Ó Tiománaidhe, *Targaireacht Bhriain Ruaidh Uí Chearbháin.*

207. IFC 523:374–75, 380; IFC 528:2; Hayes, *Last Invasion,* 212; Ó Moghráin, "Gearr-Chunntas," 7, 8, 16, 34, 36, 37, 43.

208. 1 Samuel 28: 3–25.

209. Three versions were collected from Beartla Ó Conaire (["Beartla Dhonncha"], b. 1880) of Rosmuck in Connemara: two by Prionnsias de Búrca in 1940–41, and another by P. O. Hindeberg in 1949; IFC 712:61–69; IFC 739:60–66; IFC 1265:62–69.

210. Two versions were collected in 1938 by Sean Ó Flannagan who identified one informant as eighty-year-old Seán de Róiste of Gort-Adrahan (near the border of counties Clare and Galway), who claimed to have heard the story sixty years earlier from his uncle, then aged sixty; IFC 538:263–64, 512–19. Another version was collected for the Schools' Scheme by Michael Forde of Rasheen, Loughrea, county Galway, from Maureen Forde; IFC S35:350–52.

211. Collected in 1949 by Proinnsias de Búrca from seventy-seven-year-old Maitias Mac Conama of Dubhros, county Galway; IFC 1158:334–35.

212. IFC 1018:326–29; IFC S35:350–52.

213. For references see chap. 13, n. 8 (392).

214. Collected in 1946 by Liam Mac Coisdeala from Mike Tom Mhóir of Carnmore, county Clare, who claimed to have heard the story fifty years earlier from his father and the old people of the locality; IFC 1010:48.

215. For example, IFC 686:229–32; see also

references to IFC 219:245–46 and IFC 536:100–102 cited in Ó Crualaoich, "The French are on the Say," 133–36. In neighboring county Kerry, a prophecy attributed to Colum Cille about a French invasion was collected in 1937; IFC 407:401.

216. Collected by Brian Mac Lochlainn from sixty-six-year-old Caitlín Ní Chadhain of Baile Nua, Cleggan, county Galway, who claimed to have heard the verses thirty years before from Seán Ó Cadháin, then seventy years old; IFC 113:56.

217. IFC 117:89. In recognition of vernacular nomenclature, the term *druid's altar* was adopted by the nineteenth-century Ordnance Survey in Ireland as a common name for megalithic tombs; Andrews, *Paper Landscape*, 128–29.

218. Maureen Murphy, "The Noggin of Milk," 179.

219. IFC S164:253.

220. Dropmore Papers, BL MS 71589 f. 72; NAI Rebellion Papers MS 620/40/3; Charles Vane, *Memoirs and Correspondence of Viscount Castlereagh*, vol. 1, 406–9; see also *Dublin Journal*, 20 September 1798.

221. IFC S1058:185–87; Ó Dómhnaill, *Na Glúnta Rosannacha*, 115–31.

222. Anon., *A True and Circumstantial Account*; Anon., *An Historical Narrative of the Naval Victory*.

223. Mac Gabhann, *Rotha Mór and tSaoil*, 225, trans. Valentin Iremonger as Michael MacGowan, *The Hard Road to Klondike* (London: Routledge & Kegan Paul, 1962), 147.

224. Collected from Liam Mac Meanman, IFC 185:275. The naval engagement was also remembered inadvertently in a family tradition of local loyalist gentry; Stephen Gwynn, *Highways and Byways in Donegal and Antrim* (London, 1899), 163.

225. ADG B11/2. See also Françoise Van Brock, "Dilemma at Killala," *Irish Sword* 8 (1967–68): 261–73; R. B. Aldridge, "The Journal of Captain Joseph Bull," *Irish Sword* 8 (1967–68, 1967): 65–70, 109–14, 86–91, 253–60.

226. Freyer, *Bishop Stock's "Narrative" of the Year of the French*, 111–5; BL Dropmore Papers, MS 71589 ff 96–101.

227. ADG B11/2 and *Mémoires et Reconnaissances* 1 M 1420.

228. See for example letter from Lord Cornwallis to Major-General Ross from 23 July 1801; reproduced in Ross, *Correspondence of Charles, First Marquis Cornwallis*, vol. 3, 378.

229. For example, Hardwicke Papers, BL MS 357743 ff 198–202, BL MS 35758 ff 23–4; Rebellion Papers, NAI MSS 620/14/189/6, 620/46/83.

230. P. M. Kerrigan, *Castles and Fortification*, 150–247, esp. 151–56 and 212–14.

231. B. Clarke, "Joseph Stock and Killala," 66–67.

232. See chap. 8, "The French General."

233. Anon., *Irish Peasant*, 18.

234. IFC 107:157.

235. Ó Súilleabháin, *Handbook of Irish Folklore*, 92 and 142.

236. For example, Diarmuid Ó Laoghaire, *Ár bPaidreacha Dúchais. Cnuasach de Phaidreacha agus de Bheannachtaí ár Sinsear* (Dublin: FÁS, 1975), 66; Hyde, *Ahbráin Diadha Chúige Connacht or The Religious Songs of Connacht*, 356.

237. See numerous references to Jacobite toasts in Ó Ciardha, *Ireland and the Jacobite Cause*.

238. Curtin, *United Irishmen*, 251–55; see also K. Whelan, "United Irishmen, the Enlightenment and Popular Culture," 292–93.

239. Hayes, *Last Invasion*, 246.

240. Collected by Anraí Ó Braonáin and Donnla uí Bhraonáin from Anraí de Blác [Henry Blake] of Kilbaha, Carrigaholt, county Clare; IFC Tape RO 101.

241. Dinneen, *Foclóir Gaedhilge agus Béarla*, 1007, 1120.

242. Hayes, *Last Invasion*, 262. His niece (b. 1901) later recalled that according to family tradition the Dalys had provided one hundred horses to the rebels in 1798; interview with Judge John Garavan (James Daly's grand-nephew), Daly's Hotel, Castlebar, 28 February 2003.

243. IFC S760:127–33. James O'Neill's father, Edward, was a child of two weeks on the day of the battle. O'Neill also mentioned a Roscommon United Irish leader at Ballinamuck named Davis and noted, "No doubt an ancestor of our present T. D. Mat Davis of Kilteeven." See also Ó Brádaigh, ed., *Battle of Ballinamuck*, 6.

244. Attributed locally to the great-grandchildren and relatives of Patrick Coyne of Burrishoole, county Mayo, who died at Ballinamuck; Hayes, *Last Invasion*, 264.

245. IFC 815:335–37. Traditions about Gibson were written down by J. Trainor of Shercock, county Cavan, and published in *Anglo-Celt*, 16 December 1899; almost forty years later, they were retold for the Schools' Scheme; IFC S1009:133–42.

246. For example, IFC 1858:122–23; IFC S225:149–53; IFC S228:34–36a.

247. IFC 104:479. Though this account relates to treachery in county Leitrim, government records show that a James D'Arcy in Mayo passed information, which he had received in confidence from the rebel general George Blake, to the government; Brit. Lib., Hardwicke Papers, MS 35743 ff 201–2 (cited also in Hayes, *Last Invasion*, 270–71).

248. IFC 1889:37.

249. IFC S207:225–27.

250. Hayes, *Last Invasion* (2nd ed. 1939), 347.

251. IFC S89:454.

252. Hayes, *Last Invasion*, 230–31.

253. Glassie, *Passing the Time in Ballymenone*, 652.

Chapter 6

1. Ó Dónaill, *Foclóir Gaeilge-Béarla*, 1076.

2. The seminal text has long been Delargy's 1945 Sir John Rhŷs memorial lecture to the British Academy; Delargy, "The Gaelic Storyteller," but this topic has since been subject to a thorough reappraisal in Zimmermann, *Irish Storyteller*.

3. Dinneen, ed., *Poems of Eoghan Ruadh Ua Súilleabháin* (Dublin: n.p., 1923; 1st ed. 1901); referred to in Dinneen, *Foclóir Gaedhilge agus Béarla*, 1007.

4. Carleton, *Tales and Sketches* (1854 ed.), 177–88.

5. O'Rorke, *History of Sligo*, vol. 2, 567–68.

6. Report of the third annual meeting of the Irish Society (Dublin, 17 March 1821); TCD MS 7644, ff 68–69. For the Irish Society see Pádraig de Brún, "The Irish Society's Bible Teachers, 1818–27," *Éigse* 19 (1983): 281–332.

7. For a general overview of arenas of storytelling see Anne Pellowski, *The World of Storytelling* (New York: H. W. Wilson Co., 1990), 66–86.

8. "Docent von Sydow hemma igen från Irland, sagornas ö" (*Skånsk Dagbladet*, 10.3.1934); "Samarbete mellan svensk och irländsk folkminnesforskning" (*Sydsvenska Dagbladet Snällposten*, N:r 214, 10.8.1934). See also *Irish Independent*, 27 July 1934; *Irish Independent*, 10 April 1935; *Irish Press*, 10 April 1935. The woman in question was Mrs. O'Toole of Ballycumber, Ballinglen, county Wicklow, whose account was recorded by a collector in July 1934 and subsequently published; see Ó Tuathail, "Wicklow Traditions of 1798."

9. Dinneen, *Foclóir Gaedhilge agus Béarla*, 1120.

10. Written by Michael Corduff; IFC 1244:251. For additional stories collected from "Biddy Rooney" see IFC 1089:128–29, IFC 1145:138–44, esp. 140, IFC 1242:198.

11. R. Bauman, "Differential Identity and the Social Base of Folklore," in Paredes and Bauman, *Toward New Perspectives in Folklore*, 38.

12. Kirshenblatt-Gimblett, "Folklore's Crisis," *Journal of American Folklore* 111, no. 441 (1998): 312–13. See also A. B. Rooth, *On the Difficulty of Transcribing Synchronic Perception into Chronological Verbalisation* (Uppsala: Ethnologiska Institutionen, 1979).

13. Honko, "The Folklore Process," 25–47, esp. 35.

14. Archdeacon, *Connaught: a Tale of 1798*; Archdeacon, *Legends of Connaught* (Dublin: John Cumming, 1839).

15. James O'Neill MS, "A traditional history of the Battle of Ballinamuck" (written in 1938), reproduced in Ó Brádaigh, *The Battle of Ballinamuck*; Michael Connell MS (in possession of family), reproduced in Devaney, *Killoe*, 129–33.

16. IFC S225:149–53.

17. IFC S228:34–39a.

18. IFC S214:397–98.

19. Timoney's collection was acquired for the Irish Folklore Institute by Delargy and subsequently put at the disposal of the Irish Folklore Commission; IFC 1647:1–35. For biographical information on Timoney, see Breathnach and Ní Mhurchú, *Beathaisnéis*, vol. 1, 107–8; Tony Donohue, "Michael Timoney: Gaelic Scholar and Writer," *Bliainiris* 1, no 2 (1983–84): 25–26; William Mahon, "Réamhfhocal don Eagrán Nua," in Ó Tiománaidhe, *Amhráin Ghaeilge An Iarthair*, vii–viii; Welch, ed., *Oxford Companion to Irish Literature*, 461.

20. Hayes, *Last Invasion*, 222; see also "Rebel Songs and Ballads in English" in chap. 5.

21. IFC 1649:6; Michael Timoney Papers, IFC Box (unnumbered).

22. Noyes and Abrahams, "From Calendar Custom to National Memory: European Commonplaces," 77–98.

23. Jim Mac Laughlin, *Reimagining the Nation-State*, 247.

24. Ó Tiománaidhe, *Amhráin Ghaeilge An Iarthair*, 22, 84–88, 100–102.

25. Hayes, *Last Invasion*, 259, 286.

26. For a short biography of Patrick O'Donnell (appended to the biography of his brother, Fr. Martin O'Donnell) see Breathnach and Ní Mhurchú, *Beathaisnéis*, vol. 3, 93. The date of death is noted as 9 September 1937, but this is undoubtedly a mistake as he continued to correspond with Richard Hayes at least as late as April 1938; Richard Hayes Papers NLI MS 13799 (3).

27. Hayes, *Last Invasion*, 314.

28. Quinn, *History of Mayo*, vol. 5, 192.

29. Ó Moghráin, "Gearr-Chunntas," 22, n. 31.

30. Hayes, *Last Invasion*, acknowledgement.

31. See respectively: Hayes, *Last Invasion*, 314–16, 306–7, 263–64.

32. For example, NLI MS 13801 (4).

33. *Western People*, 22 February 1930.

34. Pádraic Ó Dómhnaill, "The O'Donels of Newport House and the Execution of Father Manus Sweeney"; typescript of an article "given to E. Curtis Nov. 1937" (probably Prof. Edmund Curtis); Robert Dudley Edward Papers, UCD MS LA 22/1260. In 1930 a version of this long article was serialized in a local newspaper; *Western People*, 11, 18, and 25 January and 1, 8, 15, and 22 February 1930.

35. *Connaught Telegraph*, 3 September 1898.

36. Ó Moghráin, "Gearr-Chunntas," 22.

37. P. O. D. [Patrick O'Donnell], "Buirghéis Umhall," *An Claidheamh Soluis*, vol. 3, no. 28 (September 21, 1901), 439; collected from Hugh O'Donnell of Kilmeena, county Mayo (who was acknowledged as having a "wealth of folk-lore") and attributed to a Mathew Gibbons.

38. Collected from Dennis O'Gallaher of Currane; Hayes, *Last Invasion* (2nd ed.), 350.

39. Letters dated 22 February and 7 March 1906 in Michael Timoney Papers, IFC Box (unnumbered); see also Hayes, *Last Invasion*, 316.

40. Letter from O'Donnell to Hayes dated 4 April 1936 in NLI MS 13799 (3).

41. Hayes, *Last Invasion* (2nd ed.), 331–32.

42. Gallaher's collection of Erris songs, which includes a section on folklore on the death of Fr. Manus Sweeney, was published posthumously; Ó Gallchobhair, "Amhráin ó Iorrus," 237–38.

43. Letter dated 16 October 1937; NLI MS 13799 (3).

44. Hayes, *Last Invasion* (2nd ed.), 344–50; extended sections were originally published in the *Catholic Bulletin* 28 (July 1938): 596–99.

45. *Western People*, 11 January 1930.

46. A nonhistorical folk blessing was collected from him in 1930; IFC 497:219.

47. Note by teacher Sister Padraig, 21 September 1939, IFC S88.

48. In April 1938 Delargy was in the area and attempted to meet with O'Donnell to hear Erris traditions of Ballinamuck survivors, but according to Delargy's diary, the meeting did not take place; NLI MS 13799 (3); IFC J. H. Delargy Papers. Access to the Delargy Papers was granted by kind permission of Mrs. Catríona Miles.

49. In 1941 some of his notes were acquired from his widow by Delargy and Richard J. Hayes of the National Library, IFC Box 15.

50. IFC 881:22.

51. Interview with the late Dennis [Donncha] Ó Gallachoir of Achill Island, county Mayo; Mulranny, 24 August 2001.

52. Michel-Rolph Trouillot, *Silencing the Past: Power and the Production of History* (Boston: Beacon Press, 1995), 21.

53. Samuel, *Theatres of Memory*, vol. 1, 17.

Chapter 7

1. Literally: "Time is a good storyteller," meaning "time will tell" (Ó Dónaill, *Foclóir Gaeilge-Béarla*, 1046) or "time shows up many things" (Dinneen, *Foclóir Gaedhilge agus Béarla*, 963).

2. G. J. Whitrow, *Time in History: The Evolution of Our General Awareness of Time and Temporal Perspective* (Oxford: Oxford Univ. Press, 1988), 183.

3. R. White, *Remembering Ahanagran*, 30–31.

4. See also "Mnemohistory and Mythistory" in chap. 1. For comparative anthropological and historical perspectives on time, see Jay Griffiths, *Pip Pip: A Sideways Look at Time* (London: Flamingo, 1999).

5. Vansina, "Memory and Oral Tradition," 264.

6. Henige, *Chronology of Oral Tradition*, 27–64.

7. Fentress and Wickham, *Social Memory*, 99.

8. F. Zonabend, *The Enduring Memory*.

9. See Eviatar Zerubavel, *Hidden Rhythms: Schedules and Calendars in Social Life* (Chicago: Univ. of Chicago Press, 1981).

10. Pierre Bourdieu, *Outline of a Theory of Practice* (Cambridge: Cambridge Univ. Press, 1977), 97–109.

11. The twelve months of the revolutionary calendar each had three weekly cycles of ten days (*décades*), supplemented annually by five or six days (in turn, days were broken into decimal units of ten hours, each lasting a hundred minutes of a hundred seconds). The months were *Vendémiaire, Brumaire, Frimaire, Nivôse, Pluviôse, Ventôse, Germinal, Floréal, Prairial, Messidor, Thermidor,* and *Fructidor.*

12. See Zerubavel, *Hidden Rhythms*, 82–95.

13. Nora, "Between Memory and History," in *Realms of Memory*, vol. 1, 15.

14. See Danaher, *Year in Ireland*.

15. MacNeill, *Festival of Lughnasa*.

16. Glassie, *Passing the Time in Ballymenone*, 351–52.

17. Mircea Eliade, *The Myth of Eternal Return: Or, Cosmos and History* (Princeton: Princeton Univ. Press, 1991; trans. by W. R. Trask of *Le Mythe de l'éternel retour; archétypes et répétition* [Paris: Gallimard, 1949]), 51, 85.

18. Collected for the Schools' Scheme from seventy-year-old Martin Connell of Clooncullane, Creggs, county Galway, IFC S16:20.

19. Collected by Ciarán Bairéad in 1952 from sixty-eight-year-old Mícheál Ó Síoda [Mike Silke] of Parkgarve [Páirc Gharbh], Carnmore, county Galway, IFC 1318:49.

20. Tyrrell, *Weather and Warfare*, 98–111.

21. Collected from Martin Connolly of Clooncun, Glennamaddy, IFC S261:128.

22. IFC S214:257, 328; IFC S222:2; Hayes, *Last Invasion*, 239; Devaney, "Ballinamuck in Song and Story," 77–78.

23. IFC S222:616–18; see also IFC S214:397–98.

24. NLI MS 7335.

25. Glassie, *Passing the Time in Ballymenone*, 603.

26. Gearóid Ó Crualaoich, "Responding to the Rising," 50–55.

27. See Peter Carr, *The Big Wind* (Belfast: White Row Press, 1991).

28. Augustine Birrell, *Things Past Redress*

(London, 1937), 211; *Irish Geography* 22 (1989): 38; Ó Gráda, "The Greatest Blessing of All," in *Past and Present* 175 (2002): 134–35.

29. Collected by Teresa Dullaghan of Kilbeggan, county Westmeath, IFC S733:80.

30. Mr. and Mrs. S. C. Hall, *Ireland: Its Scenery, Character, &c*, vol. 3, 381 (quoted also in Hayes, *Last Invasion*, 266). For O'Malley's failed lawsuit in the Mayo Assizes, see Ó Móráin [Ó Moghráin], *Annála Beaga Pharáiste Bhuiréis Umhaill*, 118–19.

31. *An Claidheamh Soluis*, vol. 7, no. 39 (9 December 1905): 3–4 and no. 40 (16 December 1905): 3.

32. For example, seventy-one-year-old Pádraig Ó Muirithe, a fisherman from *Cnoc an Dúin*, county Cork, referred to 1798 as "bliain na buartha" in 1933, IFC 53:133.

33. See "Ardrigh" [Francis Joseph Bigger], *An Droch-Shaoghal: The Penal Days* (Dublin: Catholic Truth Society of Ireland, 1916).

34. See S. Ó Catháin and O'Flanagan, *Living Landscape*, 2–3.

35. For earlier layers of social memory see my conclusion, 317–18.

36. IFC 1858:102; IFC S108:258–60, IFC S116:137, IFC S760:133.

37. IFC S599:173–74. Also repeated references to "volunteers" engaged in guerrilla warfare in a story collected in 1936 from sixty-nine-year-old Micheál de Búrca of Teeranea [Tír an Fhiaidh], county Galway, IFC 167:101–4.

38. IFC S962:27.

39. Collected from seventy-six-year-old Pat (Owen) Loughlin of Dowra, county Cavan, IFC S962:27.

40. Williams, "Folklore of the Troubles"; see also Glassie, *Passing the Time in Ballymenone*, 149–52 and 243–44.

41. Lover, *Legends and Stories of Ireland*, 148.

42. Collected from Séamus Ó Conghaile of Carna, county Galway, IFC 58:88; see also Hayes, *Last Invasion* (2nd ed.), 338.

43. Bartlett, "Indiscipline and Disaffection," 130.

44. For example, "A succinct narrative of the past and present risings of the Whiteboys, Right Boys, Peep of Day Boys," written by Rev. Jim Henesson of county Kilkenny, supposedly focused on Munster in 1766, but incorporated anachronistic references to the late 1790s; Townsend Papers, National Army Museum MS 6806–41/7/6 (1); see Thomas Bartlett, "An Account of the Whiteboys of the 1790s," *Tipperary Historical Journal* (1991): 141–49.

45. Letter to the Chief Secretary Lord Castlereagh, dated 4 February 1799, NAI MS 620/46/31; also: Humphrey Thomson's "Personal Narrative," BOD MS Eng. Hist. d. 155, f. 139.

46. Ridgeway, *Report of the Proceedings*. An account collected in 1938 in the area of Attymass, county Mayo, noted that although the "thrashers" were reputedly "some kind of an organisation . . . in reality they were a band of robbers"; IFC S127:424.

47. Ó Súilleabháin, *Handbook of Irish Folklore*, 532.

48. Archdeacon, preface to *Connaught: a Tale of 1798*.

49. Maxwell, *Wild Sports*, 213–14. Maxwell regularly frequented the hunting lodge of the Marquess of Sligo at Ballycroy.

50. IFC 1244:251.

51. IFC 1858:28.

52. Collected by Kathleen Hurley of Ballymoe in northeast county Galway; IFC 485:270.

53. Fennell, *Connacht Journey*, 63–64. By then, this local tradition had been dramatized in the television miniseries *The Year of the French* (1982).

54. IFC S143:43–45.

55. Collected for the Schools' Scheme by Mary Rita Darcy from ninety-seven-year-old John Darcy of Derrinkeher, Ballinamore, county Leitrim, IFC S224:415.

56. Collected by Christie Kennedy of Gantry N.S from Mrs. Clune of Craughwell, county Galway, IFC S34:171.

57. Pádraic Ó Súilleabháin of Ballintober, county Galway, IFC 164:499.

58. Michael Moran of Roslahan, Bally-

carra (near Castlebar), county Mayo, IFC S94:400.

59. Interview with Jimmy Gilvary, Ballynacola, Crossmolina, county Mayo, 10 August 2002.

60. IFC 1534:145–46.

61. See chap. 2, 45–47.

62. L. Kelly, *Flame Now Quenched*, 132.

63. The local historian Stephen Dunford of Killala informed me that he had originally heard it as a boy (in the 1970s) from Dick Corcoran of Castlebar (then in his seventies), who was originally from Lahardane, county Mayo.

64. R. M. Young, *Ulster in '98*, 74.

65. F. M. Wilson, *The Coming of the Earls and Other Verse* (Dublin, 1918). For information on the author see John McLaughlin, "Florence Wilson and the Man From God Knows Where," *Due North* 1, no. 4 (2001): 7–10.

66. Three versions of this story were collected from Beartla Ó Conaire of Rosmuck, county Galway; see IFC· 712:66; IFC 739:65–66; IFC 1265:68.

67. For example: IFC 195:312–15; IFC 227:398–400; IFC 528:6–10; IFC 662:263–66; IFC 739:66; IFC 1512:313–18; IFC S140:300–302; IFC S141:32–34; IFC S763:155–56.

68. Time-lapses measured in units of seven (years, months, or days) have been listed as an international folklore motif type AT 451 and Z72.2 (for seven as a formulaic number see Z71.5); Stith Thompson, *Motif-Index of Folk Literature*. For examples of the use of intervals of seven years in Irish folk tales see *Béaloideas* 21 (1951–52): 109–12, 222–24.

69. For post-Rebellion disturbances in the Wicklow hills, see Bartlett, "Masters of the Mountains"; O'Donnell, *Aftermath*.

70. Rebellion Papers, NAI MS 620/14/189 (ff 1–6); Hardwicke Papers, BL MS 35758 ff 23–24. See also Hayes, *Last Invasion* (2nd ed.), 329–30.

71. Hardwicke Papers, BL MS 35746, f. 21.

72. Variations of the tradition also referred to other time intervals: IFC 1480:350–55 (after three years); IFC 712:67 (after "four and six"); IFC S167:272–74 (no time specified); see also

"Willie O'Keefe and the Battle of Granard 1798," *Longford News*, 11 September 1998 (five years).

73. Alessandro Portelli, "Uchronic Dreams: Working Class Memory and Possible Worlds," in Samuel and Thompson, *The Myths We Live By*, 143–60.

74. Niall Ferguson, "Virtual History: Towards a 'Chaotic' Theory of the Past," in Ferguson, *Virtual History: Alternatives and Counterfactuals* (London: Papermac, 1998), 1–90. Ferguson criticized earlier work in the field for focusing on "a single, often trivial" event (12).

75. IFC 104:479–80; IFC 559:233–38; IFC 1858:12–13, 96; IFC S211:393–95; IFC S214: 257–58, 329; IFC S216:207; IFC S219:248–49; IFC S220:283–85; IFC S222:19–20, 248–50, 615–19, 639–40; IFC S225:146–49, 151, 153; IFC S227:85–86; IFC S758:250, 432–34, 458; IFC S759:215–17; IFC S760:127–28, 438, 476–78; IFC S761:242–43; IFC S766:305–7; IFC S986:97–99; *Béaloideas* 4 (1933/4): 393; Hayes, *Last Invasion*, 109, 231, 234, 293, 320, 327; Ó Brádaigh, *Battle of Ballinamuck*, 5; Devaney, *Killoe*, 39; *Longford Year Book 1932*, 78.

76. Ninety-five-year-old James Carroll of Mohill (six kilometers from Ballinamuck), Hayes, *Last Invasion*, 238; see also the account of eighty-year-old Mrs. Buhan of Catten (four kilometers from Ballinamuck), in Hayes, *Last Invasion*, 226.

77. Tonkin, *Narrating Our Pasts*, 114–15.

78. Maureen Perkins, *The Reform of Time: Magic and Modernity* (London: Pluto Press, 2001).

79. See thesis 18 of Walter Benjamin, "Theses on the Philosophy of History," in Hannah Arendt, ed., *Illuminations* (New York: Knopf, 1968), 253–64 (trans. by Harry Zohn); for a German version see *Gesammelte Schriften*, vol. 1, part 2 (Frankfurt am Main: Suhrkamp, 1974).

80. See "Prophecies" in chap. 5, 106–11.

81. IFC 85:299.

82. Use of the term *cubism* here refers to a breakaway from a one-point perspective, characteristic of art since the Renaissance; see

for example: E. Fry, *Cubism* (London: Thames & Hudson, 1966), 13; D. Cooper, L. Wright, *Perspective in Perspective* (London: Routledge & Kegan Paul, 1983), 308.

83. Glassie, *Passing the Time in Bally-menone*, esp. 462.

84. Alessandro Portelli, "'The Time of My Life': Functions of Time in Oral History," *International Journal of Oral History* 2, no. 3 (1981): 162–80.

85. For example, K. Whelan, "Three Revolutions and a Failure, 26–36.

86. Samuel and Thompson, *Myths We Live By* (London: Routledge, 1990), 5.

87. Karl Marx, "Manifesto for the Communist Party," in *Marx-Engels Reader*, ed. R. C. Tucker (New York: Norton, 1978), 476.

Chapter 8

1. *Connaught Telegraph*, 5 September 1953, 3.

2. For a typical example see the bicentennial Thomas Davis Lecture by the military historian Harman Murtagh, another version of which was presented at the main 1798 Bicentenary Conference in Dublin; Murtagh, "General Humbert's Campaign in the West," 115–24; Murtagh, "General Humbert's Futile Campaign," in Bartlett et al., *1798*, 174–88.

3. Madden, *United Irishmen* (1st ed. London, 1846), 3rd ser., vol. 1, 88–120. It has been pointed out that the few accounts of Connacht United Irishmen are characteristically brief and often inaccurate; see Hayes, *Last Invasion*, xxiv.

4. See Hayes, *Last Invasion*, 179–215, 301–18, and (2nd ed.) 332–35; P. K. Egan, "Progress and Suppression of the United Irishmen in the Western Counties in 1798–99"; P. C. Power, *The Courts Martial of 1798–99*, 92–107.

5. For edited collections from the French archives see Guillon, *La France et L'Irlande Pendant La Révolution* and Desbrière, *1793–1805: Projets et Tentatives de Débarquement aux Iles Britanniques*.

6. A. Nat. MAR BB/4/123.

7. A. Nat. MAR BB/4/123; ADG *Mémoires et Reconnaissances* 1 M 1420; PRO HO 100/78/383–402 and 100/82/82–86, 104–26 and 131; NAI 620/18/12. For edited versions see Joannon, *La Descente de Français*, 88–98.

8. *L'Ami des Lois, par une société de gens de Lettres* (*24 Frimaire an VII*; 8 December 1798). For edited extract see Joannon, *La Descente de Français*, 5–23; for translation see Richard Hayes, "An Officer's Account of the French Campaign in Ireland," 110–18, 161–71. Supplemented by correspondence: PRO HO 100/82/86–90; ADG B11/2.

9. Louis-Octave Fontaine, *Notice historique de la descente des Français en Irlande* (Paris: Thermidor an IX, 1801); for an edited version see Joannon, *La Descente de Français*, 72–86.

10. ADG B11/2: J. -L. Jobit, "*Détails Véritables de l'Expédition de Rochefort en Irland*." For edited versions see Paupié, "Une Descente en Irlande en 1798"; Costello, "Jobit's Journal of the French Expedition, 1798"; Joannon, *La Descente de Français*, 25–71. For a translation by Martin Sixsmith, see Cooney, *1798 Campaign by a French Lieutenant*.

11. ADG B11/2: J. -B. Thomas, "Souvenir de ma vie militaire"; for translation see F. W. Van Brock, "A Memoir of 1798."

12. Moreau de Jonnès, *Aventures de guerre au temps de la République et du Consulat* (Paris, 1858; original written c. 1840); for a translation by Cyril Hammond see Moreau de Jonnès, *Adventures in the Revolution and Under the Consulate*. Supplemented by correspondence: PRO HO 100/82/131.

13. Musgrave, *Memoirs of the Different Rebellions*, 526–93

14. Bishop Joseph Stock, "An Eyewitness," *Narrative of What Passed at Killala*. For Stock's original notes see Bishop Stock's Journal, TCD MS 1690; reproduced in part as "Private Diary of the Bishop of Killalla, From the Landing to the Surrender of the French Army," in Maxwell, *History of the Irish Rebellion*, 255–62, with the remainder reproduced in St. George Stock, "Diary of the Bishop of Killalla." For letters written by Bishop Stock to his brother Stephen (dated Killala, 23 and

26 August 1798) see Eden [Baron Auckland], *Journal and Correspondence of William, Lord Auckland*, 46–51.

15. RIA MS 3 B 51. Reproduced in Costello, "Little's Diary."

16. Humphrey Thomson, "Personal Narrative," BOD MS Eng. Hist. d. 155.

17. Mangin, *Parlour Window*, 33–45; reproduced in F. S. Bourke, "The French Invasion of 1798: A Forgotten Eyewitness," *Irish Sword* 2 (1954–56), 289–94.

18. Costello, "Little's Diary," 72.

19. Quoted in Thomas Crofton Croker, "Recollections of Cork," TCD MS 1206, chap. 9, 11–12; also reproduced in Alan Gailey, *Irish Folk Drama* (Cork: Mercier Press, 1969), 8. For Cromwell in folklore, see Dáithí Ó hÓgáin, "Nótaí ar Chromail i mBéaloideas na hÉireann," *Sinsear* 2 (1980): 73–83.

20. See "The Century of Ninety-Eight" in chap. 14.

21. See Whelan, *Tree of Liberty*, 171–72; Whelan, *Fellowship of Freedom*, 127.

22. Unlike this description from the 1930s of an old man in county Longford, whose grandfather had participated in the Rebellion, phonemic analysis of IFC sources suggests that the letters *m* and *t* of Humbert's name were usually pronounced distinctly.

23. See Baeyens, *Sabre au Clair*; Cooney, *Humbert*, 8–12; Jacotey, *Le Général Humbert ou la passion de la Liberté*; Pellet, *Vieilles Histoires*, 61–85.

24. Hayes, *Last Invasion*, 216–18. Sixty-five years later, Jack Munnelly of Ross, Killala (b. 1920), could recall from his youth George Monnelly's conversations with Hayes; interview with Jack Munnelly, Killala, 16 September 2001.

25. Hayes, *Last Invasion*, 218.

26. Stock, *Narrative of What Passed at Killala*, 26.

27. Letter dated 22 August 1798; reproduced in Hobson, *Letters of Theobald Wolfe Tone*, 128.

28. Ibid., 25.

29. Ó Catháin, *Bedside Book of Irish Folklore*, 5.

30. Stock, *Narrative of What Passed at Killala*, 27.

31. de Jonnès, *Adventures in the Revolution*, 166.

32. See for example Edgeworth and Edgeworth, *Memoirs of Richard Lovell Edgeworth*, vol. 2, 235–36; Humphrey Thomson, "Personal Narrative," BOD MS Eng. Hist. d. 155, ff 135 and 137.

33. Hayes, *Last Invasion*, 104.

34. Collected from eighty-year-old James O'Neill of Crowdromin (near Ballinamuck); Hayes, *Last Invasion*, 234.

35. Axel Olrik, *Principles for Oral Narrative Research* (Bloomington: Indiana Univ. Press, 1992; orig. ed. in Danish, 1921), 41–61.

36. See Ó hÓgáin, *Myth, Legend and Romance*, 129–30.

37. Collected by Peter Kilkenny of Sunnaghbeg, Cloone, county Leitrim, and forwarded by Delargy to Richard Hayes; Hayes, *Last Invasion*, 321.

38. Humphrey Thomson, "Personal Narrative," BOD MS Eng. Hist. d. 155, f. 137.

39. See General Sarrazin, *Philosopher*, vol. 1, 279.

40. Archdeacon, *Connaught: a Tale of 1798*, 299.

41. Collected from Patrick Mulligan of Granard; Hayes, *Last Invasion*, 295.

42. uí Ógáin, *Immortal Dan*; Diarmaid Ó Muirithe, "O'Connell in Irish Folk Tradition," in *Daniel O'Connell: Political Pioneer*, ed Maurice R. O'Connell (Dublin: Institute of Public Administration, 1991), 72–85.

43. Ó Súilleabháin, *Handbook of Irish Folklore*, 533.

44. Heyland, *Irish Rebellion of 1798*, 23.

45. Freyer, *Bishop Stock's "Narrative,"* 24.

46. Baeyens, *Sabre au Clair*, 5–7; Jacotey, *Le Général Humbert*, 16–23; Pellet, *Vieilles Histoires*, 61–85; see also Cooney, *Humbert*, 10–11. For a general study of folklore of soldiers in Lorraine see David M. Hopkin, *Soldier and Peasant in French Popular Culture, 1766–1870* (Suffolk: Royal Historical Society/The Boydell Press, 2003).

47. Ó hÓgáin, *Hero in Irish Folk History*, 194.

48. Ó Brádaigh, *Songs of 1798*, 67; translated in Hayes, *Last Invasion*, 241.

49. Quoted in O'Rourke, "County Mayo in Gaelic Folksong," 191; originally printed in Micheál agus Tomás Ó Máille, *Amhráin Chlainne Gaedheal* (Dublin, 1905), 94. Patrick Sarsfield (ca. 1655–93) was a popular Jacobite hero from the time of the Williamite wars.

50. NLI Proclamations; See Whelan, *Fellowship of Freedom*, 97.

51. Costello, "Little's Diary," 82.

52. Recorded in 1949 by Myles Dillon and Kevin Danaher from eighty-two-year-old James Duffy of Ballaghaderreen; IFC Disk 721–23.

53. Henry, *Tales From the West*, 34–35.

54. For example, see songs from county Kilkenny ("Préachán Chill Chainnigh" and "Bualadh Ros Mhic Thriúin") in Ó hÓgáin, *Duanaire Osraíoch*, 38–39. In some songs he was affectionately called "Bóna"; see Ó Buachalla, *Aisling Ghéar*, 648.

55. Two versions of the lament for Fr. Sweeney are quoted in Hayes, *Last Invasion*, 248, 316.

56. Ó Gallchobhair, "Amhráin ó Iorrus," 237; Hayes, *Last Invasion* (2nd ed.), 349.

57. Ó Buachalla, "Irish Jacobite Poetry," 49.

58. For an overview of the events of 1798 that juxtaposes Napoleon's expedition to Egypt with the Rebellion in Ireland, see Postgate, *Story of a Year*, 79–113, 114–65.

59. Vane, *Memoirs and Correspondence of Viscount Castlereagh*, vol. 1 ("The Irish Rebellion"), 386 (translation on 389) (extracts from Humbert's papers forwarded to Lord Castlereagh, Chief Secretary in Dublin Castle, 29 September 1798).

60. This version was collected in Aranmore Island, county Donegal; Ó Muirgheasa, *Dhá Chéad de Cheoltaibh Uladh*, 26–27.

61. O'Rourke, "County Mayo in Gaelic Folksong," 191. Brian O'Rourke's rhyming translation is approximate rather than literal (the original refers to the trustworthiness of Bonaparte and of "our friends coming in the midst of the enemy" and taking "satisfaction" from the "Foreign tribe").

62. Composed by the Leitrim poet Theophilus (Teige) O'Flynn and dictated sometime between 1828–35 to the Galway scribe Patrick Glynn; RIA MS 23 o 42, 38. O'Flynn's composition of the lament was remembered locally; see Tohall, "Some Connacht Traditions," 291.

63. Carleton, *Traits and Stories* (1877 ed.; orig. ed. 1833), 314; cited in Ó Buachalla, *Aisling Ghéar*, 623–24.

64. Carleton, *Tales and Sketches* (1854 ed.), 208.

65. A manuscript version of the song, signed by Michael Carolan [Micheál Ó Cearbhalláin] on 16 January 1809, appears in the papers of the Drogheda printer Bernard Tumaltey; RIA MS 3 C 4 b; reproduced in Ó Muirgheasa, *Dhá Chéad de Cheoltaibh Uladh*, 24–25.

66. Zimmermann, *Songs of Irish Rebellion*, 33, 103, 105–6, 169, 182–92 (for a brief discussion on Napoleon referred to as a potential liberator, see 32–33); Moylan, *Age of Revolution*, 131–64. For twenty-six traditional songs as performed by the balladeer Frank Harte and the musician Donal Lunny, see the album *My Name is Napoleon Bonaparte* (Hummingbird Records, 2001; 2CDs).

67. Hayes, *Last Invasion*, 248.

68. Ibid., 220.

69. Upon his return from Ireland, Humbert was assigned to a series of unrewarding postings on the Continent and was then sent to San Domingo (1800–1803), where he had an extramarital affair with Pauline Bonaparte. In 1813 he immigrated to the United States and settled in New Orleans, fighting there under General Andrew Jackson in 1815.

70. Robert Herbert, ed., *Worthies of Thomond: A Compendium of Short Lives of the Most Famous Men and Women of Limerick and Clare to the Present Day* (Limerick: n.p., 1944), 53.

71. See respectively Plowden, *An Historical Review of the State of Ireland*, 794; C. H.

Teeling, *Sequel to Personal Narrative of the "Irish Rebellion" of 1798* (Belfast, 1832), 223, fn.; Maxwell, *History of the Irish Rebellion*, 236.

72. A loyalist pamphlet described it as a setback for the Crown forces; Anon, *A True and Circumstantial Account*, 4. Lord Shannon described the engagement as a "gallant" defeat; PRO NI MS 2707/A3/3/111–112; reproduced in Hewitt, *Lord Shannon's Letters to his Son*, 147–48.

73. *Dublin Evening Post*, 18 October 1798; reproduced in McTernan, *In Sligo Long Ago*, 35.

74. E. H. O'Toole, "The Medal for Collooney, 1798."

75. Hayes, *Last Invasion*, 94–96; Snoddy, "The Limerick City Militia and the Battle of Collooney, 1798."

76. See Maurice Lenihan, *Limerick: Its History and Antiquities* (Dublin, 1866), 390–97.

77. Hayes, *Last Invasion*, 94–95.

78. Ibid., 271.

79. Collected for the Schools' Scheme in 1939 by Imelda Walsh; IFC S89:454.

80. Hayes, *Last Invasion*, 43.

81. Burke, "History as Social Memory," 104.

82. See Owens, "Nationalism Without Words."

83. A version was recorded in 1949 from eighty-two-year-old James Duffy (Séamus Ó Dubhthaigh) of Sceithín near Ballaghaderreen, then a *Gaeltacht* area in east Mayo (now in county Roscommon); IFC Disk 721–23. A fragmented version labeled "When the French came into Killala" and showing Anglophone influences was collected for the Schools' Scheme in county Galway; IFC S16:77–78.

84. Breathnach and Ní Mhurchú, *Beathaisnéis* vol. 1:41–42.

85. Mag Ruaidhrí, *Le Linn M'Óige*, 11–12.

86. See Ó Buachalla, *Aisling Ghéar*.

87. See Leerssen, *Remembrance and Imagination*. Reference to the Pale is most likely an anachronism deriving from mid-nineteenth-century romantic nationalist poetry in English.

88. Michael Corduff collected a version in 1946, from ninety-year-old Bridget Corduff ("Biddy Rooney") in Erris; IFC 1244:251. In 1959 he collected another version, which was attributed to the Erris folk poet Michael McGrath of Glengad, county Mayo; IFC 1534:522–23. In 1955 Micheal Mac Énri collected a version in the south of Achill Island from sixty-nine-year-old Micheál Mac an tSaoir of Fálmor who had heard it recited by his father fifty-five years earlier (ca. 1900); IFC 1710:197. Richard Hayes published two variants of the stanza, one from Dominick McDonnell of Muingrevagh; see *Last Invasion*, 219 and 243.

89. Richard Hayes Papers, NLI MS 13800 (5).

90. Musgrave, *Memoirs of the Different Rebellions* (4th ed.), 703.

91. Sir Charles Stanford, *Complete Collection of Irish Music*, parts 1 and 2, 254, no. 996. It was originally a Scottish air known as "Willie was a wanton wag" (first printed in 1725); Zimmermann, *Songs of Irish Rebellion*, 160–61. From the late nineteenth-century it was generally associated with Thomas Davis's "Clare Dragoons"; Moylan, *Age of Revolution*, 85.

92. Lever, *Maurice Tierney*, 220; see also repeated references in J. J. Gibbons, *Slieve Bawn and the Croppy Scout*.

93. Including an air by the celebrated harpist Turlough Carolan (1670–1738) about a seventeenth-century Antrim swordsman (Sir Richard O'Cahan of Deneane, "Slasher O'Kane"), which was later associated with a song by Thomas Campbell about a "Wounded Hussar" named Henry O'Kane (1797); see Donal O'Sullivan, *Carolan: The Life Times and Music of an Irish Harper* (London: Routledge & Kegan Paul, 1958), vol. 1, 235; Moylan, *Age of Revolution*, 133–35. Also a tune written down in the mid-nineteenth century by the song collector William Forde; RIA MS 24 O 24, 193.

94. The first edition of the United Irishmen's song book *Paddy's Resource* (1795) includes the song "Vive la Liberté," 51–52, and the second edition (1796) includes the song "Vive la Peuple," 85.

95. See Costello, "Jobit's Journal of the French Expedition, 1798," 40, 54–55; also General Jean Sarrazin's account in *L'Ami des Lois* (Paris, 8 December 1798), translated in Hayes, "An Officer's Account," 111.

96. Thuente, "Folklore of Irish Nationalism," 56–57.

97. C. G. Duffy et al., *Spirit of the Nation: 1845*, 70–73.

98. See C. G. Duffy, *Short Life of Thomas Davis, 1840–1846*, 126–27.

99. Stock, *Narrative of What Passed at Killala*, 58.

100. Hayes, *Last Invasion*, 243.

101. Collected by his son, James McKenna of Kiltycreevagh (Ballinamuck); IFC S758:457.

102. Stock, *Narrative of What Passed at Killala*, 58.

103. Mag Ruaidhrí, *Le Linn M'Óige*, 40.

104. Hayes, "Priests in the Independence Movement," 268; Keogh, *French Disease*, 182; Swords, *Hidden Church*, 65; Swords, "Irish Priests and Students of Revolutionary France," in Swords, *Protestant, Catholic and Dissenter*, 20 and 37.

105. ADG XL 16a.

106. A. Nat. MAR bb/4/123. See also Bertaud, "Forgotten Soldiers," 225.

107. Letter signed in Paris, 29 Nivôse Year 8 (1800); in the private possession of Pierre Joannon. My thanks to Prof. Thomas Bartlett of the Department of Modern Irish History, UCD, for providing me with a photocopy of this document.

108. Similar pleas were advanced to no avail on behalf of the more senior United Irishman Bartholomew Teeling, who also held a French commission.

109. ADG XL 16a.

110. Byrne, *Memoirs of Miles Byrne*, vol. 3, 64–66.

111. Stock, *Narrative of What Passed at Killala*, 58–59.

112. Byrne, *Memoirs of Miles Byrne*, vol. 3, 65–66.

113. Stock, *Narrative of What Passed at Killala*, 58–60.

114. Musgrave, *Memoirs of the Different Rebellions* (4th ed.), 546–47, 560–61, 565.

115. BOD MS Eng. Hist. d. 155, f. 137. In contrast, Bridget Thompson (the wife of the Anglican Dean of Killala) briefly met *Major Keen* before the rebel's last stand and described him as "a great ruffian," whose boasts of courage were based on false grounds; Ormsby Papers, NLI microfilm P8162; reproduced in *Cornhill Magazine* (1898): 475.

116. S. Hannan, "Two Patriot Priests of 1798," *Ballina Herald*, 28 April 1928; A. D. (Tony Donohue), "Father Henry O'Keon: The Green Horseman," *Bliainiris* 2 (1983–84): 48; Mulloy, "The Clergy and the Connacht Rebellion," 263.

117. *Dublin Penny Journal*, vol. 1, no. 49 (1 June 1833): 392; reproduced also in Croker, *Popular Songs*, part 4, 75; *Shan Van Vocht*, vol. 3, no. 8 (1 August 1898): 137–38. The greeting "Cad é mar atá tú" is typical of the Donegal dialect and is also familiar in northwest Mayo.

118. Mag Ruaidhrí, *Le Linn M'Óige*, 11.

119. *Dublin Journal*, 1 September 1798.

120. See Alvin M. Josephy Jr, ed., *The American Heritage Book of Indians* (New York: Dell Publishing Co., 1982), 84–85; Margareta Bowen, "Interpreters and the Making of History," in *Translators Through History*, eds. Jean Deslisle and Judith Woodsworth (Amsterdam: John Benjamins, 1995), 260–62, 280, fig. 20.

121. For example, it was recalled that Fr. Dunne of Cloone spoke French with the visiting troops (and even recognized an old schoolmate in their ranks); Hayes, *Last Invasion*, 108, 319–20, 327; IFC S225:148–49.

122. After the defeat of the rebels, Fr. Gannon went into hiding in Connemara. Arrested in November 1799, he was imprisoned in Castlebar and then transported to New Geneva, from where he escaped to Portugal and made his way to France. He became a curé in the diocese of Versailles (1803), transferred between different parishes, and eventually became a chaplain in the French army (requesting in 1810 to join the Irish Legion). A grant from the Ministry of Interior rescued him from destitution in Paris follow-

ing his suspension in 1819 and allowed him to take up a position in the diocese of Autun. ADG Xh b; Hayes, *Last Invasion*, 194–95; Swords, "Irish Priests," 37 and 41.

123. IFC S164:255.

124. Hayes, *Last Invasion*, 219.

125. See chap. 10, 191–92.

126. Collected in 1938 by Áine Ní Ghiorraidhe [Annie Hare] from her father, James Hare of Knockanillaun; IFC S148:241.

127. Musgrave, *Memoirs of the Different Rebellions in Ireland* (4th ed.), 456.

128. For example, IFC S766:257.

129. *Dublin Journal*, 4 September 1798; reproduced in *Saunders's News-Letter, and Daily Advertiser*, 5 September 1798. Subsequently, Blake was the target of unfounded hostile loyalist propaganda, which depicted him as a ruthless rebel who wished to massacre Protestant prisoners; *Dublin Journal*, 18 September 1798.

130. Hayes, *Last Invasion*, 33.

131. See M. J. Blake, *Blake Family Records, 1600–1700*, 2nd ser., 199–200.

132. See *Dublin Journal*, 18 September 1798.

133. Mangin, *Parlour Window*, 39.

134. Mrs. Buhan of Cattan; Hayes, *Last Invasion*, 227.

135. Hayes, *Last Invasion*, 268–71. Blake's activities in the area of Ballinrobe were described in reports by Captain Taylor and Colonel Crawford; PRO HO 100/82 ff. 19, 25–26.

136. "Return of the French army taken prisoners at the Battle of Ballinamuck, September 8, 1798"; PRO HO 100/82/58.

137. Ó Súilleabháin, *Handbook of Irish Folklore*, 533.

138. For example, IFC Box S759a: copybooks of James Hughes (7th grade), Peter Maguire (7th grade), Mark Mimnagh (6th grade), John Rogers (5th grade), Willie Rogers (6th grade).

139. Hayes, *Last Invasion*, 269.

140. *Dublin Journal*, 4 September 1798; subsequently reproduced in *Saunders's News-Letter, and Daily Advertiser*, 5 September 1798.

For the conservative politics of the *Dublin Journal* (established by George Faulkner in 1728 and edited in 1798 by John Giffard), see R. R. Madden, *History of Irish Periodical Literature*, vol. 2, 1–163; for the slightly more liberal politics of the loyalist *Saunders's News-Letter* see ibid., 253–68.

141. Shannon Papers, PRO NI D 2707/A3/3/105; reproduced in Hewitt, *Lord Shannon's Letters*, 141. At the time, Richard Boyle, 2nd Earl of Shannon (1728–1807), was First Lord of the Treasury.

142. *Freeman's Journal*, 13 June 1799, 3. At the time, the *Freeman's Journal* was a government organ, under the proprietorship of Francis Higgins (an informant who regularly reported to Dublin Castle on the United Irishmen).

143. Collected from eighty-six-year-old Michael Grimes of Kiltycreevagh, county Longford, in May 1938 by James McKenna, the principal of Kiltycreevagh N.S.; IFC 1457:655.

144. See Robert Duffy, *One Hundred Years Too Soon: Hacketstown and 1798* (Hacketstown: Hacketstown Area Community Council, 1998); my thanks to Dr. Thomas O'Grady, Director of Irish Studies at the University of Massachusetts, for this reference.

145. Hayes, *Last Invasion*, 269.

146. Ibid., 270.

147. Quinn, *History of Mayo*, vol. 1, 147–50; see also Hayes, *Last Invasion*, 271. Dr. Marley Blake was also the source of information on General Blake in "An Eyewitness of '98," *Irish Press*, 6 June 1935.

148. Hobsbawm, *Bandits*, 125.

149. See P. M. Hogan, "Undoing of Citizen John Moore"; Freyer and Mulloy, "The Unfortunate John Moore"; Mulloy, "John Moore of Moorehall (1767–99)."

150. Hayes, *Last Invasion*, 284.

151. Joseph Hone, *Moores of Moore Hall*, 43–45.

152. Hayes, *Last Invasion*, 191.

153. See "Commemoration into the Mid-Twentieth Century" in chap. 14.

154. Auckland Papers, BL MS 34454 f. 485; Shannon Papers, PRO NI MS D 2707/

A3/3/116 and 117; Anon., *Impartial relation of the military operations*, 40; Heyland, *Irish Rebellion*, 23; soldier's letter (signed W. H. G. and dated Ballina, 3 October 1798) in Jones, *An Impartial Narrative*, 272 (also quoted in Gribayédoff, *French Invasion*, 136); Maxwell, *History of the Irish Rebellion*, 235 and 248; Mangin, *Parlour Window*, 38–39.

155. Musgrave, *Memoirs of the Different Rebellions* (4th ed.), 573.

156. Ibid., 585.

157. Though a reward of one hundred pounds sterling was offered for his arrest, McDonnell escaped to Connemara and sailed on to France, where he joined other United Irishmen in exile. Appointed a captain in the French army's Irish Legion, he reestablished contacts with rebels in Connemara (1803) but then moved to Spain and emigrated to the United States, where he was eventually appointed a judge in Hudson County, New Jersey (1843). In the twentieth century, a memorial was erected in his honor at Carnacon house. See ADG XL 16c; NAI MS 999/49 ff 1–22 (the originals are kept by McDonnell's descendent, Mrs. Josephine Phillips, Freaghvallen, Miltown Malbay, county Clare); NLI MS 7335 (reproduced in Mulloy, "James Joseph MacDonnell, 'The Best-Known of the United Irish Chiefs of the West,'" *Cathair na Mart* 5, no 1 [1985]: 72–76); Byrne, *Memoirs of Miles Byrne*, vol. 3, 52–54; NAI State of the County Papers no. 1023/3–5 (letters from Richard Martin of Ballinahinch, county Galway, dated 4 and 30 August 1803; and from Denis Browne of Westport, dated 30 October 1803), no. 3493 (letter from Richard Martin of Ballinahinch, dated 23 July 1803).

158. Madden, *United Irishmen*, 3rd ser., vol. 1, 103.

159. Quinn, *History of Mayo*, vol. 1, 147–48.

160. Hayes, *Last Invasion*, 268.

161. *Dublin Journal*, 18 September 1798.

162. See "Recalcitrant Traditions" in chap. 9.

163. Ninety-five-year-old James Carroll of Mohill (four miles from Ballinamuck) told Hayes of Lashlie [Leslie] the informer "that spied on General Blake"; Hayes, *Last Invasion*, 238. Seán Ó hEslin of Ballinamore collected from District Justice J. H. Rice a song that tells the story of Blake's betrayal without revealing the informer's name; IFC S225:151, 153.

164. Hayes, *Last Invasion*, 157–58.

165. Ibid., 245. Another version was submitted to the Schools' Scheme by the schoolteacher Seán Ó hEslin of Ballinamore, county Leitrim; IFC S225:151.

166. See R. M. Young, *Ulster in '98*, 65; Zimmermann, *Irish Songs of Rebellion*, 156. More specifically, the reference to bribing "a false traitor" with a watch appears in the early-nineteenth-century poem "The Colonel's Retreat" by a respected weaver poet; Francis Boyle, *Miscellaneous Poems* (1811), 154–58.

167. Collected by Peter Duignan of Gaigue from Patrick Duignan of Derawley, Drumlish in county Longford, who cited as his source the famous local parish priest Fr. Tom Conefry (who in 1881 led the agitated tenants in the Drumlish Land War); IFC S758:169.

168. Collected from Patrick Gill of Edenmore; Hayes, *Last Invasion*, 231 and *Béaloideas* 4 (1933/4): 393.

169. Written down by Bridget Cassidy of Ballinamuck from her father Thomas Cassidy, aged fifty-five (original author was unknown); see DeVaney, "Ballinamuck in Song and Story," 88.

170. Collected by James McKenna from eighty-six-year-old Michael Grimes of Kiltycreevagh, Ballinamuck; IFC S758:434.

171. For example, Peter Duignan of Gaigue preceded the information he provided Maureen O'Rourke by stating "according to one version"; IFC 1858:25.

172. IFC 1858:24–25, 96–97; IFC S758:434–35, 455–6, 458–59; IFC S760:133, 477; IFC S761:244; IFC S766:307.

173. Hayes, *Last Invasion*, 227–29; IFC S758:434.

174. Hayes was referred to the house of Jack Griffin in Kiltycrevagh, later the house of Mrs. Devine; Hayes, *Last Invasion*, 230, 233.

Thirty years later, Maureen O'Rourke was shown a different location in Dinniny Street (by Mae Mc Eoin's house); IFC 1858:25.

175. IFC Box S759a: copybook of Mary Cullum.

176. Hayes, *Last Invasion*, 227. The trees were also associated with Saint Patrick, who is the patron of the site; the place-name Tubberpatrick derives from the Irish for "Patrick's Well."

177. See a contemporary newspaper report reproduced in Quinn, *History of Mayo*, vol. 1, 147; also *Longford Year Book 1929*, 54–55.

178. Seamus Mac Ciarnáin, ed., *Last Post*, xxv. See also MacNerney, *From the Well of St. Patrick*, 82.

179. "Blake's Grave" was collected by James McKenna of Kiltycrevagh from approximately sixty-year-old Michael Cassidy and attributed to the Poet Higgins of Cloncoose; IFC S758:455–56. "Tone's Grave" was originally published in the *Nation*, 25 November 1843; republished in Martin MacDermott, *Songs and Ballads of Young Ireland* (London: Downey, 1896), 253–54.

180. Collected from Patrick Gill of Edenmore; Hayes, *Last Invasion*, 233.

181. "The Betrayal of Blake at Cloone," in Devaney, "Ballinamuck in Song and Story," 88.

182. Bernard Thompson and his wife, Margaret (maiden surname Reilly), were from Creelaughter, Ballinamuck, and Patrick Joe Reilly was from Edenmore, Ballinamuck; IFC 1858:97–98.

183. See for example Mosse, *Fallen Soldiers* (New York: Oxford Univ. Press, 1990); Winter, *Sites of Memory, Sites of Mourning*. For Ireland, see Keith Jeffery, *Ireland and the Great War* (Cambridge: Cambridge Univ. Press, 2000), 107–43.

184. David Thelen, "Memory and American History," *Journal of American History* 75 (1989): 1117–29; see also Bodnar, *Remaking America*, 3–9. For an Irish example, see David Officer, "'For God and for Ulster': The Ulsterman on the Somme," in I. McBride, *History and Memory*, 160–84, esp. 181.

185. IFC S758:447.

186. Mac Gréine, "Traditions of 1798," 393–95; Hayes, *Last Invasion*, 231–33.

187. IFC S758:48–50 and 446–47; IFC 1858:120.

188. For example, an account collected for the Schools' Scheme by a pupil of Gaigue Boys N.S. can also be traced back to Patrick Gill; IFC Box S758b: copybook of Francis Lenehan.

189. Hayes, *Last Invasion*, 234–5; also IFC S760:129–30; Ó Brádaigh, *Battle of Ballinamuck*; *Longford Leader*, 29 December 1928, 2.

190. IFC S758:32–34.

191. Collected in 1938 from seventy-two-year-old Joe Larkin of Gaigue, Ballinamuck; IFC Box S758b: copybook of Pat Cunningham.

192. IFC 1858:0–11, 100–101.

193. Interview with Clára Ní Ghiolla, Falls Hotel, Ennistymon, county Clare, 21 August 2003; Clára Ní Ghiolla, *Dóchas* (Belfast, 1998; orig. ed. 1987), 22–24.

194. "An Eyewitness of '98," *Irish Press*, 6 June 1935.

195. *Longford News*, 6 July 1979.

196. See my epilogue.

197. For example, IFC 538:518–19; IFC 772:68–69; IFC 969:178; IFC S209:484–86; IFC S758:53, 437–38; IFC S760:130–31; Horgan, *James Berry*, 137–38.

198. Conal Cearnach, "A Story of the French Invasion in '98," *Celt*, August 1858, 271.

199. Whitney, *Legends of Mount Leinster*, 134–35; cited in Ó hÓgáin, *Hero in Folk History*, 198–99.

200. Traditions of Bryan O'Neill were promulgated by his grandnephew James O'Neill of Crowdrummin (near Ballinamuck); IFC S760:130–31; Hayes, *Last Invasion*, 236; Ó Brádaigh, *Battle of Ballinamuck*, 6.

201. IFC 1858:11; IFC S758:45; IFC S760:131–32.

202. *A Return of Killed and Wounded in Certain Regiments from the 20th of August to 20th September inclusive* [signed by several doctors headed by George Renny, the Army's

Chief Medical Officer, dated October 1st, 1798]; Hardwicke Papers BL MS 35,919, f. 89. See Hogan, "Casualties Sustained by Government Forces During the Humbert Episode, August–September, 1798."

203. Gribayédoff, *French Invasion*, 138.

204. Traditions about Gunner Magee are widespread in folklore sources. For example: IFC 1858:11–12; 100–102; IFC S219:248–49; IFC S221:5a; IFC S222:619–20; IFC S225:149–50; IFC S758:56–58, 462–63; IFC S760:133, 476–78; Hayes, *Last Invasion*, 227–28, 229, 231–32, 235, 324; *Béaloideas* 4 (1934/5): 393–94; Farrell, *Historical Notes*, 106; Michael Connell MS reproduced in Devaney, *Killoe*, 129–33; *Longford Year Book 1928*, 103.

205. Through consultations with historians and folklorists, the trophy was designed to resemble Magee's actual cannon; Lt. Dave Hathaway, "Gunner Magee and the Defence Forces Connection," in Rehill, *Ballinamuck Bi-Centenary*, 119–22.

Chapter 9

1. Quinn, *History of Mayo*, vol. 1, 170.

2. Hayes, *Last Invasion*, 311–12; letters dating 24 February and 21 July 1935, 4 and 8 February 1936 in Richard Hayes Papers, NLI MS 13799 (6).

3. Dorson, "The Oral Historian and the Folklorist," 289.

4. Collected from Pat Rogers of Currygrane; IFC S766:64–65.

5. IFC 1457:443–48, 655–58; IFC 1480: 60–61, 350–55; IFC 1858:122; IFC S741:179; IFC S758:130, 145, 173, 178; IFC S759:209–11; IFC 761:195–98; IFC S762:338–41; IFC S763:141–44, 154–56; IFC S764:36–37, 221–5; IFC S765:23–25, 46–47, 407–8; IFC S766:64–65, 301–2. Other names of Granard rebels remembered in local folklore include Philip Brady of Rosduff Castle, Brian Crummy, the blacksmith Harry Farrelly, Flynn, John Kiernan, Mackan, Patrick Mac Namee, Maguire, Partholán Masterson, Johnnie Stephenson, Kit and Arthur Timmins, and Rogers and Hanlan of Derrycassan.

6. Hayes, *Last Invasion*, 294–95.

7. Fontaine, *Notice historique;* reproduced in Joannon, *La Descente de Français*, 82; translated in Hayes, *Last Invasion*, 106. For a more accurate contemporary account of the Rebellion in Granard see an extract of a letter (dated Granard, 11 September 1798) published in *Saunders's News-Letter, and Daily Advertiser*, 14 September 1798.

8. Collected by James Delaney from Thomas Monahan, who was related to O'Keefe through his great-grandmother and cited as his source Mary Kiernan (née Kenny) of Gallid, county Longford (ca. 1862–1940); IFC 1480:350–55.

9. Recounted by Dick Monahan of Muckerstaff, Coolarty, Granard, Willie O'Keefe's great-grandnephew; *Longford News*, 11 September 1998.

10. IFC 1480:350–55; IFC S742:21–25; IFC S743:254–55, 291; IFC S758:173; S759:215–17; S765:407–8; S766:64–65; IFC Box S759A: copybook of James Hughes. Folklore about "Hempenstall" remains strong in the eastern parishes of county Westmeath; see Flynn and McCormack, *Westmeath 1798*, 66. There is a dispute over how his name is spelled (Hempenstall, Hepenstal, etc.), but the variant spellings refer to the same person.

11. See O'Donnell, *Rebellion in Wicklow, 1798*, 98; Chambers, *Rebellion in Kildare, 1790–1813*, 53. Woods, *Annals of Westmeath*, 21–29; Cox, "Westmeath in the 1798 Period," 6–7.

12. *Press*, 16 November 1797 and 11 January 1798 (republished in *Extracts from The Press* [Philadelphia, 1802]).

13. Madden, *United Irishmen* (2nd ed.; Dublin, 1858), vol. 1, 308–9. Lecky listed Hempenstall among the most militant loyalists involved in the terror that preceded the Rebellion; Lecky, *History of Ireland*, vol. 277.

14. Collected in 1938 by thirteen-year-old Mathew Kearney from his mother, forty-two-year-old Mrs. Kearney of Mullaghmeelan, Ballymore, county Westmeath; IFC 743:243–44.

15. W. J. Fitzpatrick, *"The Sham Squire,"* 225.

16. Oral traditions of him were noted as far off as Ulster; Margaret Dobin (née Cochrane) letters, TCD MS 10354.

17. Walford, *County Families of the United Kingdom*, 306. The 1901 census for county Longford notes two Dopping-Hepenstals living in Longford; Leahy, *County Longford and its People*, 57. For a colorful history of the family see Columb, *Lough Gowna Valley*, 85–146.

18. Sinn Féin Election leaflet: South Longford, 1917 (NLI ILB 300 P 9 f. 74); cited in Novick, "The Advanced Nationalist Response to Atrocity Propaganda, 1914–1918," 145–46.

19. IFC S207:225–27.

20. Collected from eighty-year-old Mrs. Buhan of Catten; Hayes, *Last Invasion*, 227.

21. IFC S599:306–7.

22. Several verses were recited to Maureen O'Rourke in 1964 by Bernard Thompson of Creelaughter, Ballinamuck; IFC 1858:99.

23. Madden, *Literary Remains*, 240–42; Zimmermann, *Irish Political Ballads*, 103.

24. Hayes, *Last Invasion*, 242.

25. Moylan, *Age of Revolution*, 52–53.

26. IFC 1534:530–31.

27. A letter by Fr. Thomas Sweeney of Brooklyn mentions family traditions from Muingwar, Castelconnor (on the border of Mayo and Sligo), where the rebel priest Fr. Owen Cowley of Crossmolina took refuge in 1798; see E. MacHale, *The Parishes in the Diocese of Killala* (Killala: n.p., 1985), 1:138–39.

28. In 1937 Michael O'Gallaher [Ó Gallchobhair] of Chicago, who was reared in Bellacorick, county Mayo, and immigrated to the United States in 1888, recalled traditions about his rebel grandfather Cathaoir Ó Gallchobhair of Tawnagh, county Mayo (d. 1845); see *Last Invasion* (2nd ed.), 344–49; letter dated 16 October 1937 in Richard Hayes Papers NLI MS 13799 (3); *Catholic Bulletin* 28 (July 1938): 596–98. O'Gallaher collected Erris folklore in America as early as 1895, when he took down oral traditions from Mayo emigrants in Elroy, Wisconsin; Ó Gallchobhair, "Amhráin ó Iorrus," 226–27, 233–35, and 258–62.

29. Michael O'Mullally, who was born in 1848 in Glenaughill, Clon, county Longford, and immigrated to Nebraska, recalled stories told by his grandparents; Mullally Family Papers (compiled ca. 1938); my thanks to Fr. Owen Devaney of Mullahoran, Kilcogy, county Cavan, for allowing me access to copies of the papers. See also Fr. Owen Devaney, "A Time and a Half Time," in Rehill, *Ballinamuck Bi-Centenary*, 108–10.

30. The stories of Katherine Flannery (née Davitt), who was born in Mayo in 1792 and died in Whetstone Run, Marion County, West Virginia, in 1869, were recalled by her granddaughter; "Mayo and American Memories of Mrs. M. Kennedy" (41 typescript pages, dated 29 December 1908), ff 3 and 7; my thanks to Prof. Kevin Whelan of the University of Notre Dame for providing me with a copy of Mrs. Kennedy's papers.

31. Alice Patricia DeVaney, who was born in Hubbar, Ohio, in 1900 and whose grandparents hailed from Westport, county Mayo, recalled hearing stories of a DeVaney who piloted a French vessel into Killala Bay in 1798; information communicated to the author by her grandson, James D. Nealon, currently residing in Montevideo, Uruguay. For stories about "Paddy the Rebel" Flynn of county Mayo recalled in Concord, New Hampshire, see Elizabeth Gurley Flynn, *The Rebel Girl* (New York: International Publishers, 1973), 23–26.

32. Richard Hayes Papers, NLI MS 13799 (7); *Connaught Telegraph*, 10 June 1899.

33. Quinn, *History of Mayo*, vol. 1, 158.

34. In 1977 a Castlebar-born general practitioner in Rumcorn, Cheshire, in England inadvertently referred to local enmities between Castlebar and Killala that date back to 1798; interview with Olive Kennedy, Killala, 17 September 2001.

35. In the early 1980s Alan Judge Holt from Australia investigated family traditions about the death of his great-grandfather John Judge, the steward of the Knox's estate at Rappa Castle (eight kilometers south of Killala), and discovered that they matched a local tradition of a killing in 1798 (bloodstains were said to be visible at the kennels of

the North Mayo Hunt at Rappa until the building was demolished in 1925); C. G. Knox, "The Knox Family in Tyrawley North Mayo" (unpublished typescript in the Knox Family Papers); interview with Jimmy Gilvary, Ballynacola, Crossmolina, county Mayo, 10 August 2002.

36. The Dublin schoolteacher Eamonn Henry (son of the Mayo storyteller Seán Henry) collected in 1997 a ballad, "The Year of '98," from John Joseph Howley of Ontario, who had heard it sung by his mother, Dorothy Howley (née Clifford, b. 1910), who in turn had learned it from her mother, Bridget Lillian Clifford (b. 1865); reproduced in the online internet newsletter the *Mayo Gazette;* www.mayogazette.com/folk/year98.html. In 1997 Pat McGoldrick heard from his uncle, Father Desmond McGoldrick of Toronto, family traditions that recalled that his great-grandfather, Patrick Goldrick of Annageliffe [Aghnacliff] in county Longford, was the sole survivor of a family burned alive in their hut after the battle of Ballinamuck; *Irish Times,* 17 November 1998.

37. BBC Northern Ireland, 1998.

38. IFC S760:439–40.

39. Hayes, *Last Invasion,* 168, 275; IFC S123:211. My thanks also to his descendent, Eamonn Horkan of Castlebar, for providing me with additional information based on local tradition.

40. Collected from John McNeeley of Lahardane, county Mayo; Richard Hayes Papers, NLI MS 13799 (2) (orange covered notebook); Hayes, *Last Invasion,* 223. The story of Larry Gillespie appeared in mid-nineteenth-century popular print; *Celt,* August 1858, 271–76.

41. Collected by Alice Boland from Ian Carroll of Letterhane, Aclare, county Sligo; IFC S173:267–70; a printed version appeared in L. M., "The Shanachie Talks: The Folklore Commission at Work," *Irish Press,* 27 February 1936.

42. Collected by William F. Gill of Leamonish, Fenagh, county Leitrim; IFC S212:334.

43. Collected from Bernard Thompson of Creelaughter; IFC 1858:105.

44. IFC S968:146; IFC S976:102.

45. Collected by James Delaney from Patrick Connell of Drumlish; IFC 1457:658.

46. Hayes, *Last Invasion,* 295.

47. Collected by Peter Kilkenny; Hayes, *Last Invasion,* 322–23; IFC S221:1b–2a.

48. IFC S225:151.

49. For references to Tom Gilheany and Jack O'Hara see "Rebel Songs and Ballads in English" in chap. 5

50. Hayes, *Last Invasion,* 174.

51. Collected by Kathleen Devaney from Martin Loughney of Market Street, Killala; IFC S142:338.

52. Otway, *Sketches in Erris and Tyrawley,* 302. This tradition may refer to Captain Kirkwood of the Killala yeomanry, who hid with his family in caves in Erris and was helped by local Catholics, among them the rebel leader Ferdinand (Ferdie) O'Donnell of Pollathomas; Stock, *A Narrative of What Passed at Killala* (1800 ed.), 12.

53. Collected from Mathew McManus of Driney, Drumcong, Carrick-on-Shannon; IFC S211:394. For another example, see chap. 10, 194.

54. For the argument that accounts of sectarian violence have been exaggerated, see K. Whelan, "United and Disunited Irishmen"; K. Whelan, "Reinterpreting the 1798 Rebellion in County Wexford," 9–36; Dáire Keogh, "Sectarianism in the Rebellion of 1798," 37–47. For the counterargument that sectarianism was at the heart of the Rebellion, see Donnelly, "Sectarianism in 1798," 15–37.

55. For example, see letter to George Lenox-Conyngham (27 April 1799), PRO NI D.1449/12/292.

56. See Kelly, "We Were All To Have Been Massacred," 325–26.

57. TCD MS 871. The records of the Commission were subsequently destroyed in 1922, yet two reports on their work were printed in the Irish *Commons' Journals* in 1799 (vol. 18) and 1800 (vol. 19); see W. N. Osbor-

ough, "Legal Aspects of the 1798 Rising, its Suppression and its Aftermath," in Bartlett et al., *1798*, 462–63.

58. Musgrave, *Memoirs of the Different Rebellions* (4th ed.), 591–94.

59. Anon., *List of Persons who have suffered Losses* (for a reproduced extract see Hayes, *Last Invasion* [2nd ed.], 356–61; reproduced in full in E. D. MacHale, "Official List of Claims"); also RIA MS 12/D/26.

60. See O'Rorke, *History of Sligo*, vol. 1, 376–76; vol. 2, 593–99.

61. See Kelly, "We Were All To Have Been Massacred," 323–24.

62. Including Rev. James Burrowes (the tutor of Stock's children), Dr. Thomas Ellison of Castlebar, Rev. James Little of Lackan, curate Robert Nixon of Killala, Dean Thomas Thompson of Killala, and Mr. Marshall, the Presbyterian minister of Multifarragh (near Ballina); see Stock, *Narrative of What Passed at Killala*, 18–19 and 95–96.

63. There were probably other considerations that stalled Stock's promotion; see Richard Henry [Lord Holland], *Memoirs of the Whig Party During My Time*, vol. 1 (London, 1852), 136–37.

64. Letter by Bishop Stock, dated 29 September 1798; TCD MS 3390.

65. Stock, *Narrative of What Passed at Killala*, 93–96. Rev. Little also referred to the looting of a Protestant church; Costello, "Little's Diary," 114.

66. The records of the vicarage of Ardnaree in Ballina apparently list 214 killed and 178 injured during August 1798; Tony Donohue Papers, Creevy, county Mayo. My thanks to Tony Donohue for allowing me access to his papers.

67. Costello, "Little's Diary," esp. 97, 104.

68. See Mulloy, "Clergy," 253–73; Hayes, *Last Invasion*, 191–97; Hayes, "Priests in the Independence Movement"; "Priests Associated with the Rising in 1798," *Connaught Telegraph*, 29 August 1953, 4 (based on the work of Richard Hayes); Hoban, "Dominick Bellew, 1745–1812," esp. 363; E. MacHale, "Some Mayo Priests of 1798."

69. Including Fr. Fitzgibbon (who after the Rebellion settled in Turlough, county Galway), IFC 712:67; Fr. O'Brien of Killasser (near Swinford) in county Mayo, IFC 117:90; Fr. Michael Gleeson of Ballyconnell in county Cavan (who was remembered locally as a miracle worker and martyr), IFC S968:142–43.

70. For remembrance of Fr. Conroy see chap. 12 (217–18) and chap. 13 (262–63).

71. Hewitt Papers, National Army Museum MS 5910-198 f. 150; Rebellion Papers, NAI MS 620/14/189/1–4; State of the Country Papers 1803, NAI MS 1023/3–5; Hardwicke Papers, BL MS 35730 ff 317–19 and 386–87; MS 35758, ff 23–24. See also McManus, *Sketches of the Irish Highlands*, 78; Carroll, "Myles Prendergast OSA," 60–69; J. Gibbons, "Father Myles Prendergast"; Lavelle, "The Mayo Rebels of '98 in Connemara." See also Hayes, *Last Invasion*, 192–94.

72. See "Amhráin na ndaoine" in chap. 5 (88–89), and "Mapping Commemorative Micro-toponymy" in chap. 12 (214). In the mid-twentieth century, the civil servant, historian, and author Leon Ó Broin (b. 1902), who was also a member of the Irish Folklore Commission, wrote a one-act play in his honor; L. Ó Broin, *Slán le Muirisg*.

73. IFC 523:371–85 (reproduced and edited in Ó Duilearga, "Seanchas Phádraig," 225–60); IFC 528:1b–6; IFC 528:106–9; IFC 770:432–37; IFC 1710:197–98; IFC 1318:114–15; IFC S142:189–90; Michael Timoney Papers, IFC Box (unnumbered); Hayes, *Last Invasion*, 212–13, 313–16; Mac Coisdealbha, "Seanchas Ó Iorrus," 223–26; Ó Gallchobhair, "Amhráin ó Iorrus," 237 (reproduced in part in Hayes, *Last Invasion* [2nd ed.], 344–49); Ó Moghráin, "Gearr-Chunntas," 3–57 (reproduced and translated in Uí Mhaoluaidh, *Father Manus Sweeney*).

74. See Ó hÓgáin, *Hero in Irish Folk History*, 204–15.

75. See Alan Ford, "Martyrdom, History and Memory in Early Modern Ireland," in I. McBride, *History and Memory*, 43–66; Clodagh

Tait, "Adored for Saints: Catholic Martyrdom in Ireland c. 1560–1655," *Journal of Early Modern History* 5, no. 2 (2001): 128–59.

76. The mistaken private name probably derived from confusion with a Fr. Hugh Conway of Ballycroy, who was the parish priest in Islandeady in the early nineteenth century (ca. 1825).

77. Collected by Prionnsias de Búrca from Pádraic Mac Manamoin of Ballycroy, Erris; IFC 523:371–85; reproduced in Ó Duilearga, "Seanchas Phádraig," 255–260. See also Hayes, *Last Invasion* (2nd ed.), 347; Ó Moghráin, "Gearr-Chunntas," 13, 34–35. Stories of Fr. Conway were still recounted in north Mayo until recent times; interview with seventy-one-year-old Jimmy Gilvary, Ballynacola, Crossmolina, county Mayo, 10 August 2002.

78. IFC 523:378.

79. Rev. E. MacHale, *The Parishes in the Diocese of Killala* (Killala: n.p., 1985), vol. 2, 65.

80. Costello, "Little's Diary," 128–29.

81. Collected from Dominick McDonnell of Muingrevagh (in Kilbride); Hayes, *Last Invasion*, 219.

82. Hayes, *Last Invasion*, 110. See also reference to Fr. O'Flanagan of Granard in "An Insurgent General" in chap. 8 (158).

83. IFC S225:148–49; Hayes, *Last Invasion*, 108, 319–20, and 327.

84. For relations between rebellious laity and loyalist priests in the late eighteenth–early nineteenth centuries, see S. J. Connolly, *Priests and People in Pre-Famine Ireland, 1780–1845* (Dublin, 2001; orig. ed. 1982), 208–44, esp. 214–16.

85. Commentary by Lord Carleton on a letter by Lord Cornwallis to the Duke of Portland, dated St. Johnstown, 9 September 1798; Hugh Carleton Papers, NLI MS 4290.

86. Hayes, *Last Invasion*, 320.

87. *First Report of the Commissioners of Public Instruction in Ireland*, H.C. 1835, vol. 33. My thanks to Dr. Liam Kennedy of QUB for sharing with me the population figures calculated by himself and Dr. Kerby Miller.

88. Kennedy, Miller, and Graham, "Protestants, Economy and Society," esp. 39–50. See also Lenehan, "Memories of Ballinamuck," 48; F. O'Farrell, "History of the Ballinamuck Land War 1835–39."

89. Collected by Moira Keaveny of Cora Droma Rúisc, county Leitrim; IFC S209:304.

90. Séamas Mac Philib, "The Irish Landlord System in Folk Tradition—Impact and Image" (PhD thesis, UCD, 1990), 159–60, 250–69.

91. IFC 1710:197. Many traditions about the rebel priest Fr. Sweeney recall Bingham's role in his arrest and conviction.

92. IFC 528:6–10; IFC 1206:364–65; IFC 1512:313–18; Hayes, *Last Invasion*, 264.

93. See "Amhráin na ndaoine" in chap. 5 (88–89). In one account, Browne was labeled an informer (*spíadóir*); IFC 202:73. This heavily stigmatized title proves to be historically accurate because he received payment from Secret Service funds for giving information on local rebels; Madden, *United Irishmen* (1st ed. London, 1846), 3rd ser., vol. 1, 112.

94. IFC S758:458–59; Hayes, *Last Invasion*, 158–59, 233, 238, 293, and 324.

95. IFC 494:339–40.

96. Columb, *Lough Gowna Valley*, 131. For traditions of Hempenstall see chap. 9, 170–71.

97. The claim that demographic decline was the result of deliberate sectarian policy has been forcefully put forward in a study of West Cork but disputed in a study of Sligo. See Peter Hart, *The I.R.A. and Its Enemies: Violence and Community in Cork, 1916–1923* (Oxford: Oxford Univ. Press, 1998), 273–92 and 312–15; Michael Farry, *The Aftermath of Revolution: Sligo 1921–23* (Dublin: UCD Press, 2000), 177–201.

98. McDowell, *Crisis and Decline*, 98.

99. See Bartlett and Jeffery, *Military History of Ireland* (Cambridge: Cambridge Univ. Press, 1996), 401. "The Men of the West" was also the title of a well-known painting from 1916 by Seán Keating (1889–1997), whose depiction of Irish separatist "citizen soldiers" crossed associations of 1798 with idealized

perceptions of Irish rural life and the American frontier.

100. For north Longford, see Marie Coleman, *County Longford and the Irish Revolution, 1910–1923* (Dublin: Irish Academic Press, 2002), 160, 177–78.

101. Terence Dooley, *The Decline of the Big House in Ireland: A Study of Irish Landed Families, 1860–1960* (Dublin: Wolfhound Press, 2001), 190, 235–38.

102. The novelist George Augustus Moore (1852–1933), Maurice Moore's elder brother, provocatively declared himself a Protestant in the *Irish Times* (1903).

103. Interview with Sean Murphy (b. 1919) from the area of Moorehall; Daly's Hotel, Castlebar, 28 February 2003.

104. A commemorative plaque "In memory of John Moore, First President of Ireland, and the men of this parish who gave their lives for Ireland in the rising of 1798" was later placed on the gate of the estate by Maurice Moore of California (son of Colonel Maurice Moore); for a photograph see Murray and Cullen, *Epitaph of 1798*, 95. Toward the bicentennial of Ninety-Eight, a local community group campaigned for the restoration of Moore Hall, and on 12 December 1998, Minister of State Éamonn Ó Cuiv laid a wreath on the site; *Irish Times*, 18 April 1997 and 14 December 1998.

105. "Déaradh cuid de na daoiní go ndeachaigh páirtí as na bailte seo, go ndeachaigh sin go Cill Ala san am ar tháinig na Franncaigh ann, ach mhothaigh mise m'athair mór a rá má fuaigh, ach, nár mhothaigh sé féin ariamh é. Ara, bhí na daoiní a bhí anseo chomh mór le cúl agus nach raibh a fhios acu i gceart cé chaoi a raibh aon rud. Ní le troid ná achrann is mó a bhí aird acu ach oiread lena chéilí ach ag iarraidh greim a sholáthar dófa féin agus iad a fháil a seansáith le déanamh agus a' greim sin féin a choinneáil leath an ama. Ach sílim nach raibh aon láimh mhór ag éinne acu i ngraithe Chill Allaidh ná Chaisleáin a' Bharraigh." Collected by Tomás a Burc from Seán a Goireachtaigh [Geraghty] of Carrowteige [Ceathrú Thaidhg]; IFC 770:205–6.

106. Collected from Dominick McDonnell of Muingrevagh; Hayes, *Last Invasion*, 218–19.

107. Hayes, *Last Invasion*, 222.

108. "Nuair a rith gáir na Francaigh (1798) a scaipeadh ar fud na mbailte bhí scanradh agus crith-eagla ar na daoine. Bhí faitíos orthu nach bhfágfaí greim bídh acu dhá dtigidís an bealach. Bhí na daoine san áirdeall orthu ar feadh i bhfad ach níor tháinigeadar go Gleann Chuilinn mar sin féin. Le linn an ama a rabhthas san áirdeall ar na Francaigh . . . 'Thug na Francaigh roille mór do na daoiní thart anseo' a deir Patsy liom. Chuir siad trína chéile go mór iad. Bhí scáth acu roimh an arm Sasanach agus roimh an arm Francach." Collected by Liam Mac Coisdeala from Patsy Carey [Páraic Ó Cioraín] of Doolough [Dubhloch]; IFC 662:20–21.

109. Collected in 1939 by Liam Mac Coisdeala from seventy-four-year-old Micheál Ó Rodaigh of Muiningawn, Bangor in Erris, county Mayo; IFC 625:197–98.

110. Collected from Michael McGough of Polonore, Cummer, county Galway; IFC S21:161–62.

111. Collected in 1947 by Liam Mac Coisdeala from seventy-year-old Mícheál Ó Coileáin [Mike Tom Mhóir] of Carnmore [Carn Mór] and originally told by his father (ca. 1900); IFC 1106:376–77.

112. Collected in 1938 by Seán Ó Flanagáin from Seán de Róiste of Gort-Adrahan; IFC 538:516–18.

113. Gribayédoff, *French Invasion* (94–97); cited in Ó Moghráin "Gearr-Chunntas," 46.

114. NLI MS 7335, f. 5; see also Hayes, *Last Invasion*, 275–78; Mulloy, "James Joseph MacDonnell," 67–79.

115. Hayes categorically dismissed this tradition as not having "very much support"; Hayes, *Last Invasion*, 214, 316. Yet tracing the original source to Henry Taafe (alias "Senex" of Knock) reveals that apparently moral censorship, nationalist sentiment, and local patriotism were the considerations for disqualifying this tradition; Richard Hayes Papers, NLI MS 13799 (7) (purple covered notebook); *Connaught Telegraph*, 27 August 1898, 5.

116. Hayes, *Last Invasion*, 292–93; for traditions about Thomas O'Cahan ("Captain Rock"), see Diarmaid Ó Catháin, "Tomás Ó Catháin," *Teathbha* 2, no 4 (1997): 276–78; *Longford Year Book 1929*, 40.

Chapter 10

1. NLI MS 4290.

2. The most celebrated of these heroines include Mary Doyle (New Ross), Suzy Toole the "moving magazine" (Wicklow), Teresa Malone (Kilcumney), Molly Weston (Tara), and Betsy Gray (Ballynahinch).

3. MacNeill received international recognition following the publication of her seminal monograph *The Festival of Lughnasa*.

4. See Mahon, *While Green Grass Grows*, 44.

5. See chart 2 (chap. 2, 53). Women who collected traditions of *Bliain na bhFrancach* include Cáit Ní Chafraidh of Ballinamore in county Leitrim; Sarah Foley of Ardmore, Carna in county Galway (who originally submitted her collections to *Moore's Almanac*); Brígid M. Ní Ghamhnáin of Baile-an-Dúin (near Boyle) in county Sligo, Kathleen Hurley of Ballymoe in county Galway, Eileen H. Loughlin of Mohill in county Longford, and Monica Ní Mhaodhbh of Galway. In addition, during the mid-1960s the American folklore student Maureen O'Rourke (later Murphy) collected in the area of Ballinamuck an entire volume of relevant material (IFC 1858).

6. Michael Gorkin, Marta Pineda, and Gloria Leal, *From Grandmother to Granddaughter. Salvadoran Women's Stories* (Berkeley: Univ. of California Press, 2000), 6–7. This observation also takes into account the experience of an earlier study; Michael Gorkin and Rafiqa Othman, *Three Mothers, Three Daughters—Palestinian Women's Stories* (Berkeley: Univ. of California Press, 1996).

7. In addition to principal teachers, this figure includes assistant teachers and members of religious orders; *An Roinn Oideachais Turasgabháil / Report of the Department of Education 1937–38* (Dublin: n.p., 1938), 122.

8. Seosamh O'Neill, *National Tradition and Folklore*. As the evident insider's familiarity with the discipline suggests, the booklet was actually written by a folklorist—Énrí Ó Muirgheasa (1874–1945).

9. These local figures slightly exceed the national ratio of 51.8 percent female pupils; *An Roinn Oideachais Turasgabháil*, 134–35.

10. Séamas Ó Catháin, "Oral History: The Folklore Perspective" (paper presented at the Economic and Social History Society of Ireland's conference on Oral History, Royal Irish Academy, Dublin, 20 November 1999).

11. His conservative views on women's issues came to the fore during his tenure as Film Censor (1940–54), at a time when the extensive censorship authorized by the Censorship of Films Acts 1923 and 1930 was enhanced under Article 52 of the Emergency Powers Order (1939); see "The Bellman," "Meet Dr. Hayes."

12. Hayes, *Last Invasion*, 225, 226–27, and 230.

13. Zimmermann, *Irish Storyteller*, 432.

14. Delargy, "Gaelic Storyteller," 181.

15. Arensberg and Kimball, *Family and Community*, 196.

16. IFC 1858.

17. C. R. Farrer, ed., *Women and Folklore* (Austin: Univ. of Texas Press, 1976), vii.

18. Sayers's autobiographical reflections were published in *Peig* (Dublin: Talbot Press, 1936), trans. by Bryan McMahon as *Peig: The Autobiography of Peig Sayers of the Great Blasket Island* (Dublin: Talbot Press, 1973); *Machtnamh Seana-Mhná* (Dublin: Oifig an tSoláthair, 1939), trans. by Séamus Ennis as *An Old Women's Reflections* (Oxford: Oxford Univ. Press, 1962); *Beatha Pheig Sayers* (Dublin: Foilseacháin Náisiúnta Tta, 1970). For collections of her stories available in print see *Scéalta ón mBlascaod* (Dublin: Cumann le Béaloideas Éireann, 1998; orig. publ. in *Béaloideas* 8 [1938]), and *Oral Literature from Dunquin* (Belfast: Institute of Irish Studies, QUB, 1983). Her public image suffered in consequence of compulsory teaching of *Peig* in the Irish language school curriculum.

19. Marc Bloch, *The Historian's Craft* (Manchester: Manchester Univ. Press, 1954), 40; see also Marc Bloch, "Mémoire collective, tradition et coutume," 79.

20. Hayes, *Last Invasion*, 233; *Béaloideas* 4 (1933/4), 393–95.

21. IFC 1430:91–95.

22. Hayes, *Last Invasion*, 269.

23. Ibid., 274–75.

24. Collected by John J. Mulligan of St. Patrick's N.S. in Aughnacliffe in county Longford from eighty-seven-year-old John Reilly of Rathmore, Collumcille, county Longford; IFC S761:243–44.

25. For example: IFC 1858:97; *Béaloideas* 4, 393; Hayes, *Last Invasion*, 28, 231, 323–24.

26. Collected from John Clancy of Faughill (d. 1936); Hayes, *Last Invasion*, 322.

27. Collected from Mrs. Buhan of Catten in county Leitrim; Hayes, *Last Invasion*, 227. Another version of this tradition was written down for the Schools' Scheme in Cloone by the schoolteacher A. Ó Corraidhin; IFC S222:2.

28. Devaney "Ballinamuck in Song and Story," 69.

29. Two versions were collected for the Schools' Scheme in county Longford: one from eighty-seven-year-old Mrs. Patrick Doyle of Aughnacliffe, Granard; IFC S766:304; and another from eighty-seven-year-old John Reilly of Rathmore, Collumcille; IFC S761:245.

30. Joannon, *La Descente de Français*, 18; for an English version see Hayes, "An Officer's Account," 166.

31. Ormsby Papers, NLI microfilm P8162; reproduced in *Cornhill Magazine* (1898), 477.

32. Classified as Q42 (generosity rewarded) and Q111 (riches as reward) in Thompson, *Motif-Index*.

33. Collected by Peter Kilkenny of Sunnaghbeg, a teacher at Dromloughan N.S, from ninety-year-old Mary McKeown, née Cassidy (d. ca. 1916), of Drumbad, near Gorthlettera in county Leitrim (seven kilometers west of Ballinamuck); IFC S221:2a; Hayes, *Last Invasion*, 323–24.

34. Collected by John Duignan from Pat Duignan of Kiltycreevagh; IFC S758:50.

35. Collected by Maureen O'Rourke from Peter and Biddy Duignan; IFC 1858:9.

36. Collected by James Delaney from James Dolan of Kiltycreevagh; IFC 1480:181.

37. Collected from seventy-seven-year-old M. Denning of Derrycassan; IFC S763:143.

38. Seán de Búrca, "An Echo of 1798," *Cathair na Mart* 19 (1999), 47.

39. Collected by Bridie Beirne of Cloonmorris, Johnston's Bridge, Bornocoola (on the Leitrim-Longford border) from forty-two-year-old Patrick Reynolds of Bornacoola; IFC S219:136.

40. James McKenna of Lear, Mohill, county Leitrim, heard this story from his mother Mrs. B. McKenna (d. 1912 at the age of sixty-four); IFC S214:397–98. Another version was collected by Máire Bí Bhrádaigh of Caol-Doire, Mohill, county Leitrim from her father; IFC S222:618.

41. Joannon, *La Descente de Français*, 22; for English version see Hayes, "An Officer's Account," 171; orig. pub. in Jean Sarrazin, "Notes sur l'Expédition d'Irlande," *L'Ami des Lois*, 8 December 1798.

42. Stock, *Narrative of What Passed at Killala*, 17.

43. Thuente, "Liberty, Hibernia and Mary Le More: United Irish Images of Women," in Keogh and Furlong, *Women of 1798*, 9–25.

44. William Drennan, "Wail of the Women After the Battle," in Madden, *Literary Remains*, 46.

45. A. Kinsella, "Nineteenth-Century Perspectives," in Keogh and Furlong, *Women of 1798*, 198.

46. See Eileen Reilly, "Rebel, Muse and Spouse: The Female in '98 Fiction," *Éire-Ireland* 34, no. 2 (1999): 135–54.

47. Kinsella "Nineteenth-Century Perspectives," 187.

48. IFC 54:132–33; IFC 437:132–33.

49. F. Kavanagh, *Popular History of the Insurrection of 1798*, 334–37. For this book's impact in reshaping popular memory see K. Whelan, *Tree of Liberty*, 171–72.

50. IFC 1134:473; IFC 1457:656–57; IFC 1858:8–10; IFC S207:145; IFC S220:148–49; IFC S758:47, 252–53, 436–38; IFC S760:127–33; S766:305–8; Hayes, *Last Invasion*, 236 and 321.

51. Judges 4:17–22 and 5:24–27.

52. Murphy, "Noggin of Milk," 183–85.

53. For example, an account collected from Mrs. Lynn of Cortoon, Killala; IFC S144:22–23.

54. IFC S220:148–49; IFC S986:96–97. The local historian Jude Flynn, originally from Gortletteragh, recalled his father tell the story of "the Highlander" in the late 1940s, and he later heard another version in Drumlish parish, south of Ballinamuck; interview with Jude Flynn, Longford, 15 September 2001.

55. Murphy, "Noggin of Milk," 185–86.

56. IFC 1858:120 (this version, collected in 1964 from Patrick Reilly of Edenmore, is a story adaptation of the ballad of Robin Gill, which was collected in 1938 from Patrick Gill Jr. of Edenmore; IFC S758:446–47); IFC Box S758b: copybook of Pat Cunningham.

57. Collected from seventy-three-year-old Pat Chambers of Greenan, Castlebar; IFC S94:247–48; and Mrs. Loftus of Barnaderrig, Ballina (who lived to the age of one hundred); IFC S146:298.

58. For example, traditions collected in Connemara in 1952 by Ciarán Bairéad about the popular outlaw hero Fr. Myles Prendergast include several references to women who assisted him; IFC 1318:105–7 and 111–15. See also Mac Giollarnáth, *Annála Beaga*, 64–81 (for a partial translation see Hayes, *Last Invasion* [2nd ed.], 341–44).

59. Collected by the local historian Seán de Búrca of Pollatomish from Micheál Ó Donnchadha of Bellmullet; de Búrca, "An Echo of 1798," 47.

60. Labeled as R152.3 in Thompson, *Motif-Index*, vol. 5, 283.

61. For example, Peter Gibbons of Newport probably escaped Castlebar prison by boring a wall in the cell; folklore had him dressed as a woman; Hayes, *Last Invasion*, 185.

62. Collected in 1965 by James Delaney from seventy-four-year-old Patrick Reilly of

Shanmullagh (near Ballinamuck); IFC 1457:444.

63. For example, IFC 1858:122.

64. Bartlett, "Bearing Witness," in Keogh and Furlong, *Women of 1798*, 64–87.

65. *Last Invasion*, 223; *Celt*, August 1858, 271–76.

66. Collected from Myles Tiernan of Drumshanbo; Hayes, *Last Invasion*, 292.

67. Classified as P711 in Thompson, *Motif-Index*.

68. 2 Maccabees 7 and 4 Maccabees 8–18. The woman (identified in Jewish tradition as Hanna) was declared a martyr by the Catholic Church.

69. IFC 1380:88–162; see also E. G. Brandt, *Memoirs of the Staker Wallace* (Chicago: J. S. Hyland, 1909; repr. 1989 by E. T. Wallace), 40; Mainchín Seoighe, *Staker Wallis: His Life and Times and Death* (Cill Fhiontáin, county Limerick: Coiste Scoil na Seoigheach, 1994), 41; Murray and Cullen, *Epitaph of 1798*, 82.

70. "Anecdote of a Mrs. Hill of Castlecomer," *Irish Magazine*, November 1811, 510.

71. See Munnelly, "1798 and the Balladmakers," 164.

72. Madden, *United Irishmen* (3rd ed.), vol. 10, ix.

73. Charles Gavan Duffy, *Ballad Poetry of Ireland*, 116–17.

74. See for example Denis Devereux, *Songs and Ballads of '98* (Dublin: B. Doyle, 1898), 7; *The Emmet Song Book: Specially compiled for the Irish Patriot's Centenary* (Dublin, 1903), 19.

75. Though set in 1798, the ballad has autobiographical resonance, as the poetess encouraged her fiancée not to cooperate with the authorities when he was prosecuted for his involvement in the Young Ireland insurrection of 1848 and subsequently their marriage was postponed for many years due to his transportation to Australia; Justin McCarthy, "Biographical Sketch," in *Poems by "Eva" of "The Nation,"* ed. Seumas Mac Manus (Dublin: M. H. Gill & Son, 1909), xv–xvi; see also *Irish Book Lover* 1, no. 12 (July 1910): 163.

76. Reproduced online in the *Mayo Gazette*; http://www.mayogazette.com/folk/year98.html.

77. Collected for the Schools' Scheme by Frankie McQuaide from seventy-five-year-old Patrick Brady of Gaigue (who identified his father and uncle as the source); IFC 758:45.

78. Written in February 1938 by eighty-year-old James O'Neill of Crowdrummin; IFC S760:131–32; see also Ó Brádaigh, *Battle of Ballinamuck*, 6–7.

79. See chap. 16, 307–8.

80. Collected for the Schools' Scheme from M. J. Kenny, Ballygilcash; IFC S166:355–56.

81. Collected from Michael Clyne of Mohill; Hayes, *Last Invasion*, 238.

82. Collected from Michael Kiernan of Mullinroe, Granard, county Longford; IFC S763:154–55.

83. Collected by the schoolteacher Pádhraic Maguidhir from Thomas Kiernan (ca. 1831–1913) of Cloughla, Carrigallen, county Leitrim, and later submitted to the Schools' Scheme; IFC S228:39.

84. Collected in 1938 by James McKenna from eighty-six-year-old Michael Grimes of Kiltycreevagh (near Ballinamuck); IFC S758:436.

85. Bartlett, "Bearing Witness," 80–83.

86. Lyons, "Races of Castlebar," 19.

87. Collected from George Monnelly; Hayes, *Last Invasion*, 217.

88. Collected by Nell Loftus from Mrs. Nealon of Banagher, county Mayo; IFC S141:304.

89. Hayes, *Last Invasion*, 90.

90. *Irish Citizen*, 6 November 1915, 150.

91. O'Rorke, *History, Antiquities* 73. While O'Rorke's account may well be the source for Hayes's reference, O'Rorke's source remains unspecified.

92. J. J. Moran, *Stories of the Irish Rebellion*, 50–69.

93. Daniel Savary, *Carnet de la Sabretache* no. 67; A. Nat. MAR BB/4/123; reproduced also in Desbrière, *Projets et Tentatives*, vol. 2, 83.

94. See Gasty, "L'Étonnante de L'Armée d'Irlande," n. 19; Joannon, *La Descente de Français*, viii.

95. de Jonnès, *Adventures in the Revolution*, 184.

96. An example can be found in a hand-colored etching by Thomas Rowlandson, who depicted "French Liberty" as a depraved French woman; see Diana Donald, *The Age of Caricature: Satirical Prints in the Reign of George III* (New Haven: Yale Univ. Press, 1996), 153.

97. Meredith, "Shan Van Vocht: Notes from the North," in Kelly and Gillis, *Critical Ireland*, 173–81.

98. *Irish Citizen*, 6 November 1915 (150–51), 13 November 1915 (161), 20 November 1915 (168–69), 27 November 1915 (177–78), and 4 December 1915 (183).

99. Talbot Press declined to publish Markievicz's manuscript; NAI, MS 1948/1/46, letter 63. My thanks to Joanna Susan Wydenbach of QUB for references to the papers of Talbot Press.

100. Concannon, *Women of 'Ninety-Eight*.

101. Keogh and Furlong, *Women of 1798*; Keogh, "Women of 1798: Explaining the Silence," 512–28. See also Ó Saothraí, *Heroines of 1798*, which is partially based on an earlier booklet in Irish: Séamas Ó Saothraí, *Mná calma '98* (Dublin: Cló Grianréime, 1966).

102. M. Cullen, "Partners in Struggle," 159.

103. For further discussion based on the case of remembrance of Ninety-Eight in Ulster, see Guy Beiner, "Oral Herstoriography," in *Ireland (Ulster) Scotland: Concepts, Contexts, Comparisons*, eds. Eamonn Hughes, Edna Longley, and Des O'Rawe (Belfast: Queen's University Belfast, 2003), 86–93.

104. For "bricolage" as an anthropological concept, see Claude Lévi-Strauss, *The Savage Mind* (Chicago: Univ. of Chicago Press, 1966), 1–33.

Chapter 11

1. V. C. Uchendo, "Ancestoricide! Are African Ancestors Dead?" in *Ancestors*, ed. W. H. Newell (Hague: Mouton, 1976), 283–96;

J. S. Mbiti, *African Religions and Philosophy* (London: Ibadan Heinemann, 1969), 25 (cited also in Lowenthal, *Past is a Foreign Country*, 195).

2. Robert Hertz, *Death and the Right Hand* (Aberdeen: Cohen & West, 1960), 27–86 (trans. by Rodney Needham and Claudia Needham of "Contribution à une étude sur la représentation collective de la mort," *Année Sociologique* 10 (1907): 48–137).

3. Halbwachs, *On Collective Memory*, 73–74.

4. R. R. Madden, "Memorials of the Dead," in T. M. Madden, *Memoirs (Chiefly Autobiographical)*, 256.

5. See Bergson, *Matter and Memory* (London: Swan Sonnenscher & Co., 1911), 86–105.

6. Explaining how memory is "sedimented in the body," Connerton distinguished between "incorporating" memory, which is reenacted in habitual activity, and "inscribing" memory, which is stored and retrieved through various media; Connerton, *How Societies Remember*.

7. Neal Ascherson, "The centralisation of memorials and memory," in Bort, *Commemorating Ireland*, 202–3.

8. See for example the analysis of Israeli commemorations at Massada, alongside other Zionist myths, in Zerubavel, *Recovered Roots*, esp. 60–79. A northern Irish example can be found in studies of commemorations of the siege of Derry; for example, Ian McBride, *The Siege of Derry in Ulster Protestant Mythology* (Dublin: Four Courts Press, 1997); Walker, *Past and Present*, 1–28; William Kelly, ed., *The Sieges of Derry* (Dublin: Four Courts Press, 2001).

9. See Winter, *Sites of Memory*.

10. Prominent examples can be found in the case of Australian remembrance of Anzac participation at the battle of Gallipoli or the Vietnam Veteran's Memorial in the United States. See Alistair Thomson, *Anzac Memories: Living with the Legend* (Oxford: Oxford Univ. Press, 1994); Marita Sturken, "The Wall, the Screen, and the Image: The Vietnam Veterans Memorial," *Representations* 35 (Summer 1991): 118–42; Thelen, "Memory and American History," 1117–29. For a penetrative discussion on

how traumatic memories of veteran combatants and relatives of casualties can challenge official commemoration at national memorials see Jenny Edkins, *Trauma and Memory of Politics* (Cambridge: Cambridge Univ. Press, 2003), 57–110.

11. T. W. Laqueur, "Memory and Naming in the Great War," in Gillis, *Commemorations*, 150–67. For the earlier case of naming casualties in monuments of the American Civil War see Piehler, *Remembering War*, 51–53.

12. Patricia Lysaght, "Caoineadh os Cionn Coirp: The Lament for the Dead in Ireland," *Folklore* 108 (1997): 66–70.

13. T. C. Croker, *The Keen of the South of Ireland as Illustrative of Irish Political and Domestic History, Manners, Music and Superstitions* (London: The Percy Society, 1844).

14. O'Rourke, "County Mayo in Gaelic Folksong," 185–86. A long version of the lament was collected by Tomás de Búrc in 1943; IFC 914:434–38; reproduced in Tomás Ó Concheanainn, *Nua-Dhuanaire* (Dublin: Institiúd Ardléinn, 1981), vol. 3, 6–7. The song was first collected in Connacht in several versions shortly after the 1798 Rebellion by Patrick Lynch and Edward Bunting; Edward Bunting Papers, QUB MSS 6/103, 10/60, 14/59, 17/50–51, 28/103. Though the lament probably originated in northwest Mayo, its popularity spread along the coastline and it entered the traditional singing repertoire of Donegal, south Mayo and Connemara. In 1895 a version was collected among Mayo emigrants in Elroy, Wisconsin; Ó Gallchobhair, "Amhráin ó Iorrus," 258–60. For an English translation titled "The Lament for Yellow-Haired Donough," see Frank O'Connor, *Kings, Lords, and Commons* (Dublin: Gill & Macmillan, 1959), 120–21.

15. Paul Ricoeur, "Memory and Forgetting," in *Questioning Ethics: Debates in Contemporary Philosophy*, eds. Richard Kearney and Mark Dooley (London: Routledge, 1999), 5–11. For the original essays see *The Standard Edition of the Complete Psychological Works of Sigmund Freud* (London: Hogarth, 1962), vol. 12, 147–56 and vol. 14, 237–58.

16. See Ulla-Maija Peltonen, "The Return of the Narrator," in *Historical Perpectives on Memory*, ed. Anne Ollila (Helsinki: SHS, 1999), 115–38; Peltonen, "Sisällisota ja naiset: Sosiaalinen muisti ja kerronta," in *Telling, Remembering, Interpreting, Guessing*, eds. Maria Vasenkari, Pasi Enges, and Anna-Leena Siikala (Joenuu: Suomen kansantietouden Tutkijain Seura, 2000).

17. IFC 202:65–73; IFC 314:507–9; IFC 793:83–87; IFC 819:175–79; IFC 1280:347–48, 595–96, 616; Richard Hayes Papers NLI MS 13801 (3) (dated 5 August 1899); *Gaodhal* (February 1886); *Gaelic Journal* no. 3, vol. 6 (1895 [no. 63 of the old series]), 37–38; *An Claidheamh Soluis* 1 (1899), 326–27; Ó Máille, *Amhráin Chlainne Gaedheal*, 127; Ó Máille, *Micheál Mhac Suibhne*, 61–63; Hayes, *Last Invasion*, 249–50; (reproduced in Tomás Ó Concheanainn, *Nua-Dhuanaire*, Cuid 3 [Dublin, 1978], 17–18; O'Rourke, "County Mayo in Gaelic Folksong," 190).

18. Horgan, *James Berry*, 137.

19. Bourke, "Lamenting the Dead," in *Field Day Anthology*, vol 4, 1365.

20. IFC 202:71. This version was collected locally by Sarah Folley of Ardmore, Carna, county Galway, in response to a request published in *Moore's Almanac* for "Irish songs, stories etc."; IFC 202:33–34.

21. Hayes, *Last Invasion*, 249.

22. Collected by Brian Mac Loughlin from Michael Toole of Clare Island; IFC 819:178–79. Five years earlier (ca. 1937), Mac Loughlin collected another version of the lament from Pádraic Ó hÉiniú [Seathrún] of Claonuane, Renvyle, county Galway.

23. See L. M. Cullen, "The Contemporary and Later Politics of *Caoineadh Airt Uí Laoire*," *Eighteenth-Century Ireland* 8 (1993): 10.

24. Bourke, "Lamenting the Dead," 1367.

25. Translated in Hayes, *Last Invasion*, 248.

26. See Ó Gallchobhair, "Amhráin ó Iorrus," 237–38; Hayes, *Last Invasion* (2nd ed.), 348–49.

27. See the critique of Breandán Ó Buachalla's influential monograph *An Caoine agus an Chaointeoireacht* (Dublin: Cois Life

Teoranta, 1998) by S. E. McKibben, "Angry Laments and Grieving Postcoloniality," in *New Voices in Irish Criticism*, ed. J. Mathews (Dublin: Four Courts Press, 2000), 216.

28. Bourke, "Keening as Theatre: J. M. Synge and the Irish Lament Tradition," in *Interpreting Synge: Essays from the Synge Summer School, 1991–2000*, ed. Nicholas Grene (Dublin: Lilliput Press, 2000), 67–79.

29. See n. 73 in chap. 9 (377).

30. Larkin, *Historical Dimensions of Irish Catholicism*, 57–89.

31. See Liam Ua Cadhain, *Knock Shrine* (Galway: O'Gorman printinghouse, 1935).

32. James S. Donnelly, Jr., "The Marian Shrine at Knock: The First Decade," *Éire-Ireland* 28, no. 2 (1993): 54–97.

33. Halbwachs, *On Collective Memory*, 88.

34. Owens, "Nationalist Monuments in Ireland," 111–15.

35. Lyons, "Races of Castlebar," 44; interview with Ken Lyons, Castlebar, 21 August 2001.

Chapter 12

1. Vansina, *Oral Tradition as History*, 45.

2. Seosamh Ó Tuathalláin of Garryroe; IFC S119:518.

3. Joanne Rappaport, *The Politics of Memory: Native Historical Interpretation in the Columbian Andes* (Cambridge: Cambridge Univ. Press, 1990), 198.

4. Glassie, *Passing the Time in Ballymenone*, 201.

5. Kent C. Ryden, *Mapping the Invisible Landscape: Folklore, Writing, and the Sense of Place* (Iowa City: Univ. of Iowa Press, 1993), 63.

6. Maurice Halbwachs, *La Topographie légendaire des Evangiles en Terre Sainte* (Paris: Presses Universitaires de France, 1941); for an English translation see Halbwachs, *On Collective Memory*, 193–235.

7. Simon Schama, *Landscape and Memory* (London: Harper Collins, 1995).

8. Flower, *Irish Tradition*, 1. In modern Irish *dinnseanchas* is translated as topography, while *logainm* and *áitainm* are terms used for

place-names and the verbal noun *logainmníocht* means the naming of places, i.e., toponymy. For a general overview of Irish toponymic research see Diarmuid Ó Murchadha and Kevin Murray, "Place-names," in Buttimer, Rynne, and Guerin, *Heritage of Ireland*, 146–55.

9. Welch, *The Oxford Companion to Irish Literature*, 150.

10. Ó hÓgáin, *Myth, Legend and Romance*, 363.

11. Evans, *Personality of Ireland: Habitat, Heritage and History*.

12. Raphael Samuel, *Theatres of Memory*, vol. 1, *Island Stories*, 367.

13. K. Whelan, "The Region and the Intellectuals," 126–27.

14. J. B. Jackson, "The Vernacular Landscape," in *Landscape Meaning and Values*, eds. E. C. Penning and David Lowenthal (London: Allen & Unwin, 1986), 65–81; see also J. B. Jackson, *Discovering the Vernacular Landscape* (New Haven: Yale Univ. Press, 1984), 149–54.

15. Witoszek and Sheeran, *Talking to the Dead*, 77.

16. K. Whelan, "Place-name Change."

17. S. Ó Catháin and O'Flanagan, *Living Landscape*.

18. J. Duffy, "Heritage and history: exploring landscape and place in county Meath," *Ríocht na Midhe* 11 (2000): 206–8.

19. Ó Catháin and O'Flanagan, *Living Landscape*, 71.

20. McParlan, *Statistical Survey*, 154.

21. For example, see entries for Castlebar and Killala in Anon., "An English-Gentleman aided by the communication of several friends," *The Scientific Tourist*; Trotter, *Walks Through Ireland*, 459–60; Fraser, *Handbook for Travellers*, 472; Mr. and Mrs. Hall, *Ireland*, 379–81 (reproduced [without acknowledgement] and popularized in Measom, *Official Illustrated Guide to the Midland . . . Railways*, 329–31).

22. Leerssen, *Remembrance and Imagination*, 102.

23. See Andrews, *Paper Landscape*, esp. 123–29 and 156–68; for a reappraisal see Doherty, *Irish Ordnance Survey*.

24. Cronin, "Memory, story and balladry," 116.

25. For examples from county Longford, see chap. 4, 71–72.

26. Cronin, "Memory, Story and Balladry," 122–26.

27. Gillian Smith, "An Eye on the Survey," 41.

28. *Irish Press*, 3 April 1935; *Irish Times*, 3 April 1935.

29. See Yates, *Art of Memory*.

30. See Nora, "Between Memory and History," in Nora, *Realms of Memory*, vol 1, 1–20.

31. White, *Remembering Ahanagran*, 52.

32. Ben-Amos and Weissberg, *Cultural Memory*, 298.

33. Collected for the Schools' Scheme by Nell Loftus of Banagher, county Mayo, from her seventy-eight year old grandmother; IFC S141:304. Also heard by Hayes from George Monnelly of Kilcummin, county Mayo; Hayes, *Last Invasion*, 217.

34. My thanks to the local historian Sean Lavin for showing me the site identified in an account he had heard in the 1980s from seventy-year-old Paddy Kelly of Church village, Kilcummin; interview on 22 August 2001.

35. My thanks to Wendy Lyons of Collooney (whose house is on Camp Hill) for showing me the site; interview in Collooney, 31 October 2001.

36. IFC S222:248–50; IFC S222:615–19; numerous other references appear in the copybooks of pupils from the area: IFC Boxes S222a, S222b, S222d.

37. Lyons, "Races of Castlebar," 20. The route taken through Cloonawilliam farm in Crossmolina, county Mayo, was also known as a "French road"; IFC S152:73–74.

38. IFC Box S222a: copybook of Lizzie A. MacNally; IFC Box S222b: copybooks of Michael Higgins and Francis O'Neill; IFC Box S222d: copybooks of Annie Josephine Mitchell, Bride O'Carroll, and Mary Reynolds.

39. IFC S207:219.

40. For example, Dr. Shane Butler of the Department of Social Studies at TCD

informed me in 2002 that he recalled how in December 1973, when driving in county Mayo from Swinford to Foxford, a local man pointed out a side road near the river Moy and offhandedly exclaimed that this was where "the *Frinch* came."

41. Hayes, *Last Invasion*, 27–28. The Irish word for wisp of straw [*sop*] is also used as a verb meaning "to light with straw"; Ó Dónaill, *Foclóir Gaeilge-Béarla*, 1135.

42. Interview with Jimmy Gilvary, Ballynacola, Crossmolina, county Mayo, 10 August 2002. This place-name was also found elsewhere and a variant of a children's rhyme in Connemara refers to a local *bóthar na sop*; IFC 73:493; reproduced in Williams, *Cniogaide Cnagaide*, 76.

43. IFC S758:254–55, 438, 460. Copybooks of pupils from the Ballinamuck area mention two different locations known as "Croppy's Gap"; IFC Box S222a: copybooks of Mary Ann Garvey, Thomas O. Garvey, Mary O. Boy, and Annie O'Neill; IFC Box S222b: copybooks of John Higgins and Patrick Mahon. From the 1980s, "the Croppies' Gap" at Kiltycreevagh is marked with a sign, whereas the other sites are neglected and mostly forgotten.

44. IFC S758:438.

45. Interview with Jimmy Breslin, Ballinamuck, 15 September 2001.

46. Collected for the Schools' Scheme from Jim Halloran of Ballina; IFC S146:298.

47. Hayes, *Last Invasion*, 43.

48. Interview with the local historian Ernie Sweeney (February 2003), who had heard this tradition in the early 1980s from Mick Kearney, a resident of Sion Hill.

49. IFC S94:244; Hayes, *Last Invasion*, 47–48; see also *Celt*, August 1858, 271.

50. IFC S89:445; Lyons, "Races of Castlebar," 44. Lyons suggests that the name may actually have originated from a slaughterhouse known as "Stabb Hall."

51. IFC S89:454. The building is currently marked with a plaque; for a photograph see Murray and Cullen, *Epitaph of 1798*, 96.

52. Hayes, *Last Invasion*, 53; IFC 1649:5.

53. See *Adventures of Captain Blake*, 95; Maxwell, *History of the Irish Rebellion*, 235.

54. Hayes, *Last Invasion*, 16 and 258.

55. IFC 1584:563. Collected by Micheál Mac Énrí from Seán Ó hÉilí of Glencalry, Ballycastle, county Mayo.

56. Hayes, *Last Invasion*, 262.

57. Glenree traditions about Rory were collected for the Schools' Scheme from forty-six-year-old M. J. Ruane and sixty-four-year-old John Carberry; IFC S128:533–34, 561.

58. Hardwicke Papers, BL MS 35758, ff 23–24.

59. McManus, *Sketches of the Irish Highlands*, 78; see also Carroll, "Myles Prendergast OSA," 60–69.

60. NAI MS 620/14/189.

61. Collected in 1952 in Letterfrack, county Galway, by Ciarán Bairéad from fifty-year-old Mark Coyne (a fisherman from Mullach Glas) and eighty-year-old Willie Lavelle; IFC 1318:105–7, 111–15. See also Hayes, *Last Invasion*, 303–4.

62. Mac Giollarnáth, *Annála Beaga*, 64–81, esp. 78–79—translated in part in Hayes, *Last Invasion* (2nd ed.), 341–44; Mac Giollarnáth, "Sliocht de Sheanchas Mhicheál Bhreathnaigh," 122–23.

63. Lavelle, "The Mayo Rebels of '98 in Connemara," 74.

64. IFC 1318:107 and 114.

65. Horgan, *James Berry*, 136.

66. MacNeill associated this motif, which is found throughout the British Isles, with the Celtic festival of Lughnasa; MacNeill, "The Musician in the Cave."

67. Collected from forty-five-year-old Patrick Quinn of Brackla, who repeated stories he had heard as a young boy from Catherine Noone of Ballyheigue; IFC S261:129.

68. The original name of the place was identified as Tóin Léibe; IFC S261:130. In 1938 the collector Kathleen Hurley was informed that the estate was already called Tobinstown in the time of John Tobin, Mick's father; IFC 485:37.

69. See MacDonald, "South Ulster," 241–42.

70. IFC 815:335–37; IFC S1011:124 and S1012:141.

71. IFC 815:335.

72. Collected from J. O'Reilly of Church Street, Ballyconnell, county Cavan; IFC S968:146.

73. Padraig Rehill, "People and Places," in Rehill, *Ballinamuck Bi-Centenary*, 143.

74. For references to Ninety-Eight folklore in the Irish diasporas see "Local Heroes and Their Constituencies" in chap. 9.

75. Collected by the sixteen-year-old pupil Kathleen Dawson from forty-six-year-old Patrick Dawson of Carrickduff, Granard; IFC S764:36–37.

76. More attention has been given to Alexander Denniston, who was an outlaw for a considerable time and later escaped to America; Hayes, *Last Invasion*, 293–95.

77. IFC 1480:60–61. IFC S763:145–46; IFC S765:46–47; see also an account collected from Dick Monahan of Muckerstaff, Coolarty, county Longford, in *Longford News*, 11 September 1998, 19.

78. Collected by James McKenna of Mohill, county Leitrim, from his mother Mrs. B. McKenna (1848–1912) and the Cloone parish priest Fr. Conefry (1837–1917); IFC S214:328.

79. Collected from Pat Duignan of Kiltycreevagh; IFC S758:50.

80. For example: PRO HO 100/82/47; Dropmore Papers, BL MS 71589, ff 66–67; Auckland Papers, BL 34454 f. 485.

81. Humphrey Thomson, "Personal Narrative," BOD MSS Eng. Hist. d. 155 f. 138.

82. Letter by Joshua Kemmis, Ballina, 25 September 1798, NLI Frazer MS II/89. Massacres of Irish rebels following the fall of Killala are confirmed in several government reports; PRO HO 182/100/172–75; Dropmore Papers, BL MS 71589, ff 78 and 81.

83. Hayes, *Last Invasion*, 173.

84. "Pollnashantona" (*Poll na Sean Toinne*, the Hole of the Big Wave) is a common name for "blow-holes" on the north Mayo coast; see Westropp, "Promontory Forts," 102–3, 197, 204; MacNeill, "Poll na Seantuinne."

85. Hayes, *Last Invasion*, 117; IFC 1140:29–30.

86. *Dublin University Magazine*, vol. 18 (1841), 300–301; republished as Otway, *Sketches in Erris and Tyrawley*, 216–18. This story was recounted locally in the 1930s and '40s; Hayes, *Last Invasion*, 117; IFC 1140:29–30.

87. In an alternative version the fugitives were shot down by soldiers; see Lyons, "Races of Castlebar," 48. In another version, the event occurred on Halloween night and only three fugitives drowned (identified as Ó Brádaigh, an Ó Dúbháin, and an Ó Muinghile); Mag Ruaidhrí, *Le Linn M'Oíge*, 13–14. The site is now marked with a plaque; for a photograph see Murray and Cullen, *Epitaph of 1798*, 92.

88. IFC S148:117, 137.

89. IFC S94:400.

90. O'Flynn, *History of Leitrim*, 72–73. The trees used to hang the selected men were identified; IFC 559:237–38; IFC S209:227. A vivid description of the lottery was recounted by Ian Carroll of Letterhane, Aclare, county Sligo; IFC S173:268–69. In an account collected in 1933 from Patrick Gill of Edenmore, execution by lottery was located in Kiltycreevagh, near Ballinamuck; Mac Gréine, "Traditions of 1798," 394–95.

91. Hewitt Papers, National Army Museum MS 5910–198 f. 143. A contemporary account noted that one-fifth of courts-martial death sentences were "executed by lot"; Humphrey Thomson, "Personal Narrative," BOD MS Eng. Hist. d. 155 f. 137. See also Maxwell, *History of the Irish Rebellion*, 243–44; Lecky, *History of Ireland*, vol. 5, 63; Falkiner, "French Invasion of Ireland," 317–18.

92. IFC S738:209.

93. Lady Gregory, *Kiltartan History Book*, 60.

94. IFC S207:143–45.

95. IFC S214:257.

96. IFC S214:328.

97. IFC 1480:397.

98. Hayes, *Last Invasion*, 230, 233; IFC S758:434–35 and numerous accounts in the

copybooks of pupils from schools in neighboring parishes, for example Drumgownagh N.S. in Annaghmore [Eanach Mór], county Leitrim; IFC Box S222a and S222b.

99. IFC S766:207.

100. Devaney, *Killoe*, 128.

101. Collected from Michael Moran of Roslahan, Belcarra [Ballycarra]; IFC S94:400–402.

102. Collected from Martin Joyce of Lahardane, county Mayo; Hayes, *Last Invasion*, 273–74.

103. Quoted in Nuala Costello, *John MacHale, Archbishop of Tuam* (Dublin: Talbot Press, 1939), 15.

104. *Connaught Telegraph*, 19 August 1961.

105. IFC S89:436–37 (the year of the tree's uprooting is mistakenly given as 1921). See also D'Alton, *History of the Archdiocese*, vol. 1, 369; Ní Cheannain, *Heritage of Mayo*, 76; MacHale, "Some Mayo Priests of 1798," 11.

106. See Quinn, *History of Mayo*, vol. 1, 165 and 168.

107. *Mayo News*, 12 June 1948. It is currently held in St. Angela's Girls N.S., Castlebar; information provided by the local historians Noel O'Neill and Stephen Dunford. Another photograph of this "Hanging Tree Cross" is available online, courtesy of Noel O'Neill (Mayo Historical & Archaeological Society), at the Castlebar Community News and Information website: http://www.castlebar.ie/news/article_221.shtml.

108. The cross is currently in the possession of Fr. McEvilly's nephew in Dublin; my thanks to Michael McEvilly for providing me with a photograph of this souvenir. A photograph was also published in the *Castlebar Parish Magazine*, Christmas 1976.

109. *Exhibition Programme. '98 Commemoration Ceremonies, Castlebar, August 1, 1948* ('98 Commemoration Committee, county Mayo; Castlebar, 1948); see also photo caption in *Connaught Telegraph*, 5 September 1953, 3.

110. Hayes, *Last Invasion*, 305; IFC S138:161.

111. Hayes, *Last Invasion*, 159.

112. IFC S128:564.

113. Collected by Nora Kelly of Templeligan, Bonniconlon (Bunnyconnelan) from sixty-year-old Bernard Mullen of Newtown, Bonniconlon; IFC S128:236.

114. Hayes, *Last Invasion*, 289–90; see also P. O'Connor, *"French Are in Killala,"* 28.

115. Ó Brádaigh, *French Graves*, 2.

116. Conversation with Michael Murphy of Killasser, Swinford, county Mayo; Castlebar, 28 February 2003.

117. My thanks to Ernie Sweeney for showing me the site, which was originally identified by the owner of the property, the late John Murray.

118. My thanks to Ernie Sweeney for showing me the site.

119. Ó Brádaigh, *French Graves*, 2.

120. IFC 79:634; Hayes, *Last Invasion*, 222; see also Lyons, "Races of Castlebar," 23.

121. My thanks to the local historian Sean Lavin for showing me the site. In 1986 a monument was erected there, though the original grave has since been demolished. See epilogue, 329.

122. IFC S119:518.

123. IFC S123:211.

124. O'Hara, *Killasser*, 33.

125. Hayes, *Last Invasion*, 290; P. O'Connor, *French Are at Killala*, 28–29.

126. IFC S202:131.

127. IFC 104:479–80.

128. Collected from Michael Reilly of Enaghan, who heard this tradition from his grandfather John Reilly (1845–1927); Devaney, "Ballinamuck in Song and Story," 77–78. See also MacNerney, *From the Well of St. Patrick*, 83.

129. "Lough Gowna's French Graves," *Longford Leader*, 5 June 1998.

130. IFC S116:157 and 181; IFC S117:67.

131. IFC S116:137.

132. Collected by Robert Cawley of Garracloonagh from James Reilly of Scotchfort; IFC S148:117.

133. *Irish Sword* 3 (1957–58): 286.

134. Interview with Ken Lyons, Castlebar, 21 August 2001.

135. Hayes, *Last Invasion*, 282.

136. My thanks to the local historian Ken Lyons for sharing with me this information based on his own inquiries and conversations with people in the locality.

137. My thanks to the local historian Ernie Sweeney for showing me the grave.

138. McGowen was related to Mangan by marriage. In 1935 Hayes collected an account of Captain's Mangan's death from his grandniece, Mrs. McGowan of Linen Hall Street, Castlebar; Hayes, *Last Invasion*, 225.

139. Lyons, "Races of Castlebar," 44–45; interview with Ken Lyons, Castlebar, 21 August 2001.

140. Lyons, "Races of Castlebar," 22. The controversy over the widening of the road was recalled in 2003 by Peter Kearney, who had lived nearby. My thanks to Ken Lyons and Ernie Sweeney for showing me the site.

141. Archdeacon, *Legends of Connaught*, 354–71.

142. IFC S222:618; IFC S758:254, 320–22, 434; IFC S759:216; IFC S760:127–33; IFC S765:25; IFC S766:306. See also Devaney, *Killoe*, 136.

143. IFC S222:616; S759:216; IFC S766:207, 307; IFC Box S759a: copybooks of Teresa Brady (6th grade), James Hughes (7th grade), Peter Maguire (7th grade); Mac Gréine, "Traditions of 1798," 395; *Longford Year Book 1940*, 123. The old graveyard at Ballinalee is currently derelict, and most of the gravestones are illegible. A bicentennial Ninety-Eight memorial was erected in August 1998 by the main road.

144. Peter Duignan of Gaigue; IFC 1858:27.

145. Collected from John Traof Soran, Ballinalee, county Longford; IFC S759:211.

146. IFC S225:144–45; IFC S758:438–41; IFC 1858:41–42.

147. Scully, *Irish Catholic's Advice*, 12.

148. Collected from Patrick Cross of Kiltycreevagh; Hayes, *Last Invasion*, 229.

149. Interview with Jimmy Breslin, Ballinamuck, 15 September 2001.

150. Pádhraic Maguidhir of Carrigallen, county Leitrim; IFC S228:37–38a.

151. Patrick Tohall, "A Croppy's Grave," *Béaloideas* 14 (1944): 291.

152. Collected by Kate Dolan of Kilduff N.S. from seventy-six-year-old Pat (Owen) Ui Lough Lin [Lochlainn] of Unshenagh, Dowra, county Cavan; IFC S962:27–28.

153. IFC 733:4 and 81.

154. IFC S765:25.

155. Collected in 1935 from eighty-year-old Patrick Mulligan of Granard; Hayes, *Last Invasion*, 295.

156. In September 1998 a plaque erected in Cortnawilliam Lane was dedicated to the memory of "Bonny Pat Farrell and the United Irishmen who were defeated and slain at this site in the Battle of Granard, Sept. 5th 1798"; for a photograph see Murray and Cullen, *Epitaph of 1798*, 89.

157. Noted on heritage-tourist information signs in Ardagh. See also the account of Fr. John Quinn, parish priest of Gortletteragh, county Leitrim, himself a descendent of a Granard rebel who died in 1798; *Longford News*, 11 September 1998.

158. See Murray and Cullen, *Epitaph of 1798*, 95.

159. From the poem "The Croppies' Grave" reproduced in the souvenir program booklet *1798 Commemoration at Ballinamuck* (Longford: n.p., 1938).

160. IFC S760:133.

161. IFC 1858:27–28.

162. Rehill, "People and Places," 143.

163. Ó Brádaigh, *French Graves*, 2.

164. Lyons, "Races of Castlebar," 47; interview with Kenneth Lyons, Castlebar, 21 August 2001. My thanks to Ernie Sweeney and Ken Lyons for showing me the site at the Pontoon Road junction (on the property of Seamus Neary).

165. See MacNeill, "Wayside Death Cairns in Ireland." See also sections on "Graves and Tombs," "Memorials of the Dead," and "Stone-Heap Memorials," in Ó Súilleabháin, *Handbook of Irish Folklore*, 20–22.

166. Gibbons, *Slieve Bawn and the Croppy Scout*, 3–4.

167. C. G. Knox, "The Knox Family in

Tyrawley North Mayo," unpublished type-script in the Knox family papers (private possession).

168. My thanks to Sean Lavin for showing me the site, which he was originally shown by a local resident (Paddy McHale) in 1984.

169. Collected from sixty-nine-year-old Peter McGuire of Dunbeggan, Granard, county Longford; IFC S759:215–16. Collected for the Schools' Scheme also by other pupils of the locality: IFC Box S759a: copybooks of John Brady (5th grade), Teresa Brady (6th grade), John Gibna (7th grade), James Hughes (7th grade), Teresa Mac Manus (6th grade), Mark Mimnagh (6th grade).

170. Collected from seventy-three-year-old uncle John Traof Soran; IFC S759:211–10. The site was also identified as a mass grave in other accounts collected for the Schools' Scheme; IFC Box S759a: copybooks of Peter Maguire (7th grade), Patrick Sheeran (7th grade).

171. IFC S759:211–10; IFC Box S759a: copybooks of Teresa Brady (6th grade), Mark Mimnagh (6th grade), Teresa Mac Manus (6th grade), and Patrick Sheeran (7th grade). No explanation was offered as to why this ritual took place specifically in June.

172. IFC 523:384; IFC 1318:114; P. J. Joyce, *Forgotten Part of Ireland*, 83; Hayes, *Last Invasion*, 314; Henry, *Tales From the West*, 42–44.

173. A description of this grave was originally taken down in 1938 by pupil Frank Lenahan of Gaigue N.S. from his seventy-one-year-old grandfather. In 1964 his teacher Peter Duignan repeated the account to Maureen O'Rourke; IFC 1858:27.

174. Devaney, *Killoe*, 136.

175. Collected in March 1938 by pupil Annie Hare [Áine Ní Ghiorraidhe] of Knockanillaun from her father, James Hare; IFC S148:241.

176. Collected from forty-five-year-old Mrs. Gill of Leamonish, Fenagh, county Leitrim; IFC S212:334.

177. Collected for the Schools' Scheme from eighty-seven-year-old Miss Ellen Langan of Russagh, Rathowen, county West-

meath. Eighty-year-old Tom Weir of Rathowen noted that one member of Katie Daly's family had fought at Granard and managed to escape; IFC S741:144.

178. Rehill, "People and Places," 144; Murray and Cullen, *Epitaph of 1798*, 116. Farrell's wake at Kilmore Cross (near Clondra) was recalled locally and recounted in 1998 by Mrs. Willie Glennon of Longford, who had two ancestors who died at Ballinamuck; *Longford News*, 11 September 1998.

179. The memorial was restored by Frank O'Dowda of Tallagh, Dublin in 1995; Dowds, *French Invasion*, 83.

180. T. Donohue, "Some Recollections," 37–38.

181. Ó Moghráin, "Gearr-Chunntas," 21–22.

182. *Irish Independent*, 21 July 1939.

183. Collected from seventy-year-old Martin Connell of Clooncullane, Creggs, IFC S16:20; and from sixty-five-year-old Martin Connolly of nearby Clooncun, Glenmaddy; IFC S261:128.

184. Rehill, "People and Places," 144–45; also: IFC S752:309–10. For a photograph see Murray and Cullen, *Epitaph of 1798*, 88.

185. Hoban, "Dominick Bellew," 364–65; Patrick Hogan, "Some Observations."

186. Collected by James McKenna from Michael Grimes of Kiltycreevagh; IFC S758:438.

187. Collected from John Brady of Crowdromin; IFC S758:47.

188. IFC S214:415.

189. Wallace, *Multyfarnham Parish History*, 72.

190. IFC S220:283–85.

191. Ben-Amos and Weissberg, *Cultural Memory*, 298.

192. Collected by James Delaney in 1956 from Thomas Monahan and originally told by Mary Kieran of Gallid, county Longford (d. 1940); IFC 1480:350–51. This story was repeated in 1998 by Dick Monahan of Muckerstaff, Coolart, Granard; see *Longford News*, 11 September 1998, 19.

193. IFC 1430:85.

194. IFC S752:309–10.

195. Forwarded to Hayes by Patrick O'Donnell of Newport; Hayes, *Last Invasion,* 307.

196. Hayes, *Last Invasion,* 229.

197. Ibid., 233.

198. IFC S766:307.

199. Hayes, *Last Invasion,* 231.

200. IFC S758:434–35. An account of Blake's execution, wake, and burial was also collected from sixty-year-old John Farrell of Clonakelly; IFC S760:477.

201. MacNerney, *From the Well of St. Patrick,* 82.

202. Cited in *Bliainiris* 2 (1983/84): 24.

203. Collected from Martin Loughney of Killala; IFC S142:338–39.

204. Collected from Thomas Moran of Cortoon, who spoke of "a lot of bones, skulls and teeth exposed in the sand yet"; IFC S144:24–25.

205. Collected from Patrick Allen of Drumshanbo; IFC S207:145.

206. Collected from Patrick Dolan of Kiltycreevagh Cross; IFC S758:255 and 460; Hayes, *Last Invasion,* 229.

207. Vansina, *Oral Tradition as History,* 45.

208. Ó Catháin and O'Flanagan, *Living Landscape.*

209. Ó Súilleabháin, *Handbook of Irish Folklore,* 245–46. As a rule, the Irish Folklore Commission's collectors did not profess to personally believe in "superstitions" or ghosts; see Mahon, *While Green Grass Grows,* 89, 95.

210. See Tóibín, "Irish Famine," 23–24.

211. Angela Bourke, "The Virtual Reality of Irish Fairy Legend," *Éire-Ireland* 31, nos. 1–2 (1996): 7–25.

212. Angela Bourke, *The Burning of Bridget Cleary* (London: Pimlico, 1999).

213. Hayes, *Last Invasion,* 312.

214. See L. Gibbons, "Republicanism and Radical Memory," 221.

215. Hayes, *Last Invasion,* 291–92.

216. Collected by Tadhg Ó Rabhartaigh from Mary Gaffney of Arigna, county Roscommon; IFC 104:479.

217. IFC S969:239.

218. IFC 202:145–49.

219. Collected from John Giblin of Drumshanbo; IFC S225:129–30.

220. For a general discussion on folklore of ghosts as a popular expression of bereavement see Gillian Bennett, *"Alas, Poor Ghost!": Traditions of Belief in Story and Discourse* (Logan, UT: Utah State Univ. Press, 1999).

221. IFC S765:23–25.

222. IFC S599:159.

223. Interview with Jude Flynn, Longford, 15 September 2001.

Chapter 13

1. T. O. Ranger, *Revolt in Southern Rhodesia 1896–7: A Study in African Resistance* (London: Heinemann, 1967), 385.

2. Hayes-McCoy, "Irish Pike," in particular 110–17.

3. Costello, "Little's Diary," 87, 112.

4. Richard Hayes Papers, NLI MS 13799 (2) (orange notebook).

5. See *Descriptive Catalogue of the Collection of antiquities and other Objects, Illustrative of Irish History, exhibited in the Museum, Belfast on the Occasion of the Twenty-Second Meeting of the British Association for the Advancement of Science, September, 1852* (Belfast, 1852).

6. Griffin, "Scallions, Pikes and Bog Oak Ornaments."

7. IFC 1858:2.

8. IFC 770:204–5; IFC 969:178; IFC 1480:60–61, and 350–55; IFC 1018:326–29; IFC 1858:17, 103; IFC S35:350–52; IFC S167:272–74; IFC S222:619–20; IFC S742:21–22; IFC S758:52 and 435–36; IFC S759:209–11; IFC S760:127–33; IFC S763:141–43; IFC S1009:133–42; Hayes, *Last Invasion,* 234, 319; *Béaloideas* 14 (1944): 291.

9. IFC S23:25; IFC 1142:1–10; Hayes-McCoy, "Irish Pike," 120–21, 128; Hayes, *Last Invasion* (2nd ed.), 339; see also *An Claidheamh Soluis* 2, no. 45 (19 January 1901): 706. Pike drills in Ireland stem back to the seventeenth century; for example, Ormonde Papers, NLI MS B 5353; reproduced in *Irish Sword* 1 (1953): facing 180.

10. Peter Duignan of Gaigue, Ballinamuck; IFC 1858:17. This is the opening verse of the popular Fenian ballad "Rory of the Hill" by Charles Joseph Kickham.

11. Hayes-McCoy, "Irish Pike," 123. For Fenians displaying "old Croppy pikes" as an act of defiance see O'Donovan Rossa, *Rossa's Recollections*, 243–46.

12. For 1938, see "Wexford Makes Pikes Again for Ceremonies," *Irish Independent*, 16 May 1938. For 1998, see "Pike People" (RTÉ, 2000: director Angela Ryan); also *Irish Times*, 11 March 2000.

13. H. G. Leask, *Ancient Objects in Irish Bogs and Farm Lands: A Guide for the Finders / Neithe Ársa i bPortachaibh nó i bFeirmeachaibh Éireann* (Dublin: Department of Education, 1942).

14. Irish folk-life artifacts from the nineteenth and twentieth centuries were only given permanent exhibition space with the opening of the Museum of Country Life in Turlough Park, near Castlebar (2001).

15. The musket, inscribed "Mre. Rle. de St. Etienne," is stored in the National Museum's holdings and is not on public display. My thanks to Stephen Dunford of Killala for uncovering its whereabouts.

16. IFC 1858:104.

17. Collected by Bridie Beirne of Cloonmorris, Johnston's Bridge, Barnacoola, county Longford, from sixty-year-old Patrick McGlynn of Cloonart, Barnacoola; IFC S219:105, 110.

18. IFC 1858:14.

19. Collected from Patrick Dolan of Kiltycreevagh Cross; Hayes, *Last Invasion*, 229; IFC S758:460.

20. IFC S758:457; IFC S207:145.

21. For example, in 2001 Jimmy Breslin of Ballinamuck showed me a lead musket ball, which he found in a field sometime around 1968.

22. "Retracing Humbert's Footsteps," *Longford News*, 11 September 1998.

23. See *1798 Commemoration at Ballinamuck, County Longford: Sunday, September 11th, 1938: Souvenir Programme* (Longford: n.p., 1938).

24. In 1979 the exhibition was held in Ballymahon and prior to that it had been displayed for two years in Longford town and one year in Granard; *Longford News*, 13 July 1979.

25. IFC 1858:14.

26. Interview with Jimmy Breslin (b. 1934), Ballinamuck, 15 September 2001.

27. Interview with the former curator Mary MacNamara, Ballinamuck, 16 August 1999.

28. *Connaught Telegraph*, 17 June 1899, 4.

29. *Irish Sword* 3 (1957–58): 286.

30. Lyons, "Races of Castlebar," 44.

31. The cannon shell was discovered by Jarlath Dunford of Newport and has since been deposited in the Mayo County Library. The musket balls were found near Lannagh Lake and have since been lost. Information provided by Stephen Dunford, Killala.

32. Collected from Jim Halloran of Ballina; IFC S146:298.

33. Lyons, "Races of Castlebar," 43–44; interview with Ken Lyons, Castlebar, 21 August 2001.

34. K. Whelan, *Fellowship of Freedom*, 143.

35. Tonkin, *Narrating Our Pasts*, 94–96. For a pioneering study of Irish material culture and its folklore, see E. E. Evans, *Irish Folk Ways* (London: Routledge & Paul, 1957). Ireland's folk-life heritage was explored visually in the documentary series "Hidden Treasures" (RTÉ and BBC: 1998; director Anne O'Leary).

36. See for example G. E. Evans, *Where Beards Wag All* (London: Faber, 1970), 36–48.

37. *Longford News*, 17 May 1985.

38. John Carthy, "The McGee Gun—Jack McHale's Story," *Longford News*, 28 October 1983, 20; Terry Reilly, "Gunner McGee's Cannon," reprinted from the "Old Ballina" series in *Western People*; Rehill, "Years Before," in Rehill, *Ballinamuck Bi-Centenary*, 11.

39. Interview with Jimmy Gilvary, Ballynacola, Crossmolina, county Mayo, 10 August 2002.

40. Alan Radley, "Artefacts, Memory and a Sense of the Past," in Middleton and Edwards, *Collective Remembering*, 46–59.

41. Collected by Evelyn Geelan from Coote Geelan of Cloonagher, Barnacoola, county Longford; IFC S219:110 and 113–14.

42. Collected by Resa Carroll of Enniscrone [Inishcrone], county Sligo IFC S164:61.

43. Radley, "Artefacts, Memory and a Sense of the Past," 52.

44. Peter Collins, *Who Fears to Speak of '98?*, 49.

45. See for example *Connaught Telegraph*, 8, 22, 29 January and 5 February 1898.

46. *Mayo News*, 12 June 1948.

47. I am grateful to the Castlebar historian Ken Lyons for setting the record straight and to Ernie Sweeney for facilitating a visit to see the relic.

48. My thanks to Ms. Mary Gibbons of the staff of Westport House for allowing me access to this relic.

49. Mhac Ruaidhrí, *Lúb na Caillighe agus Sgéalta Eile*, 74–75.

50. Lavin, *History of the Civil Parish of Kilcummin*, 10; my thanks to local historian Sean Lavin for showing me these sites.

51. Collected by Nell Loftus from her grandmother, Mrs. Nealon of Banagher; IFC S141:303–4.

52. "The Bishop and the Castle," *Connaught Telegraph*, 11 September 1897, 1 (orig. pub. in the *Ballina Herald*).

53. IFC 1649:6.

54. See for example Patrick Geary, "Sacred Commodities: The Circulation of Medieval Relics," in *The Social Life of Things: Commodities in Cultural Perspective*, ed. Arjun Appudrai (Cambridge: Cambridge Univ. Press, 1986), 169–91.

55. Interview with eighty-one-year-old Jack Munnelly of Ross near Killala; Humbert Lodge pub, Killala, 16 September 2001.

56. Nealon's pub was demolished in the mid-1950s. The new public house in Banagher was later named the General Humbert and is currently the Kerryman's Inn. Humbert's Stone (which was split in two by the local blacksmith Tom Collins) can still be found in the parking lot and is marked with a sign; Lavin, *History of the Civil Parish of Kilcummin*, 42.

57. Hayes, *Last Invasion*, 216–17.

58. *Mayo News*, 28 August 1948. Also reported in *Western People*; see Carmel Hughes "150th Anniversary Commemorated in Ballina and Killala," *Bliainiris* 2 (1983–84): 35.

59. For Parnell's monument, see O'Keefe, "Art and Politics of the Parnell Monument."

60. Owens, "Nationalist Monuments," 110.

61. Hill, *Public Sculpture*, 135, 142–45.

62. Mac Giollarnáth, *Annála Beaga*, 65.

63. Barbara Kirshenblatt-Gimblett, "Objects of Memory: Material Culture as Life Review," in *Folk Groups and Folklore Genres: A Reader*, ed. Elliot Oring (Logan, UT: Utah State Univ. Press, 1989), 331.

64. Collected by Tony Donohue from John McNamara of Crossmolina; see Donohue, "Some Recollections," 37–38.

65. Collected by James Delaney from the child's great-grandnephew, seventy-six-year-old Patrick O'Reilly of Dromard, county Longford; IFC 1430:84–86.

66. Hayes, *Last Invasion*, 28.

67. See chap. 14, 243.

68. Noted by the schoolteacher Martin C. Dodd of St. Patrick's N.S. in Aughnacliffe, county Longford; IFC S761:195.

69. Lyons, "Races of Castlebar," 20.

70. Hayes, *Last Invasion*, 268.

71. Collected by Patrick Tohall from fifty-five-year-old Patrick Travers of Derrinvoney Lower (on the north shore of Lough Allen), county Leitrim; *Béaloideas* 14 (1944): 290–91.

72. IFC S195:315–16.

73. IFC 1858:102.

74. Otway, *Sketches in Erris and Tyrawley*, 219–20.

75. McTernan, *In Sligo Long Ago*, 512.

76. Interview with John Banks of the Teeling Sport's Centre, Collooney, 31 October 2001.

77. Donohue, "Some Recollections," 37.

78. Ó Loinsigh, *1798 Rebellion in Meath*, 56. My thanks to Mrs. Méadhbh Ní Chonmhidhe Pisorski for providing me with information that she had originally heard from her grandmother, the local historian Mrs. Margaret Conway.

79. See Stuart Semmel, "Reading the Tangible Past: British Tourism, Collecting, and Memory After Waterloo," *Representations* 69 (2000): 9–37.

80. Jill Hamilton, *The Myth of Napoleon's Horse* (London: Fourth Estate, 2001). The skeleton is currently on display at the National Army Museum in London.

81. Letter from Dr. Baldwin of Lancaster to the author Shan F. Bullock; reproduced in *Irish Book Lover* 5, no. 9 (April, 1914): 165–66.

82. See Shils, *Tradition*, 63–77.

83. See Igor Kopytoff, "The Cultural Biography of Things: Commodization as Process," in Appudrai, *Social Life of Things*, 64–91.

84. Semmel, "Reading the Tangible Past," 14.

Chapter 14

1. My thanks to John Daly for showing me the relics.

2. Police files include a biography of Daly that notes his central involvement in fundraising for the monument; NAI Crime Branch Special file 16005/S.

3. *Nation*, 13 May 1876. This report was based on an article in the *Connaught Telegraph*, 6 May 1876 (no existing copies remain), and descriptions of the coins were preserved in the newspaper's files; see Michael Mullen, "1876: A New Spirit," *Connaught Telegraph*, 19 and 26 December 1976.

4. Maurice Agulhon, "La 'statuomanie' et l'histoire," *Ethnologie Française* 3–4 (1978): 145–72.

5. For a general European overview see Hobsbawm, "Mass-Producing Traditions," 263–307; for the United States, see Piehler, *Remembering War*, 47–91.

6. See Yvonne Whelan, *Reinventing Modern Dublin: Streetscape, Iconography and the Politics of Identity* (Dublin: UCD Press, 2003), 53–80.

7. J. Hill, "Ideology and Cultural Production: Nationalism and the Public Monument in Mid-Nineteenth-Century Ireland," in Foley and Ryder, *Ideology and Ireland*, 55–68.

8. Potterton, *O'Connell Monument*.

9. For correspondence relating to this monument, see John Morisy, *A Wreath for the O'Brien Statue: Its Origin, Its Inauguration* (Dublin: N. Harding, 1871).

10. For a survey of nineteenth-century monuments, see J. Hill, *Irish Public Sculpture*, 84–118.

11. For a study of French national funerals, see Avner Ben-Amos, *Funerals, Politics, and Memory in Modern France, 1789–1996* (Oxford: Oxford Univ. Press, 2000).

12. See Robert Kee, *The Laurel and the Ivy: The Story of Charles Stewart Parnell and Irish Nationalism* (London: Hamish Hamilton, 1993), 5–12.

13. Hobsbawm, "Mass-Producing Traditions," 263.

14. O'Keefe, "1898 Efforts to Celebrate the United Irishmen."

15. O'Keefe, "Who Fears to Speak of '98?"

16. Paseta, "1798 in 1898." For the "New Nationalism," see Foster, *Modern Ireland*, 431–60.

17. Bull, "The Centenary of 1798 and the 'Old Nationalism,'" in Bull, Devlin-Glass, and Doyle, *Ireland and Australia*, 80–89.

18. See Patrick Maume, *The Long Gestation: Irish Nationalist Life 1891–1918* (Dublin: Gill & Macmillan, 1999), 48–49.

19. *Freeman's Journal*, 6 March 1897.

20. *Connaught Telegraph*, 24 April 1897.

21. Ibid., 29 May 1897.

22. NAI Crime Branch Special file 15200/S (1898).

23. For example, the Castlebar committee met on a monthly basis over the second half of 1897; *Connaught Telegraph*, 29 May, 3 July, 21 August, and 2 October 1897.

24. Jordan, *Land and Popular Politics in Ireland*, 313.

25. Originally appeared in *Contemporary Review* 73 (1898): 14–34.

26. Fergus Campbell, *Land and Revolution*, 30; William O'Brien, *An Olive Branch in Ireland and Its History* (London: Macmillan, 1910), 89.

27. For example, *Connaught Telegraph*, 22 January 1898; *Freeman's Journal*, 28 January 1898; *United Ireland*, 29 January 1898; *Nation*, 10 February 1898; *Sligo Champion*, 12 November 1898. See also Bull, "Centenary of 1798," 85–87.

28. Paul Bew, *Conflict and Conciliation in Ireland, 1890–1910* (New York: Oxford Univ. Press, 1987), 34–69.

29. Campbell, *Land and Revolution*, 30.

30. William O'Brien, *Recollections* (London: Macmillan, 1905), 225; cited in Marie-Louise Legg, *Oxford Dictionary of National Biography* (Oxford: Oxford Univ. Press, 2004), s.v. "Daly, James" (ca. 1840–1911).

31. Lee, *Modernisation of Irish Society*, 69.

32. See *Connaught Telegraph*, 25 March 1911; Bew, *Land and the National Question*; Philip Bull, *Land, Politics and Nationalism* (Dublin: Gill & Macmillan, 1996), 136; Jordan, *Land and Popular Politics*, 265–77; Moody, *Davitt*; G. Moran, "James Daly"; O'Hara, *Mayo*, 260–61. See also biographical information on Daly on the *Connaught Telegraph* website: http://www.connaughttelegraph.net.

33. For the importance of the *Connaught Telegraph* in spreading Land League activities, see Legg, *Newspapers and Nationalism*, 16, 119, and 139–40.

34. Fr. Conefry is credited as the primary author of *A Short History of the Land War in Drumlish in 1881, by An Irish Priest* (Dublin: James Duffy, 1892); see John Carthy, "Who Wrote 'The Land War,'" *Longford News*, 28 December 1979. His contribution was acknowledged in the centennial of the Land War in county Longford, celebrated in July 1981; *Longford Leader*, 17 July 1981. See also John Carthy, "Soggarth Aroon," in Rehill, *Ballinamuck Bi-Centenary*, 52–54.

35. *Freeman's Journal*, 16 August 1898.

36. See *Connaught Telegraph*, 21 August, 2 and 23 October 1897.

37. *Irish Independent*, 10 January 1898; *Connaught Telegraph*, 15 January and 19 February 1898.

38. *Sligo Champion*, 8 January 1898.

39. *Freeman's Journal*, 1 and 5 January 1898; *Sligo Champion*, 5 and 8 January 1898; referred to also in the *Connaught Telegraph*, 22 January 1898.

40. NAI Crime Special Branch, Box 13 (1898).

41. *Sligo Champion*, 28 May and 4 June 1898.

42. See Gribayédoff, *French Invasion*, 106.

43. See Danaher, *Year in Ireland*, 134–44.

44. Information from the *Longford Leader*, researched by Paul Davis and incorporated in Padraig Rehill, "Who Fears to Speak of '98," in Rehill, *Ballinamuck Bi-Centenary*, 126.

45. *Connaught Telegraph*, 3 July 1897, 4.

46. Ibid., 22 January 1898.

47. Ibid., 22 May 1897.

48. O'Keefe, "Who Fears to Speak of '98?" 69 and 86.

49. TCD Dillon Papers, Elizabeth Dillon's Diary, 30 August 1898; cited in Kinsella, "Who Feared to Speak in '98?" 229.

50. *Westmeath Examiner*, 11 December 1897.

51. *Connaught Telegraph*, 27 August 1898.

52. Ibid., 3 September 1898. A monster meeting was held in Castlebar in 1843; Owens, "Nationalism without Words," 243.

53. O'Keefe, "Who Fears to Speak of '98?" 75–77.

54. C. J. Woods, "Tone's Grave at Bodenstown."

55. *Nation*, 7 February 1898.

56. See C. J. Woods, "R. R. Madden, Historian of the United Irishmen," in Bartlett et al., *1798*, 497–511. For the publication of Madden's magnum opus see T. M. Madden, *Memoirs . . . of Richard Robert Madden*, 163–66.

57. *United Ireland*, 16 March 1895.

58. Whelan, *Tree of Liberty*, 169–72; Kinsella, "1798 Claimed for the Catholics"; see also Kinsella, "'Who Fears to Speak of '98?'" (MLitt thesis, TCD, 1985).

59. For example, *Nation*, 4 February 1898.

60. See Turpin, "1798 . . . Sheppard's Monuments."

61. Hill, *Public Sculpture*, 118–36, esp. 133–34; N. C. Johnson, "Sculpting Heroic Histories."

62. Owens, "Nationalist Monuments," 110, 112–15.

63. *Western People*, 11 May 1899.

64. A prominent example in Dublin is the moving of the William Smith O'Brien statue in 1929 to O'Connell Street, where it was overshadowed by O'Connell's monument; see Hill, *Public Sculpture*, 103–4.

65. Hill, *Public Sculpture*, 135.

66. *Freeman's Journal*, 3 October 1898.

67. McTernan, *In Sligo Long Ago*, 499–500.

68. *Sligo Champion*, 8 October 1898.

69. Ibid., 9 September 1899; see also McTernan, *In Sligo Long Ago*, 504–7, 510.

70. *Sligo Champion*, 27 August 1898.

71. See Bruce Arnold, *Jack Yeats* (New Haven: Yale Univ. Press, 1998), 78–79.

72. *Sligo Champion*, 10 September 1898 and 8 July 1899; see also McTernan, *In Sligo Long Ago*, 501–4, 506, 509.

73. *Sligo Champion*, 10 June 1899.

74. Interview with Attracta Brownlee, Research Officer at the Teeling Center in Collooney, 31 October 2001.

75. Gonne had raised funds on the committee's behalf in the United States (1897). See "The Centennial Association," in Gould, Kelly, and Toomey, *Collected Letters of W. B. Yeats*, vol. 2, *1896–1900*, 695–707; Toomey, "Who Fears to Speak of Ninety-Eight?" 209–61.

76. Anna MacBride White and A. N. Jeffares, eds., *Gonne-Yeats Letters*, 93.

77. *Irish Independent*, 10 January 1898; *Connaught Telegraph*, 15 January 1898.

78. NAI Crime Special Branch, Box 13 (1898).

79. *Freeman's Journal*, 22 August 1898; *Connaught Telegraph*, 27 August 1898. See also Margaret Ward, *Maud Gonne: Ireland's Joan of Arc* (London: Pandora, 1990), 49–51 and 53.

80. See for example *Connaught Telegraph*, 8 and 15 January 1898.

81. *Connaught Telegraph*, 19 February 1898; appeared originally in the *Shan Van Vocht* 3, no. 2 (7 February 1898): 25.

82. For a photograph see Murray and Cullen, *Epitaph of 1798*, 91.

83. Collected by Margaret Lynn of Cortoon in Killala from her mother, Mrs. A. Lynn; IFC S144:21.

84. Griffith, *Poems and Ballads*, ix. See also J. Mathews, "A Battle of Two Civilizations? D. Moran and William Rooney," *Irish Review* 29 (2002): 21–37.

85. Griffith, *Poems and Ballads*, 125.

86. Ibid., 146–48. Translated into Irish by Conchúr Mag Uidhir as "Muintir an Iarthair," the ballad won a prize in Feis Mhaigh Eo, 1903; Ó Brádaigh, *Songs of 1798*, 5–6. It was sung to the air of "Eoghan Cóir," a song attributed to the eighteenth-century Mayo poet Richard Barrett, who was incarcerated in 1798; see Williams, *Riocard Bairéad*, 70–71.

87. Seán Ó hEislin of Ballinamore Boys School in county Leitrim; IFC S225:147.

88. *Connaught Telegraph*, 3 September 1898.

89. See Schwartz, "Reconstruction of Abraham Lincoln," in Middleton and Edwards, *Collective Remembering*, 81–107.

90. From the resolutions proposed by the chairman Fr. Thomas Conefry and adopted unanimously at the main commemorative meeting in Ballinamuck; *Westmeath Examiner*, 10 September 1898.

91. For example, see "French Invasion of Ireland," *Connaught Telegraph*, 27 August 1898 (originally published in the influential Irish-American newspaper *Irish World*).

92. McTernan, *In Sligo Long Ago*, 501–4.

93. *Sligo Champion*, 10 September 1898.

94. *Freeman's Journal*, 6 September and 3 October 1898.

95. See McTernan, *Here's To Their Memory*, 397–401.

96. For a collection of his poetry see John O'Dowd, *Lays of South Sligo: A Few Wild Flowers of National Poetry*, 2nd ed. (Dublin: M. H. Gill & Son, 1889).

97. *Connaught Telegraph*, 27 August 1898.

98. Collected in 1936 by Elizabeth Benson; IFC S185:26–30.

99. See Joannon, *La Descente de Français*, 16 (General Sarrazin), 79–80 (General Fontaine), 38–39 (Captain Jobit); Van Brock,

"A Memoir of 1798," 201–2 (Sergeant-Major Thomas)—which confuses Collooney with Cloone.

100. Teeling Papers, TCD R. R. Madden Papers MS 873, nos. 8a–25; Teeling, *History of the Irish Rebellion*, 314–22; also: J. B. Daly, ed., *Ireland in '98*, 375–400.

101. See Jones, *An Impartial Narrative*, 266–7 (report of Colonel Charles Vereker written in Sligo on 30 September 1798); *Dublin Journal*, 18 September 1798 (letter written in Sligo, dated 6 September 1798); Hewitt Papers, National Army Museum 5910–198 f. 133a (Captain Cripps of the Limerick Militia); Humphrey Thomson, "Personal Narrative," BOD MS Eng. Hist. d. 155, f. 132; see also *Sligo Journal*, 14 September 1798 (reproduced in *Dublin Journal*, 18 September 1798, and *Saunders's News-Letter*, 19 September 1798).

102. O'Rorke, *History of Sligo*, vol. 1, 375.

103. Teeling, *History of the Irish Rebellion*, 307.

104. Letters of Margaret Dobin (née Cochrane), written in 1875, TCD MS 10354; see also *Some Recollections of Hugh McCall* (Lisburn: J. E. Reilly, 1899), 8–9.

105. IFC S760:129; IFC 1858:8, 103.

106. See for example "How Bartholomew Teeling Behaved at Carrig-na-Gat," *Irish Packet* 12, no. 300 (1909): 403 (based on O'Rorke's history).

107. Richard Hayes Papers, NLI MS 13799 (9).

108. See "Local Politics and Nation-building: The Grassroots of Nationalist Hegemony," in Mac Laughlin, *Reimagining the Nation-State*, 247–77.

109. *Longford Leader*, 14 May 1960, 11; Ó Suilleabháin, *A Biographical Dictionary*.

110. Farrell, *Historical Notes*, 104–6 and 112.

111. *Freeman's Journal*, 6 March 1897.

112. "Great Meeting at Ballinamuck," *Westmeath Examiner*, 10 September 1898. John Redmond (1856–1918), leader of the Parnellite faction and soon to be leader of the reunited Irish Parliamentary Party, sent his apologies, and a telegram from Maud Gonne was read publicly.

113. Collected from forty-year-old Alice McLoughlin of Kiltycreevagh; IFC S758:323–25; and also from John Brady of Kiltycon (5 kilometers from Ballinamuck); S760:435–37. McLouglin's version mentions an attendance of 50,000 whereas Brady refers to 30,000 people.

114. IFC S760:437.

115. *Record of the Ballinamuck Bicentenary Commemoration 1798–1998*, 29 and 33.

116. Collected by Brígid M. Ní Ghamhnáin from her fifty-four-year-old father Séan O'Ghamhnáin of Baile-an-Dúin, Manistear [Mainistir] na Buaile, county Sligo, who had originally heard it performed by Tomás O'Láingin of Baile na gCarraigh, county Sligo, ca. 1907; IFC 339:290–92.

117. O'Keefe, "Who Fears to Speak of '98?" 71.

118. *Anglo-Celt*, 16 December 1899; IFC S1009:133–42.

119. Notes written by Henry Taaffe and given by his son John to Richard Hayes; Richard Hayes Papers, NLI MS 13799 (7) (purple notebook).

120. *Connaught Telegraph*, 27 August 1898, 5.

121. Ibid., 28 September 1899, 3.

122. Ibid., 27 May 1899, 5. For a brief account of James (Jamsie) Morris, a member of the committee who ran for a seat on the Mayo County Council, see Willie Costello, *A Connacht Man's Ramble: Recollections of Growing Up in the Rural Ireland of the Thirties and Forties* (Dublin: Edmund Burke, 1999), 94–96.

123. For example, *Connaught Telegraph*, 10 and 24 June, 3 and 22 July, 16 and 28 September, 21 October, and 18 November 1899. Notices also include acknowledgements for publicity given in the *Weekly Freeman*, *Mayo News*, *Western People*, and *Irish World*.

124. Hill, *Public Sculpture*, 122, 132, 149.

125. See Owens, "Constructing the Martyrs."

126. For a photograph see Murray and Cullen, *Epitaph of 1798*, 93.

127. Collected from sixty-five-year-old

James O'Connell of Wingfield, Knock, county Mayo; IFC S108:258–60.

128. Henry Taaffe insisted that he met Cunniffe at the age of ninety, "though in crutches when I saw him"; Richard Hayes Papers, NLI MS 13799 (7).

129. Quinn, *History of Mayo*, vol. 1, 158. Contrary to a claim advanced by the folklore collector Pádraig Ó Moghráin, the hall was not demolished in 1918 but remained intact until the late 1920s; Ó Moghráin, "Gearr-Chunntas," 22; T. Hughes, "Fr. Manus Sweeney," 42.

130. A photograph of the monument is available on the website: www.achill247.com/pictures/burrishoole-7.html.

131. Quinn, *History of Mayo*, vol. 1, 157–59 (the ceremony is mistakenly dated to 1922); *Mayo News*, 15 June 1912.

132. *Mayo News*, 15 June 1912. Extracts from a similar lecture delivered three days later (12 June 1912) were preserved by Fr. Martin O'Donnell's brother; Patrick O'Donnell Papers, IFC Box 15.

133. Hill, *Public Sculpture*, 136.

134. See Kinsella, "Who Feared to Speak in 1898?" 229.

135. See L. Gibbons, "Where Wolfe Tone's Statue Was Not."

136. Rehill, "Who Fears to Speak of '98," 128–29.

137. *Longford Leader*, 9 and 15 September 1928. For contemporary photographs of the monument and the unveiling ceremony see *Longford Year Book 1929*, 48–49.

138. Donohue, "Michael Timoney," 25–26.

139. *Irish Independent*, 30 July 1937.

140. IFC 1649:3–6; Michael Timoney Papers, IFC Box (unnumbered).

141. MacHale, "Some Mayo Priests of 1798," 11–12.

142. Griffith, *Poems and Ballads*, 141–45. For an early historical account of Fr. Conroy's involvement in the Rebellion see Musgrave, *Memoirs of the Different Rebellions*, 543–44.

143. Patrick Bradey, introduction to Griffith, *Poems and Ballads*, xxiv–v.

144. Donohue, *Local Songs*, 9–10.

145. For example, IFC S89:435–37; IFC S94:244; IFC S141:22–23; Hayes, *Last Invasion*, 222.

146. *Connaught Telegraph*, 20 August 1938, 5.

147. See "Sites of Death, Burial, and Supernatural Encounters" in chap. 12.

148. See Trotter, *Walks Through Ireland*, 476.

149. See "Priests Associated With the Rising in 1798," *Connaught Telegraph*, 29 August 1953, 4.

150. "níl aon ní dá gcuidíonn le ainm agus gníomhartha na dtír-ghrádhuitheoirí a chuaidh romhainn a choinneáil go buan i gcuimhne do na daoine, nach dtuilleann a mholadh"; Ó Moghráin, "Gearr-Chunntas," 23.

151. See Scott, *Domination and the Arts of Resistance*.

152. Ballinamuck Community Association Minute Book, 18 May 1982. My thanks to Jimmy Breslin of Ballinamuck, the secretary of the association at the time, for allowing me access to select documents.

153. Owens, "Nationalist Monuments," 108–9. For a discussion on the importance of monuments for the study of national identity, see Nuala Johnson, "Cast in Stone: Monuments, Geography and Nationalism," *Environment and Planning D: Society and Space* 113 (1995): 51–65.

154. Written by Seán de Eintlár; IFC 172:493.

155. Novick, *Holocaust and Collective Memory*, 276.

156. J. E. Young, "The Biography of a Memorial Icon."

157. IFC 1858:97–98; IFC S758:255; IFC S759:211; IFC S760:477; IFC S760:477; IFC Box S759a: copybook of James Hourican; IFC Box S761d: copybook of Peter Sheridan.

158. *Longford Leader*, 15 September 1928; see also Patrick Murray, *Oracles of God: The Roman Catholic Church and Irish Politics* (Dublin: UCD Press, 2000), 120–21.

159. Rehill, "Who Fears to Speak of '98," 130.

160. Other sites maintained by the NGA

include Wolfe Tone's grave at Bodenstown in county Kildare, the Roddy McCorley memorial at Toomebridge in county Antrim, and the pikeman monument at Tralee in county Kerry. See Collins, "The Contest of Memory," 44–45.

161. *Longford Leader*, 17 September 1938.

162. This is particularly apparent in copybooks from Annaghmore [Eanach Mór]; IFC Box S222a: copybook of Mary O'Boy (5th grade); IFC Box S222b: copybooks of Kathleen O'Brien (6th grade), and Charles Bohan (7th grade).

163. *Longford Leader*, 25 September 1948.

164. Recollections of Dick Monahan of Muckerstaff, Coolarty, county Longford; "Remembering 1798," *Longford News*, 11 September 1998, 19.

165. See the booklet *Granard in 1798* (published by the Granard Harp Festival); reproduced in the Local Ireland website at http://longford.local.ie/content/765.shtml/granard/history/ general. For a photograph see Murray and Cullen, *Epitaph of 1798*, 89.

166. *Sligo Champion*, 9 October 1948; *Sligo Independent*, 9 October 1948.

167. My thanks to the Collooney Research Officer Attracta Brownlee for presenting me with a copy of the transcript of an interview with Pat Noone from 22 April 1998 and for information on other local people who recalled the commemoration in 1948 (including Pat Joe McNulty and the local TD Mattie Brennan).

168. See McTernan, *In Sligo Long Ago*, 508.

169. "Mayo in '98," (letter to the editor by Seamus O'Rian, dated 5 August 1936) *Irish Press*, 10 August 1936.

170. M. C. Boyer, *The City of Collective Memory: Its Historical Imagery and Architectural Entertainments* (Cambridge, MA: Harvard Univ. Press, 1996).

171. Samuel, "Reading the Runes," 354.

172. Maoz Azaryahu, "German Reunification and the Politics of Street Names: The Case of East Berlin," *Political Geography* 16, no. 6 (1997): 481.

173. See Maoz Azaryahu, "The Power of Commemorative Street Names," *Environment and Planning D: Society and Space* 14 (1996): 311–30.

174. For a case study based in the southern United States see Derek H. Alderman, "A Street Fit for a King: Naming Places and Commemoration in the American South," *Professional Geographe*, 52, no. 4 (2000): 672–84, and Alderman, "Street Names and the Scaling of Memory: The Politics of Commemorating Martin Luther King Jr Within the African American community," *Area* 35, no. 2 (2003): 163–73.

175. For objections to the renaming of Sackville Street to O'Connell Street see Yvonne Whelan, *Reinventing Modern Dublin*, 101–3.

176. See Linnane et al., *Heritage Trail of Castlebar*; my thanks to the Castlebar historian Ernie Sweeney for forwarding me this material.

177. Hayes, *Last Invasion*, 282.

178. Letter to the editor from Henry Hoban of Pearse Street in Castlebar; *Irish Press*, 3 June 1938.

179. An article on Humbert appeared in *Connaught Telegraph*, 27 August 1938; a piece on O'Kane (syndicated from *Irish Independent*) appeared in *Connaught Telegraph*, 10 September 1938.

180. *Connaught Telegraph*, 20 August 1938.

181. Hayes, *Last Invasion*, 281.

182. *Connaught Telegraph*, 7 August 1948.

183. *Irish Independent*, 2 August 1948; *Connaught Telegraph*, 7 and 14 August 1948; *Mayo News*, 7 August 1948. Photographs of the dignitaries visiting Castlebar were later published in *Castlebar Parish Magazine*, Christmas 1988, 23.

184. *Connaught Telegraph*, 28 August 1948.

185. *Mayo News*, 7 August 1948.

186. *Exhibition Programme: '98 Commemoration Ceremonies, Castlebar, August 1, 1948* ('98 Commemoration Committee, county Mayo; Castlebar, 1948).

187. For a photograph see Murray and Cullen, *Epitaph of 1798*, 96.

188. J. S. Donnelly, "The Peak of Marian-

ism in Ireland, 1930–60," in *Piety and Power in Ireland 1760–1960: Essays in Honour of Emmet Larkin,* eds. Stewart J. Brown and David W. Miller (Notre Dame, IN: Univ. of Notre Dame Press, 2000), 252–83.

189. *Connaught Telegraph,* 5 September 1953.

190. For example, *Connaught Telegraph,* 8, 22, and 29 August, and 5 September 1953.

191. *Connaught Telegraph,* 5 September 1953.

192. See Hayes, *Last Invasion of Ireland,* 243 and 328.

193. For a photograph see Murray and Cullen, *Epitaph of 1798,* 122.

194. Thirty-seven years later, in the bicentenary, a monument to John Moore was unveiled in Muinebheag; *Irish Times,* 7 September 1998; for a photograph see Murray and Cullen, *Epitaph of 1798,* 12.

195. Quoted from the inscription on the monument in the Castlebar Mall.

196. *Connaught Telegraph,* 19 August 1961. For excerpts from the commemorative booklet issued for the event see *Connaught Telegraph,* 12 August 1961.

197. Interviews with Judge John Garavan (b. 1933), who had been a member of the local commemoration committee in 1961, and Sean Murphy (b. 1919) from the area of Moorehall; Daly's Hotel, Castlebar, 28 February 2003.

198. *Connaught Telegraph,* 11 March 1998.

199. Kiberd, "Elephant of Revolutionary Forgetfulness," 1–20; see also interview with Catriona Crowe of the National Archives of Ireland in *Seven Ages* (RTÉ: 2000, producer Seán Ó Mórdha), episode 5.

200. An examination of academic citations in the social sciences (SSCI) and in the arts and humanities (A&HCI) indices confirms the canonical status of the "Invention of Tradition" thesis associated with an influential collection of essays edited by Hobsbawm and Ranger, which from the mid-1980s has been referred to axiomatically in hundred of articles and books. See Hobsbawm and Ranger, *Invention of Tradition.*

201. See Michael Schudson, "The Present in the Past versus the Past in the Present," *Communication* 11 (1989): 105–13.

202. Anthony D. Smith, "The Nation: Invented, Imagined, Reconstructed?" in *Reimagining the Nation,* eds. Marjorie Ringrose and Adam J. Lerner (Buckingham: Open Univ. Press, 1993), 9–28, esp. 16; A. D. Smith, "Gastronomy or Geology? The Role of Nationalism in the Reconstruction of Nations," *Nations and Nationalism* 1, no. 1 (1995): 3–23, esp. 16–17.

203. For examples based on studies of the Middle East, see Bernard Lewis, *History: Remembered, Recorded and Invented* (Princeton: Princeton Univ. Press, 1975).

204. Ó Duignéain, "Ballinamuck and '98," 43.

205. Interview with Jimmy Gilvary of Ballynacola (b. 1931), 10 August 2002.

206. See *An Claidheamh Soluis* 4, no. 27 (13 September 1902): 447.

207. For older photographs of the monument see NLI William Lawrence Photograph Collection, Royal 6046–7 (a photo listed in the index of the Crime Branch Special files appears to have been misplaced; CBS 18502/S 8.2.1899).

208. See Séamas S. de Vál, *Bun Clóidí: A History of the District down to the Beginning of the Twentieth Century* (Bunclody: Séamas S. de Vál, 1966), 250; for a photograph, see Murray and Cullen, *Epitaph of 1798,* 147.

209. *Connaught Telegraph,* 15 January 1898.

210. D'Alton, "The French in Mayo, 1798," 225.

211. Hayes, *Last Invasion,* 281.

Chapter 15

1. See Daly and Dickson, *Origins of Popular Literacy in Ireland.*

2. H.C. 1912–13, vol. 117, 238.

3. See Kevin Whelan, "Writing Ireland: Reading England," in *Ireland in the Nineteenth Century: Regional Identity,* eds. Leon Litvack and Glen Hooper (Dublin: Four Courts Press, 2000), 185–98.

4. Ó Ciosáin, *Print and Popular Culture*, esp. 75–78.

5. Penny Fielding, *Writing and Orality: Nationality, Culture and Nineteenth-Century Scottish Fiction* (Oxford: Oxford Univ. Press, 1996).

6. Leerssen, *Remembrance and Imagination*; Leerssen, "1798: Recurrence of Violence."

7. Aki Nikolai Kalliomäki, "Who Dares To Write of '98? " (MLitt thesis, TCD, 2000), 6–41.

8. Letter 7, originally published in the Edinburgh Review (1807) and reissued in a collection (1808), which quickly ran through sixteen editions. See *The Works of the Rev. Sydney Smith* (Boston: Sampson & Company, 1857), 468–69.

9. Mitchel, *History of Ireland*, 349–55.

10. Froude, *English in Ireland*, 538–40.

11. Lecky, *History of Ireland*, vol. 5, 41–68 (quotation from page 47; for list of sources see page 42 n. 2).

12. See D. Sampson, "The French Expedition to Ireland in 1798," *Dublin Review*, 4th ser., 121, no. 23 (July 1897): 60–79.

13. *Macmillan's Magazine* 77 (1898): 227.

14. Falkiner, *Studies in Irish History*, 251.

15. *Nation* [New York], 86, no. 2225 (20 February 1908), 162. Gribayédoff saw himself as following in the footsteps of others; Valerian Gribayédoff, "Pictorial Journalism," *Cosmopolitan* 11, no. 4 (August 1891): 471–81.

16. Gribayédoff, *French Invasion of Ireland*, 66–69; see chap. 15, 288 and fig. 34.

17. *Western People*, 23 and 30 May 1891.

18. *Irish Weekly Independent*, 22 and 29 December 1894.

19. Including *Aegis and Western Courier* (Castlebar, 1841–42), *Ballina Advertiser, Mayo and Sligo Commercial Gazette* (Ballina, 1840–43), *Ballina Chronicle* (1849–51), *Ballina Herald* (1844–1962), *Ballina Journal and Connaught Advertiser* (Ballina, 1880–95), *Ballinrobe Chronicle and Mayo Advertiser* (Ballinrobe, 1866–1903), *Connaught Telegraph* (Castlebar, 1834–present), *Connaught Watchman* (Ballina, 1851–63), *Mayo Examiner and West of Ireland Agricultural and Commercial Reporter and Advertiser* (Castlebar, 1868–1903), *Mayo Mercury and Connaught Advertiser* (Castlebar, 1840–41), *Mayo News* (Westport, 1892–present), *Telegraph, Or Connaught Ranger* (Castlebar, 1830–70), *Tyrawley Herald, Or Mayo and Sligo Intelligencer* (Ballina, 1844–70), *Western Gem* (Ballina, 1843), *Western People* (Ballina, 1883–present), and *Western Star* (Ballina, 1835–37). See J. O'Toole, *Newsplan*.

20. Including the *Longford Independent and Westmeath Advertiser* (1868–1900), *Longford Journal* (1839–1937), *Longford Leader, Cavan, Leitrim, Roscommon and Westmeath News* (1897–present), *Longford Messenger and General Advertiser for the Counties of Longford, Westmeath, Cavan and Leitrim* (1837), and the *Midlands Counties Gazette* (1853–63). See J. O'Toole, *Newsplan*.

21. Most notably the *Westmeath Examiner* (published in Mullingar from 1882).

22. For distribution in Mayo based on the records of the prominent newsagent D. Wynne of Castlebar see Legg, *Newspapers and Nationalism*, 149–55.

23. See L. W. McBride, "Nationalist Constructions," 117–18, n. 4.

24. See Mac Laughlin, *Reimagining the Nation-State*, 187–209, esp. 203–6; Legg, *Newspapers and Nationalism*; Paul A. Townend, "'Academies of Nationality': The Reading Room and Irish National Movements, 1835–1905," in L. W. McBride, *Reading Irish Histories*, 19–39.

25. See James Loughlin, "Constructing the Political Spectacle: Parnell, the Press and National Leadership, 1879–86," in *Parnell in Perspective*, eds. D. George Boyce and Alan O'Day (London: Routledge, 1991), 221–41; Anne Kane, "The Ritualization of Newspaper Reading and Political Consciousness: The Role of Newspapers in the Irish Land War," in L. W. McBride, *Reading Irish Histories*, 40–61.

26. Greer, *Windings of the Moy*, 15.

27. *Ballina Herald*, 27 August–22 October 1927; *An Phoblacht*, 29 April–15 October 1927.

28. *Western People*, 19 September 1931.

29. Joseph McGarrity, "The French at Killala in '98," *Clan-na-Gael Emmet Anniversary Magazine* (14 March 1914): 11–27.

30. Joseph McGarrity Papers NLI MS 17559.

31. *Moore's Irish Melodies* (10 vols.; 1808–34) continued the literary tradition of the United Irishmen; see Thuente, *Harp Restrung*, esp. chaps. 6 and 7. Moore also wrote *The Life and Death of Lord Edward Fitzgerald* (1831) and the anonymously published *Memoirs of Captain Rock* (1824), which incorporated subtle references to the Rebellion; see T. O'Sullivan, "Violence of a Servile War," 74–76, 82–87.

32. *Nation*, 13 April 1844. The newspaper reached a peak of 13,000 copies per issue under its founding editor, Charles Gavan Duffy; see Barbara Hayley, "Reading and Thinking the Nation: Periodicals as the Voice of Nineteenth-Century Ireland," in *Three Hundred Years of Irish Periodicals*, eds. Barbara Hayley and Enda McKay (Mullingar: Lilliput Press, 1987), 40–41.

33. *Nation*, 22 July 1843.

34. See Foster, *Modern Ireland*, 311–13.

35. Ryder, "Speaking '98"; republished in a revised version as "Young Ireland and the 1798 Rebellion," in Geary, *Rebellion and Remembrance*, 135–47.

36. See McCormick, *Irish Rebellion*, 18–19.

37. Originally published in the *Weekly Freeman* and reproduced in the *Connacht Telegraph*, 4 September 1897, 1.

38. For a bibliography of Irish political ballads including collections of broadside ballads and song books and a list of nationalist newspapers that published songs, see Zimmermann, *Irish Songs of Rebellion*, 321–28.

39. For example, Denis Devereux, *Songs and Ballads of '98* (Dublin: J. Duffy, 1898); Charles Welsh, *Who Fears to Speak of Ninety-Eight Song Book* (London, 1910); Rev. Joseph Ranson, *Songs and Ballads of '98* (Wexford, 1938); M. J. Murphy, *The Ninety-Eight Song Book* (Dublin, 1942).

40. Thuente, "Folklore of Irish Nationalism," 42–43.

41. *Nation*, 1 April 1843. For the ballad's reception and the ambivalent attitude of the author, who was associated with Young Ireland but became a Unionist, see J. R. McKeown, "The Memory of the Dead," *Irish News*, 16 September 1948.

42. Duffy et al., *Spirit of the Nation*, 44–45; see also Zimmermann, *Irish Songs of Rebellion*, 227.

43. See Owens, "Popular Mobilisation," 54.

44. O'Keefe, "Who Fears to Speak of '98?" 74–75. Two loyalist songs titled "Who Fears to Speak of '98" were written in response and published in the *Crimson Ballad Song Book* (Belfast: J. Nicholson, 1911), 61–63 and 106–7; see Zimmermann, *Irish Songs of Rebellion*, 303.

45. *Connaught Telegraph*, 27 August 1898.

46. Hill, *Public Sculpture*, 127.

47. See Curtis, *Images of Erin*.

48. See Owens, "Nationalist Monuments," 114–15.

49. Hill, *Public Sculpture*, 128–32.

50. See McTernan, *In Sligo Long Ago*, 510–11; for a photograph see Murray and Cullen, *Epitaph of 1798*, 94.

51. Lucas, *Infernal Quixote*, 319 and 345.

52. Mangin, *Oddities and Outlines*, 104–6. For his eyewitness account, see Mangin, *Parlour Window*, 33–45.

53. See Dunne, "Representations of Rebellion," in *Ireland, England and Australia: Essays in Honour of Oliver MacDonagh*, ed. F. B. Smith (Cork: Cork University Press, 1990), 14–40.

54. Echoes of the Edgeworth family's experiences in county Longford at the time of the French invasion can be detected in Maria Edgeworth's *Castle Rackrent* (Dublin, 1800), and the Rebellion appears more overtly in her *Ennui* (London, 1809).

55. Having spent time in the West of Ireland, Maturin located in Connacht a fictional rebellion described in *The Milesian Chief* (London, 1812, 4 vols.), although the only scenes that resemble historical events from 1798 are descriptions of defeated rebels taking

refuge in caves in Connemara and resorting to banditry (vol. 3).

56. Owenson, *The O'Briens and the O'Flahertys* (London, 1827), 4 vols.

57. Colburn published a British edition of the *Memoirs of Wolfe Tone* (1827), of Charles Hamilton Teeling's *Personal Narrative of the Irish Rebellion of 1798* (1828), and of Thomas Crofton Croker's edited version of the *Memoirs of Joseph Holt* (1838).

58. McHenry, *O'Halloran*, 476–86. The title slightly varies in different editions.

59. Anon. [Matthew Archdeacon], *Connaught.*

60. Archdeacon, *Legends of Connaught* (Dublin: John Cumming, 1839), 354–71.

61. W. H. Maxwell, *Adventures of Captain Blake*, 65–116.

62. W. H. Maxwell, *O'Hara; or, 1798* (London: Andrews, 1825), 2 vols.

63. Maxwell, *History of the Irish Rebellion*, 220–71.

64. See chap. 5, 88.

65. Lever, *Maurice Tierney*, 161–319.

66. Hayes, *Last Invasion*, 16 and 258. Kerrigan is also mentioned in an eyewitness account of the French landing probably written by a son of Bishop Joseph Stock; see Anon. [A. I.], "Landing of the French at Killala," 392 (reproduced also in Croker, *Popular Songs*, part 4, 75).

67. *Dublin University Magazine* 18 (September 1841): 300–301; republished in Otway, *Sketches in Erris and Tyrawley*, 216–18. For Lever's involvement with the journal, see Wyne E. Hall, *Dialogues in the Margin: A Study of the Dublin University Magazine* (Buckinghamshire: n.p., 2000), esp. 108–36 and 167–68.

68. Eileen Reilly, "Who Fears to Speak of '98?" esp. 125, 119, 126 n. 7.

69. J. Murphy, *Shan Van Vocht*, 301.

70. McDonnell, *Kathleen Mavourneen*, 181–83.

71. Bram Stoker, *The Snake's Pass* (Dingle: Brandon, 1990; orig. ed. 1890), see in particular 24–25. For a brief discussion on this novel and its representation of Irish history, see L. Gibbons, "'Some Historical Hatred,'" 13–16.

72. Aiden Brett of Garryduff, Castlebar, a local historian and collector of 1798 lore and memorabilia, recounted this story in August 2001, noting that he had originally heard it from Michael Fergus, a Christian Brother of De La Salle order.

73. Martin J. Blake traced the marriage of Bram Stoker's grandfather to Matilda Blake, George's sister; see Quinn, *History of Mayo*, vol. 1, 470–71.

74. Patrick C. Faly, *Ninety-Eight*, esp. 305–13.

75. Fowler, *Chapters in '98 History*.

76. Bodkin, *Rebels*, 257–358.

77. J. J. Moran, *Stories of the Irish Rebellion*, 27–49 and 50–69.

78. Lawless and Bullock, *The Race of Castlebar*.

79. Lawless considered Stock's *Narrative* to be "by far the best account" and superior to "any of the official records of the time," but was also familiar with other contemporary sources; see Emily Lawless, *Maria Edgeworth* (New York: Macmillan, 1904), 68–85.

80. Timothy G. McMahon, "'To Mould an Important Body of Shepherds': The Gaelic Summer Colleges and the Teaching of Irish History," in L. W. McBride, *Reading Irish Histories*, 121.

81. Ua Ruaidhrí, *Bliadhain na bhFranncach*.

82. J. J. Gibbons, *Slieve Bawn*; see in particular xiii, 3–5, 135, 141, 217, 256–57, 259, 262.

83. See Herr, *The Land They Loved*.

84. S. J. Brown, *Guide to Books on Ireland*, 254 and 314.

85. D. E. S. Maxwell, "Irish Drama 1899–1929: The Abbey Theatre," in Deane, *Field Day Anthology*, vol. 2, 597. For the co-authorship see James Pethica, "'Our Kathleen': Yeats's Collaboration with Lady Gregory in the Writing of *Cathleen Ni Houlihan*," in *Yeats Annual 6*, ed. Warwick Gould (London, 1988): 3–31.

86. See Toomey, "Who Fears to Speak of Ninety-Eight," 209–61; Gould, Kelly, and Toomey, *Collected Letters of W. B. Yeats*, 695–707.

87. Lady Gregory, *Kiltartan Poetry Book* (London: G. P. Putnam, 1919), 4.

88. For Casey's ballad see "Rebel Songs and Ballads in English" in chap. 5.

89. See Fogarty, "Where Wolfe Tone's Statue Was Not"; L. Gibbons, "Where Wolfe Tone's Statue Was Not."

90. Reilly, "Beyond Gilt Shamrock," 112.

91. L. W. McBride, "Historical Imagery," 24.

92. See also L. W. McBride, "Nationalist Constructions of the 1798 Rebellion," 117–34, and "Visualizing '98."

93. Shamrock, *Christmas*, 1887.

94. Ibid., 1 August 1891.

95. For example, the MacEvilly household, a prominent republican family in Castlebar, kept a framed poster of "Died for Ireland"; interview with Michael MacEvilly, Dublin, 14 February 2002.

96. For the original see Gribayédoff, *French Invasion*, 67.

97. Madden, *United Irishmen*, vol. 5, 98.

98. National Gallery of Ireland, *Cuimhneachán 1916*, 19.

99. Maguire, Up in Arms, 252.

100. P. O. D. [Patrick O'Donnell], "Buirghéis Umhall," *An Claidheamh Soluis* 3, no. 28 (21 September 1901): 439.

101. *Celt*, August 1858, 271–76. The author used a nom de plume ["Conal Cearnach of Ballina"], named after a mythological warrior hero of the Ulster Cycle.

102. Hayes, *Last Invasion*, 223.

103. *Western People*, 11 January to 22 February 1930. See chap. 6, n. 36.

104. For republished relevant articles in Quinn's series, the "History of Mayo" (orig. published in the 1930s), see Quinn, *History of Mayo*, vol. 1, 109–51, 204–5 and 208–9.

105. For example, Matt H. Matsuda, *The Memory of the Modern* (New York: Oxford Univ. Press, 1996), esp. 55–56.

106. Seosamh Ó Tuathalláin of Garryroe; IFC S119:518–20.

107. Bridie Hopkins of Liscromwell; IFC S89:435–37.

108. Imelda Walsh of Snugboro; IFC S89:454–55.

109. See J. Dowling, *The Hedge Schools of Ireland* (London: Longman, Greens & Co., 1935); Antonia McManus, *The Irish Hedge School and Its Books, 1695–1831* (Dublin: Four Courts Press, 2002).

110. Connolly, *Oxford Companion to Irish History*, 237–38.

111. See McParlan, *Statistical Survey*, 97–100.

112. Figures extracted from the "Second Report," H. C. 1826–27, vol. 12 (in particular see appendix 1, 27–34; parochial returns, 688–705 and 1191–323). For earlier figures see "First Report of the Commissioners of Irish Education," H. C. 1825, vol. 12, appendix 268, 856–57, and 858–59.

113. James S. Donnelly, Jr., "The Whiteboy Movement, 1761–5," *Irish Historical Studies* 21, no. 81 (1978): 40; also McManus, *Irish Hedge School*, 9, 25–26, 32–33, 79–81.

114. Smyth, *Men of No Property*, 115.

115. McManus, *Irish Hedge School*, 35.

116. Croker, *Researches in the South of Ireland*, 329.

117. Carleton, *Traits and Stories*, vol. 1, 232–33.

118. McManus, *Irish Hedge School*, 11.

119. "First Report of the Commissioners of Irish Education," H. C. 1825, vol. 12, appendix 1; reproduced in McManus, *Irish Hedge School*, see esp. 248–53.

120. See McManus, *Irish Hedge School*, 124.

121. These figures are calculated from lists in an appendix of the *Report of the Society of Promoting the Education of the Poor in Ireland* (Dublin, 1826); several schools did not submit their rolls of pupils.

122. *Report of the Committee to the Annual Meeting of the Society of Promoting the Education of the Poor in Ireland*; held at Kildare-Place, Dublin, 1st February, 1832 (Dublin, 1832).

123. M. Daly, "Development of the National School System," 150–63.

124. See D. H. Akenson, *The Irish Education Experiment: The National System of Edu-*

cation in the Nineteenth Century (London: Routledge & K. Paul, 1970); Norman Atkinson, *Irish Education: A History of Educational Institutions* (Dublin: Allan Figgis, 1969), 90–120; John Coolahan, *Irish Education: Its History and Structure* (Dublin: Institute of Public Administration, 1981), 3–51.

125. *Second Report for the Commissioners of National Education in Ireland for the Year Ending 31st March 1835*, H.C. 1836, vol. 36.

126. *Sixty-Seventh Report for the Commissioners of National Education in Ireland for the Year 1900*, H.C. 1901, vol. 21. From that time on, the number of girl pupils exceeded the number of boys.

127. T. J. McElligott, *Education in Ireland* (Dublin: Institute of Public Administration, 1966), 11–12.

128. Figures from the 1901 census reproduced in the *Seventy-sixth Report for the Commissioners of National Education in Ireland for the Year 1910–11*, H.C. 1911, vol. 21.

129. McElligott, *Education in Ireland*, 20–22.

130. *An Roinn Oideachais Turasgabháil / Report of the Department of Education 1937–38* (Dublin, 1938).

131. T. J. Durcan, *History of Irish Education* (Bala: Dragon Books, 1972), 38–52.

132. John Logan, "Sufficient to their Needs: Literacy and Elementary Schooling in the Nineteenth Century," in Daly and Dickson, *The Origins of Popular Literacy*, 113–37.

133. John Logan, "Book Learning: The Experience of Reading in the National School 1831–1900," in *The Experience of Reading: Irish Historical Perspectives*, eds. Bernadette Cunningham and Máire Kennedy (Dublin: Economic & Social History Society of Ireland, 1999), 173–95.

134. McManus, *Irish Hedge School*, 229–30.

135. For the teaching of history in France see Brigitte Dancel, *Enseigner l'histoire à l'école primaire de la IIIe République* (Paris, 1996). In this context, it would seem that the Irish experience could be compared to that of Brittany.

136. *Royal Commission of Inquiry into Primary School Education* (Ireland), H. C. 1870, xviii. "Evidence taken before the Commis-

sioners" is collected in vols. 3 and 4; the comments cited above appear in vol. 4, 962 (Rev. Menamin) and 1189 (Cardinal Cullen). The final report on "School Books" appears in vol. 1, 348–59. The recommendations were "implemented piecemeal and slowly"; Akenson, *Irish Education Experiment*, 316. For a brief discussion on the commission's debates over teaching history see L. W. McBride, "Young Readers and the Learning and Teaching of Irish History, 1870–1922," in McBride, *Reading Irish Histories*, 84–87.

137. Martin Haverty, *The History of Ireland, Ancient and Modern, for the use of Schools and Colleges. With questions for examination at the end of each chapter* (Dublin: Duffey, 1860), 716–18.

138. Townsend Young, *The History of Ireland, from the earliest records to the present time: for the use of schools with questions suited for classes* (Dublin: McGlashan & Gill, 1865; orig. ed. 1863), v, 256–57, and 304.

139. M. F. Cusack, *An Illustrated History of Ireland* (London: Bracken, 1995; orig. ed. 1868), 631.

140. W. F. Collier, *History of Ireland for Schools* (London: Marcus Ward, 1885, orig. ed. 1884), 229–30.

141. There were forty-five Christian Brothers in 1831, 105 in 1845, and almost 1,000 at the turn of the century. In 1899 it was estimated that they taught 25,000 pupils (of which 21,000 were at primary level). See Barry M. Coldrey, *Faith and Fatherland: The Christian Brothers and the Development of Irish Nationalism, 1838–1921* (Dublin: Gill & Macmillan, 1988), esp. 113–39.

142. Lorcan Walsh, "Nationalism in the Textbooks of the Christian Brothers," *Irish Educational Studies* 6, no 2 (1986–87): 1–16.

143. Christian Brothers, *Historical Class-Book, comprising Outlines of Ancient and Modern History, abridged from Dr. Fredet with Outlines of English and Irish History* (Dublin: William Powell, 1859). Coverage of the Rebellion was not improved in subsequent revisions; see for example *Historical Class-Book 7 ed. revised* (1876), 594.

144. See T. J. McElligott, *Secondary Education in Ireland 1870–1921* (Dublin: Irish Academic Press, 1981).

145. *Report of the Intermediate Education Board for Ireland for the Year 1879*, H.C. 1880, vol. 23.

146. *Report of the Intermediate Education Board for Ireland for the Year 1900*, H.C. 1901, vol. 21. In 1904 there were 728 intermediate school pupils in Connacht; see E. Brian Titley, *Church, State, and the Control of Schooling in Ireland 1900–1944* (Kingston: McGill-Queen's Univ. Press, 1983).

147. 1051 intermediate pupils in Connacht and 81 in Longford were presented for exams in 1920; *Report of the Intermediate Education Board for Ireland for the Year 1920*, H.C. 1921, vol. 11.

148. McElligott, *Education in Ireland*, 78.

149. See L. W. McBride, "Young Readers," 93–94.

150. *Intermediate Education (Ireland) Commission: Final Report of the Commissioners* (Dublin, 1899), see the "Minutes of Evidence" in the appendix.

151. P. W. Joyce, *Child's History of Ireland*, 470. In addition to numerous studies of social history, music, linguistics, and geography, Joyce also wrote the *Handbook of School Management and Methods of Teaching* (orig. ed. Dublin: McGlashan & Gill, 1863), which ran to eighteen editions and was considered an essential text for teachers until the end of the nineteenth century; see Logan, "Book learning," 184–85.

152. Gwynn, *Stories from Irish History*, 153.

153. Gabriel Doherty, "National Identities," 330–32.

154. D. Fitzpatrick "The Futility of History," in *Ideology and the Historians*, ed. Ciaran Brady (Dublin: Lilliput Press, 1991), 173–74.

155. Mac Shamhráin, "Ideological Conflict."

156. Corkey, *Church of Rome and Irish Unrest*, 36–37 (reprinted from the Belfast paper *Witness*).

157. Christian Brothers [Br. O'Brien], *Irish History Reader* (Dublin: M. H. Gill & Son, 1916; orig. ed. 1905), 264–66.

158. See Titley, *Church, State*, 114–15.

159. Holohan, "History Teaching."

160. An Roinn Oideachais [Department of Education], *Notes for Teachers: History* (Dublin: Stionary Office, 1933), 5.

161. D. Fitzpatrick "The Futility of History," 182–83.

162. An Roinn Oideachais, *Notes for Teachers: History*, 6–8, 24.

163. C. Maxwell, *School History of Ireland*, 112; C. Maxwell, *A Short Bibliography of Irish History* (London: Historical Association, 1921).

164. An Roinn Oideachais, *Notes for Teachers: History*, 30.

165. Ibid., 8.

166. IFC Box S222a: copybooks of Mary O. Boy (2), Mollie Brady (2 copybooks), Rose Brennan, Joan Costello (2), Rose Flynn, Kathleen Gray, Maggie Gray, Thomas O. Garvey (2), Mary Ann Garvey, Michael Higgins, Paddy McGovern, Lizzie A. MacNally, Kathleen McGovern, Brigid A. Mulloy, Eileen O'Brien, Kathleen O'Brien Annie O'Neill, Mary E. O'Neill, and Brigid A. Ward (2); IFC Box S222b: copybooks of Charles Bohan, Eddy Brady, Thomas Garvey, John Higgins, Michael Higgins, Patrick Mahon, Brigid A. Molloy, Kathleen O'Brien, Francis O'Neill (2), Mary D. Sorrohan, Mary Ward.

167. IFC S222.

168. Grant Bage, *Thinking History 4–14: Teaching, Learning, Curricula and Communities* (London: Taylor and Francis, 2000), 27.

169. Trouillot, *Silencing the Past*, 71–72.

170. Callan, "Aspects of the Transmission of History."

171. L. W. McBride, *Images, Icons*, 9.

172. L. Gibbons, "Constructing the Canon: Versions of National Identity," in Deane, *Field Day Anthology*, vol. 2, 999 n. 9.

173. Coldrey, *Faith and Fatherland*, 138.

174. A. S. Mac Shamhráin, "Ideological Conflict," 236–37.

175. R. F. Foster, *Irish Story*, 1–22, esp. 6 (orig. published as Foster, "Story of Ireland").

176. L. Gibbons, *Transformations in Irish Culture* (Cork, 1996), 15.

177. A. M. Sullivan, *Story of Ireland*, 519.

178. L. W. McBride, "Young Readers," 105 (see also 105–13).

179. Scott and Hodge, *Round Tower*.

180. Coldrey, *Faith and Fatherland*, 125–28.

181. Interview with Fr. Owen Devaney, Mullahoran, Kilcogy, county Cavan, 25 August 2001. The source of inspiration was "The Bells of Clonmoyne," *Our Boys* (December, 1947). For Devaney's writings on Ballinamuck lore, see Devaney, *Killoe*; "Ballinamuck in Song and Story"; "Ballinamuck and '98."

182. IFC S1009:133–42.

183. See Owens, "Nationalist Monuments," 106, 108.

184. Comments by M. J. Lord paraphrased in *Sinn Féin*, 8 December 1906.

185. *Connaught Telegraph*, 27 August 1898; recited for the Schools' Scheme in 1936, IFC S185:26–30.

186. *Connaught Telegraph*, 28 August 1948.

187. James Joyce, *Portrait of the Artist as a Young Man* (London: Penguin, 1992; orig. ed. 1916), 195.

188. FÁS Scheme interview, 22 April 1998; Teeling Centre Research Archive, Collooney, county Sligo.

189. McLoughlin, "A Sense of History," 112.

190. Interview with Ken Lyons, Castlebar, 21 August 2001.

191. Interview with Michael MacEvilly, Dublin, 14 February 2002.

192. Longford Leader, 17 September 1938.

193. IFC 1858:100.

194. For collections undertaken and supervised by Peter Duignan of Gaigue, Ballinamuck, see IFC S758:45–69, 141–42, 145, 168–70, 173–78; by James McKenna of Kiltycreevagh, Ballinamuck, see IFC S758:432–63.

195. Written by A. Ó Corraidhin of Cloone; IFC S222:2.

196. See Grant Bage, *Narrative Matters: Teaching and Learning History through Story* (London: Taylor and Francis, 1999).

197. An Roinn Oideachais, *Notes for Teachers: History*, 5–6, 8.

198. See for example Bage, *Thinking History*, 4–14.

199. Micheál Breathneach of Headford; IFC S23:25.

200. *An Claidheamh Soluis* 2 (1901), no. 45, 707; no. 52, 823; Hayes-McCoy, "The Irish Pike," 120–11, 128. A 1943 questionnaire on pike order drills produced three additional versions from around Tuam in county Galway; IFC 1142:1–10. See also Hayes, *Last Invasion* (2nd ed.), 339.

201. Mac Laughlin, *Reimagining The Nation-State*, 187–88.

Chapter 16

1. Burke, "History as Social Memory," 106.

2. See Ernest Renan, "What is a Nation?" in *Nation and Narration*, ed. Homi K. Bhabha (London: Routledge, 1990), 8–22 (trans. and annotated by Martin Thom).

3. Milan Kundera, *The Book of Laughter and Forgetting* (London: Faber, 2000), 4 (trans. by Aaron Asher from *Le Livre du Rire et de L'oubli* [Paris, 1979]; orig. pub. as *Kniha Smíchu a Zapomnění* [1978]).

4. William Graham Sumner, *Folkways* (Boston: Ginn, 1907; orig. ed. 1906), 636.

5. Ricoeur, "Memory and Forgetting," 5–11. For detailed discussion see Paul Ricoeur, *Memory, History, Forgetting* (Chicago: Univ. of Chicago Press, 2004).

6. See D. W. Blight, *Race and Reunion: The Civil War in American Memory* (Cambridge, MA: Harvard Univ. Press, 2001); Kirk Savage, "The Politics of Memory: Black Emancipation and the Civil War Monument," in Gillis, *Commemorations*, 127–49.

7. See Bartlett, "Indiscipline and Disaffection," 121 and 128; T. Bartlett, "Defence, Counter-Insurgency and Rebellion: Ireland, 1793–1803," in Bartlett and Jeffery, *Military History of Ireland*, 271.

8. Peter Stewart, "The Destruction of Statues in Late Antiquity," in *Constructing Identities in Late Antiquity*, ed. Richard Miles (London: Routledge, 1999), 159–89, esp. 167; C. W. Hedrick Jr., *History and Silence: Purge*

and *Rehabilitation of Memory in Late Antiquity* (Austin: Univ. of Texas Press, 2000), 88–130, esp. 93.

9. Mona Ozouf, *Festivals and the French Revolution* (Cambridge, MA: Harvard Univ. Press, 1988), 166–86.

10. For a discussion on Foucault's concept of "history as countermemory" see Hutton, *History as an Art of Memory*, 106–23.

11. Philippe Joutard, *La Légende des Camisards: Une sensibilité au passé* (Paris: Gallimard, 1977); Joutard, "The Museum of the Desert: The Protestant Minority," in Nora, *Realms of Memory*, 1, 353–78.

12. Scott, *Domination and the Arts of Resistance*, 227.

13. See Raymond Williams, *Marxism and Literature* (Oxford: Oxford Univ. Press, 1977), 108–27.

14. Johnson, "Sculpting Heroic Histories," 92.

15. For example, the Intelligence Branch of Dublin Castle compiled copies of all press coverage of the centennial commemoration events; see Chief Secretary's Office, *Irish News Cuttings*, NLI vols. 56–57, "1798 Centenary" (Dublin, 1898).

16. See David Fitzpatrick, "Commemoration in the Irish Free State," 184–203. See also Anne Dolan, *Commemorating the Irish Civil War: History and Memory, 1923–2000* (Cambridge: Cambridge Univ. Press, 2003).

17. Leerssen, "Monument and Trauma," 204–22; Leerssen, "1798: The Recurrence of Violence," 37–45.

18. Maguire, *Up in Arms*, 259–60.

19. *Dublin Journal*, 13 and 18 of September 1798.

20. Leerssen admitted that "like any schematisation it is overly facile and black-and-white" and that "the distinction between community and society remembrance is blurring even as I am making it"; Leerssen, "Monument and Trauma," 215 and 218–19.

21. TCD MS 871; Musgrave, *Memoirs of the Different Rebellions*.

22. Whelan, *Tree of Liberty*, 136–37.

23. "Sketches of Life and Manners; From

the Autobiography of an English Opium Eater," *Tait's Edinburgh Magazine* 1 (1834): 200–204 and 263–66.

24. See *Dublin University Magazine* 28, no. 167 (Nov. 1846): 546–48.

25. W. H. Maxwell, *Adventures of Captain Blake*, 84–91.

26. Maxwell, *Wild Sports*, 256–59.

27. See Otway, *Sketches in Erris and Tyrawley*, 219–21, 302.

28. Edgeworth, *Memoirs of Richard Lovell Edgeworth*, vol. 2, 209–38; reproduced in Beatty, *Protestant Women's Narratives*, 240–56.

29. Hare, *Life and Letters of Maria Edgeworth*, 54–59.

30. NLI MS 18756.

31. *Cornhill Magazine* (1898), 463–78 (dated Castlebar, 17 October 1798); for the original text see Miller and Ormsby Family Papers, NLI microfilm P8162. Another letter dated Castlebar, 10 October 1798, has survived in incomplete form; NLI MS 8283.

32. I. McBride, "Reclaiming the Rebellion," 406–7. Noteworthy exceptions include Allan Blackstock, *An Ascendancy Army: The Irish Yeomanry, 1796–1834* (Dublin: Four Courts Press, 1998); Blackstock, "The Irish Yeomanry and the 1798 Rebellion," in Bartlett et al., *1798*, 331–44; James Wilson, "Orangeism in 1798," in Bartlett et al., *1798*, 345–62.

33. Dunne, "1798 and the United Irishmen," 65 (italics in original). A noteworthy exception is the work of John D. Beatty; see Beatty, "Protestant Women of County Wexford"; Beatty, *Protestant Women's Narratives*.

34. See Jane Leonard, "The Twinge of Memory: Armistice Day and Remembrance Sunday in Dublin since 1919," in *Unionism in Modern Ireland*, eds. Robert English and Graham Walker (Houndsmill: Macmillan Press 1996), 99–114; Leonard, "Facing 'the Finger of Scorn': Veterans' Memories of Ireland after the Great War," in *War and Memory in the Twentieth Century*, eds. M. Evans and K. Lunn (Oxford: Oxford Univ. Press, 1997), 59–72.

35. Nuala C. Johnson, *Ireland, the Great War and the Geography of Remembrance* (Cambridge: Cambridge Univ. Press, 2003).

See also Keith Jeffery, "The Great War and Modern Irish Memory," in *Men, Women and War*, eds. T. G. Fraser and Keith Jeffery (Dublin: Lilliput Press, 1993), 136–57.

36. Y. Whelan, *Reinventing Modern Dublin*, 192–213.

37. See Jim Higgins, "1798: Some Galway–Mayo Links," *Cathair na Mart* 22 (2002): 77–80.

38. McParlan, *Statistical Survey*, 154.

39. Mangin, *Parlour Window*, 43–44.

40. Archdeacon, *Connaught: a Tale of 1798*, 218. See also Hayes, *Last Invasion*, 281–82.

41. In 1998 a new plaque was put up with the inscription: "Site of last royalist defended position. Fraser Fencibles buried within"; for a photograph see Murray and Cullen, *Epitaph of 1798*, 96.

42. Interview with Cathleen MacLoughlin, whose source of information was Andy Jackson of Castlebar (b. ca. 1880); Castlebar, 27 February 2003.

43. See McCoy, *Ulster's Joan of Arc*; A. T. Q. Stewart, "The Ghost of Betsy Gray," in *1798 Rebellion in County Down*, eds. Myrtle Hill, Brian Turner, and Kenneth Dawson (Newtownards: Colorpoint Books, 1998), 251–57; Marianne Elliot, *The Catholics of Ulster: A History* (London: Allen Lane, 2000), 263.

44. J. R. Gillis, "Memory and Identity: The History of a Relationship," in Gillis, *Commemorations* 10.

45. See Crossman, "Shan Van Vocht."

46. See Síghle Bhreathnach-Lynch, "Commemorating the Hero," 164–65.

47. See P. Novick, *Holocaust and Collective Memory*, 192–97.

48. See Margaret Kelleher, "Hunger and History: Monuments to the Great Irish Famine," *Textual Practice* 16, no. 2 (2002): 249–76.

Conclusion

1. Hobsbawm, "Mass-Producing Traditions," 263–307.

2. Eugen Weber, *Peasants into Frenchmen: The Modernization of Rural France, 1870–1914* (London: Chatto & Windus, 1977).

3. See Nora, "Between Memory and History," 1–20.

4. A survey of studies suggests that "memory" in the twentieth century is commonly considered as a modern phenomenon; Peter Fritzsche, "The Case of Modern Memory," *Journal of Modern History* 73, no. 1 (2001): 87–117.

5. Hayes, *Last Invasion*, xxv.

6. Halbwachs, *Les Cadres Sociaux de la mémoire*, 18.

7. Jacques Derrida, *Archive Fever: A Freudian Impression* (Chicago: Univ. of Chicago Press, 1996), 22. For a reappraisal, see Carolyn Steedman, *Dust* (Manchester: Manchester Univ. Press, 2001), 66–88.

8. See Shils, *Tradition*. For a critique of this seminal analysis of tradition, which argues that it lacks a critical "historical perspective," see Michael S. Roth, *The Ironist's Cage: Memory, Trauma and the Construction of History* (New York: Columbia Univ. Press, 1995), 177–79.

9. Amin, *Event, Metaphor, Memory*, 189.

10. Christian J. Emden, "Nachleben: Cultural Memory in Aby Warburg and Walter Benjamin," in *Cultural Memory: Essays on European Literature and History*, eds. Richard Caldicott and Anne Fuchs (Oxford: Oxford Univ. Press, 2003), 209–24. See also Kurt Forster, "Aby Warburg's, History of Art: Collective Memory and the Social Mediation of Images," *Daedalus* (1976): 239–59; Gombrich, *Aby Warburg*, 239–59.

11. Vansina, *Oral Tradition as History*, 29, 196.

12. Tosh, *Pursuit of History*, 186.

13. Gross, *Past in Ruins*, 116–19.

14. In archaeology, *terminus ante quem* marks the last period up to which evidence can be dated, and *terminus post quem* describes the earliest period; see Ian Shaw and Robert Jameson, eds., *A Dictionary of Archaeology* (Oxford: Oxford Univ. Press, 1999), 570.

15. Ó Grianna, *Rann na Feirste*, 58–59.

16. For historical context see L. M. Cullen, "The Smuggling Trade in Ireland in the Eigh-

teenth Century," *Proceedings of the Royal Irish Academy*, 67C, no. 5 (1969): 149–75.

17. IFC S752:309–10; IFC S968:142–43.

18. IFC 969:180–82; IFC S34:413.

19. IFC S143:157; IFC S152:74.

20. Collected from sixty-nine-year-old Éamonn Ó Finneadha of Spiddal, county Galway; IFC 72:33. For "bog butter" see A. T. Lucas, "Irish Food Before the Potato," *Gwerin* 3, no 2 (1960): 30.

21. Told by seventy-four-year-old Micheál Ó Rodaigh, a farmer from Bangor, Erris, county Mayo, to the collector Liam Mac Coisdeala in 1939; IFC 625:197–98.

22. IFC 572:55–64; IFC 625:330–33; IFC 665:520–21; IFC 743:450–54; IFC 1242: 263–65; see also John O'Donovan, *"Letters Containing Information,"* vol. 1, typescript 5 (orig. RIA MS, 14).

23. IFC S962:27. See also associations in traditions of the burial place of the insurgent General George Blake in Tubberpatrick, by the holy "Well of Saint Patrick" [Tobar Pádraig]; see chap. 8, n. 176. For prophecies attributed to Saint Columcille see chap. 5.

24. For references to dolmens as "druids' altars" see "Prophecies" in chap. 5 (109).

25. See Ó Ciosság, "Famine memory," 95–117.

26. L. B. Namier, "Symmetry and Repetition," in Namier, *Conflicts: Studies in Contemporary History* (London: Macmillan, 1942), 69–70 (orig. pub. in *Manchester Guardian*, 1 January 1941).

27. For Protestant commemoration in the seventeenth and eighteenth centuries, see T. C. Barnard, "The Uses of 23 October 1641 and Irish Protestant Celebrations," *English Historical Review*, 106, no. 421 (1991): 889–920; James Kelly, "'The Glorious and Immortal Memory': Commemoration and Protestant Identity in Ireland 1660–1800," *Proceedings of the Royal Irish Academy*, 94C (1994): 25–52.

28. Humphrey Thomson, "Personal Narrative," BOD MS Eng. Hist. d. 155, f. 183.

29. See Whelan, *Tree of Liberty*, 135–36; see also Kelly, "We Were All To Have Been Massacred," 325–29.

30. See Farrel Corcoran, "Technologies of Memory," in *Memories of the Present: A Sociological Chronicle of Ireland, 1997–1998*, eds. Eamonn Slater and Michel Peillon (Dublin: Institute of Public Administration, 2000), 25–34.

31. Ó Dómhnaill, *Na Glúnta Rosannacha*, 124.

32. O'Rourke, "County Mayo in Gaelic Folksong," 193; Ó Broin, *Songs of Past and People*, 33; uí Ógáin, "Béaloideas 1798 Thiar," 150. For references to the song, see "Amhráin na ndaoine" in chap. 5 (90).

33. McFarland, "Scotland and the 1798 Rebellion," 568–70.

34. C. H. Teeling, *Personal Narrative of the "Irish Rebellion" of 1798* (London: H. Colburn, 1828), 220, note. See also Madden, *United Irishmen* (2nd ed.; Dublin, 1860), vol. 3, 283, note.

35. IFC 72:31–33; IFC S220: 148–49; IFC S761:195–98; IFC S986:97–99; IFC S997:59–60; IFC S1058:185–87.

36. Letter dated 11 April 1938 in Richard Hayes Papers, NLI MS 13799 (3).

37. Foucault, *Discipline and Punish* (trans. from *Surveiller et punir: Naissance de la prison* [Paris: Gallimard, 1975]), 218.

38. Whelan, *Tree of Liberty*, 133.

39. Smyth, *Men of No Property*, 178.

Epilogue

1. For a more detailed discussion see Guy Beiner, "The Decline and Rebirth of 'Folk Memory': Remembering 'The Year of the French' in the Late Twentieth Century," *Éire-Ireland* 38, no. 3–4 (2003): 7–32.

2. Interviews with Jimmy Breslin, Ballinamuck, 15 September 2001; Padraig Rehill (whose grandfather had previously owned the field), Dublin, 25 October 2001.

3. Interview with Jude Flynn (whose father owned the property), Longford, 15 September 2001; see also "Sites of Death, Burial, and Supernatural Encounters" in chap. 12 (230).

4. Lyons, "Races of Castlebar," 44–55; interview with Ken Lyons, Castlebar, 21 August 2001.

5. Interview with Padraig Rehill.

6. For an obituary, see *Saoirse—Irish Freedom*, 6 March 2001. In April 2006 it was announced that the Jackie Clarke Collection, which contains more than 15,000 histrorical documents, has been donated to Mayo County Council and is to be permanently exhibited at the former site of the Moy Hotel in Ballina. See *Connaught Telegraph*, 5 April 2006; *Irish Times*, 12 April 2006; *Mayo News*, 12 April 2006; *Western People*, 15 March 12 and 19 April 2006.

7. Ó Tuairisc, *L'Attaque*.

8. Nic Eoin, *Eoghan Ó Tuairisc*, 161–62; for the use of Hayes as a source, see Ó Flathartha, "Gnéithe Comparáideacha."

9. J. M. Cahalan, *Great Hatred, Little Room: The Irish Historical Novel* (Dublin: Gill & Macmillan, 1983), 171–75.

10. Ó Tuairisc, *Lux Aeterna*; the poem originally appeared in *Feasta* (October 1949); republished in Seán Ó Tuama, ed., *Nuabhéarsaíocht 1939–1949* (Dublin: Sáirséal agus Dill, 1950), 97–98. For an English translation (missing a stanza) by Lt. Col. Denis Burke, former commander of Magee Barracks in county Kildare, see Rehill, *Ballinamuck Bi-Centenary*, 123.

11. Of these, 23 percent lived in designated *Gaeltachts* (as defined by the Gaeltacht Areas Order of 1956), including 11,599 in county Mayo and 22,877 in county Galway; *Census of Population of Ireland 1961* (Dublin, 1966), vol. 9: "Irish Language."

12. A second edition was issued in 1980, a third edition came out for the bicentenary in 1998, and a new edition appeared in 2005.

13. Benedict Kiely, *A Raid into Dark Corners and Other Essays* (Cork: Cork Univ. Press, 1999), 162.

14. Flanagan, *Irish Novelists 1800–1850*.

15. See Nuala O'Farrell, "Who Fears To Speak of '98?" Flanagan visited the battle site of Ballinamuck together with the poet Seamus Heaney and so had an opportunity to hear Ninety-Eight oral traditions first-hand; see Jennifer Clarke, "Q and A with Tom Flanagan," *Irish Literary Supplement* 7, no. 1 (1988): 26–27.

16. IFC S 142: 189; IFC S164: 253–56.

17. Flanagan, *Year of the French*, 557. For O'Kane in folk history see "A Franco-Irish Officer " in chap. 8.

18. S. J. White, "A Week in The Year of the French," 27.

19. For an account of the production see Michael Garvey, "Recreating 1798," in Freyer, *Bishop Stock's "Narrative,"* vii–xv. The discussion on the film has benefited from an interview with the director Michael Garvey and from consultation with Louis Lentin, former Director of Drama at RTÉ.

20. The Chieftains, *The Year of the French* (Claddagh Records, 1982).

21. John Walsh, "Brave Irishmen, Our Cause is Common," *RTÉ Guide*, vol. 6, no. 46 (12 November 1982): 14–15.

22. Kevin Rockett, Luke Gibbons, and John Hill, *Cinema and Ireland* (London: Croom Helm, 1987), 90.

23. Sheehan, *Irish Television Drama*, 314, 410, and 418.

24. See Garry Redmond, ed., *RTÉ Comóradh 1962–1987* (Dublin, 2 January 1987).

25. *Westmeath Examiner*, 4 and 11 July 1981.

26. Michael Mullen, "The Year of the French, 1981," *Connaught Telegraph*, 2 September 1981, 9.

27. Fennell, *Connacht Journey*, 62.

28. Interview with Michael Garvey, Dublin, 8 May 2002.

29. Joseph Lacken, "The Year of the Extra (A diary from the filming)," *Western People*, 12 August 1981, 9.

30. "Killala to Retain '98 Look?" *Connaught Telegraph*, 2 September 1981, 1.

31. Brendan Hoban, "When the French Came to Killala," *Western People*, 9 September 1981, 5 (continued in *Western People*, 16 September 1981).

32. *Western People*, 2 September 1981.

33. See chap. 15, 279, 288, and fig. 34 (290).

34. Conversation with Stephen Dunford, Killala, April 2002.

35. Freyer, *Bishop Stock's "Narrative"*; for an obituary of Freyer, see *Cathar na Mart* 4, no. 1: 57.

36. Ó Brádaigh, *Songs of 1798*.

37. Interview with Seán Ó Brádaigh, Dublin, 12 April 2001. For the text of a lecture on a similar topic delivered around that time, see Ó Brádaigh, *French Revolution*.

38. For Cooney's relevant publications, see "Two French Revolutionary Soldiers"; *Humbert's Expedition—A Lost Cause?*; *Humbert*; "En Campagne Avec L'Armée D'Humbert." See also Cooney, *1798 Campaign by a French Lieutenant*.

39. *Sunday Independent*, 1 August 1993.

40. Interviews with John Cooney, Dublin, 24 October 2001, and Tony McGarry (chairman of the Humbert Summer School), Killala, 16 September 2001. The proceedings of the summer school have been published, and a full set is available at the Mayo County Library.

41. Interviews with John Cooney and Tony Donohue, Creevy, county Mayo, 22 August 2001.

42. For a photograph, see Murray and Cullen, *Epitaph of 1798*, 93.

43. Interview with Sean Lavin, Lackan, county Mayo, 22 August 2001. For a photograph, see Murray and Cullen, *Epitaph of 1798*, 92.

44. Ballinamuck Community Association Minute Book, 18 May 1982. My thanks to Jimmy Breslin (the association's founding secretary) for sharing his recollections of the events and for allowing me access to select documents. For photographs, see Murray and Cullen, *Epitaph of 1798*, 87.

45. *Longford News*, 7 October 1983, 7.

46. Ibid., 7 and 14 October 1983. A souvenir booklet was published for the event.

47. For photographs, see Murray and Cullen, *Epitaph of 1798*, 86.

48. *Longford News*, 17 May 1985.

49. Longley, "Northern Ireland," 529. For a description of the bicentennial commemorative events across Ireland see Collins, *Who Fears to Speak of '98?*, 84–154.

50. For a more detailed discussion see Guy Beiner, "Commemorating Ninety-Eight in 1998: A Reappraisal of History-Making in Contemporary Ireland," in *These Fissured*

Isles: Ireland, Scotland and British History, 1798–1948, eds. Terry Botherstone, Anna Clark, and Kevin Whelan (Edinburgh: John Donald Publishers, 2005), 221–41.

51. 1798 Bicentenary Files in Roinn an Taoisigh [Department of the Taoiseach] Library.

52. *1798 The Year of the French: Calendar of Commemorative Events* (produced in association with Ireland West Tourism, North West Tourism, Midlands-East Tourism, and Mayo County Council).

53. Interviews with Wendy Lyons, Collooney Bicentenary Committee; and Attracta Brownlee, Research Officer, Teeling Centre, Collooney, county Sligo, 31 October 2001. My thanks to Ms. Brownlee for providing me with copies of local bicentenary literature. See "Collooney in '98: Bicentenary Commemoration 1798–1998" (video: Collooney Bicentenary Committee: 1998).

54. See Ballinamuck, *Record of the Ballinamuck Bicentenary Commemoration 1798–1998* (Longford, 1999); Lennon, "The Spirit of '98." See also the video "Who Fears to Speak of '98: Bicentenary Commemoration of the Battle of Ballinamuck 1798–1998" (Ballinamuck Bicentenary Committee, 1998).

55. Castlebar 1798 Commemorative Committee, eds., *1798: A Commemorative Booklet* (Castlebar, 1998). My thanks also to Patricia Fitzgerald for an interview on the bicentennial commemoration at Killala, and for providing me with copies of publications and allowing access to the papers of the organizing committee (17 September 2001, Killala).

56. For a photographic record of all the monuments, see Murray and Cullen, *Epitaph of 1798*.

57. Dunne, "Wexford's *Comoradh '98*." For further critique of commemorative heritage, see also Foster, "Remembering 1798," in McBride, *History and Memory;* and "Themeparks and Histories," in Foster, *Irish Story*, 211–34, 25–36.

58. Samuel, *Theatres of Memory*, vol. I, esp. 16–17 and 259–73.

59. Statement by An Taoiseach, Mr. Bertie

Ahern, TD, on "The Bicentenary of the 1798 Rebellion," Dáil Éireann Debates, vol. 493, 3 July 1998.

60. See *Irish Times*, 11 and 14 July 1998.

61. "Tour de Humbert" (Westport: Westport Tourist Office, 1998). Tour packages were made available for cyclists who preferred an organized group experience; *Mayo News*, 18 March 1998; *Western People*, 28 January 1998. See also http://www.anu.ie/mayocycling/Pages/ page7.html.

62. See for example Guckian, *Leitrim & Longford 1798*; Mac Atasney, *Leitrim and the Croppies*, 54–61; Kelly, *Flame Now Quenched;* Ó Brádaigh, *Songs of 1798* (1998, 2nd ed.); Padraic O'Farrell, *'98 Reader*, 127–38; Sheila Mulloy [Síle Uí Mhaoluaidh], *Father Manus Sweene;* M. Whelan, *Parish of Aughavas*, 75–87. See also in local history journals: T. Hughes, "Fr. Manus Sweeney," and McDermott, "Tree of Liberty" and "1798 and Newport"; de Búrca, "Echo of 1798," 47; Comer, "Humbert in Swinford"; Ó Catháin, "Tomás Ó Catháin," *Teathbha* 2, no. 4 (1997): 276–78.

63. *Western People*, 2 September 1981, 18.

64. This process affected other communities along the route of the Franco-Irish army, such as Tubbercurry in county Sligo, which was twinned with Viarmes. See *Chauvé -Infos*, Numéro 3 (October 1996) and Numéro 8 (February 1998); *Connaught Telegraph*, 18 November 1998; *L'Est Républicain*, 10 May 1997; *Le Télégramme*, 24 January, 2 February, 17 April 1998, and 19 January, 11 March and 6 April 1999; *Longford News*, 4 September 1998; *Longford Leader*, 4 September; *Western People*, 26 August 1998.

65. See for example: *Longford Leader*, 4 September 1998; *Sligo Champion*, 23 September 1998; *Killala Remembering 1798* (Killala: Killala Bi-Centenary Commemoration Committee, 1998).

66. For example, interviews in county Mayo with eighty-three-year-old Sean Burke, Poolathomas (23 August 2001); eighty-one-year-old Tony Donohue, Creevy (22 August 2001); eighty-one-year-old Jack Munnelly, Ross, Killala (16 September 2001); eighty-seven-year-old Séamus Mór Ó Mongáin, Dohooma (24 August 2001).

67. Ó Giolláin, *Locating Irish Folklore*, 180.

68. Honko, "Folklore Process," 42–45.

69. *Irish Times*, 16 July 1998; *Longford Leader*, 17 and 24 July.

70. Proposal for Ballinamuck Visitor Centre, Roinn an Taoisigh Library: 1798 Bicentenary files, county Longford, S110/05/03/0042; "The Battle of Ballinamuck Battlefield Centre" leaflet (Longford Community Resources). My thanks to Mary MacNamara (curator in 1998) and Betty Creegan for facilitating visits to the Centre and to the consultant Jonathan Mason from Heritage Planning and Design Services for a conversation on its design.

71. "The Battle of Ballinamuck Remembered" (audio tape: Heritage Planning & Design Services, 1998). The accounts include "Tom Gilheany and the Yeoman" and Peggy Waugh's "Story"; "Breakfast for Two," "Grey Pat's Stories," and "John Clancy's Stories." They originally appeared in *Béaloideas* 4 (1933/34): 393–95; Hayes, *Last Invasion*, 291–93, 319–22, 325–26 (Kilkenny's account was first submitted to the Schools' Scheme in 1936; IFC S221:1a–10a).

72. McLouglin, a local schoolteacher and member of a drama society, is familiar with local folk history; see McLoughlin, "Sense of History," 111–18. The Dublin actress Felicity Stewart was coached in the local dialect.

Selected Bibliography

ARCHIVAL SOURCES

References to nonarchival private papers, inter-
views, and audio-visual material are listed in
footnotes.

Irish Folklore Collection, Department of
Irish Folklore, UCD (IFC)
    Main Manuscript Collection
    Schools' Manuscript Collection
    Audio Tape Collection
    J. H. Delargy Papers
    Michael Timoney Papers
    Patrick O'Donnell Papers
    "Tuarascáil an Choimisiún" (typescript
    report, 1970)
National Library of Ireland (NLI)
    Orders for French Troops, NLI MS 707
    Hugh Carleton Papers, NLI MS 4290
    J. J. McDonnell Manuscript, NLI MS 7335
    Mrs. B. Thompson letter, NLI MS 8283
    F. S. Bourke Papers, NLI 9897
    Richard Hayes Papers, NLI MSS
    13799–13801
    W. J. Fitzpatrick Papers, NLI MS 15486
    Joseph McGarrity Papers NLI MS 17559
    Elizabeth Edgeworth Journal, NLI MS
    18756
    Bartholomew Teeling Correspondence,
    NLI MS 36094 (4)
    Miller and Ormsby Family Papers, NLI
    Microfilm P8162
    Kilmainham Papers
    Chief Secretary's Office (Intelligence
    Branch) *Irish News Cuttings,* "1798
    Centenary" (1898)
National Archives of Ireland (NAI)
    Rebellion Papers [620/-]

Crime Special Branch Box 13 (1898)
Chief Secretary's Office files
Outrage Papers
State of the Country Papers
James Joseph McDonnell Papers, MS
    999/49
Royal Irish Academy (RIA)
    Rev. James Little's Diary, RIA MS 3 B 51
    Bernard Tumaltey Papers, RIA MS 3 C 4 b
    Forde-Pigot Collection, RIA MS 24 o 24
    Theophilus (Teige) O'Flynn Papers, RIA
    MS 240 1934; 23 o 42
    Printed 1798 Bulletins, RIA MSS 3/B/54;
    3/B/59; 12/D/26; 12/D/54;
    24/Q/37
Trinity College Dublin (TCD)
    Richard Musgrave Depositions, TCD MS
    871
    Bartholomew Teeling Papers in R. R. Mad-
    den Collection, TCD MS 873: 8a–25
    Joseph Stock Diary, TCD MS 1690
    Bishop Stock Letters, TCD MSS 3390,
    3903
    Crofton Croker Papers, TCD MS 1206
    Minutes of the Irish Society, TCD 7644
    Margaret Dobin Letters, TCD MS 10354
University College Dublin (UCD)
    Robert Dudley Edwards Papers, UCD
    MSS LA 22/452–55, 1128, 1195, 1260
Roinn an Taoisigh
    1798 Bicentenary Commemoration Files
Belfast Central Library
    Francis Joseph Bigger MSS Collection
Public Record Office, Northern Ireland
(PRO NI)
    Dublin Castle Correspondence, MS D
    162/101

Shannon Papers, MS D 2707/A3/3
Young Papers, MS D 2930
Queens' University Belfast (QUB)
   Edward Bunting Papers, MS 4
Public Record Office, Kew Gardens, London
(PRO)
   Home Office Papers, PRO HO
      100/78/171–422; PRO HO 100/82
British Library (BL)
   Thomas Crofton Croker Papers, MS
      20094
   Auckland Papers, MS 34454
   Morley Papers, MS 48252
   Hardwicke Papers, MSS 35728–68
   Dropmore Papers, MS 71589
National Army Museum, London
   Hewitt Papers, MS 5910–198
   Cornwallis Letters, MS 6602–45
   Townsend Papers, MS 6806–41/7/6 (1)
   Nugent Papers, MSS 6807–174, 6807–175
Bodleian Library (BOD)
   Humphrey Thomson, "Personal Narra-
      tive," MS Eng Hist d. 155
   Thomas Crofton Croker Letters
   Hughendon Papers MS Dep. Hughendon
      243/3
   MS Eng 3.32
   MS Eng lett d. 169
Archives Nationales Paris (AN)
   MAR BB/4/123
Archives de la Guerre, Château de Vin-
cennes, Paris (ADG)
   Mémoires et Reconnaissances 1M 1420,
      1M1422
   B 11/1, B11/2
   Troop registers: 18 YC 170–171; 21 YC
      782; Xb 290

OFFICIAL PUBLICATIONS
House of Commons Parliamentary Papers,
United Kingdom (H.C.)
   Reports of the Commissioners of Educa-
      tion in Ireland, 1825–27
   Reports for the Commissioners of
      National Education in Ireland,
      1834–1921
   Reports of the Intermediate Education
      Board for Ireland, 1880–1921

Royal Commission of Inquiry into Pri-
   mary School Education (Ireland),
   1870
Censuses of Ireland (for the years 1841,
   1851, 1861, 1871, 1881, 1891, 1901,
   1911)
Department of Education [An Roinn
Oideachais], Irish Free State
   Yearly reports, 1922–38.
   Notes for Teachers: History (orig. ed. 1933)
Department of Industry and Commerce (sta-
tistics branch), Irish Free State
   Census of Population of Ireland (for the
      years 1926 and 1936)
Department of Social Welfare, Republic of
Ireland
   Commission on Emigration and Other
      Population Problems 1948–54:
      Reports
General Statistics Office, Republic of Ireland
   Census of Population of Ireland (1961)
Department of the Taoiseach [Roinn an
Taoisigh], Republic of Ireland
   "Government's 1798 Commemoration
      Committee National Programme"
      (1998) and associated speeches, press
      releases, and documents (circulated
      by the Government Information
      Services)
   *Irelands' Famine: Commemoration and
      Awareness* (Famine Commemoration
      Committee, 1995)
Dáil and Seanad Éireann Debates, Republic
of Ireland
   1798 Bicentenary (1998)

NEWSPAPERS AND MAGAZINES
   Anglo-Celt
   Ballina Herald
   Castlebar Parish Magazine
   Celt
   Connaught Telegraph
   Contemporary Review
   Cornhill Magazine
   Dublin Evening Post
   Dublin Journal
   Dublin Penny Journal
   Dublin Review

Selected Bibliography

Dublin University Magazine
Father Mathew Record
Fortnightly Review
Freeman's Journal
Ireland of the Welcomes
Ireland's Own
Irish Book Lover
Irish Citizen
Irish Emerald
Irish Fireside
Irish Independent
Irish Magazine
Irish News
Irish Packet
Irish Penny Journal
Irish Press
Irish Republican Info Service
Irish Times
Irish Weekly Independent
Irish World
Leitrim Advertiser
Leitrim Observer
Longford Leader
Longford News
Longford Year Book
Macmillan's Magazine

Mayo Examiner
Mayo News
Nation
An Phoblacht
The Press
Roscommon Herald
RTÉ Guide
Saoirse
Saunders's News-Letter
Shamrock
Shan Van Vocht
Sinn Féin
Sligo Champion
Sligo Independent
Sunday Business Post
Sunday Independent
Sunday Tribune
Tait's Edinburgh Magazine
United Ireland
Walker's Hibernian Magazine
Western People
Westmeath Examiner

Irish-Language Journals
An Claidheamh Soluis
Fáinne an Lae
The Gaelic Journal

PRINTED SOURCES

While most of the 1,300 books and articles consulted can be traced through footnotes, the listed bibliography is confined to Irish folk history and remembrance of the 1798 Rebellion, alongside selected general items.

Anon. *Paddy's Resource: Being a Select Collection of Original and Modern Patriotic Songs, Toasts and Sentiments, Compiled for the Use of the People of Ireland*. Belfast, 1795.

———. *An Account of the Late Insurrection in Ireland*. London, ca. 1798; 12 ed.

———. *An Historical Narrative of the Naval Victory in the Irish Coast by Sir J. B. Warren*. 1798.

———. *A True and Circumstantial Account of the French in Ireland and Their Total Defeat and Surrender to General Lake. Also A list of the killed and wounded of his Majesty's Forces; ordnance, arms, ammunition & c. taken; and the number of French made prisoners. To which is added An account of the defeat of the rebels and the capture of* Roach, Teeling, *and* Holt, *the Rebel leaders, by which the tranquillity is happily restored*. ca. 1798.

———. *A True and Circumstantial Account of the Total Defeat of the French Fleet off the Coast of Ireland on the 12th by Sir John Borlese Warren*. 1798.

———. *Vain Boastings of the Frenchmen. The Same in 1386 as in 1798. Being an Account of the Threatened Invasion of England by the French. The 10th Year of King Richard II. Extracted from Ancient Chronicles*. London, 1798.

———. ["An officer who served in the corps under command of his excellency Marquis

Cornwallis"]. *Impartial Relation of the Military Operations which took place in Ireland, in consequence of the landing of a body of French troops, under General Humbert, in August, 1798*. Dublin, 1799.

———. *List of Persons who have suffered Losses in their Property in the County of Mayo, and who have given in their Claims on or before the 6th of April, 1799, to the Commisioners for enquiring into the Losses sustained by such of His Majesty's Loyal Subjects as have suffered in their Property by the Rebellion*. Dublin, 1799.

———. *Constitutional Songs*. ca. 1800.

———. *The Last Speech and Dying Words of Martin McLoughlin*. Cork, 1800.

———. *Proceedings of a Court of Inquiry held at Castlebar, the 1st of December, 1800 pursuant to an order from His Excellency the Lord Lieutenant to investigate certain charges made against James Moore O'Donel, Esq. Captain of the Newport-Pratt Cavalry and Connel O'Donel, Esq. First Lieutenant of the said corps by the Rev. John Benton, Doctor of Law, and Chaplain to the South Mayo Militia contained in a letter to Major Gen. Sir James Duff, Bart. With an appendix containing different letters and other papers referred to in the court of the trial*. Dublin, 1801.

———. ["An English-Gentleman aided by the communication of several friends"]. *The Scientific Tourist Through Ireland by which the Traveller is Directed to the Principal Objects of Antiquity, Art, Science and the Picturesque; Arranged by Counties*. London, 1818.

———. *Narrative of a Private Soldier in His Majesty's 92nd Regiment of Foot, Written by Himself. Retailing many circumstances relative to the Irish Rebellion in 1798; the Expedition to Holland in 1799; and the Expedition to Egypt in 1801; and giving a particular account of the Religious History and Experience*. Glasgow, 1820; 2nd ed.

———. [A. I.]. "Landing of the French at Killala: By an Eye Witness." *Dublin Penny Journal* 1, no. 49 (1833): 391–92.

———. ["A Guardian of the Poor"]. *The Irish Peasant: A Sociological Study*. London, 1892.

Abrahams, Roger D. "Personal Power and Social Restraint in the Definition of Folklore." In Paredes and Bauman, *Toward New Perspectives in Folklore*, 16–30.

Aarne, Antti, and Stith Thompson. *The Types of the Folk-Tale: A Classification and Bibliography*. Helsinki: Academia Scientiarum Fennica, 1961; orig. ed. 1928.

Aldridge, R. B. "The Journal of Captain Joseph Bull." *Irish Sword* 8 (1967): 65–70, 109–14, 86–91, 253–60.

Amin, Shahid. *Event, Memory, Metaphor: Chauri Chaura 1922–1992*. Berkeley: Univ. of California Press, 1992.

Andrews, J. H. *A Paper Landscape: The Ordnance Survey in Nineteenth-Century Ireland*. Oxford: Oxford Univ. Press, 1975.

Archdeacon, Matthew. *Connaught: a Tale of 1798*. Dublin, 1830.

Arensberg, Conrad M., and Solon T. Kimball. *Family and Community in Ireland*. Ennis: Clasp Press, 2001; orig. ed. 1940.

Baeyens, Jacques. *Sabre Au Clair: Amable Humbert, Général de la République*. Paris: Albatros, 1981.

Ballinamuck Bicentenary Committee. *Record of the Ballinamuck Bicentenary Commemoration 1798–1998*. Longford, 1999.

Ballinamuck Commemoration Committee. *1798 Commemoration at Ballinamuck, County Longford: Sunday, September 11th 1938, Souvenir Programme*. Longford, 1938.

Barrington, Sir Jonah. *Historic Memoirs of Ireland; comprising of secret records of the national convention, the rebellion and the Union; with delineations of the principal characters connected with the transactions*, 2 vols. London, 1835; orig. ed. vol. 1, 1809; vol. 2, 1815.

Barry, Michael Joseph. *The Songs of Ireland*. Dublin, 1846; orig. ed. 1845.

Bartlett, Thomas. "Indiscipline and Disaffection in the Armed Forces in Ireland in the 1790s." In Cornish, *Radicals, Rebels and Establishments*, 115–34.

———. "General Humbert Takes His Leave." *Cathair na Mart* (Journal of the Westport Historical Society) 11 (1991): 98–104.

———. "'Masters of the Mountains': The Insurgent Careers of Joseph Holt and Michael Dwyer, County Wicklow 1798–1803." In *Wicklow: History and Society*, edited by Ken Hannigan and William Nolan, 379–410. Dublin: Geography Publications, 1994.

———. "Defence, Counter-Insurgency and Rebellion: Ireland, 1793–1803." In Bartlett and Jeffery, *A Military History of Ireland*, 247–93.

———. "Bearing Witness: Female Evidences in Courts Martial." In *The Women of 1798*, edited by Dáire Keogh and Nicholas Furlong, 64–86. Dublin: Four Courts Press, 1998.

———, ed. *Life of Theobald Wolfe Tone: Compiled and Arranged by William Theobald Wolfe Tone*. Dublin: Lilliput Press, 1998.

———. "Representing the Rebellion in County Longford." In Rehill, *Ballinamuck Bi-Centenary, 1798–1998*, 151–59.

———. "The 1798 Rebellion in Perspective." In Bull, Devlin-Glass, and Doyle, *Ireland and Australia, 1798–1998: Studies in Culture, Identity and Migration*, 13–23.

———. "Why the History of the 1798 Rebellion Has yet to Be Written." *Eighteenth-Century Ireland* 15 (2000): 181–90.

———. "Informers, Informants and Information: The Secret History of the 1790s Reconsidered." In Bartlett et al., *1798: A Bicentenary Perspective*, 406–22.

Bartlett, Thomas, and Keith Jeffery, eds. *A Military History of Ireland*. Cambridge: Cambridge Univ. Press, 1996.

Bartlett, Thomas, Kevin Dawson, and Dáire Keogh. *Rebellion: A Television History of 1798*. Dublin: Gill & Macmillan, 1998.

Bartlett, Thomas, David Dickson, Dáire Keogh, and Kevin Whelan, eds. *1798: A Bicentenary Perspective*. Dublin: Four Courts Press, 2003.

Beatty, John B. "Protestant Women of County Wexford and Their Narratives of the Rebellion of 1798." In Keogh and Furlong, *The Women of 1798*, 113–36.

———. *Protestant Women's Narratives of the Irish Rebellion of 1798*. Dublin: Four Courts Press, 2001.

Becket, J. C. *The Study of Irish History*. Belfast: Queens Univ. Belfast, 1963.

"The Bellman." "Meet Dr. Hayes or The Genial Censor." *Bell* 3, no. 2 (1941): 106–14.

Ben-Amos, Dan, and Liliane Weissberg, eds. *Cultural Memory and the Construction of Identity*. Detroit: Wayne State Univ. Press, 1999.

Bertaud, Jean-Paul. "Forgotten Soldiers: The Expedition of General Humbert to Ireland in 1798." In Gough and Dickson, *Ireland and the French Revolution*, 220–28.

Bew, Paul. *Land and the National Question in Ireland, 1858–82*. Dublin: Gill & Macmillan, 1978.

Bhreathnach-Lynch, Síghle. "Commemorating the Hero in Newly Independent Ireland: Expressions of Nationhood in Bronze and Stone." In L. W. McBride, *Images, Icons and the Irish Nationalist Imagination*, 148–65.

Blake, Martin J. *Blake Family Records, 1600–1700*. London: Elliot Stock, 1905.

Bodkin, Mathias McDonnell. *The Rebels*. London: Ward, Lock & Co., 1899.

Bort, Eberhard, ed. *Commemorating Ireland: History, Politics, Culture*. Dublin: Irish Academic Press, 2004.

Bourke, Angela, et al., eds. *The Field Day Anthology of Irish Writing*. Vol. 4. Cork: Cork Univ. Press and Field Day, 2002.

Bourke, F. S. "The French Invasion of 1798: A Forgotten Eyewitness." *Irish Sword* 2 (1954): 289–94.

Boyce, D. G. "'No Lack of Ghosts': Memory, Commemoration, and the State in Ireland." In I. McBride, *History and Memory in Modern Ireland*, 254–71.

Boylan, Henry, ed. *A Dictionary of Irish Biography*. Dublin: Gill & Macmillan, 1998.

Boyle, Francis. *Miscellaneous Poems.* 1811.

Bradley, P. Brendan. *Bantry Bay: Ireland in the Days of Napoleon and Wolfe Tone.* London: Williams & Norgate, 1931.

Brady, Ciaran, ed. *Interpreting Irish History: The Debate on Historical Revisionism, 1938–1994.* Dublin: Irish Academic Press, 1994.

Breathnach, Diarmuid, and Máire Ní Mhurchú. *Beathaisnéis 1882–1982.* 5 vols. Dublin: An Clóchomhar Tta, 1986.

Brown, Stephen J. *A Guide to Books on Ireland.* Dublin: Hoggis Figgis, 1912.

———. *Ireland in Fiction: A Guide to Irish Novels, Tales, Romances, and Folklore.* Dublin: Maunsel & Co., 1916.

Brown, Terence. *Ireland: A Social and Cultural History 1922–1985.* London: Fontana, 1985.

Buchanan, Robert, *The "Peep 'O Day Boy": A Story of the "Ninety-Eight."* London: John Dicks, 1900.

Bulfin, William. *Rambles in Eirinn.* Dublin: M. H. Gill & Son, 1907.

Bull, Philip, Frances Devlin-Glass, and Helen Doyle, eds. *Ireland and Australia, 1798–1998: Studies in Culture, Identity and Migration.* Sydney: Crossing Press, 2000.

Burke, Peter. "History as Social Memory." In *Memory: History, Culture and the Mind,* edited by Thomas Butler, 97–113. Oxford: Basil Blackwell, 1989.

———, ed. *New Perspectives on Historical Writing.* Cambridge: Cambridge Univ. Press, 1991.

Burne, Charlotte Sophia. *The Handbook of Folklore.* London: Sidgewick & Jackson, 1957; orig. ed. 1913.

Butler, Harriet Jessie, and Harold Edgeworth Butler, eds. *The Black Book of Edgeworthstown and Other Edgeworth Memories 1585–1817.* London: Faber & Gwyer, 1927.

Buttimer, Neil, Colin Rynne, and Helen Guerin, eds. *The Heritage of Ireland.* Cork: Collins Press, 2000.

Byrne, Fanny. *Memoirs of Miles Byrne, Edited by His Widow.* Dublin: Maunsel, 1907; orig. ed. Paris, 1863.

Callan, Patrick. "Aspects of the Transmission of History in Ireland During the Latter Half of the Nineteenth Century." *Irish Educational Studies* 6, no. 2 (1986–87): 56–75.

Campbell, Fergus. *Land and Revolution: Nationalist Politics in the West of Ireland 1891–1921.* Oxford: Oxford Univ. Press, 2005.

Carleton, William. *Tales and Sketches Illustrating the Character, Usages, Traditions, Sports and Pastimes of the Irish Peasantry.* Dublin: James Duffy, 1854.

———. *Traits and Stories of the Irish Peasantry.* 2 vols. London: George Routledge & Sons, 1877; orig. ed. 1833.

Carolan, Nicholas. "Irish Political Balladry." In *The French Are in the Bay: The Expedition to Bantry Bay, 1796,* edited by John A. Murphy, 138–44. Cork: Mercier Press, 1997.

Carrigbyrne Pike Group, ed. *Footsteps of '98.* Carrigbyrne County Wexford: Carrigbyrne Pike Group, 1998.

Carroll, Denis. "Myles Prendergast OSA." In *Unusual Suspects: Twelve Radical Clergymen,* edited by Denis Carroll, 60–69. Blackrock, Co. Dublin: Columba Press, 1998.

Carter, Erica, and Ken Hirschkop, eds. "Cultural Memory." Special issue, *New Formations* 30 (Winter 1996–97).

Casey, Jimmy, John Carthy, and Sean Cahill. *Primary Schools in County Longford.* Longford, 2000.

Castlebar 1798 Commemorative Committee, eds. *1798: A Commemorative Booklet.* Castlebar, 1998.

"Cearnach, Conal." "A Story of the French Invasion in '98." *Celt* (1858): 271–76.

Chambers, Liam. *Rebellion in Kildare 1790–1813.* Dublin: Four Courts Press, 1998.

Christian Brothers [Br. O'Brien]. *Irish History Reader.* Dublin: M.H. Gill & Son, and London: Burns & Oates, 1916; orig. ed. 1905.

Clarke, Basil. "Joseph Stock and Killala." *Éire—Ireland* 20, no. 1 (1985): 58–72.

Cloney, Sean. "The Hessians." *Journal of the Wexford Historical Society* 14 (1992–93): 113–28.

Colleran, Gabriel. "The Year of the French." In O'Hara, *Mayo: Aspects of its Heritage*, 88–95.

Collins, Peter. "The Contest of Memory: The Continuing Impact of 1798 Commemoration." *Éire-Ireland* 34, no. 2 (1999): 28–50.

————. *Who Fears to Speak of '98?: Commemoration and the Continuing Impact of the United Irishmen*. Belfast: Ulster Historical Foundation, 2004.

Columb, Frank. *The Lough Gowna Valley*. Oxford: Gasan Academic Publishing Company, 2003.

Comer, Michael. "Humbert in Swinford." *Swinford Echoes* (1997): 95–97.

Comer, Michael, and Nollaig Ó Muraíle, eds. *Béacán/Bekan: Portrait of an East Mayo Parish*. Ballinrobe: Michael Comer, 1986.

Concannon, Mrs. Thomas [Helena]. *Women of 'Ninety-Eight*. 2nd ed. Dublin: M. H. Gill & Son, 1920; orig. ed. 1919.

Connerton, Paul. *How Societies Remember*. Cambridge: Cambridge Univ. Press, 1989.

Connolly, S. J. "Aftermath and Adjustment." In *A New History of Ireland*, vol. 5, edited by W. E. Vaughan, 1–23. Oxford: Oxford Univ. Press, 1989.

————., ed. *The Oxford Companion to Irish History*. Oxford: Oxford Univ. Press, 1998.

Cooney, John. "Two French Revolutionary Soldiers in Rebel Ireland." *Études Irlandaises* 13, no. 2 (1988): 101–7.

————. *Humbert's Expedition—a Lost Cause?* Ballina: Bicentennial Humbert School and *Western People*, 1989.

————. "En Campagne Avec L'Armée D'Humbert." *Études Irlandaises* 23, no. 2 (1998): 137–49.

————. *Humbert: A French General in Rebel Ireland, 1798*. Ballina: Humbert Publications, 1998.

————, ed. *The 1798 Campaign by a French Lieutenant*. Westport: Westprint Ltd., n.d.

Cooney, John, and Tony McGarry. eds. *The General Humbert Addresses 1987–1989*. Ballina, 1989.

————, eds. *The Irish-French Alliance: Papers of the Humbert Summer School, Mayo, 1987*. Ballina: Western People, 1988.

————, eds. *Post Mastricht Papers of the 1992 Humbert Summer School*. Dublin: Humbert Publications, 1993.

————, eds. *Who Rules Europe?: Papers of the 1993 Humbert Summer School*. Dublin: Humbert Publications, 1993.

————, eds. *Spin-Doctors: A Threat to Democracy? Papers of the 1994 Humbert Summer School*. Dublin: Humbert Publications, 1994.

————, eds. *A New Ireland Quest for Peace: Papers of the 1995 Humbert Summer School*. Dublin: Humbert Publications, 1995.

————, eds. *Humbert Papers 1996: From Lemass to the Millennium*. Dublin: Humbert Publications, 1996.

————, eds. *Peace in Ireland: Humbert Bicentenary Papers*. Dublin: Humbert Publications, 1998.

Corkey, William. *The Church of Rome and Irish Unrest: How Hatred of Britain Is Taught in Irish Schools*. Edinburgh: William Bishop, 1918.

Cornish, Patrick J., ed. *Radicals, Rebels and Establishments*. Belfast: Appletree Press, 1985.

Cosgrove, Art, and Donal McCartney, eds. *Studies in Irish History*. Dublin: Univ. College Dublin Press, 1979.

Costello, Nuala. "Jobit's Journal of the French Expedition, 1798." *Analecta Hibernica*, no. 11 (1941): 7–55.

————. "Little's Diary of the French Landing in 1798." *Analecta Hibernica*, no. 11 (1941): 59–168 (ed. text of RIA MS 3 B 51).

Cox, Liam. "Westmeath in the 1798 Period." *Irish Sword* 9 (1969): 1–15.

Croker, Thomas Crofton. *Researches in the South of Ireland: Illustrative of the Scenery, Architectural Remains and the Manners and Superstitions of the Peasantry with an Appendix Containing a Private Narrative of the Rebellion of 1798*.

Shannon: Irish Academic Press, 1969; orig. ed. London, 1824.

———, ed. *Popular Songs Illustrative of the French Invasions of Ireland*. Parts 3–4: *The Bantry Bay and Killala Invasions*. London: Richards, 1847.

Crone, John S., and F. C. Bigger, eds. *In Remembrance: Articles & Sketches, Biographical, Historical, Topographical, by Francis Joseph Bigger, M.A., M.R.I.A., F.R.S.A.I.* Dublin, Cork: Talbot Press, and Belfast: Mullan & Son, 1927.

Cronin, Maura. "Memory, Story and Balladry: 1798 and Its Place in Popular Memory in Pre-Famine Ireland." In Geary, *Rebellion and Remembrance in Modern Ireland*, 112–34.

Crooke, Elizabeth. "Exhibiting 1798: Three Recent Exhibitions." *History Ireland* 6, no. 4 (1998): 41–45.

Crossman, Virginia. "The Shan Van Vocht: Women, Republicanism, and the Commemoration of the 1798 Rebellion." *Eighteenth Century Life* 22, no. 3 (1998): 128–39.

Crossmolina Historical and Archaeological Society. *The Deel Basin: A Historical Survey*. Ballina, 1990.

Cullen, Louis M. "Poetry, Culture and Politics." *Studia Celtica Japonica*, no. 8 (1996): 1–26.

Cullen, Mary. "Partners in Struggle: The Women of 1798." In Póirtéir, *The Great Irish Rebellion of 1798*, 146–59.

Curtin, Nancy J. *The United Irishmen: Popular Politics in Ulster and Dublin, 1791–1798*. Oxford: Clarendon Press, 1998.

Curtis, L. Perry, Jr. *Images of Erin in the Age of Parnell*. Dublin: National Library of Ireland, 2000.

D'Alton, E. A. "The French in Mayo, 1798." *Journal of the Galway Archaeological and Historical Society* 4 (1905): 219–25.

———. *History of the Archdiocese of Tuam*. Dublin, 1928.

Daly, J. Bowles, ed. *Ireland in '98. Sketches of the Principal Men of the Time. Based Upon the Published Volumes and Some Unpublished Mss of the Late Dr. Richard Robert Madden*. London: Swan Sonnenschein, Lowrey & Co., 1888.

Daly, Mary. "The Development of the National School System, 1831–40." In Cosgrave and McCartney, *Studies in Irish History*, 150–63.

Daly, Mary, and David Dickson, eds. *The Origins of Popular Literacy in Ireland: Language Change and Educational Development 1700–1920*. Dublin: Department of Modern History, Trinity College Dublin, 1990.

Danaher, Kevin (Ó Danachair, Caoimhín). "The Questionnaire System." *Béaloideas* 15 (1945): 203–17.

———. "The Irish Folklore Commission." *Folklore and Folk Music Archivist* 4, no. 1 (1961): 1, 4.

———. "Folk Tradition and Literature." *Journal of Irish Literature* 1, no. 2 (1972): 63–76.

———. *The Year in Ireland: A Calendar*. Cork: Mercier Press, 1972.

———. "The Death of a Tradition." *Studies* 63, no. 251 (1974): 219–30.

———. *A Bibliography of Irish Ethnology and Folk Tradition*. Dublin: Mercier Press, 1978.

———. "The Progress of Irish Ethnology, 1783–1982." *Ulster Folklife* 29 (1983): 3–17.

Danaher, Kevin, and Patricia Lysaght. "Supplement to a Bibliography of Irish Ethnology and Folk Tradition." *Béaloideas* 48–49 (1980): 206–17.

Davis, Natalie Zemon, and Randolph Stern. "Introduction: Memory and Counter-Memory." *Representations* 26 (1989): 1–6.

Deane, Seamus, gen. ed. *The Field Day Anthology of Irish Writing*. Vol. 2. Derry: Field Day, 1991.

de Búrca, Seán. "An Echo of 1798." *Cathair na Mart* 19 (1999): 47.

de Jonnès, Moreau. *Adventures in the Revolution and under the Consulate*. London: Peter Davies, 1969; orig. ed. 1929.

Delargy, James Hamilton [Ó Duilearga, Séamas]. "Editorial." *Béaloideas* 1 (1928): 3–6.

———. "Editorial: The Importance of Irish

Popular Tradition." *Béaloideas* 3 (1932): 103–4.

———. "The Gaelic Storyteller. With Some Notes on Gaelic Folk Tales." *Proceedings of the British Academy* 31 (1945): 177–221.

———. "Seanchas Phádraig Mhic Meanaman." *Béaloideas* 16 (1946): 215–79.

Department of Irish Folklore NUI Dublin, *The Department of Irish Folklore and its Archive*. Dublin, 1993.

de Quincey, Thomas. "Sketches of Life and Manners; From the Autobiography of an English Opium Eater." *Tait's Edinburgh Magazine* 1 (1834): 200–204 and 263–66.

Desbrière, Édouard. *1793–1805: Projets et Tentatives de Débarquement aux Iles Britanniques*, Vol. 2. Paris: Librairie Militaire R. Chapelot, 1900–02.

Devaney, Owen. *Killoe: History of a County Longford Parish*. Cavan: Abbey Printers, 1981.

———. "Ballinamuck in Song and Story." In Rehill, *Ballinamuck Bi-Centenary, 1798–1998*, 57–81.

———. "Ballinamuck and '98." In *To the Memory of Ballinamuck on 8th September 1798*. Ballinamuck, 1998 (souvenir booklet).

Dickson, David, Dáire Keogh, and Kevin Whelan, eds. *The United Irishmen: Republicanism, Radicalism and Rebellion*. Dublin: Lilliput, 1993.

Dinneen, Patrick S. *Foclóir Gaedhilge agus Béarla: An Irish-English Dictionary*. Dublin, 1937.

Doherty, Gabriel. "National Identities and the Study of Irish History." *English Historical Review* 111 (1996): 324–49.

Doherty, Gillian. *The Irish Ordnance Survey: History, Culture and Memory*. Dublin: Four Courts Press, 2004.

Donnelly, James S., Jr. "Propagating the Cause of the United Irishmen." *Studies* 69 (1980): 5–23.

———. "The Peak of Marianism in Ireland, 1930–60." In *Piety and Power in Ireland 1760–1960: Essays in Honour of Emmet Larkin*, edited by Stewart J. Brown and

David W. Miller, 252–83. Belfast: Institute of Irish Studies, and Indiana: Univ. of Notre Dame, 2000.

———. "Pastorini and Captain Rock: Millenarianism and Sectarianism in the Rockite Movement of 1821–4." In *Irish Peasants: Violence and Political Unrest 1780–1914*, edited by Samuel Clarke and James S. Donnelly, Jr., 102–37. Dublin: Gill & Macmillan, 1983.

———. "Sectarianism in 1798 and in Catholic Nationalist Memory." In *Rebellion and Remembrance in Modern Ireland*, edited by Laurence M. Geary, 15–37. Dublin: Four Courts Press, 2001.

Donnelly, James S., Jr., and Kerby A. Miller, eds. *Irish Popular Culture, 1650–1850*. Dublin: Irish Academic Press, 1998.

Donoghue, Denis. *We Irish*. Brighton Sussex: Harvester Press, 1986.

Donohue, Tony. "Some Recollections of Local Involvement in the 1798 Rebellion: Crosmollina and Addergoole." *Bliainiris* 1, no. 1 (1982): 36–40.

———. "Michael Timoney: Gaelic Scholar and Writer." *Bliainiris* 1, no. 2 (1983): 25–26.

——— (signed A.D.). "Father Henry O'Keon: The Green Horseman." *Bliainiris*, 2 (1983–84): 48.

———, ed. *Local Songs, Poems and Ballads from the Shadow of Nephin*. Ballina: Ballina Printing Co., n.d.

Dorson, Richard M., ed. *Folklore Research around the World: A North American Point of View*. Bloomington: Indiana Univ. Press, 1961.

———. "Oral Tradition and Written History." *Journal of the Folklore Institute* (1964): 200–34.

———. "The Question of Folklore in a New Nation." *Journal of the Folklore Institute* 3 (1966): 277–98.

———. *The British Folklorists: A History*. Chicago: Univ. of Chicago Press, 1968.

———. "The Debate over the Trustworthiness of Oral Traditional History." In *Volksüberlieferung, Festschrift für Kurt*

Ranke, edited by Fritz Harkot, Karel C. Peeters, and Robert C. Wildhaber, 19–35. Göttingen: O. Schwartz, 1968.

———, ed. *Folklore and Folklife: An Introduction.* Chicago: Univ. of Chicago Press, 1972.

———. *Folklore and Fakelore:* Cambridge, MA: Harvard Univ. Press, 1976.

———. "The Oral Historian and the Folklorist." In Dunaway and Baum, *Oral History: An Interdisciplinary Anthology,* 283–91.

Dowds, Thomas J. *The French Invasion of Ireland in 1798.* Stillorgan, Co. Dublin: IHR Publications, 2000.

Doyle, Danny, and Terence Folan. *The Gold Sun of Irish Freedom: 1798 in Song and Story.* Cork: Mercier Press, 1998.

Dublin 1798 Commemorative Committee, *Dublin '98 Programme.* Dublin, 1998.

Dudley Edwards, Robert. "An Agenda for Irish History, 1978–2018." In Brady, *Interpreting Irish History,* 54–67.

Duffy, Charles Gavan, ed. *The Ballad Poetry of Ireland.* Dublin: James Duffy & Sons, 1866; orig. ed. 1845.

———. *Short Life of Thomas Davis, 1840–1846.* London, 1895.

Duffy, Charles Gavan et al. *The Spirit of the Nation: 1845.* Washington, D.C.: Woodstock Books, 1998 (reprint of 3rd ed.); orig. ed. 1843.

Duffy, Patrick. "Locality and Changing Landscape: Geography and Local History." In *Doing Irish Local History,* edited by Raymond Gillespie and Myrtle Hill, 24–46. Belfast: Institute of Irish Studies, QUB, 1998.

Dunaway, David K., and Willa K. Baum, eds. *Oral History: An Interdisciplinary Anthology.* Walnut Creek, CA: Alta Mira, 1996.

Dunne, Tom. "Popular Ballads, Revolutionary Rhetoric and Politicisation." In Gough and Dickson, *Ireland and the French Revolution,* 139–55.

———. "Representations of Rebellion: 1798 in Literature." In *Ireland, England and Australia: Essays in Honour of Oliver Macdonagh,* edited by F. B. Smith, 14–40. Canberra: Australian National Univ., and Cork: Cork Univ. Press, 1990.

———. "1798: Memory, History, Commemoration." *Journal of the Wexford Historical Society* 16 (1996): 5–39.

———. "1798 and the United Irishmen." *Irish Review* 22 (1998): 46–53.

———. "Wexford's Comoradh '98: Politics, Heritage and History." *History Ireland* 6, no. 2 (1998): 49–53.

———. "Subaltern Voices? Poetry in Irish, Popular Insurgency and the 1798 Rebellion." *Eighteenth Century Life* 22, no. 3 (1998): 31–44.

———. "Rebel Motives and Mentalities: The Battle for New Ross, 5 June 1798." *Éire-Ireland* 34, no. 2 (1999): 5–27.

———. "'Tá Gaedhil Bhocht Cráidhte': Memory, Tradition and the Politics of the Poor in Gaelic Poetry and Song." In Geary, *Rebellion and Remembrance in Modern Ireland,* 93–111.

Eden, William [Baron Auckland]. *Journal and Correspondence of William, Lord Auckland,* Vol. 4. London: Richard Bentley, 1862.

Edgeworth, Robert Lovell, and Maria Edgeworth. *Memoirs of Richard Lovell Edgeworth: Begun by Himself and Concluded by His Daughter Maria Edgeworth.* Shannon: Irish Univ. Press, 1969; org. ed. London, 1820.

Edwards, R. D., and T. D. Williams, eds. *The Great Famine: Studies in Irish History, 1845–52.* Dublin: Lilliput Press, 1957.

Egan, Patrick K. "Progress and Suppression of the United Irishmen in the Western Counties in 1798–99." *Journal of the Galway Archaeological and Historical Society* 25, no. 3–4 (1953–54): 104–34.

Elliott, Marianne. *Partners in Revolution: The United Irishmen and France.* New Haven: Yale Univ. Press, 1982.

———. *Wolfe Tone. Prophet of Irish Independence.* New Haven: Yale Univ. Press, 1989.

Evans, Emyr Estyn. *The Personality of Ireland: Habitat, Heritage and History.* Cambridge: Cambridge Univ. Press, 1973.

Faculty of Celtic Studies, NUI Dublin, *Commemorative Programme for the Centenary of the Birth of James Hamilton Delargy, 25.6.1899–26.5.1980*. Dublin, 1999.

Falkiner, C. Litton. "The French Invasion of Ireland in 1798." *Macmillan's Magazine* 77 (1898): 227–40 and 301–13.

———. *Studies in Irish History and Biography, Mainly of the Eighteenth Century.* London: Longmans, Green & Co., 1902.

Faly, Patrick C. [John Hill]. *Ninety-Eight: Being the Recollections of Cormac Cahir O'Connor Faly (late Colonel in the French Service) of that awful period. Collected and Edited by his grandson Patrick C. Faly, Attorney-at-Law Buffalo, N.Y. and illustrated by A.D. McCormick.* London: Downey, 1897.

Fanning, Ronan. "'The Great Enchantment': Uses and Abuses of Modern Irish History." In Brady, *Interpreting Irish History*, 146–60.

Farrell, James P. *Historical Notes and Stories of the County Longford.* Dublin: Dollard, 1886.

Fennell, Desmond. *A Connacht Journey.* Dublin: Gill & Macmillan, 1987.

Fentress, James, and Chris Wickham. *Social Memory.* Oxford: Blackwell, 1992.

Ferriter, Diarmaid. "Archives Report." *Irish Economic and Social History* 25 (1998): 91–95.

Finnegan, Ruth. *Literacy and Orality: Studies in the Technology of Communication.* Oxford: Oxford Univ. Press, 1988.

Fitzpatrick, David. "Class, Family and Rural Unrest in Nineteenth-Century Ireland." In *Irish Studies 2; Ireland: Land, Politics and People*, edited by P. J. Drury, 37–75. Cambridge: Cambridge Univ. Press, 1982.

———. "The Futility of History: A Failed Experiment in Irish Education." In *Ideology and the Historians*, edited by Ciaran Brady, 168–82. Dublin, 1991.

———. "Commemoration in the Irish Free State: A Chronicle of Embarrassment." In I. McBride, *History and Memory in Modern Ireland*, 184–203.

Fitzpatrick, W. J. *"The Sham Squire" and the Informers of 1798: with Jottings about Ireland a Century Ago.* 2nd ed. Dublin: M. H. Gill & Son, 1865.

Flanagan, Thomas. *The Irish Novelists 1800–1850.* Westport, CT: Greenwood Press, 1976; orig. ed. 1959.

———. *The Year of the French.* New York: Holt, Reinhart & Winston, 1979.

Flower, Robin. *The Irish Tradition.* Oxford: Oxford Univ. Press, 1947.

Flynn, Kathleen, and Stan McCormack. *Westmeath 1798: A Kilbeggan Rebellion.* Kilbeggan: K. Flynn & S. McCormack, 1998.

Fogarty, Anne. "'Where Wolfe Tone's Statue Was Not': Joyce, 1798 and the Politics of Memory." In "Études Irlandaises." Special issue, *Irlande: Fins de Siècles* 24, no. 2 (1999): 19–32.

Foley, Tadhg, and Seán Ryder, eds. *Ideology and Ireland in the Nineteenth Century.* Dublin: Four Courts Press, 1998.

Foster, R. F. *Modern Ireland, 1600–1972.* London: Allen Lane, 1988.

———. *The Story of Ireland: An Inaugural Lecture Delivered before the University of Oxford on 1 December 1994.* Oxford: Clarendon Press, 1995.

———. "Remembering 1798." In I. McBride, *History and Memory in Modern Ireland*, 67–94.

———. *The Irish Story: Telling Tales and Making It up in Ireland.* London: Allen Lane, 2001.

Foucault, Michel. *The Archaeology of Knowledge.* London: Tavistock, 1972.

———. *Discipline and Punish: The Birth of the Prison.* London: Penguin Books, 1991; orig. ed. 1977.

Fowler, Joseph H. *Chapters in '98 History.* London: St. Giles Bookshop, 1938.

Fraser, James. *Handbook for Travellers in Ireland, Descriptive of Its Scenery, Towns, Antiquities, Etc.* Dublin: McGlashen & Gill, 1854; orig. ed. 1838.

Freyer, Grattan, ed. *Bishop Stock's "Narrative" of the Year of the French: 1798.* Ballina: Irish Humanities Centre, 1982.

Freyer, Grattan, and Sheila Mulloy. "The Unfortunate John Moore." *Cathair na Mart* 4 (1985): 51–68.

Friel, Brian. *Plays*. London: Faber & Faber, 1999.

Froude, James Anthony. *The English in Ireland in the Eighteenth Century*, Vol. 3. London: Longmans, Green & Co., 1887; orig. ed. 1874.

Furlong, Nicholas. *Fr. John Murphy of Boolavaogue: 1753–1798*. Dublin: Geography Publications, 1991.

Gasty. "L'Étonnante De L'Armée d'Irlande." *Revue Historique de L'Armée* 8, no. 4 (1952): 19–32.

Geary, Laurence M., ed. *Rebellion and Remembrance in Modern Ireland*. Dublin: Four Courts Press, 2001.

Gibbons, John. "Father Myles Prendergast." *An Coinneal*, no. 12 (1980): 79–82.

Gibbons, Luke. "'Some Historical Hatred': History, Hysteria and the Literary Revival." *Irish University Review* 27, no. 1 (1997): 7–23.

———. "Radical Memory." *Index on Censorship* 27, no. 5 (1998): 141–43.

———. "Alternative Enlightenments. The United Irishmen, Cultural Diversity and the Republic of Letters." In *1798: 200 Years of Resonance*, edited by Mary Cullen, 119–27. Dublin: Irish Reporter Publications, 1998.

———. "Republicanism and Radical Memory: The O'Conors, O'Carolan and the United Irishmen." In Smyth, *Revolution, Counter-Revolution and Union*, 211–37.

———. "'Where Wolfe Tone's Statue Was Not': Joyce, Monuments and Memory." In I. McBride, *History and Memory in Modern Ireland*, 139–59.

Gibbons, Rev. J. J. *Slieve Bawn and the Croppy Scout: A Historical Tale of Seventeen Ninety-Eight in North Connaught*. Denver: Kistler Press, 1914.

Gillespie, Raymond, and Gerald Moran, eds. *"A Various Country": Essays in Mayo History, 1500–1900*. Westport: Foilseacháin Náisiúnta Teoranta, 1987.

Gillis, John R., ed. *Commemorations: The Politics of National Identity*. Princeton: Princeton Univ. Press, 1994.

Glassie, Henry. "Folklore and History." In *The Use of Tradition: Essays Presented to G. B. Thompson*, edited by Alan Gailey, 68–74. Holywood: Ulster Folk & Transport Museum, 1988.

———. *Passing the Time in Ballymenone: Culture and History of an Ulster Community*. Bloomington: Indiana Univ. Press, 1995.

Gordon, James. *History of the Rebellion in Ireland, in the Year 1798, Containing an Impartial Account of the Proceedings of the Irish Revolutionists, from the Year 1782 till the Suppression of the Rebellion*. Dublin: William Porter, 1801.

Gough, Hugh. "France and the 1798 Rebellion." In Póirtéir, *The Great Irish Rebellion*, 37–48.

Gough, Hugh, and David Dickson, eds. *Ireland and the French Revolution*. Dublin: Irish Academic Press, 1990.

Gould, Warwick, John Kelly, and Deirdre Toomey, eds. *The Collected Letters of W. B. Yeats*. Vol. 2. Oxford: Clarendon Press, 1997.

Graham, Tommy. "The Colossus of Clonegal." *History Ireland* 9, no. 4 (2001): 42–45.

Greer, James. *The Windings of the Moy with Skreen and Tireragh*. Dublin: Alex Thom & Co., n.d.

Gregory, Lady. *The Kiltartan History Book*. London: T. Fisher Unwin, 1926; orig. ed. 1909.

———. *The Kiltartan Poetry Book*. London: G. Putnam's Sons, 1919; orig. ed. 1918.

Gribayédoff, Valerian. *The French Invasion of Ireland in '98: Leaves of Unwritten History That Tell of an Heroic Endeavor and a Lost Opportunity to Throw Off England's Yoke*. New York: Charles P. Somerby, 1890.

Griffin, Brian. "'Scallions, Pikes and Bog Oak Ornaments': The Irish Republican Brotherhood and the Chicago Fenian Fair, 1864." *Studia Hibernica*, no. 29 (1995): 85–97.

Griffith, Arthur, ed. *Poems and Ballads by William Rooney (Fear na Muinntire)*. Dublin: M. H. Gill & Son, 1901.

Groeger, J. A. *Memory and Remembering: Everyday Memory in Context*. Essex: Longman, 1997.

Gross, David. *The Past in Ruins: Tradition and the Critique of Modernity*. Amherst: Univ. of Massachusetts, 1992.

Guckian, Des. *Leitrim and Longford, 1798: Undaunted by Gibbet and Yeos*. Longford: Rapid Press, 1998.

Guillon, Édouard. *La France et L'Irlande Pendant La Révolution*. Paris: Armand Colin, 1888.

Gwynn, Mrs. Stephen. *Stories from Irish History*. Dublin: Browne & Nolan, 1904.

Halbwachs, Maurice. *Les Cadres sociaux de la mémoire*. Paris: F. Alcan, 1925.

———. *The Collective Memory*. New York: Harper & Row, 1980.

———. *On Collective Memory*. Chicago: Univ. of Chicago Press, 1992.

Hall, Mr. and Mrs. S. C. *Ireland: Its Scenery, Character, &C*. London: Jeremiah How, 1843.

Hardiman, James. *The History of the Town and County of Galway, from the Earliest Period to the Present Time*. Dublin, 1820.

———. *Irish Minstrelsy or Bardic Remains of Ireland with English Poetical Translations*. 2 vols. Shannon: Irish Univ. Press, 1971 (facsimile of orig. ed., London, 1831).

Hare, Augustus J. C., ed. *The Life and Letters of Maria Edgeworth*. Vol. 1. London: Edward Arnold, 1894.

Harvey, Clodagh Brennan. *Contemporary Irish Traditional Narrative: The English Language Tradition*. Berkeley: Univ. of California Press, 1992.

Hayes, Richard. *Ireland and Irishmen in the French Revolution*. Dublin: Phoenix Pub. Co, 1932.

———. *The Last Invasion of Ireland: When Connacht Rose*. Dublin: M. H. Gill & Son, 1937.

———. "Priests in the Independence Movement of '98." *Irish Ecclesiastical Record* 66 (1945): 258–70.

———. *Biographical Dictionary of Irishmen in France*. Dublin: M. H. Gill & Son, 1949.

———. "An Officer's Account of the French Campaign in Ireland." *Irish Sword* 2 (1955): 110–18, 61–71.

———. "The Battle of Castlebar, 1798." *Irish Sword* 3 (1957): 107–14.

Hayes-McCoy, G. A. "Fencible Corps in Ireland 1782–1803." *Irish Sword*, no. 2 (1954–56): 140–43.

———. "The Irish Pike." *Journal of the Galway Archaeological and Historical Society* 20, no. 3–4 (1943): 99–128.

Heaney, Seamus. "The Sense of the Past." *History Ireland* 1, no. 4 (1993): 33–37.

Henige, D. P. *Chronology of Oral Tradition: Quest for a Chimera*. Oxford: Oxford Univ. Press, 1974.

Henry, Seán. *Tales from the West of Ireland*. Dublin: Mercier Press, 1980.

Herr, Cheryl. *The Land They Loved: Irish Political Melodramas, 1890–1925*. Syracuse: Syracuse Univ. Press, 1993.

Hewitt, Esther, ed. *Lord Shannon's Letters to His Son: A Calendar of the Letters Written by the 2nd Earl of Shannon to His Son, Viscount Boyle, 1790–1802*. Belfast: PRO NI, 1982.

Heyland, Langford. *The Irish Rebellion of 1798: From the Journal of Colonel Heyland of Glendarargh with Copy of Address to the United Irishmen by the Brothers Sheares, and General Humbert's Address to the Army*. London: Glencock, 1913.

Hickey, D. J., and J. E. Doherty, eds. *The Dictionary of Irish History*. Dublin: Gill & Macmillan, 1980.

Higgins, Jim. "1798: Some Galway—Mayo Links." *Cathair na Mart* 22 (2002): 77–83.

Hill, Judith. *Irish Public Sculpture: A History*. Dublin: Four Courts Press, 1998.

Hoban, Brendan. "Dominick Bellew, 1745–1812. Parish Priest of Dundalk and Bishop of Killala." *Seanchas Ard Mhacha* 6, no. 2 (1972): 333–71.

Hobsbawm, Eric. *Bandits*. Harmondsworth: Penguin, 1972.

———. "Mass-Producing Traditions: Europe, 1870–1914." In Hobsbawm and

Terence Ranger, *The Invention of Tradition*, 263–307.

Hobsbawm, Eric, and Terence Ranger, eds. *The Invention of Tradition*. Cambridge: Cambridge Univ. Press, 1983.

Hobson, Bulmer, ed. *The Letters of Theobald Wolfe Tone*. Dublin: M. Lester, Ltd., 1920.

Hogan, Patrick M. "Some Observations on Contemporary Allegations as to Bishop Dominick Bellew's (1745–1813) Sympathies During the 1798 Rebellion in Connaught." *Seanchas Ard Mhacha* 10, no. 2 (1982): 417–25.

———. "The Undoing of Citizen John Moore—the President of the Provisional Government of the Republic of Connacht, 1798." *Journal of the Galway Archaeological and Historical Society* (1981–82): 59–72.

———. "Casualties Sustained by Government Forces During the Humbert Episode, August-September 1798: A Re-Appraisal." *Journal of the Galway Archaeological and Historical Society* 55 (1998): 1–9.

Holohan, Francis T. "History Teaching in the Irish Free State 1922–35." *History Ireland* 2, no. 4 (1994): 53–55.

Hone, Joseph M. *The Moores of Moore Hall*. London: Jonathan Cape, 1939.

Honko, Lauri. "The Folklore Process." *Folklore Fellows' Summer School [FFSS]* (1991): 25–47.

Horgan, Gertrude M., ed. *James Berry, Tales of the West of Ireland*. Dublin: Dolmen, 1966.

Hughes, Carmel. "'98 Celebrations in Ballina." *Bliainiris* 1, no. 1 (1982): 59–71.

———. "'98 Celebrations: 150th Anniversary Commemorated in Ballina and Killala." *Bliainiris*, no. 2 (1983): 27–35.

Hughes, Tommy. "Fr. Manus Sweeney and the Rebellion of 1798." *Back The Road: Recollections of Burrishoole and Newport* 1, no. 2 (1998): 37–42.

Hutton, Patrick H. *History as an Art of Memory*. Hanover, NH: Univ. Press of New England, 1993.

Hyde, Douglas. *Abhráin Atá Leagtha Ar an Reachtúire or Songs Ascribed to Raftery*. Dublin: Gill, 1903.

———. *Abhráin Diadha Chúige Connacht or the Religious Songs of Connacht*. 2nd ed. London: T. Fisher Unwin, and Dublin: M. H. Gill & Sons, n.d.

Jacotey, Marie-Louise. *Le Général Humbert Ou La Passion De La Liberté*. Mirecourt: Imp. de la Plaine de Vosges, 1980.

Joannon, Pierre, ed. *La Descente De Français en Irlande—1798*. Paris: La Vouivre, 1998.

Johnson, Nuala C. "Sculpting Heroic Histories: Celebrating the Centenary of the 1798 Rebellion in Ireland." *Transactions of the Institute of British Geographers* 19 (1994): 78–93.

Jones, John. *An Impartial Narrative of the Most Important Engagements which Took Place between His Majesty's Forces and the Rebels During the Irish Rebellion of 1798*. Dublin, 1799.

Jordan, Donald E., Jr. *Land and Politics in Ireland: County Mayo from the Plantation to the Land War*. Cambridge Univ. Press, 1994.

Joyce, P. J. *A Forgotten Part of Ireland*. Tuam, 1910.

Joyce, Patrick Weston. *A Child's History of Ireland*. London: Longmans, Green & Co. and M. H. Gill & Son, 1903; orig. ed. 1897.

———. *Old Irish Folk Music and Songs*. Dublin: Univ. Press, 1909.

———. *English as We Speak It in Ireland*. London: Longmans, Green & Co., 1910.

Kalliomäki, Aki Nikolai. "Who Dares To Write of '98? The Historiography of the 1798 Rebellion in Ireland 1798–1868." MLitt thesis, TCD, 2000.

Kansteiner, Wulf. "Finding Meaning in Memory: A Methodological Critique of Collective Memory Studies." *History and Theory* 41 (2002): 179–97.

Kavanagh, Partick F. *A Popular History of the Insurrection of 1798: Derived from Everyday Record and Reliable Tradition*. Cork, 1898; orig. ed. Dublin, 1870.

Kelly. Aaron, and A. A. Gillis, eds. *Critical Ire-*

land. *New Essays in Literature and Culture.* Dublin: Four Courts Press, 2001.

Kelly, James. "'The Glorious and Immortal Memory': Commemoration and Protestant Identity in Ireland 1660–1800." *Proceedings of the Royal Irish Academy* 94C (1994): 25–52.

———. "'We Were All to Have Been Massacred': Irish Protestants and the Experience of Rebellion." In Bartlett, Dickson, Keogh, and Whelan, *1798: A Bicentenary Perspective,* 312–30.

Kelly, Liam. *A Flame Now Quenched: Rebels and Frenchmen in Leitrim, 1793–1798.* Dublin: Lilliput Press, 1998.

Kelly, Michael. "The Bekan Area in 'the Year of the French'." In Comer and Ó Muraíle, *Béacan/Bekan: Portrait of an East Mayo Parish,* 146–47.

Kennedy, Liam, Kerby A. Miller, and Mark Graham. "Protestants, Economy and Society, 1660–1926." In *Longford: Essays in County History,* edited by Raymond Gillespie and Gerald Moran, 31–62. Dublin: Lilliput Press, 1991.

Kennedy, Patrick. *Legendary Fictions of the Irish Celts.* London, 1866.

Keogh, Dáire. *The French Disease: The Catholic Church and Irish Radicalism 1790–1800.* Blackrock, Co. Dublin: Four Courts Press, 1993.

———. "Sectarianism in the Rebellion of 1798: The Eighteenth-Century Context." In Keogh and Furlong, *The Mighty Wave,* 37–47.

———. "The Women of 1798: Explaining the Silence." In Bartlett, Dickson, Keogh, and Whelan, *1798: A Bicentenary Perspective,* 512–28.

Keogh, Dáire, and Nicholas Furlong, eds. *The Mighty Wave: The 1798 Rebellion in Wexford.* Dublin: Four Courts Press, 1996.

———, eds. *The Women of 1798.* Dublin: Four Courts Press, 1998.

Kerrigan, Paul M. *Castles and Fortifications in Ireland 1485–1945.* Cork: Collins Press, 1995.

Kiberd, Declan. "The Elephant of Revolutionary Forgetfulness." In Ní Dhonnchadha and Dorgan, *Revising the Rising,* 1–21.

Kilgannon, Tadhg. *Sligo and Its Surroundings: A Descriptive and Pictorial Guide to the History, Scenery, Antiquities, and Places of Interest in and around Sligo.* Sligo: Kilgannon Press & Sons Ltd., 1926.

Kinsella, Anna. "'Who Fears to Speak of '98?' The Nineteenth Century Interpretation of 1798." MLitt thesis, TCD, 1985.

———. "1798 Claimed for Catholics: Father Kavanagh, Fenians and the Centenary Celebrations." In Keogh and Furlong *The Mighty Wave,* 139–55.

———. "Nineteenth-Century Perspectives: The Women of 1798 in Folk Memory and Ballads." In Keogh and Furlong, *The Women of 1798,* 187–200.

———. "Who Feared to Speak in 1898?" *Journal of the Wexford Historical Society* 17 (1998): 221–34.

Kneafsey, Moya. "A Landscape of Memoirs: Heritage Tourism in Mayo." In *Landscape, Heritage and Identity,* edited by Ullrich Kockel, 135–53. Liverpool: Liverpool Univ. Press, 1995.

Larkin, Emmet. "The Devotional Revolution in Ireland, 1850–75." In *The Historical Dimensions of Irish Catholicism,* edited by Emmet Larkin, 57–89. Washington, D.C.: Catholic Univ. of America Press, and Dublin: Four Courts Press, 1997.

Lavelle, Rory. "The Mayo Rebels of '98 in Connemara." *Connemara* (Journal of the Clifden and Connemara Heritage Group) 1, no. 1 (1993): 70–75.

Lavin, Sean. *History of the Civil Parish of Kilcummin.* n.p., 1986.

Lawless, Emily, and Shan F. Bullock. *The Race of Castlebar: Being a Narrative by Mr. John Banbury, Attached to His Brittanic Majesty's Embassy in Florence, October 1798, and Now for the First Given to the World.* London: John Murray, 1913.

Leahy, David. *County Longford and Its People: An Index to the 1901 Census for County Longford.* Glenageary Co. Dublin: Flyleaf Press, 1990.

Lecky, W. E. H. *A History of Ireland in the Eighteenth Century.* Vol. 5. London: Longmans, Green & Co., 1913; orig. ed. 1896.

Lee, Joseph. *The Modernisation of Irish Society, 1848–1918.* Dublin: Gill & Macmillan, 1989; orig. ed. 1973

Leerssen, Joep. *Mere Irish and Fíor Ghael: Studies in the Idea of Irish Nationality, its Development and Literary Expression Prior to the Nineteenth Century.* Cork: Cork Univ. Press and Field Day, 1996.

———. *Remembrance and Imagination: Patterns in the Historical and Literary Representation of Ireland in the Nineteenth Century.* Cork: Cork Univ. Press and Field Day, 1996.

———. "1798: The Recurrence of Violence and Two Conceptualizations of History." *Irish Review* 22 (1998): 37–45.

———. "Monument and Trauma: Varieties of Remembrance." In I. McBride, *History and Memory in Modern Ireland,* 204–22.

Legg, Marie-Louise. *Newspapers and Nationalism: The Irish Provincial Press 1850–1892.* Dublin: Four Courts Press, 1999.

Le Goff, Jacques. *History and Memory.* New York: Columbia Univ. Press, 1992.

Lenehan, John F. "Memories of Ballinamuck." *Teathbha* 1, no. 1 (1969): 47–50.

Lennan, Michael. "The Spirit of '98." In Rehill, *Ballinamuck Bi-Centenary, 1798–1998,* 5–10.

Lever, Charles. *Maurice Tierney, the Soldier of Fortune.* Boston: Little, Brown & Co., 1894; orig. ed. New York, 1852.

Lewis, Samuel. *A Topographical Dictionary of Ireland.* New York, 1837.

Linnane, Margaret, Burke Deirdre, Anne Marie McHale, Joanne Murphy, and Kathleen O'Toole. *Heritage Trail of Castlebar.* Castlebar, 1996.

Logan, John. "Book Learning: The Experience of Reading in the National School 1831–1900." In *The Experience of Reading: Irish Historical Perspectives,* edited by Bernadette Cunningham and Máire Kennedy, 173–95. Dublin: Rare Books Group of the Library Association of Ireland, 1999.

Longley, Edna. "Northern Ireland: Commemoration, Elegy, Forgetting." In I. McBride, *History and Memory in Modern Ireland,* 223–53.

———. "The Rising, the Somme and Irish Memory." In Ní Dhonnchadha and Dorgan, *Revising the Rising,* 29–49.

Lover, Samuel. *Legends and Stories of Ireland.* Westminster: Archibold Constable, 1899; orig. ed. Dublin, 1834.

Lowenthal, David. *The Past Is a Foreign Country.* Cambridge: Cambridge Univ. Press, 1985.

———. *The Heritage Crusade and the Spoils of History.* Cambridge: Cambridge Univ. Press, 1998.

Lucas, Charles. *The Infernal Quixote: A Tale of the Day,* edited by M. O. Grenby. Peterborough, Ont.: Broadview Editions, 2004; orig. ed. 4 vols., London, 1801.

Lyons, Ken. "The Races of Castlebar." In *1798: A Commemorative Booklet,* 13–48.

Mac Atasney, Gerald. *Leitrim and the Croppies 1776–1804.* n.p., 1998.

MacBride White, Anna and A. N. Jeffares eds. *The Gonne-Yeats Letters, 1893–1938: Always Your Friend.* London, 1992.

Mac Ciarnáin, Seamus, ed. *The Last Post.* Dublin: National Graves Association, 1986; orig. ed. 1932.

Mac Coisdealbha, Liam. "Seanchas Ó Iorrus." *Béaloideas* 13 (1943): 173–237.

MacDonald, Brian. "South Ulster in the Age of the United Irishmen." In Bartlett, Dickson, Keogh, and Whelan, *1798: A Bicentenary Perspective,* 226–42.

Mac Gabhann, Micí. *Rotha Mór an tSaoil.* Dublin: Foilseacháin Náisiúnta Teoranta, 1959.

Mac Giollarnáth, Seán. *Annála Beaga ó Iorrus Aithneach.* Dublin: Oifig an tSoláthair, 1941.

———. "Sliocht De Sheanchas Mhicheál Bhreathnaigh." *Béaloideas* 13 (1943): 102–29.

Mac Gréine, Pádraig. "Traditions of 1798, the Battle of Ballinamuck." *Béaloideas* 4 (1933): 393–94.

MacHale, Conor. "Colonel Baron James

O'Dowda, Bonniconlon (1765–1798): The Real Corney O'Dowd." *Bliainiris* 2, no. 2 (1988): 11–20.

MacHale, E. "Official List of Claims for Loss and Damage in the County of Mayo in the Year 1798." *Bliainiris* 2, no. 2 (1988): 21–45.

———. "Some Mayo Priests of 1798." *Bliainiris* 2, no. 5 (1991): 7–20.

Mac Laughlin, Jim. *Reimagining the Nation-State: The Contested Terrains of Nation-Building*. London: Pluto Press, 2001.

MacNeill, Máire. "Wayside Death Cairns in Ireland." *Béaloideas* 16 (1946): 49–63.

———. *The Festival of Lughnasa*. Oxford: Oxford Univ. Press, 1962.

———. "Poll Na Seantuinne and Poll Tigh Liabáin." *Béaloideas* 39–41 (1971): 206–11.

———. "The Musician in the Cave." *Béaloideas* 57 (1989): 109–32.

MacNerney, James P. *From the Well of St. Patrick. Dromard Parish*. Longford: St. Mel's Diocesan Trust and Dromard History Group, 2000.

Mac Philib, Séamas. "The Irish Landlord System in Folk Tradition—Impact and Image." PhD thesis, Univ. College Dublin, 1990.

Mac Shamhráin, A. S. "Ideological Conflict and Historical Interpretation: The Problem of History in Irish Primary Education, ca. 1900–1930." *Irish Educational Studies* 10, no. 1 (1991): 229–40.

Madden, Richard Robert, *The History of Irish Periodical Literature, from the End of the 17th to the Middle of the 19th Century, Its Origins, Progress and Results; with Notices of Remarkable Persons Connected with the Press in Ireland During the Past Two Centuries*. 2 vols. London: T. C. Newby, 1867.

———, ed. *Literary Remains of the United Irishmen of 1798 and Selections from Other Popular Lyrics of Their Times with an Essay on the Authorship of "the Exile of Erin."* Dublin: James Duffy, 1887; orig. compiled in 1846.

———. *The United Irishmen: Their Lives and Times*. 3rd. ed. 12 vols. New York: The Catholic Publication Society, 1910–16. Orig. issued in 2 "editions" (installments). 1st ed.: 1st ser., 2 vols. (London, 1842); 2nd ser., 2 vols. (London, 1843); 3rd ser., 3 vols. (Dublin, 1846). 2nd ed.: 1st ser. (Dublin, 1857); 2nd ser. (Dublin, 1858); 3rd ser. (London, 1860); 4th ser. (London, 1860).

Madden, Thomas. "Book Review of Rebellion in Kildare 1790–1803 by Liam Chambers." *Maynooth University Record* (1998): 14–124.

Madden, Thomas More, ed. *The Memoirs (Chiefly Autobiographical) from 1798 to 1886 of Richard Robert Madden, M.D., F.R.C.S.* London: Ward & Downey, 1891.

Mag Ruaidhrí, Micheál. *Le Linn M'Óige*. Dublin: Coiscéim, 2001; orig. ed. 1944.

Maguire, W. A. *Up in Arms: The 1798 Rebellion in Ireland: A Bicentenary Exhibition*. Belfast: Ulster Museum, 1998.

Mahon, Bríd. *While Green Grass Grows: Memoirs of a Folklorist*. Dublin: Mercier Press, 1998.

Mangin, Edward. *Oddities and Outlines*. 2 vols. London: J. Carpenter, 1806.

———. *The Parlour Window; or, Anecdotes, Original Remarks on Books, Etc*. London: Edward Lumley, 1841.

Matthews, James H. *Voices: A Life of Frank O'Connor*. Dublin: Gill & Macmillan, 1983.

Maxwell, Constantia. *A School History of Ireland*. 2nd ed. Dublin: The Educational Company of Ireland, 1925.

Maxwell, William Hamilton. *Wild Sports of the West, with Legendary Tales and Local Sketches*. London: Richard Bentley, 1832.

———. *The Adventures of Captain Blake; or, My Life*. London: Richard Bentley, 1838.

———. *The Irish Movements: Their Rise, Progress, and Certain Termination; with a Few Broad Hints to Patriots and Pikemen*. London: Baily Brothers, 1848.

———. *Erin-Go-Bragh, or Irish Life Pictures*. London: Richard Bentley, 1859.

———. *History of the Irish Rebellion in 1798; with Memoirs of the Union and Emmett's Insurrection in 1803*. London: George Bell & Sons, 1881; orig. ed. 1845.

McAnally, Henry. "The Government Forces Engaged at Castlebar in 1798." *Irish Historical Studies* 4 (1944): 316–31.

McBride, Ian. "Reclaiming the Rebellion: 1798 in 1998." *Irish Historical Studies* 31, no. 123 (1999): 395–410.

———, ed. *History and Memory in Modern Ireland*. Cambridge: Cambridge Univ. Press, 2001.

———. "Memory and Forgetting: Ulster Presbyterians and 1798." In Bartlett, Dickson, Keogh, and Whelan, *1798: A Bicentenary Perspective*, 478–96.

McBride, Lawrence W. "Historical Imagery in Irish Political Illustrations, 1880–1910." *New Hibernia Review* 2, no. 1 (1998): 9–25.

———. "Visualizing '98: Irish Nationalist Cartoons Commemorate the Revolution." *Eighteenth Century Life* 22, no. 3 (1998): 103–17.

———. "Nationalist Constructions of the 1798 Rebellion: The Political Illustrations of J.D. Reigh." *Éire-Ireland* 34, no. 2 (1999): 117–34.

———. "Young Readers and the Learning and Teaching of Irish History, 1870–1922." In L. W. McBride, *Reading Irish Histories: Texts, Contexts, and Memory in Modern Ireland*, 80–117.

———, ed. *Images, Icons and the Irish Nationalist Imagination*. Dublin: Four Courts Press, 1999.

———, ed. *Reading Irish Histories: Texts, Contexts, and Memory in Modern Ireland*. Dublin: Four Courts Press, 2003.

McCabe, Desmond. "Law, Conflict and Social Order: County Mayo 1820–1845." PhD thesis, Univ. College Dublin, 1991.

McCarthy, Patrick. "Remembering 1798: A Bibliographical Essay." *Irish Sword* 21 (1999): 232–38.

McCormick, James, ed. *The Irish Rebellion*. 2nd ed. Dublin: James McCormick, 1844.

McCoy, Jack. *Ulster's Joan of Arc: An Examination of the Betsy Gray Story*. Bangor: North Down Borough Council Visitors and Heritage Centre, 1987.

McDermott, Joe. "1798 and Newport." *Back The Road: Recollections of Burrishoole and Newport* 1, no. 2 (1998): 8–11.

———. "The Tree of Liberty." *Back The Road: Recollections of Burrishoole and Newport* 1, no. 2 (1998): 5.

McDonald, Theresa. *Achill Island*. Tullamore, Co. Offaly: I.A.S. Publications, 1997.

McDonnell, Randal. *Kathleen Mavourneen: A Memory of the Great Rebellion. From the Record of Hugh Talent, Rebel to King George the Third, in the Year of Grace One Thousand Seven Hundred and Ninety-Eight*. London: T. Fisher Unwin, and Dublin: Sealy, Bryers & Walker, 1898.

McFarland, Elaine. "Scotland and the 1798 Rebellion: The Limits of "Common Cause."" In Bartlett, Dickson, Keogh, and Whelan, *1798: A Bicentenary Perspective*, 565–76.

McGuffie, T. H. "A Sketch-Map of Castlebar 27th August, 1798." *Journal of the Society for Army Historical Research* 26 (1948): 88–90.

McHenry, James. *O'Halloran; or the Insurgent Chief: An Irish Historical Tale of 1798*. London: J.S. Pratt, 1842; orig. ed. 1824.

McHugh, Roger. "The Famine in Irish Oral Tradition." In Edwards and Williams, *The Great Famine: Studies in Irish History, 1845–52*, 389–436.

McKelvie, Colin. "Notes Towards a Bibliography of William Hamilton Maxwell (1792–1850)." *Irish Booklore* 3, no. 1 (1976): 32–42.

McLoughlin, Pat Joe. "A Sense of History." In Rehill, *Ballinamuck Bi-Centenary, 1798–1998*, 111–18.

McManus, Henry. *Sketches of the Irish Highlands: Descriptive, Social and Religious. With Special Reference to Irish Missions in West Connaught since 1840*. London: Hamilton Adams & Co., 1863.

McParlan, James. *Statistical Survey of the County of Mayo with Observations on the Means of Improvement; Drawn up in the Year 1801, for the Consultation and under the Direction of the Dublin Society*. Dublin: Graisberry & Campbell, 1802.

McRedmond, Louis, ed. *Modern Irish Lives: Dictionary of 20th-Century Biography.* Dublin: Gill & Macmillan, 1996.

McTernan, John C. *Here's To Their Memory: Profiles of Distinguished Sligonians of Bygone Days.* Dublin and Cork: Mercier Press, 1977.

———. "Bartholomew Teeling (1774–1798)—a Hero of 1798." *Corran Herald,* no. 31 (1998): 14–16.

———. *In Sligo Long Ago: Aspects of the Town and County over Two Centuries.* Sligo: Avena, 1998.

McVegh, John. *Irish Travel Writing: A Bibliography.* Dublin: Wolfhound Press, 1996.

Measom, George S. *The Official Illustrated Guide to the Midland Great Western, and Dublin and Drogheda Railways with a Description of Dublin and an Account of Some of the Most Important Manufactories in Dublin & in the Towns on the Lines.* London: C. Griffin, 1866.

Méith, Muireadhach [Laurence Murray]. *Amhráin Chúige Uladh.* Dublin: Gilbert Dalton, 1977.

Meredith, Robbie. "The Shan Van Vocht: Notes from the North." In Kelly and Gillis, *Critical Ireland: New Essays in Literature and Culture,* 173–81.

Mhac an Fhailigh, Éamonn. *The Irish of Erris, Co. Mayo.* Dublin: The Dublin Institute for Advanced Studies, 1968.

Mhac Ruaidhrí, Mícheál. *Lúb na Caillighe agus Sgéalta Eile.* Dublin: Clódhanna Teo, 1910.

Middleton, David, and Derek Edwards, eds. *Collective Remembering.* London: Sage Publications, 1990.

Miller, Kerby A. "Introduction." In "Ireland, 1798-1998: From Revolution to Revisionism and Beyond." Special issue, *Eighteenth Century Life* 22, no. 3 (1998): 1–6.

Mims Wall, Drucilla. "1998 Constructions of Irish Identity in Enniscorthy: Personal Reflections on the 1798 Uprising and Its Legacies." *Eighteenth Century Life* 22, no. 3 (1998): 140–52.

Mitchel, John. *The History of Ireland, from the Treaty of Limerick to the Present Time.* New York: D. and J. Sadlier & Co., 1868.

Moloney, Colette. *The Irish Music Manuscripts of Edward Bunting (1773–1843): An Introduction and Catalogue.* Dublin: Irish Traditional Music Archive, 2001.

Moody, T. W. *Davitt and Irish Revolution 1842–82.* Oxford: Clarendon Press, 1981.

———. "A New History for Ireland." In Brady, *Interpreting Irish History,* 38–53.

———. "Irish History and Irish Mythology." In Brady, *Interpreting Irish History,* 71–86.

Moore, John. *Diary.* Edited by J. F. Maurice. London, 1904.

Moran, Gerald. "James Daly and the Land Question 1876–1879." *Retrospect* (Journal of the Irish Student's Association) (1980): 33–40.

———. "James Daly and the Rise of the Land League in the West of Ireland 1879–82." *Irish Historical Studies* 29, no. 114 (1994): 189–207.

Moran, J. J. *Stories of the Irish Rebellion, 1798.* Aberdeen: Moran & Co., and London: Simpkin & Co., 1898.

Moran, Seán Farrell. "Images, Icons and the Practice of Irish History." In L. W. McBride, *Images, Icons and the Irish Nationalist Imagination,* 166–78.

———. "History, Memory and Education: Teaching the Irish Story." In L. W. McBride, *Reading Irish Histories: Texts, Contexts, and Memory in Modern Ireland,* 212–19.

Moylan, Terry, ed. *The Age of Revolution: 1776–1815 in the Irish Song Tradition.* Dublin: Lilliput Press, 2000.

———. *Songs Composed During the Irish Rebellion of 1798 by the Late William Ball Esqr. Dublin.* Ennistymon, Co. Clare: Clare Festival of Traditional Singing, 2001.

Mulcahy, Richard, W. T. Cosgrave, and Charles Petrie. "Dr. Richard Hayes." *Irish Sword* 3 (1958): 210–12.

Mulloy, Sheila (Síle Uí Mhaoluaidh). "James Joseph Macdonnell, 'The Best-Known of the United Irish Chiefs of the West.'" *Cathair na Mart* 5, no. 1 (1985): 67–79.

———. "John Moore of Moorehall (1767–99): The General Who Wasn't." *Irish Sword* 18 (1990–92): 264–70.

———. "Father Manus Sweeney (1763–1799)." *Cathair na Mart* 1, no. 14 (1994): 27–38.

———. "The Clergy and the Connacht Rebellion." In *Protestant, Catholic and Dissenter,* edited by Liam Sword, 253–73. Blackrock, Co. Dublin: Columba Press, 1997.

———. "The Radical Cleric and the French Invasion of Connacht: Father Manus Sweeney (1763–99)." In *Radical Irish Priests, 1660–1970,* edited by Gerard Moran, 79–90. Dublin: Four Courts Press, 1998.

———. "1798 igConnachta." In *Éirí Amach 1798 in Éirinn,* edited by Gearóid Ó Tuathaigh, 107–22. Indreabhán Connemara: Cló Iar-Chonnachta, 1998.

———, ed. *Father Manus Sweeney, a Mayo Priest in the Rebellion of 1798 / an tAthair Mánus Mac Suibhne, Sagart Ó Mhaigh Eo in Éirí Amach 1798 le Pádraig Ó Móráin.* Westport: Westport Historical Society, 1999.

Munnelly, Jack. *The French Invasion of Connaught.* Killala: Western People, 1998.

Munnelly, Tom. "1798 and the Balladmakers." In Póirtéir, *The Great Irish Rebellion of 1798,* 160–70.

Murphy, James. *The Shan Van Vocht: A Story of the United Irishmen.* Dublin: M. H. Gill & Son, 1889; orig. ed. 1883.

Murphy, Maura. "The Ballad Singer and the Role of the Seditious Ballad in Nineteenth-Century Ireland: Dublin Castle's View." *Ulster Folklife* 25 (1979): 79–101.

Murphy, Maureen. "'The Noggin of Milk': An Old Testament Legend and the Battle of Ballinamuck." In Keogh and Furlong, *The Women of 1798,* 177–86.

Murray, Bill, and John Cullen, eds. *Epitaph of 1798: A Photographic Record of 1798 Memorials on the Island of Ireland and Beyond.* Enniscorthy, Co. Wexford: Carrigbyrne Film Productions and The Carrigbyrne Pikegroup, 2002.

Murtagh, Harman. "Irish Soldiers Abroad, 1600–1800." In Bartlett and Jeffery, *A Military History of Ireland,* 294–314.

———. "General Humbert's Campaign in the West." In Póirtéir, *The Great Irish Rebellion of 1798,* 115–24.

———. "General Humbert's Futile Campaign." In Bartlett, Dickson, Keogh, and Whelan, *1798: A Bicentenary Perspective,* 174–88.

Musgrave, Richard. *Memoirs of the Different Rebellions in Ireland from the Arrival of the English: Also a Particular Detail of That Which Broke out the 23rd of May, 1798 with the History of the Conspiracy Which Preceded It.* 4th ed., edited by Steven W. Myers and Delores E. McKnight. Fort Wayne, IN: Round Tower Books, 1995; orig. 3rd ed. London, 1802.

National Gallery of Ireland, *Cuimhneachán 1916: A Commemorative Exhibition of the Irish Rebellion 1916.* Dublin: National Gallery of Ireland, 1966.

Neville, Grace. "'He Spoke to Me in English; I Answered Him in Irish': Language Shift in the Folklore Archives." In *L'Irlande et ses langues,* edited by Jean Brihault, 19–32, 1992.

Ní Cheannain, Áine. *The Heritage of Mayo.* Dublin: Foilseacháin Náisiunta Teoranta, 1982.

Ní Dhonnchadha, Máirin, and Theo Dorgan, eds. *Revising the Rising.* Derry: Field Day, 1991.

Nic Eoin, Máirín. *Eoghan Ó Tuairisc: Beatha agus Saothar.* Dublin: An Clóchomhar Tta, 1988.

Ní Fhlathartaigh, Ríonach. *Clár Amhrán Bhaile na hInse.* Dublin: An Clóchomhar Tta, 1976.

Ní Ghiolla, Clára. *Dóchas.* 2nd ed. Belfast: Glandore Publishing, 1998.

Nora, Pierre, ed. *Realms of Memory: Rethinking the French Past.* 3 vols. New York: Columbia Univ. Press, 1996–98; orig. pub. as *Les Lieux de Memóire.* 7 vols. Paris: Galimard, 1984–1992.

Novick, Peter, *That Noble Dream: The "Objec-*

tivity Question" and the American Historical Profession. Cambridge; Cambridge Univ. Press, 1988.

———. *The Holocaust and Collective Memory: The American Experience.* London: Bloomsbury, 2000.

Noyes, Dorothy, and Roger D Abrahams. "From Calendar Custom to National Memory: European Commonplaces." In Ben-Amos and Weissberg, *Cultural Memory,* 77–98.

Ó Brádaigh, Seán. *The French Revolution and the Irish Struggle.* Longford: Seán Lynch on behalf of County Longford Branch of the National Graves Association, 1985.

———, ed. *The Battle of Ballinamuck: A Traditional History by James O'Neill of Crowdrummin.* Longford: Seán Lynch, 1986.

———. *Songs of 1798: Bliain na bhFrancach—The Year of the French.* Dublin: Irish Freedom Press, 1998; orig. ed. 1982.

———. *French Graves in Connacht,* n.d.

O'Brien, William. *Who Fears to Speak of Ninety-Eight?* Dublin: 1898.

Ó Broin, Leon. *Slán Le Muirisg.* Dublin: Oifig an tSoláthair, 1944.

Ó Broin, Seosamh. *Songs of Past and People: Singers from East Mayo.* Ballinrobe: Family Research D.T.P., 1994.

Ó Buachalla, Breandán. *I mBéal Feirste Cois Cuain.* Dublin: An Clóchomhar Tta, 1968.

———. *Aisling Ghéar: Na Stíobhartaigh agus an tAos Léinn.* Dublin: An Clóchomhar Tta, 1996.

———. "From Jacobite to Jacobin." In Bartlett, Dickson, Keogh, and Whelan, *1798: A Bicentenary Perspective,* 75–96.

Ó Canainn, Pádraig, and Seán Ó Deaghdha. *Filíocht na nGael.* Dublin: An Press Náisiúnta, 1958.

O'Carroll, Paddy. "Re-membering 1798." In *Memories of the Present: A Sociological Chronicle of Ireland, 1997–1998,* edited by Eamonn Slater and Michel Peillon, 15–23. Dublin: Institute of Public Administration, 2000.

Ó Catháin, Diarmaid. "Tomás Ó Catháin." *Teathbha* 2, no. 4 (1997): 276–78.

Ó Catháin, Séamas. *The Bedside Book of Irish Folklore.* Dublin: Mercier Press, 1980.

———. "Súil Siar ar Scéim na Scol 1937–1938." *Sinsear* 5 (1988): 19–30.

———. "The Irish Folklore Archive." *History Workshop Journal* 31 (1991): 145–48.

———. "Sceim Na Scoil." In *It's Us They're Talking About,* edited by Margaret Farren and Mag Hoken (13 pages, unnumbered). Clonmany, Co. Donegal: McGlinchey Summer School, 1998.

Ó Catháin, Séamas, and Patrick O'Flanagan. *The Living Landscape: Kilgalligan, Erris County Mayo.* Dublin: Comhairle Bhéaloideas Éireann, 1975.

Ó Ciosáin, Niall. *Print and Popular Culture, 1750–1850.* Houndmills: Macmillan, and New York: St. Martin's Press, 1997.

———. "Famine Memory and the Popular Representation of Scarcity." In *History and Memory in Modern Ireland,* edited by Ian McBride, 95–117. Cambridge: Cambridge Univ. Press, 2001.

Ó Coigligh, Ciarán. *Raiftearaí: Amhráin agus Dánta.* Dublin: An Clóchomhar Tta, 1987.

Ó Conaire, Breandán, ed. *Language, Lore and Lyrics: Essays and Lectures by Douglas Hyde.* Dublin: Irish Academic Press, 1986.

O'Connor, Frank. *Leinster, Munster and Connaught.* London: R. Hale, [1950?].

O'Connor, Pat. *"The French are in Killala." 1798: An Account of Humbert's Campaign from Kilcummin to Ballinamuck.* P. O'Connor, 1998.

Ó Crualaoich, Gearóid. "The Primacy of Form: A 'Folk Ideology' in de Valera's Politics." In *De Valera and His Times,* edited by J. P. O'Carroll and J. A. Murphy, 47–61. Cork: Cork Univ. Press, 1983.

———. "Responding to the Rising." In Ní Dhonnchadha and Dorgan, *Revising the Rising,* 50–71.

———. "'The French Are on the Say.'" In *The French Are in the Bay: The Expedition to*

Bantry Bay, 1796, edited by John A. Murphy, 120–38. Dublin: Mercier Press, 1996.

O Cuinneagain, Seosamh. *Lecture on the Tones in a Decade of Irish History: Delivered at the Curragh Concentration Camp on Sunday, 27th April, and Sunday, 4th May, 1958.* Enniscorthy: North Wexford Printing & Publishing Co., 1970.

Ó Domhnaill, Niall. *Na Glúnta Rosannacha.* Dublin: Oifig an tSoláthair, 1952.

Ó Dónaill (Ó Dómhnaill), Niall. *Foclóir Gaeilge-Béarla.* 2nd ed. Dublin: An Gúm, 1992.

O'Donnell, Ruán. *1798 Diary.* Dublin: Irish Times, 1998.

———. *Insurgent Wicklow 1798: The Story as Written by Luke Cullen, O.D.C.* Bray, Co. Wicklow: Kestrel Books, 1998.

———. *The Rebellion in Wicklow, 1798.* Dublin: Irish Academic Press, 1998.

———. *Aftermath: Post Rebellion Insurgency in Wicklow, 1799–1803.* Dublin: Irish Academic Press, 2000.

O'Donnell, Ruán, and Bob Reece. "'A Clean Beast': Crofton Croker's Fairy Tale of General Holt." *Eighteenth Century Ireland* 7 (1992): 7–42.

O'Donovan Rossa, Diarmuid (Jeremiah). *Rossa's Recollections, 1838–1898.* Shannon: Irish Univ. Press, 1972; orig. ed. New York, 1898.

O'Donovan, John. *Letters Containing Information Relative to the Antiquities of the County of Longford: Collected during the progress of the Ordinance Survey in 1837.* Dublin: Royal Irish Academy, 1837.

O'Dowd, Liam, ed. *On Intellectuals and Intellectual Life in Ireland: International, Comparative and Historical Contexts.* Belfast: Institute of Irish Studies, QUB, 1996.

Ó Drisceoil, Donal. *Censorship in Ireland, 1939–1945: Neutrality, Politics and Society.* Cork: Cork Univ. Press, 1996.

O'Dubhthaigh, LeSean. "Riocard Bairead, File Iorrais (1740–1819)." *Bliainiris* I, no. 2 (1983): 18–22.

Ó Duignéain, Peadar. "Ballinamuck and '98: A Talk to the Society." *Teathbha* 1, no. 1 (1969): 41–46.

———. "The Battle of Granard." *Teathbha* 2, no. 2 (1971): 145.

O'Farrell, Fergus. "History of the Ballinamuck Land War of 1835–39." *Teathbha* 2, no. 2 (1983): 104–9.

O'Farrell, Nuala. "Who Fears to Speak of '98?" *Hibernia* (1979): 4.

O'Farrell, Padraic, ed. *The '98 Reader: An Anthology of Song, Prose and Poetry.* Dublin: Lilliput Press, 1998.

O'Farrell, Patrick. *O'Farrell's Collection of National Music for the Union Pipes,* London, 1804.

Ó Flathartha, Peadar. "Gnéithe Comparáideacha den Stair agus de Thraidisiún an Úrscéil Stairiúil i *L'Attaque.*" *Comhar* 44, no. 10 (1985): 54–58.

O'Flynn, T. M. *History of Leitrim.* Dublin: C.J. Fallon Ltd., 1937.

Ó Gallchobhair, Micheál. "Amhráin ó Iorrus." *Béaloideas* 10 (1940): 210–84.

Ó Giolláin, Diarmuid. "An Béaloideas agus an Stát." *Béaloideas* 57 (1989): 151–63.

———. *Locating Irish Folklore: Tradition, Modernity, Identity.* Cork: Cork Univ. Press, 2000.

Ó Gráda, Cormac. *Ireland: A New Economic History 1780–1939.* Oxford: Clarendon Press, 1994.

———. *An Drochshaol: Béaloideas agus Amhráin.* Dublin: Coiscéim, 1994.

———. *Black '47 and Beyond: The Great Famine in History.* Princeton: Princeton Univ. Press, 1999.

———. "Famine, Trauma and Memory." *Béaloideas* 69 (2001): 121–43.

Ó Grianna, Séamus. *Rann Na Feirste.* Dublin: An Press Násiúnta, 1942.

O'Hara, Bernard. *Killasser: a History.* Galway: B. O'Hara, 1981.

———, ed. *Mayo: Aspects of its Heritage.* Galway: Archaeological, Historical & Folklore Society, 1982.

Ó hÓgáin, Dáithí. "Nótaí Ar Chromail i mBéaloideas na hÉireann." *Sinsear* 2 (1980): 73–83.

———. "An Stair Agus an Seanchas Beil." *Léachtaí Cholmcille* 14 (1983): 173–96.

———. *The Hero in Irish Folk History*. Dublin: Gill & Macmillan, 1985.

———. *Dunaire Osraíoch: Cnuasach D'fhilíocht na nDaoine ó Cho*. Chill Chainnigh. Dublin: An Clóchomhar Tta, 1990.

———. *Myth, Legend and Romance: An Encyclopaedia of Irish Folk Tradition*. London: Prentice Hall, 1990.

O'Keefe, Timothy. "The Art and Politics of the Parnell Monument." *Éire-Ireland* 19 (1984): 6–25.

———. "The 1898 Efforts to Celebrate the United Irishmen: The '98 Centennial." *Éire-Ireland* 23 (1988): 51–73.

———. "'Who Fears to Speak of '98?' The Rhetoric and Rituals of the United Irishmen Centennial, 1898." *Éire-Ireland* 27 (1992): 67–91.

Olick, Jeffrey K., and Joyce Robbins. "Social Memory Studies: From 'Collective Memory' to the Historical Sociology of Mnemonic Practices." *Annual Review of Sociology* 24 (1998): 105–40.

Ollivier, Sophie. "Les Historiens Irlandais et Le Bicentenaire de 1798." *Études Irlandaises* 24, no. 2 (1999): 139–53.

———. "Presence and Absence of Wolfe Tone During the Centenary Commemoration of the 1798 Rebellion." In Geary, *Rebellion and Remembrance in Modern Ireland*, 175–84.

O Lochlainn, Colm. *Irish Street Ballads*. Dublin: Three Candles, and London: Constable, 1939.

———. *More Irish Street Ballads*. Dublin: Three Candles, 1965.

Ó Loinsigh, Séamus. *The 1798 Rebellion in Meath*. Nobber, Co. Meath: Meath Archaeological & Historical Society, 1997.

Ó Máille, Tomás S. *Sean-Fhocla Chonnacht*. Dublin: Oifig an tSoláthair, 1948.

———. *Micheál Mhac Suibhne agus Filidh an tSléibhe*. 2nd. ed. Dublin: Oifig Dhíolta Foilseachán Rialtais, 1969; orig. ed. 1934.

Ó Maonaigh, Pádraig A. *Claisceadal na n-Óg*. Dublin: Foillseachán Rialtais, 1945.

Ó Moghráin (Ó Móráin), Pádraig. "Gearr-Chunntas ar an Athair Mánus Mac Suibhne." *Béaloideas* 17 (1947): 3–57.

———. *Annála Beaga Pharáiste Bhuiréis Umhaill: A Short Account of the History of Burrishoole Parish*. P. Ó Móráin, 1957.

Ó Muirgheasa, Énrí. *Dhá Chéad de Cheoltaibh Uladh*. Dublin, 1934.

Ó Muraíle, Nollaig. "Mayo Placenames." In O'Hara, *Mayo: Aspects of its Heritage*, 55–83.

Ó Murchadha, Diarmuid, and Kevin Murray. "Place-Names." In Buttimer, Rynne, and Guerin, *The Heritage of Ireland*, 146–55.

O'Neill, Francis. *Irish Folk Music*. Chicago: Regan, 1910.

———. *Irish Minstrels and Musicians with Numerous Dissertations on Related Subjects*. Chicago: Regan, 1913.

O'Neill, Seosamh. *National Tradition and Folklore*. Dublin: Department of Education, 1934.

O'Rorke, Terence. *History, Antiquities and Present State of the Parishes of Ballysadare and Kilvarnet in the County of Sligo*. Dublin: James Duffy, 1878.

———. *The History of Sligo: Town and County*. Dublin: James Duffy, 1889.

O'Rourke, Brian. "County Mayo in Gaelic Folksong." In O'Hara, *Mayo: Aspects of its Heritage*, 153–200.

Ó Saothraí, Séamas. *Heroines of 1798*. Bray: Bray Heritage Centre, 1998.

Ó Súilleabháin, Seán. *Irish Folklore and Tradition*. Dublin: An Roinn Oideachais, 1937.

———. *A Handbook of Irish Folklore*. Dublin: Education Company of Ireland, 1942.

———. *Folktales of Ireland*. London: Routledge & Kegan Paul, 1966.

———. *Storytelling in the Irish Tradition*. Cork: Mercier Press, 1973.

———. *A Biographical Dictionary of Longford Authors*. Mullingar: Longford/Westmeath Joint Library Committee, 1978.

Ó Súilleabháin, Seán, and Reidar Th. Christiansen. *The Types of the Irish Folktale*. Helsinki: Academia Scientiarum Fennica, 1967.

O'Sullivan, Donal J. *The Bunting Collection of Irish Folk Music and Songs.* Part 5. London: C. J. Farncombe & Sons, 1936.

O'Sullivan, Tadhg. "'The Violence of a Servile War': Three Narratives of Irish Rural Insurgency Post 1798." In Geary, *Rebellion and Remembrance in Modern Ireland,* 73–92.

Ó Tiománaidhe (Timoney), Micheál. *Targaireacht Bhriain Ruaidh Uí Chearbháin agus Stair-Sheanchas Le Cois* [Red Brian Carabine's Prophecy and Other Interesting Historical Matter]. Dublin: M. H. Gill & Son and Gaelic League, 1906.

———. *Amhráin Ghaeilge an Iarthair.* 2nd ed. Indreabhán, Conamara: Cló Iar-Chonnachta, 1992; orig. ed. Dublin, 1906.

O'Toole, E. H. "The Medal for Collooney, 1798." *Orders and Medals* (Journal for the Orders and Medals Research Society) 24, no. 1 (1985): 19–23.

O'Toole, James. *Newsplan: Report of the Newsplan Project in Ireland.* London: British Library, and Dublin: National Library of Ireland, 1998.

Ó Tuairisc, Eoghan. *L'Attaque.* Dublin, 1962.

———. *Lux Aeterna.* Dublin: Allen Figgis, 1964.

Ó Tuathail, Pádraig. "Wicklow Traditions of 1798." *Béaloideas* 5 (1935): 154–88.

Otway, Caesar (Terence O'Toole). *A Tour in Connaught: Compromising Sketches of Clonmacnoise, Joyce County and Achill.* Dublin: William Curry Jun. & Co., 1839.

———. *Sketches in Erris and Tyrawley, Illustrative of the Scenery, Antiquities, Architectural Remains, and the Manners and Superstitions of the Irish Peasantry.* 2nd ed. Dublin: Thomas Connolly, and London: Longman, Brown & Co., 1850; orig. serialized in *Dublin University Magazine* 18 (1842).

Owens, Gary. "Nationalist Monuments in Ireland, ca. 1870–1914: Symbolism and Ritual." In *Ireland: Art into History,* edited by Raymond Gillespie and Brian P. Kennedy, 103–17. Dublin: Town House, and Niwot, Colorado: Robert Rinehart, 1994.

———. "Constructing the Martyrs: The Manchester Executions and the Nationalist Imagination." In L. W. McBride, *Images, Icons and the Irish Nationalist Imagination,* 18–36.

———. "Nationalism without Words: Symbolism and Ritual Behaviour in the Repeal 'Monster Meetings' of 1843–5." In Donnelly and Miller, *Irish Popular Culture, 1650–1850,* 242–70.

———. "Popular Mobilisation and the Rising of 1848: The Clubs of the Irish Confederation." In Geary, *Rebellion and Remembrance in Modern Ireland,* 51–63.

Pakenham, Thomas. *The Year of Liberty: The Story of the Great Irish Rebellion.* London: Weidenfeld & Nicholson, 1997; orig. ed. 1969.

Paredes, Américo, and Richard Bauman, eds. *Toward New Perspectives in Folklore.* Austin: Univ. of Texas Press, 1972.

Paseta, Senia. "1798 in 1898: The Politics of Commemoration." *Irish Review* 22 (1998): 46–53.

Paupié. "Une Descente En Irlande En 1798, Journal Du Capitane Jobit." *Bulletin de la Société de Géographie de Rochefort* 28 (1906): 155–76.

Pearse, H. W. "The French Raid in Ireland, 1798, and Short Sketches of Other Attempts and Landings on the Coast of the United Kingdom." *Journal of the United Service Institution* 53 (1909): 1153–73.

Pellet, Marcellin. *Vieilles Histoires.* Paris: Ocantania, 1930.

Perks, Robert, ed. *Oral History: An Annotated Bibliography.* London: The British Library National Sound Archive, 1996.

Perks, Robert, and Alisdair Thompson. *The Oral History Reader.* London: Routledge, 1998.

Piehler, G. K. *Remembering War the American Way.* Washington, DC: Smithsonian Institution Press, 1995.

Plowden, Francis. *An Historical Review of the State of Ireland from the Invasion of the Country Under Henry II to its Union with Great Britain.* Vol. 2, part 2. London: C. Roworth for T. Egerton, 1803.

Póirtéir, Cathal. *Famine Echoes.* Dublin: Gill & Macmillan, 1995.

———. "Folk Memory and the Famine." In *The Great Irish Famine,* edited by Cathal Póirtéir, 219–31. Dublin: Mercier Press and RTÉ, 1995.

———. *Glórtha ón nGorta: Béaloideas na Gaeilge agus an Gorta Mór.* Dublin: Coiscéim, 1996.

———, ed. *The Great Irish Rebellion of 1798.* Dublin: Mercier Press and RTÉ, 1998.

Postgate, Raymond. *Story of a Year: 1798.* London: Longmans, 1969.

Potterton, Homan. *The O'Connell Monument.* Ballycotton, Co. Cork: Gifford & Craven, 1973.

Power, Patrick C. *The Courts Martial of 1798–9.* Kilkenny: Irish Historical Press, 1997.

Quin, E. G., ed. *Contributions to a Dictionary of the Irish Language.* Dublin: Royal Irish Academy and Hoggis Figgis, 1953.

Quinlan, Carmel. "A Punishment from God: The Famine in the Centenary Folklore Questionnaire." *Irish Review* 19 (1996): 68–86.

Quinn, J. F. *History of Mayo.* 5 vols. Ballina: Brendan Quinn, 1993–2002; orig. serialized in *Western People.*

Rehill, Padraig, ed. *Ballinamuck Bi-Centenary, 1798–1998.* Longford: Turner Print Group, 1998.

Reilly, Eileen. "Who Fears to Speak of '98? The Rebellion in Historical Novels, 1880–1914." *Eighteenth Century Life* 22, no. 3 (1998): 118–27.

———. "Beyond Gilt Shamrock: Symbolism and Realism in the Cover Art of Irish Historical and Political Fiction, 1880–1914." In L. W. McBride, *Images, Icons and the Irish Nationalist Imagination,* 95–112.

———. "Rebel Muse and Spouse: The Female in '98 Fiction." *Éire-Ireland* 34, no. 2 (1999): 135–54.

Reilly, Terry. "Gunner McGee's Cannon." *Bliainiris,* no. 2 (1983): 23–24; reprinted from the "Old Ballina" series in *Western People.*

———. *Dear Old Ballina.* Ballina: Western People, 1993.

Richard, Henry [Lord Holland]. *Memoirs of the Whig Party During My Time.* Vol. 1. London: Longman, 1852.

Ricoeur, Paul. "Memory and Forgetting." In *Questioning Ethics: Debates in Contemporary Philosophy,* edited by Richard Kearney and Mark Dooley, 5–11. London: Routledge, 1999.

———. *Memory, History, Forgetting.* Chicago: Univ. of Chicago Press, 2004.

Ridgeway, William. *A Report of the Proceedings under a Special Commission of Oyer and Terminer and Gaol Delivery for the Counties of Sligo, Mayo, Leitrim, Longford and Cavan in the Month of December, 1806.* Dublin: Graisberry & Campbell, 1807.

Robinson, Henry A. *Further Memories of Irish Life.* London: H. Jenkins, 1924.

Roche, Richard. "Local History Publications on 1798." *History Ireland* 6, no. 2 (1998): 59–60.

Roe, Owen. *Reliques of John K. Casey ("Leo").* Dublin: Richard Pigott, 1878.

Ross, Charles, ed. *Correspondence of Charles, First Marquis Cornwallis.* London: John Murray, 1859.

Rouvier, Charles. *Histoire des Marins Français sous la République (de 1789–1803).* Paris: Arthur Bertrand, 1868.

Ryder, Sean. "Speaking of '98: Young Ireland and Republican Memory." *Éire-Ireland* 34, no. 2 (1999): 51–69.

Sampson, D. "The French Expedition to Ireland in 1798." *The Dublin Review* 121, no. 23 (4th ser.) (1897): 60–79.

Samuel, Raphael. *Theatres of Memory.* Vol. 1: *Past and Present in Contemporary Culture.* London: Verso, 1994.

———. *Theatres of Memory.* Vol. 2: *Island Stories: Unravelling Britain,* edited by Alison Light, Sally Alexander, and Gareth Stedman Jones. London and New York: Verso, 1998.

Samuel, Raphael, and Paul Thompson, eds. *The Myths We Live By.* London, 1990.

Sarrazin, General. *Reply of General Sarrazin to*

the Narrative Made by General Clarke, Minister of War to General Bonaparte. London, 1810.

———. *The Philosopher; or, Historical and Critical Notes.* 2nd ed. London, 1812.

Scott, Florence Mary Seymour, and Alma Hodge. *The Round Tower: A Story of the Irish Rebellion in '98.* London: Thomas Nelson & Sons, 1904.

Scott, James C. *Domination and the Arts of Resistance: Hidden Transcripts.* New Haven: Yale Univ. Press, 1990.

Scully, Denys. *An Irish Catholic's Advice to His Brethren, How to Estimate Their Present Situation and Repel French Invasion, Civil Wars and Slavery.* 2nd ed. Dublin: M. Mahon, and London: G. Gordon, 1803.

Seoighe, Mainchín. *From Bruree to Corcomahide.* Bruree, Co. Limerick: Bruree/Rockhill Development Assoc., 2000.

Searleman, Alan, and Douglas Hermann. *Memory from a Broader Perspective.* New York: McGraw-Hill, 1994.

Sheehan, Helena. *Irish Television Drama: A Society and Its Stories.* Dublin: RTÉ, 1986.

Shields, Hugh. *Narrative Singing in Ireland: Lays, Ballads, Come-All-Yes and Other Songs.* Dublin: Irish Academic Press, 1993.

Shils, Edward. *Tradition.* London: Faber & Faber, 1981.

Smith, Gillian. "'An Eye on the Survey': Perceptions of the Ordnance Survey in Ireland 1824–1842." *History Ireland* 9 (2001): 37–41.

Smyth, Jim. *The Men of No Property.* Dublin: Gill & Macmillan, 1992.

———, ed. *Revolution, Counter-Revolution, and Union: Ireland in the 1790s.* Cambridge: Cambridge Univ. Press, 2000.

Snoddy, Oliver. "The Limerick City Militia and the Battle of Collooney, 1798." *North Munster Antiquarian Journal* 9, no. 3 (1964): 117–22.

Stanford, Charles Villiers. *The Complete Collection of Irish Music as Noted by George Petrie.* London: Boosey, 1902–05.

Stead, William T. *The Centenary of 1798 and its Bearing on the Practical Politics of To-Day.* London: Review of Reviews, 1898.

Stewart, A. T. Q. *The Summer Soldiers: The 1798 Rebellion in Antrim and Down.* Belfast: Blackstaff Press, 1995.

Stock, Joseph. *A Narrative of What Passed at Killala in the County Mayo and the Parts Adjacent During the French Invasion in the Summer of 1798 by an Eyewitness.* London: R.E. Mercier & Co., 1800.

Stock, St. George. "The Diary of the Bishop of Killalla, 1798." *The Fortnightly Review* 70 (1898): 984–1001.

Stoker, Bram. *The Snake's Pass.* Dingle: Brandon, 1990; orig. ed. 1890.

Stuart Jones, E. H. *An Invasion That Failed: The French Expedition to Ireland in 1796.* Oxford: Basil Blackwell, 1950.

Sullivan, Alexander Martin. *New Ireland: Political Sketches and Personal Reminisces of Thirty Years of Irish Public Life.* London: Cameron & Ferguson, 1882.

———. *The Story of Ireland.* Dublin: M. H. Gill & Son, 1909; orig. ed. 1867.

Swords, Liam. *The Green Cockade: The Irish in the French Revolution, 1789–1815.* Dublin: Glendale, 1989.

———. *A Hidden Church: The Diocese of Achonry, 1689–1818.* Blackrock Co. Dublin: Columba Press, 1997.

———, ed. *Protestant, Catholic and Dissenter.* Dublin: Columba Press, 1997.

Taithe, Bertrand, and Tim Thornton, eds. *Prophecy: The Power of Inspired Language in History, 1300–2000.* Stroud: Sutton, 1997.

Teeling, Charles Hamilton. *History of the Irish Rebellion of 1798 and Sequel to the History of the Irish Rebellion of 1798.* Shannon: Irish Univ. Press, 1972; facsimile of 1876 ed. orig. pub. as *Personal Narrative of the "Irish Rebellion" of 1798* (London, 1828) and *Sequel to Personal Narrative of the "Irish Rebellion" of 1798* (Belfast, 1832).

Thelen, David. "Memory and American History." *Journal of American History* 75(1989): 1117–29.

Thompson, Mrs. B. "The Siege of Killala." *Cornhill Magazine* (1898): 463–78.

Thompson, F. Glen. *The Uniforms of*

1798–1803. Dublin: Four Courts Press, 1998.

Thompson, Paul. *The Voice of the Past: Oral History*. Oxford: Oxford Univ. Press, 1978.

Thompson, Spurgeon. "The Politics of Photography: Travel Writing and the Irish Countryside, 1900–1914." In L. W. McBride, *Images, Icons and the Irish Nationalist Imagination*, 113–29.

Thompson, Stith. *Motif-Index of Folk Literature*, 6 vols. Bloomington: Indiana Univ. Press, 1955.

Thuente, Mary Helen. "A Bibliography of W. B. Yeats's Sources for Fairy Tales of the Irish Peasantry and Irish Fairy Tales." *Irish Booklore* 3, no. 1 (1976): 43–49.

———. *W. B. Yeats and Irish Folklore*. Dublin: Gill & Macmillan, 1980.

———. "The Folklore of Irish Nationalism." In *Perspectives on Irish Nationalism*, edited by Thomas E. Hachey and Lawrence J. McCaffrey, 42–60. Kentucky: Univ. Press of Kentucky, 1989.

———. *The Harp Re-Strung: The United Irishmen and the Rise of Irish Literary Nationalism*. Syracuse: Syracuse Univ. Press, 1994.

Tohall, Patrick. "Some Connacht Traditions." *Béaloideas* 14 (1944): 289–91.

Tóibín, Colm. "The Irish Famine." In *The Irish Famine: A Documentary*, edited by Colm Tóibín and Diarmaid Ferriter. London: Profile Books, 2001.

Tonkin, Elizabeth. *Narrating Our Pasts: The Social Construction of Oral History*. Cambridge: Cambridge Univ. Press, 1992.

Toomey, Deirdre. "Who Fears to Speak of Ninety-Eight." In Warwick Gould, ed., "Yeats and the Nineties." Special issue, *Yeats Annual* 14 (1998): 209–61.

Tosh, John. *The Pursuit of History: Aims, Methods and New Directions in the Study of Modern History*. Essex: Longman, 1984.

Tracy, Robert. "Who Fears to Speak of '98, '63, '64, '65, '66, '67, '68, '69, '70? *The Year of the French* and the Nineteen Sixties." *Irish University Review* 28, no. 1 (1998): 1–10.

Trotter, John Bernard. *Walks through Ireland in the Years 1812, 1814 and 1817: Described in a Series of Letters to an English Gentleman*. London: Sir Richard Phillips, 1819.

Trouillot, Michel-Rolph. *Silencing the Past: Power and the Production of History*. Boston: Beacon Press, 1995.

Turpin, John. "1798, 1898 and the Political Implications of Sheppard's Monuments." *History Ireland* 6, no. 2 (1998): 44–48.

Tyrrell, John. *Weather and Warfare: A Climatic History of the 1798 Rebellion*. Cork: Collins Press, 2001.

ua Ruaidhrí, Seaghán. *Bliadhain na bhFranncach*. Dublin: Connradh na Gaedhilge, 1907.

uí Ógáin, Ríonach. *Immortal Dan: Daniel O' Connell in Irish Folk Tradition*. Dublin: Geography Publications, 1995.

———. "Béaloideas 1798 Thiar." In *Éirí Amach 1798 in Éirinn*, edited by Gearóid Ó Tuathaigh, 137–53. Indreabhán Connemara: Cló Iar-Chonnachta, 1998.

Van Brock, F. W. "Dilemma at Killala." *Irish Sword* 8 (1967): 261–73

———. "A Memoir of 1798." *Irish Sword* 9 (1969): 192–207.

———. "Morres's Memorial, 1798." *Irish Sword* 15 (1982): 36–44.

Vane, Charles, Marquess of Londonderry, ed. *Memoirs and Correspondence of Viscount Castlereagh, Second Marquess of Londonderry*. London: Henry Colburn, 1848.

Vansina, Jan. *Oral Tradition as History*. London: James Currey, and Nairobi: Heinemann Kenya, 1985.

———. "Memory and Oral Tradition." In *The African Past Speaks*, edited by J. C. Miller, 262–79. Kent: Archan Books, 1980.

Vendryes, J. *Lexique Étymologique de l'Irlandais Ancien*. Dublin: Institute for Advanced Studies, and Paris: Centre National de la Recherche Scientifique, 1974.

Walford, Edward. *The County Families of the United Kingdom, or Royal Manual of the Titled and Untitled Aristocracy of Great Britain and Ireland*. 6th ed. London: R. Hardwicke, 1871.

Walker, Brian M. *Parliamentary Election Results in Ireland, 1918–1992*. Dublin: Royal Irish Academy, 1992.

———. *Past and Present: History, Identity and Politics in Ireland*. Belfast: Institute of Irish Studies of Queen's Univ. Belfast, 2000.

Wallace, Peter. *Multyfarnham Parish History*. Mullingar, 1987.

Walsh, Edward. *Reliques of Irish Jacobite Poetry, with Metrical Translations*. 2nd. ed. Dublin, 1866; orig. ed. 1844.

Walsh, Lorcan. "Nationalism in the Textbooks of the Christian Brothers." *Irish Educational Studies* 6, no. 2 (1986): 1–16.

Ward, Catherine. "Thomas Flanagan's The Year of the French: A Cautionary Tale." *Éire—Ireland* 22, no. 1 (1987): 59–71.

Welch, Robert, ed. *The Oxford Companion to Irish Literature*. Oxford: Clarendon Press, 1996.

Westropp, T. J. "The Promontory Forts and Early Remains of the Coasts of Mayo." *Journal of the Royal Society of Antiquaries in Ireland* 42 (1912): 51–59, 186–216.

Whelan, Kevin. "Place-name Change—an Index of Value Systems in Transition." *Sinsear* 1 (1979): 44–49.

———. "The United Irishmen, the Enlightenment and Popular Culture." In Dickson, Keogh, and Whelan, *The United Irishmen: Republicanism, Radicalism and Rebellion*, 269–96.

———. "United and Disunited Irishmen: The Discourse of Sectarianism in the 1790s." *Studies on Voltaire and the 18th Century* 335 (1995): 231–47.

———. *The Tree of Liberty: Radicalism, Catholicism and the Construction of Irish Identity 1760–1830*. Cork: Cork Univ. Press and Field Day, 1996.

———. "Reinterpreting the 1798 Rebellion in County Wexford." In Keogh and Furlong, *The Mighty Wave*, 9–36.

———. "The Region and the Intellectuals." In Dowd, *On Intellectuals and Intellectual Life in Ireland*, 116–31.

———. *Fellowship of Freedom: The United Irishmen and 1798*. Cork: Cork Univ. Press, 1998.

———. "Three Revolutions and a Failure." In Póirtéir, *The Great Irish Rebellion of 1798*, 26–36.

Whelan, Michael. *The Parish of Aughavas, Co. Leitrim: Its History and its People*. Ferbane, Co. Offaly: Brosna Press, 1998.

Whelan, Yvonne. *Reinventing Modern Dublin: Streetscape, Iconography and the Politics of Identity*. Dublin: Univ. College Dublin Press, 2003.

White, Richard. *Remembering Ahanagran: Storytelling in a Family's Past*. New York: Wing & Wang, 1998.

White, Sean J. "A Week in the Year of the French." *Ireland of the Welcomes* 31 (1982): 25–32.

Whitney, Harry. *Legends of Mount Leinster*. Dublin: P. Kennedy, 1855.

Whyte, J. H. *Church and State in Modern Ireland*. Dublin: Gill & Macmillan, 1971.

Wilde, William R. *Irish Popular Superstitions*. Shannon: Irish Univ. Press, 1972; orig. ed. Dublin, 1852.

Williams, Nicholas J. *Riocard Bairéad: Amhráin*. Dublin: An Clóchomhar Tta, 1978.

Winter, Jay. *Sites of Memory, Sites of Mourning: The Great War in European Cultural History*. Cambridge: Cambridge Univ. Press, 1995.

Witoszek, Nina, and Pat Sheeran. *Talking to the Dead: A Study of Irish Funerary Traditions*. Amsterdam: Radopi, 1998.

Wood-Martin, William Gregory. *History of Sligo, County and Town*. 3rd ed. Dublin: Hodges Figgis, 1892.

Woods, C. J. "Tone's Grave at Bodenstown: Memorials and Commemorations, 1798–1913." *Irland Gesellschaft und Kultur* 6 (1989): 138–48.

Woods, James. *Annals of Westmeath: Ancient and Modern*. Dublin: Sealy, Bryers & Walker, 1907.

Yates, Frances. *The Art of Memory*. London: Routledge & Paul, 1966.

Yeats, W. B. *Cathleen Ní Houlihan.* Dublin, 1902.

Young, James E. "The Biography of a Memorial Icon: Nathan Rapaport's Warsaw Ghetto Memorial." *Representations* 26 (1989): 69–106.

———. *The Texture of Memory: Holocaust Memorials and Meaning.* New Haven: Yale Univ. Press, 1993.

Young, Robert M. *Ulster in '98: Episodes and Anecdotes.* Belfast: Marcus Ward, 1893.

———. "Edward Bunting's Irish Music and the McCracken Family." *Ulster Journal of Archaeology* 2nd ser., 4, no. 3 (1898): 175–78.

Zerubavel, Yael. *Recovered Roots: Collective Memory and the Making of Israeli National Tradition.* Chicago: Univ. of Chicago Press, 1995.

Zimmermann, Georges Denis. *The Irish Storyteller.* Dublin: Four Courts Press, 2001.

———. *Songs of Irish Rebellion: Irish Political Street Ballads and Rebel Songs, 1780–1900.* Dublin: Four Courts Press, 2002; orig. ed. 1967.

Zonabend, Françoise. *The Enduring Memory: Time and History in a French Village.* Manchester: Manchester Univ. Press, 1984.

FILMOGRAPHY

1798 Agus Ó Shin (TnaG: 1998, director Louis Marcus).

1798. The Comedy (BBC Northern Ireland: 1998, *The Hole in the Wall Gang*).

A Patriot's Fate (BBC Northern Ireland: 1998, director Moore Sinnerton).

Collooney in '98: Bicentenary Commemoration 1798–1998 (Collooney Bicentenary Committee: 1998)

Hidden Treasures (RTÉ and BBC: 1998, director Anne O'Leary).

Killala Remembering 1798: Bicentenary Commemoration Video August 22nd–27th 1998 (Killala Bicentenary Committee: 1998).

Pike People (RTÉ: 2000, director Angela Ryan).

Rebellion (RTÉ: 1998, producer Kevin Dawson).

Seven Ages (RTÉ: 2000, producer Sean Ó Mordha).

The Year of the French (RTÉ director Michael Garvey, 1982).

Who Fears to Speak of '98: Bicentenary Commemoration of the Battle of Ballinamuck 1798–1998 (Ballinamuck Bicentenary Committee: 1998).

Index

HISTORY *of* IRELAND
and the IRISH DIASPORA

James S. Donnelly, Jr., and Thomas Archdeacon, Series Editors

Remembering the Year of the French: Irish Folk History and Social Memory
Guy Beiner

*Ireland's New Worlds: Immigrants, Politics,
and Society in the United States and Australia, 1815–1922*
Malcolm Campbell

The Slow Failure: Population Decline and Independent Ireland, 1920–1973
Mary E. Daly

The Eternal Paddy: Irish Identity and the British Press, 1798–1882
Michael de Nie

Old World Colony: Cork and South Munster 1630–1830
David Dickson

Sinn Féin: A Hundred Turbulent Years
Brian Feeney

Stakeknife: Britain's Secret Agents in Ireland
Martin Ingram and Greg Harkin

New Directions in Irish-American History
Edited by Kevin Kenny

The Same Age as the State
Máire Cruise O'Brien

*The Bible War in Ireland: The "Second Reformation" and the Polarization
of Protestant-Catholic Relations, 1800–1840*
Irene Whelan

*Tourism, Landscape, and the Irish Character:
British Travel Writers in Pre-Famine Ireland*
William H. A. Williams